STRATEGIC MANAGEMENT

AWARENESS AND CHANGE

Second edition

John L. Thompson

University of Huddersfield
Queensgate
Huddersfield
UK

CHAPMAN & HALL
University and Professional Division
London · Glasgow · New York · Tokyo · Melbourne · Madras

Published by Chapman & Hall, 2–6 Boundary Row, London SE1 8HN

Chapman & Hall, 2–6 Boundary Row, London SE1 8HN, UK

Blackie Academic & Professional, Wester Cleddens Road,
Bishopbriggs, Glasgow G64 2NZ, UK

Chapman & Hall Inc., 29 West 35th Street, New York, NY10001, USA

Chapman & Hall Japan, Thomson Publishing Japan, Hirakawacho
Nemoto Building, 6F, 1–7–11 Hirakawa-cho, Chiyoda-ku, Tokyo 102,
Japan

Chapman & Hall Australia, Thomas Nelson Australia, 102 Dodds
Street, South Melbourne, Victoria 3205, Australia

Chapman & Hall India, R. Seshadri, 32 Second Main Road, CIT East,
Madras 600 035, India

First edition 1990
Second edition 1993

© 1990, 1993 John L. Thompson

Typeset in 10/12 pt Times by Photoprint, Torquay, Devon.
Printed in Great Britain at the Alden Press, Oxford

ISBN 0 412 46340 7

A catalogue record for this book is available from the British Library

Library of Congress Cataloging-in-Publication data

Thompson, John L.
    Strategic management : awareness and change / John L. Thompson.
– 2nd ed.
        p.   cm.
    Includes bibliographical references and indexes.
    ISBN 0–412–46340–7 (pbk.)
    1. Strategic planning. 2. Industrial management. I. Title.
HD30.28.T56   1993   92–44936
658.4′012–dc20   CIP

CONTENTS

Preface   xiii

Acknowledgements   xxiv

Part One **The Strategy Process**   **2**

1 Exploring strategic management   5

   Learning objectives   5
   Introduction   5
   The scope of strategic management   6
   Strategic management in perspective   7
   Aspects of strategic management   8
   E–V–R congruence   15
   Strategy statements   18
   The management of strategic change   18
   Strategic change in practice   23
   Summary   23
   Checklist of key terms and concepts   25
   Questions and research assignments   25
   References   30

2 A strategic management framework   31

   Learning objectives   31
   Introduction   31
   Models of strategic management   32
   The framework for the book   34
   Strategic leadership and values   38
   Applying the framework of questions   41
   Summary   44
   Research assignment   44
   Recommended further reading to Chapters 1 and 2   44

3 Strategic leadership and decision making   45

   Learning objectives   45
   Introduction   45
   Strategic leadership   46
   Risk   56

Decision making 61
Decision making and problem solving 61
Entrepreneurship 69
Summary 72
Checklist of key terms and concepts 75
Questions and research assignments 75
Recommended further reading 76
References 76

4 Culture and values 77

Learning objectives 77
Introduction 77
Culture and the organization 78
Culture and strategy creation 79
Culture, structure and styles of management 83
Culture and power 88
Determinants of culture 90
Aspects of culture 91
Levels of culture 92
The search for excellence 93
Changing culture 99
The Japanese culture 102
Summary 112
Checklist of key terms and concepts 112
Questions and research assignments 112
Recommended further reading 114
References 114

Interlude: Strategic awareness 116

Introduction to strategic awareness 117

Part Two **Situation Assessment** 118

5 Where are we going? 121

Learning objectives 121
Introduction 121
Definitions, terminology and examples 122
Mission statements 126
Objectives: what should they be; and what are they? 127
Objectives of not-for-profit organizations 140
The impact of personal objectives 145
Social responsibility and business ethics 149
Summary 155
Checklist of key terms and concepts 156
Questions and research assignments 156
Recommended further reading 156
References 157

6   How are we doing?   158

   Learning objectives   158
   Introduction   158
   How are we doing?   159
   Financial analysis   163
   The measurement of success in not-for-profit organizations 175
   Summary   178
   Checklist of key terms and concepts   180
   Questions and research assignments   180
   Recommended further reading   180
   References   181

7   Analysing competition   183

   Learning objectives   183
   Introduction   183
   Competition: an introduction   184
   Competition and the structure and regulation of industry
     in the United Kingdom   187
   Analysing an industry   198
   Competitive advantage   210
   Concluding comments   221
   Summary   224
   Checklist of key terms and concepts   225
   Questions and research assignments   225
   Recommended further reading   226
   References   226

8   What causes a company to fail?   227

   Learning objectives   227
   Introduction   227
   Symptoms of decline   228
   Causes of decline   229
   Predicting a failure   235
   Summary   235
   Questions and research assignments   235
   Recommended further reading   236
   References   236

Part Three   **Situation Analysis**   **238**

9   Where are our opportunities and threats?   247

   Learning objectives   247
   Introduction   247
   Understanding the environment   248

Managing the environment   259
The UK business environment   266
Do our resources match up well?   279
Summary   283
Checklist of key terms and concepts   284
Questions and research assignments   285
Recommended further reading   285
References   285

Resources and competitive advantage: an overview of Chapters 10–14   287

10   Marketing as a strategic resource   290

Learning objectives   290
Introduction   290
Understanding marketing   291
Understanding product and service management   295
The marketing mix   316
Marketing in service, not-for-profit and small businesses   320
Summary   321
Checklist of key terms and concepts   322
Questions and research assignments   322
Recommended further reading   323
References   323

11   Operations as a strategic resource   325

Learning objectives   325
Introduction   325
The strategic importance of operations   326
Marketing and operations management   327
Manufacturing management and strategy   333
Service businesses   340
Service and total quality management   343
Research and development and innovation   347
Summary   355
Checklist of key terms and concepts   355
Questions and research assignments   355
Recommended further reading   356
References   356

12   People as a strategic resource   358

Learning objectives   358
Introduction   358
Integrating people   359
Management and leadership   369
Summary   373
Checklist of key terms and concepts   374

Questions and assignments   374
Recommended further reading   374
References   375

13   Finance as a strategic resource   376

Learning objectives   376
Introduction   376
Financial strategy   377
Financing the business   378
Investments and capital budgeting   387
Finance and competitive advantage   397
Summary   400
Checklist of key terms and concepts   401
Questions and research assignments   401
Recommended further reading   402
References   402

14   Information as a strategic resource   403

Learning objectives   403
Introduction   403
Information, information systems and information technology   404
The impact of information systems and information technology
     on organizations   407
Information technology and competitive advantage   415
Information in context   424
Summary   424
Checklist of key terms and concepts   424
Questions and research assignments   425
Recommended further reading   425
References   425

15   Where is our competitive advantage?   427

Learning objectives   427
Introduction   427
The value chain   429
The value chain and competitive advantage   434
Speed and competitive advantage   439
Summary   442
Checklist of key terms and concepts   443
Questions and research assignments   443
References   444

Interlude: Strategic change   446

Introduction to strategic change   447

Part Four   **Changes in Corporate Strategy**   **450**

16   Where do we want to go?   453

   Learning objectives   453
   Introduction   453
   Planning and planning systems   456
   Strategic planning techniques   468
   Strategy formulation   474
   Strategic change and systems thinking   482
   Strategy statements   489
   Summary   491
   Checklist of key terms and concepts   492
   Questions and research assignments   492
   Recommended further reading   493
   References   493

17   What strategic alternatives are available?   494

   Learning objectives   494
   Introduction   494
   The do-nothing alternative   496
   Internal growth strategies   496
   External growth strategies   501
   Disinvestment strategies   506
   The international alternative   510
   Strategic means   515
   The selection of a strategy   519
   Summary   520
   Checklist of key terms and concepts   520
   Questions and research assignments   520
   References   522

18   Growth strategies: diversification, acquisition and joint venture   523

   Learning objectives   523
   Introduction   523
   Diversification and acquisition by UK companies   525
   Research into diversification and acquisition   531
   Effective acquisition strategies   537
   Joint ventures and strategic alliances   545
   Summary   550
   Checklist of key terms and concepts   550
   Questions and research assignments   551
   Recommended further reading   552
   References   552

19   Recovery, recession and divestment strategies   553

   Learning objectives   553
   Introduction   553
   The feasibility of recovery   554

Retrenchment strategies   559
Turnaround strategies   560
Divestment strategies   563
Managing in a recession   568
Strategies for declining industries   569
Implementing recovery strategies   572
Summary   572
Checklist of key terms and concepts   573
Questions and research assignments   573
Recommended further reading   573
References   573

20   Management buy-outs   574

Learning objectives   574
Introduction   574
Management buy-outs in the United Kingdom   576
The parties involved and their expectations   580
Financing a buy-out   583
Management buy-ins   587
Summary   590
Checklist of key terms and concepts   590
Questions and research assignments   590
Recommended further reading   591
References   591

21   What constitutes a good choice?   592

Learning objectives   592
Introduction   592
Strategy evaluation   593
Criteria for effective strategies   596
Judgement   603
Summary   606
Checklist of key terms and concepts   608
Questions and research assignments   608
Recommended further reading   608
References   608

Part Five   **Strategy Implementation**   **610**

22   Strategy and structure   621

Learning objectives   621
Introduction   621
Structural forms   623
Structure: determinants and design   645
Structure and styles of management: management style at the corporate level   655
Structure and styles of management: the role of general managers   657

Measuring and rewarding performance   661
Summary   662
Checklist of key terms and concepts   663
Questions and research assignments   663
Recommended further reading   664
References   664

23   Resource management and control   666

Learning objectives   666
Introduction   666
The operational aspects of strategy implementation   667
Corporate resource planning   670
Functional resource planning: an introduction   672
Policies, procedures, plans and budgets   675
Allocating resources   680
Issues of measurement and control systems   684
Crisis management   690
Summary   694
Checklist of key terms and concepts   695
Questions and research assignments   695
Recommended further reading   696
References   696

24   Managing change   697

Learning objectives   697
Introduction   697
Issues in the management of change   698
Strategies for implementation and change   709
Power and politics   717
Summary   725
Checklist of key terms and concepts   726
Questions and research assignments   726
Recommended further reading   726
References   727

25   Final thoughts   728

Learning objectives   728
The major themes   729
Essential aspects of corporate strength   730
Strategic effectiveness   732
Final thoughts: the challenge for the future   733
References   733

Author index   735
Subject index   739

PREFACE

This preface outlines the content and approach of this book and explains how it is appropriate both for managers and for students who will become future managers. There are suggestions about how different types of reader might make effective use of the material.

STRATEGIC AWARENESS AND CHANGE

This book is about strategic awareness and the management of strategic change. It looks at how managers can become strategically aware of their company's position and opportunities for change; at how changes often happen in reality; and at how the process might be managed more effectively.

It is in five parts. The first part looks at the strategy process as a whole and includes in Chapter 2 a comprehensive framework of the process, around which the book is structured. This part also includes chapters on strategic leadership and decision making and on culture and values as these are forces which determine how strategy is managed within organizations.

Parts II and III comprise a study of strategic awareness, and Parts IV and V relate to issues involved in strategic change. Part II, entitled 'Situation assessment', analyses where the organization is going by considering objectives; how well the company is performing, and how success might be measured; how competition and competitiveness can be evaluated; and what causes companies to fail.

Part III considers how a situation analysis might be carried out. The emphasis is on understanding the firm's environment and its resources. The functional subjects which relate to the management of organizational resources and which under-pin a study of **competitive** strategy, namely marketing, operations, human resources and finance, are examined. Whilst these subjects are normally studied separately, it is my experience that many students fail to integrate them. In addition they often fail to relate the strategic aspects of these functional areas to their studies of strategic management and to the strategy cases they analyse as part of their studies. Therefore chapters on these functional subjects are included in the book,

---

The manager's job is change. It is what we live with. It is what we are to create. If we cannot do that, then we are not good at the job. It is our basic job to have the nerve to keep changing and changing and changing again.

Sir Peter Parker, Executive Chairman, Rockware Group, speaking at a BIM Workshop in London, February 1986

---

together with a chapter on information and information technology.

Part IV is a consideration of how changes in **corporate** strategy are formulated, followed by a study of the various strategic alternatives which a firm might consider and the determinants of a good choice.

The issues involved in strategy implementation are evaluated in Part V. Organization structures, resource management and the complexities of managing change are included. Pressures to change are always present in the form of opportunities and threats. At any point in time the significance of these pressures will vary markedly from industry to industry and from organization to organization. Managers may be aware of them and seek to respond positively; they may recognize opportunities and threats and choose to do little about them other than perhaps to avert crises; or they may be totally unaware of them. A lack of awareness can mean that potentially good opportunities are also lost; it may mean businesses fail if they are not able to react and respond to the threats and problems when they arise. Whilst all businesses must react to pressures from the environment such as supply shortages, new products from competitors or new retailing opportunities, some will be very proactive and thereby seek to manage their environment.

It must be emphasized that no single approach, model or theory can explain the realities of strategic change in practice for all organizations; different organizations and managers will find certain approaches much more relevant to their circumstances and style. All approaches will have both supporters and critics. It is therefore important to study the various approaches within a sound intellectual framework so that they can be

---

Box 1
KEY TERMS

MISSION The essential purpose of the organization, concerning particularly why it is in existence, the nature of the business(es) it is in, and the customers it seeks to serve and satisfy.

OBJECTIVES (or **GOALS**) are desired states or results linked to particular time-scales and concerning such things as size or type of organization, the nature and variety of the areas of interest, and levels of success.

STRATEGIES The MEANS by which organizations meet, or seek to meet, OBJECTIVES. There can be a strategy for each product or service, and an overall strategy for the organization.

STRATEGIC MANAGEMENT is the process by which an organization establishes its objectives, formulates actions designed to achieve these objectives in the desired time-scale, implements the actions and assesses progress and results.

STRATEGIC CHANGE concerns changes which take place over time to the strategies and objectives of the organization. Change can be gradual or evolutionary; or more dramatic, even revolutionary.

STRATEGIC AWARENESS is the understanding of managers within the organization about (a) the strategies being followed by the organization and its competitors, (b) how the effectiveness of these strategies might be improved and (c) the need for, and suitability of, opportunities for change.

Box 2
EXAMPLES OF STRATEGY C

Lex Service Group, sizeable dis[
Austin Rover, Rolls Royce and Vo
the main, felt too dependent on o
business and sought to find suitabl
cation opportunities. Lex chose fo
star hotels in the UK and USA but [
to sell them when the results were
desired.

W H Smith, desiring growth b[
scope offered from its current bu[
(wholesaling and retailing of news[
magazines; stationery; books an[
diversified into do-it-yourself with
Do-It-All stores, introduced trave[
into a number of its existing [
acquired related interests in C[
America. Travel has since been divested,
along with investments in cable television, to
enable greater concentration on books,
sounds and videos.

The Burton Group sold the last of its
manufacturing interests in 1988. Once one of

problems and situations which this book w[
cover, Box 2 gives some examples of str[
changes which have occurred in[
notable firms or industry secto[
detailed analysis or discussion o[
ples will be found in later ch[

**DIFFERENT VIEW[
MANAGEMENT[**

Early stra[
sequenti[
where[
tio[

National Bus Company was privatized
during the mid-1980s mostly by splitting it
into small local or regional companies which
were bought out by their existing management teams.

evaluated by readers and students. The
framework developed for this book encourages an assessment and evaluation of what
happens in practice against a more theoretical
model of how the total process of strategic
change might be managed. This framework,
built around a series of logical questions, is
outlined briefly below and fully explained in
Chapter 2.

Practising managers and students of business and management must work out for
themselves the intricacies and difficulties of
managing organizations at the corporate level
and of managing strategic change. It is no
good being told how to be prescriptive when
it is patently obvious that there is no univer-

sal model. Observations of practice in isolation are equally limited in their usefulness.
However, an attempt to find explanations
which can be utilized does make sense.
Testing and evaluating reality against a theoretical framework helps this process.

Preliminary definitions of key terms which
will be used in the book are presented in Box
1. These terms are explained or discussed in
much more detail in later chapters, but since
they will necessarily be used on several
occasions in the preface and early chapters it
will be useful to have brief working definitions for you to refer to at this point.

Strategic management is a rich and diverse
field. As a foretaste of the sort of issues,

ll
tegy
some
rs. More
these exam-
pters.

S OF STRATEGIC

egy theory concentrated on
models of corporate planning
by sound forecasting enabled organiza-
s to set realistic objectives and then to
valuate strategies to achieve them. Such
models implied that organizations could and
should manage change; but they were criticized for concentrating on planning and for
ignoring, to a large extent, how the plans
would be implemented. In other words the
managerial aspects were not sufficiently considered, mainly because the planning was
often carried out by specialist planners who
'sold' their plans to the board.

Nevertheless, corporate planning was
popular in the 1960s. The period enjoyed
economic stability and planners were able to
convince both themselves and their directors
that they could predict the future several
years ahead. The oil crisis of 1973 proved
them wrong. The outcome was that corporate
planning was criticized as organizations
found themselves in turbulent change and
long-range plans were of little use.

One important method to emerge from the
early approaches was SWOT (strengths,
weaknesses, opportunities, threats) analysis,
and the usefulness of this has endured. The
organization's resources (its strengths and
weaknesses) are evaluated alongside the
external environment (the source of opportunities and threats) before finalizing objectives
and strategies. This approach encourages
the view that strategic management is
about managing the external environment,
which might well be dynamic, complex and
uncertain. Whilst the fit between an organization and its environment is very important, it must not be overlooked that decisions
concerning change may be stimulated internally rather than as the result of external
pressures.

During the 1970s a number of other techniques for strategic analysis emerged, including the Boston Consulting Group Matrix,
PIMS (Profit Impact of Market Strategy) and
Porter's work on industry analysis and competitive strategy. All these will be discussed
in later chapters.

The emphasis of these has been termed
'market oriented' for they require an organization clearly to address the question 'what
business(es) are we in?' and to seek to satisfy
the needs of their market(s). Emphasis is
placed on the appropriate management of
products and services at different stages in
their lives and on how they compete within
particular industries.

These are valuable tools of analysis, but
they ignore many aspects of implementation.
Some authors prefer instead to consider
strategic management from a process viewpoint. In particular they look at how strategic
decisions are made, at how changes arise and
at the values that are fundamental to the
most successful companies. Inevitably process approaches are more anecdotal than
prescriptive – they consider what does happen in practice rather than suggest ways of
managing an organization strategically.

A FRAMEWORK FOR THIS BOOK

When planning this book I found it useful to
develop a series of questions which strategists should be asking as they analyse their
company's position and formulate strategy.
These questions have provided a framework,
or model, which has suggested an order and
structure for the subject matter of the book.
The framework of questions is given in
Figure 1. It is explained and expanded in
Chapter 2.

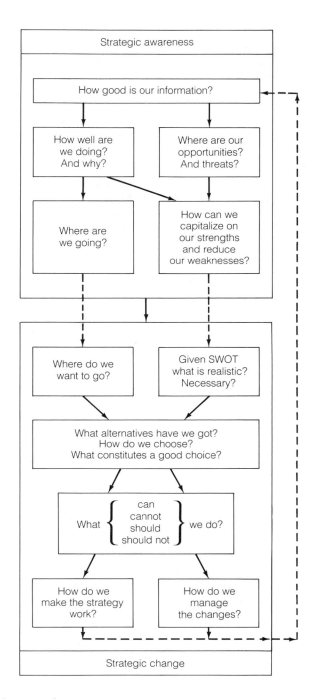

Figure 1 A strategy framework.

All that needs to be said at this stage is that the process suggested by the framework or model should be seen as a series of iterations, involving constant re-assessment of whether the objectives and strategies are appropriate. Whilst the questions can be presented in a logical order, and followed through as a decision-making process, the model illustrated in Figure 1 also represents a 'picture' of the organization at any time which effective managers will be constantly up-dating. This point is expanded later in the Preface.

CHANGES FOR THE SECOND EDITION

Strategic management is a complex and dynamic subject, and since the first edition of this book was published a number of new ideas have emerged. In addition, certain practices and priorities have changed to reflect developments around the world, particularly in Europe, and the economic recession of the early 1990s. These changes have been incorporated into this second edition. The whole text has been reviewed, and some chapters substantially rewritten, but the basic structure of the book has remained the same.

Feedback on the first edition from my students and from teachers in many universities and polytechnics has been most positive and helpful, and several valuable suggestions have been made. As a result, the second edition has a more international focus and the number of short case studies has been increased substantially. The model of E–V–R Congruence (environment–values–resources), introduced in Chapter 1 has been developed and used as a more central theme throughout the text. The major additions are listed below:

☐ Chapter 1: outline of key strategic challenges for the 1990s – developed through text
☐ Chapter 3: new section on corporate governance

☐ Chapter 4: section on 'organizational philosophies' added to the culture debate
☐ Chapter 5: strengthened sections on the long-termism versus short-termism debate, and on ethics and environmental issues
☐ Chapter 6: new key concept box on efficiency and effectiveness to strengthen treatment of this topic; more material on performance measures in service businesses and privatized organizations
☐ Chapter 7: new section on deregulation; assessment of latest work by Porter on international competitive advantage
☐ More comprehensive section on synergy
☐ Chapter 9: up-dated to take more account of the issues raised by 1992 in Europe
☐ Chapter 10: new section on the value of branding in marketing and strategy
☐ Chapter 11: stronger on service and total quality management
☐ Chapter 12: rewritten to include more on performance management and the hard versus soft human resource management debate
☐ Chapter 13: new section on re-structuring strategies and the breaking up of conglomerates
☐ Chapter 15: new section on speed and competitive advantage
☐ Chapter 16: up-dated section on strategic management in local government
☐ Chapter 17: stronger section on international strategies
☐ Chapter 18: more up-to-date treatment of strategic alliances and joint ventures
☐ Chapter 19: new section on managing in a recession
☐ Chapter 21: small section on judgement added to this chapter on strategy selection
☐ Chapter 22: new key concept box on empowerment; more detailed treatment of control issues
☐ Chapter 23: new section on crisis management; lengthier discussion of performance measurement
☐ Chapter 24: evaluation of the learning organization

In addition a Lecturer's Resource Manual has been developed to accompany the second edition. This book, available from the publishers and free to lecturers adopting the text, includes a selection of full-length cases, industry and competitive analyses, strategic leader profiles and longer discussions on contemporary issues in specific contexts. OHP slide masters for the most important diagrams are also provided.

THE AUDIENCE FOR THIS BOOK

The main purpose of the book is to help managers, and students who aim to become managers, (a) to develop their strategic awareness, (b) to increase their understanding of how the functional areas of management (in which they are most likely to work) contribute to strategic management and to strategic changes within organizations and (c) to appreciate how strategic change is managed in organizations.

The content is broad and the treatment is both academic and practical, in order to provide value for practising managers as well as full- and part-time students. The subject matter included is taught in a wide variety of courses including courses for the MBA and other postgraduate master's degrees, courses for the DMS and other post-experience management courses, courses for a number of professional qualifications, undergraduate courses in business studies and related areas and BTEC Higher National Diploma courses. The subject can be entitled strategic management, business policy, corporate strategy, business planning, organizational policy or managerial analysis.

The material is relevant for all types of organizations: large and small businesses, manufacturing and service organizations, and both the public and private sectors. The examples included relate to all of these. Although the topics discussed are broadly applicable, there are certain issues which are sector-specific, and these are discussed individually.

KEY FEATURES OF THE BOOK

Learning Objectives.   At the beginning of each chapter I have listed the main tasks which you should have mastered by the end of the chapter.

Key Concepts.   The most significant concepts which under-pin an understanding of strategic management and change are featured separately within the relevant chapter for special emphasis and easy reference.

Key Readings.   A selection of important ideas from leading writers on strategy have been summarized and presented separately as key readings.

Cases.   In addition to numerous references in the main text to organizations and events, over 100 short case examples are included. These relate to a wide variety of organization types from throughout the world. Inevitably some of the cases will 'date' in the sense that the strategies and fortunes of the companies featured in the examples will change. Strategies have life cycles, and strategies which prove effective at certain times will not always remain so. Companies who fail to change their strategies at the right time are likely to experience declining fortunes. Occasionally I have included questions at the ends of chapters which encourage you to research and analyse the subsequent fortunes of companies included as cases. The cases are designed to illustrate points in the main text. They are also intended to supplement your own experiences and reading.

Quotations.   Short and pithy quotations from a variety of senior managers in the private and the public sectors are sprinkled throughout the text to illustrate a spectrum of opinions. These are useful for provoking class discussion and examination questions.

Checklist of Key Terms and Concepts.   At the end of every chapter there is a summary of the chapter content and a checklist of key terms and concepts. This is included to enable you to evaluate whether you understand the main points covered in the chapter before moving on.

Questions and Research Assignments.   These questions relate to the ideas contained in the text and the illustrative cases, and some are examples of the type that feature in non-case-study examinations of this subject. A number of research assignments, mostly library based, are included to encourage you to develop your knowledge and understanding further. The library-based assignments assume access to a library in the UK. Lecturers in other countries will be able to advise students on similar, more local, companies which can be substituted and researched.

The book itself does not contain any long case studies. Whilst I believe that these are an essential feature of most teaching programmes on the subject, lecturers typically have their own preferred cases, many of which they will have written themselves. However, a selection are included in the support pack. The short cases included are ideal for illustrating the main points in the text, and the book provides an ideal back-up for teachers who concentrate on using case studies.

HOW TO USE THE BOOK

Strategic management is concerned with understanding, as well as choosing and implementing, the strategy or strategies that an organization follows. It is a complex process which can be considered from a number of different perspectives. For example one can design prescriptive models based upon a series of logical stages which look at how to choose and implement strategies aimed at achieving some form of long-term success for the organization. This is a systematic approach designed to bring about optimum results. An alternative paradigm, or conceptual framework, is a systemic approach which concerns understanding what is happening in reality and thinking about how things might be improved. The emphasis is on learning about how strategic management is practised by looking at what organizations actually do and by examining the decisions they make and carry out.

In this book we consider both these perspectives, linking them together. Whilst it is always useful to develop models which attempt to provide optimizing solutions, this approach is inadequate if it fails to explain reality. Strategic management and strategic change are dynamic, often the result of responses to environmental pressures, and requently not the product of extensive deliberations involving all affected managers.

Managers should be aware of the issues and questions which must be addressed if changes in strategy are to be formulated and implemented effectively. At the same time they should be aware of the managerial and behavioural processes which take place within organizations in order that they can understand how changes actually come about.

Prescriptive models are in fact found quite frequently in business and management teaching. For example, there are models for rational decision making built around the clear recognition and definition of a problem and the careful and objective analysis and evaluation of the alternative solutions. There are economic models of various market structures showing how an organization can maximize profit. However, decision making invariably involves subjectivity and short-cutting; and organizations do not always seek profit maximization as their top priority. Although organizations and individuals rarely follow these models slavishly – quite often they cannot, and sometimes they choose not to – this does not render them worthless. Far from it; they provide an excellent framework or yardstick for evaluating how people reach their decisions, what objectives are being pursued and how situations might be improved. The argument is that if managers observe what is happening and seek to explain it and evaluate it against some more ideal state then they will see ways of managing things more effectively. In this way managerial performance can be improved. Note the use of the expression 'more effectively'. For a whole variety of reasons situations cannot be managed 'perfectly'.

You will probably have personal experience of organizations, management and change. This experience might be limited or extensive, broad or specialized. You should use this experience to complement the examples and cases described in the book. Ideally the experience and the cases will be used jointly to evaluate the theories and concepts discussed. There is no universal approach to the management of strategy and strategic change. You must establish for yourself what approaches and decisions are likely to prove most effective in particular circumstances, and why. This is a learning experience which can be enhanced (a) by evaluating the theoretical and conceptual contributions of various authors, (b) by considering practical examples of what has proved successful and unsuccessful for organizations and (c) by examining these two aspects in combination to see which theories and concepts best help an understanding of reality.

Managers perform a number of activities, including planning and organizing the work of their subordinates, motivating them, controlling what happens and evaluating results.

All managers are planners to some degree; and it is extremely useful if they can develop an ability to observe clearly what is really happening in organizations and reflect on how things might be improved. Kolb (1979) calls this the learning cycle, and it can be usefully applied to a study of strategic management and change. Managers and students build on their own experiences when they read about theories and concepts and think about case study examples. They should reflect upon all these experiences continually and seek to develop personal concepts which best explain for them what happens in practice. Wherever appropriate they should experiment with, and test out, these concepts to establish how robust they are. This, of course, constitutes added experience for further reflection. In other words:

$$\text{experience} \rightarrow \text{reflection} \rightarrow \text{theory}$$
$$\searrow \qquad \qquad \nearrow$$
$$\text{pragmatism and experimentation}$$

This approach is illustrated in more detail in Figure 2. Experiences, theories and concepts generate awareness. This, with reflection, improves understanding. Constant evalu-

---

I believe the single most important contribution to competitiveness is the ability of managers and management to *think strategically* about the business or businesses they are in. Although this capability is vital for general management, functional management should also be encouraged and trained in this approach at an early stage in their careers so that they can both contribute to the overall strategic assessment of a business or group of businesses and understand the key objectives.

Sir Trevor Holdsworth, when Group Chairman,
Guest Keen & Nettlefolds plc

Quoted in *Improving Managerial Performance,* BIM and Professional Publishing, 1985

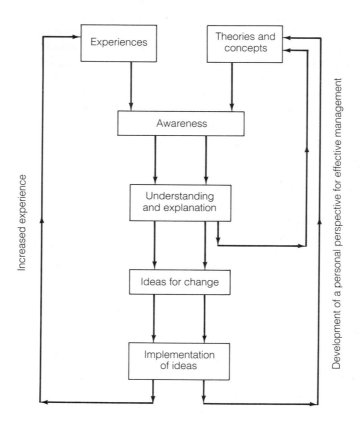

Figure 2   A learning cycle for strategic management.

This approach is illustrated in more detail in Figure 2. Experiences, theories and concepts generate awareness. This, with reflection, improves understanding. Constant evaluation helps develop a personal perspective of effective management. This process is enhanced by trying out ideas which generate new experiences.

Finally it is important to point out that students of strategic management may not be, or may not become, key strategic decision makers in their organizations but instead may specialize in one particular function, perhaps marketing, perhaps production or finance. Similarly their experience may be with only one product or one division of

Experience is a wonderful thing, but not a useful one; when you are young, you don't trust others' experience, and if you trust it, this paralyses you; when you get old, it is too late to use it, and you cannot transmit it for the reasons quoted before.

Jacques Calvet, Le Président du Directoire,
PSA Peugeot Citroën

a multi-product or multi-divisional organization. Nevertheless the decisions they make or contribute to can affect the strategy for a particular product or service and in turn affect the organization. It is vital that they appreciate exactly how their function operates within an organizational context, and how decisions made in their area of interest can affect both other functions and the organization as a whole.

REFERENCE

Kolb, D A (1979) *Organizational Psychology*, Prentice Hall.

ACKNOWLEDGEMENTS

It is impossible to acknowledge individually everyone who has contributed to this book; and I am indebted to numerous teachers, colleagues and past and present students for providing me with ideas and for helping me to develop the perspective for, and revise the content of, *Strategic Management: Awareness and Change*. I would specifically like to thank the following people. Linda Bennett, a past student, and now a colleague at Huddersfield who gave me a detailed appraisal of the book from a user's point of view; Jeremy Swinfen Green, who, whilst at Chapman and Hall, encouraged me to tackle a second edition and provided valuable feedback on the first edition; Mark Wellings, also of Chapman and Hall, for helping me to develop the text; and, finally, my wife Hilary for her constant support and also for working long hours to allow me the space and opportunity to write.

PART ONE

Good management is the means by which a leader creates a united team which achieves agreed objectives within the required time and with economy in the use of resources . . .

Good management exists when:

☐ the organization has defined its purpose
☐ in order to achieve its purpose, objectives have been determined for the organization and for its constituent parts
☐ strategy and policies are determined and formulated for obtaining these objectives
☐ plans and targets are set for the achievement of these objectives
☐ responsibilities and accountability are clearly defined
☐ progress is monitored, and action taken as necessary, to ensure achievement within defined timescales and allocated resources.

(British Institute of Management)

Quotations taken from *Improving Management Performance: Report of a BIM Panel*, BIM and Professional Publishing, 1985.

I think one of our problems as a nation is that we are apt to be somewhat complacent. We have been content with things as they are and have not been aware sufficiently early of progress and changes taking place in other countries which are going to result in their over-taking us if we don't change ourselves. In business one has constantly to be looking at ways of adapting to change in terms of technology, marketing, and possibly also financial structure. We need to see opportunities developing and take bold steps to ensure that we are in the vanguard of change. This requires vision and courage, and good communication with shopfloor people so that they understand the benefits of change, and welcome new technology and new working practices with enthusiasm.

Sir Hector Laing, Chairman, United Biscuits plc

THE STRATEGY PROCESS

Organizations, their strategies, their structures and the management of them become ever more complex. Among the reasons for this are the increasing turbulence and propensity to change in the business environment, and the tendency for multi-product multi-national organizations to become commonplace. Organizations need to know where they are, where they are going and how to manage the changes. Managers in these organizations need to know where their roles fit in relation to the whole and how they can contribute to strategic developments and changes. These are the issues addressed by a study of strategic management.

This first part is designed to provide a broad appreciation of strategic management and to develop the framework used in the book. Specifically the objectives are:

- [ ] to outline the scope and complexity of the study area;
- [ ] to provide an initial overview of some major contributors to the subject in order to illustrate what is meant by, and included in, strategic management, and to show that there is no single universally accepted approach;
- [ ] to develop a framework, built around simple questions, which will provide a model for the structure and content of the book;
- [ ] to illustrate and discuss the importance of strategic leadership and decision making, and culture and values, in every aspect of strategic management.

A number of issues and topics will be raised and discussed in brief in Chapters 1 and 2 and will then be explored in greater depth in the following chapters.

EXPLORING STRATEGIC MANAGEMENT

1

LEARNING OBJECTIVES

After studying this chapter you should be able to

☐ define strategic management and strategic change;
☐ explain what is meant by E–V–R congruence;
☐ define key success factors and give examples of these;
☐ explain the term competitive advantage;
☐ distinguish between corporate, competitive and functional strategies;
☐ summarize briefly the views of a number of strategy authors;
☐ identify a simple framework for an outline strategy statement.

In this chapter we develop a deeper understanding of the subject and scope of strategic management and explore what is involved in managing the strategies of an organization.

INTRODUCTION

The need for all managers to be able to think strategically was stressed in the Preface, and the approach taken in this book concentrates on the development of strategic awareness. While strategic management incorporates major changes of direction, such as diversification and growth overseas, for the whole business, it also involves smaller changes in the strategies for individual products and services and in particular functions such as marketing and operations. Decisions by managers in relation to their particular areas of product or functional responsibility have a strategic impact and contribute to strategic change.

There are three aspects to strategic management: firstly the **strategy** itself, which is concerned with the establishment of a clear direction for the organization and a means of getting there, and which requires the creation of strong competitive positions; secondly **excellence** in the implementation of strategies in order to yield effective performance; thirdly **innovation** to ensure that the organization is responsive to pressures for change and that strategies are improved and renewed.

Strategic management builds upon studies of individual management functions, seeking to integrate them so that managers in one part of the business consider the implications of their decisions for other activities and managers. Strategic management is normally taught as a capstone subject on a variety of business and management courses, drawing widely upon other subject areas, studied previously, and seeking to integrate them.

Important themes, introduced here and developed later in the book are:

☐ strategic leadership and organization culture
☐ environmental fit
☐ corporate, competitive and functional strategies
☐ competitive advantage
☐ key success factors and core competencies
☐ E–V–R (environment–values–resources) congruence
☐ the management of strategic change.

THE SCOPE OF STRATEGIC MANAGEMENT

Constable (1980) has defined the area addressed by strategic management as 'the management processes and decisions which determine the long-term structure and activities of the organization'. This definition incorporates five key themes.

Management processes. Management processes relate to how strategies at all levels are created and changed. The term encompasses both formal structured processes (the prescriptive approach) and informal unstructured processes (how strategies emerge through gradual change). It incorporates planning activities as well as manager intuition, and it is dependent on the values held by the managers, their ability to spot oppor-

tunities for, and threats to, the organization in a changing environment and their ways of managing the organization's resources to deal with these.

Management decisions. Information is an input into the processes, and decisions are an output. But the decisions, to be valuable, must relate clearly to a solution of perceived problems (how to avoid a threat; how to capitalize on an opportunity). They also require support from other managers and they must be capable of implementation – the requisite resources must be available.

Time-scales. The definition above uses the expression 'long-term' but what is long term? The strategic time horizon for a company in real trouble can be very short; the strategic investment decisions made by the Central Electricity Generating Board looked more than 10 years ahead.

Structure of the organization. An organization is managed by people within a structure. Issues of how functions are related to each other and of whether power is centralized or decentralized are important. The structure can be designed and changed to ensure that desired changes in strategy can be implemented effectively; but the decisions which result from the way that managers work together within the structure can result in strategic change.

Activities of the organization. This is a potentially limitless area of study. We shall normally focus on products or services and markets and examine such issues as vertical integration in particular product areas, the degree, scope and pace of diversification and the relative desirability and potential for internal development and acquisition to achieve growth and/or diversification. This theme encapsulates the organization's attitudes towards the various stakeholders – shareholders, employees, financial institutions, customers, suppliers – which affect the priorities attached to certain activities.

STRATEGIC MANAGEMENT IN PERSPECTIVE

It is worth mentioning that strategic management is not something that British companies are thought to be very good at. In the last 40 or so years, Britain has performed less well industrially than many of her major competitors in a number of key sectors. This conclusion has been reached by measuring such factors as relative world and European market shares won by British companies, investment expenditure, productivity and the proportion of revenue allocated for research and development. A lack of marketing skills, low productivity, inadequate investment and poor management generally have all been identified as causes, but in many cases these have actually improved in the last few years. Another important aspect is the general failure to assess properly how to compete best.

Discussing this theme, Peter Beck, the Chairman of the British Strategic Planning Society during 1984–6, was critical of British companies as a whole:

Far too many companies either have no goals at all, other than cost reduction, or their boss hides them in his head. There's no hope for companies in Britain unless more top managements accept the need for a widely communicated set of clear objectives.

(Beck, 1987)

Strategic clarity is absent, Beck argues, for essentially three reasons: the difficulties of forecasting in today's business environment (but difficulty is no excuse for not trying!); the lack of managerial competence in many companies; and above all the frequent absence of strong leadership from the top.

Part of the problem is the distinction between established views hostile towards the formal and elaborate strategic planning systems that were in vogue during the 1960s and 1970s, but which failed to work in many cases, and the idea of 'strategic thinking'. It is perfectly possible for any organization to address a number of key questions about how well the company is doing, and why, and where it should seek to develop in the future, and how. It will be argued in this book that the most successful companies strategically are likely to be those that are aware of where they are and of what lies ahead, those that understand their environment and those that seek to achieve and maintain competitive advantage. By way of illustration the following points have been developed from a *Financial Times* article (Morrison and Lee, 1979).

Whatever their strategy, companies that are adept at strategic thinking seem to be distinguished from their less successful competitors by a common pattern of management practices.

☐ First, they identify more effectively than their competitors the key success factors inherent in the economics of each business. For example, in the airline industry, with its high fixed costs and relatively inflexible route allocations, a high load factor is critical to success. A certain pack-

---

The flame of competition has changed from smokey yellow to intense white heat. For companies to survive and prosper they will have to have a vision, a mission and strategy. They will pursue the action arising from that strategy with entrepreneurial skill and total dedication and commitment to win.

Peter B Ellwood, Chief Executive, TSB Group

age tour operator achieves a high load factor by limiting his product line (although many travel operators do exactly the opposite), choosing high density routes, consolidating under-subscribed tours and using special price deals to fill marginal capacity. He achieves a higher load factor than his competitors and his business is profitable.

☐ Second, they segment their markets so as to gain decisive competitive advantage. The strategic thinker bases his market segmentation on competitive analysis. Thus he may separate segments according to the strengths and weaknesses of different competitors. This enables him to concentrate on segments where he can both maximize his own competitive advantage and avoid head-on competition with stronger competitors.

☐ Third, successful companies base their strategies on the measurement and analysis of competitive advantage. Essential to this is a sound basis for assessing a company's advantages relative to its competitors.

☐ Fourth, they anticipate their competitors' responses. Good strategic thinking also implies an understanding of how situations will change over time. Business strategy, like military strategy, is a matter of manoeuvring for superior position and anticipating how competitors will respond, and with what measure of success.

☐ Fifth, they exploit more, or different, degrees of freedom than do their competitors. They seek to stay ahead of their rivals by looking for new competitive opportunities.

☐ Finally, they give investment priority to businesses (or areas) that promise a competitive advantage.

Challenges

There are a number of major challenges for organizations in the 1990s:

☐ The need for many businesses to develop a culture of change orientation without losing internal cohesion and stability. This implies an explicit and shared vision of where the organization is heading.

☐ The need to decentralize and give managers more delegated authority whilst not losing sight (at chief executive level) of the changes they are introducing.

☐ The trade-off between such empowerment (designed to make the business more effective in its relations with all its stakeholders) and the greater efficiencies often yielded by centralized control and systems which harness the latest information technology.

☐ The need to act quickly in response to opportunities and threats, but not at the expense of product and service quality – achieving high quality at the same time as cutting costs and improving efficiencies.

These four challenges are all related.

☐ Finally, the dilemma of the recession. Organizations must cut back, control their costs and accept lower margins as supply potential exceeds demand in many industries. Profits fall. Paradoxically those organizations which are able to consolidate and invest strategically during the recession will be best prepared for the economic up-turn.

ASPECTS OF STRATEGIC MANAGEMENT

Strategic leadership

It has been pointed out that a major aim of this book is to encourage readers to be more strategically aware. Long-term strategic success requires that the efforts of managers are co-ordinated. This is the task of the Chief Executive or Managing Director of the whole organization and in turn of general managers of subsidiaries or divisions in the case of large complex organizations. For simplicity in this book we shall use the term strategic leader to refer to this role. The theme of strategic leadership is the subject of Chapter 3, whilst Chapter 22 considers the specific role of general managers of subsidiaries and divisions.

The role is analogous to that of the captain of a ship. In a sailing race, for example, the captain must sail the ship possibly in uncertain or dangerous waters, with one or more clear goals in sight. His chosen strategy or strategies will be decided upon in the light of these goals, and the risks of any actions will be assessed. Nevertheless the captain's success will depend upon the crew. It is vital that the crew act in a co-ordinated way, and therefore it is crucial that the strategies are communicated and understood.

Lee Iacocca, who became chairman of the Chrysler Corporation in America in the early 1980s and succeeded in turning it round, provides a useful example. Chrysler, faced with competition from General Motors, Ford and Japan, was nearly bankrupt and had lost its way. Iacocca changed some of his crew, but essentially his success lay in persuading his managers to think about how to succeed in the 1980s and to forget the strategies of the 1960s and 1970s. Cars were re-designed, marketing was improved, labour costs were lowered, productivity and quality were improved and government support was obtained. Chrysler recovered.

The strategic leader must build and lead a team of managers – and establish the goals or objectives. Styles will vary enormously, as will the scope of the objectives. Some leaders will be autocratic, others entrepreneurial. Some, arguably like Henry Ford of Ford Motor Company and Ray Kroc who started McDonald's, will be visionaries; others will set more modest goals.

The leader and his or her managers should be clear about where the organization is going, where they want to go and how they are going to get there. This requires an appreciation of the environment and an understanding of the organization's resources.

Environmental fit

Several authors have defined strategy in terms of the relationship between an organization and its environment. One such definition is:

The positioning and relating of the firm/ organization to its environment in a way which will assure its continued success and make it secure from surprises. (Ansoff, 1984)

Figure 1.1, which takes an open systems perspective and considers the organization in the context of its environment, illustrates the implications. The organization draws its resources (employees, managers, plant, supplies, finance etc.) from a competitive business environment. It has to compete with other firms for labour, supplies, loans etc. It must then use these inputs in some organized way to produce products and services which can be marketed effectively and in many cases profitably. It must succeed in a competitive marketplace. As well as appreciating market demand and the strengths, weaknesses and strategies of its competitors, it must also respond to fundamental changes in society and the economy. Over time people's tastes change, their discretionary purchasing power rises and falls, luxuries can become necessities and previously popular products can become unfashionable. The economy is not static, and it is strongly affected by government policy. Whilst some companies influence government policy, many do not.

Therefore strategic management involves the following:

☐ a clear awareness of environmental forces and the ways in which they are changing;
☐ an appreciation of potential and future threats and opportunities;

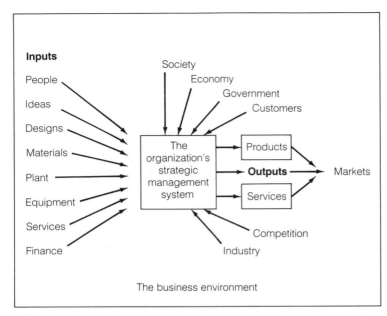

Figure 1.1   The strategic perspective. This model has been adapted from one used by the General Electric Co., USA.

☐ decisions upon appropriate products and services for clearly defined markets;
☐ the effective management of resources to develop and produce these products for the market – achieving the right quality for the right price at the right time.

Functional, competitive and corporate strategies

Organizations choose to produce one or more related or unrelated products or services for one or more markets or market segments. The organization itself should be structured to encompass this range of product markets or service markets. As the number and diversity of products increases the structure is likely to be centred upon divisions which are typically referred to as **strategic business units** (SBUs). SBUs are responsible individually for developing, manufacturing and marketing their own product or group of products. Each SBU will therefore have a

strategy, which Porter (1980) calls a competitive strategy.

Competitive strategy is concerned with 'creating and maintaining a competitive advantage in each and every area of business' (Porter, 1980). It can be achieved through any one function.

For each functional area of the business, such as production, marketing and personnel, the company will have a **functional strategy**. It is important that functional strategies are designed and managed in a coordinated way so that they interrelate with each other and at the same time collectively allow the competitive strategy to be implemented properly.

Corporate strategy, essentially and simply, is deciding what businesses the organization should be in and how the overall group of activities should be structured and managed. It has been described by Porter as 'the overall plan for a diversified business', although it is perfectly acceptable for a business to elect to stay with only one product or service. This

ASPECTS OF STRATEGIC MANAGEMENT 11

Key Concept 1.1
COMPETITIVE ADVANTAGE

Business strategy is all about competitive advantage. Without competitors there would be no need for strategy, for the sole purpose of strategic management is to enable the company to gain, as effectively as possible, a sustainable edge over its competitors – to alter a company's strength relative to that of its competitors in the most efficient way.

Actions affecting the health of a business (value engineering or improved cash flow which improve profitability) widen the range of alternative strategies the company may choose to adopt *vis-à-vis* its competitors.

A good strategy is one by which a company can gain significant ground on its competitors at an acceptable cost to itself. There are basically four ways.

☐ Identify the key success factors in an industry (explored later in this chapter) and concentrate resources in a particular area where the company sees an opportunity to gain the most significant strategic advantage over its competitors.

☐ Exploit any area where a company enjoys relative superiority. This could include using technology or the sales network developed elsewhere in the organization for other products or services.

☐ Aggressively attempt to change the key success factors by challenging the accepted assumptions concerning the ways business is conducted in the industry or market.

☐ Innovate. Open up new markets or develop new products.

The principal concern is to avoid doing the same thing, on the same battleground, as competition.

The aim is to attain a competitive situation in which your company can (a) gain a relative advantage through measures its competitors will find hard to follow and (b) extend that advantage further.

Taken from Ohmae, K (1982) *The Mind of the Strategist*, McGraw-Hill.

---

does happen in many companies, especially small businesses. In this case the corporate and competitive strategies are synonymous.

Corporate strategy for a multi-business group is concerned with maintaining or improving overall growth and profit performance through acquisition, organic investment (internally funded growth), divestment and closure. At the level of each of the distinct businesses which form the group, the strategic plan must embrace markets, products (or services) and competitors. This needs an analysis of strengths, weaknesses, opportunities and threats of both one's own business and one's competitors.

The term **strategic perspective** is often used to describe the range and diversity of activities, in other words the corporate strategy. Each activity then has a **competitive position** or strategy.

Competitive advantage

Competitive advantage is important for the organization and for every product and service that it markets. The topic is defined in Key Concept 1.1. Kenichi Ohmae stresses that strategy relates to the 3Cs – customers, competitors and the corporation. Success, he argues, is about doing things better than one's competitors. Organizations should seek to create and then sustain a clear competitive advantage (Ohmae, 1982).

☐ CUSTOMERS will ultimately decide whether or not the business is successful by buying or not buying the product or service. But customers cannot be treated *en masse*. Specific preferences should be sought and targeted. Products should be differentiated to appeal to defined market segments.

The corporation will be successful and profitable if it can meet customer needs more effectively than its competitors do. Differentiation is used to add value to a product or service, a value for which the market is willing and able to pay a premium price.

There are opportunities for low cost, low price, no frills products, but there can be only one least cost producer in any market. The least cost producer is the one who is able to manufacture goods of comparable quality to those of his competitors but at a lower cost, so that when he prices similarly to his competitors he makes more profit per item.

☐ CORPORATIONS are organized around particular functions (production, marketing etc.). The way that they are structured and managed determines the cost of the product or service.

There are opportunities to create competitive advantage in several areas of business, such as product design, packaging, delivery, service and customizing. Such opportunities achieve differentiation, but they can increase costs. Costs must be related to the price that customers are willing to pay for the particular product, based to some extent upon how they perceive its qualities – again in relation to competitors.

☐ COMPETITORS will similarly differentiate their products, goods and services, and again incur costs in doing so.

Competition can be based upon price, image, reputation, proven quality, particular performance characteristics, distribution or after-sales service, for example.

Strategic success, in the end, requires a clear understanding of the needs of the market, especially its segments, and the satisfaction of targeted customers more effectively and more profitably than by competitors.

Opportunities for change

It is therefore vital that managers are strategically aware both of potentially threatening developments and of opportunities for profitable change, and that they seek to match and improve the fit between the environment and the organization's resources.

A wise man will make more opportunities than he finds.   (Francis Bacon)

There is no single recommended approach for seeking out and pursuing new opportunities. There is a broad spectrum ranging from what might be termed entrepreneurial opportunism to what Quinn (1980) calls 'logical incrementalism'. These are analogous to the Bird and Squirrel approaches described in Box 1.1.

In Box 1 in the Preface it is apparent that strategic change can be relatively evolutionary or gradual, or much more dramatic or revolutionary. The nature of the opportunities (and threats) is directly related to both the general and the specific industry environments; and the approach that particular organizations take in seeking to match resources to the environment is dependent on the basic values of the organization and the style of the strategic leader. However, as will be seen it does not follow that the strategic leader is the sole manager of strategic change.

Any organization improves its chances of strategic success if it can successfully relate its culture, values and styles of management to the environment in which it competes. 'Culture' is defined in Key Concept 1.2 and is explored more fully in Chapter 4.

In summary it is vitally important to consider the human element together with

---

Box 1.1
APPROACHES TO STRATEGIC MANAGEMENT

THE BIRD APPROACH

Start with the entire world – scan it for opportunities to seize upon, trying to make the best of what you find.

You will resemble a bird, searching for a branch to land on in a large tree. You will see more opportunities than you can think of. You will have an almost unlimited choice. But your decision, because you cannot stay up in the air for ever, is likely to be arbitrary, and because arbitrary, it will be risky.

THE SQUIRREL APPROACH

Start with yourself and your company – where you are at with the skills and the experience you have – and what you can do best.

In this approach you will resemble a squirrel climbing that same large tree. But this time you are starting from the trunk, from familiar territory, working your way up cautiously, treefork by treefork, deciding on each fork the branch that suits you best.

You will only have one or two alternatives to choose from at a time – but your decision, because it is made on a limited number of options, is likely to be more informed and less risky.

In contrast with the bird who makes single big decisions, the squirrel makes many small ones. The squirrel may never become aware of some of the opportunities the bird sees, but he is more likely to know where he is going.

Adapted from Cohen, P (1974). *The Gospel According to the Harvard Business School*, Penguin. Originally published by Doubleday, New York, 1973.

---

analysis if strategy and strategic change are to be managed effectively.

Key success factors

The environment dictates key success factors that an organization really needs for long-term competitive advantage and strategic success. They will vary, and include risk, innovation, production technology, distribution or change orientation.

Risk taking, which will be explored further in Chapter 3, can manifest itself in a number of ways; certain dynamic industry environments offer more opportunities for the risk taker. Other more stable industries can be more resistant to change, and therefore are more suitable for risk-averse managers. Risk

increases as the potential actual loss involved in any decision increases. Consequently industries requiring substantial investments with no guarantee of success involve high levels of risk.

All businesses are taking risks when managers decide what products or services to produce and how to market them. Decisions, though, vary dramatically in the degree of inherent risk. Perceptions of the risk involved, and the willingness to accept the risk, also vary enormously between different managers. Thresholds of risk, i.e. the levels of risk that individual managers find acceptable, are not consistent. An entrepreneurial manager might see the risk in a particular option as being perfectly acceptable; another more cautious person might regard the same option as too risky to proceed with.

Just as the personal characteristics of parti-

Key Concept 1.2
CULTURE

Culture is 'the deeper level of **basic assumptions** and **beliefs** that are shared by members of an organization, that operate unconsciously, and that define in a basic "taken for granted" fashion an organization's view of itself and its environment'.

Culture is 'learned, evolves with new experiences, and can be changed if one understands the dynamics of the learning process'.

Culture is 'a pattern of basic assumptions that works well enough to be considered valid, and therefore is taught to new [organization] members as the correct way to perceive, think and feel in relation to problems of external adaptation and internal integration'.

In the very simplest terms it is the way organizational members behave and the values that are important to them.

Culture is considered further in Chapters 2 and 4.

Quotations from Schein, E H (1985) *Organization Culture and Leadership*, Jossey Bass.

---

cular individuals are suited to certain organizations (their values, perceptions and so on are complementary), so certain organizational values determine how well companies fit their environment.

In a company as truly global as ICI, with manufacturing facilities in approximately 40 countries, and a sales organization in over 150 markets, facing up to continuous change must be the norm to survive in today's fiercely competitive world. We are therefore continuously reviewing the shape of our businesses so as to focus them better on core strengths which allow us to identify the best opportunities for our expertise. We place enormous emphasis on our people, constantly seeking to develop them by broadening their experience and testing their skills. We encourage constructive criticism and rapid independent decision making within ICI strategies as a whole. Promotion will come from a clearly demonstrable track record over the years.

Sir Denys Henderson, Chairman, ICI plc

Attitudes towards change can be viewed similarly. Many managers, and hence their organizations, are wary of change, and whilst this may be appropriate generally in particular industries, it can be highly inappropriate in dynamic circumstances. Where the environment is turbulent, for any reason, organizations must be ready, willing and able to change. It could be argued, for example, that a large number of professional football clubs have been slow to change their overall product package as crowds diminished from the late 1940s to the mid-1980s. In the same way the UK machine tool industry was slow to react to foreign innovation and competition, and as a result a number of organizations have either been taken over or have gone out of business.

Innovation is a vital factor for success in other industries such as aerospace and consumer electronics. Companies which fail to allocate sufficient resources to a sound research and development programme have little prospect of long-term success.

In industries such as semiconductor manufacture low cost, reliable and high quality production is essential, and so investment in production technology is a key success factor.

For a number of consumer products, such as beer and motor cars, distribution and availability are key factors – but these are achieved in different ways.

It is of course essential that the whole organization is appreciative and supportive of the appropriate values. These values must be shared – not just held by the strategic leader. Certain aspects of strategy may well be available to top management only – sometimes, for example, there will be a need for secrecy about proposed acquisitions or changes in competitive positioning – but the fundamental values must become part of the organization's culture.

Core competencies

In order to meet their key success factors organizations must develop core competencies (Prahalad and Hamel, 1990). These are distinctive skills which yield competitive advantage, and ideally they:

(a) provide access to important market areas or segments;
(b) make a significant contribution to the perceived customer benefits of the product or service; and
(c) prove difficult for competitors to imitate.

Once developed they should be exploited, as, for example, Honda have exploited their skills at engine design and technology. Core competencies must, however, be flexible and responsive to changing customer demands and expectations. Canon have developed core competencies in precision mechanics, fibre optics and microelectronics, and these are spread across a range of products, including cameras, calculators, printers and photocopiers. There is constant product innovation.

Strategic capabilities

Stalk *et al.* (1992) argue that rather than competencies, strategic success is based upon capabilities – **processes** which enable the company to be an effective competitor. Distribution networks which achieve both high service levels (effectiveness) and low costs (efficiency) would be an example. Typically these processes will cut across whole organizations, rather than be product-specific, and they will rely heavily on information systems and technology.

E–V–R CONGRUENCE

If one wished to claim that an organization was being managed effectively from a strategic point of view, one would have to show, first, that its managers appreciated fully the dynamics, opportunities and threats present in their competitive environment, and that they were paying due regard to wider societal issues; and, second, that the organization's resources (inputs) were being managed strategically, taking into account its strengths and weaknesses, and that the organization was taking advantage of its opportunities. Key success factors and core competencies would be matched. This will not just happen, it needs to be managed. Moreover, potential new opportunities need to be sought and resources developed. It is also important, therefore, that the values of the organization match the needs of the environment and the key success factors. It is the values and culture which determine whether the environment and resources are currently matched, and whether they stay congruent in changing circumstances. Values are traditionally subsumed as a resource in a SWOT (strengths, weaknesses, opportunities, threats) analysis, but I believe they need to be separated out. This notion of E–V–R (environment–values–resources) congruence is illustrated in Figure 1.2 and Case 1.1 on The National Trust.

Pümpin (1987) uses the term **strategic excellence positions** (SEPs) to describe 'capabilities which enable an organization to

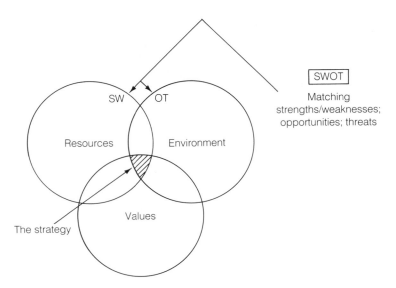

Figure 1.2 E–V–R congruence. The greater the congruence the greater the likelihood that the organization is managing its resources effectively to match the key success factors dictated by the environment.

produce better-than-average results over the longer term compared with its competitors'. SEPs imply that organizations appreciate the views of customers and develop the capabilities required to satisfy these needs. Moreover, they are perceived by their customers to be a superior competitor because of their skills and accomplishments.

It is important to deploy resources and to focus the drive for excellence (an aspect of the organization's culture) on issues which matter to customers. IBM, for example, have succeeded by concentrating on service, Rolls Royce (Motor Cars) on image and quality, and Procter and Gamble on advertising and branding.

Businesses should seek to develop competitive advantage and a strategic excellence position for each product and service. Overall E–V–R congruence then depends upon these SEPs together with any corporate benefits from linkages and interrelationships.

The development of SEPs and E–V–R congruence takes time, and requires that all the functional areas of the business appre-

ciate which factors are most significant to customers. Once achieved, though, it cannot be assumed that long-term success is guaranteed. Situations change, and new windows of opportunity open (Abell, 1978). The demand for guaranteed overnight parcel deliveries anywhere in the country, and immediate services within cities, opened up the opportunity for couriers; new technologies used in lap-top computers and facsimile machines have created demand changes. Competitors may behave unexpectedly, and consequently there is a need for strategic awareness and for monitoring potential change situations.

Vigilance should help an organization decide where it should be concentrating its resources at the moment, how it might usefully invest for the future, and where it needs to divest as existing windows of opportunity start to close. New market needs may imply a change of values, and this again will take time and prove challenging. It is not easy, for instance, to change a strong cost culture into one that is more innovatory.

A new book by Pümpin (1991) contains

Case 1.1
THE NATIONAL TRUST

The National Trust acquires and preserves countryside and historic places of interest 'for the benefit of us all', generally allowing access to members and fee-paying visitors. At the end of 1990 the National Trust was responsible for over half a million acres of land, 500 miles of coastline and some 200 houses and gardens. The Trust relies heavily on members' subscriptions to help fund its various activities; and gifts and endowments, together with some (limited) government funding, enable new acquisitions. Maintenance standards are high (and expensive) and conservation is seen as more important than commercial exploitation, and, where necessary, access. On occasions, but not very often, the numbers of visitors will be restricted either directly or indirectly, by, for example, limiting the parking facilities.

Stakeholders and interested parties – those whose interests the Trust must serve.

- ☐ National Trust members and visitors
- ☐ Donors of properties
- ☐ Conservation agencies and ramblers' associations
- ☐ Financial benefactors
- ☐ NT employees
- ☐ Government, and
- ☐ The nation as a whole.

Skills required

- ☐ Property management – both upkeep of the buildings and the management of land resources. Large areas of farmland are leased
- ☐ Expertise in arts and furnishings
- ☐ Public relations and marketing
- ☐ Financial skills – the Trust has substantial funds invested to yield income streams.

Values

The National Trust has proved successful in developing and deploying resources to meet the needs and expectations of its stakeholders. Staff are typically more 'property management' oriented than they are marketing oriented, but they are knowledgeable and expert. Preservation and the presentation of the properties to the standard maintained by their original owners are seen as important aspects of the service by both the Trust employees and its members. Theme parks and activities have no place in the National Trust; and there is a high moral tone to every activity, including the National Trust shops which tend to sell high-quality selected products at premium prices.

In addition, Trust staff appear to share an ethos (typically shared by people who work for other charities) which combines the feeling of working for a good cause, clear identification with its purpose and principles, and a certain readiness to accept lower rewards than those normally earned in manufacturing and service businesses.

National Trust membership doubled from 1 million to 2 million during the 1980s. A dilemma and a new challenge for the National Trust would arise if a more commercial orientation became necessary in order to fund desired activities.

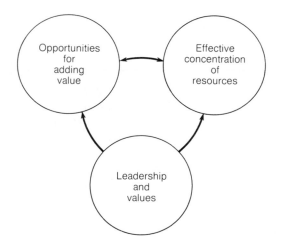

Figure 1.3 E–V–R congruence re-stated.

that multiplication – strategic consistency and performance improvement by concentrating on certain important strategies and learning how to implement them more effectively – promotes growth. The matching process is led and championed by the strategic leader, who is responsible for establishing the key values. Whilst striving to improve performance with existing strategies the organization must constantly search for new windows of opportunity. McDonald's, which is featured in Case 1.3 later in this chapter, provides an excellent example. Ray Kroc spotted an opportunity in the growing fast food market and exploited it by concentrating on new product ideas and franchised outlets, supported by a culture which promoted 'quality, service, cleanliness and value'.

ideas which enable the basic E–V–R congruence model to be redrawn, as in Figure 1.3. Opportunities for adding value which attracts customers must be sought and exploited. Numerous possible opportunities exist at corporate, competitive and functional strategy levels, and these are listed in Table 1.1, cross-referenced to the relevant chapters in the text. Resources must be deployed to exploit these opportunities. Pümpin argues

STRATEGY STATEMENTS

Having looked briefly at the key elements of strategy, and before considering how strategy and strategic change are managed, it is appropriate to summarize how the strategy of an organization might be stated in outline. This is illustrated simply in Figure 1.4.

Table 1.1 Opportunities for adding value

	Chapter
☐ Marketing (segmentation; globalization)	10
☐ Operations (technology → cost reduction	11
→ service and quality	11
procurement and linkages with suppliers)	15
☐ Finance (globalization of financial markets; better use of assets)	13
☐ Information (exploiting the potential of information technology)	14
☐ People (exploiting expertise; encouraging innovation)	12
☐ Acquisition and re-structuring strategies	18 and 13
☐ Co-operation strategies	18
☐ Opportunities from changes in industry regulation	7
☐ Cost-cutting and concentration	19
☐ Synergy – greater return from assets	Part III
☐ Organizational changes (re-structuring; new processes)	22

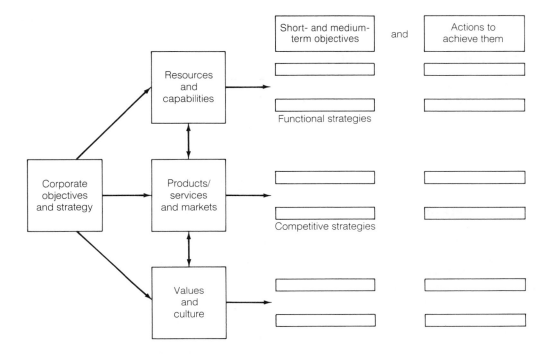

Figure 1.4 A strategy statement framework.

One starts with the strategic leader's vision of the future of the organization, its long-term objectives and corporate strategy. These are developed from the 'mission'. The major aspects of three contributing factors should be summarized in the strategy statement:

☐ the organization's resources, its strengths and weaknesses, which determine any distinctive capabilities that can generate competitive advantage and will normally be capable of improvement
☐ its products, services and markets (current and future)
☐ the organization's essential values and culture, which affect the implementation of strategy.

These three determinants should be co-ordinated. The selected markets should be appropriate for the capabilities and values of the organization and the capabilities and values should be compatible with the key success factors.

Competitive strategies for individual product markets and service markets, and functional strategies for various areas of the business, will be stated in the form of short- and medium-term objectives and actions being undertaken to achieve them. In arriving at these attention should have been given to environmental opportunities and threats.

This introductory strategy statement framework will be developed further and refined in Chapters 5 and 16.

THE MANAGEMENT OF STRATEGIC CHANGE

The following section has been written in the light of a number of different definitions of strategic management by a variety of authors. These definitions have been categorized into three separate approaches by Chaffee (1985) (see Key Reading 1.1).

Key Reading 1.1
THREE MODELS OF STRATEGY

Numerous authors have written about strategy, and whilst they agree on a number of points there are three quite distinct approaches.

AREAS OF AGREEMENT

Organizations use strategy to deal with changing environments.

The study of strategy includes both the actions taken, or the content of strategy, and the processes by which actions are decided and implemented.

Intended, emergent and realized strategies may differ from one another.

Firms may have both corporate strategy ('what businesses shall we be in?') and competitive strategies ('how shall we compete in each business?').

The making of strategy involves conceptual as well as analytical exercises. Some authors stress the analytical dimension, but most affirm that the heart of strategy making is the conceptual work done by leaders of the organization.

APPROACH 1: LINEAR STRATEGY

This approach focuses on planning such that goals, and the means of achieving them, are the results of strategic decision making.

A sample definition is:

Strategy is the determination of the basic long-term goals of the enterprise, and the adoption of courses of action and the allocation of resources necessary for carrying out these goals.   (Chandler, 1962)

APPROACH 2: ADAPTIVE STRATEGY

This approach corresponds to the notion of incrementalism.

Strategy is concerned with the development of a viable match between the opportunities and the risks present in the external environment and the organization's capabilities and resources for exploiting these opportunities. (Hofer, 1973)

This approach is more continuous and iterative than Approach 1; attention is focused more on means with goals seen as an alignment of the organization and environment; lower level changes, say in style, marketing or quality, are seen as strategically important; and although top managers are still seen as responsible for guiding strategy, other managers are clearly involved.

APPROACH 3: INTERPRETIVE STRATEGY

Like adaptive strategy this approach sees the organization and its environment as clearly related, but the emphasis is placed on managers 'holding a cognitive map that provides a view of the world, helps interpret the changes the organization faces, and provides appropriate responses' (Weick, 1983).

In other words the culture and values of the organization are seen as important, as is management motivation. Managers are motivated to believe and act in ways that are expected to produce favourable results for the organization; and it is one role of the strategic leader to create the appropriate organizational climate to encourage this.

Taken from Chaffee, E E (1985) Three models of strategy, *Academy of Management Review*, **10** (1).

Further reading relevant to the above is listed at the end of Chapter 2.

Major changes in corporate strategy will generally be the result of decisions made by the strategic leader, possibly in collaboration with his Board of Directors. These decisions can be the outcome of a thorough and comprehensive planning and evaluation exercise, but they can also be much more *ad hoc* and opportunistic. Quite literally an opportunity may be spotted or offered to the organization. The opportunity may offer potentially high rewards, and it may require a speedy decision and fast action. Impulses may prove to be well founded or ill founded. Similarly plans require forecasts, and they can be right or wrong, good or bad.

Much depends upon the awareness, insight and sometimes the intuition of the strategic leader, and upon the scope of the organization's information system. There is simply no one way of tackling the issue. Changes in top management can often result in dramatic strategic change, not surprisingly.

Trafalgar House plc is one example. From a base of property and construction Trafalgar diversified into shipping with the purchase of Cunard in 1971, and later into newspapers, acquiring the *Daily Express* group, Beaverbrook, in 1977. The *Star* was launched by Trafalgar, but newspapers were in fact sold off quite quickly. Change of this magnitude, however, is relatively uncommon for many organizations. Ansoff (1984) refers to it as discontinuous change and sees it as entrepreneurial behaviour. Major changes, though, may or may not be tied to a planning system, and as we shall see later (in Chapter 4) the more they are planned the less they are viewed as 'entrepreneurial'.

Changes also occur in competitive and functional strategies as managers lower down in the organization quite correctly recognize opportunities and react to threats. Changes may also be introduced as managers learn from experience, become more aware and quite simply see better ways of doing things. Generalizing, this results in more gradual changes over a period of time. Both strategies and objectives evolve as problems are identified and resolved and opportunities are identified and exploited. Such 'coal-face' managers, as one might call them, are close to their suppliers, customers and competitors, and they are expected to handle short-term unexpected problems and opportunities with quick responses. Realistically they are in the best position to make decisions concerning their functions or products in relation to the environment. It is appropriate that they should have authority delegated to them; it is also incumbent on them to consider and deal with the implications of their decisions on other managers in the company. This will work more effectively if there is a set of common shared values.

Mintzberg (1989) argues that organizations should be structured and managed to ensure that formulators of strategies (managers whose decisions lead to strategic change) have information, and that implementers of strategies and changes have the appropriate degree of power to ensure that the desired changes are brought about.

Logical incrementalism

This more gradual process of change relates closely to what Quinn (1980) has termed 'logical incrementalism'.

When I was younger I always conceived of a room where all these [strategic] concepts were worked out for the whole company. Later I didn't find any such room. . . . The strategy [of the company] may not even exist in the mind of one man. I certainly don't know where it is written down. It is simply transmitted in the series of decisions made.

(James B. Quinn, 1980)

Quinn argues that organizations *test out* relatively small changes and develop with this approach rather than go for major changes. An example would be Marks & Spencer testing a proposed new line in a selected and limited number of stores before deciding to launch it nationally. Lex Group (mentioned in the Preface, Box 2) followed an incremental approach when they diversified into hotels, building and buying properties one by one rather than acquiring a chain of hotels.

An organization can, of course, use more than one means of bringing about strategic changes at any one time. During the 1980s, for example, Asda, the major food retailer, acquired, and later sold, the kitchen furniture group MFI. At the same time they developed and pursued strategies of opening new stores, re-designing and refurbishing existing stores, developing own label goods, introducing more fresh foods and non-food items, using information technology and streamlining their distribution system.

Strategy, therefore, can result from a stream of decisions and information fed upwards from the lower management levels of the organization. Quinn contends that this is sensible, logical and positive. . . .

The most effective strategies of major enterprises tend to emerge step by step from an iterative process in which the organization probes the future, experiments and learns from a series of partial (incremental) commitments rather than through global formulations of total strategies. Good managers are aware of this process and they consciously intervene in it. They use it to improve the information available for decisions and to build the psychological identification essential to successful strategies. The process is both logical and incremental. Such logical incrementalism is not 'muddling' as most people understand that word. Properly managed it is a conscious, purposeful, proactive, executive practice.

Thus strategic change can be brought about in a number of ways; and in any one organization change will not always be the outcome of a single process.

The place of corporate planning

A number of books have been written on the subject of corporate planning. It is generally agreed that strategic change is the outcome of objective, systematic decision making which establishes objectives and then seeks and chooses ways of achieving them. Change is a planned activity.

Corporate planning is therefore prescriptive in its approach. It would be churlish to argue that formal planning has no role to play in strategic management but, quite simply, there is more to strategic management and strategic change than planning.

Planning activity will consider opportunities and threats (although this is not the only way they should be spotted); it will allow a thorough evaluation of strengths and weaknesses; it will allow an assessment of where competitive advantage is or is not and how it might be achieved; and future scenarios can be tested. Planning can be used to help decide where the organization's scarce resources (for example, future investment capital) should be concentrated; and it can be used to establish tactics (actions) for carrying out strategies.

There are a number of useful planning techniques and these will be considered in a later chapter. But the overall role and relative importance of planning remains a controversial and disputed issue. As mentioned by Mintzberg (1982), strategy 'need not always be a conscious and precise plan'. Indeed, Mintzberg argues, 'strategy can emerge, almost unconsciously, as a pattern from a fits-and-starts stream of entrepreneurial decisions and actions' (Quinn re-stated). 'Complex planning processes are not always needed, either at corporate headquarters or in the divisions and business units. Nor is there much point in a company re-assessing its strategy every year as part of its annual planning cycle. It is like asking every year "Why am I married?" What is important is the entrepreneurial ability suddenly to respond to changes in the environment after having followed the same strategy, whether agreed or implicit, for several years.' Whilst well supported, this view is not adhered to wholeheartedly.

Bruce Henderson, founder of the technique-oriented Boston Consulting Group, argues differently:

Most companies don't have a strategy. They just talk about it, like they do about the weather.

Companies need more tools and techniques if they are to survive and prosper. If companies really had been able to produce sophisticated strategies, would so many of them all have jumped together into the computer business? Many of the entrants who are now fighting for their lives had not even worked out relatively simple things . . . how they were going to secure their technical talent, develop their software and so on. If they wanted to have a strategy worth the name they would have to go very much further than that. For instance, into highly complex mapping of competitor strengths and weaknesses.   (Henderson, 1983)

Finally it is quite plausible to argue that the outcome of planning need not be a plan. Rather than trying to produce a watertight document covering the next ten years, planning, as an exercise, should concentrate on identifying and evaluating alternative courses of action for the business, so that more opportunities are created. Planning therefore increases awareness.

In this section we have outlined the views of a number of contributors on strategy. It can usefully be summarized as follows. Strategic management is concerned with

☐ deciding the future direction and scope of the business, in line with perceived opportunities and threats. This will clearly require awareness and planning. The planning, however, may be more cerebral and visionary than detailed, formal and quantitative.

☐ ensuring that the required resources are, or will be, available in order that the chosen strategies can be implemented.

☐ ensuring that there is innovation and change. These changes can be in relation to corporate, competitive or functional strategies. Equally, innovation can take place throughout the organization. If this is to happen then an appropriate organization structure and culture must be in place.

Ansoff (1987) restates these points by suggesting that strategic management involves:

☐ strategic planning
☐ management capability planning
☐ the overall process of strategic change.

STRATEGIC CHANGE IN PRACTICE

Three short case histories of Marks & Spencer, McDonald's and Virgin, all successful and visible organizations in quite different industries, illustrate a number of the points made above (see Cases 1.2, 1.3 and 1.4).

McDonald's and Marks & Spencer change gradually and incrementally, whilst Virgin has been more opportunistic. Being more entrepreneurial Virgin has changed direction more than once. In all three cases a clear set of values or principles established the parameters for development; and in each case it is fair to claim that these values were recognized and understood throughout the whole organization.

Case 1.2
MARKS & SPENCER PLC

Marks & Spencer (M & S) is a major 'High Street' retailer of clothing (UK market leader), food and homewear.

M & S strategy is concerned with diversification of their product ranges within these broad product groups, but at the same time seeking to specialize where their St Michael label can be used effectively. All M & S products carry their own brand label. They seek to innovate whilst upgrading and adding value to their existing ranges. During the 1980s, for example, M & S successfully introduced furniture – a limited range of middle-of-the-road designs. Products are displayed in selected stores and delivered to customers' homes within three weeks. From the outset demand exceeded supply.

M & S have found that many of their long-established stores in town and city centres are simply too small. An expansion programme has therefore developed along several lines. Adjacent units have been acquired when practical and new larger stores created; if land has been available, buildings have been extended; and new sales floors have been opened up by converting stockrooms and moving stock to outside warehouses. This brings its own logistics problems, of course. Satellite stores – smaller branches some distance away from the main branch – have been opened in certain towns. These satellites carry complete ranges – it might be men's fashions, ladies' clothes, or children's items. The choice depends upon the square footage available and the local prospects for particular lines. In similar vein, in towns considered too small to support a full branch, specialist stores, perhaps just for food, are being opened. Finally, new, larger, edge-of-town stores for car-bound customers are also being built. The selection of products within the whole M & S range varies between stores.

Other strategic changes are:

☐ Constant improvements in displays, partly to present products better, and also to get more items into the stores. 'Sales per square foot' is a vital measure of success.

☐ Electronic point-of-sale. Information technology has been harnessed to improve productivity and to enable M & S to respond faster to market changes – particularly relevant for fashion items. Thanks in part to technology, M & S staff costs as a percentage of their turnover are less than those of their competitors, but the quality of service has remained high.

☐ The development of support financial services, such as unit trusts, building upon the success of the M & S Chargecard, the third most popular credit card in the UK.

☐ International growth in France, Belgium, Canada, America and Hong Kong. The development has been gradual, with one of the objectives being to introduce new types of competition. Some mistakes have been made as part of the learning process, but the risks have been contained in order not to threaten the UK interests.

Whilst there have been, and continue to be, strategic changes, the fundamental principles or values of the business have remained constant. These are:

- [ ] High-quality, dependable products, styled conservatively and offering good value for money.
- [ ] Good relations with employees, customers, suppliers and other stakeholders. During the late 1980s M & S has become more dynamic and progressive, seeking to change to a meritocracy instead of being perceived as a 'safe, jobs-for-life-type organization'.
- [ ] The development and maintenance of an efficient supply network of good-quality British goods. Not all goods are of British origin, but a high proportion are.
- [ ] Simple operations.
- [ ] Comfortable stores.
- [ ] Financial prudence. Most properties, for example, are freehold – they have not been sold and leased back to fund the expansion.

Case 1.3
McDONALD'S

McDonald's is known for its instantly recognizable and popular fast food, widely available around the world, and the corporation has become something of an institution. The company is an industry leader and contends that there are five main reasons behind this.

- [ ] Visibility: to this end substantial resources are devoted to marketing. The golden arches symbol is instantly recognizable.
- [ ] Ownership or control of real-estate sites: McDonald's argue that this factor differentiates it from its competitors who lease more.
- [ ] A commitment to franchising: some three-quarters of McDonald's restaurants around the world are operated by local business people.
- [ ] It is world wide, with restaurants in over 40 countries.
- [ ] It is a growth company: 'Our strategy focuses on adding 500 new restaurants per year; maximizing sales at existing restaurants through reinvestment, new product development and marketing; and improving international profitability through economies of scale achieved by market penetration.'

McDonald's has not diversified or sought to offer any different 'food' concept. But it does change the product mix (for example, breakfasts and, in America, salads) and it does seek out new markets, opening branches (again in America) in hospitals, military bases, college campuses and zoos.

Opportunity. Recognizing it. Creating it. Maximizing it. That's what McDonald's has always done.

Continued overleaf

For over 30 years the basic goal has been to 'serve customers, better, faster, friendlier than competitors, whilst building sales volume and dollar profits'.

Unquestionably McDonald's is market oriented and defines its competitive advantage as 'Q, S, C, and V': 'QUALITY food products; fast friendly SERVICE; restaurants known for CLEANLINESS; and a menu which provides VALUE.' This basic philosophy was established by McDonald's founder, the late Ray Kroc.

One key feature of McDonald's is the fast, friendly and efficient service. Many employees are young, under 21, and part time. They work a closely prescribed system, operating internationally established rules and procedures for preparing, storing and selling food, and various incentive schemes operate. Labour turnover is high, however, and consequently McDonald's has its critics as well as supporters. Nevertheless it is obvious that some competitors seek to emulate McDonald's in a number of ways – products, systems and employee attitudes. McDonald's response:

Our competitors can copy many of our secrets, but they cannot duplicate our pride, our enthusiasm and our dedication for this business.

Sources: annual reports of the McDonald's Corporation and Gapper, J (1987) Crew system done to a turn, *Financial Times*, 14 September.

Case 1.4
VIRGIN

The Virgin group of companies is headed by its founder, Richard Branson, a widely self-publicized entrepreneurial businessman, who holds world records for Atlantic crossings by both power boat and balloon. Founded in 1970 the business developed rapidly from selling popular records by mail order to a full stock exchange listing in December 1986 as a leading entertainment company.

The flotation prospectus claimed:

The Directors aim to develop Virgin into the leading British international media and entertainment group. Virgin will continue to expand those activities in which it has proven skills, knowledge and depth management. . . . the core of the Group's activities will continue to be primarily concerned with the acquisition and marketing of creative rights. The Directors are confident that by recognizing changes in consumer tastes Virgin can expand successfully and profitably in this field.

A number of strategic investments, in particular an attempt to penetrate the American popular music market with the Virgin label (rather than have Virgin-contracted artists released on American labels under licensing agreements) caused short-term profits to suffer. The share price fell well below the December 1986 offer price, and as a result Virgin (in July 1988) decided to buy back its own shares (at the offer price) and return to being a private company.

It has been argued that culturally Virgin was wrong to become a public company. Branson has a particularly individual style of informal, entrepreneurial management which did not lend itself to the more formal expectations of the City and institutional shareholders, although, it should be said, Virgin had a high proportion of individual investors.

Three years later, in 1991, the Virgin group comprised:

☐ Virgin Music (recording and music publishing, and the largest of the businesses)
☐ Virgin Retail
☐ Virgin Communications (including computer games, television, books and magazine publishing)
☐ Voyager (including Virgin Atlantic Airways and Virgin Holidays)

plus investments in broadcasting. Richard Branson was influential, if not wholly active, in all of these businesses, each of which contained a number of separate Virgin subsidiary companies.

The Virgin group consisted of some 200 companies. Each time a company grows beyond about 80 staff it is split up, and people separated (say, into new premises) in order to prevent impersonality and to maintain motivation.

The heart of the business had always been music – recording, publishing and retailing. Virgin has recorded some of the world's leading pop stars and influenced the marketing of their work around the world.

Recording cannot realistically offer consistent and rapid growth because of changes in fashion and tastes which can be unpredictable. Spotting future star performers and producing a series of hit records for those stars involves a little luck and a lot of good management. With stars like Phil Collins, Culture Club, Mike Oldfield and UB40 amongst their 100 or so contracted artists, Virgin can boast an excellent track record.

Retailing has allowed Virgin to benefit in part from the success of artists contracted to other recording companies; and it also offers opportunities for diversification into associated products. Virgin have successfully introduced such products as computer games, videos and books into their retailing operations. The company developed four types of outlet: single-product record stores; multi-product leisure interest megastores; specialist computer games stores; and concessions within such stores as Debenhams. In June 1988, because they were relatively unprofitable in a very competitive market, Virgin sold over 70 single-product stores to W H Smith who incorporated them into their Our Price chain. In September 1991 Virgin and W H Smith formed a 50 : 50 partnership to develop Virgin's chain of 12 megastores and 7 games centres. Thirty-five new stores were being considered, with WHS providing both finance and retail expertise. Since going private Virgin sought to raise money for expansion by a series of joint ventures – Fujisankei (Japan) bought 25% of Virgin Music, and Seisu Saison (also Japan) owns 10% of Virgin Atlantic Airways.

In February 1992 Branson sold Virgin Music to Thorn–EMI, who had earlier bought Chrysalis Records to add to their established record labels. This acquisition (which valued Virgin Music at 1000 times its 1991 after-tax earnings) offered scale economies and synergy potential (see Key Concept III.1) to Thorn–EMI, by increasing their global

continued overleaf

market share. Virgin was paid over £500 million in cash, some 60% of which went directly to Branson. It was assumed that much of this would be re-invested in his airline.

In 1984 *The Economist* argued: 'Mr. Branson has followed four rules throughout the growth of Virgin. He is determined to stick to all of them even as his business expands and matures.' They are:

☐ *Keep overheads low*. There is no grand centralized Head Office and the Group's divisions are allowed considerable autonomy.

☐ *Encourage entrepreneurship*. If employees came up with good ideas that were likely to be profitable, Branson on occasions put up venture capital and established new companies within the Virgin Group. Those with the ideas were given shares in the new business, but not Virgin overall. Examples include a traditional pub, night clubs and the development of an electronic synthesizer controller. In 1991 Virgin established a new venture to develop airships for such markets as corporate advertising and aerial observation and policing.

☐ *Buy, don't make*. Although Virgin Music owned a number of recording studios they avoided major capital investments wherever possible, preferring instead to act as 'publishers of entertainment' and distributors. In the record business world wide there are, of course, numerous licensing opportunities. Similarly, aeroplanes have been leased rather than bought, although, as a result of low prices in the recession, it was speculated that Virgin Atlantic would buy additional planes in 1992.

☐ *Never move far from your core market*. This would be defined as 15–35 year olds with income to spend on enjoying themselves.

Virgin also diversified into the production of feature films, but withdrew from this in 1986, concentrating instead on the acquisition of distribution rights for films and videos. More recent moves into cable and satellite television complement this and arguably offer genuine music and communication linkages for the market Virgin traditionally appeals to. In 1991 Virgin bid for, but failed to win, a franchise for a regional independent television station.

Virgin Atlantic Airways was founded in 1984, initially flying between Gatwick and the New Jersey side of New York. Branson aimed to offer better value for money than the major transatlantic carriers. Learning from the earlier problems of Sir Freddie Laker's Skytrain (case featured in Chapter 8), the Virgin strategy was one of affordable quality, not the lowest possible price. There are fewer seats to give more leg room, on-board services are considered superior, and prices are generally lower than the major airlines. The venture has proved extremely successful with passengers, albeit on a limited scale. Virgin has won a number of international awards for service and quality and now flies out of Heathrow and to destinations such as Miami, Los Angeles and Tokyo. The airline is now Richard Branson's main business interest, and he aims to fly more international routes and challenge the predominance of British Airways in the UK.

Source: 'What Size Virgin Does Richard Branson Want?', *The Economist*, 24 November 1984.

SUMMARY

In this chapter we have

☐ outlined the scope of the subject area of strategic management;
☐ mentioned the factors required for strategic success;
☐ introduced the idea of E–V–R congruence by reference to environmental fit and key success factors;
☐ discussed the importance of organization culture as a feature of strategic management, and the need for strategic leadership;
☐ defined competitive advantage, and shown the relationship between corporate, competitive and functional strategies;
☐ summarized the different approaches, definitions and models that are relevant for our study of the subject;
☐ argued that strategic change can be the result of a prescriptive planning process, or emerge from the decisions and actions of managers.

CHECKLIST OF KEY TERMS AND CONCEPTS

At this stage you should feel confident that you have a basic understanding of the following terms and ideas:

☐ Objectives (at this stage only as an idea)
☐ Strategic management
☐ Strategic change
☐ Environmental fit
☐ Key success factors
☐ Core competencies
☐ Strategic excellence positions
☐ Strategic leadership
☐ Culture
☐ Competitive advantage
☐ E–V–R congruence
☐ SWOT analysis
☐ Corporate, competitive and functional strategies
☐ Logical incrementalism
☐ Corporate planning.

QUESTIONS AND RESEARCH ASSIGNMENTS

Text related

1. How do Marks & Spencer seek to attain and maintain competitive advantage? What do you think their objectives might be?
2. Assess McDonald's in terms of E–V–R congruence.
3. What might be the key success factors required in the popular music business? How do you feel Virgin embraced these? How important a factor is 'risk taking'?

Library based

4. Sainsbury's first became market leader for 'packaged groceries' in 1983, with some 16% market share. Tesco and the Co-op each had 14.5% and Asda 8%.

   ☐ In ten years the Company's share price had risen by 900% against 175% for the FT All Shares index.
   ☐ The performance combines 'profitability, productivity and a sense of social purpose' (*Financial Times* comment).
   ☐ There was no 'grand strategy'.

   We did not sit down in the early 70s and work out any corporate plan, or say that by a particular time we intended to be in a particular business, or to be of a particular size.

(Roy Griffiths, Managing Director)

☐ Rather, Sainsbury's has identified and 'obsessively pursued' opportunities that fitted the company's corporate values, the 'basics of the business'. These are:

☐ selling quality products at competitive (though not necessarily the cheapest) prices

☐ exacting quality control standards

☐ extensive research of competitors and customers

☐ strict financial management

☐ tight control of suppliers

☐ planned staff involvement

From your own observations and/or library research:

☐ How successful, strategically, do you believe Sainsbury's is?

☐ What is their competitive strategy?

☐ What changes have they made since 1983, and how successful have they been?

REFERENCES

Abell, D F (1978) Strategic windows, *Journal of Marketing*, **42** (July)

Ansoff, H I (1984) *Implanting Strategic Management*, Prentice Hall.

Ansoff, H I (1987) *Corporate Strategy*, revised edition, Penguin.

Beck, P, quoted in Lorenz, C (1987) Crusading for a clear strategy, *Financial Times*, 25 February.

Burns, T and Stalker, G M (1961) *The Management of Innovation*, Tavistock.

Chaffee, E E (1985) Three models of strategy, *Academy of Management Review*, **10** (1).

Chandler, A D (1962) *Strategy and Structure*, MIT Press.

Constable, J (1980) Business strategy, Unpublished paper, Cranfield School of Management.

Henderson, B (1983) Lecture to the Annual Conference of the Strategic Management Society, Paris, October.

Hofer, C W (1973) Some preliminary research on patterns of strategic behaviour, *Academy of Management Proceedings*, pp. 46–59.

Mintzberg, H, quoted in Lorenz, C (1982) Strategic doctrine under fire, *Financial Times*, 15 October. The themes are developed extensively in Quinn, J B, Mintzberg, H and James, R M (1987) *The Strategy Process*, Prentice Hall.

Mintzberg, H (1989) *Mintzberg on Management*, Free Press.

Morrison, R and Lee, J (1979) From planning to clearer strategic thinking, *Financial Times*, 27 July.

Ohmae, K (1982) *The Mind Of The Strategist*, McGraw-Hill.

Porter, M E (1980) *Competitive Strategy*, Free Press.

Prahalad, C K and Hamel, G (1990) The core competence of the corporation, *Harvard Business Review*, May/June.

Pümpin, C (1987) *The Essence of Corporate Strategy*, Gower.

Pümpin, C (1991) *Corporate Dynamism*, Gower.

Quinn, J B (1980) *Strategies for Change: Logical Incrementalism*, Richard D Irwin.

Stalk, G, Evans, P and Shulman, L E (1992) Competing on capabilities: the new rules of corporate strategy, *Harvard Business Review*, March/April.

Weick, K E (1983) Managerial thought in the context of action. In *The Executive Mind* (ed. S Srivastra), Jossey Bass.

A STRATEGIC MANAGEMENT FRAMEWORK

2

LEARNING OBJECTIVES

After studying this chapter you should be able to

☐ summarize strategic management in terms of three interrelated aspects: analysis, choice and implementation;

☐ identify a series of questions concerning strategic awareness and decisions about strategic change; and

☐ apply these to the outline framework around which this book has been structured;

☐ justify the role of strategic leadership, values and culture as central in this framework.

In this chapter we explore strategic management by expanding and explaining the model (Figure 1) which was introduced in the Preface and which has been used to provide a framework for the order and content of the book. You may wish to use this chapter as a reference to check where later chapters fit into the book as a whole.

INTRODUCTION

Models of strategic management are generally built around three themes: analysis, choice and implementation. The model for the present text relates specifically to strategic awareness and change, but the compatibility between the two approaches is explained.

Effective strategic management requires that managers address a number of important issues continuously and simultaneously. This can be achieved by constantly seeking answers to a number of questions. The questions are included in this chapter and linked to the structure of the text.

All strategic decisions are affected by the nature and style of strategic leadership in the organization together with the prevailing culture and values.

MODELS OF STRATEGIC MANAGEMENT

Various models of the strategic management process already exist and, whilst there are differences between them, many tend to follow a pattern based on the following outline:

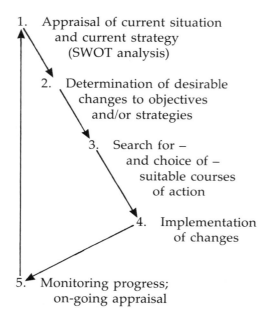

1. Appraisal of current situation and current strategy (SWOT analysis)

2. Determination of desirable changes to objectives and/or strategies

3. Search for – and choice of – suitable courses of action

4. Implementation of changes

5. Monitoring progress; on-going appraisal

By a series of analyses and decisions an organization can determine the directions that its future strategy should follow. This approach is adequate on a prescriptive basis, but realistically it will fail to explain all that happens in practice. For example, in Chapter 1 the notion of incrementalism was introduced. Strategy changes which are gradual cannot be encapsulated into the above model. The process of strategic management should not be thought of as having a linear form exclusively.

Hence an alternative way of modelling the

process is to follow the approach of Johnson and Scholes (1984) and base it upon three areas of decision – strategic analysis; strategic choice and strategic implementation – which should be seen as interrelated and linked to a monitoring and information system. The functional change discussed above would constitute both evaluation and implementation at the same time, for in many respects the manager is actually trying out something to see whether it works. He progresses in gradual steps, learning from experience all the time.

Figure 2.1, described below, has been derived from this approach; and it features the major areas of decision and analysis.

Strategic analysis was introduced in Chapter 1, Figure 1.1. If an organization understands the nature of its market and is generally aware of, and responsive to, changes in the environment as a whole, it can be a successful competitor and achieve profit and growth. The levels of success that it is achieving with current strategies should be assessed, and future targets, which may imply more or even less of the same, or activities which are different, determined.

This requires an analysis of current results, an evaluation of current resources (strengths and weaknesses) and an assessment of opportunities and threats present and developing in the environment. The values held by the organization and its key managers are a crucial factor to include in this.

Strategic choice is concerned with establishing just what courses of strategic action are available to an organization and how these might be evaluated and one or more selected. Whilst strategic choice decisions are important for determining future courses of action, other strategic changes may emerge from a more gradual process of trial and error.

Additionally, managers may not be able to identify a feasible course of action. Competition might be too intense; legislation may prevent it; pressure groups may mount an effective opposition to the proposals; or the

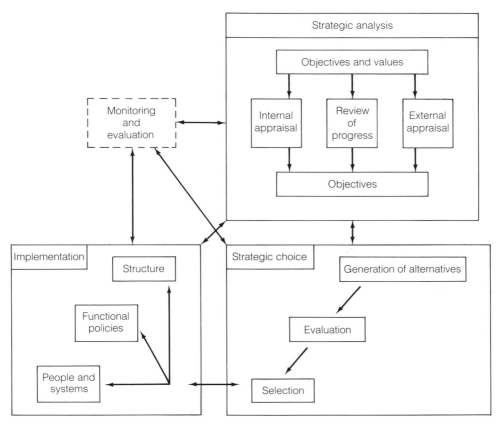

Figure 2.1   The elements of strategic management.

necessary resources may not be available. It would then be necessary for the organization to re-appraise its target objectives and set new ones.

Strategic implementation: a strategy is only useful when it has been implemented, and hence the organization must have an appropriate structure, clear and contributory functional strategies and systems which ensure that the organization behaves in a cohesive rather than a fragmented way. The larger, or more diverse the organization becomes, the more likely it is that this becomes a problem. In multi-product multi-national organizations with considerable interdependence between the products or services and between subsidiaries, for exam-ple, divisions may become competitive with each other and not pull together.

The way that an organization is structured into divisions and/or functions, and the amount of authority that is delegated to individual managers must inevitably influence day-to-day decision making. These 'coal-face' decisions determine (as suggested in Chapter 1) the actual strategies pursued and the levels of success. The objectives that an organization is pursuing in reality there-fore stem from strategy implementation.

Hence the 'strategic analysis' box in Figure 2.1 contains an assessment of both the objectives currently being pursued and the desired objectives. In order to appreciate properly just how well an organization is doing relative to both its objectives and its competitors, to explore opportunities and threats, to appraise strengths and weaknesses, to evaluate alternative courses of action and so on, it is vital to have an effective information system. How an organization gathers and uses information is therefore another important aspect of strategic management.

The present text is not structured directly around the model illustrated in Figure 2.1 but around a model which concentrates on awareness and change.

The most important management technique is to understand the real situation in which you are operating.

Sir Paul Girolami, Chairman, Glaxo – quoted in Accountancy, *March 1987, p.133.*

THE FRAMEWORK OF THE BOOK

This book explores strategic management by considering a number of basic questions or decision areas, divided into two groups:

☐ **strategic awareness questions** and
☐ **strategic change questions**.

These are presented in a sequential form in Boxes 2.1 and 2.2, and the related Figures 2.2 and 2.3 to provide a framework for the text. They should not, however, be seen as a step-by-step model, but rather as a set of issues which managers and organizations should be addressing at all times. If managers seek answers to these questions continuously, and make and carry out appropriate strategic decisions, they will improve the performance and effectiveness of their organization by

☐ generating increased strategic awareness;
☐ ensuring that functional managers appreciate the strategic environment and the implications of decisions concerning indi-

vidual products, services and markets; as well as
☐ making decisions about the need for, and appropriateness of, particular change opportunities.

The questions relate to strategic decision models like that illustrated in Figure 2.1. Figure 2.4 has been designed to illustrate the linkages in the model. The questions (Parts II to V) are grouped around a central core of styles of corporate decision making and leadership, and values (Part I). These parts correspond to the parts of the book, and they are linked to the following analyses and decisions, which constitute the main elements of strategic management:

II. Situation assessment
III. Situation analysis (including SWOT)
IV. Objective setting
    Strategic alternatives
    Strategic choice
V. Strategic implementation
    plus
    Measurement and control systems

The strategic change part of the model (Parts IV and V) primarily reflects changes in the corporate strategy of the organization. Incremental changes to competitive and functional strategies by general and specialist managers as opportunities arise, and in reaction to strategic changes by competitors, are shown in the top section of Figure 2.4. These changes will affect the strategic situation on an on-going basis.

The annotations to Figure 2.4 are essentially a summary of the questions detailed in boxes 2.1 and 2.2 laid out in the order that they are treated in the book. Case 2.1 is an illustration of how the questions might be applied. But

---

The best way to predict the future is to invent it.

Rosabeth Moss Kanter quoting an unnamed American chief executive

---

Box 2.1
STRATEGIC AWARENESS QUESTIONS

SITUATION ASSESSMENT

Where are we going? (Chapter 5)

☐ What strategies are we pursuing?
☐ What objectives are we seeking to achieve?
☐ What is our fundamental mission as an organization?

How are we doing? (Chapter 6)

☐ Are we implementing the strategies we decided to pursue?
☐ If so, what are we learning?
☐ If not, why not?
☐ How successful is the implementation?
☐ Where are we experiencing difficulties?
☐ What are our levels of success?
☐ How do these compare with our targets or stated objectives?
☐ What are our financial results?
☐ How do these compare
  ☐ with budgets?
  ☐ with last year?
  ☐ with our competitors?
  ☐ with our industry average?
☐ Do we need to change?
☐ What will happen if we carry on as before?

SITUATION ANALYSIS

Generally,

Where and why are we doing well? Where and why are we doing badly? (Chapter 7)

☐ What is the nature of our industry?
☐ How good a competitor are we? And why?

SWOT ANALYSIS

Where are our opportunities and threats? (Chapter 9)

☐ What are our key success factors?
☐ What are our competitors doing? Planning?
☐ What is happening on our supply side?
☐ Should we change any of our previous 'make or buy' decisions?
☐ Should we change any of our suppliers?
☐ What is happening in our distribution channels? – and so on
☐ Do any general political, social, economic changes provide us with new opportunities, threats etc.?
☐ Basically – are we properly aware of the changes in our environment?
☐ And are we doing enough about it?
☐ And particularly – do we really appreciate the nature of competition in our market(s)?

Do our resources match up well? How can we capitalize on our strengths and reduce our weaknesses? (Chapters 10–13). This requires an identification and evaluation of how effectively the organization is using all its resources:

☐ Marketing management – where are our products in their life cycles?
☐ Operations management
☐ Research and development – innovation
☐ Human resources management
☐ Financial management

. . . and identifying appropriate changes

How good is our information system? (Chapter 14). This relates to being able to provide good quality answers to all the questions, and incorporates an element of forecasting.

Where is our competitive advantage? (Chapter 15) – for all our products and services

☐ Is it sustainable, and appropriate for the future?
☐ If not, what are we doing/should we be doing about it?

Box 2.2
QUESTIONS CONCERNING STRATEGIC CHANGE

OBJECTIVES AND DIRECTION

Where do we want to go to? (Chapter 16)
Objectives for the future:

☐ What type of organization do we want to be?
☐ How big?
☐ How global?
☐ How diversified?
☐ How fast do we want to change things?
☐ How big a gap exists between where we are and where we want to be?
☐ Are we basically satisfied with minimal change?

Given our SWOT what is realistic? And maybe necessary?

Particularly important is an honest appreciation of strengths and weaknesses, and recognition of competition and the importance and feelings of key stakeholders in the business.

☐ Do we face any constraints?
☐ Is time an issue for any reason?

STRATEGIC ALTERNATIVES

What alternatives are available? (Chapters 17–20)

☐ What opportunities for change exist?
☐ With current products/services?
☐ With new products/services?
☐ Could/should we divest any businesses?
☐ Could/should we diversify?
☐ Could/should we merge?
☐ How risky are our opportunities?
☐ Have we any previous experiences we can learn from?

STRATEGIC CHOICE

How do we choose?

This links in to how the organization plans change –

the processes, the people etc. (Chapter 16)

What constitutes a good choice? (Chapter 21)
What can/cannot, should/should not we do?

☐ Ability
☐ Opportunity
☐ Risk (wisdom of accepting the risks; desire to take risks etc.)
☐ Acceptability to decision makers and stakeholders
☐ Appropriateness (considering resources, competition, time-scales etc.)

STRATEGIC IMPLEMENTATION

How do we make the strategy work (Chapters 22–23)

☐ What would be an appropriate structure?
☐ What functional strategies do we need to implement our corporate and competitive strategies?
☐ What do we need to do to ensure that we harness all necessary resources?
☐ How do we ensure commitment and support from all our managers?
☐ What measurement and control systems do we need?

How do we manage the changes? (Chapter 24)

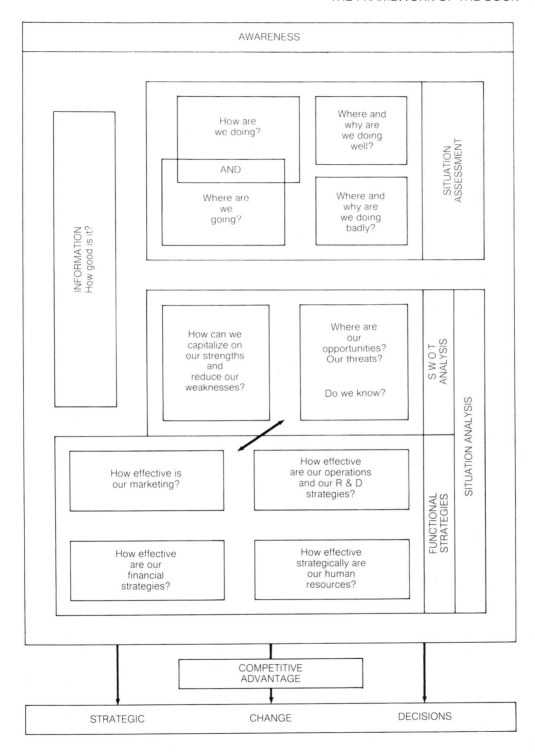

Figure 2.2 Strategic awareness.

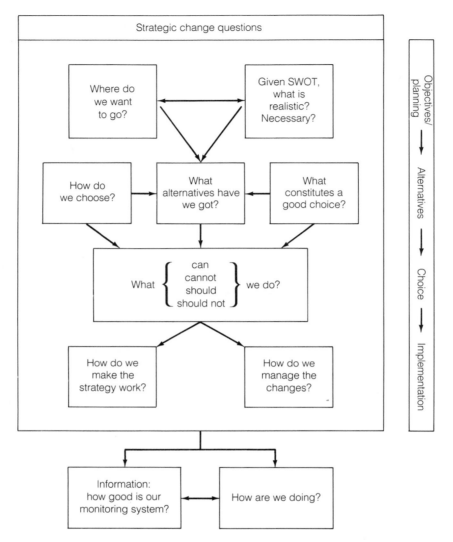

Figure 2.3 Strategic change.

first it is important to explain why the model is built around the Part I core of strategic leadership, decision making and values.

STRATEGIC LEADERSHIP AND VALUES

In the above lists of questions one key strategic element is missing: the values of the organization. In Chapter 1, in explaining E–V–R congruence, I emphasized the contri-

bution of the strategic leader in establishing corporate values and in managing the process of matching resources with environmental opportunities and threats. Values dictate the way decisions are made, the objectives of the organization, the type of competitive advantage sought, the organization structure and systems of management, functional strategies and policies, attitudes towards managing people, and information systems. Many of these are interrelated.

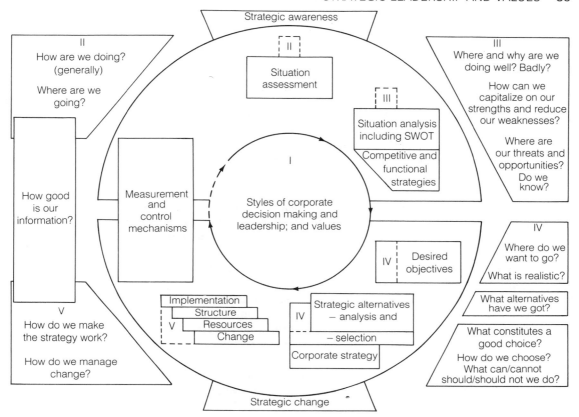

Figure 2.4 Dimensions of strategic management.

Topic	Chapter	Relevant questions
I THE STRATEGY PROCESS		
Styles of corporate decision making and leadership;	3	How is strategy managed within the organization?
values and culture	4	How important are culture and values?
STRATEGIC AWARENESS (How is the business being managed strategically?)		
II SITUATION ASSESSMENT	5	Where are we going?
	6	How are we doing?
	7	Where and why are we . . . doing well? doing badly?
III SITUATION ANALYSIS	9	Where are our opportunities and threats?
SWOT analysis	10–13	How can we capitalize on our strengths and reduce our weaknesses?
Competitive and functional strategies	14	How good is our information system?
	15	Where is our competitive advantage?
STRATEGIC CHANGE (How to manage changes in the corporate strategy)		
IV CHANGES IN CORPORATE STRATEGY	16	Where do we want to go? and, given our SWOT, What is realistic?
STRATEGIC ALTERNATIVES AND	17–20	What alternatives have we got? and
STRATEGIC CHOICE	16	How do we choose?
	21	What constitutes a good choice? What can/cannot should/should not we do?
V STRATEGIC IMPLEMENTATION	22–24	How do we make the strategy work? How do we manage the changes?

Case 2.1
MARGARET BROOKE

Mrs Margaret Brooke, the wife of a successful American businessman resident in the UK, loved buying and collecting antiques from auction sales. Unfortunately by early 1985 her house in Henley-on-Thames was 'overflowing' and beginning to look like a museum. She was restless for something to do and her husband was pressurizing her into getting rid of at least some of her antiques.

A friend gave her an idea. A converted derelict building in the West End of London was home for a large number of antique dealers (some 40 in all) who were able to rent small stalls (150 square foot floor area) for £30 per week. Arguing that she already had stock, would enjoy going out and buying more and that the rent was cheap, Margaret Brooke went into business.

After six months Mrs Brooke was unsure about her next move. She was certainly enjoying herself, she had learnt a lot about the antique trade, and her house was more orderly. But she felt that she should at least be breaking even and she did not know whether she was or not. For one thing she could not remember all the purchase prices of antiques she had owned before 1985. Additionally she had bought items she simply could not sell – but all the time she was doing less of this.

In future, she promised her husband, she would employ clear policies rather than simply buying and selling opportunistically as she had been doing.

So far she had taken few real risks. By concentrating on relatively inexpensive Victoriana she overcame her inexperience to a great extent. Unlike the scarce Queen Anne period furniture, for example, Victorian antiques were plentiful and there were very few 'fakes' on the market. For this reason she was not really in competition with the major dealers; but neither had she the opportunity for substantial profits. She never spent very much on any one article, and felt she could afford to make the odd mistake.

Margaret Brooke worked most days of the week and although she enjoyed selling she preferred spending her time at small auction sales. Her neighbour in the market frequently looked after her stall while she was away. Quite often Mrs Brooke sold her goods (furniture, pictures and other *objets d'art*) to other dealers in the market for a fast turnover, but this meant low mark-ups. For sales to non-dealers she tended to price halfway between the price she would happily pay for an article at auction and the amount she felt was the maximum a keen customer would pay. This represented a mark-up of around 100%.

At the end of six months she knew enough dealers to feel confident that she could sell on virtually all the furniture and oil paintings she might buy. However, she got very little satisfaction from dealing in articles that she herself did not like.

About one-third of the other stall holders seemed to be extremely knowledgeable; they specialized far more than Margaret Brooke did, and they appeared to be making a lot of money. Two, in particular, concentrated on renovated grandfather clocks and Georgian silver. The majority seemed not unlike Mrs Brooke – enthusiastic but not expert.

This analysis has been adapted from a short case written originally by Mr Kenneth Ambrose.

Questions

1. Where is Margaret Brooke going?
2. How is she doing?
3. Where and why is she doing well? Badly?
4. What are the opportunities and threats?
5. How might she capitalize on her strengths and reduce her weaknesses?
6. Where is her competitive advantage? Where might it be?
7. What might/should her future objectives be? What is realistic?
8. What choices does she have?
9. What would constitute a good choice?
10. What are the implementation aspects?

In the late 1980s, Woolworths (the High Street retailers now known as the Kingfisher Group) identified their customer service as being a weakness, particularly compared with their main rivals. People, they argued, are a major strategic resource, and they reflect the values of the organization. In common with many other service organizations, Woolworths introduced a customer care training programme entitled 'Excellence', and linked it to staff rewards. There have been two achievements. First, customer perception of staff helpfulness has increased, and second, there have been financial gains.

For these reasons, styles of corporate decision making, leadership and values should be a central driving force in the model in Figure 2.4. They are always important, and they are not easily changed without the appointment of a new chief executive. It seems appropriate that a study of strategic management should start with a consideration of their nature and implications.

Hence two additional questions can be added to the list:

☐ *How is strategy managed within the organization?* (Chapter 3)
☐ *How important are culture and values?* (Chapter 4)

APPLYING THE FRAMEWORK OF QUESTIONS

Case 2.1 is a very simple example of a small service business, and it is included to illustrate how the framework of questions might be applied. It demands a consideration of various change opportunities developing from a clear awareness of the current situation.

Suggested answers are provided below for the ten questions which follow the case. Before studying these you should attempt to answer the questions yourself.

1. Where is Margaret Brooke going?

Mrs Brooke appears to be developing her business incrementally, learning about marketing opportunities and prices as she goes along. She has not properly sorted out how to divide her time between buying and selling, and as a result of this she seems happy to sell goods on at low margins rather than to hold stock longer for greater gains. She chooses to deal in antiques that she herself likes – and whilst this must result in profitable opportunities being lost, it also means that she would probably keep any articles she failed to sell in her own home.

2. How is she doing?

Her house is emptier and less cluttered, and she is enjoying herself and learning more about antiques and the antique trade all the time. She has almost certainly achieved all she originally set out to do.

However, she is not sure how well she is doing financially. As one of the major reasons for this is that she has been selling antiques that she originally bought to keep and cannot remember all the purchase prices, it seems likely that by simple record keeping she can quickly overcome this as she buys more and more for the business.

3. Where and why is she doing well? Badly?

She is making fewer mistakes as she learns more, and she seems to be reaching a stage where she understands certain lines well enough to know that she can sell on all she buys, albeit at limited profit. Mark-ups of 100% seem satisfactory, and her concentration on 'safe' Victoriana has probably been wise.

However, she must be limited in what she can handle by physical and transportation constraints. By relying on other stall holders to watch her stall and sell for her on an *ad hoc* basis she is neglecting a major aspect of her business. She also does not appear to put a realistic value on her time.

4. Where are her opportunities and threats?

She is in a market full of opportunities, but one that is competitive because there are few barriers to entry. She could expand . . . but might require assistance. She could specialize more and consider the more profitable segments – but this would require more professionalism and imply greater risks.

At the moment she faces very few threats.

But maybe she really wants to develop the business, and if so she could face threats from more knowledgeable dealers, from 'fake' antiques and from customers who might have greater knowledge and expertise than she has herself. Her husband, or bank manager, might constitute a threat if she starts investing more money in expensive specialized stock.

5. How might she capitalize on her strengths and reduce her weaknesses?

The areas she could look at are the following:

☐ *Products*	extending her knowledge
☐ *Stock control*	clearly deciding whether she is buying to sell to customers or to other dealers, and how long she should hold on to articles
☐ *Pricing*	related to the above
☐ *Financial records*	including valuing her time for profit calculations

More particularly, she must assess how effectively she is using her time – and how she wants to use it. If she wants to concentrate on buying and still run something of a successful profitable business she will need either a partner or an assistant . . . and this would bring a new dimension to the business.

6. Where is her competitive advantage? Where might it be?

At the moment she really has none. She would not appear to have many prospects with either products, service or delivery.

She might consider using low prices, especially if the financial side is of secondary importance to her. But she then runs the risk of antagonizing the other stall holders, one of whom she is dependent upon.

As she seems to prefer buying to selling, could she seek competitive advantage by looking to 'buy to order' in some way? (Developed below.)

7. What might/should her future objectives be? What is realistic?

To determine these she will have to address the following issues:

- [ ] How much does she want to develop a 'real' business?
- [ ] How much time is she happy/willing to devote to it on a long-term basis?
- [ ] How profitable does she want it to be? Would she be happy to just break even?
- [ ] How much risk is she willing (and able) to take on products, money and other people?
- [ ] Where does she want to concentrate her effort?

Less ambitious objectives would seem to be more realistic.

8. What choices does she have?

- [ ] She could give it all up! After all, her house is emptier.
- [ ] She could stay roughly as she is, making sure she keeps proper records and assesses just how well she is doing financially.
- [ ] She could look to expand whilst staying in relatively safe Victoriana. Maybe she could join forces with another dealer, concentrating herself on buying. As partners they might be able to operate a larger stall. They might also be able to increase profits by better marketing – display, selling effort and pricing.
- [ ] She could specialize more, either in antiques with a higher profit margin or in just one type of good.

- [ ] She could act as essentially a buying agent – buying for other dealers who prefer to concentrate on selling or buying for individual clients. To accomplish the latter she would have to build an order book for particular customers and then go around the auctions buying for them.
- [ ] Finally, she could think of opening an antique shop, although for a number of reasons this would seem improbable.

9. What would constitute a good choice?

Simplistically, a good choice would be one which would achieve her objectives.

It will be seen, at this stage, how important her values are in this evaluation. Margaret Brooke started buying and selling antiques for a number of reasons, none of them apparently concerned with making substantial profits from a commercial venture. She has enjoyed the experience and has done things in a relatively informal *ad hoc* way. If she wishes to continue in much the same way her likely choice of direction will be very different from the one she might select if she decides that now is the time to view the business as a real business.

Her ability is a constraint, but it is becoming less of one. She has a number of opportunities with varying degrees of risk. Arguably her choice must be acceptable to her, her husband and, possibly, the bank manager.

10. What are the implementation aspects?

These must centre upon knowledge and any need for new knowledge; money if expansion is planned; the amount of time involved; and possibly the need for additional assistance with the business.

There could well be implications for the fundamental values if outside help and/or commercial finance is introduced into the business.

SUMMARY

In this chapter we have

- ☐ shown the component stages of a very simple prescriptive model of strategic management
- ☐ illustrated how strategic management can be seen as three interrelated aspects: strategic analysis, strategic choice and strategic implementation
- ☐ developed a series of questions designed to provide insight into strategic awareness and strategic decision making – emphasizing that organizations should be addressing some or all of these on an on-going basis
- ☐ used these questions to illustrate the dimensions of a study of strategic management, and to provide a framework for the content and order of the book
- ☐ reinforced the importance of styles of decision making, corporate leadership, values and culture
- ☐ worked through a simple example using the questions.

RESEARCH ASSIGNMENT

Library based

Take any organization that you are reasonably familiar with, for example the one you work for, the one you study in, one you have worked for, or maybe one that a member of your family works for, and

EITHER apply to it the ten questions provided after Case 2.1

OR write down what you already know and can find out about it under the headings: environment, values and resources.

RECOMMENDED FURTHER READING TO CHAPTERS 1 AND 2

On linear strategy

Chandler, A D (1962) *Strategy and Structure*, MIT Press.
Drucker, P F (1974) *Management: Tasks, Responsibilities, Practices*, Harper and Row.
Learned, E P, Christensen, C R, Andrews, K R and Guth, W R (1969) *Business Policy*, Richard D Irwin.

On adaptive strategy

Ansoff, H I, Declerck, R P and Hayes, R L (eds) (1976) *From Strategic Planning to Strategic Management*, Wiley.
Glueck, W F and Jauch, L R (1984) *Business Policy and Strategic Management*, McGraw-Hill.
Hofer, C W and Schendel, D (1978) *Strategy Formulation: Analytical Concepts*, West.
Johnson, G and Scholes, K (1984) *Exploring Corporate Strategy*, Prentice Hall.
Mintzberg, H (1987) Crafting strategy, *Harvard Business Review*, July–August, pp. 66–75.
Quinn, J B (1980) *Strategies for Change: Logical Incrementalism*, Richard D Irwin.

On interpretive strategy

Pettigrew, A M (1977) Strategy formulation as a political process, *International Studies of Management and Organization*, 7, 78–87.
Schein, E H (1985) *Organizational Culture and Leadership*, Jossey Bass.

STRATEGIC LEADERSHIP AND DECISION MAKING

3

LEARNING OBJECTIVES

After studying this chapter you should be able to

☐ define strategic leadership and identify the key roles of a strategic leader in the creation and implementation of strategy;
☐ identify factors which contribute towards effective strategic leadership;
☐ describe and evaluate the rational approach to decision making;
☐ summarize a number of alternative theories of decision making;
☐ define risk; and describe why different strategic leaders will have varying perceptions of what is an acceptable level of risk;
☐ explain the significance of entrepreneurship, and describe entrepreneurial strategy making.

This is the first of two chapters which concentrate on the central core of the strategy framework (Figure 2.4). The nature, role and significance of strategic leadership are discussed, and issues of risk and entrepreneurship are explored. In addition we consider how decisions might be made in an organization.

INTRODUCTION

The quotation in Box 3.1 emphasizes the need for a clear direction for the organization. It is the responsibility of the chief executive to clarify the mission and objectives of the organization, to define the corporate strategy which is intended to achieve these and to establish and manage the organization's structure. 'Mission' means the long-term objectives of the organization related to the strategic leader's vision of the nature and scope of the business or businesses that he feels would be appropriate and desirable.

The corporate strategy will be implemented within the structure, and this will

---

Box 3.1
QUOTE FROM STRATEGIC LEADER – I

The task of leadership, as well as providing the framework, values and motivation of people, and allocation of financial and other resources, is to set the overall direction which enables choices to be made so that the efforts of the company can be focused.

(Sir John Harvey-Jones, Chairman, ICI plc. 1982–7)

---

introduce changes in competitive and functional strategies. The chief executive will also be a major influence on the organization's culture and values, which are key determinants of the ways in which strategies are created and implemented.

However, the chief executive is not the only creator of strategic change. Managers who are in charge of divisions or strategic business units (normally referred to as 'general managers') are also responsible for strategic changes concerning their own products, services or geographic territories. Functional managers will make and carry out decisions which result in strategic change. In many firms the chief executive will also act as chairman of the board, but in others he will be supported by a part-time, non-executive chairman who will contribute actively to corporate strategy decisions, and external relations. In a limited number of large companies, particularly those which are diverse and multi-national, a chief operating officer will report directly to the chief executive. He or she will be responsible for ensuring that the operating parts of the business perform effectively, and consequently will influence changes in competitive and functional strategies. Throughout this book the term **strategic leader** is used to describe the managers who head the organization and who are primarily responsible for creating and implementing strategic change.

Whilst the strategic leader has overall responsibility for managing strategy in the organization it should not be thought that he

or she is the sole source of thoughts and ideas. All employees can make a contribution, and should be encouraged to do so. The more that people are invited to participate in debate and discussions concerning products, services, markets and the future the more likely they are to accept changes.

The strategic leader, however, is in a unique position to gather and receive information about all aspects of the business, and it is encumbent upon him to monitor the environment and the organization and watch for opportunities and threats. He or she will need both analytical skills and insight (or 'awareness') to provide an intuitive grasp of the situation that faces the organization. The way the organization manages to grasp opportunities and overcome potential threats will be very dependent upon the personal qualities and values of the strategic leader.

STRATEGIC LEADERSHIP

The role of the strategic leader

The strategic leader is responsible directly to the Board of Directors of the organization, and, through the Board, to the stakeholders in the business. The responsibilities of the Board, and, in effect, the strategic leader, are featured in Box 3.2. The role of strategic leadership is illustrated in Figure 3.1.

The strategic leader must **direct** the organ-

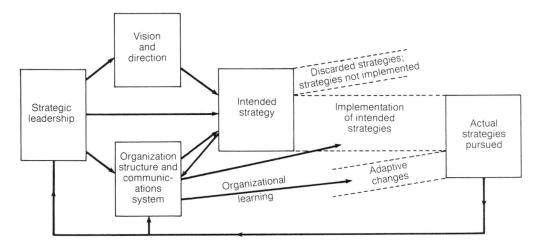

Figure 3.1   Strategic leadership and strategic change.

ization. He or she must ensure that long-term objectives and strategies have been determined and that they are understood and supported by managers within the organization who will be responsible for implementing them. The more feasible and achievable the objectives and strategies seem, the more likely they are to be supported.

These intended strategies will be implemented through the **organization structure** the strategic leader adopts. Some intended strategies will prove not to be feasible – the assumptions on which they are based may be wrong, and circumstances can change – and they will be discarded or postponed. Decisions taken by general and functional managers within a decentralized structure will lead to new, adaptive changes in competitive and functional strategies. A third

major responsibility of the strategic leader is a system of **communications** which, first, enables managers throughout the organization to be strategically aware, and, second, ensures that the strategic leader stays informed of the changes that are taking place.

As an analogy, the strategic leader is providing managers with a survival kit. There is a map (the mission and intended strategies), but managers also need a compass, emergency provisions, and ways of summoning assistance when, for whatever reason, the map proves inadequate. The structure, policies and communication networks provide this necessary flexibility.

Corporate governance

Box 3.2 summarizes the main responsibilities of the Board of Directors of an organization. The execution of these responsibilities is normally through the appointment of a chief executive; but the Board will also have a chairman to oversee decision making and operations. The chairman will additionally be responsible for ensuring that the structure and composition of the Board is appropriate.

There are two contentious issues. First:

I believe that increasing shareholder value is the key to profitable industrial growth. The choice, motivation and direction of management is crucial. Leaders should not be slow constantly to encourage change. They should see all problems as solvable and all questions as answerable.

Lord Hanson, Chairman, Hanson plc

Box 3.2
THE RESPONSIBILITIES OF THE BOARD OF DIRECTORS

1. Manage the business on behalf of all the stakeholders (or interested parties)
2. Provide direction in the form of a mission or purpose
3. Formulate and implement changes to corporate strategies
4. Monitor and control operations, with special reference to financial results, productivity, quality, customer service, innovation and new products and services and staff development

5. Provide policies and guidelines for other managers to facilitate both the management of operations and changes in competitive and functional strategies.

Responsibility 5 is achieved through the organization structure; 2 and 4 are dependent upon an effective communications network.

---

should the roles of chairman and chief executive be separated or combined? This is debated in Box 3.3. Second, what contribution should be made by non-executive directors, i.e. members of the Board who are not employed as executives within the firm? There are conflicting opinions on these issues, and no straightforward answers. The challenge is to ensure that there is effective leadership and control, and objectivity. This requires strong and capable leaders, but also opportunities for debate amongst the key executives who are responsible for both the creation and implementation of strategic change. Objectivity can often be improved by the appointment of outside non-executive directors with the ability to contribute particular skills and expertise. The Guinness affair in the mid-1980s, which concerned illegal share support operations during an acquisition, has been partially blamed on a Board which was not properly informed and objective. Strong and independent non-executive directors might have alleviated the difficulties.

A 1992 report by the Committee on Financial Aspects of Corporate Governance (chaired by Sir Adrian Cadbury) recommended that

☐ Board authority should be divided between a chairman and chief executive – but if Boards chose to combine the roles they should ensure 'the presence of a strong independent element with an appointed leader';
☐ more decisions should be deferred to non-executive directors – who should also constitute an audit and remuneration committee;
☐ more information should be given to shareholders.

The Committee and its findings are supported by the Confederation of British Industry, the Stock Exchange and the Institutional Shareholders Committee, but the recommendations are voluntary.

The role of management is to maximize within a given environment. The role of the Board is to change the environment to the benefit of the company.

The best Boards have a mix of experiences, backgrounds, qualifications and ages, giving the strength of the mongrel, rather than the weakness of the pedigree.

Roy Watts, Chairman, Thames Water

Box 3.3
CORPORATE GOVERNANCE

The topic for debate: *Should organizations separate the roles of chairman and chief executive, or combine them?*

If they are separated the chairman could be either executive (full-time) or non-executive (part-time). Typically a non-executive chairman would act as a sounding board for the chief executive, manage Board meetings and liaise with institutional shareholders. The chief executive would be in charge of both strategy and control. An executive chairman would accept responsibility for corporate strategy, with the chief executive controlling the business.

The majority of institutional shareholders in the UK favour a split in the roles for public companies; but not all large companies agree. Over 25% of the largest 100 UK companies combine the roles, many of them, including BOC, Grand Metropolitan and Kingfisher (Woolworths), successfully.

The case for the combined role

☐ Allows for clear, strong and accountable leadership
☐ Part-time, non-executive, chairmen are unsuitable for large, complex, multinational businessess – the job is too demanding
☐ A non-executive deputy chairman is an ideal compromise

☐ The strength of the Board as a whole, in terms of both executive and non-executive directors, is a more critical issue
☐ The executive workload can be spread amongst all the executive directors, allowing for greater cohesion.

However: It is important to ensure that the strategic leader does not become lonely and isolated.

The case for splitting the roles

☐ More likely to guarantee proper checks and balances
☐ Ideal way of tightening control over strategic decision making without placing it in the hands of one person – large Boards are not always going to agree
☐ Allows for complementary skills, with each role requiring different expertise
☐ Succession issues are likely to be less complicated.

However: It is critical that the two people involved generally agree with each other and can work together.

Clearly there is no single answer which is appropriate for all companies. Strategic demands vary and individual abilities differ. The challenge is to establish both clear leadership and objectivity.

Adapted from: Morrison, R (1991) 'Two views on a split personality', *Financial Times*, 4 October.

Corporate governance varies between countries, and it could impact increasingly on corporate strategies as companies become more global, and seek to acquire businesses, or set up joint ventures, more widely. Germany, for example, employs a two-tier Board structure to introduce checks and balances and ensure that employees, as well as shareholders, are properly represented. In France and Italy executives wield significant power and are rarely challenged by shareholders. In Japan, shareholders again tend to be passive, and the Board, essentially an extension of management, has no independent powers.

The contribution of non-executive directors

In thinking about the future direction of the organization, strategic leaders can, and will, seek advice and ideas from a variety of people, including fellow managers, outside contacts and non-executive directors.

Historically there has been some tendency to regard non-executive directors as people who contribute little more than their actual presence at Board meetings. However, I believe that this represents a wasted opportunity. It can prove useful, for example, to appoint an external director who understands the mood and mentality of the City, in addition to having contacts who might help with financing arrangements. The potentially significant role of City analysts and institutional investors is discussed later in the book.

Smaller companies, who may not employ experts in every functional area, can obtain their expertise from non-executives. New businesses, run by young managers, can obtain experience by appointing older or even retired businessmen who understand their products, services and markets. Most companies, in fact, could benefit from fresh insights from people whose perspective is different from that of the executive directors and managers. However, it will be important for the strategic leader to make use of their expertise by keeping them informed and discussing matters with them, rather than simply inviting them along to Board meetings.

Ideally there will be only limited interference from non-executives when things are progressing well, but they will be there when they are needed. A final essential contribution they can make is to stand aside and appraise the performance of the strategic leader and the other executive directors more objectively than they can do it themselves.

In the UK one might expect one-third of the Board to be non-executive, whilst two-thirds would be the norm for a large American company. SmithKline (of America) and Beecham merged in 1989 to form a major international pharmaceuticals, animal health and consumer products company. On 1 January 1991 a new Board was appointed, comprising seven executive directors and nine non-executives – both British and American. It was stated that the non-executives would be expected 'to conduct a penetrating interrogation of management, looking at performance and how it is accomplished'. They were to be in a majority so that 'they can ensure that the proper management is in place'. Of course, the performance of the non-executive directors should also be appraised.

Falls from grace

Institutional shareholders own 66% of all UK shares (1991), with private shareholdings amounting to 21%. Twenty years earlier the respective percentages were 39 and 54. Institutions have their own shareholders, and consequently they pay close attention to the performance of the businesses in which they have invested. Institutional pressures can

---

The traditional British unitary board structure is at its least effective in the strategy debate. It is essential for non-executive directors to play a positive and leading role when the issue of 'change' and 'response to change' is, or should be, on the agenda. Non-executive directors are more normally outnumbered in manufacturing industry and often prefer to remain low-key in the face of executive self-assurance. This is fundamentally wrong, since it is in the areas of broad-brush strategy, economic overviews, political evolution and the like, that experienced non-executive directors can offer most; while executives may have a narrower focus.

Moral   More non-executives and ensure that they speak their minds.

Alick Rankin, Chairman, Scottish & Newcastle Breweries plc

ensure that the strategic leader is held accountable for his or her strategic decisions and the performance of the company. Three years after the Stock Market crash of 1987, only one chief executive from the ten worst performing companies (measured by their share price movements) was still in post. The 'losers' included Sir Ralph Halpern of Burton (Halpern had earlier been responsible for turning Burton around after a poor performance during the 1970s – see Case 21.2), George Davies, the creator of Next, and Tony Berry who had built Blue Arrow into the world's largest employment agency. The lone survivor was Brian Beazer of Beazer (Construction) which was acquired by Hanson in 1991. Case 3.1, Coloroll, describes the rise and subsequent fall of John Ashcroft.

Although described as 'losers', many such chief executives resign and receive generous golden handshakes. The real losers are the employees who also lose their jobs in the contraction, and sometimes the shareholders.

Leadership qualities

Box 3.4 lists a number of qualities and skills for effective strategic leadership.

Bennis (1988) contends that vision is crucial and that the most effective leaders are people with ideas. This accords with the view of Sir Winston Churchill who believed that the 'emperor of the future will be the emperor of ideas'. Short-term success can be determined by market forces, and some highly pragmatic chief executives are very successful at turning around organizations that are experiencing difficulties and decline, but long-term success also requires a clear vision of where the organization is going. Different situations require particular strategies. Companies looking to grow quickly are likely to behave aggressively with competitive, higher-risk strategies. Those that are seeking to maximize the earnings from the existing portfolio of activities by increasing productivity, and

those which choose, or need, to rationalize and prune will typically follow lower-risk, less competitive strategies. Some strategic leaders will be flexible and able to change as circumstances alter; others will prove more inflexible. The Coloroll case also illustrates this point.

Bennis believes that successful organizations are those that are well led rather than those that are well managed, thus emphasizing the need for a clear vision. Without a vision an organization may be very efficient and may carry out certain tasks very well, but it is less likely to be effective (doing the right things very well) than those organizations with a clear and shared direction.

Bennis further argues that three other factors are extremely important:

☐ the ability to communicate and sell the vision and ideas
☐ trust: the need for followers to trust and believe in the leader
☐ the ability and willingness to learn from experience and to adapt.

In many respects the first two issues are related to the organization culture.

In addition, Bennis comments, it is important to believe more in success than in failure. In other words, strategic leaders should understand clearly where the strengths of the organization are, concentrate on them and develop them to make the company more successful.

Management style

Management style incorporates a number of factors such as risk taking, autocracy, democracy, reliance on planning, willingness to change as opportunities arise and awareness of opportunities. There is no single recommended style; different leaders all behave individually. But the activity and relative success of the organization is strongly influenced by the style adopted.

Some strategic leaders will be entrepreneur-

Case 3.1
COLOROLL

Coloroll was based in Manchester and after John Ashcroft became Managing Director in 1979 at the age of 30 (and subsequently Chairman) it increased its share of the UK wallpaper market from 3% to 30%, and diversified into pottery and earthenware, bed linen and finally carpets (Kosset) with the acquisition of John Crowther in 1988.

The company was very market oriented and concerned to give the customer 'what he wants when he wants it'.

I've geared the business towards generic growth, which means exploiting market trends and knocking out competitors by pushing them off the shelf.   (Ashcroft)

There was a clear and coherent strategy. Coloroll successfully identified and exploited an opportunity for providing a range of attractive and affordable household products for young consumers who were either first-time home owners or removing for the first time. The Coloroll brand name, though, was stamped upon some famous and well-established products including Denby pottery and Edinburgh crystal.

Acquisitions were handled in three stages: 'assessment, reconstruction and rehabilitation'. Companies were acquired if Coloroll believed they could improve the performance, and they began by changing the culture.

Symbols are regarded as important in making the change of culture. Staffordshire Potteries had a wood-panelled boardroom and a directors' snug complete with bar. Both were ripped apart by Coloroll (alcohol is not allowed anywhere within the group) and turned into meeting rooms for the workforce. At Fogarty [duvets and bedlinen], where there were three grades of toilet – one for the chairman, one for the other directors, and one for the ranks – there was a similar ritual demolition.   (Ashcroft)

Reconstruction was designed to simplify the job of management, accelerate decision making and reduce unnecessary overheads. Structures were altered, and Coloroll ensured that managers understood the objectives they were being set, and offered incentives to make them worthy of achievement. The most senior managers from the acquired company were likely to be replaced, often by managers from within the company, and Coloroll introduced tight financial monitoring systems. Clear targets were set for key financial measures. Up-to-date sales and financial information was collected weekly, and any variations from budgets were acted upon quickly.

We have a very small head office team of four directors. The rest of the company is divided into businesses that all have their own managing directors who operate autonomously. These MDs have big salaries, big bonuses, big cars and big prestige positions, and they are the people who make all the decisions.   (Ashcroft)

To operate smoothly, I need to have a clear perception of where the business is going. Every year we debate it, but once I decide, then everybody has to go along with it. There's a lot of nonsense talked about democracy. I believe management democracy is everybody agreeing to do what the leader wants.   (Ashcroft)

Sales of £6 million in the late 1970s increased 100 times in ten years. Profits grew at a comparable rate and exceeded £50 million in the 1988/9 financial year. However high rates of interest in 1989 led to a slowing down in the rate of growth of Coloroll's sales, aggressive pricing policies by both Coloroll and its competitors, and substantial increases in the cost of borrowings. The financial difficulties were compounded by Coloroll having paid too high a price for John Crowther. Interim profits for the six months to September 1989 collapsed.

Ashcroft's strategy had proved extremely successful in buoyant market conditions, but growth was too fast. The company was not sufficiently robust financially to withstand adverse trading conditions.

We got carried away with the concept and lost sight of the cash.   (Ashcroft)

In March 1990 John Ashcroft resigned, and his replacement was described as a 'doctor handed an incurable patient'. Within weeks Coloroll was in receivership, and the business was subsequently offered for sale either as a whole or up to 11 separate parts. Finally five divisions were sold to their respective managers, three to other companies, and three were closed down.

Ashcroft himself started a new business – Survival Aid – in the Lake District in 1991, selling outdoor clothing by mail order, but with plans to expand into retailing.

Adapted from: Ashcroft, J (1987) Coloroll's blueprint for acquisitions, *Financial Decisions*, April; Rawsthorn, A (1990) Coloroll comes unstuck over high interest rates, *Financial Times*, 24 January; Nash, T (1991) When Coloroll's rainbow faded, *Director*, February. Quotations mainly from:
John Ashcroft's wall-to-wall confidence, an interview with Marina Cantacuzino, *Telegraph Sunday Magazine*, 1988.

Box 3.4
QUALITIES AND SKILLS FOR EFFECTIVE LEADERSHIP

☐ A vision – articulated through the culture and value systems.

☐ The ability to build and control an effective team of managers.

☐ The ability to recognize and synthesize important developments, both inside and outside the organization. Requires strategic awareness, the ability to judge the significance of an observed event, and conceptualization skills.

☐ Effective decentralization, delegation and motivation.

☐ Credibility and competence. 'Knowing what you are doing' and having this recognized. Requires the abilities to exercise power and influence and to create change.

☐ Implementation skills; getting things done. Requires drive, decisiveness and dynamism.

☐ Perseverance and persistence in pursuing the mission or vision, plus mental and physical stamina.

Sources: Kets de Vries, M F R (1989) *Prisoners of Leadership*, Wiley; and Boyle, D and Braddick, B (1981) *The Challenge of Change: Business Leaders for the 1980s*, Gower in association with Ashridge Management College.

ial – by nature they will seek out opportunities for change or growth, and they will be willing to take the necessary risks. Entrepreneurialism is considered in detail later in this chapter. Other leaders will be more conservative, unlikely to take any major risks, and concerned to preserve the status quo; and in relatively stable environments this can prove both appropriate and successful. The organization will be less dynamic, some would say less exciting, but this is no argument against such a style. The proper congruence between environment, values and resources is the crucial issue.

The strategic leader similarly may adopt an autocratic or a democratic style. One might expect small companies which have been started and developed by one person to be run autocratically by that person, who may remain the major shareholder. In a sense it is that person's company, and hence it is logical that he or she should make all major decisions. It is also possible, however, for large companies to be run successfully along similar lines. Lonrho, the multi-national conglomerate, has been very dependent upon chief executive Roland 'Tiny' Rowland for many years, and he is the major shareholder. At one stage Rowland was described as running Lonrho as a personal fiefdom, but he has remained firmly in charge for over 20 years and the company has undoubtedly been successful. Equally it is possible for chief executives to be very democratic and consult other senior managers extensively. Furthermore it is not necessary for the overall control function to be solely one person's responsibility. Trafalgar House, which was mentioned in Chapter 1 and which has developed into shipping and shipbuilding from a base in property and construction, has arguably been successful because the responsibilities for strategy creation and strategy execution and implementation have been separated. Sir Nigel Broakes, who founded the company and remained as chairman until 1992, is regarded as primarily a successful creator.

The style of leadership also relates to the role of planning and the importance of incremental change in strategic management. Some strategic leaders will rely quite heavily on information systems, forecasts and plans for determining strategic change, and this could be linked to a strict adherence to financial targets. Hanson plc, run by Lord Hanson, is regarded as a company which has grown by a strategy of acquisition and appropriate divestment, and is strongly controlled through central direction. Subsidiaries are given clear financial targets to achieve.

Where organizations are divisionalized much depends upon the amount of freedom and encouragement that the strategic leaders of each division are given. In some cases they are constrained from changing things in any major way, and in other cases they are encouraged to make changes if competitive pressures or opportunities arise.

Objectives and ambitions

The strategic leader may be very ambitious to create a certain type of organization. Size, international scope, involvement in certain industries, public image and reputation are all possible issues. Some leaders have a very clear remit, perhaps being appointed to rescue a company in difficulties; others may have considerable freedom to choose their own terms of reference. As a result organizations can change markedly with changes of strategic leader. In the 1970s, Heywood Williams, a company which enjoys a low profile as far as the general public is concerned but which is nevertheless a leading UK supplier of glass and associated products, operating in most segments of the glass market, followed a strategy of diversification in both the UK and USA, buying amongst other things a chain of hotels. At the end of the decade there was a change of leader when the chief executive died suddenly, and a dramatic change of overall direction. Heywood Williams divested itself of all interests not directly related to glass and aluminium, its core businesses.

Where a new strategic leader is appointed and is determined to make changes the results could be either positive or negative. Much will depend upon the need to change, the directions for change that are chosen, and how well they match existing skills and values. Long-term success requires that the development of resources and any changes in culture complement conditions and changes in the external environment.

Equally some companies will experience difficulties when a strong and possibly charismatic leader departs. He or she may be 'impossible to follow' and there can be temporary or even permanent decline.

Values and the strategic leader

The strategic leader may have very clear or specific values which influence his or her style and the culture of the organization. For example if the leader has a financial background and orientation, this may prove important. Financial targets and analysis may be crucial elements in the management of strategy. Similarly if the leader has a marketing background this could result in a different style of leadership, with perhaps more concentration on consumers and competition. An engineer may be very committed to product design and quality. These comments are generalizations and will not always prove to be true, however.

If a new strategic leader is appointed from another company it is inevitable that he or she will bring values which have been learned elsewhere, and these may involve change. Logically the person will be chosen because of his or her successful record in one or more previous companies, and as a newcomer he or she may be determined to establish his or her presence by introducing changes.

Strategic leadership and strategic change

It has already been emphasized that strategies can **form** or **emerge** as well as be **formulated** or **prescribed**. The role of the strategic leader must be examined in this context.

Strategic change results from decisions taken and implemented in response to perceived opportunities or threats. The management of change therefore requires strategic awareness and strategic learning, which implies the ability to recognize and interpret signals from the environment. Signals from the environment come into the organization all the time and in numerous ways. It is essential that they are monitored and filtered in such a way that the important messages reach decision makers. If strategic change is to some degree dependent upon a planning system, then that planning system must gather the appropriate data. Equally, if there is greater reliance on strategic change emerging from decisions taken within the organization by managers who are close to the market, their suppliers and so on, these managers must feel that they have the authority to make change decisions. In both cases appropriate strategic leadership is required to direct activity.

Planning systems can be used for a number of reasons. Their role is determined by the strategic leader, but basically they are a part of the decision-making process. It is feasible to have a planning system within the organization which follows an annual cycle. Data in terms of results, forecasts and proposals can be collected from all parts of the organization and then evaluated by senior management before they establish future objectives and strategies and allocate corporate resources to enable the strategies to be implemented. In this situation, the greater the number of managers that are consulted in some way and whose opinion, related to their product or market knowledge, is asked for, the more detailed the insight is likely to be. Planners, in other words, can facilitate an input from a wide range of knowledgeable managers into a decision-making system. However, it is possible for planners to carry out their own data gathering and forecasting without involving many other functional managers, but it is generally believed that this is less effective. The planning process should result in plans, objectives and strategies to which managers are committed because they have had an input, rather than a set of plans that never get implemented.

The major decisions fall to the strategic leader, and therefore he or she must decide upon the most appropriate planning system and manage it. The planning and management system of ICI is detailed in Case 3.2. Planning will be explored in greater detail later in the book.

The ICI system is designed to balance the need for central control of a complex group of interdependent divisions with the desirability of giving freedom to managers with responsibilities for geographic areas and product types. Sir Denys Henderson, the current Chairman of ICI, believes that a deliberate lack of rigidity in the management structure allows this flexibility, and enables the company to be quick to react to new technical and marketing opportunities. The delegation of more authority to managers has switched the emphasis from formal planning towards implementation and emergent change, but a

planning system still exists to co-ordinate efforts.

Strategic change can emerge from day-to-day decisions, as has already been discussed. Managers who are aware and alert to changes in the environment realize when a development is occurring that needs to be reacted to. This is change in response to some discontinuity. Managers can also be constantly alert to new ways of producing or marketing their product or service so as to improve or strengthen their competitive advantage. If this is to happen effectively then the strategic leader must ensure that the managers feel encouraged, motivated and rewarded for acting accordingly. The strategic leader must design and manage an appropriate organization structure to ensure this.

RISK

It was emphasized in Chapter 1 that certain business environments involve higher risks than others. High technology industries, where there is constant innovation and technological change, involve high levels of risk. In pharmaceuticals it takes a number of years to develop and test a new drug before it can be introduced on to the market, and for much of this time there will be a real possibility that the new drug may never become a commercial success. Again, therefore, there is a high level of risk. A third example is oil exploration. The oil companies drilling in the North Sea, for example, have had to invest several million pounds in the hope of finding oil. Whilst they can reduce their risk with sophisticated geological surveys before full exploration is embarked upon, there is again a risk of failure and loss of investment.

What then is risk? Risk occurs whenever anyone must make a choice and the potential outcomes involve uncertainty. In other words if a manager is faced with a decision and the alternative choices involve estimated potential gains and losses which are not

---

As a strategic leader . . .

One must organize oneself to have as much time as possible to see colleagues in the firm, and to be known to be available to them, for talking face-to-face is more valuable than a long memo. One must go and see others in their offices.

This is the only way to stay in touch with what is going on and to ensure that an agreed plan is being carried out.

François Michelin, PDG, Michelin et Cie

Case 3.2
STRATEGIC MANAGEMENT AT ICI

ICI produces a wide range of products from petrochemicals to pharmaceuticals in some 40 countries and markets them throughout the world. Turnover exceeds £12 billion (1991).

In the 1970s ICI over-invested in commodity chemicals and a supply surplus in the early 1980s caused prices and profits to collapse. This, in conjunction with the problems resulting from the economic recession in the UK, caused ICI 'to re-appraise the role of executive directors in directing, planning and managing the company'.

Profit and operating responsibility for business units was delegated to a level of management below the Main Board, who would concentrate on group financial performance and corporate direction as a whole, allocating resources to the chief executives of the business units. In other words more authority was delegated than had been the case in the past.

Business units have a ten year strategic planning horizon and three year profit and cash budgets. This is appropriate as it takes at least ten years to develop a new drug from synthesis to market.

Twice a year the executives at Main Board level meet to review the overall strategy, progress, and needs for change. Strengths and weaknesses within the portfolio of products are assessed, as is the resource allocation. More resources will be put in if products or businesses are felt to deserve it; and similarly business unit chief executives are encouraged to divest certain poor performers. Particular concern is placed on comparisons with competition.

Periodically, not to a set timetable, each business unit undergoes a thorough strategic review when the Main Board feels that the existing strategy for the unit is no longer viable or the chief executive of the unit wishes to offer new strategic options for consideration.

Each business unit has 'milestones' or measures of performance in terms of cash and profit.

Budgets are reviewed annually and monitored quarterly.

The key element will always be competent, experienced, determined managers who are 'winners'. And they have to demonstrate their winning ability by consistently performing well against both budgets and strategies.

(This system was introduced by Sir John Harvey-Jones and has been continued by his successor, Sir Denys Henderson, the current Chairman of ICI. In 1992 plans were announced for a radical re-structuring. Case 22.4).

Taken from Henderson, D (1987) Corporate direction of ICI, *First*, **1** (2).

---

certainties, the situation involves risk. The outcome of a typical decision will be depen-

dent upon a number of factors, such as customer reaction, levels of demand and competitor reactions. Some managers will understand the situation better than others might, and partly for this reason be happier to accept the risk involved in a particular choice. Personality also affects the willingness to accept and take a particular risk.

It is important that there is compatibility between the strategic leader's attitude towards risk and the demands of the industry. A risk-averse strategic leader in a high risk industry may miss valuable opportunities.

Risk increases as the amount of potential loss increases. For example a person might be offered a ticket in a raffle which costs £1.00, and the chance of winning the first prize of £150 might be 1 in 200. Another person might be offered the opportunity to invest £100 with a 1 in 200 chance of winning £15 000. Although the odds of winning and losing are identical, the risk involved in each situation is different. The potential loss in the second case is 100 times greater than in the first, and it consequently involves greater risk.

The willingness to take the risk is affected by the amount and by its relative importance to the decision taker. For many people the loss of £1.00 would be an acceptable risk, especially as they might win £150, but fewer people would feel the same about £100. The utility of the potential gain and the potential loss, the relative worth to the decision maker, relates to his or her particular circumstances, needs and aspirations.

Consider as an example a manager in a secure job, earning £20 000 per year, who inherits £100 000 which he or she can invest and earn £10 000 per year interest with very little risk of losing the capital. He or she is given the opportunity to buy a significant shareholding in a small company which currently yields £50 000 per year to the owner who is retiring. The business could fail if the new owner makes strategic mistakes, and the whole investment might be lost. Some would take the risk; others would not. The risk would not be the same, however, if the manager concerned had inherited £500 000

and was being invited to invest just 20% of this.

The following criteria are important in the decision:

☐ the attractiveness of each option to the decision maker;
☐ the extent to which he or she is prepared to accept the potential loss in each alternative;
☐ the estimated probabilities of success and failure;
☐ the degree to which the decision maker is likely to affect the success or failure.

Hence in considering risk and strategic leadership in an organization a number of factors are worth investigating. It may well have an effect if the strategic leader is a significant shareholder rather than a minor one. Similarly, in the case of managers throughout the organization who are involved in strategic decisions in various ways, the culture and values of the organization with regard to reward for success and sanction for failure will be important. So too will be the personality of the managers and their **awareness** of the relative pay-offs and probabilities of success and failure.

Attitudes towards risk also affects the way managers make decisions.

Dunnette and Taylor (1975), whose research involved industrial managers, concluded: 'high risk takers tended to make more rapid decisions, based on less information than low risk takers, but they tended to process each piece of information more slowly . . . although risk-prone decision makers reach rapid decisions by the expedient of restricting their information search, they give careful attention to the information they acquire.'

Environmental factors may prove significant. The availability and cost of finance, forecasts of market opportunities and market buoyancy, and feelings about the strengths and suitability of internal resources will all be important. For other managers within the organization the overall culture and styles of

Case 3.3
THE LIGHT AIRCRAFT INDUSTRY: TWO PROFILES

The **Norman Aeroplane Company** was founded by Desmond Norman in 1976 after Britten–Norman Ltd, of which he was co-founder, had gone into receivership and been sold. Britten–Norman had designed the Islander and Trislander light aircraft, which were marketed successfully around the world. The company had experienced cash flow problems.

Norman received a grant of almost £1 million from the British Technology Group to pay for part of the research and development costs of the Fieldmaster, a versatile agricultural aircraft, useful for both crop spraying and fire fighting. During development the world market for agricultural aircraft collapsed. Over the same period the company also developed the Freelance, a general-purpose five-seater plane with folding wings, which is ideal for take-off and landing on unimproved fields, and which can be stored easily. By 1987 both aircraft had received certificates of air-worthiness, but the company had received no major orders.

In the early 1980s the Firecracker was also developed and, together with an associate company, a bid was made for the Royal Air Force contract for air trainers. The order was worth £150 million, but the company was unsuccessful.

Whilst none of the three Norman aeroplanes is unique in itself, they all have distinctive features. The Fieldmaster has a unique spraying system, integral within the wings, which allows for an extra-wide ground coverage, and a unique spray container tank which is fully integrated into the fuselage. The agricultural market segment is intensely competitive, and dominated by American producers. The distinctive aspects of the Freelance make it a very versatile plane, but with little real competitive advantage. The Firecracker also has a number of special features. It has a speed brake, unusual for this type of aircraft; a raised rear seat, allowing for better passenger visibility; and a rocket-assisted ejection system. It was targeted at a very unpredictable market where political judgement can over-ride technical and commercial issues.

Over £3 million was invested in the Fieldmaster and Freelance, and it was reported that some £5 million more in private capital was spent on the Firecracker.

Norman went into receivership in August 1988.

*   *   *   *   *

The unique **Optica** spotter plane was designed by John Edgley, who built the prototype in a house he owned in North London, before taking it for final assembly and testing to an airfield in Bedfordshire. The plane received substantial publicity when the first production model, under test by the Hampshire Police for observation duties, crashed on its maiden flight in May 1985. The subsequent investigation cleared the Optica of any design faults.

The Optica is revolutionary, having a three-seater observation cockpit at the very front, with the engine, propellor and wings all behind. It can cruise at slow speed and turn tightly. It is designed to compete with helicopters, and it enjoys a substantial cost advantage for both purchase and running. The business was design-led, with the market investigated properly only after the prototype was flying. Forecasts for potential demand have always proved over-optimistic.

Continued overleaf

Edgley and his institutional backers invested an estimated £8 million in building a sophisticated production facility, using computer-controlled machine tools, at Old Sarum Airfield near Salisbury before any definite orders were received.

In October 1985 Edgley Aircraft (the company) went into receivership, was sold, and renamed Optica Industries. The wisdom of building a capital-intensive production facility without orders for aircraft was questioned.

The premises, however, were destroyed by a mysterious fire early in 1987, and subsequently re-built. The company was re-named Brooklands Aerospace. The first order, in March 1988, came nine years after the Optica had first flown. In July 1989 an American order for 132 aircraft was received, and the company also diversified into manufacturing additional planes (including the Norman Fieldmaster) under licence. Financial difficulties led to a second receivership in April 1990.

These summaries are edited from 'The Norman Aeroplane Company' and 'The Optica' case studies, written by John L Thompson, and available from the European Case Clearing House at Cranfield Institute of Technology.

leadership and the reward systems will influence their risk taking.

Case 3.3 looks at elements of risk in the light aircraft industry, where substantial investment is required. Both examples illustrate entrepreneurial behaviour.

The industry key success factors relate to design, manufacture and marketing. In a very competitive industry with high development costs and reasonably lengthy development lead times (ten years is not abnormal for small companies from conception to airworthiness), it is essential to have some competitive edge in the design. However, customers must be persuaded that these special features create competitive advantage if companies are to penetrate the market in any significant way.

The manufacturing facility must be able to produce to high quality standards because of the safety factor. The more sophisticated the factory and the tooling, the more money is required to establish it, possibly before any orders are received. Edgley took the risk; Norman did not, at least not to the same extent. Norman subcontracted much of their parts and components manufacture and concentrated on design and assembly.

Desmond Norman and John Edgley are both entrepreneurs. They believe in their own ability to succeed; they are achievement motivated (defined below), willing to take the necessary risks and able to persuade backers to invest with them. Both had government grants, and Norman have received support from the Welsh Development Agency as they were located at Rhoose Airport in Cardiff. However, it is generally felt that insufficient equity capital is available for these innovatory businesses, and the dependence on loan capital can put pressure on the business.

Investment finance does seem to be available for the 'right' person with the 'right' idea, but it is often a long struggle to acquire it. Both companies raised money, but experienced some difficulties in doing so. Certain backers are willing to accept the risk – the potential pay-offs are substantial, but so are the potential losses.

Managing risk

Organizations will often pursue strategies which seek to manage or minimize risk.

Hanson, an extremely successful and profitable company which is discussed in detail in Chapter 13, always investigates 'the downside' in any strategy or proposed deal. Lord Hanson has said of his partner, Lord White: 'We would actually have done a lot more deals if Gordon did not have so many worries. He is constantly looking for the potential trouble in a deal.' When Richard Branson started Virgin Atlantic Airways, clearly a high-risk venture, he was cautious. He began with just one Boeing plane on sale or return for one year. Issues of risk in the airline industry are featured in Case 3.4, 'GPA – Guinness Peat Aviation'.

DECISION MAKING

Whatever the nature of the decision and the level in the organization at which it is taken, it will only be regarded as **effective** if it is supported by the people who must implement it, if it is implemented and if it achieves the objective it is related to. In other words an effective strategic decision will be one that is understood and supported within the organization, that is feasible and is implemented and that achieves the strategic objectives it relates to. Communications within the organization will be discussed later in this chapter; objectives are the subject of a later chapter. In this section we shall look at decision making in practice, at how decisions are taken and might be taken, and at why some bad decisions are made.

DECISION MAKING AND PROBLEM SOLVING

Decision making is a process related to the existence of a problem, and it is often talked about in terms of problem solving. A problem, in simple terms, exists when an undesirable situation has arisen which

requires action to change it. In other words a problem exists for someone if the situation that they perceive exists is unsatisfactory for them. They would like to see something different or better happening and achieving different results.

However, in many instances the problem situation is very complex and can only be partially understood or controlled, and therefore decisions are not so much designed to find ideal or perfect answers but to improve the problem situation. In other instances, managers may find themselves with so many problems at any time that they can at best reduce the intensity of the problem rather than systematically search for a so-called right answer.

Russell Ackoff (1978) distinguishes between solving, resolving, dissolving and absolving problems. A **solution** is the optimum answer, the best choice or alternative, and rational decision making (developed below) is an attempt to find it. A **resolution** is a satisfactory answer or choice, not necessarily the best available, but one that is contingent upon circumstances, such as time limitations, or lack of real significance of the problem. This will again be developed below. A **dissolution** occurs when objectives are changed in such a way that the problem no longer seems to be a problem. Feelings about what should be happening are changed to bring them in line with what is happening; current realities are accepted. If problems are **absolved** they are ignored in the hope that they will disappear.

The notion of rational decision making

The outcome of the rational model for decision making is the optimum solution. In reality, or in terms of explaining what happens in practice, the model can only be hypothetical because of the assumptions it makes: the problem can be stated clearly and unambiguously; the decision maker has all the information he or she needs to make the

Case 3.4
GPA – GUINNESS PEAT AVIATION

GPA is an unquoted company based in the low-tax zone of Shannon in Ireland. Its owners include airlines such as Aer Lingus and Air Canada, together with various banks and financial institutions. The majority shareholder (with 12%) is Mitsubishi; GPA's Chairman and founder, Tom Ryan, holds 8%.

GPA has been described as a supermarket for aircraft. In mid-1991 the company owned over 300 commercial aircraft, which it leases to airlines around the world. One hundred more were due for delivery before mid-1992. GPA has firm orders and options for a further 700 planes (10% of world manufacturing capacity) with deliveries scheduled into the next century. The penalties for any postponements or cancellations vary between deals. This level of ordering involves huge sums of money. In 1991 a Boeing 737 cost $33 million and a 747 between $125 and $145 million depending upon the specification. GPA conducts all its business in American dollars.

During the boom years of the late 1980s GPA was very successful. Profits increased ten-fold from $25 to $250 million over five years, but they slumped when the impact of the Gulf War was felt on travel and tourism.

The GPA strategy is to buy planes in bulk for price discounts of up to 25%, lease them on normally five- to seven-year non-cancellable agreements, and then sell used aircraft once the lease expires. The business is inevitably high risk, but GPA attempt to manage the downside in a number of ways.

☐ GPA has become skilled at re-leasing aircraft which are returned from airlines in liquidation or receivership.
☐ The customer base is diverse. It includes some 88 airlines in 45 countries world wide, and both state-owned carriers and smaller, private companies with low credit ratings, who are both required and prepared to pay higher lease charges.
☐ Most of the planes are modern and fuel-efficient, which is ideal when fuel prices are rising or are uncertain.

One dilemma is that in an air travel recession the value of used aircraft falls, and most of GPA's profits are from sales rather than lease charges. Moreover, airlines often delay or cancel new purchases – but at the same time, when planes have to be replaced, they may well switch to leasing instead of buying.

The risk inherent in GPA was illustrated by the failure of the planned global flotation of a minority of the shares in June 1992. Institutional demand, especially in America, was not forthcoming and the flotation was withdrawn. Whilst the relative gloom in world stock markets generally was an issue, there were real concerns about the stability of the world airline industry. The flotation aimed to reduce GPA's dependency on debt, and the assumption was that the company would then have to borrow more to meet its commitments in respect of new planes on order and due for delivery.

Over 75 banks have lent money to GPA, and some would argue that they have already been too generous. It has been commented that the banking system cannot afford to let GPA collapse.

Base Source: GPA comes down to earth; Cope, N (1991) *Business*, May.

Figure 3.2   The rational approach to decision making as part of the overall process of problem solving. (*Source*: The Open University Course P670, *The Effective Manager* p. 52.)

optimum decision; a complete list of possible alternatives can be drawn up and evaluated against the objectives; the decision maker has the time and inclination to search for the ideal solution. However, if it does not explain decision making in reality, the rational model does provide a very useful framework for examining reality and seeking explanations for how managers do make decisions.

Figure 3.2 illustrates the model as a series of ten stages, as follows.

Decision making

1. Sense the existence of a problem.
2. Clarify the nature and dimensions of the

problem and fully analyse the problem situation.

3. Specify objectives and identify any constraints which may determine the feasibility of certain objectives. Determine the criteria for achieving the objectives.
4. Generate a list of alternative solutions to the problem.
5. Evaluate all these alternatives using the criteria detailed in 3.

Decision taking
6. Select the **best** solution.

Implementation and control
7. Plan and schedule appropriate actions for the people who will be involved in implementation.
8. Communicate the decision clearly and unambiguously. Motivate and reward accordingly.
9. Implement the actions determined.
10. Monitor progress; control; review.

The rational model is based on the premise that the decision maker is primarily seeking to maximize his own satisfaction in making the decision. Having complete knowledge of the way to achieve this and of the exact reaction of other people and organizations, such as customers and competitors, to the decision, an objective evaluation of all the alternatives is quite feasible. In reality, although it is perfectly appropriate to consider organizations and individual decision makers as having objectives, it is not at all certain that they will be aimed at maximizing satisfaction. In many cases the decision will not be made by an individual alone but by a team of managers working together. At other times the single decision maker will be relying upon information provided to him by colleagues, and this information may be biased to a particular point of view rather than perfectly objective. For the rational model to work the information has to be accurate, complete, understandable, relevant and available in the appropriate form at the appropriate time, which in reality is idealis-

tic, despite advances in information technology. The generation of a wide range of alternative solutions is often also rare for a number of reasons. Managers may not have enough time, or be sufficiently creative, and they may be reluctant to change from behaviour patterns they already follow. They may suffer from what is termed tunnel vision, concentrating their thoughts in narrow well-defined channels. Explicit in the model is the ability to predict outcomes and anticipate competitor reactions, but forecasts are not very accurate. For a number of reasons, then, the model has weaknesses as far as practical application and use is concerned.

The alternative theories of decision making which follow are based on the premise that in reality there is more subjectivity and irrationality present. Simplification is used to reduce the complexity of problems and lessen the information handling.

It should be mentioned that there are strong similarities between the rational model of decision making and the outline model of strategic management presented at the beginning of Chapter 2. This particular model was described as being prescriptive, but not ideal for explaining all that happens in practice. Just as many decisions are affected by simplification and subjectivity, strategic decisions are similarly influenced in many instances.

Decision making is additionally linked to the skills and attributes of the person charged with making the decision.

Table 3.1 features the key skills required to accomplish each stage of the rational model, and it will be apparent that, individually, many managers will possess only some of them.

Alternative theories

Satisficing behaviour

Herbert Simon (1976) contends that satisficing consists of finding a course of action that is acceptable in the light of the intended

Table 3.1 The rational model of decision making: stages and skills required

Stage	Key skill required
Sensing the problem	Problem clarity; clarity of thought
Analysing the problem	Information handling
Specifying objectives	Objectives clarity; precision of thought
Generating alternatives	Creativity
Assessing probable outcomes	Forecasting
Selecting the best solution	Judgement and decisiveness
Implementation and evaluation	Leadership and management

objective. A satisfactory rather than an optimal course of action is chosen because of internal and external constraints: time pressure, lack of information, the influence of other interested parties, and so on. A satisfactory course exists, according to Simon, when there are criteria present which describe minimally satisfactory alternatives and when the alternative in question meets or exceeds all those criteria. It follows that rather than evaluate and select from a range of alternatives, only one need be considered if it meets the minimally satisfactory criteria. Simon argues that this approach is in fact rational within specified limits. Using the term **bounded rationality** he argues that the decision is bounded by three factors: the skills, habits and reflexes of the decision maker, which may no longer be conscious acts; the decision maker's values and motives; and his or her knowledge of issues relevant to the job. This approach therefore allows for limitations on information gathering and bias or focus on particular values. Simon does argue that in the case of extremely important or far-reaching decisions time will be found to make the evaluation of alternatives as exhaustive as possible.

It is easy to see how this could be reflected in certain strategic decisions. If, for example, the objective was to increase sales of a particular product by 5% in real terms, there would probably be a number of ways of achieving this. Increased advertising would be one; a new bonus scheme for the salesforce might be another; a price reduction may work; and marketing the product through additional channels of distribution could also achieve the objective. There may or may not be a profitability constraint in the decision. In the rational approach all four and possibly more would be evaluated. In Simon's approach only one need be considered and chosen if it is predicted to yield the desired result.

Bounded discretion

Shull and his associates (1970) have developed Simon's concept of bounded rationality to encompass what they call bounded discretion. Decision makers, they argue, are bounded by a discretionary area comprising social norms, formal rules and policies, moral and ethical norms and legal restrictions. The decision maker accepts these restrictions and perceives that 'certain alternatives will be judged acceptable, whereas other activities will be deemed illegitimate and inappropriate'.

The basic values and culture of the organization, and the personal values of the decision maker, are essential aspects of both these approaches.

The science of muddling through

Lindblom (1959) describes an incremental approach to decision making, and he has subtitled it 'muddling through'. Contrast James Quinn's (1980) idea that incrementalism can be perfectly logical.

Lindblom's research was concerned with policy decision making in the public sector, but the lessons have a wider application. He differentiates between what he terms the **root** and the **branch** approaches. The former can be likened to the rational model, as the decision maker starts from fresh and stated assumptions (objectives) each time that he evaluates alternatives and seeks to make a decision. However, Lindblom argues that this approach is unworkable for complex issues where various interested parties are involved and where there is no clear agreement amongst them on objectives.

The branch approach, in contrast, looks at alternative policies in terms of their various implications without any stated and predetermined objectives. The interested parties reach agreement on one particular policy, although for each of them the reasons for the choice may be different. The choice is one which receives a wide measure of agreement rather than one which clearly meets stated objectives.

Implicit in this approach are firstly that the evaluation is likely to concentrate on options that are most closely related to those already being followed, as they will already be enjoying some measure of support, secondly that a number of possible alternatives may never be considered, especially if they involve radical change, and thirdly that certain consequences will be ignored if they are not significant for the decision makers, however much they might affect some outsider.

Hence, over a period of time groups of managers will make minor and incremental changes to the way that certain tasks are managed and so on. Minor adjustments apparently carry little immediate threat to working practices, and so this approach is also useful for busy managers who, at any time, are faced with several problematical issues and have a number of relatively minor decisions to make. The decisions, being limited in scope, may not work if the problem has been misjudged or under-estimated, and they may have certain adverse effects as they have not been thought through in detail. But they can be corrected quickly by further minor changes. Hence there is incremental progress towards an optimum solution.

In summary, as far as strategic management is concerned, Lindblom's approach helps explain how new competitive and functional strategies will emerge over time through minor incremental changes, as managers make a series of low risk decisions when problems arise or environmental changes are noted. It also highlights the need for clear and strong strategic leadership if major changes are to be managed effectively.

The mixed scanning model

Etzioni (1967) has tried to reconcile the rigid formality of the rational approach with the more undisciplined approach of the incrementalists. Features of his model are as follows.

☐ When decisions have to be made concerning new courses of action, prior decisions will be made to determine how much time, money and effort should be devoted to the search and evaluation. This takes place within the context of a ranking of objectives.
☐ Alternatives are evaluated by sequentially rejecting those which contain some 'crippling objection'.
☐ When the selected alternative is implemented it should be a planned process such that the least costly and most reversible aspects are introduced first, and the most costly and least reversible last. Such incremental changes can be monitored appropriately.

Fundamental to the model is the ranking of objectives, and so again its relevance for a particular organization will be related to the issue of strategic leadership and whether or not there are clearly stated, understood and supported objectives.

Good and bad decisions

At the beginning of this section on decision making an effective decision was described as one which is supported by the people who

---

Box 3.5
POSSIBLE REASONS FOR BAD DECISIONS

☐ Tunnel vision; restricting the scope of analysis

☐ Personal, even selfish, objectives or ambitions

☐ No real framework; and the consequent grasp of the first or easy alternative

☐ Lack of information

☐ Deliberately ignoring information

☐ Failure to consider or generate alternatives; lack of creativity; insufficient time

☐ Inability or reluctance to appreciate consequences of certain actions

☐ Failure of a group to reach or agree a decision; or reaching a decision which no individual really supports, but which nobody fundamentally objects to

☐ Indecisiveness

Notes

A bad decision can arise at any stage within the overall process.

The more widely people think and consider implications in relation to their effect on other people the less likely it is that the above factors will be present.

---

must implement it, which is implemented and which achieves pre-determined objectives. In the previous section on alternative theories (to the notion of the rational approach, which in theory is the attempt to make effective decisions), it was shown that, if objectives are not clearly stated and understood, then decision making will be constrained. Satisficing alternatives may be chosen, or change may be accomplished gradually and incrementally with constant learning. Whilst these may not be optimizing approaches, they may result in perfectly satisfactory decisions. But the reasons which cause the approach to be non-optimizing may in fact lead to bad decisions, i.e. decisions which cause undesirable results which may be detrimental to the organization as a whole. A bad decision may be made if the problem is wrongly diagnosed or misunderstood, or if available and relevant information is ignored, or if personal objectives are allowed to take precedence over the real interests of the organization.

Box 3.5 is an extended list of possible reasons for poor or bad decision making.

Decision making involves both **information** and **people**. Whilst the strategic leader

must develop an appropriate information system, he or she must also ensure that a good team of people has been gathered and manage them well.

The conductor is only as good as his orchestra. (André Previn)

Considerable research has been carried out into group behaviour and it is not within the scope of this book to examine it in detail. But no leadership style is universally better than the others. Much depends on the personality, power and charisma of the leader.

The **implementation aspects** of the decision are also of vital importance. It may prove very sensible to spend time arriving at a decision by, say, involving the people who must implement it, aiming to generate a

---

Strategic awareness and change involves

Becoming aware – listening, being on the shop floor more than in the office, and, most important of all, staying humble.

Taking action – sharing with others.

Michel Bon, PDG, Carrefour SA

commitment at this stage even though it may be time consuming. Such a decision is likely to be implemented smoothly. One alternative to this, the speedy decisive approach, may prove to be less effective. If it is not supported, the alternative chosen may result in controversy and reluctance on the part of others to implement it. Vroom and Yetton (1973) have developed a model of five alternative ways of decision making.

Vroom and Yetton's model

A short summary of the five approaches is as follows.

☐ The leader solves the problem or makes the decision him or herself using information available at the time.
☐ The leader obtains necessary information from subordinates and then decides on the solution to the problem himself or herself. Subordinates are not involved in generating or evaluating alternative solutions.
☐ The leader shares the problem with relevant subordinates individually, obtaining their ideas and suggestions without bringing them together as a group. Then the leader makes the decision, which may or may not reflect the influence of subordinates.
☐ The leader shares the problem with the subordinates as a group, collectively obtaining their ideas and suggestions. Then he or she makes the decision, which again may or may not reflect their influence.
☐ The leader shares the problem with the subordinates as a group, and together the leader and subordinates generate and evaluate alternatives and attempt to reach an agreement on a solution.

(Vroom and Yetton use the expression 'solve' throughout.) Vroom and Yetton contend that the choice of style should relate to the particular problem faced, and their model includes a series of questions which can be used diagnostically to select the most appropriate style.

Whilst the model is useful for highlighting the different styles and emphasizing that a single style will not always prove to be the most appropriate, it is essentially a normative theory ('this is what you should do') and in this respect should be treated with caution.

Communicating the decisions

Strategic leaders need to be effective communicators (see Box 3.6). At the annual symposium of the European Management Forum in Davos, Switzerland, in 1984, John Young from Hewlett-Packard, the US computer and electronics company, claimed that 'successful companies have a consensus from top to bottom on a set of overall goals. The most brilliant management strategy will fail if that consensus is missing.' Sir John Harvey-Jones, Chairman of ICI plc from 1982 to 1987, supported this, saying that the 'problem is not to get people to work. It is to get them working together for the same damn thing.'

Having introduced the topic of strategic leadership and considered decision making in organizations we now consider the impact of risk and entrepreneurship on strategic management.

Two-way communication is at the heart of successful management of change.

Top management must beware of the conceit that it has all the answers. Having identified a problem, it will often be very rewarding to put to those in middle management a challenge to suggest a solution. Being nearer to the 'sharp-end' of the business in practical terms, it is surprising how frequently and rapidly they will provide an answer; and, since it comes from the heartland of the business, its implementation, will find easier acceptance.

Peter Smith OBE, Chairman, Securicor Group plc

Box 3.6
QUOTES FROM STRATEGIC LEADERS – II

Faced with the question of how to improve their competitiveness a dozen heads of business would, more than likely, provide a dozen different answers. But, whatever their preferred solutions, the fact is there would be no hope of success unless the management team was wholeheartedly committed to its objective.

That, I believe, is a fundamental truth in any business. There is no progress without leadership, and that has to come from the very top.

(Sir John Egan, then Chairman, Jaguar plc)

I believe the starting point for all management improvement is the opening up of **communications** both inside and outside the company.

(Sir John Harvey-Jones, Chairman, ICI plc, 1982–7)

Quotations taken from *Improving Management Performance: Report of a BIM Panel*, BIM and Professional Publishing, 1985.

ENTREPRENEURSHIP

It was argued in Chapter 1 that strategic management is concerned with environmental fit. It is important to achieve congruence between environment, values and resources for both existing and potential future products and services.

The management of existing businesses focuses attention on costs and prices (as they determine profits) and on ways of reducing costs by improving productivity. Technology changes, and new operating systems, may reduce costs; equally they may improve product quality for which premium prices might be charged.

Future developments might concern new products (or services) or new markets or both, and they might involve diversification. For different alternatives the magnitude of the change implied and the risk involved will vary.

For both areas the changes which take place can be gradual or incremental, or they can be more dynamic or individually significant. Real innovation can be costly in terms

of investment required, as we have seen in Case 3.3, and consequently can involve a high level of risk, but sometimes it is necessary. Entrepreneurship is concerned with dynamic change and growth.

Entrepreneurial strategy

Mintzberg (1973) contends that there are four chief characteristics of entrepreneurial strategy making:

☐ Strategy making is dominated by the active search for new opportunities.
☐ In entrepreneurial organizations, power is centralized in the hands of the chief executive.
☐ Strategic change is characterized by dramatic leaps forward in the face of uncertainty.
☐ Growth is the dominant goal of the organization.

Implicit is an attempt to be proactive and manage the environment.

		Independence/power	
		Dominant need for independence	Dominant need for power
Need to create	Weak	Marginal businesses Professional people	Company executives
	Strong	Independent entrepreneurs	Entrepreneurs — organization makers

Figure 3.3   Typology of the entrepreneur. Adapted from Ettinger, J C (1983) Some Belgian evidence on entrepreneurial personality, *European Small Business Journal*, **1** (2). Reproduced with permission.

Achievement and power motivation

McClelland and Winter (1971) have argued since the 1950s that all managers, in fact all workers, are influenced and motivated by three desires: the desire to achieve, the desire for power, and the desire for affiliation at work. The relative strength of each of these three desires or motives will vary from individual to individual, and what matters as far as management is concerned is to understand what does motivate people rather than to believe that all people can be motivated in the same way.

Entrepreneurial behaviour is characterized by high achievement motivation, supported by a power motive, and with affiliation very much third.

Achievement motivation is characterized by concern to do a job well, or better than others, with the accomplishment of something unusual or important, and with advancement. Such managers thrive where they have personal responsibility for finding answers to problems, and they tend to set moderate achievable goals and take calculated risks. If the targets are too modest, there is little challenge and little satisfaction, but if they are too high they are too risky.

Actually achieving the goal is important. They also prefer constant feedback concerning progress. Achievement motivation is closely linked to the desire to create something.

Entrepreneurial behaviour also features a desire for power, influence and independence.

Ettinger (1983) has developed this thesis, and argues that there are two types of entrepreneur (Fig. 3.3). Independent entrepreneurs are intent on creating and developing their own organization and retaining control, as they are more concerned with independence than power. Where power is stronger organization makers are looking for growth opportunities, because growth and size yields power. Arguably they will accept a loss of independence if they can build something important.

Obviously some strategic leaders will exhibit more entrepreneurialism than others. The management style, the nature of objectives set and chased, and the type and magnitude of change within the organization will all be influenced.

Entrepreneurs need both creativity and confidence if they are to seek out and exploit new ideas; and they must be willing to take risks. Whilst McClelland and Winter describe achievement-motivated people as those who take very measured risks, there are some entrepreneurs who thrive on uncertainty and are successful because they take chances and opportunities that others would and do reject. They will not always succeed of course.

Why entrepreneurialism is important

Entrepreneurs develop new ideas and new businesses. They are therefore crucial for economic growth. They are the people who choose to start new businesses, and who seek growth opportunities for existing businesses. As certain industries go into decline and jobs are lost, as has been the case with steel, coal mining, shipbuilding and certain sectors of textiles, then new opportunities must be created to replace the lost jobs. Similarly as certain products and services near the ends of their profitable lives they need to be replaced by new ones. Different organizations will respond to this need in various ways. Some will be essentially reactive, responding to the threat posed by the decline; others will have anticipated the decline well in advance and have prepared for change. The latter companies could be said to be more proactive.

As far as the UK is concerned the decline of the traditional industries has caused economic depression in certain areas of the north, where once they were dominant, and the major growth opportunities have been localized. In the south of England, for example, high technology industries have developed to the west of London near the M4 motorway, and similar companies have been established in southern Scotland, in Silicon Glen as it is called. There has also been strong growth in a number of service businesses, such as building societies, fast food outlets and retailing as relative wealth, life-styles and preferences have changed.

In the article summarized in Key Reading 3.1 it is argued that the UK, and in fact the whole of Europe, is generally less entrepreneurial than the USA and Japan. Case 3.5 David Bruce, describes the success of one British entrepreneur.

Entrepreneurship is closely linked to innovation, and it will be considered further when we examine innovation in Chapter 11.

Intrapreneurship

Entrepreneurial activity, innovation and growth is affected greatly by the ambition and style of the strategic leader, his or her values, and the culture he or she creates, but arguably it should be spread throughout the organization.

Intrapreneurship is the term given to the establishment and fostering of entrepreneurial activity within large organizations. Many new ideas for innovation, for product or service developments, can come from managers within organizations if the structure and climate encourages and allows them to contribute. There are a number of ways. Special task forces and development groups are one alternative. Allowing individual managers the opportunity, freedom and, if necessary, the capital to try new ideas is another.

Three large American companies are all noted for their success at intrapreneurial activity: Procter and Gamble (soap, detergents, food and edible oils); Johnson and Johnson (hygiene, health care and baby products) and 3M (who produce a variety of consumer and industrial products, and who are probably best known for their Scotch branded products such as sticky tape, videos and cassettes). Whilst there are differences in approaches, a common feature is the fact that once managers have come forward with ideas the new venture becomes a separate business

Key Reading 3.1
ENTREPRENEURSHIP IN EUROPE

Although a considerable amount of venture capital is available for investment in Europe, there are insufficient entrepreneurs with the drive, vision and management flair to turn today's small firms into tomorrow's big businesses. Only a small number of companies with growth potential are run by people with a growth mentality. As a result as much as 50% of the investment capital available might go to American companies.

A key issue is whether the reason why European companies lag behind the Americans in particular lies primarily in government policies and the economic climate or is because Europeans are less competitive people.

There are signs of improvement, though, particularly in the UK. Essential features have been the growth in the number of management buy-outs (see Chapter 20) and the creation of the Unlisted Securities Market in 1980. Under this small companies can have shares issued and traded on the Stock Exchange without a more costly full listing. Its success has led to similar developments in France and Holland. Although equity funding is scarce in West Germany a number of small high-technology companies have sprung up, and in Italy managers from such companies as Olivetti and Fiat have left to start on their own.

The problem is not so much in stimulating new business start-ups but in encouraging them to grow.

A fair proportion of the change has been a spin-off from America, where entrepreneurial activity has been seen to be successful. It has been estimated that some two-thirds of new jobs created in the early 1970s in America were in small businesses. Small American companies have been very successful in diffusing technology and in turning ideas into products more rapidly than large bureaucratic organizations.

Another reason for the sluggish growth has been a tendency for large companies to buy from other large companies rather than switch to newer smaller companies. Consequently it is difficult for some companies to penetrate their markets.

However, the main cause lies with management errors. High-tech start-ups fail in the UK mainly because managers under-estimate development times, under-finance the company or concentrate more on engineering than marketing.

A final difficulty is the desire of small businessmen to retain control; they refuse equity funding if the implication is that they lose total control.

Summarized from Jonquières, G. de (1985) A conspicuous shortage of vision and flair, *Financial Times*, 19 June.

with a project manager in charge. Success brings appropriate rewards.

Success in this field requires that change is perceived more as an opportunity than a threat, that the company is aware of market opportunities and is customer oriented and that the financial implications are thought through.

SUMMARY

The strategic leader of an organization affects both strategy creation and strategy implementation. He or she is responsible for establishing the basic direction of the

Case 3.5
DAVID BRUCE

In March 1988 Midsummer Leisure, an expanding public house, snooker club and discotheque business with some 130 outlets, bought Bruce's Brewery, comprising 11 outlets and one site for development, from David Bruce for £6.6 million in cash.

David Bruce was in his late twenties when he opened his first pub-brewery in 1979. He had previously worked for such companies as Courage and Theakstons and felt that there was a market opportunity for a pub which brewed its own beer on site. He bought the lease on a site at the Elephant and Castle in London, an existing pub which was being closed down, and renamed it the Goose and Firkin. The pub was completely remodelled with one large bar with wooden seats, bare floor boards and several decorations such as a stuffed goose. The aim was to re-create a traditional drinking house. Brewing took place in the cellar, which had a production capacity of 5000 pints per week. Additionally other real ales were sold. Lloyds Bank lent £10 000 for this new venture, but Bruce was turned down by others he approached. He had to take a second mortgage on his house to provide collateral for his overdraft and he borrowed some money from a friend of his wife.

Three types of real ale were brewed and sold, all with individual brand names and varying in strength. These were Bruce's Borough Bitter, Bruce's Dog Bolter and Bruce's Earth Stopper, which at o.g. 1075 was claimed to be the strongest draught beer in Britain. Traditional food of high quality supplemented the beer. Success came instantaneously and the turnover was into the thousands of pounds within weeks of opening. It quickly reached an annual quarter of a million pounds. A manager and a team of seven, including a brewer, were employed to run the pub.

A second outlet was opened in 1980; by 1985 there were seven, with the total reaching 11 in 1987. All 11 were in the Greater London area, and nine of them had in-house breweries. The last two were called the Fuzzock and Firkin and the Flamingo and Firkin. By the mid-1980s Bruce was the fifth largest operator of breweries in the UK. All the pubs had Firkin in the name, and by this time a number of new real ale brands had been introduced including Spook, brewed exclusively in the Phantom and Firkin. Bruce had also developed a reputation for promotional slogans for each pub. The Flounder and Firkin was a 'plaice worth whiting home about' and at the Phantom and Firkin you could 'spectre good pint when you ghost to the Phantom'.

Sales in 1986–7, with eight outlets operating, were £4 million. Bruce had sold 10% of the equity to Investors in Industry for £120 000, and they also provided additional loan facilities.

There had been difficulties, however.

In 1982 Bruce had obtained a pub-brewery with additional warehouse capacity in Bristol. His aim was to distribute his real ales to West Country pubs. But the company was already experiencing problems from the rapid growth. Beer quality was inconsistent; there were cash flow problems; and David Bruce's own role was unclear. A microbiologist and an accountant were brought into the business, which relieved the first two of these. But Bruce still faced the problem that, whilst there were managers in every outlet, he was personally responsible for ensuring that his original success formula at the Goose and Firkin was implemented and maintained in all the

Continued overleaf

pubs and at the same time was seeking new opportunities for growth and development. Once the company spread outside London Bruce felt that he was no longer able to give sufficient attention to detail throughout the organization. Essentially the problem was one of managing growth and at the same time retaining the 'personal touch', a key success factor for this type of service business.

The Bristol site was sold.

Bruce had hoped to take the company to the Unlisted Securities Market in 1987, but this never happened. Further growth, he felt, was inhibited by a lack of equity capital and the problems of interest charges on loans.

After paying off loans and capital gains tax, Bruce was left with £1 million, part of which he used to establish a charitable trust to provide canal holidays for disabled people.

In 1990 David Bruce started brewing again. Two pubs, both named The Hedgehog and Hogshead, and offering beers such as Hogbolter and Prickletickler, were opened in Hove and Southampton. The conditions of sale of Bruce's Brewery prevented Bruce from opening in Greater London. Key staff have been recruited back from Midsummer Leisure (now owned by Stakis); the sites are leased rather than freehold; and borrowing has been kept to a minimum. Bruce has personally invested £500 000.

Figure 3.4 Strategic leadership and decision making.

organization, the communications system and the structure. These influence the nature and style of decision making within the firm. In addition decision making and change is affected by the personal ambitions of the strategic leader, his or her personal qualities such as entrepreneurialism and willingness to take risks, the style of management adopted and the management systems used. These responsibilities and issues are summarized in Figure 3.4, and they have all been discussed in this chapter.

Specifically in this chapter we have

☐ considered the role of the strategic leader as a creator and an implementor of strategy, emphasizing the need for an appropriate organization structure and effective communications;
☐ looked at styles of leadership in terms of risk taking, autocracy, democracy and change orientation;
☐ introduced the topical debate on corporate governance;
☐ discussed how the personal ambitions of the strategic leader will influence the objectives, direction and strategy of the organization;
☐ defined risk and looked at risk in relation to strategies;
☐ introduced the rational model of decision making and compared it with other approaches to provide some insight into how decisions concerning strategy might be reached in practice;
☐ emphasized that decision making involves both information and people, and by reference to Vroom and Yetton's model shown that there are a number of approaches for handling this;
☐ discussed how bad decisions might be reached;
☐ examined entrepreneurship in relation to economic aspects and particularly decisions concerning strategic change.

CHECKLIST OF KEY TERMS AND CONCEPTS

You should feel confident that you understand the following terms and ideas:

☐ Styles of leadership
☐ Corporate governance
☐ The rational model of decision making
☐ Alternative satisficing and incremental approaches

☐ Risk
☐ Entrepreneurship and intrapreneurship.

QUESTIONS AND RESEARCH ASSIGNMENTS

Text related

1. Case 3.5: David Bruce.
   (a) Do you think David Bruce's approach to growth and change was appropriate for the business he was in? Do you see it as opportunistic or incremental or planned?
   (b) Why do you think Bruce's breweries have been successful?
   (c) Do you think David Bruce's style of managing the organization was also appropriate?
2. Considering the points raised in the ICI case, what do you think are the key issues involved in ensuring that strategic change at corporate, competitive and functional levels is managed effectively in large complex international organizations comprising several interdependent businesses?

Library based

3. Select at least one well-established large corporation which is quoted on the Stock Exchange, together with one of the companies privatized during the 1980s.
   (a) Examine the composition of the Board of Directors in terms of executive and non-executive members.
   (b) Determine whether the roles of chairman and chief executive are split or combined.
   (c) What conclusions might you draw concerning strategic leadership and corporate governance in these organizations?
4. The following facts relate to Alan Sugar, founder and chief executive of Amstrad,

and one of Britain's richest businessmen. You are required to research the growth and success of Amstrad in the consumer electronics and microcomputers markets in order to answer the same questions as Questions 1(a), 1(b) and 1(c) above.

1947 Born Hackney, East London
1963 Left school
1966 Began selling car aerials from a van
1968 Founded Amstrad to sell plastic covers for record players
Involvement in televisions, video receivers and CB radio led to
1985 Launch of a low cost word processor and compact disc player
1986 Acquisition of the intellectual property rights of Sinclair computers from Clive Sinclair and launch of an IBM-compatible microcomputer
1988 Entered satellite dish market

In 1987 turnover exceeded £500 million, almost half that of Britain's largest computer company ICL, which at the time was less profitable than Amstrad.

RECOMMENDED FURTHER READING

It would be useful at this stage to read Mintzberg (1973) on the three modes of strategy creation. An ideal introduction to the topic of decision making can be found in the section 'Making Decisions' in the Open University *The Effective Manager* module (Course Code P670).
Harrison, E F (1981) *The Managerial Decision Making Process*, Houghton Mifflin, provides a comprehensive summary of the theories and concepts introduced in this chapter; the managerial perspective is covered well in Heirs, B and Farrell, P (1987) *The Professional Decision Thinker*, Sidgwick and Jackson.
Bennis, W and Nanus, B (1985) *Leaders: The Strategies of Taking Charge*, Harper and Row,

supplements the comments of Bennis included in this chapter.
The semi-autobiographical books on business written by such British authors as Sir John Harvey-Jones (previously chairman of ICI), George Davies (Next) and Debbie Moore (Pineapple), together with American authors such as Lee Iacocca (Chrysler) and Victor Kiam (Remington), provide insight into the perspective and strategies of individual strategic leaders.
Readers interested in corporate governance are referred to: Cadbury, Sir Adrian (1990), *The Company Chairman*, Director Books.

REFERENCES

Ackoff, R (1978) *The Art of Problem Solving*, Wiley.
Bennis, W, Interview recorded in Crainer, S (1988) Doing the right thing, *The Director*, October.
Dunnette, M D and Taylor, R N (1975) Influence of dogmatism, risk taking propensity and intelligence on decision making strategy for a sample of industrial managers, *Journal of Applied Psychology*, **59** (4).
Ettinger, J C (1983) Some Belgian evidence on entrepreneurial personality, *European Small Business Journal*, **1** (2).
Etzioni, A (1967) Mixed scanning: a third approach to decision making, *Public Administration Review*, **27**, December.
Lindblom, C E (1959) *The Science of Muddling Through*; 2nd edn, reprinted in Pugh, D S (ed.) (1987) *Organization Theory*, Penguin.
McClelland, D and Winter, D (1971) *Motivating Economic Achievement*, Free Press.
Mintzberg, H (1973) Strategy making in three modes, *California Management Review*, **16**(2), Winter.
Quinn, J B (1980) *Strategies for Change: Logical Incrementalism*, Richard D Irwin.
Shull, F A, Delbecq, A L and Cummings, L L (1970) *Organizational Decision Making*, McGraw-Hill.
Simon, H A (1976) *Administrative Behaviour: A Study of Decision Making Processes in Administrative Organizations*, 3rd edn, Free Press.
Vroom, V and Yetton, P (1973) *Leadership and Decision Making*, University of Pittsburgh Press.

CULTURE AND VALUES

4

LEARNING OBJECTIVES

After studying this chapter you should be able to

☐ explain the impact of corporate culture on the management of an organization, and on managers and other employees;

☐ distinguish between the entrepreneurial, adaptive and planning modes of strategy creation;

☐ define Handy's four organizational cultures and list and define different sources of power;

☐ assess the conclusions of normative researchers concerning 'excellence';

☐ appreciate important aspects of the Japanese business culture.

This chapter explores the role of organizational culture in strategic management since (i) the prevailing culture is a major influence on current strategies and future changes and (ii) any decisions to make major strategic changes may require a change in the culture. Culture is therefore a vital element in both strategy creation and strategy implementation.

INTRODUCTION

Institutional strategy is a term used to describe the vision and culture of an organ-ization. The vision, influenced substantially by the strategic leader, should provide the foundation for the corporate and competitive strategies; the culture, values and norms of behaviour affect the implementation of these strategies and the management of change in the organization.

Visionary strategic leaders communicate their views of the future, and their main values for the business, throughout the organization, thereby influencing the culture. Their values concern customers and service, people management within the organization, and management systems and procedures. Not every manager will readily share the perspective and values of the strategic leader, and so any potential conflicts must be dealt with if the organization is to be cohesive and benefit from shared values.

E–V–R congruence was introduced in Chapter 1. The culture and values of the organization are crucial for matching the organization's resources to its environment.

The established culture, which is generally slow and difficult to change, is very important in strategic decision making that involves major changes of direction. The established culture also helps to determine the freedom and the willingness or reluctance of managers to make changes as they spot opportunities and threats. But the organization's structure is designed by the strategic leader, and the styles of management, communication and decision making that he or she encourages will become part of the culture.

Strategy in an organization can only be analysed effectively, and understood, if one appreciates the basic culture and values that influence of key strategic elements. Strategy changes cannot be implemented successfully without due regard to culture.

CULTURE AND THE ORGANIZATION

Culture is reflected in the way that people in an organization perform tasks, set objectives and administer resources to achieve them. It affects the way that they make decisions, think, feel and act in response to opportunities and threats. Culture also influences the selection of people for particular jobs, which in turn affects the way that tasks are carried out and decisions are made. Culture is so fundamental that it affects behaviour unconsciously. Managers do things in particular ways because it is expected behaviour.

The culture present in an organization will reflect the strength and style of the strategic leader. If the leader is strong he will have clear views about what should be done and how. If strategic leadership is weak the culture may centre on decision making to accomplish low level objectives.

I suggested in Chapter 1 that culture influences how resources are administered, managed and co-ordinated, and that for strategy to be managed effectively, there must be E–V–R congruence. Figure 4.1 shows

that culture is a central driving force with a number of linked elements.

Styles of decision making were explored in Chapter 3. The more autocratic the strategic leader, and the more power is centralized with him or her, the more the culture is likely to inhibit initiative in other managers. Thus opportunities that functional managers perceive may be missed as the strategic leader never becomes aware of them and other managers do not have the authority or inclination to act on them.

Objectives will be examined in Chapter 5. Delivering on time, or attention to detail in production, may be stated objectives of the organization, and if they are shared and followed they can become fundamental values. As an example, McDonald's **competitive advantage** (featured in Case 1.3) has been summarized as 'Quality, service, cleanliness and value' which are basic values and part of the company culture, as well as objectives.

Structure is closely tied to leadership and decision making. The extent to which the organization is decentralized and managers are held accountable and rewarded for success (and sanctioned for failing) will affect the culture. The willingness to take risks is an example.

Management systems will include communications, both formal and informal, which in turn affect the way managers work together. This is an important aspect of the culture.

The **management of people** includes communications, motivation and, as mentioned above, rewards and sanctions. The more managers are aware of what is expected of them and of the objectives and strategies of the organization, and the more motivated they are to help achieve them, the more the basic values will be shared and adhered to.

Functional strategies and policies reflect the values and culture. In marketing and production functions, delivery on time and emphasis on quality are examples.

Information systems refers to both com-

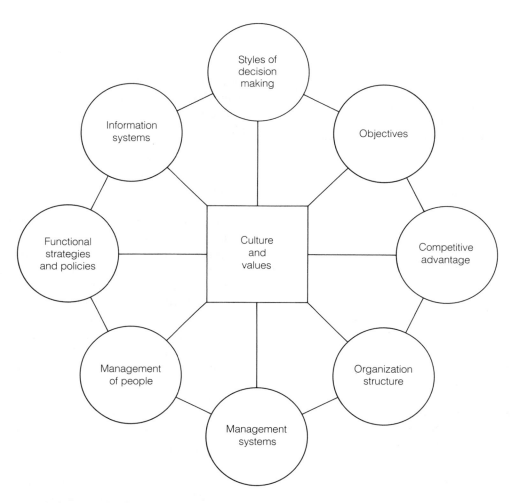

Figure 4.1 Culture and values.

munications within the organization and from the environment. A basic value might be concerned with satisfying customers, making sure that attention is given to checking how well the company is doing relative to competitors, and making sure that the importance of the market is appreciated throughout the organization.

The way that managers work with each other, whether there is collaboration or conflict, and how much they exchange and share information and keep each other informed will affect the culture. This example encap-

sulates structural aspects, the management of people, and information systems.

CULTURE AND STRATEGY CREATION

The link between culture and strategy creation or formation has already been mentioned. The boldness and magnitude of strategic changes, whether they result essentially from planning systems or from incremental change, the risk inherent in them, and the degree to which they are entrepreneurial will all reflect basic values and the culture of the organization.

The four characteristics of entrepreneurial strategy were detailed in Chapter 3, page 69. Mintzberg (1973) contends that there are two other main modes – adaptive and planning – and that each exhibits particular features.

Modes of strategy creation

The planning mode

Russell Ackoff (1970) has summarized the three main characteristics of the planning mode.

☐ Planning is anticipatory decision making and is carried out in advance of taking action.
☐ Planning is undertaken when the future state desired requires a number of interdependent decisions.
☐ Planning is a process directed towards producing one or more desired states which are unlikely to occur without action.

The key features of the planning mode are the following.

☐ The 'analyst' plays a major role.
☐ The focus is on systematic analysis, particularly in the assessment of the costs and benefits of competing proposals.

Whether the analysis is designed to address existing problems or search for new opportunities, the process will always be systematic and structured.

☐ The planning mode aims to integrate strategies and decisions. In other words in complex multi-activity organizations there is a need for integration and co-ordination, and this must be planned rather than expected to happen without direction.

Adaptive strategy

Adaptive strategy is closely linked to the views of Lindblom and Quinn which have been described earlier.

The four major characteristics of an adaptive organization are as follows.

☐ Clear goals do not exist. Strategy making reflects a division of power among members of a complex coalition. In other words managers may differ in their perspective of which issues and values are important, and their relative power in the organization will influence the strength of individual objectives. An example might be a production manager who is concerned with cost reduction and production efficiency and a sales manager anxious to please a customer and increase costs by enhancing the product or service in some way which is either costly or disruptive. This point also relates to Cyert and March's *A Behavioural Theory of the Firm* which is featured in Chapter 5. As a result the organization will be pursuing a number of goals at any time and there may be inconsistencies between them.
☐ Strategy making is characterized more by a reaction to problems and threats than by a proactive search for new opportunities.
☐ Decisions are made in incremental, serial, steps.
☐ Disjointed decisions are commonplace. Consequently strategy making is fragmented and not well co-ordinated.

Planning is an important aspect of strategic management, but not everything can or should be planned systematically. Major changes in the corporate strategy (the strategic perspective) are likely to require thorough analysis and planning; equally the allocation and management of resources, especially finance, should be planned in detail. But plans should be flexible, and the existence of formal planning activities should not inhibit opportunistic and incremental changes, particularly in competitive and functional strategies, in a dynamic environment.

Peters (1988) states that 'managers have to learn how to make mistakes faster'. In turbulent and uncertain environments managers must experiment with new ideas and changes. Not every hunch will prove to be right first time, and further changes and improvements will be required. This is the operation of a learning cycle in a decentralized organization. Managers learn by doing, and their decisions concerning what to do are based upon their awareness and perception of situations and their willingness to take certain risks. In turn they must be rewarded appropriately for success. These are all aspects of the culture.

Hampden-Turner (1990) argues that culture is based upon communication and learning. The strategic leader's vision must be communicated and understood; events and changes affecting the organization also need to be communicated widely. Managers should be encouraged to seek out new opportunities by learning about new technology and customer expectations, and to innovate. The organization should help them to share their experiences and their learning. British Airways, for example, has established 'Customer First' teams, where groups of staff meet regularly. If organizations expect their employees to care about, and look after, customers, they must in turn look after their staff. The internal culture will affect external relationships.

The link between strategy creation and culture

The entrepreneurial mode requires strong leadership in an environment offering growth opportunities, and risk is an inherent aspect.

The adaptive mode is the most suitable approach if the environment is dynamic and unstable, and if managers enjoy decentralized power and perhaps compete with each other for rewards in the form of promotion or investment capital. Disagreement about certain priorities and the need for conflict resolution become key aspects and of course this can affect customers. Sometimes the conflict can divert attention away from environmental issues and focus it on internal disputes, and the resulting strategy will be somewhat *ad hoc* and unco-ordinated.

The planning mode is most suitable in a

Strategic analysis on its own may improve the perception of leadership but have little influence on the nature, pace and direction of corporate decisions, since there is a natural tendency for corporate behaviour to follow the past momentum.

The power of 'corporate culture' should not be underestimated, both for a company's success, and, if it is inappropriate, in frustrating change. Values, strategies, systems, organization and accountabilities – the components of culture – are a very strong mix which can either make a company successful or alternatively, lead to its decline.

The task of corporate leadership is to apply energy and judgement to the corporate culture to ensure its continued relevance. And the art of Strategic Management is to bring forward, at the very least, the same energy that arises at times of crisis, and to address the potential culture barriers to renewal, early enough, whilst options are still available, before the trend of performance turns downwards. Typically this requires clear leadership signals, reinforced by changes in organization, systems and people.

Sir Allen Sheppard, Chairman,
Grand Metropolitan plc

Table 4.1 Organizations values and strategies

Type	Characteristics	Strategy formation
Defenders	Conservative beliefs Low risk strategies Secure markets Concentration on narrow segments Considerable expertise in narrow areas of specialism Preference for well-tried resolutions to problems Little search for anything really 'new' Attention given to improving efficiency of present operations	Emphasis on planning
Prospectors	Innovative Looking to break new ground High risk strategies Search for new opportunities Can create change and uncertainty, forcing a response from competitors More attention given to market changes than to improving internal efficiency	Entrepreneurial mode
Analysers	Two aspects: stable and changing Stable: formal structures and search for efficiencies Changing: competitors monitored and strategies amended as promising ideas seen (followers)	Planning mode Adaptive mode
Reactors	Characterized by an inability to respond effectively to change pressures Adjustments are therefore forced on the firm in order to avert crises	Adaptive mode

reasonably stable and predictable environment but a reliance on it in a more unstable situation can lead to missed opportunities. It can also mean that threats which were not forecast are not dealt with at the appropriate time. Reliance is placed on implementing the plans and flexibility to change quickly is lost.

Elements of all three modes could be present in the same organization, and certainly the mode may change over time. The basic mission and long-term objectives and decisions about desirable products, services and markets could be the result of entrepreneurial decisions. Appropriate strategies to achieve the objectives could have resulted from a planning system; and as these have been implemented and changed in line with environmental pressures, an adaptive mode may have been adopted.

Miles and Snow (1978), whose research has been used to develop Table 4.1, have suggested a typology of organizations which can be looked at in relation to culture and strategy formation. The typology distinguishes organizations in terms of their values and objectives, and different types

will typically prefer particular approaches to strategy creation. Defenders, prospectors and analysers are all regarded by Miles and Snow as positive organizations; reactors must ultimately adopt one of the other three approaches or suffer long-term decline. As examples of each type, I suggest that GEC, despite being in high technology industries, is relatively conservative and a defender. The risk-oriented innovative Amstrad is a prospector. The respective strategic leaders of these organizations, Lord Weinstock and Alan Sugar, adopt different styles of management and exhibit different corporate values. Historically many public sector bureaucracies have been stable analysers, whilst Marks & Spencer is a changing analyser. Prior to its decline and acquisition by BTR, Dunlop, in the 1970s, exhibited many of the characteristics of a reactor organization, and failed to change sufficiently in line with environmental changes.

Miles and Snow argue that, as well as being a classification, their typology can be used to predict behaviour. For example, a defender organization, in a search for greater

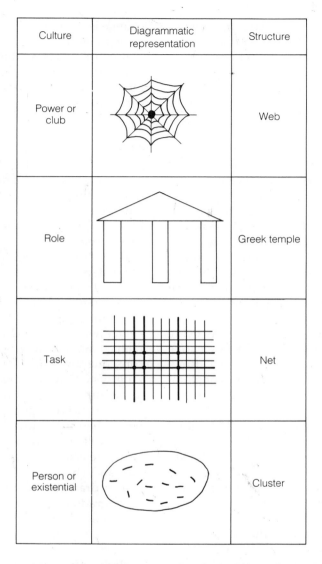

Culture	Diagrammatic representation	Structure
Power or club		Web
Role		Greek temple
Task		Net
Person or existential		Cluster

Figure 4.2   Handy's four cultures. Adapted from Handy, C B (1976) *Understanding Organizations*, Penguin.

operating efficiency, might consider investing in the latest technology, but reject the strategy if it has high risk attached.

CULTURE, STRUCTURE AND STYLES OF MANAGEMENT

Charles Handy (1976), building on earlier work by Harrison (1972) has developed an alternative classification of organizations based on cultural differences, and this is illustrated in Figure 4.2.

The club culture or power culture

In the club culture type of organization, work is divided by function or product and a diagram of the organization structure would be quite traditional. There would be departments for sales, production, finance and so on, and possibly product-based divisions or strategic business units if the organization was larger. However, this structure is mostly found in smaller firms.

These functions or departments are represented in Handy's figure by the lines radiating out from the centre; but the essential point is that there are also concentric lines representing communications and power. The further away from the centre, the weaker is the power and influence. This structure is dominated from the centre and therefore is typical for small entrepreneurial organizations. Decisions can be taken quickly, but the quality of the decisions is very dependent upon the abilities of managers in the inner circle.

Lonrho, mentioned in Chapter 3 as being very strongly influenced by its chief executive and major shareholder Roland 'Tiny' Rowland, despite being an international conglomerate, is an illustration of a large company with a power culture. The case also exhibits one of the major problem areas of this culture – that of succession. Rowland was 70 years old in 1987. This issue is exacerbated by the fact that typically very little is formalized; on the contrary, much depends on informality.

Similarly, Hanson has been described by a former director as a 'solar system, with everyone circling around the sun in the middle, Lord Hanson' (see Leadbeater and Rudd, 1991). This analogy suggests both movement and dependency.

Decisions depend a great deal on empathy, affinity and trust both within the organization and with suppliers, customers and other key influences. Using Lonrho as an example again, the early growth was very much influenced by Rowland's ability to reach agreement with leaders of a number of African States. For this reason the culture can be designated either 'club' or 'power'.

Employees are rewarded for effort, success and compliance with essential values; and change is very much led from the centre in an entrepreneurial style.

A culture such as this may prevent individual managers from speaking their minds, but decisions are unlikely to get lost in committees.

The role culture

The role culture is the more typical 'organization' as the culture is built around defined jobs, rules and procedures and not personalities. People fit into jobs, and are recruited for this purpose. Hence rationality and logic are at the heart of the culture, which is designed to be stable and predictable.

The design is the Greek Temple because the strengths of the organization are deemed to lie in the pillars, which are joined managerially at the top. One essential role of top management is to co-ordinate activity, and consequently it will be seen that both planning systems and incremental changes can be a feature of this culture. Although the strength of the organization is in the pillars, power lies at the top.

As well as being designed for stability the structure is also designed to allow for continuity and changes of personnel, and for this reason dramatic changes are less likely than more gradual ones. Handy quotes insurance companies, the Civil Service and local authorities as all being typical exponents of the role culture.

High efficiency is possible in stable environments, but the structure can be slow to change and is therefore less suitable for dynamic situations. In situations of greater turbulence this structure will need intrapreneurship, or aspects of the task culture could be incorporated.

The task culture

Management in the task culture is concerned with the continuous and successful solution of problems, and performance is judged by the success of the outcomes.

The culture is shown as a net, because for particular problem situations people and other resources can be drawn from various parts of the organization on a temporary basis. Once the problem is dealt with people will move on to other tasks, and consequently discontinuity is a key element. Expertise is the major source of individual power and it will determine a person's relative power in a given situation. Power basically lies in the interstices of the net, because of the reliance on task forces.

The culture is ideal for consultancies, advertising agenices, and for research and development departments. It can also be useful within the role culture for tackling particularly difficult or unusual problem situations.

In dynamic environments a major challenge for large organizations is the design of a structure and systems which allow for proper management and integration without losing the spirit and excitement typical of small, entrepreneurial businesses. Elements of the task culture superimposed over formal roles can help by widening communications and engendering greater commitment within the organization. One feature is cost. This culture is expensive as there is a reliance on talking and discussion, experimentation and learning by trial. Although Handy uses the expression problem solving, there can be problem resolutions or moves towards a solution along more incremental lines, as well as decisions concerning major changes. If successful changes are implemented the expense can often be justified.

The person culture or existential culture

The person culture is completely different from the other three, for here the organization exists to help the individual rather than the other way round. Groups of professional people, such as doctors, architects, dentists and solicitors, provide excellent examples. The organization with secretarial help, printing and telephone facilities and so on provides a service for individual specialists and reduces the need for costly duplication. If a member of the circle leaves or retires, he or she is replaced by another who may have to buy in.

Some professional groups exhibit interdependences and collaboration, allocating work amongst the members, although management of such an organization is difficult because of individual expertise. However, in an environment where government is attempting to increase competition between professional organizations, and in some cases to reduce barriers to entering the profession, it is arguable that effective management, particularly at the strategic level, will become increasingly necessary. Efforts will need co-ordinating and harnessing if organizations are to become strong competitors.

Management philosophies

Press (1990) suggests that the culture of an organization is based upon one or more philosophies. I have developed his ideas into Figure 4.3. The specific philosophies are related to the various stakeholders in the business, and are determined by two intersecting axes. One relates to whether the business is focused more internally or externally; the other is based upon performance measures. Do they concentrate more on resource management and efficiency, or outcomes and effectiveness? This creates four discrete philosophies:

☐ **the resource focus** which concentrates upon internal efficiencies and cost management
☐ **the shareholder focus** which sees the business as a portfolio of activities which should be managed to maximize the value of the business for its shareholders

Figure 4.3 Organizational philosophies.
Adapted from Press, G (1990) Assessing
competitors' business philosophies,
Long Range Planning, **23**, 5.

□ **the people focus** which emphasizes the
skills and contribution of employees, and
their needs and expectations
□ **the market focus** which stresses the
importance of satisfying customers by
adding value and differentiating products
and services.

All of these are important; none of them can
be ignored. The culture can be analysed in
terms of how these four philosophies are
perceived and prioritized.

A company which relies heavily upon
formal strategic planning, for example, is
likely to concentrate more upon shareholders
and resources. Hanson at a corporate level is,
I would argue, similarly inclined; the individual subsidiary businesses will have a
resource focus supported by people and
market philosophies (see Chapter 13 for a
detailed discussion of the Hanson strategy).
General Electric (GE) of America (see Chapter
22) is another diversified conglomerate but
with a different policy from Hanson on
empowerment and decentralization. GE places
most emphasis upon people and shareholders. Japanese companies, discussed later
in this chapter, exhibit a particular blend of
people, markets and resources.

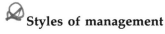 **Styles of management**

Styles of management were described in
Chapter 3 when the important role of strategic leadership was discussed. It is important to emphasize that the style adopted by
the strategic leader can have a strong
influence on the culture of the organization.
Case 4.1, Scott Bader, is included as an
illustration of an unusual culture resulting
from a very individual style of management.
Strategic changes do take place but they
involve more consultation with the total
workforce than will be normal for most
organizations. However, whilst Scott Bader is
very unusual, it should not be thought that
the basic principles cannot be found elsewhere.

The John Lewis Partnership, Britain's third
largest department store chain after Debenhams and House of Fraser, practises worker
participation and democracy. John Lewis is
also diversified into supermarkets with its
Waitrose chain. The company has a chairman, a board of directors and a management
structure, as do most companies, but parallel
to this commercial structure stands a second
structure which represents the interests of
the ordinary worker who is also a partner in
John Lewis. Whilst a partner working in a
department in a store cannot directly

My belief is that common trusteeship of our
total assets is the only viable and honourable
way forward in industry, because it provides
an advanced socio-industrial structure in
which man's spirit can be more free and
where he is motivated to become more
creative, productive and responsible.

Godric E. S. Bader, Chairman,
Scott Bader Company Ltd

At Scott Bader there is a belief 'that the way
the City operates, and their share holding
activities, do not bring out the best in human
beings'.

Case 4.1
SCOTT BADER COMPANY LTD

Scott Bader Co. Ltd is a private industrial chemical company with a radically different approach to ownership and management.

Scott Bader was started as a private company in 1923 by Ernest Bader to be the sole agent in the UK for a Swiss manufacturer of celluloid. Other products in the paint industry were later imported from Germany and America, but the depression of the 1930s squeezed these merchanting activities. Bader moved into manufacturing, concentrating on a specialist niche within the chemical industry.

In 1940 the company was moved from its central London offices and dockland factory to the old Wollaston Hall in Northamptonshire. The hall itself provided office accommodation, the stables became laboratories, and a new factory was built on the 44 acre site. The company has always remained relatively small, reaching a maximum of around 450 employees, a number which has declined and risen with trade recessions and strategic changes. Scott Bader acquired a manufacturer of glass-reinforced plastic products in 1972, for which it supplied the raw materials, and a major distributor in 1978. The company has always been profitable in a very competitive industry.

Ernest Bader, a Quaker, believed that men should employ capital rather than capital employ men, and as a result he established the Scott Bader Commonwealth in 1951 as a charitable trust. Bader and his family gave 90% of the company shares to the Commonwealth, holding back the remaining 10% (which carried over half the voting shares) until 1963, when they too were transferred. All employees who have completed a probationary period with the company can apply for membership of the Commonwealth and thus share in the ownership of the company, although shares are never individually theirs to trade.

The Commonwealth has a Board of Management with members elected from company employees and its prime functions are concerned with social guidance, support of charitable causes, and encouraging similar forms of common ownership elsewhere. Scott Bader has a proper management structure with a Board of Directors, similar to that of other companies except that there are the equivalent of four employee directors.

The Community Council with elected members from all parts of the company can investigate and discuss any matters referred to it by any individual or group and can recommend a course of action to the Company Board. In the past members of the Community Council have been actively involved in the selection of a new managing director for the company. In addition there is a Board of Trustees (two Directors, two from the Community Council and three external to the company) to deal with such things as constitutional changes.

No group has overall authority, so that ultimately they have to move together as one body even though they may push and pull against each other in representing particular interests.

The principles of the Commonwealth include:

Continued overleaf

☐ opportunities for personal growth and development
☐ releasing the best in all employees
☐ recognizing and sharing talents
☐ to render the best possible service as a corporate body to one's fellow men
☐ to produce goods beneficial to the community
☐ management by consent and not coercion.

Things have not gone completely smoothly. Whilst many employees have participated, some have chosen not to. It has been claimed that the company has lost dynamism because there is too much concern with the quality of working life.

People are allowed to serve on Boards for limited periods of time only and are not allowed to stand for re-election, so that individual power bases cannot be developed. Newly elected members have often had to be trained for their new roles.

Most significantly Scott Bader bought a Unilever subsidiary, Synthetic Resins (Speke, Liverpool) in 1982. Although some Scott Bader employees are members of trade unions, the unions are not active within the company. But Synthetic Resins was different. It was conventionally managed and traditionally unionized. Despite efforts to integrate the companies and introduce common ownership at Synthetic Resins Scott Bader failed to persuade the Liverpool workers to accept the new culture. Synthetic Resins was closed in 1985 and the essential parts of the business were transferred to Northamptonshire.

Further reading on Scott Bader

Bader, G (1986) The Scott Bader Commonwealth: putting people first, *Long Range Planning*, **19** (6).
McMonnies, D S (1984) Trade unions and co-ops? A Merseyside case study: the Scott Bader–Synthetic Resins saga, *Working Paper 6*, Department of Political Theory and Institutions, University of Liverpool.
Hoe S (1978) *The Man Who Gave His Company Away* (a biography of Ernest Bader), Heinemann.

influence management decisions, as a result of the partnership and its constitution the ordinary workers are again in ultimate control of the company they work for. This is supplemented by a profit-sharing scheme.

Decision making and communications within the organization must be affected by high levels of participation. John Lewis's motto of 'never knowingly undersold' is based on value for money which is helped by employee involvement. Through its work-force the company can relate well to its customers.

CULTURE AND POWER

In Charles Handy's classification of organizations in terms of their culture, power is an important element which needs further consideration. Whilst an introduction to the topic is included here, the subject of power is explored more fully in Chapter 24 when its impact on strategy implementation is considered.

Power is related to the potential or ability to do something. Consequently strategic change will be strongly influenced by the

Box 4.1
POWER LEVERS

☐ **Reward power** is the ability to influence the rewards given to others. These can be tangible (money) or intangible (status). Owner managers enjoy considerable reward power, managers in larger public sector organizations very little. For reward power to be useful, the rewards being offered must be important to the potential recipients.

☐ **Coercive power** is power based upon the threat of punishment for non-compliance, and the ability to impose the punishment. The source can be the person's role or position in the organization, or physical attributes and personality.

☐ **Legitimate power** is synonymous with authority, and relates to an individual manager's position within the structure of the organization. It is an entitlement from the role a person occupies. The effective use of legitimate power is dependent upon three things: access to relevant information; access to other people and communication networks inside the organization; and approaches to setting priorities – this determines what is asked of others.

☐ **Personal power** depends upon individual characteristics (personality) and physical characteristics. Charm, charisma and flair are terms used to describe people with personality-based power. Physical attributes such as height, size, weight and strength also affect personal power.

☐ **Expert power** is held by a person with specialist knowledge or skills in a particular field. It is particularly useful for tackling complex problem areas. It is possible for people to be attributed expert power through reputation rather than proven ability.

☐ **Information power** is the ability to access and use information to defend a stance or viewpoint – or to question an alternative view held by someone else – and is important as it can affect strategic choices.

☐ **Connection power** results from personal and professional access to key people inside and outside the organization, who themselves can influence what happens. This relates particularly to information power.

bases of power within an organization and by the power of the organization in relation to its environment.

Internal power

Change is brought about if the necessary resources can be harnessed and if people can be persuaded to behave in a particular way. Both of these require power. Power results in part from the structure of the organization, and it needs exercising in different ways in different cultures if it is to be used effectively. At the same time power can be a feature of an individual manager's personality, and managers who are personally powerful will be in a position to influence change.

The ways in which managers apply power are known as 'power levers'; Box 4.1 describes seven major sources of power. The classifications of power bases produced by a number of authors differ only slightly. Box 4.1 has been developed from a classification by Andrew Kakabadse (1982), who has built on the earlier work of French and Raven (1959).

In order to understand the reality of change in an organization and to examine how change might be managed, it is important to consider where power lies, which managers are powerful, and where their sources of power are. Whilst a visible, powerful and influential strategic leader is often a feature of an entrepreneurial organization, the nature and direction of incremental change will be influenced significantly by which managers are powerful and how they choose to exercise their power.

A power culture has strong central leadership as a key feature and power lies with the individual or small group at the centre who control most of the activity in the organization. In contrast, role cultures are based on the legitimacy of rules and procedures and individual managers are expected to work within these. Task cultures are dependent upon the expertise of individuals, and their success, in some part, depends upon the ability of the individuals to share their power and work as a team. Managers are expected to apply power levers in ways that are acceptable to the predominant culture of the organization, and at the same time the manner in which power levers are actually used affects what happens in the organization. Power is required for change; change results from the application of power. Hence the implementation of desired changes to strategies requires the effective use of power bases; but other strategic changes will result from the exercise of power by individual managers. It is important for the organization to monitor such activity and ensure that such emergent changes and strategies are desirable or acceptable.

The relative power of the organization

The ability of an organization to effect change within its environment will similarly depend on the exercise of power. A strong competitor with, say, a very distinctive product or service, or with substantial market share, may be more powerful than its competitors. A manufacturer who is able to influence distributors or suppliers will be similarly powerful. The issue is the relative power in relation to those other individuals, organizations and institutions upon whom it relies, with whom it trades, or which influence it in some way. These other influences are known as stakeholders, and their impact is discussed in Chapter 5.

DETERMINANTS OF CULTURE

Deal and Kennedy (1982) have conducted research into American companies in an attempt to ascertain what factors lead to consistently outstanding (above average for the industry) performance. They found that over the long term the companies that are the most successful are those that **believe in something** and those where the belief or beliefs have permeated through the whole organization, i.e. they are communicated and understood. Examples quoted are progress via innovation and technology and 'excellence' in something that customers value, say service or delivery on time.

Deal and Kennedy argue that employees must be rewarded for compliance with the essential cultural aspects if these values are to be developed and retained over time; and they conclude that people who build, develop and run successful companies invariably work hard to create strong cultures within their organizations.

From their research Deal and Kennedy isolated five key elements or determinants of culture.

☐ The environment and key success factors: what the organization must do well if it is to be an effective competitor. Innovation and fast delivery are examples quoted.

☐ The values that the strategic leader considers important and wishes to see adopted and followed in the organization. These should relate to the key success factors, and to employee reward systems.

☐ Heroes: the visionaries who create the culture. They can come from any background and could be, for example, product or service innovators, engineers who build the appropriate quality into the product, or creative marketing people who provide the slogans which make the product or brand name a household word.

☐ Rites and rituals: the behaviour patterns in which the culture is manifest. Again there are any number of ways that this can happen, including employees helping each other out when there are difficulties, the way sales people deal with customers, and the care and attention that goes into production.

☐ The cultural network: the communications system around which the culture revolves and which determines just how aware employees are about the essential issues.

When the culture is strong, people know what is expected of them and they understand how to act and decide in particular circumstances. They appreciate the issues that are important. When it is weak time can be wasted in trying to decide what should be done and how. Moreover it is argued that employees feel better about their companies if they are recognized, known about and regarded as successful, and these aspects will be reflected in the culture.

There can be a number of separate strands to the culture in any organization, which should complement each other. For example there can be aspects relating to the strategic leader, the environment and the employees. There could be a strong power culture related to an influential strategic leader who is firmly in charge of the organization and whose values are widely understood and followed. This could be linked to a culture of market orientation, which ensures that customer needs are considered and satisfied, and to a work culture if employees feel committed to the organization and wish to help achieve success.

ASPECTS OF CULTURE

Pümpin (1987) suggests that seven aspects comprise the culture of an organization, and that the relative significance of each of these will vary from industry to industry. The seven aspects are:

1. The extent to which the organization is marketing oriented, giving customers high priority.
2. The relationships between management and staff, manifested through communication and participation systems, for example.
3. The extent to which people are target oriented, and committed to achieving agreed levels of performance.
4. Attitudes towards innovation. It is particularly important that the risks associated with failure are perceived as acceptable by all levels of management if innovation and entrepreneurship is to be fostered.
5. Attitudes towards costs and cost reduction.
6. The commitment and loyalty to the organization felt, and shown, by staff.
7. The impact of, and reaction to, technology and technological change and development. One major issue concerns whether or not the opportunities offered by information technology are being harnessed by the firm.

Many of these aspects are developed further in later chapters of the book.

Hampden-Turner (1990) believes that the culture is a manifestation of how the organization has chosen to deal with specific dilemmas and conflicts. Each of these can be viewed as a continuum, and the organization needs a clear position on each one. One dilemma might be the conflict between, on the one hand, the need to develop new products and services quickly and ahead of competitors, and, on the other hand, the need for thorough development and planning to ensure adequate quality and safety. Another dilemma is the need for managers to be adaptive and responsive in a changing environment, but not at the expense of organization-wide communication and awareness. Such change-orientation may also conflict with a desire for continuity and consistency of strategy and policy.

LEVELS OF CULTURE

Edgar Schein (1985) contends that it is important to consider culture as having a number of levels, some of which are essentially manifestations of underlying beliefs.

The first and most visible level Schein terms 'artefacts'. These include the physical and social environment and the outputs of the organization. Written communications, advertisements and the reception that visitors receive are all included.

Values are the second level, and they represent a sense of 'what ought to be' based on convictions held by certain key people. For example if an organization has a problem such as low sales or a high level of rejections in production, decisions might be made to advertise more aggressively or to use high quality but more expensive raw materials. These are seen initially as the decision maker's values, which can be debated or questioned. Many of the strategies followed by organizations start in this way, and many will reflect values held by the strategic leader.

If the alternative is successful it may well be tried again and again until it becomes common practice. In this way the value becomes a belief and ultimately an assumption about behaviour practised by the organization. These basic underlying assumptions are Schein's third level, and they represent

Table 4.2 Corporate culture: underlying assumptions

Assumption	Example
Relationship to nature	The corporate mission, and the understanding of it throughout the organization Whether it is, say, aiming for market dominance or finding an appropriate niche
Nature of reality	Objectivity or subjectivity in decision making; whether consensus is sought
Nature of time	Is the organization most concerned with past or present successes?
Nature of human nature	Aspects of motivation
Nature of human activity	Is the organization proactive or reactive to change? This is concerned with 'the right things to do'
Nature of human relationships	How people work together; how power is exercised

Source: Schein E H (1985) *Organizational Culture and Leadership*, Jossey Bass.

the 'taken-for-granted ways of doing things or solutions to problems'.

Group behaviour amongst members of the organization may evolve in a similar way, but this will be less tangible. It is also important to appreciate that certain organizations may state that they have particular values but in reality these will be little more than verbal or written statements or aspirations for the future.

Schein argues that cultural paradigms are formed which determine 'how organization members perceive, think about, feel about, and judge situations and relationships' and these are based on a number of underlying assumptions. Table 4.2 is based on his work.

Schwartz and Davis (1981) argue along similar lines. For them culture is 'a pattern of beliefs and expectations shared by the organization's members, and which produce norms that powerfully shape the behaviour of individuals and groups in the organization'. They argue that the beliefs held by the company are seen as major aspects of corporate policy as they evolve from interactions with, and in turn form policy towards, the marketplace. As a result rules or norms for internal and external behaviour are developed and eventually both performance and reward systems will be affected.

Success is measured by, and culture therefore becomes based on, past activities. Current decisions by managers reflect the values, beliefs and norms that have proved beneficial in the past and in the development and growth of the organization. Moreover they reinforce the corporate culture and expected behaviour throughout the organization.

The culture affects suppliers and customers, and their reactions are important. They will feed back impressions about the organization, and their views should be sought. Successful organizations will ensure that there is congruence between these environmental influences and the organization culture. In this way key success factors can be met if resources are administered, controlled and developed appropriately.

Organizations need a cohesive blend of the philosophies introduced earlier. A cohesive culture would exhibit strong leadership, whereby the strategic leader is sensitive to the degrees of decentalization and informality necessary for satisfying customer needs efficiently – and managing change pressures – in order to keep the business strong and profitable. At the same time a centralized information network will ensure that communications are effective and that managers are both kept aware and rewarded properly for their contributions. A fragmented culture, on the other hand, would suggest that the needs of certain stakeholders were perhaps not being satisfied adequately, or that strategies and changes were not being co-ordinated, or that managers or business units were in conflict and working against each other, or that the most deserving people were not being rewarded.

Some years ago British Airways was seen to be fragmented. Leadership was to an extent 'military' with strict rules and procedures and top-down communications. Cabin staff were essentially powerless, and insufficiently customer-oriented. Customer attitudes and reactions were not fed back into the organization, and BA was seen as less friendly than many of its rivals. Case 4.2 describes how BA has attempted to become more cohesive. Front-line staff have been given more authority to use initiative, on the assumption that they will behave more warmly to passengers. Positive and negative responses (complaints) are now fed back through formalized channels, aided by increased use of information technology. Staff became more professional, and the organization more effective and more profitable. However the Gulf War led to a slump in air travel, and, together with the world recession at the end of the 1980s, caused BA to become less profitable and less efficient. Conscious of the need to remotivate staff and restore morale and efficiency, BA have introduced new service campaigns called 'Winning for Customers' and 'Managing Winners' (1992).

THE SEARCH FOR EXCELLENCE

Research into American companies

McKinsey and Company, well-known American management consultants, initiated an investigation in the 1970s into why certain companies were more successful than their rivals. The findings were published in 1980 in a *Business Week* article and they eventually became the basis for the book *In Search of Excellence* (Peters and Waterman, 1982). The research emphasizes the important contribution of culture and values to organizational success.

Some 40 companies were surveyed in a cross-section of industries and included IBM, Texas Instruments, Hewlett Packard, 3M,

Case 4.2
SCANDINAVIAN AIRLINES SYSTEM (SAS) AND BRITISH AIRWAYS (BA) – CHANGES IN CULTURE AND STRATEGIES

SAS was losing money in 1981 when Jan Carlzon (then 39 years old) was appointed Chief Executive Officer. Morale was low and employees were being laid off. Within one year he had changed the corporate culture and the strategy and made the airline profitable. Carlzon 'simply' improved customer service, insisting that customers received priority treatment. Behind Carlzon's success was the creation of awareness and enthusiasm for his vision of service throughout the organization, which employed 20 000 people around the world. This entailed:

☐ an assessment of the nature and needs of the market;
☐ the development of a strategy which concentrated on providing the right service for travelling businessmen – and which earned for SAS the reputation for being the preferred airline for businessmen;
☐ an evaluation of activities performed throughout the organization with the objective of improving service;
☐ extensive personal communication by Carlzon supplemented by training programmes – managers were encouraged to provide support for those employees who dealt with customers and who in turn were expected to take more decisions and solve problems without reference upwards.

In the financial year to 31 March 1983 British Airways recorded a pre-tax profit of £74 million on a turnover of £2.5 billion. In the previous year BA had lost over £100 million. Colin Marshall (now Sir Colin) became Chief Executive of BA in 1983, and he set 'giving the best service' as a key objective. He argued that this involved:

☐ appreciating what the market wants;
☐ being able to respond quickly to changes in customer demand and expectations by
  ☐ having an appropriate organization structure and
  ☐ being adequately resourced.

These were to be achieved by ensuring that employees throughout BA were committed to providing a high level of customer service and that managers were equally aware of the needs and expectations of employees. Marshall sought to change the culture of BA to one of service orientation by

☐ issuing a new mission statement reflecting the revised objectives and values;
☐ a management training programme entitled 'Managing People First', designed to 'substantially enhance the participant's personal performance as a manager of others' by concentrating on developing a sense of urgency, vision, motivation, trust and a willingness to take responsibility;
☐ improving both performance appraisal and a linked reward system;
☐ customer service training for all employees who dealt directly with customers – entitled 'Putting People First'.

In both 1984 and 1985 BA was awarded the title 'Airline of the Year' by *Executive Travel* magazine, and was credited as the most preferred transatlantic carrier and the airline with the best overall cabin staff and the best food and wine.

Profits doubled in 1984 and they have continued to grow. In 1987 British Airways was privatized successfully by the UK government.

Sources: 'The Art of Loving'. An interview with Jan Carlzon, *Inc Magazine*, May 1989; Sadler P, *Managerial Leadership in the Post-Industrial Society*, Gower, 1988.

Procter and Gamble, Johnson and Johnson, and McDonald's. The companies were selected for being 'well-run and successful organizations'. Most of the companies were well established and large. In the selection process 20 years of financial data were analysed and the companies under consideration were evaluated relative to competitors in their industry. In addition a subjective assessment of their innovation records was used as a final screen. The research concluded that the most successful companies exhibited eight common attributes, which are featured in Table 4.3, and that their success was based primarily on good management practice. Managers had invested time, energy and thought into doing certain important things well and those activities and values were understood by employees and appreciated by customers. In other words they had become part of the culture of the organization.

I produce the show. I think I am a strategic person. But how do I get people to grab the strategy, to get it under their skin, to get a feel for it, to **get** it? I can't write it in a manual. I must make a show of it. I motivate people through the show. Communication. And it is not manipulating – it is a way of getting the message across.

Jan Carlzon, President and Chief Executive Officer, Scandinavian Airlines System

---

In most companies the role of one or more strategic leaders had proved to be very influential in establishing and developing the values, and in many cases the values had been established early in the company's history. In other words growth had been assisted by the culture. Peters and Waterman conclude that 'the real role of the chief executive is to manage the **values** of the organization' (see Chapter 3).

Peters and Waterman argue that 'excellent' companies are successful in their management of the basic fundamentals with respect to their environment: customer service; low cost manufacturing; productivity improvement; innovation; and risk taking. In order to ensure that the key values are understood and practised throughout the organization there is an emphasis on simplicity: simple organization structures; simple strategies; simple goals; and simple communications systems.

The attributes featured in Table 4.3 are essentially quite basic rather than startling, and they are very much related to the contribution made by people. 'The excellent companies live their commitment to people.' Not all the attributes were visible in each of the companies studied, nor were they given the same priority in different organizations, but in every case there was a preponderance of the attributes and they were both visible and distinctive. In less successful companies, argue Peters and Waterman, 'far too many managers have lost sight of the basics: quick action, service to customers, practical

Table 4.3   In search of excellence: characteristics of the most successful organizations

A bias for action	Greater emphasis on trying things rather than talking about them and seeking 'solutions' rather than 'resolutions' Avoidance of long complicated business plans Use of task forces to tackle special problems (Handy's task culture)
Close to the customer	Companies are 'customer-driven, not technology-driven, not product-driven, not strategy-driven' They 'know what the customer wants, and provide it – better than competitors'
Autonomy and entrepreneurship	Managers are authorized to act entrepreneurially rather than be tied too rigidly by rules and systems
Productivity through people	Productivity improvements by motivating and stimulating employees, using involvement and communications 'Corny merit awards, like badges and stars work' if they are properly managed and not just used as a gimmick
Hands on, value driven	Values are established with good communications People must 'believe' The power and personality of the strategic leader is crucial
Stick to the knitting	Successful companies know what they do well and concentrate on doing it well
Simple form, lean staff	Simple structures
Simultaneous loose–tight properties	An effective combination of central direction and individual autonomy Certain control variables, such as a particular financial return measure or the number of employees, are managed tightly; for other things managers are encouraged to be flexible

Summarized from Peters, T J and Waterman, R H Jr (1982) *In Search of Excellence*, Harper and Row.

innovation, and the fact that you can't get any of these without virtually everyone's commitment'. The issues also relate to marketing and operations and will be considered further in Chapters 10 and 11 when the strategic role of these functions is explored. The strategic impact of human resource management is the subject of Chapter 12.

Since the book was published some of the 'excellent' companies, notably People Express and Caterpillar Tractor, have been less successful and so the findings of *In Search of Excellence* should be treated carefully. Basically the research found a number of common attributes to be present in the organizations studied rather than providing a set of recommendations concerning how unsuccessful companies could be transformed. It provided food for thought rather than answers.

In a more recent book Robert Waterman (1988), writing independently, argues that in order to become and remain successful organizations must master the management of change. As will be seen later in this book, there is often a fear of change and hostility towards it. These must be overcome, claims Waterman, because competition changes too quickly to allow companies to fall into what he calls the 'habit trap'. He further argues that strategies should be based on 'informed opportunism', developing from effective information systems which ensure that customers, suppliers and other key influences are consulted. Waterman emphasizes that for an information system to be effective it should not be allowed to become too rigid or bureaucratic.

Peters (1988) asserts that there are no long-term excellent companies. 'The pace of change has become far too rapid to make any enterprise secure. Tomorrow's winners will have to view chaos, external and internal, not as a problem, but as a prime source of

Table 4.4 Successful British companies: key issues

Leadership	**Visible** top management Clear board-level objectives Strategic 'vision' Complemented by management objectives throughout the organization and the provision of appropriate resources
Autonomy	Entrepreneurial spirit in key areas Certain initiatives decentralized, but . . .
Control	Where it matters, say in capital spending, and quality standards
Involvement	Commitment through, for example, high pay and incentives; promotion from within; equity involvement; information and communication; training
Market orientation	Linked to quality
'Zero basing'	Staying close to the fundamentals of the business – often including careful attention to detail
The innovation factor	An interest and commitment to things new Culture and values are particularly important here R & D should be market-directed
The integrity perception	**Fairness** to employees, suppliers and customers

Summarized from Goldsmith, W and Clutterbuck, D (1984) *The Winning Streak*, Weidenfeld and Nicolson.

competitive advantage.' Peters quotes Ford of Europe as an example of a company which has dealt successfully with the challenge of change by stressing a new set of basic values: world class quality and service; greater flexibility and responsiveness; continuous and rapid product and service innovation. Arguably, however, the change was forced on Ford by strong Japanese competition.

British companies

In the UK a CBI Report (1985) suggested that the key aspects of successful strategic management are deceptively simple, but neither widely understood nor applied. These are, they claim,

☐ sound financial controls
☐ decentralized decision making
☐ attention to customers and products
☐ motivation of employees.

The last point was seen as the key to improved performance.

These points relate closely to the issues that Goldsmith and Clutterbuck (1984) highlighted when they studied British companies in a replication of *In Search of Excellence*. Their

Another reason for Britain's poor economic performance is that still too few leaders of industry believe, or at least fail to implement, the policy of good human relations at work . . .

Over many years Marks & Spencer has implemented a policy of good human relations at work, treating all our employees as individuals and with respect, looking after their well-being, and making sure they share in the profitable progress of the business.

Lord Sieff of Brimpton, Honorary President,
Marks & Spencer plc, speaking at a BIM
Workshop in London, February 1986

findings are summarized in Table 4.4, and similarly to Peters and Waterman they argue that whilst not every 'winning company' practises all the winning elements the emphasis is on a 'culture of key issues which matter'.

The limits to excellence

The research of Peters and Waterman in the USA and of Goldsmith and Clutterbuck in the UK suggest that firms with above-average financial performance over several years are characterized by strong managerial values which dictate the way the business is run. These core values, which affect how employees are treated and the relationships with customers and suppliers, encourage innovativeness and flexibility. If they are combined with effective management control they are thought to yield above-average financial performance.

These findings provide valuable food for thought, but they are normative. Some firms do appear to obtain superior financial performance from their cultures, but it does not follow that firms who succeed in copying these cultural attributes will necessarily also achieve superior financial results. Organizations which pursue the excellence factors must surely improve their chances of success, but clearly there can be no guarantees. Ignoring these issues will increase the chances of failure.

In my opinion effective strategic management requires:

1. A sound strategy, which implies an effective match between the resources and the environment.
2. A well-managed execution and implementation of the strategy.
3. Appropriate strategic change. Whilst it can be important to 'stick to the knitting', firms must watch for signs indicating that strategies need to be improved or changed.

Points 2 and 3 are influenced by the culture and values of the organization, and consequently Figure 4.4 shows these three factors alongside the model of E–V–R congruence. Many of the excellence factors discussed above also affect the ways in which strategies are implemented and changed. In addition to the excellence factors, therefore, we also need to look at the quality of the strategies and ensure that a match between environment and resources is maintained. Case 4.3 (British Vita) applies these ideas.

Culture and competitive advantage

Barney (1986) has examined further the relationship between culture and 'superior financial performance'. He has used microeconomics for his definition of superior financial performance, arguing that firms record either below-normal returns (insufficient for long-term survival in the industry), normal returns (enough for survival, but no more) or superior results, which are more than those required for long-term survival. Superior results, which result from some form of competitive advantage, attract competitors who seek to copy whatever is thought to be the source of competitive advantage and generating the success. This in turn affects supply and margins and can reduce profitability to only normal returns and, in some cases, below normal. Therefore **sustained** superior financial performance requires **sustained** competitive advantage.

Barney concluded that culture can, and does, generate sustained competitive advantage, and hence long-term superior financial performance, when three conditions are met.

☐ The culture is valuable. The culture must enable things to happen which themselves result in high sales, low costs or high margins.
☐ The culture is rare.
☐ The culture is imperfectly imitable, i.e. it cannot be copied easily by competitors.

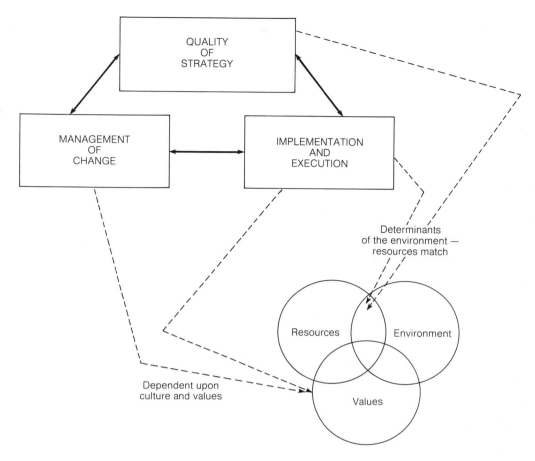

Figure 4.4 Strategic excellence and E–V–R congruence.

Hence if the cultural factors identified by Peters and Waterman are in fact transferable easily to other organizations, can they be the source of superior financial performance? Barney contends that valuable and rare cultures may be difficult, if not impossible, to imitate. For one thing it is very difficult to define culture clearly, particularly in respect of how it adds value to the product or service. For another culture is often tied to historical aspects of company development and to the beliefs, personality and charisma of a particular strategic leader.

Body Shop (Case 4.4) provides an example of a company which has created long-term superior performance with a culture-based competitive advantage. Club Méditerranée (Case 4.5) was similarly successful for many years, but more recently – faced with financial results which showed revenue and profits to be growing more slowly than the level of inflation in France – the strategy has been changed.

CHANGING CULTURE

The culture of an organization may appear to be in need of change for any one of a number of reasons. It could be that the culture does not fit well with the needs of the environment

Case 4.3
BRITISH VITA

British Vita is an international polymer, fibre and foam company based in Manchester. In the year ended December 1991 turnover was £635 million with a 27% return on capital employed. The company manufactures and trades throughout Europe and Africa.

British Vita has a distinctive management style based on 'common sense and Victorian entrepreneurial values of aggressive ambition, bold strategy and hard work'. The company believes that people work harder for enterprises where they have a financial interest, and as a result runs a share incentive scheme. On retirement, long-serving managers are likely to have amassed shares worth between one-quarter and one-half million pounds. These incentives are linked to a control system based wholly on financial performance and profit contribution. British Vita is structured around some 130 business units, the managers of which are able to change the strategies of their individual businesses, say through acquisition. Much of the company's growth is the result of acquisitions, most recently in Europe, but historically also in Africa, of **related** businesses. Quite often this involves the purchase of small subsidiaries owned by larger companies.

International chemical companies manufacture the basic polymers, and carry out technical research before developing new basic products. Companies like British Vita develop applications for the polymers and, having added value, market them in the form of semi-finished products such as foam fillings for furniture, carpet underlay and material for manufacturing leotards. British Vita therefore invest in development and marketing but not basic research, and they remain flexible to enter new market niches and opportunities quickly – and exit them when 'windows of opportunity' close.

This strategy, supported by the decentralized structure, allows British Vita to remain close to its customers.

---

or with the organization's resources, or that the company is not performing well and needs major strategic changes, or even that the company is growing rapidly in a changing environment and needs to adapt.

Ideally the culture and the strategies being pursued will complement each other, and, again ideally, the organization will be flexible and adaptable to change when it is appropriate. But these ideals will not always be achieved. Dean Berry (1983) points out some of the problems in the featured article summary – Key Reading 4.1.

Culture and strategic change are unques-tionably linked. Certain changes in strategy will force cultural change on the organization, as illustrated in Case 4.6 which considers the implications for building societies of the change from being mutual to limited companies as a response to changes in legislation and increased competition, particularly from the major High Street banks. Equally it can be argued that certain strategic change options will only be viable if they can be complemented by corresponding culture changes, and the difficulties involved may prove to be a limiting factor.

Culture is an essential element in the

Case 4.4
BODY SHOP

Body Shop, which sources, manufactures and retails (mainly through franchises) natural lotions and cosmetics, is a highly successful business with a price to earnings ratio consistently higher than the average for the retail sector. Body Shop was started in England in 1976, since when it has enjoyed revenue and profits growth of some 50% per year. Growth continued during the recession at the end of the 1980s. The business was founded by Anita Roddick and her husband, Gordon, who shortly afterwards took a sabbatical leave and rode a horse from Buenos Aires to New York. At this time the Roddicks had two young daughters. There are thought to be substantial international opportunities for Body Shop during the 1990s. Currently they have stores in some 40 countries, but 60% of the profits are still made in the UK. There are, for example, two shops in Tokyo, but Body Shop have a target of 200 Japanese stores by the year 2000.

Body Shop arouses enthusiasm, commitment and loyalty amongst those involved with it. Much of this has developed from the ethical beliefs and values of Anita Roddick, which have become manifested in a variety of distinctive policies. Gordon Roddick is now responsible for the highly efficient operational aspects of the business.

☐ Body Shop is very strong on environmental issues, offering only biodegradable products and refillable containers. Shops have been used to campaign, amongst other things, to save whales and to stop the burning of rain forests.

☐ Packaging is plain, but the shops are characterized by strong and distinctive aromas. The packages, together with posters and shelf cards, provide comprehensive information about the products and their origins and ingredients. This has created a competitive advantage which rivals have found difficult to replicate.

☐ The sales staff are knowledgeable, but they are not forceful and do not sell aggressively, offering advice only if it is requested.

☐ Marketing themes concern 'health rather than glamour, and reality rather than instant rejuvenation'.

☐ Body Shop does not advertise, preferring in-store information to attempts at persuasion.

☐ Ingredients are either natural or have been used by humans for years. There is no testing on animals.

☐ Employees are provided with regular newsletters, videos and training packages. Anita Roddick contributes regularly to the newsletters, which concentrate on Body Shop campaigns. Employees and franchisees can attend the Body Shop training centre in London free of charge. All the courses are product centred and informative – they do not focus on selling, marketing or how to make more money.

☐ Employees are given time off, and franchisees encouraged to take time off, during working hours, to do voluntary work for the community.

☐ Body Shop has integrated manufacturing and retailing and is efficient and operationally strong. Fresh supplies are typically delivered with a 24-hour lead time. As a result of acquisition Body Shop has the capacity to manufacture most of its product range.

Continued overleaf

> ☐ 'Profits are perceived as boring, business as exciting.'
> ☐ 'The company must never let itself become anything other than a human enterprise.'
>
> These strategies, policies and beliefs have, of course, generated substantial growth and profits. In the year ended 28 February 1991 turnover exceeded £100 million with trading profits of some £22 million. One dilemma is whether this culture and quirky management style will still be wholly appropriate when Body Shop becomes a much bigger multi-national business.
>
> *Source*: Burlingham, B (1990) Body Shop bares its soul, *Business*, December.

strategy process. The potential for changing the culture of an organization is affected by the strength and history of the existing culture, how well it is understood and the strategic leader. If culture is changed as part of strategic change it becomes an essential implementation aspect; if the culture remains as it is it will act as a determinant of strategy (through its influence on decisions) and possibly as a constraint on certain strategic change options.

A great deal depends upon strategic leadership. A change in strategic leadership often brings a change in strategy. It can also mean cultural change. However, as we shall explore in later chapters, change pressures may well be resisted, and it may be that top management in an organization is not able to effect cultural change of the magnitude they desire. Equally aspects of the culture may be indeterminate and for that reason very difficult to influence. Another problem is conflicting subcultures. There can be several strands to the culture in an organization; it does not follow that all the strands will complement each other.

Cultural change needs effective leadership to provide vision and direction, but the changes need to be bottom-up. Individual employees must be motivated to change, and rewarded. Du Pont in America have successfully developed a service culture by, amongst other things, encouraging blue collar workers to visit customers and discuss their requirements with them. Many companies, especially American and Japanese, single out employees who have performed well, or better than their colleagues, and provide them with appropriate badges. This requires a belief at the head of an organization that, left to it, employees can be responsible and innovative. As the incidences of this increase organizations will have fewer levels in the managerial hierarchy, thereby improving communications.

THE JAPANESE CULTURE

The Japanese economy became relatively sluggish in the mid-1980s in comparison with the past: unemployment crept up, and resistance abroad from both America and Europe became successful in restraining Japanese exports. However, the economy improved again in the late 1980s and Japanese companies 'remain the principal challengers of any Western firm serious about world markets. There is no shortcut other than to meet the challenge. In the long run the only feasible response is to do better what the Japanese are doing well already – developing management systems that motivate employees from

Case 4.5
CLUB MÉDITERRANÉE

Club Med, founded in 1950 in France, is Europe's largest tour operator with a clearly distinguished product.

Club Med represents 'beautiful people playing all sorts of sports, white sand beaches, azure sky and sea, Polynesian thatched huts, free and flowing wine at meals, simple yet superb food' (*Economist*, 12 July 1986). It is an 'organized melange of hedonism and back to nature'.

The organization is spread around the world, with some 100 holiday villages and over 60 holiday residences (hotel/sports complexes) for both summer and winter vacations. Organizers are present in a ratio of 1:5 with guests, for whom they provide sports tuition and organize evening entertainment. All tuition, food and drinks with meals are paid for in advance in the holiday cost, and guests are provided with beads which they use as they choose to buy extra drinks and so on. Clothing is permanently casual.

Club Med has traditionally charged prices above the average for package holidays, its clientele have been mainly above-average income earners, and the organization has enjoyed a reputation for delivering customer service and satisfaction. The strategy has been developed and maintained by the founder of the business, Gilbert Trigano, but he was 70 years old in 1991.

The company grew successfully for over 30 years with little change to the basic strategy. By the mid-1980s occupancy rates had fallen, and profits declined and then stagnated. Whilst the underlying concept was still sound, people's tastes were changing. Holidaymakers increasingly sought higher quality facilities than the straw huts provided. Many Americans wanted televisions and telephones – 'it was the absence of these which helped make Club Med unique'.

Building on the original concept and strategy, Club Med has developed new products in order to better satisfy selected audiences around the world. In addition to the traditional villages, where in some cases straw huts have been replaced by bungalows, there are now both cheaper, half-board holidays available in newly acquired hotels and villages, and more expensive properties. This latter development was pioneered at Opio, near Cannes, which opened in 1989. Opio has expensive rooms with facilities, and, unusually, is open twelve months of the year. The international conference trade is being targeted. A limited number of villages now have a multi-lingual staffing policy to ensure that visitors from different European countries can all be greeted in their own language. Attempts are being made to attract more American visitors, but there is some scepticism. Americans are more puritanical in their tastes and expectations, and 'Club Med's sexy image' has not proved successful in the US.

Sources: Club Med: The bourgeois holiday camp, *The Economist*, 12 July 1986; Wood, S (1990), A new life for Club Med, *Business*, January.

Key Reading 4.1
THE PERILS OF TRYING TO CHANGE CORPORATE CULTURE

After almost 20 years of emphasis on analytical techniques in strategic management, the concentration has switched to the softer aspect of culture. The emphasis is no longer on the marketplace but on what managers can do to resolve internal problems. Three ideas are implicit:

☐ culture is an important strategic matter
☐ diagnosing and understanding corporate culture is possible
☐ by using culture companies can become more strategically effective

Given certain assumptions concerning strategic problems, expectations and time, these implications could be true, but the assumptions give rise to certain doubts.

The major doubt concerns the ability to change cultures. Most successful companies develop strong cultures such as a deep commitment to product quality and fast delivery at Honda and customer service at IBM; and employees accept them. However, strong cultures can obstruct strategic changes, particularly if companies are in decline. At BL (now Rover Group), British Steel and British Airways three new Chief Executives have been appointed (Sir Michael Edwardes, Sir Ian MacGregor and Lord King respectively), and each has succeeded in creating a strong personal mythology, significant rationalization and important results. However, neither Edwardes nor MacGregor fully succeeded in changing BL and British Steel from being production oriented to being outward looking and marketing oriented; and other airlines are more service conscious than British Airways. Rationalization can reinforce certain values as people become defensive and resistant to further change.

At more successful companies strong cultures are clearly a strategic asset as internalized beliefs motivate people to unusual performance levels. Again it may be difficult to change things. A lot may be known about the culture, but not about 'how to get it'. Books such as *In Search of Excellence* are descriptive, not prescriptive.

One problem is that many managers have short time horizons (desiring results in the short term) and cultural change is thought to take between six and 15 years (Deal and Kennedy, 1982).

Given these obstacles is an understanding of culture useful?

If a strategic leader really understands his company's culture he must, by definition, be better equipped to make wise decisions. He might conclude that 'cultural change will be so difficult we had better be sure to select a business or strategy that our kind of company can handle well'. This is just as valid, and perhaps more useful, than believing that one can accomplish cultural change in order to shift the firm towards a new strategy.

Moreover, if business strategies and culture are intertwined, the ability to analyse and construct strategies and the ability to manage and inspire people are also intertwined. Hence a good strategy acknowledges 'where we are, what we have got, and what therefore managerially helps us to get where we want to be' and this is substantially different from selecting business options exclusively on their product/market dynamics. In other words developing and implementing strategy is a human and political process that starts as much with the visions, hopes and aspirations of a company's leaders as it does with market or business analysis. Ideas drive organizations.

With ever-shortening product life cycles, intense global competition and unstable economies and currencies the future is going to require organizations that are ready to commit themselves to change. Strategy is going to be about intertwining analysis and adaptation. The challenge is to develop more effective organizations.

Source: Berry, D (1983) *Financial Times*, 14 December.

Case 4.6
BUILDING SOCIETIES

In March 1988, following changes in legislation, the Board of the Abbey National Building Society decided to recommend to its members that it should convert itself from a mutual society into a limited company. Four months later the Halifax, Britain's largest society (the Abbey is second), decided to retain mutual status. By changing, the Abbey National would become owned by equity shareholders rather than its depositors (members) and would take out a banking licence. Much of the argument for and against change has concentrated on values and the effect on customers.

The chairman of the Halifax argued that mutual status was the best guarantee of service to customers. Press comments speculated that it was because Abbey National had opted to become more of a bank by offering cheque book services and paper-based money transmission, whereas Halifax had not, relying instead on electronic payment methods, and that by becoming a bank Halifax feared it would compromise its traditional customer-friendly image.

Opponents of conversion amongst the Abbey National members quickly formed a lobby group, arguing that 'a mutual building society is owned by, and run for the benefit of, its members. A PLC is run for the benefit of its shareholders. A building society's rates are as favourable as possible for its members.'

The society claimed that a flotation would raise equity capital which could be used to fund growth and an overhaul of the branch network, including more investment in information technology, to provide better facilities and services for members. Growth may well include more estate agencies, into which Abbey National had already diversified. Some of these changes were a defence against the high street banks which now compete aggressively in the mortgage market.

Conscious of the arguments about the effect on customer service, Sir Campbell Adamson, chairman of the Abbey National, wrote to members and commented: 'We would ensure we maintain the present secure and friendly image. The aim must be to concentrate on personal financial services and not commercial banking services, and we would not, for example, expect to lend to "Third World" countries.' (Certain high street banks have had to write off unpaid debts from certain countries, thus depleting profits.) 'We would not become just another bank, but will remain Abbey National and all that has traditionally meant, and in addition will offer as wide a range of personal financial services as our customers require now and in the future. We will continue to be innovative and will provide value and high standards of service and safety for all investors and borrowers.'

During the early 1990s Abbey National has re-structured its operations and re-designed individual branches to improve customer service. The administration of mortgages, a primary activity of building societies, has been regionalized for efficiency. Branches are open for normal business six full days a week.

top to bottom to pursue growth-oriented, innovation-focused competitive strategies' (Pucik and Hatvany, 1983).

Deal and Kennedy (1982) have argued that 'Japan Inc.' is a culture, with considerable co-operation between industry, the banking systems and government. For this reason certain aspects of the Japanese culture are difficult to imitate. For example banks in the UK are public companies with their own shareholders and they borrow and lend money in order to make profit; this is their basic 'mission'. The current UK government favours competition rather than protectionism. However, there are a number of lessons to be learned from the Japanese and from their record of economic growth since World War II. It will be seen that cultural aspects are very much a driving force in the Japanese strategy process.

In Japan the focus is on human resources (Pucik and Hatvany, 1983) and this becomes the basis for three key strategic thrusts which are expressed as a number of management techniques. These act as key determinants of the actual strategies pursued (Figure 4.5). The three strategic thrusts are the notion of an internal labour market within the organization, a unique company philosophy, and intensive socialization throughout the working life.

The internal labour market is based on the tradition of lifetime employment whereby young men (not females) who join large companies after school or university are expected to remain with them for life and in return are offered job security. Commitment and loyalty to the employer result. With recession in recent years this practice has been less widespread.

The articulated and enacted unique philosophy is again designed to generate commitment and loyalty with the argument that familiarity with the goals of a company helps establish values and provides direction for effort and behaviour. YKK's 'Cycle of Goodness' (Box 4.2) is an excellent example.

The potential benefits of a company philosophy will only be gained if the philosophy is communicated to employees and demonstrated by managers. Hence this is a key aspect of company socialization in Japan, which starts with initial training and continues with further training throughout the working life.

These three strategic thrusts are closely linked to six management techniques used extensively in Japanese firms.

Open communication and sharing information across departmental boundaries aims to develop a climate of trust and a team spirit within the organization. This is enhanced by close integration between managers and employees. Job rotation and the internal training programmes supplement this communication system because through them employees become more aware of what happens throughout the organization. Because of very low labour turnover, promotion opportunities are very limited and advancement is slow and often based on seniority. However, performance is essential, and employees are carefully and regularly appraised in their abilities to get things done and to co-operate with others.

The core of management is the art of mobilizing every ounce of intelligence in the organization and pulling together the intellectual resources of all employees in the service of the firm. We know that the intelligence of a handful of technocrats, however brilliant and smart they may be, is no longer enough. Only by drawing on the combined brain power of all its employees can a firm face up to the turbulence and constraints of today's environment.

Mr Konosuke Matsushita, Matsushita Electrical Industrial Company Ltd

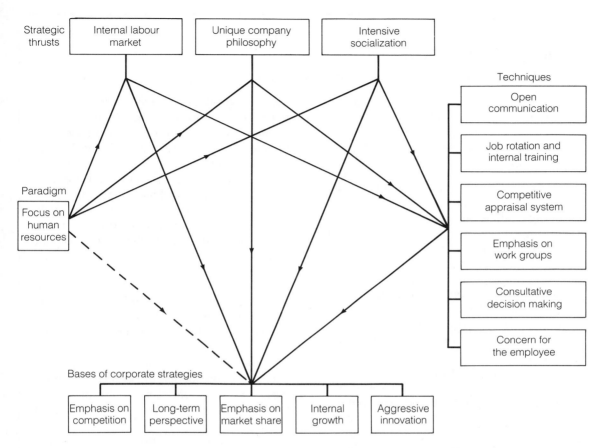

Figure 4.5 The Japanese management system. Developed from Pucik, V and Hatvany, N (1983) *Management Practices in Japan and their Impact on Business Strategy*, JAI Press.

This is particularly important as Japanese companies revolve around groups rather than individuals, with work being assigned to teams of employees. This, together with the use of Quality Circles (whereby groups of employees are encouraged to discuss issues and problems and suggest improvements), is seen as a key motivator. There is considerable emphasis on consultative decision making, involving these working groups, and a desire for consensus decisions. This generates greater loyalty to the decisions and to implementation. Finally, managers are encouraged to spend time with employees discussing both performance and personal problems. Companies also provide housing and various other services for employees.

A number of Japanese companies have invested in manufacturing plants in the UK (as well as in America and other countries in Europe) in recent years. In a number of cases they have selected industries where the UK had already ceased to manufacture products because of an inability to compete (e.g. television sets and video recorders) or where the competitive edge had declined. Motor vehicles is an example of the latter. The British car industry fell behind the Japanese

Box 4.2

THE CYCLE OF GOODNESS
Attributed to Tadeo Yoshida, President, YKK

YKK is the world's leading manufacturer of zip fasteners. YKK produces and markets zips throughout the world, and is vertically integrated, designing and manufacturing much of its own machinery.

I firmly believe in the spirit of social service.

Wages alone are not sufficient to assure our employees of a stable life and a rising standard of living. For this reason we return to them a large share of the fruits of their labour, so that they may also participate in capital accumulation and share in the profits of the firm. Each employee, depending upon his means, deposits with the company at least ten per cent of his wages and monthly allowances, and fifty per cent of his bonus; the company, in turn, pays interest on these savings. Moreover, as this increases capital, the employees benefit further as stockholders of the firm. It is said that the accumulation of savings distinguishes man from animals. Yet, if the receipts of a day are spent within that day, there can be no such cycle of saving.

The savings of all YKK employees are used to improve production facilities, and contribute directly to the prosperity of the firm.

Superior production facilities improve the quality of the goods produced. Lower prices increase demand. And both factors contribute to the prosperity of other industries that use our products.

As society prospers, the need for raw materials and machinery of all sorts increases, and the benefits of this cycle spread out not just to this firm, but to all related industries. Thus the savings of our employees, by enhancing the prosperity of the firm, are returned to them as dividends that enrich their lives. This results in increased savings which further advance the firm. Higher incomes mean higher tax payments, and higher tax payments enrich the lives of every citizen.

In this manner, business income directly affects the prosperity of society; for businesses are not mere seekers after profit, but vital instruments for the improvement of society.

This cycle enriches our free society and contributes to the happiness of those who work within it. The perpetual working of this cycle produces perpetual prosperity for all. This is the cycle of goodness.

and German producers in terms of quality and productivity and has struggled to catch up. The first Japanese car plant was built by Nissan, and Case 4.7 describes the human resources strategies which have contributed markedly to its early success.

Competition

Although there are close supporting links between companies, government and the banking system, there is intense and aggressive competition between the individual firms in an industry, fostered by growth objectives and the loyalty of employees to their firm.

C K Prahalad of the University of Michigan and Gary Hamel of London Business School have suggested (1985) that the Japanese 'rewrite the rules of the game to take their competitors by surprise'. Through technology, design, production costs, distribution and selling arrangements, pricing and service

Case 4.7
NISSAN UK

Milestones

1984   Agreement with UK Government concerning location and development incentives.

1985   Wearside (Sunderland) factory completed on schedule.

1986   First Bluebird cars sold.

1987   Production and sales both ahead of targets.

1988   Decision to develop additional engine and body shops. Left-hand drive models exported into Europe.

1990   Target of 80 000 cars per year set – with an 80% local content (i.e. British components and materials).

1992   Expansion announced. New target: 300 000 cars per year – approaching the output levels of the long-established companies.

Key human resources aspects of the strategy

☐ Single union agreement – with the AEU.

☐ All employees (including managers) have the same conditions of employment, and wear similar blue overalls at work.

☐ There are no (inflexible) written job descriptions.

☐ There is no clocking on and no privileged parking.

☐ Absenteeism has remained very low.

☐ There are daily communications meetings – searching for continuous improvement.

☐ Employees often go to Japan for training – skilled workers learn both operational and maintenance skills.

☐ The training budget, equivalent to 14% of sales revenue, is exceptionally high for a British company. A typical employee will receive 9 days on-the-job and 12 days off-the-job training each year.

☐ Supervisors are empowered managers. They recruit and select their own staff (individually they are responsible for about 20 employees), and they control the layout and operation of their own part of the production line.

Source: Hill, R (1990) Nissan and the art of people management, *Director*, March.

they seek to build 'layers of competitive advantage' rather than concentrate on just one aspect. Many competitors in the West think more narrowly. Prahalad and Hamel suggest that Japanese companies are successful in part because they have a clear 'mission' and statement of strategic intent, and a culture which provides both opportunity and encouragement to change things incrementally.

Internationally Japanese companies may not be consistent with their strategies;

instead they will seek the best competitive opportunities in different places and they will change continually as new opportunities arise and are created.

Long-term perspective

We shall consider this further in Chapter 5 when we look at objectives. Whilst many Western companies concentrate on short-term strategies, influenced often by financial pressures, the Japanese take a long-term perspective.

Emphasis on market share

Japanese companies are competitive, growth oriented and anxious to build and sustain high market shares in world markets. This will enable them to provide the job security that is a fundamental aspect of the culture. They often use their experience curve (which we shall examine in detail later) to develop strategies aimed at market dominance with a long-term view of costs and prices.

Company directors should be optimistic. But they should also be realistic. I agree with Michael Crozier who said in his *Day-to-day Management* (InterEditions) that the greatest danger for managing directors is the 'temptation to run on' and to completely lose touch with reality.

Common denominator in all this is pragmatism. The common thread running through the advice given is the paramount importance of everyday concerns and of the care given to detail.

Bernard Arnault, Group Chairman, LVMH,
Moët Hennessy. Louis Vuitton.

Internal growth

Mergers, acquisitions and divestitures are relatively uncommon in Japan – the Japanese favour the internal production system and innovation.

In a book on Japanese manufacturing techniques Schonberger (1984) argues that a major reason for Japan's success is their ability to use their resources well, better in fact than many Western competitors. In many factories, he contends, the equipment is no better than that used elsewhere in the world, but wherever they can Japanese companies invest in the best equipment available. Managerial skills are used in improvement drives, a search for simple solutions and, in particular, a meticulous attention to detail. Simplicity is important since management and shopfloor can relate better to each other; and flexible techniques and workforces result in low stock production systems, efficiency and lower costs. However, suppliers and manufacturers are strongly dependent on each other if stocks are kept low (more frequent deliveries are required) and, as a result, global expansion could be hindered.

Innovation

Research and development is deemed important and funded appropriately. As a result much of Japan's technology is advancing quickly, and firms who fail to innovate go out of business. Ohmae (1985) has described Japan as a 'very unforgiving economy', with some 19 000 corporations destroyed every year through bankruptcy. He points out that Japan is selective about the industries in which research and development will be concentrated. Japan spends a relatively high proportion of its research and development money in ceramics and steel and as a result of past (and continuing) expenditure it has become a world leader in fibre optics, ceramics and mass-produced large-scale integrated circuits. For similar reasons America is

Box 4.3
INNOVATION IN JAPAN: TWO EXAMPLES

Camcorders

Sony launched the first miniaturized camcorder (hand-held video camera and recorder) in June 1989. Weighing 1.5 lb it was one-quarter the size of existing camcorders.

Within six months Matsushita and JVC had introduced lighter models. Within a further six months there was additional competition from Canon, Sanyo, Ricoh and Hitachi. Sony itself introduced two new models in Summer 1990. One was the lightest then available; the other had superior technical features.

Motor cars

The Japanese car industry has established a reputation for high quality and cost efficiency. They entered initially with competitively priced small cars, but they have sequentially moved futher upmarket and the top models from companies such as Toyota and Honda now compete in the executive car market.

In recent years the new product development lead time for Western companies has been reduced from seven years to five. Japanese companies generally take four years; Honda have trimmed their lead time to three years.

This faster model replacement is linked to an ability to break even financially with fewer sales of each model. Japan has achieved this with efficient and flexible manufacturing systems and a greater willingness to utilize common, rather than model-specific, components.

---

world leader in biotechnology and specialized semiconductors, and Europe in chemicals and pharmaceuticals.

Product innovation in Japan is fast and competitive, as illustrated in Box 4.3. This provides an important lesson for Western companies seeking to establish a presence in Japan. Individual companies have proved that it is possible, with determination and distinctive products, to launch brands and obtain significant market shares. In the 1980s Unilever were successful with Timotei shampoo, achieving a position of market leadership with a 15% share and a 75% retail coverage. As a result of local response and competition Unilever was unable to retain its position, and within four years its position was eroded substantially.

Table 4.5 Traditional American, Type Z and Japanese organizations

	Traditional American	*Z*	*Japanese*
Employment prospects	Short term	Long term	Life
Promotion prospects	Frequent	Infrequent	Slow
Career pattern	Specialized	General	General
Control systems	Formal	Informal	Informal
Decision making	Individual	Group	Group
Focus of responsibility	Individual	Individual	Group
Focus on human resources	Limited	Organization wide	Organization wide

The Japanese culture in the West

Ouchi (1981) has described a number of successful American companies as 'Type Z' because of the presence of certain characteristics which distinguish them from more traditional, and, often less successful, companies. The companies quoted are typically those researched by Peters and Waterman. Ouchi contends that the dominant Type Z characteristics are very similar to those of a Japanese company. Table 4.5 has been derived from Ouchi's work.

SUMMARY

It has been argued in this chapter that the organizational culture and the values held by managers and other employees within the organization are key influences on strategies and change. In turn the values and culture are influenced markedly by the values and style of the strategic leader. Decision making with regard to major changes, and adaptive changes, is influenced by culture and values, and equally the culture and values affect the decision makers.

Specifically we have

☐ recapped (from Chapter 2) how culture and values influence a number of essential elements of the strategy process and are therefore a central driving consideration in strategy creation and change;
☐ introduced the adaptive and planning modes of strategy creation, to supplement the entrepreneurial mode featured in Chapter 3;
☐ illustrated the typologies of organizations developed by Handy and by Miles and Snow in relation to cultural aspects;
☐ emphasized the relationship between culture and strategic leadership, and featured the case of Scott Bader as an unusual, but nevertheless successful, style of leadership;
☐ looked at the relationship between culture and power;
☐ considered the determinants and levels of culture;
☐ summarized the normative research work in both America and Britain into successful companies, emphasizing the role of culture, and pointing out the limitations of this work;
☐ briefly looked at the relationship between culture and long-term sustained competitive advantage;
☐ discussed the difficulties involved in changing culture;
☐ looked at the strategies of typical Japanese companies, emphasizing how they are culture based, and considering the possible lessons for Western organizations.

CHECKLIST OF KEY TERMS AND CONCEPTS

You should feel confident that you understand the following terms and ideas:

☐ Entrepreneurial, planning and adaptive modes of strategy creation, and their relationship with culture
☐ Power, role, task and person cultures, and their influence on strategy and strategic change
☐ Power levers – how they affect culture, and the links with strategic leadership
☐ Normative 'excellence' factors.

QUESTIONS AND RESEACH ASSIGNMENTS

Text related

1. Take an organization with which you are familiar and evaluate it in terms of Handy's and Miles and Snow's typologies.

2. List other organizations that you know which would fit into the categories not covered in your answer to Question 1.

For both Questions 1 and 2 you should comment upon whether or not you feel your categorization is appropriate.

3. Considering the organization that you used for Question 1 assess the power levers of the strategic leader and other identifiable managers.

Library and assignment based

4. Find out where your nearest John Lewis or Waitrose store is and if possible visit it. Can you detect any differences in attitude between the John Lewis staff and those who work in similar stores?
5. Carry out a similar exercise with the Abbey National, and compare the branch you visit with another major building society which has not become a plc.
6. The following notes refer to Wedgwood plc, manufacturers of high-quality china and pottery.
   (a) After reading them, research both Wedgwood and London International Group and consider whether their cultures might have been compatible or potentially conflicting. Could Wedgwood have benefited from acquisition by London International Group?
   (b) From your research do you feel that Wedgwood's strategy and the values under-pinning it are appropriate for their industry?

In the early 1980s Wedgwood (16% UK market share) was one of three main companies in its industry. Royal Doulton (17%) and Royal Worcester (9% of the fine china market) were the others. In 1984 Royal Worcester was acquired by London International Group, best known for Durex condoms.

Wedgwood's profits were below the levels of the late 1970s, but were improving as a result of sterling-dollar movements. Two-thirds of output is exported, half of which is to America.

The *Financial Times* commented on 3 February 1983 that Wedgwood tries hard to achieve a balance between traditional designs and more modern ones. However, in export markets tradition outsells modernity by 15:1 (company figures). As the public seem to require classical designs from Wedgwood opportunities for diversification are limited unless more imaginative modern designs are marketed with a different brand name. Some marketeers feel that Wedgwood fails to exploit enough potential market opportunities because it is largely reactive to consumer demands rather than moulding them in truly proactive marketing fashion.

A later article in the *Financial Times* (28 June 1984) contended that Wedgwood faces a perpetual dilemma. If it goes too aggressively downmarket in search of volume – and it has been criticized for selling earthenware goods – it could squander its reputation for quality. Yet if it stays austerely upmarket it could fail to attract sufficient customers, especially in recessions.

In 1984 the chairman, Sir Arthur Bryant, commented: 'The company is cautious about new technology. It is standing on the sidelines while Japanese, American and West German companies pour large sums of money into "advanced technology ceramics". Nobody has made much money out of it.'

In April 1986 London International bid £150 million for Wedgwood. Wedgwood opposed the bid fiercely and in May the Financial Controller commented: 'We want to stay English and independent. We will stick to our last.'

In June the bid was referred to the Monopolies Commission for consideration. The combined market share would be 25%, the level for potential investigation.

However, in October Wedgwood, still in some financial difficulties, agreed a £253 million bid from Waterford Glass (Irish), whose Aynsley pottery represented 2% of the market. Wedgwood was now market leader.

In June 1988 London International sold Royal Worcester to Derby International, a private company established the previous year to buy Raleigh (bicycles) from Tube Investments. London International Group commented: 'Royal Worcester could no longer be considered a core business in the light of surging demand for condoms and surgical gloves.' The profitability of Royal Worcester had deteriorated in the previous three years.

RECOMMENDED FURTHER READING

Deal and Kennedy (1982) is an ideal introduction to the subject of culture, whilst Schein (1985) provides a more comprehensive treatment. Frost, P J, Moore, L F, Louis, M R, Lundberg, C C and Martin, J (1985) *Organizational Culture*, Sage, contains a number of relevant readings.

It would also be useful to read one of the books written by Tom Peters, either as an individual author (*Thriving on Chaos*, 1988) or in conjunction with Robert Waterman (*In Search of Excellence*, 1982) or Nancy Austin (*A Passion for Excellence*, Collins, 1985), in order to study the normative aspects of excellence in organizations.

Readers who are particularly interested in Japanese management are referred to Schonberger (1984).

REFERENCES

Ackoff, R L (1970) *A Concept of Corporate Planning*, Wiley Interscience.

Barney, J B (1986) Organization culture: can it be a source of sustained competitive advantage?, *Academy of Management Review*, **11** (3).

CBI (1985) *Managing for Success*, Confederation of British Industry.

Deal, T and Kennedy, A (1982) *Corporate Cultures. The Rites and Rituals of Corporate Life*, Addison Wesley.

French, J R P and Raven, B (1959) The bases of social power. In *Studies in Social Power* (ed. D Cartwright), University of Michigan Press.

Goldsmith, W and Clutterbuck, D (1984) *The Winning Streak*, Weidenfeld and Nicolson.

Hampen-Turner, C (1990) Corporate culture – from vicious to virtuous circles, *Economist*.

Handy, C B (1976) *Understanding Organizations*, Penguin. The ideas are elaborated in Handy, C B *Gods of Management*, Souvenir Press.

Harrison, R (1972) Understanding your Organization's Character, *Harvard Business Review*, May/June.

Kakabadse, A (1982) *Culture of the Social Services*, Gower.

Leadbeater, C and Rudd, R (1991) What drives the lords of the deal? *Financial Times*, 20 July.

Miles, R E and Snow, C C (1978) *Organization Strategy, Structure and Process*, McGraw-Hill.

Mintzberg, H. (1973) Strategy making in three modes, *California Management Review*, **16** (2), Winter.

Ohmae, K (1985) *Triad Power*, Free Press.

Ouchi, W. (1981) *Theory Z: How American Business Should Meet the Japanese Challenge*, Addison Wesley. Also worth reading is Ouchi, W. and Johnson, J B (1978) Types of organization control and their relationship to emotional well being, *Administrative Science Quarterly*, **23**, 293–317.

Peters, T J (1988) *Thriving on Chaos*, Knopf.

Peters, T J and Waterman, R H Jr (1982) *In Search of Excellence: Lessons from America's Best Run Companies*, Harper and Row. Original article, Peters, T J (1980) Putting excellence into management, *Business Week*, 21 July.

Prahalad, C K and Hamel, G (1985) Address to the Annual Conference of the Strategic Management Society, Barcelona, October.

Press, G (1990) Assessing competitors' business philosophies, *Long Range Planning*, **23**, 5.

Pucik, V and Hatvany, N (1983) *Management Practices in Japan and Their Impact on Business Strategy*, Advances in Strategic Management, Vol. 1, JAI Press.

Pümpin, C (1987) *The Essence of Corporate Strategy*, Gower.

Schein, E H (1985) *Organizational Culture and Leadership*, Jossey Bass.

Schonberger, R J (1984) *Japanese Manufacturing Techniques*, Free Press.

Schwartz, H and Davis, S M (1981) Matching corporate culture and business strategy, *Organizational Dynamics*, Summer.

Waterman, R H Jr (1988) *The Renewal Factor*, Bantam.

INTERLUDE

STRATEGIC

AWARENESS

I have always liked A. N. Whitehead's comment: 'The habit of foreseeing is elicited by the habit of understanding. We require such an understanding of the present conditions as may give us some grasp of the novelty which is about to produce a measurable influence on the immediate future.'

Sir Adrian Cadbury, Chairman,
Cadbury Schweppes plc (retired May 1989)

INTRODUCTION TO STRATEGIC AWARENESS

This section of the book is split into two parts: Situation Assessment (Part II) and Situation Analysis (Part III).

The situation assessment chapters question where the organization is at present, what objectives and strategies are being pursued, how well the organization is performing and how effective it is as a competitor. Chapter 5 explores objectives, and the need for organizations and managers to be clear about the current objectives being pursued, their origins and their justification is discussed. Chapter 6 looks at measures of performance, concentrating on financial ratios. The advantages and limitations of such quantitative measures are discussed. Chapter 7 is on competition. Economic aspects of competition

theory are considered, and the important concept of competitive advantage is developed. In Chapter 8 we consider the major causes of poor performance and company failure.

Part III, Situation Analysis, concentrates on the environment and the organization's resources. How can their relative match or fit be evaluated? In this part the four major functional resources – marketing, operations, people and finance – together with information systems are considered as strategic resources.

The final chapter (Chapter 15) draws upon the whole section and looks at how competitive advantage might be achieved and assessed. Chapters 7 and 10–15 thus comprise a study of **competitive strategy**.

PART TWO

SITUATION ASSESSMENT

WHERE ARE WE GOING?

5

LEARNING OBJECTIVES

After studying this chapter you should be able to

☐ explain the terms mission and objectives;
☐ identify the various stakeholders of the organization and assess their impact on objectives;
☐ summarize a number of economic theories of the firm which help explain objectives and direction;
☐ discuss the significance of profits;
☐ explain the possible objectives of certain not-for-profit organizations;
☐ differentiate between official and operative objectives, and assess the impact of personal objectives;
☐ define policies and explain how they are used to help achieve objectives;
☐ identify the key issues involved in social responsibility and business ethics.

In this chapter we consider the objectives of the organization: their nature, how they might be established, and the influence of the stakeholders in the business. Social responsibility and business ethics are also discussed.

INTRODUCTION

A voyage of a thousand miles begins with a single step. It is important that that step is in the right direction.

(Old Chinese saying, up-dated)

Life can only be understood backward, but it must be lived forward. (S Kierkegaard)

How can we go forward when we don't know which way we are facing?

(John Lennon, 1972)

This chapter is about **objectives**. Objectives should be set and communicated so that people know where the strategic leader wants the organization to be at some time in the future. At the same time it is essential that the objectives currently being pursued are clearly understood. Because of incremental changes in strategies the actual or implicit objectives may have changed from those which were established and made explicit sometime in the past. Objectives, therefore, establish direction, and in some cases set specific end points. They should have time-scales attached to them. The attainment of them should be measurable in some way, and ideally they will encourage and motivate people.

It is important, however, to distinguish between the idea of a broad purpose and specific, measurable, milestones. The organization needs direction in terms of where the strategic leader wants it to go, and how he or she would wish it to develop. This is really the 'mission' of the organization, a visionary statement concerning the future. This mission is likely to be stated broadly and generally, and it is unlikely that it can ever be achieved completely. Thus the organization pursues the mission, looking for new opportunities, dealing with problems and seeking to progress continually in the chosen direction. Improvements in the overall situation towards the stated mission are the appropriate measure of performance.

Managers at all levels are likely to be set specific objectives to achieve. These, logically, are quantifiable targets for sales, profit, productivity or output, and performance against them is measured and evaluated. Objectives then become measurable points which indicate how the organization is making definite progress towards its broad purpose or 'mission'.

Strategies are developed from the mission and the desired objectives as they are the means of achieving them. Hence a change of objectives is likely to result in changes of strategy. At the same time it is important to realize that incremental and emergent changes in strategy, whether the result of internal or external pressure, affect the levels of performance of the organization, i.e. the

growth, profit or market share, and these performance levels should be related to the objectives actually being pursued.

The central theme of the chapter is that it is essential that the most senior managers in an organization understand clearly where their company is going, and why. Ideally all managers will appreciate the overall mission and how their own role contributes to its attainment. The strategies being followed may be different from those that were originally stated, and there may be good reasons for this. Thus the situation should be reviewed constantly and the strategic leader should seek to remain informed and aware of what is happening.

DEFINITIONS, TERMINOLOGY AND EXAMPLES

In the Preface (Box 1) **mission** was defined as 'the essential purpose of the organization, concerning particularly why it is in existence, the nature of the business(es) it is in, and the customers it seeks to serve and satisfy'. **Objectives** were defined as 'desired states or results, linked to particular time scales, and concerning such things as size or type of organization, the nature and variety of the areas of interest, and levels of success'.

The expression **aims** is sometimes used as an alternative to mission. The term **goals** is

---

If you don't know where you are going, any road will take you there.

Raymond G Viault, Chief Executive Officer, Jacobs Suchard, Switzerland

---

Strategy development is like driving around a roundabout. The signposts are only useful if you know where you want to go. Some exits lead uphill, some downhill – most are one-way streets and some have very heavy traffic indeed. The trick is in picking the journey's end before you set out – otherwise you go around in circles or pick the wrong road.

Gerry M Murphy, Chief Executive Officer, Greencore plc, Ireland

seen as synonymous with objectives, and in this book the terms are used interchangeably. Specifically, where other works are being referred to and those authors have used the term goal as opposed to objective, their terminology is retained. It is also important to distinguish between long-term and short-term objectives or goals. Thompson and Strickland (1980) provide a useful distinction. They argue that objectives overall define the specific kinds of performance and results which the organization seeks to produce through its activities. The **long-term object-ives** relate to the desired performance and results on an on-going basis; **short-term objectives** are concerned with the near-term performance targets that the organization desires to reach in progressing towards its long-term objectives. Making use of such techniques as management by objectives, discussed in Chapter 12, these performance targets can be agreed with individual managers, who are then given responsibility for their attainment, and held accountable.

Measurement can be straightforward for an objective such as 'the achievement of a minimum return of 20% of net capital employed in the business, but with a target of 25%, in the next 12 months'. If the objective is less specific, for example, 'continued customer satisfaction, a competitive return on capital employed and real growth in earnings per share next year', measurement is still possible but requires a comparison of competitor returns and the monitoring of customer satisfaction through, say, the number of complaints received. Richards (1978) uses the terms 'open' and 'closed' to distinguish between objectives which are clearly measurable and typically finance based (closed) and those which are less specific and essentially continuing.

Box 5.1 features a number of examples of statements of corporate missions and objectives. These examples are designed to show that

☐ there needs to be a mission for each division or business unit of a large diversified corporation, as well as for the organization as a whole;
☐ the corporate strategy is derived from the mission;
☐ certain objectives are measurable directly whereas others require indirect measures.

The examples were not selected because they are considered to be specifically good or bad examples, but to illustrate many of the points developed in the forthcoming parts of this chapter. They should be evaluated in that light.

The examples of statements of objectives featured in Box 5.1 can usefully be related to the strategy statement framework introduced in Chapter 1 (Figure 1.4). Long-term corporate objectives are used as a basis for corporate strategies. Short-term objectives, such as those for Marks & Spencer's product development and store modernization programmes, contribute to long-term growth and success. The specific objectives for the next 12 months become short-term competitive and functional strategies respectively. In turn the success of these short-term functional and competitive strategies helps to determine the sales revenue (growth) and

---

Arne Ness said, when he climbed Everest, 'I had a dream. I reached it. I lost the dream, and I miss it.'

When we reached our dream we didn't have another long term objective. So people started to produce their own new objectives – not a common objective, but different objectives depending on where they were in the organization.

I learned that before you reach an objective you must be ready with a new one, and you must start to communicate it to the organization. But it is not the goal itself that is important . . . it is the fight to get there.

Jan Carlzon, Chairman and Chief Executive Officer, Scandinavian Airlines System

Box 5.1
EXAMPLES OF MISSIONS AND STATEMENTS OF OBJECTIVES

A MISSION STATEMENT FOR ONE FORTE HOTEL

☐ To maintain position as the most profitable provincial UK hotel in the company based on profit per room.

☐ To lead the Forte brand initiative by taking advantage of our opportunity to capitalize on a prime location.

☐ To improve reputation as employers through improved living and working conditions and promotional opportunities.

☐ To respond to increased demands of clientele in terms of improved standards of accommodation, food and beverage and meeting facilities. To improve standards of service and hospitality.

A CHANGING MISSION FOR YORKSHIRE WATER

Historically it has essentially been 'to provide acceptable levels of water services at a price customers are able to pay'.

In 1986 it was established that water quality was a paramount concern of consumers and this was encapsulated.

In 1988, prior to privatization, the mission was extended further, to include 'developing the skills of our people, our assets, technology, and other resources so that we can increase earnings outside the core water services business'.

Since privatization (1989) Yorkshire Water has created two divisions: YW Services and YW Enterprises (non-core commercial activities), each with a distinctive mission. YW Services is charged with 'the provision of drinking water and waste water management services at a quality, standard and cost which meets both the requirements of our domestic and industrial customers and the approval of our regulators'. The mission for YW Enterprises develops a focus on improvements to the environment, serving new customers with quality service and achieving satisfactory returns for shareholders.

A MISSION STATEMENT FOR AN ORGANIZATION (VIRGIN GROUP) AND ONE OF ITS DIVISIONS

The Directors aim to develop Virgin into the leading British international media and entertainment group.

(Prospectus for Stock Exchange listing, 1986)

The linked strategies were highlighted in Chapter 1, Case 1.4.

A possible mission statement for the music business within the Virgin Group might conceivably have been the following.

We aim to be recognized as the premier recorder and publisher of popular music by providing the very best in technology, facilities and service to our artists and other employees in order to increase our shareholder wealth.

Virgin Music was sold to Thorn–EMI in 1992

A CORPORATE VISION AND THE RELATED OBJECTIVES FOR W H SMITH

Vision
Our goal is to be the leader in every one of our chosen markets. We will achieve this goal by attaining a standard of excellence in everything we do which clearly distinguishes us from our competitors. The pursuit of excellence requires a management style

throughout the organization which encourages initiative, innovation and personal fulfilment. This will be achieved through a high level of training for staff and managers. By achieving and maintaining leadership through excellence we aim to produce a consistent and competitive growth in earnings for our shareholders.

Objectives:

1. To be the leading retailer of books, magazines, stationery, recorded music and video in the UK.
2. To be the leading distributor of newspapers, magazines and office supplies in the UK.
3. To obtain profitable shares in chosen markets in the USA and Europe.
4. To become and remain a market leader in the out of town do-it-yourself market.

(W H Smith Annual Report, 1991.)

A CORPORATE VISION AND THE RELATED GROUP STRATEGY

Our strategic objective at **Reebok** is to become the No. 1 sports and fitness brand world wide. To achieve this objective, we are committed to continuing our creative energy and our strong focus on quality and customer service.

NON-SPECIFIC OPEN LONG-TERM OBJECTIVES FOR ICI

To increase shareholder value by focusing resources even more selectively, so as to exploit fully the profitable growth potential of those businesses where ICI already has or can develop strong global positions encompassing the major markets of Europe, North America and Asia Pacific.

Investment will be channelled into businesses which can play a truly global role.

(Issued March 1991.)

OPEN AND CLOSED OBJECTIVES AND STRATEGIES

In the coming year we [Marks & Spencer] will open a new store at Telford, extend 25 other stores and open nine satellite stores. By June 1988 our premier store at Marble Arch, London, will have been extended and modernized. Altogether we will increase our selling space by 500 000 square feet, and modernize 1.4 million sq. ft during the coming year.

The successful introduction of a selected range of furniture in 30 of our largest stores is encouraging. The development of the furniture range has been accompanied by the introduction of a home delivery service. We will continue our experiments in direct selling, concentrating on those household items which are too bulky for our customers to carry away by hand.

Good human relations, good working conditions and good staff welfare are essential ingredients in the company's continued success. We will continue to pay competitive salaries and provide staff with other benefits, including a Christmas bonus (of four weeks' pay for full time staff), non-contributory pension and life insurance, a share in the profits after five years' service, subsidized meals and discount on St Michael merchandise.

(Short extracts from Marks & Spencer plc, 1987 Annual Report)

The stores' modernization programme is ongoing and long term, but annual targets are set. Target increases in floor space are objectives; modernization and building projects to achieve them are strategies.

Product development is long term and linked to growth and product range objectives, but with incremental changes which determine actual achievement.

Good human relations, good working conditions and good staff welfare are all open long-term objectives. Achievement against them can be measured indirectly.

profits, essential aspects of long-term success.

MISSION STATEMENTS

The corporate mission is the over-riding *raison d'être* for the business. Ackoff (1986), however, has claimed that 'most corporate mission statements are worthless', one reason being that they consist of expressions like 'maximize growth potential' or 'provide products of the highest quality'. How, he queries, can a company determine whether it has attained its maximum growth potential or highest quality? Primarily the mission statement should not address what an organization must do in order to survive, but what it has chosen to do in order to thrive. It should be positive, visionary and motivating.

Ackoff suggests that a good mission statement has five characteristics.

☐ It will contain a formulation of objectives that enables progress towards them to be measured.
☐ It differentiates the company from its competitors.
☐ It defines the business(es) that the company wants to be in, not necessarily is in.
☐ It is relevant to all the stakeholders in the firm, not just shareholders and managers.
☐ It is exciting and inspiring.

Campbell (1989) argues that to be valuable mission statements must reflect corporate values, and the strategic leader and the organization as a whole should be visibly pursuing the mission. He argues that there are four key issues involved in developing a useful mission.

☐ It is important to clarify the purpose of the organization – why it exists. Hanson plc, for example, which is referred to at various stages in this book, is led by Lord Hanson who has said:

It is the central tenet of my faith that the shareholder is king. My aim is to advance the shareholder's interest by increasing earnings per share.

By contrast Lex Service says:

We will exercise responsibility in our dealings with all our stakeholders and, in the case of conflict, balance the interest of the employees and shareholders on an equal basis over time.

The implications of these contrasting perspectives are discussed in the next section of this chapter.

☐ The mission statement should describe the business and its activities, and the position that it wants to achieve in its field.
☐ The organization's values should be stated. How does the company intend to treat its employees, customers and suppliers, for example?
☐ Finally it is important to ensure that the organization behaves in the way that it promises it will. This is important because it can inspire trust in employees and others who significantly influence the organization.

Ackoff and Campbell's arguments are complementary, and in further support of their contentions Goldsmith and Clutterbuck (1984) argue that in successful British companies middle and junior managers know where the strategic leaders are taking the company and why. In less successful organizations there is often confusion about this. They emphasize the role of strategic leadership in establishing the mission and long-term objectives.

The mission corresponds closely to the basic philosophy or vision underlying the business, and if there is a sound philosophy, strategies which generate success will be derived from it. Sock Shop was founded in 1983, with a simple vision. One newspaper has summarized it as 'shopping in big stores for basic items like stockings is a fag, but nipping into an attractive kiosk at an Underground station, British Rail concourse or busy high street is quick, convenient and can be fun'. From this has emerged six key marketing features or strategies, which have become the foundations of the company's success and rapid growth:

☐ shops located within areas of heavy pedestrian traffic
☐ easily accessible products
☐ friendly and efficient service
☐ a wide range of quality products designed to meet the needs of customers
☐ attractive presentations
☐ competitive selling prices.

In 1989, after a number of years of growth and success, Sock Shop began to lose money. The hot summer weather and the London underground strikes were blamed for falling sales. Increasing interest rates caused additional financial problems. Moreover Sock Shop expanded into America and this had proved costly. However in February 1990 Sock Shop founder, Sophie Mirman, commented: '. . . our concept remains sound. Our merchandise continues to be not merely "lifestyle". We provide everyday necessities in a fashionable manner.'

Sophie Mirman has since lost control of Sock Shop but her vision prevails.

OBJECTIVES: WHAT SHOULD THEY BE; WHAT ARE THEY?

A full consideration of objectives incorporates three aspects:

☐ an appreciation of the objectives that the organization is actually pursuing and achieving – where it is going and why
☐ the objectives that it might pursue, and the freedom and opportunity it has to make changes
☐ specific objectives for the future.

In this chapter we look at the issues which affect and determine the first two of these.

Decisions about specific future objectives are considered further in Chapter 16.

As a background to the consideration of these points it is useful to look briefly at a number of theories of business organizations and to consider the role and importance of stakeholders.

Market models

Basic microeconomic theory states that firms should seek to maximize profits and that this is achieved where marginal revenue is equal to marginal cost. A number of assumptions under-pin this theory, including the assumptions that firms clearly understand the nature of the demand for their products, and why people buy, and that they are willing and able to control production and sales as the model demands. In reality decision makers do not have perfect knowledge and production and sales are affected by suppliers and distributors.

However, this basic theory has resulted in the development of four market models (Table 5.1) and the characteristics of these in respect of barriers to entry into the industry and the marketing opportunities (differentiation potential; price and non-price competition) determine whether or not there is a real opportunity to achieve significant profits.

In markets which approach pure competition (pure competition as such is theoretical), firms will only make 'normal' profits, the amount required for them to stay in the industry. Products are not differentiated, and so premium prices for certain brands are not possible. There are no major barriers to entry into the industry and so new suppliers are attracted if there are profits to be made. Competition results, and if supply exceeds demand the ruling market price is forced down and only the efficient firms survive.

In monopolistic competition there are again several suppliers, some large, many small, but products are differentiated. However, as there are once more no major barriers

Table 5.1 Structural characteristics of four market models

Market model	Number of firms	Type of product	Control over price by supplier	Entry conditions	Non-price competition[a]	Examples[b]
Pure competition	Large	Standardized Identical or almost identical	None	Free	None	Agricultural products; some chemicals, printing; laundry services
Monopolistic competition	Large	Differentiated	Some	Relatively easy	Yes	Clothing; furniture; soft drinks
Oligopoly[c]	Few or a few dominant	Standardized or differentiated	Limited by mutual interdependence Considerable if collusion takes place	Difficult	Yes	Standardized: cement; sugar; fertilizers Differentiated: margarine; soaps; detergents
Pure monopoly	One	Unique	Considerable	Blocked	Yes	

[a] Non-price competition occurs in many ways, e.g. by attempts to increase the extent of product differentiation and buyer preference through advertising, brand names, trade marks, promotions, distribution outlets; by new product launch and innovation etc.

[b] Useful further reading: Doyle, P and Gidengil, Z B (1977) An empirical study of market structures, *Journal of Management Studies*, **14** (3), October, pp. 316–28. The examples are taken from this.

[c] There are many oligopoly models of collusive and non-collusive type. They make varying behavioural and structural assumptions.

to entry the above situation concerning profits applies. Newcomers increase supply and
although those firms with distinctive products can charge some premium they will still
have to move in line with market prices
generally, and this will have a dampening
effect on profits.

Only in oligopoly and monopoly markets is
there real opportunity for 'super-normal'
profits, in excess of what is required to stay in
business. However, in oligopoly the small
number of large firms tend to be wary of each
other and prices are held back to some extent
for fear of losing market share. Suppliers are
interdependent and fear that a price decrease
will be met by competitors (thus reducing
profits) and price increases will not (hence
market share will be threatened). There are
two types of oligopoly, depending on
whether opportunities exist for significant
differentiation. In all these models competition is a major determinant of profit potential
and therefore objectives must be set with
competitors in mind. In a monopoly (again
somewhat theoretical in a pure sense) excess
profits could be made if government did not
act as a restraint. Although such public sector
organizations as British Gas and British Telecom have been privatized their actions in
terms of supply and pricing are monitored
(see Chapter 7).

Management of change for profit is what
distinguishes businessmen from bureaucrats.
In bureaucracies change can be the occasion
for industrial unrest, higher costs and cutbacks in customer service. In business change
should be an opportunity for improved working patterns, productivity increase and
enhanced customer service. The profit motive
conditions the business approach to managing change. Profit is earned through a proper
balance between the interests of customers,
employees and shareholders.

Peter Morgan, Director General,
The Institute of Directors

Stakeholder theory

The influence of external stakeholders will be
examined again in Chapter 9, which looks at
the environment, but it is important to
introduce the topic at this stage. A further
assumption of profit-maximizing theory is
that shareholders in the business should be
given first priority and be the major consideration in decision making, and this arose
because early economic theorists saw owners
and managers as being synonymous. But this
assumption no longer holds. As we have
already seen, a study of market models
demonstrates the important role played by
competitors and by government as a restraining force, and it was also suggested that
organizations must pay some regard to their
suppliers and distributors. In addition,
managers and employees must be considered. The decisions taken by managers
which create incremental change will be
influenced by the objectives and values that
they believe are important. Managers are
paid employees, and whilst concerned about
profits, they will also regard growth and
security as important.

These are all **stakeholders**. Freeman (1984)
defines stakeholders as any group or individual who can affect, or is affected by, the
performance of the organization.

Newbould and Luffman (1979) argue that
current and future strategies are affected by

☐ external pressures from the marketplace,
   including competitors, buyers and suppliers; shareholders; pressure groups; and
   government;
☐ internal pressures from existing commitments, managers, employees and their
   trade unions;
☐ the personal ethical and moral perspectives of senior managers.

Stakeholder theory postulates that the
objectives of an organization will take
account of the various needs of these different

Table 5.2   Examples of stakeholder interests

Shareholders	Annual dividends; increasing the value of their investment in the company as the share price increases. Both are affected by growth and profits Institutional shareholders may balance high risk investments and their anticipated high returns with more stable investments in their portfolio
Managers	Salaries and bonuses; perks; status from working for a well-known and successful organization; responsibility; challenge; security
Employees	Wages; holidays; conditions and job satisfaction; security – influenced by trade union involvement
Consumers	Desirable and quality products; competitive prices – very much in relation to competition; new products at appropriate times
Distributors	On-time and reliable deliveries
Suppliers	Consistent orders; payment on time
Financiers	Interest payments and loan repayments; like payment for supplies, affected by cash flow
Government	Payment of taxes and provision of employment; contribution to the nation's exports
Society in general	Socially responsible actions – sometimes reflected in pressure groups

(This is not intended to constitute a complete list)

interested parties who will represent some type of informal coalition. Their relative power will be a key variable, and the organization will on occasions 'trade-off' one against the other, establishing a hierarchy of relative importance. Stakeholders see different things as being important and receive benefits or rewards in a variety of ways, as featured in Table 5.2.

Stakeholder interests are not always consistent. For example, investment in new technology might improve product quality and as a result lead to increased profits. Whilst customers who are shareholders might perceptively benefit, if the investment implies lost jobs then employees, possibly managers, and their trade unions may be dissatisfied. If the scale of redundancy is large and results in militant resistance, the government may become involved.

The various stakeholders are not affected in the same way by every strategic decision, and consequently their relative influence will vary from decision to decision.

Newbould and Luffman divide the major stakeholders into four groups, arguing that their individual objectives suggest separate criteria for assessing the viability of particular strategies. The four groups are the shareholders who finance the business, the managers who manage it, the employees who work for it, and the economy. The last group represents buyers and suppliers, but also includes a consideration of the wider economic interests of the country. The reason for this is that the organization utilizes scarce resources which should be deployed where they can be used most efficiently and effectively.

Some of the key performance measures they identify, which will affect objectives, are as follows:

Shareholders
Market rate of return on their investment
Market value of their investment
Stability of dividends
(These measures are defined and discussed in Chapter 7)

Managers
Sales growth
Assets growth
Profit stability

Employees
Numbers employed
Labour intensity as opposed to capital intensity
Percentage wage increases
Wage increases in comparison with profit increases

The economy
Profitability in relation to capital employed (again a variety of measures are considered in Chapter 7)
Percentage of output exported

Cyert and March's behavioural theory

Stakeholder theory is closely related to the ideas in Cyert and March's *A Behavioural Theory of the Firm* (1963). Cyert and March argue that the goals of an organization are a **compromise** between members of a coalition comprising the parties affecting an organization. The word compromise is used as the actual choice is linked to relative power and there are inevitably conflicts of interest. Cyert and March argue that there are essentially five directional pulls to consider:

☐ production related, and encapsulating stable employment, ease of control and scheduling
☐ inventory related – customers and salesmen push for high stocks and wide choice, management accountants complain about the cost of too much stock
☐ sales related – obtaining and satisfying orders
☐ market share, which yields power relative to competitors
☐ profit, which concerns shareholders, senior management and the providers of loan capital.

This theory stresses the perceived importance of the short term, as opposed to the long term, because issues are more tangible and because decisions have to be taken as situations change. Organizations adapt over time and it is likely that changes will be limited unless it is necessary to change things more

radically. In other words, once a compromise situation is reached there is a tendency to seek to retain it rather than change it; and the goals will change as the values and relative importance of coalition members change. As a result 'organizational slack' develops. This is 'payments to members of the coalition in excess of what is required to keep them in the coalition'. It is difficult, for example, to determine the minimum acceptable reward for employees; assets are generally underexploited since it is difficult to know the maximum productivity of a person or machine; and uncertainties mean that less-than-optimal price, product and promotional policies will be pursued. The existence of slack does allow for extra effort in times of emergency. This theory can be usefully considered alongside Herbert Simon's theory of satisficing which was introduced in Chapter 3.

Developing these themes Herbert Simon (1964) makes an important distinction between objectives and constraints. For example an animal food company might wish to offer low priced feeds for livestock but be constrained by dietary requirements, which, by determining ingredients, influence costs and hence prices.

Simon further contends that one of the main reasons for an organization's collapse is a failure to incorporate the important motivational concerns of key stakeholders. Small businesses, for example, are generally weak in relation to their suppliers, especially if these are larger well-established concerns; and if they neglect managing their cash flow and fail to pay their accounts on time they will find their deliveries stopped. For any organization, if new products or services fail to provide consumers with what they are looking for, however well produced or low priced they might be, they will not sell.

Other theories of the firm

A number of other authors have offered theories in an attempt to explain the behaviour of organizations and the objectives they seek.

Baumol: sales maximization

Baumol (1959) argues that firms seek to maximize sales rather than profits, but within the constraint of a minimum acceptable profit level. It can be demonstrated that profit maximizing is achieved at a level of output below that which would maximize sales revenue and that, as sales and revenue increase beyond profit maximizing, profits are sacrificed. Firms will increase sales and revenue as long as they are making profits in excess of what they regard as an acceptable minimum. Businessmen, Baumol argues, attach great importance to sales as salaries are often linked to the scale of operations. 'Whenever executives are asked "How's business?", the typical reply is that sales have been increasing or decreasing.'

Williamson's model of managerial discretion

Williamson (1964) argues that managers can set their own objectives, that these will be different from those of shareholders and that managerial satisfaction is the key. Satisfaction increases if a manager has a large staff reporting to him or her, if there are 'lavish perks' and if profits exceed the level required for the essential development of the business and the necessary replacement of equipment. This extra profit can be used for pet projects or the pursuit of non-profit objectives. The manner in which managers reward themselves for success is discretionary.

Marris's theory of managerial capitalism

Marris (1964) again postulates growth as a key concern, as managers derive utility from growth in the form of enhanced salaries, power and status. The constraint is one of

security. If, as a result of growth strategies pursued by the firm, profits are held down, say because of interest charges, the market value of the firm's shares may fall relative to the book value of the assets. In such a case the firm may become increasingly vulnerable to take-over, and managers wish to avoid this situation.

Penrose's theory of growth

Penrose (1959) has offered another growth theory, arguing that an organization will seek to achieve the full potential from all its resources. Firms grow as long as there are unused resources, diversifying when they can no longer grow with existing products, services and markets. Growth continues until it is halted. A major limit, for example, could be production facilities either in terms of total output or because of a bottleneck in one part of the operation. Changes can free the limit, and growth continues until the next limiting factor appears. Another limit is the capacity of managers to plan and implement growth strategies. If managers are stretched, extra people can be employed, but the remedy is not immediate. New people have to be trained and integrated, and this takes up some of the time of existing managers. Penrose refers to this issue as the 'receding managerial limit' because again the limiting factor decreases over a period of time. In a climate of reasonably constant growth and change managers learn how to cope with the dynamics of change; and properly managed, given that over-ambition is constrained and that market opportunities exist, firms can enjoy steady and continuous growth.

Galbraith's views on technocracy

Finally, Galbraith (1969) has highlighted the particular role of large corporations, whose pursuit of size requires very large investments associated with long-term commitments. Because of these financial commitments the corporations seek to control their environment as far as they possibly can, influencing both government and consumer, and they in turn are controlled by what Galbraith calls 'technocrats' – teams of powerful experts and specialists. Their purposes are, first, to protect as well as control the organization, and hence they seek financial security and profit, and, second, to 'affirm' the organization through growth, expansion and market share. As is typical of oligopolists, price competition is not seen to be in their interests, and hence aggressive marketing and non-price competition is stressed. Additionally such firms will seek to influence or even control (by acquisition) suppliers and distributors, and they may well see the world as their market rather than just the UK. These issues are all explored later in the book.

Galbraith (1963) has also identified the growth of 'countervailing power' to limit this technocracy. The growth of trade unions in the past is an example of this, as is the increasing power of large retailers to counter the product manufacturers. As a result the potential for consumer exploitation is checked, and available profits are shared more widely.

Profit as an objective

Box 5.2 discusses whether profit is the ultimate objective of profit-seeking business organizations or whether it is merely a means to other ends, which themselves constitute the real objectives. (Not-for-profit organizations are considered separately later in this chapter.)

Ackoff (1986) argues that both profit and growth are means to other ends rather than objectives in themselves. He argues that profit is necessary for the survival of a business enterprise but is neither the reason for which the business is formed nor the reason why it stays in existence. Instead

---

Box 5.2
PROFIT

A business school is likely to teach that an organization must be good to people because then they will work harder. And if they work harder the business will make a profit.

They will also teach that a firm should strive to produce better products and services, because with better products the firm will make greater profits.

What if they told the story the other way round?

What if they taught managers: You have got to make a profit, because if you do not make a profit you cannot build offices that are pleasant to be in. Without profit you cannot pay decent wages. Without profit you cannot satisfy a lot of the needs of your employees. You have got to make a profit because without a profit you will never be able to develop a better product.

The profit would still be made. People would still get decent wages. Most employers would still make an effort to improve their products as they do now.

'But you would have a whole new ball game.'

Adapted from Cohen, P, *The Gospel According to the Harvard Business School*, Penguin, 1974. Originally published by Doubleday, New York, 1973.

Ackoff contends 'those who manage organizations do so primarily to provide themselves with the quality of work life and standard of living they desire . . . their behaviour can be better understood by assuming this than by assuming that their objective is to maximize profit or growth'.

However, it is also important to consider the 'quality of life' of investors (shareholders), customers, suppliers and distributors, as well as other employees of the firm who are not involved in decision making. It can be argued that employees are the major stakeholders, because if the firm goes out of business they incur the greatest losses.

Since the early 1970s Volvo, the Swedish company best known for its motor cars, has followed strategies aimed at diversification and at marketing a wider range of cars produced in places other than Sweden, which is not a member of the European Community. Amongst the developments has been the Kalmar plant (opened in 1974) where workers operate in autonomous teams rather than working alongside an assembly line. In 1981 the Chief Executive Officer, Pehr Gyllenhammar, said:

My objectives have been to reduce the Group's vulnerability in an exposed industry, to avoid losses during periods of poor economic conditions, to assure our growth and employment – and to achieve a good return on capital so that a share of Volvo stock becomes a sound long-term investment with an attractive yield. To attain these objectives investments in human beings have always been the most important: giving the Volvo employee the opportunity to develop competence and skills and to feel satisfaction in working with quality products under the toughest competitive conditions.

In many respects it does not matter whether profit is seen as an objective or as a means of providing service and satisfaction to stakeholders, as long as both are considered and not seen as mutually exclusive. Chapter 6 addresses the question of how success is measured. In simple terms an organization will succeed if it survives and meets the expectations of its stakeholders. If its objectives relate to the stakeholders, it is successful if it attains its objectives. But the most common and straightforward means of measuring success is by analysing financial results – by measuring profitability and growth relative to competitors – and this will be explored in detail in the next chapter. If profits are seen as a means to stakeholder satisfaction one could argue that service to stakeholders should be seen as the objective, and profit as the measure of success. Survival and growth are then implicit in these.

The influence of shareholders

The view is widely held by Constable (1980) and others that too many British companies are encouraged to seek short-term profits in order to please their major shareholders, and that it is only by considering the long term and the interests of all stakeholders that British companies will become more effective competitors in world markets. Constable states: 'Britain's steady relative industrial decline over the past 30 years is related to an insistence on setting purely financial objectives which have been operated in relatively short time scales.' This is also reflected in the summary of the article by Sir Hector Laing in Key Reading 5.1.

The issue of short-termism is complex, however, and achieving the ideals of Sir

---

The purpose of industry is to serve the public by creating services to meet their needs. It is not to make profits for shareholders, nor to create salaries and wages for the industrial community. These are necessary conditions for success, but not its purpose.

Dr George Carey, Archbishop of Canterbury

Key Reading 5.1
THE BALANCE OF RESPONSIBILITY: OWNERS AND MANAGERS

Ownership of United Biscuits in 1987 lies overwhelmingly with financial institutions, and they are inevitably remote. Where owners and managers are the same people, the goals and the means of achieving them are not in conflict; but institutional fund managers, themselves under pressure to perform in the short term, put pressure on public companies to pursue strategies which may be incompatible with sound long-term management.

The first priority for a business is to establish and sustain a long-term profitability level which satisfies the needs of both the business and its shareholders. If, however, a manufacturing business seeks to boost short-term profits and earnings per share for reasons of expedience, it may well reduce quality and service and fail to invest adequately for the future. The price for this is inevitable decline. This tendency is worsened if the company is under threat of take-over. Countries like Germany and Japan take a longer term view and the 'Damoclean sword of hostile take-overs is still virtually unknown'.

Managers must not be discouraged by their owners, their shareholders, from taking risks, from undertaking research, and from investing in innovation.

Fund managers cannot consult their members (quite typically employees of the manufacturing organizations in question) and they need not take a company's employees into consideration when they buy and sell shares. This is potentially dangerous.

I am seeking to encourage a change in the climate of opinion in which institutional owners of companies accept the responsibility of ownership and take a rational, informed and reasonably long-term proprietorial view.

Instead of selling shares if they feel management is under-achieving, they should seek to offer help and advice.

Future growth, future jobs and future wealth sometimes means sacrificing immediate reward for the welfare of generations to come.

Summarized from an article by Sir Hector Laing, Chairman of United Biscuits plc, in *First*, **1** (2), 1987.

Hector Laing will prove difficult. Box 5.3 investigates the debate.

Companies, obviously, cannot disregard powerful institutional shareholders.

As an example, Table 5.3 (page 138) highlights their importance for Marks & Spencer. What is crucial is to ensure that there is dialogue and mutual understanding and agreement concerning the best interests of the company, its shareholders and other stakeholders.

In his debate on the short- and long-term perspective, Constable, in Table 5.4 (page 139), contrasts two sets of objectives, ranked in order of priority. He contends that company B is likely to grow at the expense of company A, and that these objective sets, A and B, are essentially those adopted by large UK and Japanese companies respectively for much of the period since World War II. To suggest that Japanese success rests solely on a particular set of objectives is oversimplifying reality, but it has certainly contributed.

In Japan and Germany, however, shareholders do not exert pressure in the same way as they do in the UK. Cross shareholding between companies in Japan means that only 25% of shares in Japanese businesses are for trading and speculation, and this

Box 5.3
LONG- AND SHORT-TERMISM: THE DEBATE

It is generally acknowledged that companies must pursue strategies which increase the long-term value of the business for its shareholders, or eventually they are likely to be under threat of acquisition. Many companies also believe they are likely to be under threat from powerful institutional shareholders if short-term performance is poor – i.e. if sales and profits fail to grow. The result can be a reluctance to undertake costly and risky investments, say, in research and development, if the payback is uncertain. It is, however, disputed that there is a correlation between high spending on R & D and the likelihood of hostile take-overs.

Institutional shareholders clearly want to be able to exercise some control or influence over large companies where they have substantial equity interests. One dilemma is that whilst they want to rein in powerful and risk-oriented strategic leaders, they do not want to foresake the potential benefits of strong, entrepreneurial leadership. They can exert influence by:

☐ pushing for the roles of chairman and chief executive to be separated, and arguing for a high proportion of carefully selected non-executive directors;
☐ attempting to replace senior managers whose performance is poor or lacklustre, but this can be difficult [it is often argued that shareholders are too passive about this option];
☐ selling their shares to predatory bidders.

Whilst this final option is a perpetual threat, and the biggest fear of many strategic leaders, not all companies are prevented from investing in R & D. ICI, Glaxo and 'others which are well-managed and in command of where they are going' invest. In addition, institutions argue that they are objective about their investments and turn down more offers for their shares than they accept. In 1989, for instance, the Prudential (the largest institutional investor in the UK) received 84 bids for companies in which they held shares. They accepted five.

---

generates greater stability. In Germany the companies themselves hold a higher proportion of their own shares, and banks act as proxy voters for private investors. Banks thereby control some 60% of the tradable shares, again generating stability. German companies also adopt a two-tier Board structure. A supervisory board has overall control and reports to shareholders and employee unions; reporting to this board is a management board, elected for up to five years.

Objectives and priorities

The importance of employees has been stressed already in this chapter, and it is worth emphasizing that their interests can often be satisfied by growth. Jobs are preserved if a company is growing, increasing market share, investing in the UK, exporting to new markets etc. Growth through diversification and acquisition can provide a greater challenge and motivation for managers.

It is important to establish priorities amongst the several and varied stakeholders and objectives. These priorities will influence success. Storey (1988), for example, argues that research in northern England has shown that the most successful and fast growing small businesses emphasize profitability, market share and sales, while owners of slower growth businesses place greater emphasis on job satisfaction and life-style.

Undoubtedly more **communication** between directors and their shareholders concerning results, plans and philosophies, would be desirable in many cases. Would this resolve the difficulties, or is something more drastic required?

Lipton (1990) has suggested that Boards should be subject to quinquennial reviews of their performance (partially conducted by independent outsiders) and their plans for the next five years. Hostile bids could be considered at the same time, but not between reviews. Boards may or may not be re-elected, depending upon their relative performance. The idea is to generate more stability and to 'unite directors and shareholders behind the goal of maximizing long-term profits'.

Sir Gordon White of Hanson plc (1990) disagrees. He argues that if institutional shareholders are willing to sell their shares it is usually the result of poor management generally, and not merely a reluctance to invest in R & D. 'Under-performing companies are frequently typified by high top

salaries, share options confined to a handful of apparatchiks and generous golden parachutes.' Such companies are often legitimate take-over targets, and inevitably the bids are likely to be perceived as hostile.

Long-term success requires that companies and their strategic leaders are properly accountable for their performance, and, for many businesses, this really has to be to their shareholders. At the same time, shareholders must be objective and take a long-term perspective, and they must be active, not passive, about replacing poor managers and about intervening when they feel the corporate strategy is wrong.

The dilemmas relate to the implementation of these ideas and to the issue of whether institutions have advisers with enough detailed, industry-specific, knowledge to make an objective judgement.

Sources: Lipton, M (1990) An end to hostile takeovers and short termism, *Financial Times*, 27 June; White, G (1990) Why management must be accountable, *Financial Times*, 12 July.

We have introduced and discussed the notion of multiple objectives which can potentially be in conflict. Implicitly they suggest the need for an explicit statement of a wide range of objectives by the organization. If objectives are not stated clearly they are likely to be forgotten when the organization is under pressure. Stakeholders should be considered and consulted; priorities should be expressed; and crucially the objectives should be disseminated throughout the organization. Given this, the objectives can help resolve conflicts within the organization as there is clarity about where the organization is going.

An example is provided in Box 5.4, the stated objectives of H P Bulmer Holdings plc. The company's main business is cider; it is still under family control and it has invested in

employee participation and share-ownership schemes. It should be noted that objective 5 positively encourages incremental strategic changes.

The importance of the strategic leader

To conclude this section it is useful to emphasize the key role of the strategic leader, and his or her values, in establishing the main objectives and the direction in which they take the organization. Personal ambitions to build a large conglomerate or a multinational company may fuel growth; a determination to be socially responsible may restrain certain activities that other organizations would undertake; a commitment to high quality will influence the design, cost

Table 5.3   Shareholdings in Marks & Spencer plc, 1991

Size of shareholding	No. of shareholders	Percentage of total number of shareholders	Percentage of ordinary shares
Over 1 million	273		56.8
500 001–1 000 000	183		4.9
200 001–500 000	398	0.7	71.3	4.8
100 001–200 000	459		2.5
50 001–100 000	871		2.3
5001–50 000	38 167	13.0	15.6
2001–5000	66 615	22.8	7.8
2000 and under	185 444	63.5	5.3
	292 410	100.0	100.0

The 1313 shareholders owning more than 100 000 shares each are as follows:

Type of owner	Number of shareholders	Percentage of ordinary shares
Insurance companies	70	15.98
Banks (+ nominee companies)	760	37.23
Pension Funds (identifiable)	59	6.16
Individuals	286	5.80
Others	138	3.78
		68.95

Source: Annual Report.

and marketing approach for products. A strong orientation towards employee welfare, as is illustrated in the Scott Bader and John Lewis examples quoted in Chapter 4, will again influence objectives quite markedly.

After many years of success the Tomkinsons Group remains totally committed to the manufacture of excellently designed and coloured carpets which co-ordinate well with a wide range of products. Our carpets cover a wide range of price points and are sold with enthusiasm where customers really want to indulge their sense of style.

With these principles in mind the Company has been managed toward the primary objective of creating value for our shareholders through dividends and share price appreciation.

Lowry Maclean, Chairman and Chief Executive, Tomkinsons plc

The objectives and values of the strategic leader are a particularly important consideration in the case of small firms. Whilst it is possible for small firms to enjoy competitive advantage, say by providing products or services with values added to appeal to local customers in a limited geographical area, many are not distinctive in any marked way. Where this is the case, and where competition is strong, small firms will be price takers, and their profits and growth will be influenced substantially by external forces. Some small firm owners will be entrepreneurial, willing to take risks and determined to build a bigger business; others will be content to stay small. Some small businesses are started by people who essentially want to work for themselves rather than for a larger corporation, and their objectives could well be concerned with survival and the establishment of a sound business which can be passed on to the next generation of their family.

Table 5.4 Contrasting company objectives

Company A	Company B
1. Return on net assets, 1–3 year time horizon	1. Maintenance and growth of market share
2. Cash flow	2. Maintenance and growth of employment
3. Maintenance and growth of market share	3. Cash flow
4. Maintenance and growth of employment	4. Return on net assets

---

Box 5.4
H P BULMER HOLDINGS: STATEMENT OF COMPANY OBJECTIVES (EXTRACTS)

We believe that success in any company can be achieved only if every employee understands and supports the objectives which the company, and each individual in it, is striving to attain. These objectives are not necessarily all of equal importance and at different times some may require more attention than others.

1. To increase profitability and earnings per share each year through greater efficiency and increased sales.
2. To continue to make and sell products of high quality and to give the utmost consideration to the needs and interests of our customers.
3. To pay the best wages and salaries we can afford, and to ensure job satisfaction for all employees through enlightened management. To improve working conditions wherever possible . . . and promote the best possible human relations and a situation in which people really enjoy working for the company.
4. To remain an independent public company with a distinctive style.
5. To give executives the maximum freedom of action, and to encourage them to make the fullest use of it, so that they can personally influence profits.
6. To continue to encourage employee share ownership in the company.
7. To encourage participation by keeping employees informed of policy, progress and problems, to invite comments and criticisms, and to show everyone how individual effort contributes to the company's success.
8. To be flexible, and not to depend too much on any one product, customer or market. . . . To maintain an efficient research and development policy so that opportunities can be quickly recognized and speedily exploited.
9. To promote job security and to avoid compulsory redundancy by careful forward planning and by the early recognition of the effects of change.
10. To train and develop all employees and to promote from within whenever possible.
11. To ensure the economical supply of our vital raw materials.
12. To benefit the local community whenever and wherever the group can afford to do so, and to preserve the quality of life and of the environment.

Source: H P Bulmer Holdings plc, Annual Report and Accounts, 1990/91, reproduced with permission.

Each of the ideas and theories discussed in this section provides food for thought, but individually none of them explains fully what happens, or what should happen, in organizations. In my experience certain organizations are highly growth oriented, willing to diversify and take risks, whilst others, constrained by the difficulties of coping with rapid growth and implementing diversification strategies (discussed at some length in Chapter 18) are less ambitious in this respect. Each can be appropriate in certain circumstances and lead to high performance; in different circumstances they might be the wrong strategy.

Stakeholder theory is extremely relevant conceptually, but organizations are affected by the stakeholders in a variety of ways. Priorities must be decided for companies on an individual basis. Moreover the strategic leader, and in turn the organization, will seek to satisfy particular stakeholders rather than others because of their personal backgrounds and values. There is no right or wrong list of priorities. However, whilst priorities can and will be established, all stakeholders must be satisfied to some minimum level. In the final analysis the essential requirement is congruence between environment, values and resources.

So far in this chapter we have concentrated on profit-seeking organizations and considered just how important the profit motive might be. Not-for-profit organizations may be growth conscious, quality conscious or committed to employee welfare in the same way as profit seekers, but there are certain differences which require that they are considered separately.

OBJECTIVES OF NOT-FOR-PROFIT ORGANIZATIONS

If we are to understand the objectives of not-for-profit organizations and appreciate where they are aiming to go, a number of points need to be considered.

☐ Stakeholders are important, particularly those who are providers of financial support.
☐ There will be a number of potentially conflicting objectives, and quite typically the financial ones will not be seen as the most essential in terms of the mission.
☐ Whilst there will be a mix of quantitative (financial) and qualitative objectives, the former will be easier to measure, although the latter relate more closely to the mission of the organization.
☐ For this reason the efficient use of resources becomes an important objective.

These points will now be examined in greater depth, making reference to Cases 5.1 and 5.2 (The National Theatre and London Zoo) together with a number of other examples, as not-for-profit organizations are many and varied.

At one extreme, at least in terms of size, **nationalized industries** with essentially monopoly markets have been seen as nonprofit, and throughout their existence different governments have strived to establish acceptable and effective measures of performance for them. At various times both breakeven and return on capital employed have been stressed. There is an in-built objectives conflict between social needs (many of them provide essential services) and a requirement that the very substantial resources are managed commercially in order to avoid waste. The Conservative government of the 1980s has followed a policy of privatizing certain nationalized industries partly on the grounds that in some cases more competition will be stimulating and create greater efficiency.

The National Health Service can be viewed similarly. Fundamentally its purpose relates to the health and well-being of the nation, and attention can be focused on both prevention and cure. The role of the police in terms of crime prevention and the solution of crimes that have taken place can be seen as synonymous. The Health Service can spend any money it is offered, as science contin-

---

Case 5.1
THE NATIONAL THEATRE

The National Theatre is in fact three theatres in one building on the south bank of the Thames in London. A substantial proportion of revenue has to be allocated to cover the overheads on the building. The specially built theatre opened in 1976, and for 12 years it had only one Director, Sir Peter Hall. Richard Eyre became Director in 1988. Despite its name, and although it does at times tour the country, it does not attract a national audience. The plays it offers are generally different from those in the more commercial non-subsidized theatres in London's West End, and it attracts a mixture of regular theatre goers from the southeast, foreign tourists and occasional visitors.

The National receives a grant from the Arts Council (itself funded by the Treasury). At certain times during the 1980s the grant increased at less than the rate of inflation, a reflection of government policy concerning support for the arts and their belief that more private support is required. In addition the National receives private sponsorship and earns money from the box office, catering and other front-of-house sales. Sponsorship and subsidies allow ticket prices to be less than they otherwise would.

Some stakeholders, such as directors and actors, might hold the view that as the National is prestigious it should seek to offer the 'best of everything' – plays, actors, costumes, and scenery – and that it should experiment and seek to be innovative. At the same time it has to at least break even, although the types of play and musical which earn the most revenue at the box office are not necessarily those the National will seek to produce.

Sir Peter Hall has said that his main aim was to provide working conditions where actors can be at their most creative. Audiences and money matter, but they are not the primary goal.

How, then, is success measured? Audiences and revenue can certainly be measured, but 'success is something you can feel and smell when you are with an audience'.

---

ually improves what can be done for people. In a sense it is a chicken-and-egg situation. Resources improve treatments and open up new opportunities for prevention; and these in turn stimulate demand, particularly where they concern illnesses or diseases which historically have not been easily treated. However, these developments are often very expensive, and decisions have then to be made about where funds should be allocated. Quite simply the decisions relate to priorities.

Customers of the Health Service are concerned with such things as the waiting time for admission to hospital and for operations,

the quality of care as affected by staff attitudes and numbers, and arguably privacy in small wards, cleanliness and food. Doctors are concerned with the amount of resources and their ability to cope with demand; and administrators must ensure that resources are used efficiently.

There are a number of key points in this highly simplistic summary. The government funds the National Health Service, and as the major source of funds is a key influence. Pfeffer (1981) has argued that the relative power of influencers is related to the funds they provide. The less funding that is

Case 5.2
LONDON ZOO

London Zoo, in Regent's Park, is one of two zoological gardens which are controlled and administered by the Zoological Society of London. The other is Whipsnade Park, near Dunstable in Bedfordshire, and this covers 600 acres compared with 34 acres in London.

The Society's charter lays down its primary purpose as 'the advancement of zoology and animal physiology, and the introduction of new and curious subjects of the animal kingdom'. Given this scientific orientation, what should be the objectives of London Zoo? Who are the other stakeholders, and how important are they? The basic dilemma concerns how much zoos are places of entertainment and relaxation, with customers paramount, and how much they are organizations with primarily educational and scientific purposes. One constraint is the fact that Regent's Park is a Royal Park, and that bye-laws restrict certain activities such as on-site advertising.

Since 1985 the zoo has received a series of annual grants from the Department of the Environment, and in 1988 it was given £10 million as a one-off payment 'to put it on a firm financial footing'. It remains 'the only National collection in the world not publically funded on a regular basis'. Without these subsidies the zoo has a surplus of expenditure over income.

Income is essentially from visitors, the majority of whom live in comfortable travelling distance of London, and private sponsorship. Many of the visitors are on organized school trips; and weather conditions are very important in attracting or deterring people.

Many visitors are attracted by big animals, as evidenced by the commercial success of safari parks, but they are costly and dangerous, as well as well-researched and relatively safe as far as endangered species go. Quite often the most endangered species are relatively unattractive. Whipsnade is regarded as more ideal for big animals; and London Zoo has had no hippos (since the 1960s) and no bears (since 1986). Whipsnade has both. Visitors can drive around Whipsnade, parking in various places en route, but it is not a safari park.

Critics have argued that London Zoo's management has failed to exploit the zoo's conservation work by featuring it in informative displays and that much of the zoo's important (and scientifically renowned) research is not recognized by the general public. This is correct, but the fact remains that much of the important conservation work involves species which are relatively uninteresting for many public visitors. Such an example is the rare Rodriguez Fruit Bat.

The Department of the Environment paid for a report by independent consultants (1987–8), and they concluded that 'management at London Zoo did not reflect the commercial emphasis which was essential for survival and prosperity without a permanent subsidy'. They recommended the establishment of a new company to manage London and Whipsnade Zoos, separate from the scientific research of the Zoological Society. This company was established in October 1988, with the aim of reversing the falling trend in admissions and returning the zoo to profit in three years.

The numbers of visitors did increase in 1989 and 1990, but below the level required to break even. In April 1991 newspapers first reported that London Zoo might have to close, with some animals destroyed and others moved to Whipsnade. The Government refused further financial assistance, not wholly convinced of the need for urban zoos. Cost reduction, *per se*, was ruled out as this was likely to provoke a new fall in admissions. Instead rescue plans concentrated on a smaller zoo with a new concept – natural habitats such as an African rain forest complete with gorillas, and a Chinese mountain featuring the pandas. There would be less emphasis on caged animals.

Changes were made but attendances fell. The zoo's closure was announced formally in June 1992. New external funding has since provided a reprieve. It may prove only temporary.

provided by customers, the weaker is their influence over decisions. Hence a not-for-profit organization like the National Health Service may be less customer oriented than a private competitive firm. Some would argue that the private medical sector is more marketing conscious.

All organizations will seek to measure performance in some way. It was stated earlier in the chapter that performance against quantitative objectives can be measured directly whereas performance against qualitative objectives is typically indirect and more difficult. If attention is focused on the aspects that are most easily measured there is a danger that these come to be perceived as the most important objectives. Hospital administrators can easily measure the number of admissions, the utilization of beds and theatres, the cost of laundry and food and so on. Fundamentally more important is who is being treated relative to the real needs of the community. Are the most urgent and needy cases receiving the priorities they deserve? How is this measured? Performance measures therefore tend to concentrate on the **efficient use of resources** rather than the **effectiveness** of the organization. Although profit may not be an important consideration, costs are. In addition these measures may well be a source of conflict between medical

and administrative staff and this is a reflection of the fact that there is likely to be disagreement and confusion about what the key objectives are.

Given this the objectives that are perceived as important and are pursued at any time are very dependent upon the relative power of the influencers and their ability to exercise power. Linked to this point is the relationship between hospitals and area and regional health authorities. Similarly where not-for-profit organizations have advisory bodies, or Boards of trustees, the relationship and relative power is important.

Tourist attractions such as London Zoo (Case 5.2) and the country's leading museums (including the British Museum, the Natural History Museum and the Victoria and Albert, which is the National Museum of Art and Design) have a potential conflict of objectives concerning their inevitable educational and scientific orientations and the requirement that they address commercial issues. Museums can earn money from shops and cafeterias and they receive some private funding, but to a great extent they are reliant on government grants. In the 1980s these grants did not keep pace with their monetary demands and hence it has been necessary for them to seek additional revenue as well as manage resources and costs more efficiently.

Admission charges to museums have become a controversial issue. In November 1985 the Victoria and Albert Museum introduced voluntary admission charges, and in April 1987 the Natural History Museum started charging for entry. Some potential visitors are lost as they refuse to pay, and this has implications for the educational objective. It has been reported that by 1987 admissions to the Victoria and Albert had fallen to 1 million a year from a peak of 1.75 million in 1983, but they were increasing again after 1988. However, the museum was criticized by some arts lovers for a poster campaign describing it as 'an ace caff with quite a nice museum attached', although museum staff claimed that this was a major reason for the increase in attendances. Some museums, including the British Museum, adamantly oppose charging.

At *The National Theatre* (Case 5.1) the issue addresses art and finance. Subsidized theatres perceive their role to be different from that of commercial theatres and a number of them, including the Royal Shakespeare Company, English National Opera and the Royal Opera House, Covent Garden, all compete for a percentage of Arts Council funding. When the Arts Council, as a major stakeholder and provider of funds, attempts to influence the strategies of the theatres they are often accused of meddling. Again there is a potential chicken-and-egg situation. If the theatres, under pressure from reduced subsidies (in real terms), raise more revenue and reduce their costs, they may find that this results in permanently reduced subsidies. Hence, as an alternative, they may choose to restrain their commercial orientation.

Cathedrals face a similar dilemma. The costs of repairs and maintenance are forcing some to charge visitors fixed amounts rather than rely on voluntary donations. Their mission is concerned with religion and charity but they are not immune from commercial realities.

Charities like **Oxfam** have sets of interdependent commercial and non-commercial objectives. Oxfam's mission concerns the provision of relief and the provision of aid where it is most needed throughout the world. Additional objectives relate to teaching people how to look after themselves better through, say, irrigation and better farming techniques and to obtaining publicity to draw public attention to the plight of the needy. Their ability to pursue these is constrained by resource availability. Consequently Oxfam have fund-raising objectives, and strategies (including retailing through Oxfam shops) to achieve them. It is difficult to say which receives most priority as they are so interdependent.

We have discussed the issue of the displacement of objectives in not-for-profit organizations. Attention is centred on quantitative measures as they are relatively easily carried out. The efficient use of resources replaces profit as the commercial objective, and whilst this may not be an essential aspect of the mission, it will be seen as important by certain stakeholders. In reality attention has switched from evaluating outputs (the real objectives) to measuring inputs (resources) because it easier to do. Where the stakeholders are major sponsors, and particularly in the case of government departments, there will be an insistence upon cost effectiveness. Many of the organizations mentioned in this section are managed by people whose training and natural orientation is towards arts or science, and this can result in feelings of conflict with regard to objectives. Quite typically the organization will pursue certain objectives for a period of time, satisfying the most influential stakeholders in the coalition, and then change as the preferences of stakeholders – or their relative power and influence – change.

Whilst profit-seeking and not-for-profit organizations have essentially different missions, the issue of profit making is complex. As we have seen, some not-for-profit organizations rely on subsidies and these enable prices to be kept below what they would otherwise be. In nationalized industries the element of customer service has been seen to be important with prices controlled or at least influenced by government. An independent regulator has been appointed when nationalized businesses have been privatized (see Chapter 7). However, unless the providers of grants and subsidies are willing to bear commercial trading losses and at the same time finance any necessary investment, there is a necessity for the organizations to generate revenue at least equal to the costs incurred. Where investment finance also needs to be generated a surplus of income over expenditure is important. This basically is profit. Whilst profit may not therefore be an essential part of the mission it is still required.

The following comments of Ackoff (1986) relating to the objectives of American universities usefully round off this section and act as an introduction to the next section on personal objectives.

The objectives pursued by organizations frequently differ from those proclaimed. Some years ago I assumed that the principal objective of universities was the education of students. Armed with this assumption I could make no sense of their behaviour. I learned that education, like profit, is a requirement not an objective and that the principal objective is to provide their faculties with the quality of work life and the standard of living they desire. That's why professors do so little teaching, give the same courses over and over again, arrange classes at their convenience, not that of their students, teach subjects they want to teach rather than students want to learn and skip classes to give lectures for a fee.

These comments, interestingly, relate to an education system where students pay their own fees rather than enjoy government funding, as is the case in the UK. One might expect consumer resistance if students felt that their interests were not being satisfied.

British universities and polytechnics, of course, have become subject to tighter finan-

cial controls in the 1980s, resource utilization and cost efficiency have become increasingly important, and personal objectives along the lines of those above must cause conflict.

THE IMPACT OF PERSONAL OBJECTIVES

It has already been established that organizations are generally too large and complex to have only one objective. As a result, and influenced by stakeholders, there are typically several objectives with varying degrees of relative importance. It is now appropriate to consider why organizations cannot be treated separately from the people who work in them.

Objectives can be set (and changed) in any one of three ways.

☐ The strategic leader decides.
☐ Managers throughout the organization are either consulted or influence the objectives by their decisions and actions.
☐ All or some relevant stakeholders influence the organization in some way.

It is the second of these which is addressed in this section. Some organizations will have planning systems (which will be studied in a

---

You must provide a framework in which people can act. For example, we have said that our first priority is safety, second is punctuality, and third is other services. So if you risk flight safety by leaving on time, you have acted outside the framework of your authority. The same is true if you don't leave on time because you are missing two catering boxes of meat. That's what I mean by a framework. You give people a framework, and within the framework you let people act.

Jan Carlzon, President and Chief Executive Officer, Scandinavian Airlines System

Key Concept 5.1
POLICIES

☐ 'Policies' are guidelines relating to decisions and approaches which support organizational efforts to achieve **stated** objectives.

☐ They are basically **guides to thoughts** (about how things might or should be done) **and actions**.

☐ They are therefore **guides to decision making**. For example a policy which states that for supplies of a particular item three quotations should be sought and the cheapest selected, or a policy not to advertise in certain newspapers, or a policy not to trade with particular countries – all influence decisions. Policies are particularly useful for routine repetitive decisions.

☐ Policies can be at corporate, divisional (or strategic business unit (SBU)) or functional level; and they are normally stated in terms of management (of people), marketing, production, finance and research and development.

☐ If stated objectives are to be achieved, and the strategies designed to accomplish this implemented, the appropriate policies must be there in support. In other words the behaviour of managers and the decisions they take should be supportive of what the organization is seeking to achieve. Policies guide and constrain their actions.

☐ Policies can be mandatory (rules which allow little freedom for original thought or action) or advisory. The more rigid they are the less freedom managers have to change things with delegated authority; and this can be good or bad depending upon change pressures from the environment.

☐ **It is vital to balance consistency and co-ordination** (between the various divisions, SBUs and departments in the organization) **with flexibility**.

☐ Policies need not be written down. They can be passed on verbally as part of the culture.

☐ Policies **must** be widely understood if they are to be useful.

later chapter) which involve a wide range of managers throughout the organization, and they therefore have up-to-date information about products, services and competitors fed in from those managers closest to the market. This can influence the objectives and strategies that the organization states it wishes to achieve and implement respectively.

At the same time the decisions made by managers determine the actual strategies pursued, and in turn revised, implicit, objectives replace the explicit ones. The incidence or likelihood of this is affected by the culture of the organization, the relative power bases of managers, communication systems, and whether or not there are rigid policies and procedures or more informal management processes that allow managers considerable freedom. Key Concept 5.1 defines **policies** and discusses their role in strategy implementation. The following brief example illustrates the impact of policies. Consider a multiple store that sells records as one of its products and has nearby a small independent competitor that appeals to different customers. If the small store closed down there could be new opportunities for the manager of the multiple store if he changed his competitive strategy for records by changing his displays, improved his stock levels and

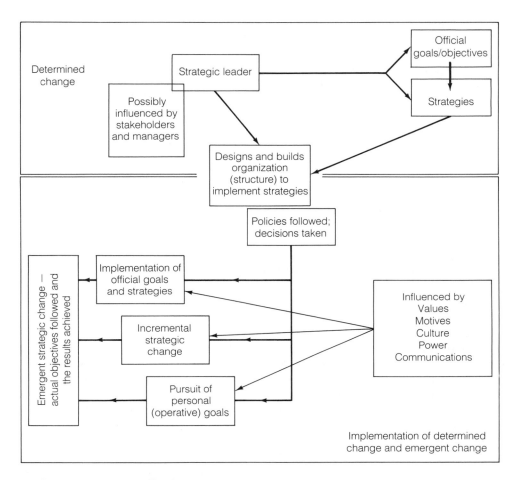

Figure 5.1   Strategy creation: official and operative goals.

supported these moves with window displays promoting the changes. Head office merchandising policies concerning stocks and displays may or may not allow him this freedom.

Figure 5.1 charts the process outlined above. The strategic leader determines and states the objectives, strategies and proposed changes for the organization. In arriving at his decisions he may be influenced in a minor or major way by stakeholders outside the organization and managers he consults. In order to ensure that the strategies are implemented (and the objectives achieved) the strategic leader will design and build an

organization structure – which may restrict managers or allow them considerable freedom – and will determine policies which may be mandatory or advisory. This will tie in to the culture of the organization and will be influenced by the style and values of the strategic leader, both of which we discussed earlier. This process is reflected in the top part of Figure 5.1.

The bottom section considers what happens in reality. The types of policy and the authority and freedom delegated to managers guides, influences and constrains decision making. The motives, values and relative power of individual managers, the

Table 5.5   Examples of official and operative goals

Type of organization	Typical official goals	Possible operative goals
Private sector firm	Profit Return on capital Customer service	Favouring certain suppliers (not lowest cost or best delivery) or customers (priority on low profit orders)
Hospital	Promotion of community health via cure and prevention	Personal ambitions of certain consultants (arguably wrong priorities) Use of more, but cheaper, unqualified nursing staff
Employment agency	Bring two interested (and ideally well-suited) parties together	Racial or other prejudice

Developed from ideas contained in Perrow, C (1961) The analysis of goals in complex organizations, *American Sociological Review*, **26**, December.

relative importance of particular functions, divisions or strategic business units in the organization, and the system of communications are also influential. The stated or *official objectives* may or may not be achieved; there may be appropriate incremental decisions which reflect changes in the environment; or managers may be pursuing personal objectives, which Perrow (1961) has termed *operative goals*. This is happening when the behaviour taking place cannot be accounted for by official company objectives and policies. The aggregation of these various decisions determines the emergent strategic changes, the actual objectives followed and the results achieved.

Official and operative goals

Perrow defines official goals as 'the general purposes of the organization, as put forth in the charter, annual reports, public statements by key executives and other authoritative announcements'. But, he argues, there are numerous ways of achieving official goals which cannot easily be accounted for; and groups and individuals may pursue unofficial goals. Operative goals, then, 'designate the ends sought through the actual operating policies of the organization; they tell us what the organization actually is trying to do, regardless of what the official goals say are the aims'.

Operative goals may complement official goals or they may conflict. A complementary situation would exist if the stated objective was in terms of a target return on capital employed, and if this was achieved through operative goals of managers and decisions taken by them regarding delivery times, quality and so on. If, however, a sales manager was favouring particular customers with discounts or priority deliveries on low profit orders, or a production manager was setting unnecessarily high quality standards (as far as customers are concerned) which resulted in substantial rejections and high operating costs, profits would be threatened. In such cases operative goals would conflict with official goals. Table 5.5 gives examples of potential conflict in different types of organization.

SOCIAL RESPONSIBILITY AND BUSINESS ETHICS

Having looked at some of the theories which are relevant for a study of objectives, and at typical objectives that organizations pursue and why, it is appropriate to conclude this chapter with a consideration of wider societal aspects. Objectives which relate to social responsibility may be affected by stake-holders; in some cases they result from legislation, but often they are voluntary actions. The issue is one of how responsible a firm might choose to be, and why. Again the particular values of the strategic leader will be very influential.

There are numerous ways that a firm can behave responsibly in the interests of society, and examples are given below. It should not be thought, though, that social responsibility is a one-way process; organizations can benefit considerably from it.

☐ **Product safety:** This can be the result of design or production and includes aspects of supply and supplier selection to obtain safe materials or components. Product safety will be influenced to an extent by legislation, but an organization can build in more safety features than the law requires. Some cars are an example of this. Volvo, for example, is promoted and perceived as a relatively safe car. Product safety will have cost implications. Some-times the safety is reflected in perceived higher quality, which adds value that the customer is willing to pay a premium for, but at other times it will be the result of the organization's choosing to sacrifice some potential profit.

☐ **Working conditions:** Linked to the pre-vious point, these can include safety at work, which again is affected by legisla-tion which sets minimum standards. Aspects of job design to improve working conditions and training to improve employees' prospects are further exam-ples.

☐ **Honesty,** including not offering or accept-ing bribes.
☐ **Avoiding pollution**.
☐ **Avoiding discrimination**.

The above points are all subject to some legislation.

☐ **Community action:** This is a very broad category with numerous opportunities, ranging from charitable activities to con-certed action to promote industry and jobs in areas which have suffered from the economic recession. Many large organiza-tions release executives on a temporary basis to help with specific community projects.
☐ **Industry location:** Organizations may locate new plants in areas of high un-employment for a variety of reasons. Whilst aspects of social responsibility may be involved the decision may well be more economic. Grants and rate concessions may be important.
☐ **Other environmental concerns** such as

Managers of today, and those who seek to succeed in the future, must have a highly-developed sense of responsibility to society and the environment. This is especially true of the chemical industry. We must under-stand and respond to public anxiety; debate, explain and listen. In Bayer's case we seek to communicate the fact that we are not only experts in what to do, but that we use our expertise in full awareness of our respons-ibilities towards the environment, our employees and neighbours, our customers and our shareholders. For us, environmental protection and safety have the same priority as high product quality and commercial success. Every one of our managers is expected to share in communicating these principles.

Hermann J. Strenger, Chairman of the Board of Management, Bayer AG, Leverkusen

Box 5.5
EXAMPLES OF ENVIRONMENTAL STRATEGIES

'The 1990s will be the decade of the environment' (The President of the Petroleum Marketers Association of America; *Fortune*, 12 February 1990, p.24).

1. **McDonald's** have taken an equity stake in a new venture for recycling the waste collected at their restaurants. Some plastic containers which cannot be recycled are being withdrawn; food scraps are used for making compost.

2. **Electricity generating** is gradually switching to gas and cleaner coal (with a low sulphur content) because coal has been shown to cause acid rain.

3. **ICI** is a leading contender in the challenge to find a replacement for chlorofluorocarbons (CFCs), gases which are used extensively in aerosols and refrigeration equipment, and which are widely blamed for depleting the ozone layer.

4. **The motor vehicle industry**. Historically, car manufacturers exploited an opportunity very successfully – increased affluence and the desire for individual freedom had generated a demand for private cars. Their success in increasing levels of ownership created a number of threats: traffic density; pollution from exhaust emissions; material waste through obsolescence; the 'waste' of scarce resources in high-consumption, inefficient,

engines; and safety problems arising from the sheer volume of traffic, congestion and hurry.

A response was needed, and this has involved both manufacturers and government.

☐ Legislation has made catalytic converters compulsory on all new cars after January 1993; maximum speed limits might be reduced some time in the future.

☐ New models invariably feature improvements in design and technology which reduce waste and increase fuel efficiency.

☐ New concept vehicles – including electric cars and others which mix the traditionally contradictory high performance with environmental friendliness – which have a long-term time-scale.

☐ Links between different forms of transport (road, rail, air and water) are being strengthened. BMW, for example, is pioneering co-operative ventures in Munich, where research has shown that in 1 square kilometre of the City Centre in busy periods 50% of the cars on the move are driving around looking for parking spaces.

☐ Old parts are being recycled. In France both Peugeot and Renault have opened plants for this, but these are small ventures in relation to the total numbers of cars being scrapped.

recycling, waste disposal, protecting the ozone layer and energy efficiency. Box 5.5 illustrates a number of specific examples. Touche Ross (1990) have reported upon investigations into environmental strategies in the chemical, heavy engineering and consumer goods industries through-

out Europe. They concluded that companies in Western Germany, Holland and Denmark were the most environmentally concerned; those in Britain, France and Belgium were the least concerned. Concern was measured against three criteria:

Case 5.3
NORSK HYDRO

Norsk Hydro is a Norwegian chemical company (with plants throughout Europe) which 'prides itself on being an environmentally responsible concern'. In 1987 activists broke into one of Norsk Hydro's plants in Norway and discovered soil impregnated with mercury. There have been other reported environmental incidences linked to Norsk, including the contamination of seafood caught in two fjords, ground water pollution and a large fire at a plastics factory. Public reaction in Norway was hostile.

The company decided upon a proactive response, carrying out an independently audited environmental appraisal of all its Norwegian operations and publishing the results.

Norsk Hydro's UK subsidiary, which manufactures nitrogen-based fertilizers and PVC and aluminium fittings, chose to replicate this strategy and the findings were published in October 1990. The appraisal concentrated on pollution, noise levels (charted over six years) and recycling issues. Most of the data were obtained from internal records, but the appraisal was evaluated independently by Lloyds Register who concluded: 'Norsk's environmental performance is generally above average.' Lloyds identified five key areas for improvement.

By publishing its findings 'Norsk is light years ahead of what many other companies in this sector are doing'.

(John Elkington, Director, SustainAbility
[environmental consultancy])

Source: Thomas D (1990) Turning over a new leaf, *Financial Times*, 24 October.

(a) Did any Board member have specific responsibility for environmental issues – as a major, not a minor, part of his or her overall responsibilities?
(b) Were the product strategies environmentally friendly?
(c) Were any environmental standards imposed on suppliers?

☐ **The attitude of food retailers** towards, for example, accurate labelling (country of origin), free range eggs, organic vegetables, biodegradable packaging, CFC-free aerosols and products containing certain dubious E number additives. It is a moot point whether retailers or consumers should decide upon these issues.

Examples of social responsibility can appear in other ways. See Case 5.3 on Norsk Hydro.

Arguably Marks & Spencer's preference for buying and retailing British made goods is an example. Scott Bader, featured in Case 4.1, include in their Commonwealth Code of Practice pledges to 'limit our products to those beneficial to the community', in particular excluding any which could become weapons of war, and 'reduce any harmful effect of our work on the natural environment by rigorously avoiding the negligent discharge of pollutants'.

Securicor, the UK's leading security company, has a number of stated aims which reflect both a concern for employees and wider social responsibilities. The philosophy was introduced by chief executive Keith Erskine, previously a 'lawyer concerned with justice'; it resulted in the slogan 'Securicor Cares' and advertising on the theme 'Securicor Cares for Customers, Co-Workers and the Common Good', and it remained intact after Erskine's death in 1974. In the 1972 Chairman's review Erskine detailed the following aims (these are selected from a longer list):

☐ to observe the highest code of business conduct;
☐ to devolve and involve; to enrich both jobs and lives; to combine private enterprise with social justice; to care for the individual;
☐ to ignore class or race; to judge only by merit; to work in comradeship.

Obviously objectives of this nature become part of the organization culture. Social responsibility is at the heart of activities and objectives because it is felt that the organization has an obligation both to the community and to society in general. However, it must not be assumed that the approach receives universal support. Milton Friedman (1979), the economist, argues that 'the business of business is business . . . the organization's only social responsibility is to increase its profit'. Friedman also comments that donations to charity and sponsorship of the arts are 'fundamentally subversive' and not in the best interests of the shareholders. Social responsibility would then be the result of legislation. Drucker (1974) argues businesses have a role in society which is 'to supply goods and services to customers and an economic surplus to society . . . rather than to supply jobs to workers and managers, or even dividends to shareholders'. The latter,

he argues, are means not ends. Drucker contends that it is mismanagement to forget that a hospital exists for its patients and a university for its students. This contrasts with the comments by Russell Ackoff about university academics quoted earlier.

The topic is complex, and although the outcome of certain decisions can be seen to be bringing benefit to the community or employees the decision may have been influenced by legislation or perceived organizational benefit (enlightened self-interest) rather than a social conscience. One could argue that the organization will benefit if it looks after its employees; equally one could argue that it will suffer if it fails to consider employee welfare. The two approaches are philosophically different, but they may generate similar results. Some organizations feature their community role extensively in corporate advertising campaigns designed to bring them recognition and develop a caring responsible image.

The pursuit of socially responsible objectives may well be costly for either or both the organization and its customers, and may be at the expense of profits, but ignoring them can in certain instances result in disaster. The inquiry into the November 1987 fire at Kings Cross Underground station (the report was published in June 1988) illustrates some interesting points. Thirty-one people were killed when a small fire on a wooden escalator 'erupted into a fireball'. Nobody had died in an underground escalator fire since 1911. A number of management failures were detailed, concerning decisions taken about safety precautions and not implemented (and not followed through by senior management) and hazards being ignored. In particular there was 'insufficient regard to public safety at stations' although safety standards were high in certain areas, particularly operations. The signalling operations were mentioned as being better managed and looked after in terms of safety. 'The business was seen to be run as a railway business first and foremost.' One conclusion of Mr Roger Henderson, QC, who chaired the inquiry, was that 'a major investment in safety is needed, and a recognition that at least as much money, and probably more public expenditure, should be devoted to safety improvements as to modernising stations'.

The argument is that in practice the balance of objectives and priorities had not been appropriate. Operative goals had not been sufficiently safety oriented. Mr Henderson also commented that 'safety had been regarded philosophically as paramount, but not unfortunately as paramount in practice'.

Business ethics

Disasters of this nature, and ones like the explosion at the chemical plant in Bhopal, India, raise the question of how far companies should go in pursuit of profits. Ethics is defined as 'the discipline dealing with what is good and bad and right and wrong or with moral duty and obligation' (*Webster's Third New International Dictionary*). Houlden (1988) suggests that business ethics encompasses the views of people throughout society concerning the morality of business, and not just the views of the particular business and the people who work in it.

Issues such as golden handshakes, insider dealing and very substantial salary increases for company chairmen and chief executives are topical and controversial. The so-called Guinness affair, and the legal action against Ernest Saunders and other businessmen and financiers, is a specific case which has received wide publicity.

Public attention is drawn to these issues, and people's perceptions of businesses generally and individually are affected. However, their responses differ markedly. Some people feel disgruntled but do nothing; others take more positive actions. Managers, however, should not ignore the potential for resistance or opposition by their customers, say through refusing to buy their products or use their services.

Another ethical concern is individual managers or employees who adopt practices which senior managers or the strategic leader would consider unethical. These need to be identified and stopped. If they remain unchecked they are likely to spread, with the argument that 'everyone does it'. Salesmen using questionable methods of persuasion, even lying, would be an example.

However, it does not follow that such practices would always be seen as unethical by senior managers – in some organizations they will be at least condoned, and possibly even encouraged.

Ethical dilemmas

One classic ethical dilemma concerns the employee who works for a competitor, is interviewed for a job, and who promises to bring confidential information if he is offered the post. Should the proposition be accepted or not? The issue, featured at the beginning of this section, is how far companies should go in pursuit of profits. In such a case as this, of course, long-term considerations are important as well as potential short-term benefits. If the competitor who loses the confidential information realizes what has happened it may seek to retaliate in some way. Arguably the best interests of the industry as a whole should be considered.

Another example is the company with a plant which is surplus to requirements and which it would like to sell. The company knows the land beneath the plant contains radioactive waste. Legally it need not disclose this fact to prospective buyers, but is it ethical to keep quiet? Petfood manufacturers, looking to expand their sales, would logically seek to differentiate their products by featuring particular benefits and satisfied, friendly pets, but they will also hope to persuade more people to become owners. Given the publicity on potentially dangerous breeds of dog, and the numbers of abandoned pets, particularly after Christmas, what would constitute an ethical approach to promotion? In 1991 a small number of ministers in the Church of England questioned whether the Church Commissioners, with £3 billion to invest to cover the future salaries and pensions of clergy, should be free to invest the money anywhere (in an attempt to maximize earnings) or whether they should be restricted to organizations which were known to be ethical in their business dealings.

In contrast, a serious dilemma faces individuals in an organization who feel that their managers are pursuing unethical practices. There are several examples of individuals who have acted and suffered as a result of their actions. An accountant with an insurance company exposed a case of tax evasion by his bosses and jeopardized his career. Stanley Adams, an employee of Hoffman la Roche, the Swiss drug company, believed that his firm was making excessive profits and divulged commercially sensitive information to the European Commission. He also lost his career and suffered financially. There are similar examples of engineers who felt that design compromises were threatening consumer safety, complained, and lost their jobs.

Many of the ethical issues which affect strategic decisions are regulated directly by legislation. Equally, many companies do not operate in sensitive environments where serious ethical issues require thought and attention. However, some companies and their strategic leaders do need a clear policy regarding business ethics. Quite often they have to decide whether to increase costs in the short run, say to improve safety factors, on the assumption that this will bring longer-term benefits. Short-term profitability, important to shareholders, could be affected. Increased safety beyond minimum legal requirements, for example, would increase the construction costs of a new chemical plant. If safety was compromised to save money, nothing might actually go wrong and profits would be higher. However, an explosion or other disaster results in loss of life, personal injury, compensation and legal costs, lost production, adverse publicity and tension between the business and local community. The long-term losses can be substantial.

Ethical standards and beliefs are aspects of the corporate culture and are influenced markedly by the lead set by the strategic leader and his or her awareness of behaviour throughout the organization. Power, for example, can be used either ethically or unethically by individual managers.

Frederick (1988) contends that the corporate culture is the main source of ethical problems. He argues that managers are encouraged to focus their professional energies on productivity, efficiency and leadership, and that their corporate values lead them to act in ways which place the company interests ahead of those of consumers or society. Schlegelmilch and Houston (1989) have ascertained that a far higher proportion of large companies in the USA have drawn up codes of ethics which are communicated to all employees than is the case in the UK. Moreover, American companies are more rigorous in ensuring that the ethical standards are adopted. They also comment that the subject is receiving more attention all the time. The typical issues covered in an ethics code include relationships with employees (the most prevalent factor in the UK codes of ethics), government (more important in the USA), the community and the environment.

Drawing on earlier points, attitudes towards bribery and inducement, and the use of privileged information, could also be incorporated in any Code. Attention might also be paid to practices which are commonplace but arguably unethical. Examples would include a deliberate policy not to pay invoices on time, and creative accounting, presenting information in the most favourable light. The extent to which audited company accounts can be wholly relied upon is another interesting issue.

In my opinion business ethics is important and worthy of serious attention. However, a consideration of ethical issues in strategic decisions typically requires that a long-term perspective is adopted. Objectives and strategies should be realistic and achievable rather than over-ambitious and very difficult to attain. In the latter case individual managers may be set high targets which encourage them to behave unethically, possibly making them feel uneasy. Results may be massaged, for instance, or deliberately presented with inaccuracies. Such practices spread quickly and dishonesty becomes acceptable. The longer-term perspective can reduce the need for immediate results and targets which managers feel have to be met at all costs. However, pressure from certain stakeholders, particularly institutional shareholders, may focus attention on the short term and on results which surpass those of the previous year. The longer-term perspective additionally allows for concern with processes and behaviour, and with how the results are obtained. The drive for results is not allowed to override ethical and behavioural concerns.

Houlden (1988) concludes that strategic leaders should be objective about how society views their company and its products, and wherever possible should avoid actions which can damage its image. If an action or decision which certain stakeholders might view as unethical is unavoidable, such as the closure of a plant, it is important to use public relations to explain fully why the decision has been taken. The need for a good corporate image should not be under-estimated.

In later chapters we discuss how organizations might achieve competitive advantage. Ethical considerations can make a significant contribution to this. A commitment to keeping promises about quality standards and delivery times, or not making promises which cannot be met, would be one example. If employees are honest and committed, and rewarded appropriately for this, then costs are likely to be contained and the overall level of customer service high, thereby improving profits.

SUMMARY

In this chapter we have explored objectives, looking at where the organization is going and considering why. We shall return to the subject in Chapter 16 when we consider the process of reviewing objectives and possibly setting new objectives as part of strategic decision making.

Specifically we have

☐ differentiated between the mission and objectives, and explained that aims and goals are frequently used as alternative expressions;

☐ considered what is required for a mission statement to be useful;

☐ recapped, from microeconomics, the four key market models;

☐ introduced the notion of stakeholder theory, and examined how this can lead to multiple objectives and priorities;

☐ briefly summarized a number of theories of the firm based upon the premise that ownership and management are separated;

☐ discussed whether profit is a means to other ends or an end (objective) in itself;

☐ considered typical objectives of UK companies, especially those influenced by shareholders, and contrasted them with those of Japanese companies;

☐ highlighted the differences between profit-seeking and not-for-profit organizations, and emphasized that for the latter it is likely that inputs (resources) will be a key measure of performance;

☐ reviewed Perrow's work on official and operative goals, and posed the question: is the organization going where it intended to go?;

☐ looked at the subject of social responsibility and business ethics.

CHECKLIST OF KEY TERMS AND CONCEPTS

You should feel confident that you understand the following terms and ideas:

☐ Mission
☐ Objectives (or goals)
☐ Stakeholder theory
☐ Official and operative goals
☐ Social responsibility and business ethics.

You should also appreciate how different market models provide opportunities for, and constraints on, competition.

QUESTIONS AND RESEARCH ASSIGNMENTS

Text related

1. Consider how the objectives of H P Bulmer Holdings, detailed in Box 5.4 might be ranked in order of priority.
   Is there a difference between an ideal ranking and the likely ranking in practice? Note: Members of the Bulmer family hold over 50% of the ordinary shares.
2. What key issues do you believe should be incorporated in a company statement on ethics?

Library based

3. When Tottenham Hotspur became the first English Football League club with a stock exchange listing (in 1983) the issue prospectus said:

The Directors intend to ensure that the Club remains one of the leading football clubs in the country. They will seek to increase the Group's income by improving the return from existing assets and by establishing new sources of revenue in the leisure field.

(a) Research the strategies followed by Tottenham Hotspur plc between 1983 and 1991. Do you believe the interests of a plc and a professional football club are compatible or inevitably conflicting?
(b) In view of the comments about social responsibility how do you view the fact that football clubs generally invest far more money in players (wages and transfer fees) than they do in their grounds (amenities and safety)?

4. Have the objectives (in particular the order of priorities) of the Natural History Museum changed since the introduction of compulsory admission charges in April 1987?
5. In view of the findings after the *Herald of Free Enterprise* disaster at Zeebrugge in March 1987, how does a company like P & O (the owners of the vessel) balance the extra costs involved in additional safety measures with the need to be competitive internationally, and the time added on to voyages by more rigorous safety procedures with customer irritation if they are delayed 'unnecessarily'?

RECOMMENDED FURTHER READING

Richards (1978) is a useful short book devoted to the subject of goals and objectives. Newbould and Luffman (1979) provides a suitable introduction to stakeholder theory; Freeman (1984) is a text on strategic management from the perspective of stakeholders.

Drucker, P F (1990) *Managing the Non-Profit Organization*, Butterworth–Heinemann, is a useful text.

Simon's article (1964) contains a number of valuable ideas and themes.

Readers interested in business ethics will find the following text provides a stimulating anecdotal discussion of the main issues: Blanchard, K and Peale, N V (1988) *The Power of Ethical Management*, Heinemann.

REFERENCES

Ackoff, R L (1986) *Management in Small Doses*, Wiley.

Baumol, W J (1959) *Business Behaviour, Value and Growth*, Macmillan.

Campbell, A (1989) Research findings discussed in Skapinker, M (1989) Mission accomplished or ignored?, *Financial Times*, 11 January.

Constable, J (1980) The nature of company objectives, Unpublished paper, Cranfield School of Management.

Cyert, R M and March, J G (1963) *A Behavioural Theory of the Firm*, Prentice Hall.

Drucker, P F (1974) *Management: Tasks, Responsibilities, Practices*, Harper and Row.

Frederick, W C (1988) An ethics roundtable: the culprit is culture, *Management Review*, August.

Freeman, R E (1984) *Strategic Management: A Stakeholder Approach*, Pitman.

Friedman, M (1979) The social responsibility of business is to increase its profits. In *Business Policy and Strategy* (eds) D J McCarthy, R J Minichiello and J R Curran, Irwin.

Galbraith, J K (1963) *American Capitalism. The Concept of Countervailing Power*, Penguin.

Galbraith, J K (1969) *The New Industrial State*, Penguin.

Goldsmith, W and Clutterbuck, D (1984) *The Winning Streak*, Weidenfeld and Nicolson.

Houlden, B (1988) The corporate conscience, *Management Today*, August.

Marris, R (1964) *The Economic Theory of Managerial Capitalism*, Macmillan.

Newbould, G D and Luffman, G A (1979) *Successful Business Policies*, Gower.

Penrose, E (1959) *The Theory of the Growth of the Firm*, Blackwell.

Perrow, C (1961) The analysis of goals in complex organizations, *American Sociological Review*, **26**, December.

Pfeffer, J (1981) *Power in Organizations*, Pitman.

Richards, M D (1978) *Organizational Goal Structures*, West.

Schlegelmilch, B B and Houston, J E (1989) Corporate codes of ethics in large UK companies: an empirical investigation of use, content and attitudes, *European Journal of Marketing*, **23** (6).

Simon, H A (1964) On the concept of organizational goal, *Administrative Science Quarterly*, **9** (1), June, pp. 1–22.

Storey, D (1988) *Fast Growth Businesses in Northern England*, Survey by the University of Newcastle, Price Waterhouse.

Thompson, A A and Strickland, A J (1980) *Strategy Formulation and Implementation*, Irwin.

Touche Ross (1990) *European Management Attitudes to Environmental Issues*, Touche Ross European Services, Brussels.

Williamson, O E (1964) *Economics of Discretionary Behaviour: Managerial Objectives in a Theory of the Firm*, Kershaw.

HOW ARE WE DOING?

6

LEARNING OBJECTIVES

After studying this chapter you should be able to

□ explain how success might be measured and assessed;
□ evaluate the significance of financial measures of performance;
□ describe the key parts of a balance sheet and a profit and loss account;
□ calculate and evaluate a number of ratios relating to investment, performance and financial status;
□ discuss how profitability might be improved;
□ identify the difficulties involved in measuring the effective performance of many not-for-profit organizations.

In this chapter we look at how the performance of a company might be measured and assessed. Important links between results, objectives and the aspirations of stakeholders are considered. The role and significance of financial ratios is discussed.

INTRODUCTION

The performance of a company is usually measured by financial ratios but a compre-hensive answer to the question 'how are we doing?' requires consideration of the follow-ing:

□ actual achievement against stated or official objectives
□ the relative success of the organization in implementing its stated strategies
□ the effect of incremental changes and the impact of any operative objectives on the organization
□ the expectations and aspirations of stake-holders.

The progress and relative success of the organization should also be evaluated against the competition. Strategies and successes of competitors could pose threats if the organ-ization fails to react or respond. Equally, this type of evaluation can reveal new opportun-ities.

HOW ARE WE DOING?

Financial measures

An analysis of financial ratios is useful for a number of reasons.

- □ It enables a study of trends and progress over a number of years to be made.
- □ Comparisons with competitors and with general industry trends are possible.
- □ It can point the way towards possible or necessary improvements – necessary if the organization is performing less and less well than competitors, useful if new opportunities are spotted.
- □ It can reveal lost profit and growth potential.
- □ It can emphasize possible dangers – for example if stock turnover is decreasing or ratios affecting cash flow are moving adversely.

However, financial analysis concentrates on **efficiency** rather than **effectiveness** unless the objectives are essentially financial or economic ones. The real measure of success, as far as the strategic leader and the various stakeholders are concerned, is whether or not the objectives *they* perceive as important are being achieved (See Key Concept 6.1.)

Outside analysts, such as students and interested readers, can gain some insight into the apparent objectives of an organization by reading annual reports, articles, press releases and so on, but only the people involved in decision making know the real objectives. Financial analysis from the published (and easily obtained) results can be very informative and lead to conclusions about how well a company is performing, but certain aspects remain hidden. Decision makers inside an organization use financial analysis as part of the wider picture, but outsiders are more restricted. Financial analysis, then, is a very useful form of analysis, and it should be used, but the wider aspects should not be overlooked.

The achievement of objectives

Financial analysis may show that a particular organization is growing at a slower rate than its major competitors but that its profitability is considerably higher (the indices and ratios in question are considered later in this chapter). One might conclude that this is perfectly satisfactory or that the declining market share is a cause for concern. It is satisfactory if profitability is a central objective; it is worrying if the organization is seeking to grow and strengthen market share in its particular industry.

Major customers and suppliers are important stakeholders, and their expectations cannot be ignored. A supplier might grant extended credit in return for regular and guaranteed orders; a different supplier might agree to substantial discounts for fast payment of invoices. Whilst one can calculate the creditor turnover ratio and look at trends over a period, one may not know the causes behind the figures.

The analysis may disclose substantial investments in research and development, or in fixed assets, and these changes will affect certain ratios in the short term. The long-term implications and expectations of these investments may not be known outside the organization, but they may relate to important long-term objectives.

If the organization is paying increased attention to quality or service, or adding value to the product or service in some other way, this may be reflected in better

---

The most important facts are not always the obvious ones. It is a key attribute of the successful manager that he can assimilate a lot of information, and identify instinctively which particular items indicate that the business may be in danger of losing its direction.

Tom W. Cain, ex-Director, Human Resources, The Channel Tunnel Group Ltd

Key Concept 6.1
EFFICIENCY AND EFFECTIVENESS

There are three important measures of performance:

☐ **Economy**, which means 'doing things cost effectively'. Resources should be managed at the lowest possible cost consistent with achieving quantity and quality targets.
☐ **Efficiency**, which implies 'doing things right'. Resources should be deployed and utilized to maximize the returns from them.

Economy and efficiency measures are essentially quantitative and objective.

☐ **Effectiveness**, or 'doing the right things'. Resources should be allocated to those activities which satisfy the needs, expectations and priorities of the various stakeholders in the business.

Effectiveness relates to outcomes and need satisfaction, and consequently the measures are often qualitative and subjective.

Where economy, efficiency and effectiveness can be measured accurately and unambiguously it is appropriate to use the expression 'performance measures'. However if, as is frequently the case with effectiveness, precise measures are not possible, it can be more useful to utilize the term 'performance indicators'.

As the following chart indicates, only efficient and effective organizations will grow and prosper. Effective but inefficient businesses will survive but under-achieve; efficient but ineffective companies will decline as they cease to meet the expectations of their stakeholders.

	Ineffective	Effective
Inefficient	Corporate collapse	Survival
Efficient	Gradual decline	Growth and prosperity

Example: British Telecom

BT is determined to continue improving service levels for all customers, and, where it falls short of its own high standards, is improving its handling of customers' complaints.

(*Report to Shareholders*, February 1991)

Measures include:

☐ % of calls connecting at the first attempt;
☐ % of public payphones properly operational at any one time;
☐ % of orders completed by customers' confirmed dates;
☐ % of residential orders/business orders completed in 8/6; working days.

Repair services

☐ % faults cleared within 2 working days;
☐ % residential/business faults cleared within 9/5 working hours.

In isolation these measures relate to efficiency; if the selected service levels are acceptable to customers they are also measures of effectiveness.

Charities: a paradox

If a charity seeks to save money by minimizing administration and promotion expenditures it is focusing on short-term efficiency. If it concentrates on long-term effectiveness it may well be able to justify investing in marketing and administration in order to raise even more money.

A charity which spends some 60% of its current income on administration and marketing (and the rest on its directly charitable activities) could well, in the long run, be more effective than one which spends only 20% in this way.

The aim is to establish the most appropriate structure, administration network and promotional expenditure to achieve the purpose – and then run it efficiently.

performance figures through lower costs, higher profits or increased profitability. These figures may not reflect the long-term value of any strengthening of competitive advantage.

Where a company has important and identifiable shareholders with a substantial or significant shareholding in the organization, an effective strategic leader will ensure that he or she fully understands their expectations. The shareholders may be more concerned with short-term earnings than long-term growth in the value of their investment, or vice versa. It is important to know. Ratios will indicate where the company is performing well or badly in this respect, and by using the share price one can judge how the stock market (and in turn the shareholders) view the company at the moment; but again outside analysts cannot be absolutely clear as to whether the organization is fully meeting shareholder expectations.

Whilst it is feasible to measure outcomes and results, and compare them with stated objectives, it may not follow that the strategies pursued by the company have themselves generated the results. Case 6.1, British Tourist Authority, explores this issue.

The implementation of stated strategies

Another measure of how well the organization is doing concerns whether the strategies it decided to pursue are in fact being implemented. Linked to this is the issue of how strategic change is taking place, the incidence of incremental change and the impact of operative objectives. This relates back to Chapter 5, Figure 5.1. The important issue is one of management and control. How aware is the strategic leader, and is he or she satisfied with what is happening? Is the change process being managed effectively? The information system has a crucial role to play if managers are to be kept informed and aware.

If this analysis suggests that the change process is not being managed effectively –

prescribed strategies are not being implemented; incremental adaptive changes are not felt to be resulting in acceptable outcomes – there should be an examination of the causes. It could be that the organization has failed to appreciate or forecast certain changes in the environment, or has been caught out by changes in competitor strategies, or has experienced difficulties in implementing strategies because appropriate resources were not available. As a result the strategies themselves may need changing, or the implementation may need rethinking.

This situation assessment and evaluation of the possible need to change should be seen as a definite learning process by the strategic leader, who should seek to be constantly aware of changes taking place and changes that might be needed.

The need for change

Constant vigilance in this respect, then, supported by an effective information system will indicate where strategies need review. If decision makers in the organization are aware of how well it is doing and of environmental threats and opportunities and internal strengths and weaknesses, they can also address the important question: what is likely to happen if we carry on with present strategies? Is change needed?

Answering this question requires insight into competitive strategies, the relative success of competitors, changes in the environment, how good the organization's resources are, and how well they are being managed. These issues are the subject of the next chapters.

Stakeholder expectations

Chapter 5 showed that the organization is influenced by a number of stakeholders whose aspirations and expectations for the business may conflict. The organization's

Case 6.1
BRITISH TOURIST AUTHORITY (BTA)

The mission of the BTA is 'to strengthen the performance of Britain's tourist industry in international markets by encouraging people to visit Britain and encouraging the improvement and provision of tourist amenities and facilities'.

BTA objectives

The BTA has agreed the following long-term objectives:

1. Maximize the benefit to the economy of tourism to Britain from abroad.
2. Ensure that the Authority makes the most cost-effective use of resources in pursuing its objectives.

Resources, of course, are constrained by grants and the ability to agree joint-venture projects; and therefore the benefits generated are inevitably limited. With more money benefits could be increased – but when do they become less cost-effective to create?

3. Identify what visitors want and stimulate improvements in products and services to meet their needs.
4. Encourage off-peak tourism.
5. Spread the economic benefit of tourism more widely, and particularly to areas with tourism potential and higher-than-average levels of unemployment.

Objectives 3, 4 and 5 may well prove contradictory. Moreover, there will always be considerable elements of subjectivity and value judgement in establishing priority areas.

Measures of corporate performance

BTA could be judged to be successful if visitors (business people and tourists) come to Britain, if they come both off-season as well as in season [Objective 4], if they spend increasing amounts of money whilst they are here, if they spend in the preferred places [Objective 5], and if they go home and tell other people to come – and over a period this increases the number of visitors and their expenditure [Objective 1 explicitly and Objective 3 implicitly].

These are all measures of effectiveness, whilst Objective 2 addresses resource efficiency. However, there is a problem of cause and effect. Whilst the criteria listed above can all be measured, the net contribution of the BTA cannot be so easily ascertained. Tourists and business people would still come, regardless of the existence of the BTA. The cause and effect of BTA initiatives is very difficult to ascertain without extensive tracking studies which are prohibitively expensive. However, recent research shows that 27% of all visitors to the UK had visited a BTA office abroad.

It is believed implicitly that the activities undertaken around the world contribute to corporate objectives and performance, but really it is the activities (efficiencies) which are measured rather than the outcomes. Are particular promotions actually implemented? Are planned brochures published? Are desirable workshops and seminars attended?

objectives should balance the interests of all the stakeholders as effectively as possible. In achieving this, such aspects as product quality, availability and delivery, reliability, productivity and company image are important measures of success, in addition to purely financial criteria. Striving for success in any area, and achieving it, may result in poor performance in another. As a result, some stakeholders are satisfied but others are less satisfied.

Admired companies

Sound profits and a strong balance sheet are very important, but alone they will not necessarily lead to a company being 'admired' (*Economist*, 1991). Admiration encourages customers to buy more and to stay loyal, employees to work harder, suppliers to be more supportive and shareholders to also remain loyal. *The Economist* carried out a research project to establish which companies were most admired by other business people, particularly those with whom they compete directly. When business people were asked to allocate marks against certain criteria for their main rivals, Marks & Spencer received the overall highest mark. The criteria used were as follows: quality of management; financial soundness; value as a long-term investment; quality of products and services; the ability to attract, develop and retain top talent; capacity to innovate; quality of marketing; and community and environmental responsibility.

Rolls Royce were seen to have the highest quality products and the greatest capacity to innovate, and Amstrad the best marketing. Marks & Spencer scored particularly highly for their ability to attract, develop and retain top talent, their value as a long-term investment and their community and environmental responsibility. They received low scores for marketing and innovation. The latter is interesting because M & S pioneered sell-by dates and cash refunds in retailing. Like many other businesses M & S suffered during the recession, laying off staff and cutting recruitment in 1991, but their underlying strategy and competitiveness is perceived to be robust.

When respondents were asked to select category winners amongst all major companies, rather than simply within their own industry, Hanson proved to be the most admired, followed by Marks & Spencer and Glaxo.

FINANCIAL ANALYSIS

The published financial accounts of a company, as long as they are interpreted carefully, can tell a good deal about the company's activities and about how well it is doing. We shall concentrate on three main aspects, examining the financial measures and what they can tell us, and consider the strategic implications. The three aspects are as follows.

☐ **Investment:** How do the results relate to shareholders and the funds they have provided, and to the company's share price?
☐ **Performance:** How successfully is the business being run as a trading concern? Here we are not so much concerned with profit as with profitability. How well is the company using the capital it employs to generate sales and in turn profits?
☐ **Financial status:** Is the company solvent and liquid? Is it financially sound?

The ratios calculated in each of these categories have relevance for different stakeholders. Shareholders, and potential investors, are particularly concerned with the investment ratios. Performance ratios tell the strategic leader how well the company is doing as a business. Bankers and other providers of loan capital will want to know that the business is solvent and liquid in addition to how well it is performing. These points will be developed throughout this chapter.

This form of analysis is most relevant for profit-seeking businesses, although some of the measures can prove quite enlightening when applied to not-for-profit organizations.

Ratios are calculated from the published accounts of organizations, but an analysis of just one set of results will only be partly helpful. Trends are particularly important, and therefore the changes in results over a number of years should be evaluated. Care should be taken to ensure that the results are not considered in isolation of external trends in the economy or industry. For example the company's sales may be growing quickly, but how do they compare with those of their competitors and the industry as a whole? Similarly, slow growth may be explained by industry contraction, although in turn this might indicate the need for diversification.

Hence industry averages and competitor performance should be used for comparisons. One problem here is that different companies may present their accounts in different ways and the figures will have to be interpreted before any meaningful comparisons can be made. Furthermore the industry may be composed of companies of varying sizes and various degrees of conglomeration and diversification. For this reason certain companies may be expected to behave differently from their competitors.

In addition it can be useful to compare the actual results with forecasts, although these will not normally be available to people outside the organization. The usefulness is dependent on how well the forecasts and budgets were prepared.

Financial statements

The two most important statements which are used for calculating ratios are the profit and loss account and the balance sheet, simplified versions of which are illustrated in Tables 6.1 and 6.2. The full accounts may be required in order to make certain adjustments.

Table 6.1 Simplified profit and loss account

			£
	Sales/turnover		
Less:	Cost of goods sold		
		equals	Gross profit
Less:	Depreciation		
	Selling costs		
	Administration costs		
		equals	Profit before interest and tax[a]
Less:	Interest on loans		
		equals	Profit before tax
Less:	Tax		
		equals	Profit after tax
Less:	Dividends		
		equals	Retained earnings (transferred to balance sheet)

[a] In published accounts this figure will not normally be shown. It is required, however, for the calculation of certain ratios.

From the **profit and loss account** (Table 6.1) we wish to extract a number of figures. **Gross profit** is the trading profit before overheads are allocated. It is the difference between the value of sales (or turnover) and the direct costs involved in producing the product(s) or service(s), which is known as the **contribution**. In the case of multi-product or multi-service organizations, where it may be difficult to attribute overheads to different products and services accurately, comparison should be made between the contributions from different divisions or strategic business units.

When depreciation and selling and administrative overheads are subtracted from gross profit the remainder is **profit before interest and before tax**. This is the net profit that the organization has achieved from its trading activities; no account has yet been taken of the cost of funding. This figure is not normally shown in published accounts; it has to be calculated by adding interest back onto profit before tax.

Profit before tax is the figure resulting

when interest charges have been removed. Tax is levied on this profit figure, and when this is deducted **profit after tax** remains. This represents the profits left for shareholders, and a proportion will be paid over to them immediately in the form of dividends; the remainder will be re-invested in the future growth of the company. It will be transferred to the balance sheet as retained earnings (or profit and loss) and shown as a reserve attributable to shareholders.

Balance sheets are now normally laid out in the format illustrated in Table 6.2. Assets are shown at the top and the capital employed to finance the assets below.

Fixed assets comprise all the land, property, plant and equipment owned by the business. These will be depreciated annually at varying rates. Balance sheets generally reflect historical costs (the preferred accounting convention), but occasionally assets may be revalued to account for inflation (land and property values can increase significantly over a number of years) and any ratios calculated from an asset figure will be affected by this issue of up-to-date valuations.

Current assets, assets which are passing through the business rather than more permanent features and which comprise stocks (raw materials, work-in-progress and finished goods), debtors (customers who are allowed to buy on credit rather than for cash), investments and cash, are added on. **Current liabilities**, short-term financial commitments, are deducted. These include the overdraft, tax payments due and trade creditors (suppliers who have yet to be paid for goods and services supplied). The resulting figure is **net assets**.

This is equal to **the total capital employed in the business**, which comprises long-term loans and shareholders' funds. **Long-term loans** are typically called 'creditors: amounts falling due after more than one year'. Shareholders' **funds** are made up of the called up share capital (the face value of the shares issued), the share premium account (money accrued as shareholders have bought shares for more than their face value, dependent on stock market prices at the time of sale), any revaluation reserve (resulting from revaluation of assets) and retained earnings (past profits re-invested in the business).

Balance sheets balance. Net assets are

Table 6.2   Simplified balance sheet

	Fixed assets (less depreciation)	(Land; property; buildings; plant and equipment)
plus	**Current assets**	(Stock; debtors; cash and investments)
less	**Current liabilities**	(Creditors: amounts falling due within one year; specifically trade creditors; overdraft; taxation not yet paid)
equals	**Net assets**	
	Long-term loans	Generally termed creditors: amounts falling due after more than one year
plus	**Shareholders' funds**	(Called-up share capital; share premium account; revaluation reserve; profit and loss account)
equals	**Total capital employed**	
Net assets	equals	**Total capital employed**

equal to the capital employed to finance them. However, it should be appreciated that the accounts of many companies include long-term loans as an asset and deduct them before calculating net assets; the 'total capital employed' used for balancing is then shareholders' funds. The ratios and calculations shown in this chapter use the Table 6.2 convention rather than this approach.

Investment ratios

The five key investment ratios are explained in Table 6.3, and the linkages between four of them are illustrated in Figure 6.1.

The **return on shareholders' funds** deals with the profit available for ordinary shareholders after all other commitments (including preference share dividends) have been met; and it is divided by all the funds provided both directly and indirectly by ordinary shareholders. 'The return on shareholders' funds is probably the most important single measure of all. It takes into account

the return on net assets, the company's tax position, and the extent to which capital employed has been supplied other than by the ordinary shareholders (for example by loans)' (Reid and Myddelton, 1974). Table 6.4 illustrates that this ratio has been steadily increasing for Marks & Spencer during the 1980s as the UK economy has become stronger. If we also look at Table 6.10 later in this chapter we can see that the improvement has coincided with a growth in turnover (in actual figures, and in real terms after accounting for inflation), albeit at a declining rate as the economy entered into recession. Table 6.4 further shows that earnings per share have increased at a faster rate than the return on shareholders' funds.

Earnings per share indicates how much money the company has earned in relation to the number of ordinary shares. Taken in isolation this measure is useful if considered over a number of years (as it is in Table 6.4). Companies can be compared with each other if the ratio is linked to the current market price of shares. This calculation provides the price-to-earnings ratio P/E.

Table 6.3 Investment ratios

Ratio	Calculation	Comments
Return on shareholders' funds (%)	$\dfrac{\text{profit after tax}}{\text{total shareholders' funds}}$	Measures the return on investment by shareholders in the company The more unstable the industry and the company, the higher this will be expected to be
Earnings per share (pence)	$\dfrac{\text{profit after tax}}{\text{number of ordinary shares issued}}$	Profit after tax represents earnings for the shareholders. It can be returned to them immediately as dividends or re-invested as additional shareholders' funds (retained earnings)
Price-to-earnings ratio P/E	$\dfrac{\text{current market price of ordinary shares}}{\text{earnings per share}}$	Indicates the multiple of earnings that investors are willing to pay for shares in the stock market The higher the ratio, the more favourably the company is perceived
Dividend yield (%)	$\dfrac{\text{dividend per share}}{\text{market price per share}}$	Equivalent to rate of interest per cent paid on the investment Shareholders will not expect it to equal say building society rates – re-invested profits should generate longer-term increases in the share price
Dividend cover (number of times)	$\dfrac{\text{earnings per share}}{\text{dividend per share}}$	The number of times the dividends *could* have been paid from the earnings The higher the better

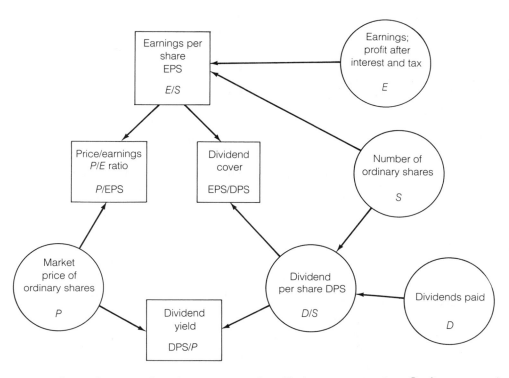

Figure 6.1 Linkages between four investment ratios: □, investment ratios; ○, figures required for calculating ratios. (Note: The two figures required to calculate each ratio are shown leading into the box.)

Table 6.4 Marks & Spencer plc: Growth in earnings, 1986–1991

Year ending 31 March	Return on shareholders' funds (%)	Earnings per 25p ordinary share (pence)
1986	15.3	8.4
1987	17.5	10.4
1988	15.0	12.2
1989	17.9	12.9
1990	17.9	14.5
1991	16.4	14.7

The price-to-earnings ratio

Table 6.5 illustrates the *P/E* for Marks & Spencer at a range of relevant share prices in relation to the 1990–1 earnings per share. Also included are the *P/Es* for a range of retailers in relation to their share prices at the end of 1991. The figures for the highly publicized and successful Body Shop chain stand out against the others.

The *P/E* ratio indicates the amount (how many times the current earnings figure) that potential shareholders are willing to pay in order to buy shares in the company at a particular time. It is affected by previous success and profits, but really it is an indication of expectations. The more confidence the market has in a company, generally the higher will be its *P/E*. It can also indicate relatively how expensive borrowing is for the company. If the company opts to raise money from existing shareholders by offering new shares in a rights issue (the shareholders are invited to buy new shares in fixed proportion to those they already hold) the higher the *P/E* is, the cheaper is the capital. A high *P/E* implies that shareholders will pay many times current earnings to obtain shares.

The *P/E* ratio is also very important in acquisition situations. Consider two companies as an example. Company A has issued

Table 6.5   Marks & Spencer plc: Price to earnings ratios

Earnings per share: year ending 31 March 1991 = 14.7 pence.

Share price: during 1990 the price ranged from 272.5 pence to 181.0 pence for 25 pence ordinary shares.

P/E ratio: at price 181.0,   P/E = 12.3
at price 220.0   P/E = 15.0
at price 272.5   P/E = 18.5

Major retailers, *P/E* ratios, end-1991

Argos	18.5	Marks & Spencer	18.1
Asda	4.4	Ratners	1.8
Body Shop	43.8	W H Smith	15.3
Boots	16.7	J Sainsbury	14.7
Dixons	19.0	Tesco	13.8
Kwik Save	12.7		

Source: *Financial Times*.

500 000 ordinary shares with a face value of 25p and their current market price is 600p. Current earnings per share are 20p (£100 000 in total). Hence the *P/E* is 600/20 = 30.

Company A looks attractive to the shareholders of company B when it makes a bid for their shares. B also has 500 000 shares issued, again with a face value of 25p, but they are trading at only 150p as company B has been relatively sleepy of late and growth has been below the average for the industry. With earnings per share of 10p (£50 000 in total) the *P/E* is 15.

A offers one new share in company A for every three shares in B (perhaps more generous than it need be), and the shareholders in B accept. A–B now has 666 667 shares issued; at the moment the combined earnings are £150 000. If the stock market, and the shareholders, are confident that A can turn B round and increase earnings significantly the current *P/E* of 30 could remain. If so the new price of shares in the combined A–B is 675p. Earnings per share are 22½p (£150 000/ 666 667 shares).

A's share price has in effect risen, possibly making it appear an even more successful company. Any company wishing to acquire A will now have to pay more. Equally A's

ability to acquire further companies on the lines above has been enhanced.

The price-to-earnings ratio and earnings per share are measures which are most applicable to companies whose shares are traded on the stock market.

Two dividend ratios

The **dividend yield** provides the rate of interest that shareholders are receiving in relation to the current market price for shares. It must be used cautiously as it takes no account of the price that people actually paid (historically) to buy their shares; and in any case shareholders are often more interested in long-term capital growth.

The **dividend cover** indicates the proportion of earnings paid out in dividends and the proportion re-invested. Company dividend policies will vary between companies, and, for example, a decision to maintain or reduce dividends in the face of reduced earnings will be influenced by the predicted effect upon share prices and in turn the valuation of the company, which as we saw above can be an issue in acquisitions.

Quoted companies can also be analysed by considering the movement of their share price against the Financial Times 100 Shares Index or the All Shares Index, and against the index of shares for their particular industry. Under- and over-performance of the shares is a further reflection of investors' confidence and expectations.

Performance ratios

Tables 6.6 and 6.8 (later) explain the various performance ratios.

Profitability

The **return on net assets** or the **return on capital employed** uses profit before interest and before tax and compares it with the assets, or capital employed, used in the business to create the profit. Actual profit is important as it determines the amount of money that a company has available for paying dividends (once interest and tax are deducted) and for re-investment. But it is also important to examine how well the money invested in the business is being used – this is **profitability**. This particular ratio ignores how the business is actually funded, making it a measure of how well the business is performing as a trading concern. It was mentioned earlier that contributions from different products or strategic business units should be compared in the case of multi-product organizations. The return on net assets should also be used to compare the profitabilities of products and strategic business units. In this way the ratio can be used for evaluating particular competitive strategies and the relative importance to the business of different products. However, this measure should not be used in isolation from an assessment of the relative importance of different products in terms of turnover. High volume products or divisions may be less profitable than smaller volume ones for a variety of reasons, which we shall examine when we look at portfolio analysis.

This ratio is particularly useful when it is examined in the light of the two ratios which comprise it. The top of Table 6.7 shows how the return on net assets is equal to the profit margin times the net asset turnover.

The **profit margin** is the proportion of sales revenue represented by profits (before interest and tax); the **net asset turnover** illustrates how well the company is utilizing its assets in order to generate sales. It can be seen from Table 6.7 that different companies exhibit different patterns even in the same industry. Case 6.2, Kwik Save, compares Kwik Save with Marks & Spencer, demonstrating how different strategies will create different ratio patterns.

Certain companies will adopt strategies which are designed to yield good profit margins on every item sold, and as a result probably add value into the product or service in such a way that their assets are not producing the same amount of sales per pound sterling as is the case for a company which uses assets more aggressively, adds less value, and makes a lower profit margin. Particular industries and businesses may offer little choice in this respect; others offer considerable choice.

If a decision is reached that for the business as a whole, or some part of it, the return on net assets (profitability) must be improved, there are two approaches. Either profits must be increased, or assets reduced, or both. Figure 6.2 illustrates the alternatives available

Table 6.6 Performance ratios

Ratio	Calculation	Comments
Return on net assets Return on capital employed (%)	$\dfrac{\text{profit before interest and before tax}}{\text{total capital employed in the business}}$	Measures the relative success of the business as a trading concern Trading profit less overheads is divided by shareholders' funds and other long-term loans Useful for measuring and comparing the relative performance of different divisions/strategic business units
Profit margin (%)	$\dfrac{\text{profit before interest and before tax}}{\text{sales (turnover)}}$	Shows trading profit less overheads as a percentage of turnover Again useful for comparing divisions, products, markets
Net asset turnover (number of times)	$\dfrac{\text{sales}}{\text{total net assets or capital employed in the business}}$	It measures the number of times the capital is 'turned over' in a year Or: the number of pounds of sales generated for every pound invested in the company

Table 6.7   An analysis of performance ratios for different companies

Sector	Company	Results (year)	Return on net assets (%)	=	Profit margin (%)	×	Net asset turnover (times)
			Profit		Profit		Sales
			Net assets		Sales		Net assets
Retailing	Tesco	1991	18.1		6.6		2.74
	Kwik Save	1990	39.5		4.7		8.4
Engineering	Weir Group	1990	25.0		6.3		3.97
	Vickers	1990	21.0		9.3		2.26
Electronics	Amstrad	1990	17.1		8.7		1.97
	GEC	1991	23.2		8.2		2.83
Chemicals	Allied Colloids	1991	26.2		16.2		1.62
	British Vita	1990	26.8		8.1		3.3
Brewing	Eldridge Pope	1990	0.7		1.3		0.54
	Scottish & Newcastle	1991	14.5		20.2		0.72
Glass	Pilkington	1991	10.4		6.9		1.51
Packaging	J Waddington	1991	18.0		7.6		2.37
Property	Mountleigh	1991	(2.8)		(10.3)		0.27
		1987	14.3		28.0		0.51
	Savills	1991	(11.3)		(5.9)		1.92
		1988	67.5		19.6		3.44
Textiles	Readicut	1991	18.6		6.6		2.82
	Sirdar	1991	16.5		10.3		1.60
	Allied Textiles	1990	25.1		6.9		3.64
	SR Gent	1991	8.2		3.6		2.28

Source: MicroExstat.

to the organization, and at the bottom the functional responsibilities. Hence a corporate or competitive strategy change will result in changes to functional strategies. This will be developed further in Chapter 19 when we consider turnaround strategies for companies experiencing difficulties.

Other useful performance ratios

Table 6.8 explains **stock turnover** and **debtor turnover** which both indicate how well the company is managing two of its current assets. The stock turnover will depend on how the company is managing its operations – different strategies will lead to higher or lower stocks. Low stocks (high stock turnover) save costs, but they can make the business vulnerable if they are reduced to too low a level in order to save money and result

in production delays. Debtor turnover, for certain types of business, looked at over a period can show whether the company is successful at persuading credit customers to pay quickly. This can affect the marketing strategy if decisions have to be taken not to supply certain customers who are slow payers.

The **gross profit margin** and the **selling and administration costs to sales ratio** are useful for indicating the percentage of turnover attributable to overheads. If a company has a high gross profit margin but is relatively unprofitable after accounting for overheads it is a sign of poor management. The product or service is able to command a price comfortably in excess of direct costs (direct labour and materials) but this contribution is being swallowed by overheads which are possibly too high and in need of reduction. Such a company is appropriate for restructuring and perhaps acquisition. Again these ratios

---

Case 6.2
KWIK SAVE

Kwik Save compete with grocery giants like Sainsbury and Tesco, but they have an individual strategy. Whilst Asda, Sainsbury and Tesco (together with other competitors) have built ever bigger stores, developed own-brand alternatives, and introduced non-food items, Kwik Save have concentrated on having a large number of smaller well-located units selling a limited range of branded products at competitive prices. Choice is therefore more limited than in some other stores, and less is invested in shopper comforts, but this is compensated for in the prices. The basic message is 'Everything is kept simple.'

The end result is lower overheads, which reduces the breakeven level in every store. Consequently Kwik Save turn over their assets approximately eight times per year, more times than their main rivals. Combined with a profit margin of some 5% (which compares quite favourably with other grocery supermarket chains) this yields a profitability of 40%. This is higher than most of their rivals.

In comparison Marks & Spencer (1990–1 figures) have a profit margin twice that of Kwik Save, but because they invest far more in their stores and offer a wider range of products (albeit under only one brand name) their asset turnover is 2.0 times, substantially less than that of Kwik Save.

Whilst the strategy has proved very successful Kwik Save are aware of one drawback. By concentrating on selling only food they are vulnerable to the introduction of Sunday trading. Stores offering a wider range of products are likely to benefit far more than food stores. In addition, their success is attracting direct competition from rivals like Aldi, the German supermarket chain which has opened a number of stores in the UK. Whilst Kwik Save offer some 2500 product lines (Sainsbury and Tesco have over 20 000) and price between 5 and 10% lower than the giants, Aldi offer just 600 lines and discounts of over 20%.

In the early 1990s Kwik Save have been opening one new store per week, financed by a strong internal cash flow. They have almost no debt.

---

should be examined over a period of years to ensure that the overhead burden is not creeping up without just cause. In terms of increasing profits (to improve profitability (Figure 6.2)) it may be easier to reduce overheads than to reduce direct costs.

Measures of financial status

Measures of financial status can be divided into two groups: solvency and liquidity. The ratios are explained in Table 6.9.

Solvency

The major ratios are the **debt ratio** and **interest cover**. The debt ratio relates to the company's gearing – how much it is funded by equity capital (shareholders' funds) and how much by long-term loans. Loans generally carry fixed interest payments, and these must be met regardless of any profit fluctuations; a company can elect not to pay dividends to shareholders if profits collapse, which gives it more flexibility.

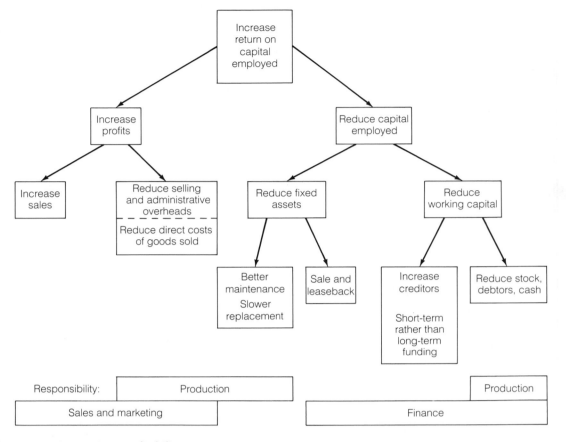

Figure 6.2 Improving profitability.

Table 6.8 Other useful performance ratios

Ratio	Calculation	Comments
Stock turnover (number of times)	$\dfrac{\text{turnover}}{\text{stock}}$	Shows how quickly stocks move through the business. Logically the quicker the better – as long as it does not result in stock shortages Most accurate measurement from *average* stock level over the year rather than the balance sheet figure
Debtor turnover (number of times; or days of credit given)	$\dfrac{\text{turnover}}{\text{debtors}}$ $\dfrac{\text{debtors}}{\text{turnover}} \times 365$	Shows how quickly credit customers pay. Again use *average* debtors Retail organizations, like Marks & Spencer, sell mostly for cash, or charge interest for credit through their credit cards A similar measure, credit purchases/average creditors, shows how much credit time is received by the company
Gross profit margin (%) and	$\dfrac{\text{gross profit}}{\text{turnover (sales)}}$	Indicates percentage profit before overheads
Selling and administration costs to sales (%)	$\dfrac{\text{selling and administration costs}}{\text{turnover (sales)}}$	Shows overheads (indirect costs) in relation to turnover

Table 6.9 Measures of financial status

Ratio	Calculation	Comments
Solvency		
Debt ratio (%)	$\dfrac{\text{long-term loans}}{\text{total capital employed}}$	The lower the debt ratio the more the company is cushioned against fluctuations in trading profits
Interest cover (number of times)	$\dfrac{\text{profit before interest and before tax}}{\text{interest on long-term loans}}$	Indicates how many times the interest is covered by earnings. Sometimes argued banks expect a figure of at least three times
Liquidity		
Current ratio (ratio *x*:1) (also known as working capital ratio)	$\dfrac{\text{current assets}}{\text{current liabilities}}$	Shows the extent to which short-term assets are able to meet short-term liabilities. 1.5:1 and 2:1 both suggested as indicative targets. Also suggested that working capital (current assets minus current liabilities) should exceed stock
Liquidity or acid test ratio (ratio *x*:1)	$\dfrac{\text{liquid assets (i.e. current assets less stock)}}{\text{current liabilities}}$	This shows how liquid the company is relative to short-term liabilities. Stock is excluded as it can take months to turn into cash

Managers and investors will both be wary of the debt ratio creeping up, as it does when companies borrow money from the banking system to finance investment or acquisitions. In fact acquisitive companies must relate their acquisition strategies to their ability to finance them. Sometimes money can be raised from shareholders, but the company must be confident that shareholders will subscribe to rights issues. If not, and the shares have to be sold to the banks who underwrite the issue (who then sell them when the price is appropriate), blocks of shares can be bought up by other acquisitive companies and this can pose a threat. The alternative is long-term loans, and the higher the proportion these constitute, the more stable profits need to be. This is taken up later in the book.

Interest cover shows by how much the interest payments are covered by profits.

Liquidity

The two main liquidity ratios, the **current ratio** and the **acid test (liquidity) ratio**, relate to working capital. Has the company sufficient money available to meet its short-term commitments? They are determined by the flow of cash in and out of the business. A shortage of cash, and commitments to meet, will push the company towards increased borrowings (say a larger overdraft), and this will increase interest commitments.

Whilst targets of 1.5:1 and 2.0:1 are sometimes quoted for the current ratio, these should be treated with some caution. Companies who trade mainly in cash, rather than allow credit, are likely to have a ratio much nearer 1:1 and still be perfectly liquid. Retailers and breweries, both used as examples in this chapter, are cases in point.

A company will experience liquidity problems if it invests in stock and then fails to win orders or if it fails to control its debtors. Conversely a successful company can have cash problems. Success at winning orders may require investment in machinery or stocks and labour, and these may have to be paid for before and during production and before the goods are delivered and paid for by customers. This can lead to temporary illiquidity, and is known as over-trading.

Cash flow, therefore, can be just as important as profitability. Where demand is seasonal for certain products production may take place when sales are low, in advance of peak demand. This puts pressure on cash

Table 6.10   Marks & Spencer plc: Turnover adjusted for inflation

Year ended 31 March	Turnover (£ million)	Index of growth (1983 = 100)	Annual year-on-year growth (%)	Value of 1983 pound (pence)	Adjusted index of growth (1983 = 100)	Annual year-on-year growth after inflation (%)
1990	5608	223	9.5	69.1	154	1.3
1989	5122	204	11.9	74.4	152	4.8
1988	4578	182	8.5	79.9	145	4.3
1987	4221	168	13	82.6	139	8.6
1986	3735	149	16	85.8	128	10
1985	3208	128	12	90.6	116	7
1984	2863	114	14	95.1	108.4	8.4
1983	2510	100		100	100	

flow in the way outlined above. This must affect corporate strategy in terms of the range of products, services and businesses selected, competitive strategies in terms of the way they are marketed (to avoid the worst implications of seasonal fluctuations) and functional production, marketing and financial strategies.

It is not unusual for companies to be slow in paying their bills when their performance is poor. This impacts upon their customers, and highlights the importance of cash flow, particularly in a recession.

Cash flow can be improved in a number of ways, for example, by

☐ increased turnover – but only if linked to:
☐ effective management of debtors and creditors;
☐ higher operating profit margins;
☐ reduced tax payments;
☐ reduced investment in working capital and/or fixed assets;
☐ improved gearing to reduce interest payments.

The movement of cash in and out of the business during a year is reflected in a Source and Application of Funds Statement, but this will not illustrate temporary illiquidity.

Accounting for inflation

It is an accounting convention to use historical costs and within the accountancy profession there is on-going debate and disagreement about how best to treat inflation. This topic is outside the scope of this book. However, it is important to take some account of inflation when looking at growth rates for actual data such as turnover and profits as otherwise companies appear to be doing far better than in reality they are.

A simple example is featured in Table 6.10. In making adjustments of this type the actual turnover (or profit) figures must be reduced by in effect taking a constant value of the pound (or other relevant currency). A 1990 pound was worth less than a 1983 pound (the base year for this comparison) as a result of inflation.

Other quantitative performance indicators

In addition to all these financial ratios, businesses will typically collect and evaluate information concerning the performance of all the activities being undertaken. For each functional area there will be a number of measures, such as the value of orders acquired by every salesperson, machine utilization, turnover at every retail outlet, output per shift, productivity per employee and absenteeism. Performance will be evaluated against targets or objectives agreed with individual managers who should be held accountable. These are measures of resource efficiency. They are important control measures which evaluate the efficiency of each functional area of the business. Improvements can strengthen the company's competitive capability. In isolation, however, these measures do not indicate how successful the company is strategically. This particular issue is very significant for not-for-profit organizations which cannot use the traditional profitability ratios sensibly and at the same time cannot readily measure their effectiveness in relation to their fundamental purpose. Consequently they often rely more on quantitative measures of efficiency. This is the subject of the next section.

Service businesses

In addition to the above measures, the ability to retain customers is a key requirement for service businesses. Retention implies customer satisfaction and probably word-of-mouth recommendation. It is likely to result in higher profits because of the high costs incurred in attracting new business. Moreover, customers are likely to increase their level of spending over time. For insurance companies the cost of processing renewals is far cheaper than the cost of finding new clients; and many people will take out additional policies with a company they feel they can rely upon.

Insurance companies have a critical and unique solvency measure concerning the ratio of balance sheet capital to non-life premium income. Legally it must be above 16%, and brokers expect it to remain above 50%. London (1991) has reported that since 1989 the ratio has been falling dramatically for some of the largest insurers; and he forecasted 1992 figures of 27% for Royal Insurance (55% in 1989), 36% for Guardian Royal Exchange (82%), and 40% (88%) for Eagle Star. These falls have been the result of property losses, especially in mortgage indemnity insurance. It is arguable that the insurers have lost rather than benefited from offering substantial commissions to building societies in return for exclusive contracts for house insurance.

Key performance measures for solicitors are their ability to achieve results for their clients, and the service they offer, measurable by, for instance, the speed with which they respond to letters and telephone calls.

THE MEASUREMENT OF SUCCESS IN NOT-FOR-PROFIT ORGANIZATIONS

It was suggested in Chapter 5 that the objectives of not-for-profit organizations are often stated in terms of resource efficiency because of the difficulty of quantifying their real purpose. As a result, the measures of their success that are utilized in practice may not be closely related to their real mission and purpose. Where this happens, financial and other quantitative measures are being used as the measures of performance, and efficiency not effectiveness is being evaluated. In other words, performance and success is being measured, but despite the usefulness of, and need for, the measures being used, they may not be assessing strategic performance directly in relation to the mission. These points are expanded below.

Drucker (1989) comments that many not-for-profit organizations are in fact more money conscious than business enterprises are because the funding they need is hard to raise. Moreover, they could invariably use more money than they have available. Money, though, is less likely to be the key element of their mission and strategic thinking than are the provision of services and the satisfaction of client needs. Given this premise, the successful performance of a not-for-profit organization should be measured in terms of outcomes and need satisfaction. Money then becomes a major constraint upon what can be accomplished and the appropriate level of expectations.

The outcomes, in turn, must be analysed against the expectations of the important stakeholders. For many organizations in this sector this involves both beneficiaries of the service and volunteer helpers as well as financial supporters and paid employees. Typically their personal objectives and expectations will differ.

But what is the case in reality? How difficult is it to measure performance and success in this way? Fundamentally the Boy Scout and Girl Guide organizations are concerned with helping youngsters develop and grow into confident and capable young men and women. But do they evaluate their success in this respect or in terms of, say, membership and monetary income which, being essentially quantitative, are far easier to measure? Similarly, it would be inadequate to claim success because of a general feeling that good was being done and that young people must be benefiting from their membership. The real measures of success concern the changes that take place outside the organization as a result of the organization's efforts.

As another example, the success of local meals-on-wheels services is related to their impact on the health and life expectancy of the elderly rather than to the number of meals served or the cost per meal.

The performance and effectiveness of the education system relates to the impact on pupils after they leave the system, their parents, the taxpayers who fund education and future employers. Their perspectives will differ, and their individual aspirations and expectations will be difficult to quantify and measure. It is far easier to measure efficiency in the way that resources are utilized – for example by class sizes, staff–student or staff–pupil ratios, building occupancy and examination performance.

Similarly, local authorities exist to serve local residents, and their mission is concerned with making the area a better place to live. Would all the residents agree on what is implied by 'a better place to live', and could changes be objectively measured and evaluated? Because of the difficulties, value for money from the resources invested is more likely to be considered, and improvements in the efficiency of service provision sought.

The not-for-profit sector is increasingly attempting to measure effectiveness in terms of impacts and outcomes rather than efficiency alone. The task is not straightforward.

Value for money looks at the relationship between the perceived value of the output (by the stakeholders involved) and the cost of inputs. Essentially it is used as a comparative measure. There are too many uncertainties for there to be any true agreement on the magnitude of 'very best value', and consequently one is seeking to ensure that good value is being provided, when measured against that of other similar, or competitive, providers.

Case 6.3 considers changes in two privatized industries, both of which are subject to external regulation, and in the NHS.

Jackson and Palmer (1989) emphasize that if performance is to be measured more effectively in the public sector, then the implicit cultural and change issues must also be addressed. The climate must be right, with managers committed to thinking clearly about what activities should be measured and what the objectives of these activities are. This may well involve different reward systems linked to revised expectations. This approach, they suggest, leads managers to move on from measuring the numbers of passengers on British Rail to analysing how many had seats and how punctual the trains were; and measuring and analysing the numbers of patients re-admitted to hospital after treatment, rather than just the numbers of patients who are admitted and the rate of usage of hospital beds. Jackson and Palmer also emphasize the importance of asking users about how effective they perceive organizations to be.

Case 6.3
EFFECTIVENESS AND PUBLIC SERVICES

YORKSHIRE WATER

Since privatization in 1989, Yorkshire Water Services (like all the other privatized water companies) has to report annually to external regulators on the service levels provided to customers. These relate to:

☐ the availability of water resources to meet supply demands;
☐ the reliability and adequacy of the water supply distribution system – i.e. water pressures and interruptions to supply;
☐ the adequacy of the sewerage system; and
☐ the speed of response to customer queries and complaints.

There are a number of specified measures and achievement targets for these service issues.

BRITISH GAS

British Gas was privatized in 1986, since when the Director General of Ofgas (Office of Gas Supply) has set standards for, amongst other things:

☐ the time it takes to respond to gas leaks; and
☐ how soon new customers can be connected.

If British Gas consistently fails to achieve its service targets, a price cut can be imposed.

In addition, there is a price formula for domestic prices, agreed between British Gas and Ofgas. After 1991 annual price changes are to be 5 percentage points less than the current rate of inflation. If inflation is below 5%, prices should be reduced. This formula is designed to drive efficiency and productivity.

THE NATIONAL HEALTH SERVICE

Prime Minister John Major announced a new Citizen's Charter in July 1991. This implied a change of attitude for the NHS – patients should be seen as customers with rights, rather than people who should be grateful for treatment, however long the wait. From April 1992 hospitals have had to set standards for maximum waiting times.

This followed on from the 1989 NHS White Paper: *Working for Patients*, which was designed to achieve:

(a) raising the performance of all hospitals and GPs to the level of the best (significant differences existed in measured performances);
(b) patients receiving better health care and a greater choice of services through improved efficiencies and effectiveness in the use of NHS resources;
(c) greater satisfaction and rewards for NHS staff.

To achieve these, a number of structural changes have since been introduced.

☐ Individual hospitals have been able to become autonomous self-governing trusts (within the NHS) instead of being administered by health authorities.

Continued overleaf

☐ Hospitals are free to treat any patient and GPs are free to book treatment at any hospital. Arrangements depend upon the prices charged by individual hospitals for the treatment, and the ability and willingness of health authorities or GPs to pay. These changes imply:

  ☐ competition between hospitals in respect of services (available beds and staff) and prices
  ☐ the opportunity for patients and their doctors to select a preferred hospital
  ☐ a need for health authorities to determine clear priorities within specified budgets.

☐ Certain General Practices, depending upon the number of patients, can apply for their own NHS budget, which they can then spend as they deem most appropriate. This also assumes that, in the long run, GPs will be able to offer a better service because it will be easier for patients to change their GPs.

In addition:

☐ Hospitals are required to give patients individual and reliable appointment times, and generally more and speedier information.
☐ Future investments have to be properly justified.
☐ There is pressure to reduce further the cost of drugs, by, say, using generic rather than branded products.
☐ Local pay arrangements have been made more flexible to provide better reward systems.

In short, hospitals and GPs have been made more accountable, and at the same time, given more responsibility and authority to encourage them to provide a better overall service for their customers. The ultimate aim: 'the best value for money'.

SUMMARY

In this chapter we considered the question: How are we doing? It has been emphasized that success should really be measured in relation to the achievement of objectives. Companies can be regarded as successful if they are achieving the objectives set by the key stakeholders. It is also important to consider the implementation of strategies created to achieve the objectives, together with the control and understanding that the strategic leader has of incremental changes.

The need for the strategic leader to be aware of what is happening and the learning process involved in evaluating the need for change were emphasized, together with the importance of considering what might happen if the organization continues with present strategies.

It has been pointed out, though, that financial measures are normally used to evaluate performance. As these may not refer to objectives held by stakeholders they may be a measure of efficiency rather than effectiveness.

Specifically

☐ a simplified profit and loss account and balance sheet have been outlined and analysed

W H SMITH GROUP PLC: DATA FOR QUESTION 1

Extracts from Profit and Loss Account and Balance Sheet, 1 June 1991

	£ million		£ million	£ million
Sales	1970.6	Fixed assets		449.4
Cost of goods sold	1404.7	Current assets:		
Gross profit	565.9	Stocks	221.4	
Overheads	453.7	Debtors	100.7	
Trading profit	112.2	Others[a]	45.3	
Other income	7.4	Cash	34.1	
Interest	30.6		401.5	
Tax	27.8	Pension prepayment	37.6	
Profit after interest and tax	61.2	Current liabilities	417.9	
Dividends paid	27.4	Working capital		21.2
Retained profit (after extraordinary				
items)	18.4	Net assets		470.6
		Long-term loans		193.8
Number of ordinary shares	211 193 000	Minority interests and provisions		24.0
Year end share price	375 pence	Shareholders' funds		252.8
		Total capital employed		470.6

[a] Assets in the course of disposal, i.e. travel and television interests.

☐ major investment, performance and financial status ratios have been explained and examples have been provided

☐ the need to consider several years, rather than one in isolation, has been emphasized and the value of intercompany comparisons (within the same industry) and interdivisional evaluations have been considered

☐ the importance of share prices and the *P/E* ratio for quoted companies has been emphasized

☐ the importance of profitability measures (rather than profit alone) has been highlighted and it has been pointed out that cash flow can be just as important as profitability

☐ a number of issues and difficulties in measuring the performance of not-for-profit organizations have been discussed.

Performance measures are also dealt with in Chapter 23.

CHECKLIST OF KEY TERMS AND CONCEPTS

You should be confident that you can calculate the major financial ratios and that you understand their meaning. The question on the W H Smith Group below includes a list of the main ratios; you should work them out before checking your answers with those provided.

QUESTIONS AND RESEARCH ASSIGNMENTS

1. W H Smith Group is a leading retailer of books, magazines, stationery, recorded music and video and a major wholesaler of

magazines and newspapers. Until 1991 W H Smith also had interests in travel and television.

Extracts from the 1990–1 Profit and Loss Account and Balance Sheet are provided above, together with a share price for the end of May 1991.

(a) Calculate the following ratios for the W H Smith Group plc:

> *Investment ratios:*
> Return on shareholders' funds
> Earnings per share
> Price/Earnings ratio
> Dividend yield
> Dividend cover
> *Performance ratios:*
> Return on net assets
> Profit margin
> Net asset turnover
> Stock turnover
> Debtor turnover
> Gross profit margin
> *Solvency ratios:*
> Debt ratio
> Interest cover
> *Liquidity ratios:*
> Current ratio
> Liquidity ratio

(*The worked ratio analysis is given on page 182.*)

Additional library questions

(b) Compare your results in (a) with those for the three previous years and for subsequent years.

(c) Obtain accounts for Boots plc, calculate the same ratios, and compare the two companies' results.

2. 'The purpose of the Metropolitan Police Service is to uphold the law fairly and firmly; to prevent crime; to pursue and bring to justice those who break the law; to keep the Queen's peace; to protect, help and reassure people in London; and to be seen to do all this with integrity, common sense and sound judgement.'

How might they measure their success?

3. The Royal Charter for the Royal National Institute for the Blind (RNIB), granted originally in 1949, states that the RNIB exists in order to:

☐ 'promote the better education, training, employment and welfare of the blind;
☐ protect the interests of the blind; and
☐ prevent blindness.'

How might they assess how well they are doing?

RECOMMENDED FURTHER READING

In addition to Reid and Myddelton the following books provide a more detailed insight into financial ratios:

Parker, R H (1972) *Understanding Company Financial Statements*, Pelican.

Sizer, J (1989) *An Insight into Management Accounting* 3rd edn, Penguin.

The Financial Times publishes a comprehensive daily summary of share prices, and the following publication provides a clear explanation of all FT statistics:

A Guide to Financial Times Statistics (regularly updated), Financial Times.

Company Financial Information is also available from Extel, Datastream and MicroExstat. Most university libraries subscribe to Extel which provides information sheets periodically, updated whenever companies publish interim and end-of-year results. Datastream is a computer service and may also be available; it is particularly useful for graphs of share movements and share index comparisons as well as ratio calculations. McCarthy's, if available, provides summaries of articles in major newspapers that relate to companies.

Annual Reports of public companies are normally provided by the company on request. In the case of private companies the data have to be purchased from Companies' House (Cardiff and London).

REFERENCES

Drucker, P F (1989) What businesses can learn from nonprofits, *Harvard Business Review*, July–August.

Economist (1991) Britain's most admired companies, 26 January.

Jackson, P and Palmer, R (1989) *First Steps in* *Measuring Performance in the Public Sector*, Public Finance Foundation, London.

London, S (1991) Repairing the balance sheet, *Financial Times*, 22 November.

Reid, W and Myddelton, D R (1974) *The Meaning of Company Accounts* 2nd edn, Gower. The quotation was taken from the second edition; there are later editions.

W H SMITH GROUP PLC: WORKED RATIO ANALYSIS

Investment ratios

Return on shareholders' funds	=	$\dfrac{61.2}{252.8}$	=	24.2%
Earnings per share	=	$\dfrac{61.2}{211.193}$	=	28.9 pence
Price/Earnings ratio	=	$\dfrac{375}{28.9}$	=	12.98
Dividend yield	=	$\dfrac{12.98*}{375}$	=	3.46%
Dividend cover	=	$\dfrac{28.9p}{12.98}$	=	2.23 times

* 12.98 = Dividends per share. It is pure coincidence that it is equal to the *P/E* ratio.

Performance ratios

Return on net assets	=	$\dfrac{112.2}{470.6}$	=	23.84%
Profit margin	=	$\dfrac{112.2}{1970.6}$	=	5.69%
Net asset turnover	=	$\dfrac{1970.6}{470.6}$	=	4.19 times
Stock turnover	=	$\dfrac{1970.6}{221.4}$	=	8.9 times (or 41 days)
Debtor turnover	=	$\dfrac{1970.6}{100.7}$	=	19.6 times (or 19 days)
Gross profit margin	=	$\dfrac{565.9}{1970.6}$	=	28.7%

Solvency ratios

Debt ratio	=	$\dfrac{193.8}{470.6}$	=	41%
Interest cover	=	$\dfrac{119.6}{30.6}$	=	3.9 times

Liquidity ratios

Current ratio	=	401.5:417.9	=	0.96:1
Liquidity ratio	=	134.8:417.9	=	0.32:1

ANALYSING COMPETITION

7

LEARNING OBJECTIVES

After studying this chapter you should be able to
☐ explain the notion of strategic life cycles and the importance of timing;
☐ define industrial concentration and describe the structure of industries in the UK;
☐ construct an experience curve and explain its significance;
☐ summarize the competition policy of the UK government;
☐ analyse two analytical models designed by Michael Porter relating to industry structure and competitive advantage;
☐ define product differentiation;
☐ explain the linkage between cost structures, break even and profits.

In this chapter we analyse the nature of the competitive environment by considering the structure of industry in the UK and the regulation of competition by government; and by exploring the concept of competitive advantage in greater detail. The need to understand the competitive environment and to seek opportunities to strengthen competitiveness is paramount for every business.

INTRODUCTION

In Chapters 5 and 6 we considered how one might assess the current position of the organization, looking at where it is going and how well it is doing. In Chapter 9 we shall examine how the environment as a whole affects the organization, and the extent to which the organization's resources match the environment, and we shall consider the usefulness of SWOT analysis (strengths; weaknesses; opportunities; threats). The present chapter, which concentrates on the competitive environment, is really part of an environmental analysis, but the issues raised are sufficiently important for the topic to merit an individual chapter.

In Chapter 1 we said that strategy is 'all about competitive advantage . . . the sole purpose of strategic management is to enable the company to gain, as effectively as possible, a sustainable edge over its competitors' (Ohmae, 1982). In the main part of this chapter we shall consider what is meant by 'doing well' in relation to competitors and look at how one might evaluate the nature of an industry. From this we shall examine how competitive strategies might be developed.

It is important here to reinforce that **corporate strategy** refers to the range of products and services offered by an organization, and the number of different industries and markets in which it competes. The company should aim to develop a distinctive competitive advantage in every area of activity. These constitute **competitive strategies**. Corporate competitiveness can sometimes be enhanced by synergy (see Key Concept III.1), and by transferring skills, sharing activities and creating effective linkages between the parts of the organization responsible for the different products and services.

When considering the appropriateness of current strategies and the need for change, managers must take account of the passage of time if their decisions are to be effective. Environmental pressures may mean that the organization needs to act quickly in response to some opportunity or threat. Equally a strategy that has been successful in the past may no longer be appropriate. This issue will be considered early in the chapter. There is a brief look at the overall business structure of the UK, and at government control of the competitive environment. Both these factors present opportunities and threats to individual organizations.

We consider how an organization can gain a deeper understanding of its competitive environment so that it may become a stronger, more effective, competitor. The emphasis is on the development of competitive advantage and effective competitive strategies.

COMPETITION: AN INTRODUCTION

According to Michael Porter of the Harvard Business School, effective strategic manage-ment is the positioning of an organization, relative to its competitors, in such a way that it out-performs them (Porter, 1980). Market-ing, operations and personnel, in fact all aspects of the business, are capable of provid-ing a competitive edge – an advantage which leads to superior performance and superior profits for profit-oriented firms.

Two aspects of the current position of an organization are important: (1) the nature and structure of the industry and (2) the position of the organization within the indus-try.

1. The number of firms, their sizes and relative power, the ways they compete, and the rate of growth must be con-sidered. An industry may be attractive or unattractive for an organization. This will depend upon the prospects for the indus-try and what it can offer in terms of profit potential and growth potential. Different organizations have different objectives, and therefore where it is able an organiza-tion should be looking to compete in industries where it is able to achieve its objectives. In turn its objectives and strat-egies are influenced by the nature of the industries in which it does compete. Porter has developed a model for analys-ing the structure of an industry. This is examined later in the chapter.

2. The position of a firm involves its size and market share, how it competes, whether it enjoys specific and recognized competitive advantage, and whether it has particular appeal to selected segments of the market.

An effective and superior organization will be in the right industry and in the right position within that industry. Obviously, an organiza-tion is unlikely to be successful if it chooses to compete in a particular industry because it is an attractive industry which offers both profit and growth potential but for which the organization has no means of obtaining competitive advantage. Equally a company should not concentrate only on creating competitive advantage without assessing the prospects for the industry. With competitive advantage a company can be profitable in an unattractive industry, but there may be very few growth opportunities if the industry is growing at a slower rate than the economy generally. Much depends upon objectives and expectations.

In the economy profit is the reward for creating value for consumers; and in individual businesses profits are earned by being more successful than competitors in creating and delivering that value. Profit may or may not be an end in itself, but profits are important for achieving other objectives and for helping finance growth. We showed (Chapter 6) that the profit remaining after interest and tax can be paid in dividends or re-invested in the firm. Obviously a firm will be healthier in the long run if it can invest as it wishes and finance the investments without building up too substantial a debt. In the same way a not-for-profit organization may not have a profit-oriented mission, but it must generate revenue to stay viable and a surplus over expenditure to develop the organization.

The most successful competitors will

☐ create value
☐ create competitive advantage in delivering that value and
☐ operate the business effectively and efficiently.

For above-average performance all three are required. It is possible to run a business well – efficiently – but never create competitive advantage. Certain products and services may have competitive advantage and yet be produced by organizations that are not run well. In both, potential is not fully exploited. Moreover, competitive advantage must be sustained. A good new product, for example, may offer the consumer something new, something different, and thus add value. But if it is easily imitated by competitors there is no sustainable competitive advantage. For example, Freddie Laker pioneered cheap transatlantic air travel but went out of

business in the face of competition and management weaknesses.

In my experience sustaining competitive advantage, rather than creating it initially, presents the real challenge. Competitive advantage cannot be sustained for ever and probably not for very long without changes in products, services and strategies which take account of market demand, market saturation and competitor activity. People's tastes change, the size of markets is limited not infinite, and competitors will seek to imitate successful products, services and strategies.

Competitive advantage can be sustained by constant innovation. Companies that are change oriented and seek to stay ahead of their competitors through innovatory ideas develop new forms of advantage. Product life cycles and new product development are considered in Chapter 10, and the importance of innovation in all areas of the business is discussed in Chapter 11. At this stage, though, it is appropriate to consider the importance of the time factor for strategies and strategic change.

If an organization is performing below average it will need to consider an appropriate turn-around strategy. This is considered in Chapter 19. The specific symptoms of, and reasons for, corporate failure are examined in Chapter 8.

The importance of timing

Products and services have finite lives, and broadly speaking they follow a life-cycle pattern. Strategies also have life cycles. Strategies which deliver value and competitive advantage will bring benefits to the organization in terms of success, growth and profits. However, if consumer preferences change, and the factors creating the advantage are no longer perceived as valuable, the advantage is lost. A change of competitive strategy is required. Similarly if the advantage is cost based and the factors generating the cost

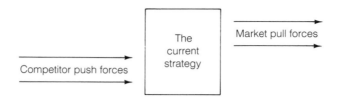

Figure 7.1 Strategy: forces for change.

advantage change, such that the advantage is lost, a new strategy is required. Again any advantage is potentially vulnerable to copying or improvements in some way by competitors, particularly if it is seen to be generating success.

Referring back to E–V–R congruence, at times particular strategies reflect a congruence between resources and the environment. However, demand can change, or investment resources to strengthen competitive advantage may not be available. The congruence may disappear, and withdrawal or divestment may well be appropriate. During the property boom of the mid-1980s civil engineering companies, such as Wimpey and Taylor Woodrow, switched their attention from competitive overseas contracts to domestic house building which proved more profitable. The building recession at the end of the 1980s caused profits to fall dramatically, encouraging the companies to switch back.

The secret is to be aware of what is happening and to be ready to change when necessary rather than be forced into changes unexpectedly. Figure 7.1 illustrates that any present competitive position must be seen as temporary. The current state could remain for some considerable time, but it will change sooner or later. If the organization is successful and profitable it will attract the attention of competitors who will seek to take over its position in the market. This pressure should make the organization vigilant and encourage a constant search for improvements and new opportunities in order to stay ahead. In addition there may be pressures for change

that originate in the marketplace. Customers may be satisfied with the value they are receiving, but probably they could be better satisfied. There will always be room for improvement with the product or service, and the organization should look for ways of creating and delivering these improvements cost effectively. An improvement is only valuable if it can be built in for a price that the customer is happy to pay and without sacrificing profits.

The two classic cases from the 1960s, featured in Case 7.1, involve well-known companies which illustrate the above point extremely well. Although dated they are still relevant examples.

One further message in these examples is that all strengths are potential weaknesses. Both Tizer and Lesney had failed to appreciate when the effective life of a particular strategy was coming to an end, as much as anything because it had proved so successful in the past. As a result the strategy became a weakness.

Taking the argument a stage further, the required changes to the strategy must also take account of the time that is available. Where a company has been caught out and is being pressurized into change it will probably have to act quickly. If the need for change is anticipated then preparations can be planned properly and alternatives tested thoroughly. The company can be proactive. If it is caught out it will have to be reactive and further mistakes could be made as a result of hurrying.

Case 7.1
TIZER AND LESNEY: THE IMPORTANCE OF STRATEGIC LIFE CYCLES

TIZER

Tizer was some 30 years old in the 1960s and it had become successful by producing its well-known fizzy drink in a number of regional plants and selling it direct to small corner shops and off-licences. Van driver salesmen collected returnable empty bottles as they sold new ones. But customer shopping habits were changing with the growth of self-service stores and supermarkets; corner shops were in decline. In addition breweries were acquiring off-licences and insisting that they stocked only brewery products. The new retailers were often part of a national chain with central rather than local buying. In addition, returnable bottles were seen as out-dated. Tizer's strategy, which had brought success to the company, was no longer appropriate; change was needed.

LESNEY

Lesney was one of the fastest growing companies in the UK in the 1960s as a result of the success of Matchbox toys. Large quantities of the small die-cast scale models of cars were produced cost effectively by using sophisticated production equipment and systems. They were priced very competitively and distributed widely through a variety of outlets rather than only toy shops. Buyers collected them, purchasing new models when they were introduced. Lesney was so busy meeting demand that they failed to innovate. An American competitor, Mattel, saw an opportunity based on how children played with the cars, and introduced a range of small cars with friction-free wheels on plastic bearings. These cars rolled further when pushed; they behaved differently in use and allowed such things as looping-the-loop. Mattel charged 30p for their cars (Matchbox cost 12½p) and they sold. Lesney's competitive strategy, similar to that of Tizer, was no longer appropriate and it needed replacement. Lesney succeeded in responding to the competition, but early in the 1980s they went into receivership. As with many UK toy producers they had been unable to withstand foreign competition.

These examples have been developed from the Tizer (A) case, written by J M Stopford and P Edmonds, and the Lesney Products and Company Ltd (A) case, written by C J Constable. Copies of both cases are available from the Case Clearing House of Great Britain and Ireland, Cranfield.

COMPETITION AND THE STRUCTURE AND REGULATION OF INDUSTRY IN THE UNITED KINGDOM

The four economic models of pure or perfect competition, monopolistic competition, oligopoly and monopoly were introduced in Chapter 5, when it was pointed out that the opportunity for substantial profits was most likely to be found in oligopoly and monopoly structures. Competition in the other models, resulting mainly from lower barriers to entry, has the effect of reducing profit margins. It is now useful to consider which models are dominant in the UK as this influences the ways firms compete. Specifically it affects the opportunities for differentiation and for the achievement of cost advantages which, as will be seen later in this chapter, are major determinants of competitive advantage.

Monopoly power

Also later in this chapter we shall consider the role of government in monitoring, policing and controlling competition. It is important to point out here that as far as the regulatory authorities are concerned a 25% market share offers opportunities for a company to exploit monopoly power. Hence, although the model of pure monopoly assumes only one producer with absolute power in the marketplace, a large producer with a substantial share will be regarded as having monopoly power. It does not follow that such power will be used against the consumer; on the contrary it can be to the consumer's advantage. Large companies with market shares in excess of their rivals may be able to produce at lower cost for any one of several reasons including the ability to invest in high output, low unit cost technology; the ability to buy supplies in bulk and receive discounts; the ability to achieve distribution savings; and the opportunity to improve productivity as more and more units are produced. In fact savings are possible in every area of the business. Economists call these savings economies of scale, and they are related to the notion of the experience or learning curve which is explained in Key Concept 7.1.

A cost advantage, then, can be a major source of competitive advantage, and this point will be developed in greater detail later. The producer who is able to produce at a lower cost than his or her rivals may choose to price very competitively with a view to driving competitors out of the market and thereby increasing his market share. Equally he or she may not; and by charging a higher price he makes a greater profit per unit and thereby seeks profit in preference to market share. In the first case the consumer benefits from lower prices and therefore monopoly power is not being used against the consumer. However, once a firm has built up a truly dominant market share it might seek to change its strategy and exploit its power more. This is when government needs to intervene in some way.

Concentration

Concentration is the measure of control exercised by organizations. There are two types.

Aggregate concentration, which we shall mention only briefly, considers the power of the largest privately owned manufacturing firms in the economy as a whole. It measures the percentage of total net output (value added), fixed assets, employment, sales value or profits in manufacturing represented by the top 100 firms. Approximately 40% of both output and employment is in the hands of the 100 largest firms (HMSO, 1978). Although this figure grew steadily throughout the first 70 years of this century it is now more stable.

Sectoral or market concentration traditionally considers the percentage of net output or employment (assets, sales or profits can also be measured) controlled by the largest firms in a particular industry, be it manufacturing or service. Typically the largest five are used, but occasionally the largest three or six are used. High concentration figures tend to encourage monopoly or oligopoly behaviour, most probably the latter, which implies substantial emphasis on differentiation and nonprice competition, with rivals seeing themselves as interdependent. Before we look at examples of market concentration it is important to appreciate that attempts to relate concentration to behaviour which is detrimental to economic performance and efficiency have generally proved inconclusive.

Key Concept 7.1
THE EXPERIENCE CURVE

A large size, relative to competitors, can bring benefits. In particular, if a company has a market share substantially greater than its competitors it has opportunities to achieve greater profitability. Lower costs can be achieved if the company is managed well and takes advantage of the opportunities offered by being larger. These lower costs can be passed on to the consumer in the form of lower prices, which in turn puts pressure on competitors' profit margins and strengthens the position of the market leader.

Lower costs are achieved through economies of scale and the experience or learning effect. In the 1960s the Boston Consulting Group in America estimated that the cost of production decreases by between 10% and 30% each time that a company's experience in producing the product or service doubles as long as the company is managed well. In other words as cumulative production increases over time there is a potential cost reduction at a predictable rate. The company learns how to do things better. The savings are spread across all value-added costs: manufacturing, administration, sales, marketing and distribution. In addition the cost of

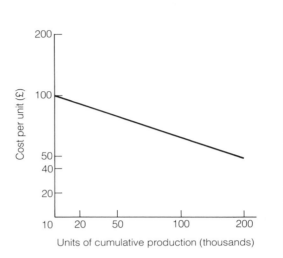

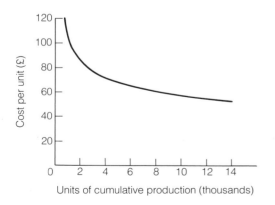

Exhibit 1   An 85% experience curve plotted on a normal scale.

Exhibit 2   The same 85% experience curve plotted in log–log form.

supplies decreases as suppliers experience the same learning benefits.

The experience effect has been observed in high and low technology industries, in new and mature industries, in both manufacturing and service businesses, and in relation to consumer and industrial markets. Specific examples are cars, semi-conductors, petrochemicals, long distance telephone calls, synthetic fibres, airline transportation, crushed limestone and the cost of administering life insurance.

The experience curve is illustrated by plotting on a graph the cumulative number of units produced over time (the horizontal axis) and the cost per unit (the vertical axis). Exhibit 1 does this. This particular curve is called an '85% experience curve' as every time output is doubled the cost per unit falls to 85% of what it was. In reality the plot will be of a least squares line but the trend will be clear. However, it is more common to plot the data on logarithmic scales on both axes, and this shows the straight line effect illustrated in Exhibit 2.

Continued overleaf

SOURCES OF THE EXPERIENCE EFFECT

☐ Increased labour efficiency through learning and consequent skills improvement
☐ The opportunity for greater specialization in production methods
☐ Innovations in the production process
☐ Greater productivity from equipment as people learn how to use it more efficiently
☐ Improved resource mix as products are redesigned with cost savings in mind

This is not an exhaustive list, and the savings will not occur naturally. They result from good management.

PRICING DECISIONS AND THE EXPERIENCE EFFECT

A market leader or other large producer who enjoys a cost advantage as a result of accumulated experience will use this as the basis for a pricing strategy linked to his or her objectives, which might be profit or growth and market share oriented. Exhibit 3 illustrates one way that industry prices might be forced down (in real terms, after accounting for inflation) as the market leader benefits from lower costs. Initially prices are below costs incurred because of the cost of development. As demand, sales and production increase prices fall, but at a slower rate than costs; the producer is enjoying a higher profit margin. This will be attractive to any competitors or potential competitors who feel that they can compete at this price even if their costs are higher. If competition becomes intensive and the major producer(s) wish to assert authority over the market they will decrease prices quickly and force out manufacturers whose costs are substantially above theirs. Stability might then be restored.

Companies with large market shares can therefore dictate what happens in a market, but there is a need for caution. If a company ruthlessly chases a cost advantage via the experience effect the implication could be ever increasing efficiency as a result of less flexibility. The whole operating system is geared towards efficiency and cost savings. If demand changes or competitors innovate unexpectedly the strategy will have run out of time as we have already seen. Companies should ensure that they are flexible enough to respond.

This material has mainly been summarized from Abell, D F and Hammond, J S (1979) *Strategic Market Planning: Problems, and Analytical Approaches*, Prentice Hall.

Exhibit 3 is adapted from *Perspectives on Experience*, The Boston Consulting Group, 1972.

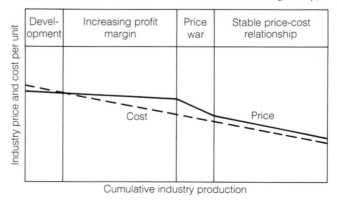

Exhibit 3   Pricing in relation to costs and the experience effect.

For example it has been argued that profits can increase after a certain level of seller concentration; but at the same time, where concentration is particularly high, profits are curbed to guard against government intervention. Similarly it has been claimed that high product differentiation generates powerful barriers to entry, high market protection and high profit rates. The converse is that high differentiation can only be achieved and maintained by intense non-price competition and that such advertising and sales promotions result in lower profits as the costs incurred are not wholly passed on to consumers (Devine *et al.*, 1979).

Concentrated industries

Government statistics, extracted from the Census of Production, provide industry concentration ratios based mainly on net output; market research companies regularly produce reports which give figures for market shares in terms of sales volumes and sales values. Both these are useful indicators of concentration, but such data alone do not fully explain reality. In Box 7.1 we examine three industries which exhibit high concentration ratios and consider the importance of diversification and market segments. There may well be marketing and distribution advantages for companies which belong to conglomerates and this could increase their relative market power. Similarly products which dominate particular market segments will yield advantages.

Many industries in the UK are essentially oligopolistic in structure, with a limited number of major competitors and barriers to entry, as highlighted in the cases of chocolate and brewing. Others are more monopolistic with just one dominant producer. The trend in the UK, parallel to the increase in aggregate concentration, has been a growth of market concentration with the emergence of oligopoly as the dominant market structure.

It was pointed out earlier that oligopoly is characterized by high barriers to entry and by interdependence and uncertainty. Competitors are aware that any change in strategy by one organization will affect the other main rivals, but because they are uncertain as to how they might react they behave cautiously in the main. Generally competition will be non-price rather than price, but price competition will be seen in situations where supply exceeds demand and there is aggressive competition for market share. Package holiday tours are an example, and this case will be looked at in greater detail later in the chapter. All kinds of competitive behaviour are in fact possible, including

- an open price war – in general the least likely because of fear as to how it might end
- hidden price competition through coupons, special offers and short-term discounts
- non-price competition, such as advertising, packaging and the provision of any additional services that might encourage customer preference and loyalty
- price leadership whereby one firm sets a new price level and the others characteristically follow – in a market there may be more than one price leader
- collusion, which might or might not be illegal, as we shall see later.

There is still opportunity for smaller companies to compete successfully in certain oligopoly markets, especially if they can differentiate their product so that it has appeal for particular segments of the market. In relation to two of the industries considered in Box 7.1, Bruce's Brewery was featured in Chapter 3, and in the chocolate industry Thornton's has been successful with a limited range of high quality products distributed through the company's own specialist outlets. In contrast, there are certain industries which exhibit very low concentration. Ladies' dresses are one example, and they are very much affected by fashion and the nature of the businesses which involve large numbers of part-time workers; leather goods are

Box 7.1
THREE CONCENTRATED INDUSTRIES

TOBACCO

In 1990 three companies, Imperial Tobacco (34% market share), Gallahers (including Benson and Hedges, 43%) and Rothmans (14%) dominated the UK market: 91% in the hands of three companies. The world market leader is BAT, British American Tobacco, which has only a relatively small presence in the UK. However, because of the declining sales of tobacco all the major companies have diversified into both related and un-related businesses. Imperial diversified into food (Ross, Golden Wonder and HP) and brewing (Courage) before it was acquired by Hanson in 1986. Hanson was already a diversified international conglomerate. Gallahers has diversified into distribution and engineering.

Although the industry is dominated by three powerful companies, there is intense competition, mainly because of falling demand. Pricing is competitive and new brands are constantly introduced. Advertising is restricted by legislation.

BREWING

In 1900 there were 1466 breweries in the UK, but this had declined to 247 in 1960 and 68 in 1986 (*source*: The Brewers' Society). In 1989 six diversified conglomerates dominated the market. As well as brewing they were actively involved in the actual sale to the consumer as they owned hotels and public houses. Some of the areas of diversification and numbers of retail outlets controlled in early 1989 are given below.

Bass	Over 7000 pubs and other outlets
	Toby Restaurants
	Holiday Inn hotel chain
Allied Lyons	Spirits: Hiram Walker-Allied Vintners
	Foods (Lyons and other brands)
	Over 6500 licensed outlets
Whitbread	Threshers off-licences (over 1000)
	Beefeater Steak Houses (over 200)
	Pizza Hut chain
Grand Metropolitan	Express Dairies; Eden Vale
	Spirits: International Distillers
	Over 6000 licensed outlets
	Pillsbury (US 'Green Giant' foods)
Scottish and Newcastle	Thistle Hotels
	Pontins Holiday Camps

A Monopolies and Mergers Commission (MMC) report into the industry (1989) concluded that no brewer should own more than 2000 on-licensed premises. The major companies lobbied against this and eventually the government allowed them to retain 2000 plus half the number currently in excess of 2000. Since this ruling:

☐ Courage has acquired Grand Metropolitan's breweries, and the two companies have established a new joint venture retailing business, Inntrepreneur Estates, comprising some 7000 pubs.

☐ In another joint venture Allied Lyons has merged its UK brewing interests with those of the Danish company Carlsberg.

☐ Three well-known regional companies, Boddington, Greenall Whitley and Devenish, have ceased brewing to concentrate on retailing.

☐ There has been a general trend to replace tenants of public houses with salaried managers – following the MMC report tenants (but not managers) have been free to stock 'guest beers' alongside those of their owner.

In the early 1990s five companies controlled 85% of this 12 billion pound market:

Bass	23%
Courage/Grand Metropolitan	20%
Allied/Carlsberg	18%
Whitbread	13%
Scottish and Newcastle.	11.5%.

Oligopoly behaviour is evident in the market. Advertising expenditure is substantial and there is little price competition. However, prices vary significantly in different regions of the country for substantially the same product. In the south of England a pint of bitter can cost over half as much again as in parts of the north.

The brewery industry is profiled in greater detail later in this chapter (see Box 7.4).

THE CHOCOLATE COMPANIES

As in the case of tobacco, three companies, Cadbury, Mars and Rowntree Mackintosh, dominate the market, with shares of 30%, 25% and 25% respectively. Cadbury, who own Trebor, Bassett, Pascall and Murray, also lead the confectionery market with a 28% share, followed by Rowntree (owned by Nestlé and including Polo) with 23% and Mars (Opal Fruits) with 18%. The leading three chocolate **brands**, however, are Kit Kat (Rowntree), Mars Bars and Twix (another Mars product). Mars is also the dominant company in the pet foods market (see Case 7.4).

---

another, and here the barriers to entry are very low.

The UK exhibits higher concentration overall than is found in rival countries such as America and Germany. However, UK com-

---

It is not acceptable for those in charge of companies trading worldwide simply to be better than their UK rivals. In all the areas that matter – research and development, product quality, price and after-sales service and support – we have to be better than our best *international* competitors. For me, that also means we have to be able to succeed in Japan.

Sir David Plastow, Chairman and Chief Executive, Vickers plc.

(Vickers manufacture Rolls Royce cars as well as defence products.)

---

panies generally compete in world markets, and therefore size is an important issue. With the further reduction of trading barriers in Europe in 1992, which will be considered in Chapter 9, this issue has become increasingly important. However, few British companies are dominant producers when considered in world terms. Britain's largest domestic motor vehicle producer is Rover and yet this company is relatively small in European terms. British Steel, created by nationalization and the amalgamation of most of the steel-making capacity in the UK, is not the largest steel company in the world, but it is a major producer. Significantly in the late 1980s British Steel became one of the most profitable steel companies as a result of rationalization.

It is also important to note that the growth in market concentration has mainly been generated by mergers and acquisition rather than by internal growth (HMSO, 1978).

When mergers and acquisition are considered later (Chapter 18) it will be seen that many mergers fail to bring benefits to either the firms involved or the consumer.

The message for organizations seems to be: know your industry, appreciate where the competitive threats and opportunities are, and appreciate which form of competitive behaviour is most appropriate. Later we shall consider how an industry might be analysed.

The dilemma for government is to encourage firms to grow in size and become powerful competitive forces in world markets but at the same time to ensure that such size and power is not used to exploit consumers in the UK. We shall consider the relevant regulatory strategies next. This issue is important for companies as it can restrict certain strategies they might propose.

The regulation of monopoly power

In the UK it is generally accepted that it is the state's role to monitor the forces of competition, to minimize any waste of resources due to economic inefficiency, to guard against any exploitation of relatively weak buyers or suppliers, and to ensure that powerful companies do not seek to eliminate their competitors purely to gain monopoly power. Government seeks to regulate competition in three basic ways: the regulation of structure, conduct and performance.

The main thrust as far as **structure** is concerned is the monitoring and possible prohibition of any large conglomerates or restrictive agreements which are intended to establish monopoly power. The approach towards **conduct** assumes that in some cases a monopoly (or large dominant producer) is potentially the most efficient organization for the market, and hence the appropriate policy is to ensure that any organization with monopoly power does not use pricing, production or marketing strategies which operate against the public interest. **Performance** regulation again assumes that monopoly

power may be justified and polices profitability, efficiency and innovation. Box 7.2 provides a summary of the competition policy of the UK government.

Restrictive practices

Restrictive practices are controlled by the Restrictive Practices Court, and the basic presumption is that they are against the public interest. A restrictive practice is defined as 'an agreement under which two or more persons accept restrictions relating to the price of goods, conditions of supply, qualities or descriptions, processes, or areas and persons supplied'. A practice may be allowed if it can be demonstrated that there is a consumer benefit, that it is being used to promote exports, or that it is necessary to counteract anticompetitive measures being taken by others. As an example cement production is analysed in Case 7.2. The prohibition of such agreements in oligopoly markets may encourage firms to consider merging their interests.

Merger investigations

The Monopolies and Mergers Commission is empowered to look at the way monopoly power is exercised in particular cases that are referred to it by the Director General of Fair Trading or an appropriate Minister of State. Similarly the Commission can be asked to investigate proposed mergers where either £30 million of assets are involved or where market share in excess of 25% would result. Each case is considered on merit, and this time the presumption is not automatically that monopoly power is against the public interest. High profitability is considered acceptable if it reflects efficiency, but not if it is sustained by artificial barriers to entry. Case 7.3 summarizes the 1986 report into the supply of salt.

It is easy to presume that there is tight

Box 7.2
UK COMPETITION POLICY

Three UK agencies regulate competition.

THE OFFICE OF FAIR TRADING

☐ Set up in 1973 the Office of Fair Trading oversees both consumer affairs and competition policy.
☐ It can initiate references to the Monopolies and Mergers Commission in the case of anticompetitive behaviour, but not proposed mergers which are referred by government.
☐ It carries out investigations into anticompetitive behaviour and practices of individual firms over a certain size which restrict, distort or prevent competition.
☐ It can refer cartels or cases of resale price maintenance to the Restrictive Practices Court.

THE MONOPOLIES AND MERGERS COMMISSION

☐ Established originally in 1948 it was extended in 1965 to cover mergers and again in 1980 to include the public sector.

☐ It has powers to decide whether situations referred to it are in the public interest or not and to make recommendations for change. The public interest is broadly defined and open to interpretation.
☐ It can investigate proposed mergers referred to it and recommend to government whether they should be allowed to proceed.
☐ The Monopolies and Mergers Commission cannot itself choose which situations or mergers should be investigated, nor are its recommendations necessarily imposed.

THE RESTRICTIVE PRACTICES COURT

☐ Set up in 1956 (with powers which have been supplemented by several further Acts) it deals with cartels and restrictive practices and seeks to outlaw them.

In addition clauses in the Treaty of Rome, relating to membership of the European Community, 'prohibit agreements which affect trade between member states and prevent, restrict, or distort competition, and prohibit abuse of a dominant position within the Community'.

---

control on proposed mergers, but this really is not the case. Only some six or seven mergers each year are referred, whilst many go through without reference. Historically more have been approved than have been turned down after investigation. Market dominance and high profits are not evidence that a firm is operating against the public interest. On the contrary it is recognized that

such firms may have cost advantages or that their dominance is justified through the development of new products or production methods.

However, the delay involved in an investigation can be important strategically. The process is likely to take at least six months and in that time a company which opposes the take-over bid against it will work hard to

---

Case 7.2
CEMENT PRODUCTION

In February 1987 British cement producers voluntarily abandoned a 53-year-old price fixing agreement which had acted to establish fixed prices throughout the industry. Three producers (Blue Circle, Rugby Portland and RTZ) shared 96% of the home market, which, although one of the largest in Europe, had been growing at only 1% per year. Capacity had been reduced since the early 1970s and it is estimated that supply still exceeds demand. Steel frames are now used in buildings as well as cement; substitute products such as pulverized fuel ash give cement better handling properties and reduce the quantity required; and there have been cutbacks in public expenditure that affect the building trade.

In 1961 the Restrictive Practices Court accepted that the cartel was in the public interest as it led to lower prices and enabled capital to be raised for modernization. However, in recent years hidden discounting has existed and it has been argued that the price fixing has in fact restricted investment in efficient new plant and inhibited efforts to reduce costs. Inefficient practices have developed. For example, producers deliver cement long distances to break into specific markets where they do not have plants whilst small local producers, with few transport costs, are unable to pass on any lower costs in the form of reduced prices.

The abandonment was aimed at making companies more competitive. Although imports were not yet significant there was fear of a threat from Greek cement, for example. A price war was not expected, but discounts for large customers were, together with reduced prices for buyers who collected their own cement. In the past there was no advantage in this. Blue Circle, the largest producer, whose market share has declined from 60% to 54% in the 1980s, was particularly keen to end the agreement.

---

improve its performance and prospects. If this results in a substantial increase in the share price the acquisitive company may withdraw on the grounds that the cost has become too high. In 1983 Trafalgar House bid for P & O; the bid was opposed and was referred to the Monopolies and Mergers Commission as Trafalgar already owned Cunard. The bid was given the go-ahead the following year but Trafalgar withdrew as the cost had increased.

Another significant strategic tactic at the time of a bid is a statement of intent by a prospective acquirer to sell off part of the company it is seeking to buy in order to

sidestep a possible reference to the Commission. In 1986, when Hanson was seeking to acquire Imperial Group, the bid was opposed and instead Imperial sought a friendly merger with United Biscuits and terms were agreed. Imperial, however, controlled 15% of the crisps market through Golden Wonder and the multi-product United Biscuits had a further 25% (through KP and own label production). United Biscuits stated that they would sell Golden Wonder. The bid was not referred, but in any case Hanson was successful.

It was announced in November 1988 that a new Companies Bill would be designed,

---

Case 7.3
WHITE SALT: AN INVESTIGATION BY THE MONOPOLIES AND MERGERS COMMISSION, 1986 (COMMAND 9778)

The Commission recommended that price control should be sought as ICI and British Salt have a virtual monopoly, and although British Salt are much more cost efficient than ICI they have not put pressure on them. Rather they have allowed ICI to raise prices, followed them and as a result achieved 'unusually high profits'.

From the mid-1970s to the mid-1980s ICI had some 45–47% market share and British Salt 50%. Over this period the prices have been close but not identical – a few pence per tonne separating them. Some of the time ICI has been more expensive, at other times British Salt. Both companies have initiated increases; more recently it has been ICI with British Salt following a few days later.

The Commission argued that 'salt prices have risen at a faster rate than prices of both the chemical industry and of manufacturing industry as a whole'. From 1980 to 1985 the respective percentage increases were 82% (salt), 40% (chemicals) and 43% (manufacturing). However, neither company had attempted to prevent other suppliers from entering the market.

The Commission felt that alternative solutions such as lower barriers to entry or strengthening the buying power of customers were impractical and recommended price regulation.

The Report concluded that British Salt's prices should be regulated for five years by a particular formula which allowed them to pass on some, but not all, anticipated cost increases.

ICI prices were not to be regulated, but in any case they were believed to be a higher cost producer than British Salt. The problem with ICI was in actually determining costs because of transfer prices throughout the organization. 'The practical effect of applying the formula to British Salt's prices is that a limit is imposed beyond which no other producer will be able to raise its prices without jeopardizing its market share.'

---

amongst other things, to speed up the clearance for proposals if companies notified the Office of Fair Trading of their intentions in advance and to allow companies formally to seek to prevent a reference by undertaking to sell off part of the businesses involved in an acquisition if competition concerns are raised.

When the conglomerate Williams Holdings bid for Racal in 1991 they undertook to sell the Chubb lock and safe businesses owned by Racal if they were successful. Williams already owned two competing businesses, Yale and Valor.

Anticompetitive behaviour

The 1980 Competition Act gave the Director General of Fair Trading powers to investigate the conduct of individual firms in order to determine whether specific practices such as discriminatory prices, predatory prices and refusal to supply non-appointed distributors were anticompetitive. If the Office of Fair Trading concludes that a firm is behaving anticompetitively reference can be made to the Monopolies and Mergers Commission for further investigation.

The effect can be dramatic. Tube Investments (TI) were investigated for refusing to supply Raleigh bicycles to cut-price retailers such as Argos, Asda, Comet and Woolworth. TI argued that they were unable to provide a comprehensive after-sales service. The Monopolies and Mergers Commission ultimately recommended that Raleigh-made bicycles, not necessarily branded with the Raleigh name, should be supplied to discount stores who could provide adequate service and spares. For a number of years Raleigh has been affected by foreign competition, and in 1987 TI sold its bicycle subsidiary as part of a rationalization programme. In 1985 Sheffield Newspapers reported the closure of the *Sheffield Morning Telegraph* because of the complete loss of estate agents' advertising to their own newspaper. In 1982 the Monopolies and Mergers Commission had found evidence of anticompetitive behaviour concerning advertising policy by Sheffield Newspapers; the estate agents had responded.

The 1980 Act also extended the work of the Monopolies and Mergers Commission to include the public sector, with the exception of health and education. A number of organizations have been investigated and criticized in relation to their management structures, financial control, pricing policies, investment appraisal techniques and their use of performance indicators.

In relation to such countries as the Federal Republic of Germany and the USA competition legislation in the UK has been relatively weak. 'There are few sanctions. If a company sees a benefit from restricting competition it may as well do so. At worst it will be found out and referred to the Office of Fair Trading. After an investigation it may be told to desist. Since there is no fine there is nothing to offset the benefits enjoyed while the restriction was in force' (Prowse, 1986).

Since September 1990 the European Commission has also been able to influence the growing number of corporate mergers and acquisitions in the European Community, with powers to intervene when:

☐ there is a proposed change in control of at least one of the companies involved;
☐ the combined worldwide turnover of the companies totals at least Ecu 5 billion (3.5 billion pounds in September 1990); and/or
☐ the aggregate EC turnover of each of at least two of the companies is Ecu 250 million or more.

These thresholds are due for revision downwards in 1993. Mergers are exempted, though, if each company has more than two-thirds of its EC-wide turnover in any one EC country.

ANALYSING AN INDUSTRY

Porter (1980) argues that five forces determine the profitability of an industry. They are featured in Figure 7.2. At the heart of the industry are rivals and their competitive

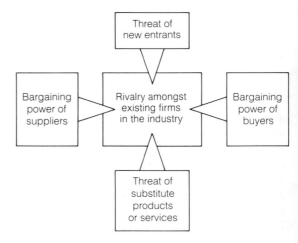

Figure 7.2 Determining industry profitability – the five forces. Adapted from Porter, M E (1980) *Competitive Strategy: Techniques for Analysing Industries and Competitors*, Free Press.

strategies linked to, say, pricing or advertising; but, he contends, it is important to look beyond one's immediate competitors as there are other determinants of profitability. Specifically there might be competition from substitute products or services. These alternatives may be perceived as substitutes by buyers even though they are part of a different industry. An example would be plastic bottles, cans and glass bottles for packaging soft drinks. There may also be a potential threat of new entrants, although some competitors will see this as an opportunity to strengthen their position in the market by ensuring, as far as they can, customer loyalty. Finally it is important to appreciate that companies purchase from suppliers and sell to buyers. If they are powerful they are in a position to bargain profits away through reduced margins, by forcing either cost increases or price decreases. This relates to the strategic option of vertical integration which will be considered in detail later in the book. Vertical integration occurs where a company acquires, or merges with, a supplier or customer and thereby gains greater control over the chain of activities which leads from basic materials through to final consumption.

Any company must seek to understand the nature of its competitive environment if it is to be successful in achieving its objectives and in establishing appropriate strategies. If a company fully understands the nature of the five forces, and particularly appreciates which one is the most important, it will be in a stronger position to defend itself against any threats and to influence the forces with its strategy. The situation, of course, is fluid, and the nature and relative power of the forces will change. Consequently the need to monitor and stay aware is continuous.

The threat of new entrants: barriers to entry

Where barriers to entry are high new entrants are likely to be deterred, and if they do attempt entry they are likely to provoke a quick reaction from existing competitors. Low barriers generally mean that responses will be slower, offering more opportunities. A number of factors can create barriers:

☐ **Economies of scale**: Some of the possible ways of achieving economies of scale were considered earlier in this chapter. In addition the experience curve can be important. If there is a need for substantial investment to allow a new entrant to achieve cost parity with existing firms this may well be a deterrent. In such a case if a newcomer enters the market with only limited investment and is not able to achieve comparable economies of scale, he or she will be at a cost disadvantage from the start, in which case substantial differentiation will be required, but this introduces another issue.

☐ **Product differentiation**: If consumers perceive rival products or services to be clearly differentiated then newcomers must also seek to establish a distinct identity. Differentiation is explained in Key Concept 7.2. Newcomers will therefore have to invest in advertising and promotion to establish their new brand, and this may be expensive. The major brewers and chocolate manufacturers, for example, spend millions of pounds each year promoting specific products and brands.

☐ **Capital requirements**: Any requirement for substantial investment capital in order to enter a market is a barrier to entry. The investment may be on capital equipment, research and development, or advertising to establish a market presence, and it may deter many aspiring competitors. However, large multi-product companies who wish to break into a market may finance the necessary investment with profits from other areas of the business.

☐ **Switching costs**: These are not costs incurred by the company wishing to enter the market but by the existing customers.

Key Concept 7.2
PRODUCT DIFFERENTIATION

A product or service is said to be **differentiated** if consumers perceive it to have properties which make it distinct from rival products or services, and ideally unique in some particular way. Differentiation is most beneficial when consumers value the cause of the difference and will pay a premium price to obtain it, and where competitors are unable to emulate it

Differentiation recognizes that customers are too numerous and widely scattered, and with heterogeneous needs and adequate spending power, for them all to prefer exactly the same product or service. Hence competitors will distinguish their brand, product or service in some way, perhaps size, quality or style, to give it greater appeal for certain customers. Those customers who value the difference will be willing to pay a premium price for it and ideally buy it consistently in preference to the alternatives.

The cause of the differentiation can be in the appearance of the product or its behaviour or both; Concorde, for example, is unique in both respects. It could result from special properties of raw materials or components used, or it could relate to quality arising from superior manufacturing, or it could be in after-sales service. It can arise from any area of the business.

The differentiation need not be clearly tangible as long as customers believe that it exists.

Where specific groups of customers with broadly similar needs can be identified and targeted they are known as **market segments**, and often products and services are differentiated to appeal to specific segments. The segmentation might be based on ages, socioeconomic groups, life-style, income, benefits sought or usage rate for consumer markets, and size of buyer and reasons for buying in the case of industrial markets. To be viable the segment must be clearly identifiable, separated from other segments, easily reached with advertising and large enough to be profitable. Given these factors and a differentiated product, prices, distribution and advertising can all be targeted specifically at the segment.

If a buyer were to change his supplier from an established manufacturer to a newcomer costs may be incurred in a number of ways. New handling equipment and employee training are examples. Buyers may not be willing to change their suppliers because of these costs, thereby making it very difficult for any newcomer to poach existing business.

☐ **Access to distribution channels**: Existing relationships and agreements between manufacturers and the key distributors in a market may also create barriers to entry. Some manufacturers may be vertically integrated and own or control their distributors. Other distributors may have established and successful working relationships with particular manufacturers and have little incentive to change. Companies aspiring to enter a market may look for unique distribution opportunities to provide both access and immediate differentiation.

☐ **Cost advantages independent of scale:** This represents factors which are valuable to existing companies in an industry and which newcomers may not be able to replicate. Essential technology may be protected by patent; the supply of necessary raw materials may be controlled; or

Case 7.4
BARRIERS TO ENTRY: PET FOODS, WET SHAVE PRODUCTS, ZANTAC AND CHAMPAGNE

PET FOODS

Canned pet foods represent over 75% of the pet foods industry and they are dominated by Pedigree Petfoods, owned by Mars. Dog foods can be divided into three segments: premium price, medium and economy. Pedigree with Chum (30% overall market share and premium price), Pal (also premium price), Bounce (medium) and Chappie (economy) has a 55% market share, followed by Spillers (14%) and Quaker (Chunky, 7%). Spillers leads in dog biscuits. The same situation is true for canned cat foods. Pedigree's Whiskas has 46% of the market (Pedigree has 52% altogether), Spillers 18% and Quaker's Felix 6%. All figures are for 1990.

   Major organizations such as Rank Hovis McDougall, General Foods (US) and Heinz have all withdrawn from an industry that is characterized with new product failures. Pet food is only profitable by exploiting economies of scale as price competition is evident despite the oligopoly structure and significant differentiation and branding. Both Mars and Spillers have made major investments in new technology and gained productivity improvements. The cost of entry is increased by the need for very substantial advertising to establish a new brand and to compete with the promotional budgets of the market leaders.

WET SHAVE PRODUCTS

A MMC report in 1989 confirmed the following UK market shares for wet shave razors and blades:

	Segments		
	Systems	Disposables	Double Edge
Share of total market (%)	46	48	6
Segment shares (%):			
Gillette	82	44	15
Wilkinson Sword	11	14	68
Bic		32	

Following the report Gillette was required to sell its shareholding in Swedish Match, owners of Wilkinson Sword.

There are a number of barriers to entry:

☐ Distributors do not encourage new manufacturers.
☐ Customers are loyal to particular products.
☐ There are no close substitutes.
☐ Products are heavily advertised.

As a result prices rose faster than inflation during the late 1980s.

ZANTAC (PATENT PROTECTION FOR GLAXO)

Sir Paul Girolami became the Chief Executive of Glaxo in 1980, and sequentially divested the non-pharmaceutical businesses: specialized chemicals and food, agricultural and horticultural products. In 1985 Glaxo was not in the leading ten world pharmaceutical companies; in 1988 it was number 2 to Merck. In 1990 half of Glaxo's worldwide revenue was contributed by Zantac, its anti-ulcer drug whose chemical name is Ranitidin. Zantac enjoys one important competitive advantage over its main rival Tagamet (SmithKline Beecham) – it is a twice daily treatment rather than four times a day.

Glaxo exploited the product successfully with two unusual strategies. First, it registered Ranitidin simultaneously in all major markets – typically drugs are registered first in their home market, followed by other countries sequentially. Second, Glaxo uniquely used other companies for manufacturing and distributing the product (including three separate companies in the US), rather than building a world sales-force. Turnover tripled in 1983/4 and then quadrupled during the next five years.

Glaxo has a definite patent barrier until 1995 and argues it has further protection until 2002, but this is disputed.

CHAMPAGNE: OVERCOMING ENTRY BARRIERS

Several barriers to entry have acted to preserve the exclusiveness of the champagne industry. In most countries, and with the notable exceptions of America and Russia, the term champagne can be applied only to wines made from grapes grown in one area, Champagne, in northwest France. The best grapes for champagne are grown on a particular type of chalky soil found only in this region. In addition, strict (and enforced) French government rules require that only three varieties of grape may be used; and after the first fermentation the wine must be matured in the bottle for at least a year to generate the bubbles.

The business is carefully regulated, generally in favour of the 19 000 growers. Growers, who operate in co-operatives, historically have accounted for approximately one-third of the champagne that is manufactured; the rest has been produced by merchants who buy the grapes from the growers at prices fixed contractually every six years.

During the early and mid-1980s demand and sales grew by some 70%. As a result, grape prices rose and growers particularly started to manufacture more. These events attracted competitors who looked for ways of overcoming the entry barriers. The real threat has come from other premium quality sparkling wines manufactured in countries such as Spain. The grower/merchant price agreement broke down in 1990, roughly at the time demand fell back. In an attempt to reinforce the image of superiority and exclusivity, and in response to the competition from other sparkling wines, champagne prices have been increased deliberately. 'Quality and image is more important than quantity.'

The most influential company in the industry is LVMH (Louis Vuitton Moët Hennessy) whose brands (including Moët & Chandon, Dom Perignon, Veuve Clicquot, Mercier and Pommery [very popular in Japan]) have a 24% market share. LVMH own 1500 prime hectares of the region's total of 35 000 hectares.

(*Sources: The Economist*, 21 June 1986; Sasseen, J (1991) Champagne's bubble bursts, *International Management*, May.)

favourable locations near to supplies or markets may not be accessible. Government restrictions on competition may apply in certain circumstances.

Case 7.4 features the powerful barriers to entry in four completely different industries.

Potential entrants, attracted by high margins in an industry and not detracted by any of the above barriers, must try and gauge any likely retaliation by existing manufacturers; and Porter argues that this can be assessed by examining

☐ past behaviour when newcomers have entered or tried to enter the market;
☐ the resource capabilities of existing companies which will affect their ability to retaliate;
☐ the investment and commitment of existing companies which may make retaliation inevitable if they are to protect their investment and position;
☐ the rate of growth of the industry – the faster it is the more possibilities for a newcomer to be absorbed.

Existing firms may be prepared to reduce prices to deter entry and protect their market shares, especially if supply already exceeds demand. As a result, even in an oligopoly, profitability can be contained.

The bargaining power of suppliers

The behaviour of suppliers, and their relative power, can squeeze industry profits. Equally the ability of a firm to control its supplies by vertical integration (acquiring its suppliers) or long-term supply arrangements can be very beneficial. The relative power is affected by five major factors.

☐ Concentration amongst suppliers *vis-à-vis* the industry they sell to: if the supply industry is very concentrated then buyers have little opportunity for bargaining on prices and deliveries as suppliers recog-

nize that their opportunities for switching suppliers are limited.
☐ The degree of substitutability between the products of various suppliers and the amount of product differentiation: a buyer could be tied to a particular supplier if his or her requirements cannot be met by other suppliers.
☐ The amount of, and potential for, vertical integration which might be initiated by either the supplier or the buyer: again government regulation on competition may prevent this.
☐ The extent to which the buyer is important to the supplier: if a buyer is regarded as a key customer he or she may well receive preferential treatment.
☐ Any switching costs that might be incurred by buyers will strengthen the position of suppliers.

The bargaining power of buyers

Any competitive action by buyers will act to depress industry profits, but specific arrangements with distributors or customers can be mutually beneficial. Vertical integration is again a possibility. Case 7.5 on the package holiday industry illustrates the increasing power of travel agents *vis-à-vis* the tour operators. Similarly the major supermarket grocery stores with their multiple outlets nationwide are in a very strong bargaining position with most of their suppliers.

This power has been strengthened by the success of private label brands. In 1990, for example, Sainsbury's introduced 1300 new privately branded products. Prices can be up to 60% below those for the recognized major brands, and private labels now account for some 33% of UK retail food sales. They have proved most successful with chilled meals, frozen vegetables, fruit juices and cheese; and least successful with pet foods, sugar, coffee and breakfast cereals. Barriers against private label products are provided

Case 7.5
RIVALRY AMONGST COMPETITORS: PACKAGE HOLIDAYS

The package holiday tour industry is dynamic and very competitive. The number of holidays offered by the major tour operators increased four-fold during the 1980s. Price competition between Thomson, the market leader, and Intasun was intense, and this contributed to the collapse of International Leisure Group (owners of Intasun). In 1991 Thomson had a 35% market share, followed by Owners Abroad (Enterprise and Sovereign) with 19% and Airtours (16%). Thomson's market leadership had been consolidated by the acquisition in 1988 of Horizon (from Bass). During the late 1980s self-catering holidays became more popular at the expense of the traditional hotel package.

The major tour operators are vertically integrated and own their own airlines. Thomson Holidays owns Britannia, frequently the most profitable part of their operation; and Owners Abroad owns Air 2000. Intasun owned Air Europe and Horizon Orion. This is one financial barrier to entry into the market. In addition, tour companies must agree hotel bedrooms with the hotel owners at least a year in advance and pay deposits; and they are required to lodge a financial bond with the Association of British Travel Agents as a form of insurance for customers.

Prices are quoted for holidays several months in advance of their being taken, and although there may be surcharges for fuel costs if the pound-to-dollar rate has been miscalculated, discounts are more common as the tour companies seek to ensure that they sell all the holidays they are committed to. Because airline seats and hotel places are fixed well in advance, they have little flexibility to reduce supply without incurring losses.

It is difficult to differentiate the product although segmentation is possible. Special holidays for young people and for old age pensioners are obvious examples. A two-week package offered by two or even three different companies, which is based on the same departure airport and the same hotel in the same resort, is obviously not regarded by the market as differentiated. Image and reputation affect customer preference but price competition must be expected. Because of the various advance payments incurred, fixed costs are a high proportion of total costs. This makes the tour operators volume dependent as explained in Figure 7.3. As they also commit themselves to large numbers of holidays to achieve economies of scale, price competition has become price warfare and this has kept profit margins low and forced smaller companies out of business.

Price competition has been imaginative and strategic throughout the 1980s. In September 1982 Thomson and Horizon launched their Summer 1983 brochures, to be followed by Intasun a few weeks later. Intasun undercut Thomson by several per cent on basically similar holidays, and expected that although Thomson would respond there would be a time delay which would work in Intasun's favour. In addition, Thomson would lose money because they had printed all their brochures. Thomson, however, had printed only a fraction of the number of brochures that they would require for the season, and having anticipated Intasun's move they very quickly relaunched their whole programme at lower prices and surprised all their rivals.

People who had already booked were given reductions of course. Throughout the 1980s Thomson and Intasun attempted to out-manoeuvre each other with their pricing strategies.

A further important aspect of competition is the role of travel agents. There are very large numbers of small independents but the concentration ratio is increasing as the bigger operators open more and more branches. The largest are Lunn Poly (owned by Thomson and with 21% market share), Thomas Cook (9% share, and sold by Midland Bank in 1992 to the German travel company, LTU), Pickfords (7% share, acquired by Airtours in 1992), Carlson Travel (US owned and incorporating A T Mays and what was W H Smith Travel) and Hogg Robinson. Since 1986 travel agents have been able to offer their own discounts on holidays, thereby increasing the complexity of price competition.

Thomson use information technology for competitive advantage. See Case 14.5.

by innovation and aggressive marketing and promotion.

The bargaining power of buyers is determined by

□ the concentration and size of buyer;
□ the importance to the buyer of the purchase in terms of both cost and quality (the more important it is the more he or she must ensure good relations with the supplier);
□ the degree of product standardization, which affects substitutability;
□ the costs, practicability and opportunity for buyers to switch supplier;
□ the possibility of vertical integration, initiated by either the supplier or the buyer.

The threat of product substitutes

The existence or non-existence of close substitutes helps to determine the elasticity of demand for a product or service. In simple terms this is price sensitivity. If there are close substitutes, demand for a particular brand will increase or decrease as its price moves downwards or upwards relative to competitors. Price changes can be initiated by any firm, but other competitors will be affected and forced to react. If products are not seen as close substitutes then they will be less price sensitive to competitor price changes.

For this reason firms will seek to establish clear product or service differentiation in order to create customer preference and loyalty and thereby make their product or service less price sensitive. Where this is accomplished industry profits are likely to rise, which of course may be attractive to prospective newcomers who will seek to create further differentiation in order to encourage customers to switch to them and enable them to establish a presence in the market.

Rivalry amongst existing competitors

Porter terms rivalry amongst existing competitors 'jockeying for position'. Competition may take the form of price competition, advertising and promotion, innovation, or service during and after sale. Where competitive firms are mutually interdependent retaliation is a key issue. Before deciding upon aggressive competitive actions firms must attempt to predict how their competitors will react; when other firms are proactive an organization must at least be defensive in

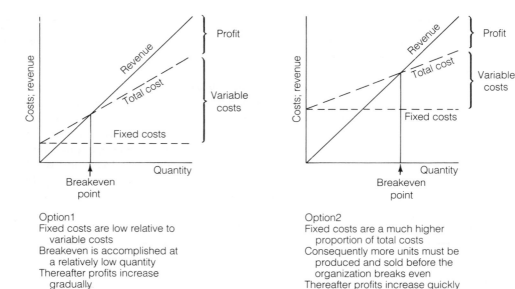

Option1
Fixed costs are low relative to
   variable costs
Breakeven is accomplished at
   a relatively low quantity
Thereafter profits increase
   gradually

Option2
Fixed costs are a much higher
   proportion of total costs
Consequently more units must be
   produced and sold before the
   organization breaks even
Thereafter profits increase quickly
This structure is more volume dependent
   and profit/(loss) increases quickly
   as output moves above/(below) breakeven

Fixed costs	Variable costs	Breakeven
Costs which remain constant over the usual range of activity, e.g. rent, rates, depreciation other overheads.	Costs which vary proportionately with output, e.g. direct labour and material costs	The point where all costs incurred have been covered by revenue from sales

Note: On the two graphs the revenue and cost schedules are shown as straight lines for simple illustration

Figure 7.3   Cost structures, breakeven points and profits.

order to protect market share and profitability. The intensity of competition is affected by the market structure and depends on
the following:

☐ the number of competitors and the degree
   of concentration
☐ the rate of growth of the industry – slow
   growth increases the pressure upon competitors to fight for market share
☐ the degree of differentiation – the less
   there is the more likely is price competition
☐ cost structures – where fixed costs are high
   relative to variable costs companies are
   very sensitive around the breakeven
   point. Profits are very dependent upon

volume. This is illustrated in Figure 7.3
which contrasts the position for companies with high and low fixed costs.

Case 7.5 on Package Holidays illustrates the
above two points. Competition for volume is
very aggressive partly as a result of the cost
structure, and price competition is a feature
because of the difficulty in differentiating the
product.

☐ The implications of changing size or
   supply capability through investment:
   although demand may be increasing at a
   relatively gradual and consistent rate,
   supply provision may increase in sizeable
   blocks as a result of the necessary investment. If a firm wishes to increase output

and it has exhausted the possibilities from increased usage of existing plant it will have to invest in new plant. When this is commissioned it may increase supply potential substantially and affect competitors as the company seeks orders to utilize its new capacity. Consider as examples a small charter airline which has three freight aeroplanes. If it buys a fourth it increases its capacity by 25% overnight. Similarly if there are two three-star hotels in a medium-sized town and a third is opened, the competitive situation changes markedly.

☐ The extent to which competitors are aware of the strategies of their rivals: one issue in this is the relative importance of the product or service to the various competitors. If a product is a by-product of another more important operation, for example, then the company concerned may compete very aggressively for sales and be far more concerned with volume than profits.

☐ The objectives of the competing firms – what matters to them. Are they more interested in profit, turnover or percentage market share? The objectives determine the strategies.

☐ Exit barriers, and the costs of leaving the industry: if these are high for any reason firms may be willing to accept low margins and limited profit opportunities in order to remain in the industry. The types of factor

---

Many companies spend a lot of time and money researching customers' views, but most spend nothing like enough on observing competitors. The main reason for change is to keep ahead of competitors or to catch up on the complacent market leaders. Companies must invest in development – it's a case of 'duck or no dinner'.

Sir Simon Hornby, Chairman,
W H Smith Group plc

---

which determine exit costs are dedicated assets which have no profitable alternative use; the costs of redundancy; interrelationships within a conglomerate, whereby a product may be either a by-product or an essential component for another division; emotional ties related to the history of the product and its association with the business; and pressure from government not to close down.

An example of dedicated assets which have no alternative use would be multiplex cinema complexes. As the number of these grows cinema audiences will have to increase if they are all to be viable. If this increase fails to materialize, the cinemas should close. But what is the alternative use for a building containing, say, ten small cinemas?

Box 7.3 provides a summary checklist of factors for industry analysis, and Box 7.4, analyses the brewery industry against Porter's model of five forces. The industry is concentrated and entry for an organization wishing to become a major force is difficult. Substantial capital would be required, and because the large brewers exercise significant control over distribution, acquisition is the most likely strategy. Competition is typically that of an oligopoly structure.

The rivalry factors discussed above, and the rivalry strategies, are both affected by any slowing down in the rate of industry growth, by acquisitions, and by changes in the marketing strategy of any one competitor resulting from the perception of new opportunities for differentiation or segmentation.

To be an effective competitor, a company must

☐ appreciate which of the five forces is the most significant (it can be different for different industries) and concentrate strategic attention in this area;
☐ position itself for the best possible defence against any threats from rivals;
☐ influence the forces detailed above through its own corporate and competitive strategies;

Box 7.3
A CHECKLIST FOR INDUSTRY ANALYSIS

☐ How many firms are in the industry, and what size are they?

☐ How concentrated is the industry?

☐ To what degree are products substitutes?

☐ Is the industry growing or contracting?

☐ What are the relative powers of suppliers?
buyers?
competitors?

☐ What are the prevailing competitive strategies?

☐ What entry barriers exist?

☐ What economies of scale are present?

☐ What experience/learning curve effects are important?

☐ What exit barriers exist (if any)?

☐ What important external factors affect competition?

☐ anticipate changes or shifts in the forces – the factors that are generating success in the short term may not succeed long term.

Much will depend upon the strategic leader, the quality of management in the organization and the prevailing culture.

The role of government

Rather than incorporation as a separate sixth factor, Porter maintains the importance of government lies in an ability to affect the other five forces through changes in policy and new legislation. The examples below are not exhaustive.

1. The introduction of competition into the National Health Service with the establishment of independent Hospital Trusts – outlined in Case 6.3.
2. A series of privatizations during the 1980s, including British Aerospace, Rolls Royce, British Airways and British Steel, along with the critically important utilities: British Telecom, British Gas and the water and electricity industries.

To prevent these utilities becoming national or local monopolies in private ownership, with enormous potential to exploit their customers, industry regulators have been

appointed, again as outlined in Case 6.3. The regulators and the newly privatized businesses have at times disagreed over important strategic issues. Late in 1991 the regulator for water (the Director General of OFWAT) expressed concern about the profits, dividends and diversification policies of certain water companies, arguing that:

☐ shareholder dividends should be restricted in order that capital developments could be properly funded;

☐ the debt ratio of some companies was too high and should be reduced; and

☐ the appropriate target return on capital employed should be reduced from the one used in the privatization.

Individual regulators are given freedom to establish specific guidelines within clear broad principles, and some would argue that this makes conflict between them and the regulated businesses inevitable. One of the reasons for the diversification strategies is that they create business activities which are outside the direct control of the regulator. Given a general trend away from diversification to a concentration on core businesses and competencies (see Chapter 18), this may prove to be risky. Maybe the impact of the regulators also needs regulating.

Privatizations have also been evident in

Box 7.4
THE BREWERY INDUSTRY: AN ANALYSIS AGAINST PORTER'S FIVE FORCES

Concentration figures were provided earlier in Box 7.1.

BARRIERS TO ENTRY

There are no major barriers to the entry of small firms which brew and retail on the same site, as evidenced in Bruce's Brewery featured in Chapter 3, Case 3.5. However, the establishment of a larger operation does require significant funding to purchase capital equipment; and the problem of distribution must be surmounted. A significant proportion of public houses are 'tied', i.e. they are controlled by the major brewers whose beers they sell. One additional problem concerns storage. Some newcomers have sought to brew real ales which are stronger than the keg varieties of the major brewers, but the former cannot be stored for long periods whereas the latter can. Therefore large-scale production of real ale would need to overcome this problem.

Breaking in might also require extensive advertising as the major brewers already promote their recognized brand names.

A company wishing to break in therefore might seriously consider an acquisition strategy; this again requires capital.

BARGAINING POWER OF SUPPLIERS

The bargaining power of suppliers is not really an issue. Beer is made from water, malt, yeast and hops, all of which are readily available.

BARGAINING POWER OF BUYERS

Consumption in public houses is controlled by the brewers as they control most of the public house licences through the 'tied house' mechanism. Additionally many of the brewers also own restaurant chains which gives them control of more outlets.

At least 50% of take-home sales are through the major supermarkets, and they provide some countervailing power to the brewers. These retailers have opposed certain mergers in brewing in the past, and some, for example Tesco, actively promote the products of smaller regional breweries.

AVAILABILITY OF SUBSTITUTES

In the last few years lager sales have been growing at the expense of the more traditional bitter beer, but the lagers are brewed by the major companies. Some brands are their own product; others are brewed under licence from foreign manufacturers. The well-advertised Foster's and Castlemaine XXXX (Australian beers), for example, are brewed by Courage and Allied respectively.

More recently alcohol-free beer has been introduced with some modest success, but again it is manufactured by the major companies.

RIVALRY AMONGST COMPETITORS

Differentiation strategies are supported by extensive advertising of brand names. Beers

Continued overleaf

and lagers are both targeted but to different buyer profiles, and image building is very important. For example a number of bitters are associated with northern regional accents and male audiences; lagers are targeted to younger customers of both sexes and occasionally celebrities are featured in the advertising. Several professional football clubs are sponsored by brewers, and brand names are featured on jerseys.

Price competition is not a major aspect, but prices of basically the same product vary in different regions of the country. All the major companies have invested in large breweries and capital equipment and therefore there are few opportunities to achieve any further cost advantages. The size of individual breweries is limited by the need to transport what is basically water long distances to the market.

Brewers have also invested substantially in improving their public houses in order to attract customers, and have again sought means of differentiating them.

(The above list of factors is not meant to be exhaustive.)

other countries. In 1991, for example, Bulgarian wine production ceased to be a State monopoly. Four State-controlled producers, who all co-operated with each other, were split into 33 independent businesses. Uncertainties concerned the ability of all 33 to survive, and their ability to maintain high quality to protect sales in the UK and Russia.

3. Deregulation of particular industries, such as air transport – see Case 7.6.

The lessening of restrictions and regulations unleashes new competitive forces and changes the nature of the industry. Some competitors will benefit; others will suffer.

In the UK the changes in air transport have created an interesting dilemma. BAA (British Airports Authority), who run most of the major airports in the UK (the exception is Manchester), was privatized in 1987. Airport charges are regulated by the Civil Aviation Authority (CAA) who have insisted on a new five-year formula covering the period April 1992 to March 1997. In Years 1 and 2 charges would change by a figure 8% below RPI (retail price index); in Year 3 by RPI less 4%; and in Years 4 and 5 by RPI less 1%. These imply a need for cost savings, together with greater efficiency and productivity. At the same time the need grows for both a fifth runway in the London area (to add to two at Heathrow and one each at Gatwick and Stansted) and a fifth terminal at Heathrow. BAA will be the developers, assuming their finances are sufficiently robust.

The forces described above determine the profitability of an industry, and hence the attractiveness of the industry for companies already competing in it and for companies who might wish to enter it. As well as understanding the nature and structure of the industry it is important for organizations to decide how best to compete. In other words, firms must appreciate the opportunities for creating and sustaining competitive advantage.

COMPETITIVE ADVANTAGE

Porter (1985) has developed his work on industry analysis to examine how a company might compete in the industry in order to create and sustain competitive advantage. In simple terms there are two basic choices.

☐ Choice one: Is the company seeking to compete
☐ by achieving lower costs than its rivals

Case 7.6
DEREGULATION AND THE INTERNATIONAL AIRLINE INDUSTRY

When governments regulated their airline industries, in order to control both national and international competition, new airlines were prevented from entering markets, existing companies could not simply offer flights into or out of any airport of their choice, routes could not be poached and prices for specified routes were fixed.

This regulation has been systematically reduced since the late 1970s. At this time domestic competition in America, where flying is as commonplace as bus and train journeys, was opened up. This has unleashed the underlying competitive nature of the industry with dramatic effects.

It is relatively easy to break into the industry if companies are allowed to do so. Planes can be leased and funded from revenue; maintenance can be bought in. Normally both fuel and planes are easily obtained. A company can enter by offering a limited service and concentrating on particular cities. Deregulation in America attracted such companies; and existing large airlines sought to expand their routes. Buyers were generally willing to fly with the airline which offered a flight at the time they wanted to travel, not differentiating, rather than building their arrangements around the schedule of their first-choice airline.

The British government has sought competition rather than monopoly control in the UK, privatizing British Airways in 1987. In 1991 the CAA (Civil Aviation Authority) relaxed certain rules, allowing new airlines to fly into and out of Heathrow for the first time since 1977. This intensified transatlantic competition as two strong US airlines (American and United, the two largest airlines in the world), which were restricted to Gatwick, acquired Heathrow/America routes from two weaker competitors, TWA and Pan Am respectively. At the same time Virgin Atlantic was: allowed to operate from Heathrow as well as Gatwick; allowed to fly to more American destinations; and given a number of BA's slots on the lucrative Heathrow to Tokyo route. All of these changes increased the competition for BA.

In June 1992 European Community transport ministers agreed a new 'open skies' policy to take effect from January 1993. There would be:

☐ Freer access for airlines to new routes throughout Europe. Previously many routes have been protected by governments to prevent competition with their national carriers. One difficulty in implementing this will be the ability of air traffic controllers to cope with more flights. European air traffic control is not fully co-ordinated and is over-stretched.

☐ Greater freedom for airlines to set their own seat prices, within certain protective safeguards. This may not mean prices will fall quickly because operating costs are already high with many flights operating below capacity.

☐ Lower barriers to entry for new carriers.

Deregulation began in Australia in 1990, when controls on prices and schedules were removed, resulting in domestic price warfare, cost-cutting measures and the entry of a new national airline, 'the first for decades'. The internal market in Australia was largely shared between Australian (owned by the government) and Ansett (owned

Continued overleaf

by TNT and Rupert Murdoch's News Corporation). In 1991 the government announced it intended to sell its 100% shareholding in Australian together with 49% of Qantas, the international carrier. In both cases it was assumed that foreign airlines would be the ultimate buyers.

EFFECTS

☐ Company winners and losers. In 1991 in America, for example, two previously major competitors, Eastern and Pan Am, went out of business. Earlier People Express, founded in America in the early 1980s (following deregulation) to offer cheaper price flights, also failed after rapid growth and profitability. Companies such as American, United and Delta, less well known before deregulation, have grown dramatically.

☐ New joint-venture agreements and cross-shareholdings. In 1991 it was mooted that BA and KLM (Holland) would form a joint venture to create the third largest airline in the world, but the two airlines have so far found it difficult to agree terms. In July 1992 BA reached an agreement with financially troubled US Air (the fourth largest American carrier) to acquire a 44% stake, and thereby gain access to American domestic routes. If the US Federal Authorities approve the deal, BA will be able to market through tickets to over 200 American cities. The largest three carriers, American, United and Delta, are trying to prevent the deal.

☐ Increased competitiveness with job losses during recession. The 1991 Gulf War had a major impact as many people were deterred from flying.

☐ Greater reliance on information technology to allow pricing flexibility in order to maximize load factors.

☐ Greater emphasis on service quality, especially punctuality and reliability, to try and establish customer loyalty.

☐ The introduction of frequent flyer promotions (free flights on particular airlines for regular travellers who accumulate points for miles). This is also aimed at generating more loyalty.

☐ New route strategies based on a 'hub and spokes' – flights are concentrated around particular regional centres. American control 65% of the slots at Dallas; United own 68% of the slots at Washington National and 48% of Chicago; and Delta 70% of Atlanta. Internationally carriers expect the same control at the major airport in their home country, but many are now seeking to establish further hubs around the world. BA lost to Air France for a joint venture with Sabena to create such a hub in Brussels. BA is also interested in a hub in Berlin.

and, by charging comparable prices for its products or services, creating a superior position through superior profitability?

or

☐ through differentiation, adding value

in an area that the customer regards as important, charging a premium price, and again creating a superior position through superior profitability?

☐ Choice two: In what arena is the company seeking competitive advantage? In a broad

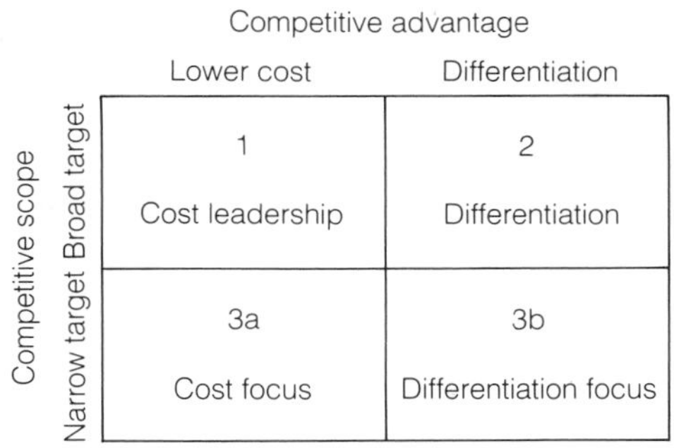

Competitive advantage

	Lower cost	Differentiation
Broad target	1 Cost leadership	2 Differentiation
Narrow target	3a Cost focus	3b Differentiation focus

Competitive scope

Figure 7.4 Porter's model of competitive advantage – the generic strategies. Adapted with permission of the Free Press, a division of Macmillan Inc., from *Competitive Advantage: Creating and Sustaining Superior Performance*, Porter, M E, Copyright 1985 M E Porter. (*Source*: Porter, M E (1985) *Competitive Advantage: Creating and Sustaining Superior Performance*, Free Press.)

Competitive advantage

	Lower cost	Differentiation
Broad target	Cost leadership Toyota	Differentiation General Motors
Narrow target	Cost focus Hyundai	Differentiation focus BMW Mercedes

Competitive scope

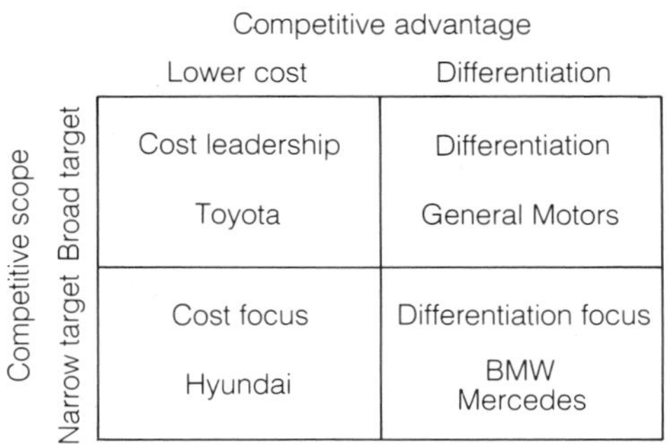

Figure 7.5 Porter's model of competitive advantage applied to the world motor industry.

Three generic strategies

These two choices lead to the three generic strategies illustrated in Figure 7.4. **Cost leadership** is where the company achieves lower costs than its rivals and competes across a broad range of segments. **Differentiation** occurs when the company has a range of clearly differentiated products which appeal to different segments of the market. **Focus strategies** are where a company chooses to concentrate on only one segment or a limited range of segments. With this approach it can again seek either lower costs or differentiation.

Motor vehicles and retailing: applications of the generic strategies

Before considering these generic strategies in greater detail it is useful to apply them to a particular industry. Porter argues that in the motor vehicle industry (Figure 7.5) Toyota is

range of segments or a narrow range, perhaps just one?

the overall cost leader. The company is successful in a number of segments with a full range of cars, and its mission is to be a low cost producer. In contrast General Motors also competes in most segments of the market but seeks to differentiate each of its products with better styling and better features. GM also offers a wider choice of models for each car in its range.

Hyundai is successful around the world with a restricted range of three small and medium size cars (Pony, Lentra and Sonata) which it produces at low cost and prices competitively. It should be noted that neither Toyota nor Hyundai market the **cheapest** cars available.

BMW and Mercedes have both succeeded by producing a narrow line of more exclusive cars for the price-insensitive quality conscious customer. There are a number of cars available from both companies but they are clearly targeted at people who are willing to pay premium prices for perceived higher quality. Jaguar would in fact be another example of a company which has a successful differentiation focus strategy. Some customers regard the unique image, styling and features of Jaguar cars as being worthy of a premium price.

Retailers similarly seek to compete on either image or cost. Image-based retailers add value to either or both the product and the service provided to customers. Success in differentiating generates customer loyalty and premium prices. Cost-based retailers operate with competitive margins, searching for strategies which balance high turnover with low costs resulting from operating efficiencies.

The cost leadership strategies of Toyota and Ikea are discussed in Case 7.7; the differentiation strategy of BMW is included in Case 7.8.

Porter argues that a company cannot achieve superior profitability if it is 'stuck in the middle' with no clear strategy for competitive advantage.

Case 7.7
TWO COST LEADERSHIP STRATEGIES: TOYOTA AND IKEA

TOYOTA

☐ Toyota enjoys a 40% plus market share in Japan, supplemented by 7.5% of the US market (where it also manufactures) and 3.0% of Europe – Toyota is following Nissan in manufacturing in the UK.

☐ Toyota sells a range of cars at prices marginally below those of comparable Ford and General Motors cars. Ford and GM both sell more cars than Toyota world wide.

☐ 'Toyota is the best car producer in the world and it keeps getting better.'

☐ In 1990 Toyota's operating profit margin was 9%. In comparison Nissan was 8.4%, Honda 6.5% and Ford (America only) 4.3%.

☐ Toyota spends 5% of sales revenue on research and development (as high as any major competitor), concentrating on a search for continuous improvements 'to inch apart from competitors', rather than major breakthroughs.

☐ There is a policy of fast new model development. In 1990 Toyota models had an average age of two years; Ford and GM cars averaged five years.

☐ Production systems, based on JIT (just-in-time supply of components – see Chapter 11), are very efficient. Toyota claims fewer defects than any other manufacturer, resulting from the vigilance of each worker on the assembly lines. The Lexus range of top-quality cars requires one-sixth of the labour hours used to build a Mercedes. The best Toyota plant assembles a car in 13 man hours, whereas Ford, Honda and Nissan all require 20.

☐ Toyota has investments of $22 billion earning interest to supplement operating profits.

☐ 'Toyota does not indulge in expensive executive facilities.'

American analysts believe that in 1992 both Ford and Chrysler can produce small cars for a lower direct cost than Toyota. But because American car plants typically operate at some 60% of capacity, and Toyota are at 95%, and also because of overheads such as pensions and healthcare, Toyota is still the industry cost leader.

(*Source*: Taylor, A III (1990) Why Toyota keeps getting better and better and better *Fortune*, 19 November.)

Case 7.7

IKEA

Ikea was started in Sweden by Ingvar Kamprad who pioneered the idea of self-assembly furniture in handy packs. The first store opened in 1958; by the late 1980s Ikea had almost 100 shops in 20 countries 'offering a wide range [11 000 products] of beautiful and functional furniture at affordable prices'. Ikea undercut their main competitors offering high quality at cheaper prices.

☐ Unlike many of their early rivals Ikea did not deliver, insisting that customers fetch their purchases.
☐ Customer traffic has always been directed through upstairs showrooms to downstairs purchase points.
☐ The furniture packs are commissioned from suppliers around the world, many from low-labour-cost countries such as Taiwan and Eastern Europe. Ikea uses 1500 suppliers in 40 countries.
☐ The organization is fundamentally informal with 'few instructions'. Dress is casual if employees wish, and periodically managers work in the warehouse or as sales personnel. 'Dynamism and a willingness to experiment will always lead us forward.'
☐ Growth has been carefully regulated. The second branch was opened only after seven years; the first branch outside Sweden was in the early 1970s; Ikea is still concentrated in Sweden and Europe. The first American store was opened in 1985 with roughly one store per year following. The gradual process is to ensure that appropriate local supply networks are properly established.
☐ In its three UK stores Ikea achieved (in 1991) sales per square foot 2.7 times the industry average.

(*Source*: Verdict Research.)

Cost leadership

To achieve substantial rewards from this strategy Porter argues that the organization must be **the** cost leader, and unchallenged in this position. There is room for only one; and if there is competition for market leadership based on this strategy there will be price competition.

Cost leadership as a generic strategy does not imply that the company will market the lowest price product or service in the industry. Quite often the lowest price products are perceived as inferior, and as such appeal to only a proportion of the market. Consequently low price related to lower quality is a differentiation strategy. Low cost therefore does not necessarily mean 'cheap' and low cost companies can have upmarket rather than downmarket appeal. Equally low cost does not imply lower rewards for employees or other stakeholders as successful cost leaders can be very profitable. Their aim is to secure a cost advantage over their rivals, price competitively and relative to how their product is perceived by customers, and achieve a high profit margin. Where this applies across a broad range of segments turnover and market share should also be high for the industry. They are seeking above-average profits with industry average prices.

Cost focus strategies can be based on finding a distinct group of customers whose needs are slightly below average. Costs are saved by meeting their needs specifically and avoiding unnecessary additional costs.

Figure 7.6 illustrates the above points and relates competitive advantage to efficiency and effectiveness.

There is little advantage in being only one of a number of low cost producers. The advantage is gained by superior management, concentrating on cost-saving opportunities, minimizing waste, and not adding values which customers regard as unimportant to the product or service. Many products do have values added which are not regarded as necessary by the market. Cost savings can generally be achieved in any and every area of the business; and quite often they begin with the strategic leader. Senior executives who enjoy substantial perks are unlikely to pursue a cost leadership strategy. Porter suggests that it is a mistake to believe that cost savings are only possible in the manufacturing function and that this strategy is only applicable to the largest producers in an industry. However, where cost leadership generates market share and volume production opportunities, economies of scale in manufacturing do apply. Key Concept 7.1, the experience curve, emphasizes that the effect is only achieved if it is managed; it is not automatic.

Differentiation

Cost leadership is usually traded off against differentiation, with the two regarded as pulling in opposite directions. Differentiation adds costs in order to add value for which customers are willing to pay premium prices.

Case 7.8 describes the differentiation focus strategy of Dunlopillo, Tomkinson's (a relatively small carpet manufacturer who are very profitable in their industry) and BMW. For a differentiation focus strategy to be successful the market must be capable of clear segmentation, and the requirements for this were highlighted in Key Concept 7.2.

Although cost leadership and differentiation may be mutually exclusive, successful strategies can be based on a mix of the two. YKK, the Japanese zip manufacturer and world market leader, achieves both cost leadership and significant differentiation. This case is explored in detail in Chapter 15. Sainsbury's argue that their strategy is based on providing good food at low cost for the broad middle ground in the market. They do not offer the cheapest food; equally they do not offer the choice or range of a specialist delicatessen. Consequently the ideas of Michael Porter can be questioned. However, they do provide an extremely useful framework for analysing industries and competitive advantage.

With differentiation superior performance

When I'm on a plane, I prowl around and talk to passengers and ask the staff about everything. I normally come back with a hundred notes in my pocket scribbled on little pieces of paper. Direct feedback is far better than market research.

Richard Branson, Chairman, Virgin Group, quoted in Ferry, J. Branson's misunderstood Midas touch, Business, November (1989)

The strategy of Virgin Atlantic Airways is built around quality service and differentiation. Virgin's 'Upper Class' aims to offer a first-class-equivalent service at business-class prices and provides, for example, electrostatic headphones which customers can keep afterwards, a selection of 30 films to watch on personal mini video-cassette players, and chauffeur-driven rides to and from airports.

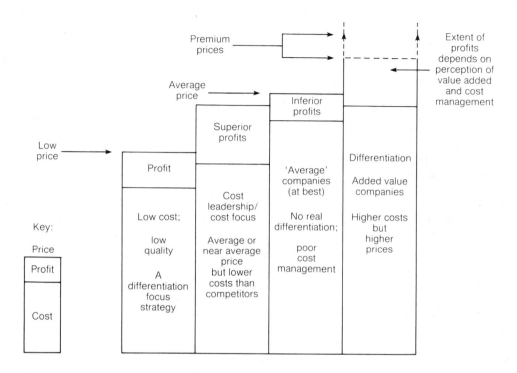

EFFICIENCY, EFFECTIVENESS AND COMPETITIVE STRATEGIES

	Cost Leadership	Differentiation
Efficiency via	Driving costs downwards	Doing things well
Effectiveness via	Knowing what is important and unimportant to customers — saving on latter	Finding and sustaining unique or different ways of competing

Figure 7.6 Competitive strategies.

is achieved by serving customer needs differently, ideally uniquely. The more unique the difference, the more sustainable is the advantage. Differentiation must inevitably add costs, which can only be recouped if the market is willing to pay the necessary premium prices. It is crucial that costs are only added in areas that customers perceive as important; and again this can relate to any area of the operation. A solicitors' practice, for example, might find competitive advantage in the manner and promptness in which

---

Case 7.8
FOCUS DIFFERENTIATION STRATEGIES: DUNLOPILLO, TOMKINSON'S CARPETS AND BMW

DUNLOPILLO

Dunlopillo is the UK bedding manufacturer subsidiary of the conglomerate BTR. Traditionally the furniture and bedding markets have been very competitive, with only limited spending on bedding products by British householders.

Dunlopillo has chosen to 'move upmarket' with a range of luxury items, looking for high prices and lower volumes. Market share overall is seen as less important than the right marketing position and image. Target customers are those 'best able to withstand any recession'.

Dunlopillo mattresses are made from latex, a spongy foam made from natural rubber, which is more flexible and resilient than springs or the more popular (and cheaper) polyurethane. Advertising, stressing benefits, is in selected magazines.

TOMKINSON'S CARPETS

Tomkinson's has only a small market share, but the company is profitable in an industry which has been depressed. Since Lowry Maclean became chief executive in 1979 the company has been turned round and made into the most profitable independent, publicly quoted, UK carpet manufacturer.

Productivity has been increased; and quality has improved, partly as a result of new policies with regard to supplies. Only good quality yarn is bought and this has resulted in fewer rejections; and the carpets are very carefully inspected for flaws.

The competitive strategy is one of medium price and high quality. The target market is the higher socioeconomic groups aged 30–55 who are likely to be interested in home decorating. The colours and patterns are selected and developed with these people in mind. Tomkinson's argue that their market segment is interested in colour (particularly), construction and performance, and is not especially price sensitive.

The carpets are not available from the large carpet warehouses but only from smaller independent shops. Specially developed display racks feature the colours and patterns. Advertisements typically list the names of suppliers. The carpets are branded 'Mr Tomkinson' and are packaged distinctively; and the advertisements have been developed around such slogans as 'Mr Tomkinson makes a better class of carpet' and 'Now . . . from Mr Tomkinson. Indulge your sense of style.'

BMW

BMW follow a number of strategies designed to protect their market niche, especially from Japanese competition. Notably these cover both the cars and the overall service package provided by BMW for its customers.

☐ Cars can be tailored and customized substantially. Customers can choose any colour they want, a benefit normally restricted to Rolls Royce and Aston Martin; and there is a wide range of interior options and 'performance extras'.
☐ BMW has chosen to ignore sports cars and hatchbacks, which they see as downmarket from luxury saloon cars. They may diversify with a 7- or 8-seater 'people carrier'.
☐ Safety, environment, economy and comfort are featured and stressed in every model.
☐ National sales companies are wholly owned together with strategically located parts warehouses. The independent distributors place their orders directly into BMW's central computer.
☐ There are fleets of specially equipped cars to go to the aid of BMW motorists who break down.
☐ BMW intends to stay independent, and, unlike many car companies, avoid joint ventures with competitors.

customer queries are dealt with, both over the telephone and in person. A fuller list might include the following possibilities:

☐ quality of materials used (related to purchasing)
☐ superior performance (design)
☐ high quality (production; inspection)
☐ superior packaging (distribution)
☐ delivery (sales; production)
☐ prompt answer of queries (customer relations; sales)
☐ efficient paperwork (administration).

Case 7.9, Crown Berger Paints, provides an example of a new differentiated product which incurred substantial development costs and was consequently launched with a premium price. The manufacturers felt convinced that the market would accept the price increase because of the added value. Competitive advantage can be built around superior performance in any of the factors listed above, but the ones selected should be key

success factors. It is very easy to add costs in areas which are unimportant to consumers and ignore those areas which really matter. The ideal means of differentiation is in an area which constitutes a key success factor, and which competitors cannot copy readily.

In the case of the Crown Berger paint container some aspects of the design are patented, and it will be interesting to see how ICI Dulux respond if the innovation proves successful in switching market shares. Interestingly the designers of the container have stated that the canister was designed by them and based upon their own perception of what was wrong with traditional paint tins, before being tested in the market. They have commented that they feel consumers cannot state clearly what is wrong with existing packaging – they need to be shown a new idea.

Furthermore it is insufficient merely to add value; customers must recognize and appreciate the difference. If it cannot be seen easily it should be communicated, perhaps through

Case 7.9
CROWN BERGER PAINTS

In January 1990 Crown Berger Paints, a subsidiary of the Williams Holdings conglomerate since 1987, launched a new paint product which was innovatory in two major ways. First, it was a one-coat emulsion called Crown Advance — typically two coats are required to cover a previous colour properly. Second, the packaging was completely new. During 1989 Crown had also introduced a gloss paint which did not require undercoat. Crown Berger are the second largest paint manufacturer in the UK; ICI are market leaders with Dulux.

The Advance container differs from the more traditional paint tin in a number of ways:

☐ It is a transparent plastic pack and consequently buyers can see the actual colour prior to purchase, rather than have to rely on colour cards. Moreover when the paint has been partly used and is in storage the level can be checked without opening up the canister.
☐ The handle is off-centre to allow for easier tipping and pouring into a paint tray.
☐ There is a special lip to prevent dripping; and the gutter around the top of tins, in which paint tends to collect, has been eradicated.
☐ The lid is deeper and easier to re-seal, and it contains a bar for wiping off surplus paint.
☐ Finally the container is basically square, although the edges are rounded. This is designed to make it easier for retailers to stack and display the product.

Crown asked Reedpack to manufacture the new containers. Both companies, incidentally, had once been subsidiaries of Reed International and had worked together. Reedpack had to invest over £1 million in new machinery and their staff had to be trained to handle them. They priced the containers at roughly double the cost of a traditional tin. Crown Berger felt convinced the market would perceive the product as superior and would accept a premium price. Advance was priced some 20% higher than existing emulsion paint.

Source: Urry M (1990) Cleaning up in the UK paint market, *Financial Times*, 4 January.

advertising. Communication between manufacturer and customer is vital, for it is only by understanding customer needs that the most appropriate value can be added. Take as an example the supplier of a component to an assembly company. At face value the supplier will seek to help the assembler lower his or her costs, or enhance the quality of his or her product, the choice depending upon the competitive strategy of the assembler. But this level of thinking alone might overlook further worthwhile opportunities. How does the assembler handle and store the components? And so on. If a supplier understands fully his or her customers' operations he might find new ways of adding value.

The differentiation strategy can be easily misjudged, however, for a number of reasons, including

☐ by choosing something that buyers fail to recognize, appreciate or value
☐ by over-fulfilling needs and as a consequence failing to achieve cost-effectiveness
☐ by selecting something that competitors can either improve on or undercut
☐ by attempting to overcharge for the differentiation
☐ by thinking too narrowly, missing opportunities and being outflanked by competitors.

CONCLUDING COMMENTS

This chapter has concentrated on how an organization can gain a deeper understanding of its competitive environment with a view to becoming a stronger more effective competitor through creating and sustaining competitive advantage. The closer a business is to its customers, the more it will understand the market and the industry. Competitive strategy, essential for every product and service that the organization makes and markets, involves a vision about how best to compete. There are a number of ways to generate competitive advantage, and the process is both logical and creative. The choice will also be influenced by the strategic leader and by the organization's culture. However, every employee contributes in some way to both lower costs and uniqueness, and therefore it is important that the competitive strategy is communicated and understood throughout the organization.

Understanding competitors

Information about competitors can be obtained in various ways. Technical journals, annual reports and press articles all help. By contrast it has been reported that Mitsubishi, the Japanese trading company, employs over 650 people in New York specifically to gather information about their American rivals and their markets.

Porter contends that competitors can be viewed as 'good' or 'bad'. Good ones differentiate, innovate and help to develop an industry; bad ones just cut prices in an attempt to drive others out of business. Good competitors should be encouraged as they sharpen their rivals and help to set up barriers against bad competitors. A good competitor seeks to increase the market by improving products, not by cutting prices. An interesting example is Polaroid who invented and patented the instant picture camera. Kodak introduced a rival product but Polaroid eventually succeeded in establishing that it broke their patent illegally. Whilst both products were in competition Polaroid became a much more effective competitor as they were unable to rely on their barrier to entry. By contrast it has been argued that certain large Japanese companies have literally bought themselves into segments of the computer and semiconductor industries by accepting very low prices until volume sales have been achieved. Where this has the effect of driving rivals out of business, as has been the experience in random access memory (RAM) chips, the question arises whether it is in the best long-term interests of consumers. Much depends upon the strategies of companies when they reach a stage of market domination.

These points are expanded further in Key Reading 7.1

How can we expect to succeed when we are playing cricket and the rest of the world is practising karate?

Sir Edwin Nixon, Chairman,
Amersham International

Key Reading 7.1
INTERNATIONAL COMPETITIVENESS

National competitiveness is not associated with factor costs, economies of scale and government protectionism. Rather it is associated with the ability to innovate – using the term in its widest sense. The search for new technologies and new ways of doing things – and this requires investment. Investment in research and development, in information technology and in marketing – and very much in people. A change in culture is implied for countries like Britain.

Sustained competitive advantage at a national level can only come about if firms are committed to change and to shifting the base of their competitive edge. The Japanese did this with motor cars, starting with basic, low-cost vehicles, progressing through mass market production to technically advanced products. Companies gain international competitive advantage, succeeding against the 'best' rivals, because they respond positively to pressure and challenge – they benefit heavily from having strong domestic rivals, aggressive home-based suppliers and demanding local customers.

The creation of this competitive advantage by certain firms in certain industries does not happen by chance. According to Porter (1990) there are four key attributes which together constitute the 'diamond of national advantage'. The term 'diamond' is used to emphasize the interrelationships and interdependencies between the factors.

THE DIAMOND OF NATIONAL ADVANTAGE

The four constituent parts are as follows:

1. **Factor conditions**, such as the availability of skilled labour. These factors, however, are not inherited, but consciously created often as a response to scarce resources. The Japanese, for example, enjoy competitive advantage in terms of delivery lead times and low costs, through JIT (just-in-time) systems, which they invented mainly as a response to the scarcity and high cost of land and space in Japan. The most valuable factor advantages tend to be specialized and require sustained investment. In fact, quite often they must be specialized in order to be sustainable – a generally well-educated workforce, for instance, is not a source of long-term advantage, but particular specialized skills may well be.

Frequently the creation of suitable factor conditions is a function of the other three forces, which facilitate the investment needed.

2. **Demand conditions**, especially in the home market. Porter argues strongly that global competitiveness actually increases the significance of the home market. A demanding clientele at home will often force firms to innovate if they are to compete successfully; and it is this which provides the basis for sustainable international advantage. If the nation's values and culture are also being exported – as has been the case with particular aspects of America to Europe, such as fast foods and credit cards – the advantage is reinforced.

3. **Related and supporting industries**, which themselves are internationally competitive. This ensures ready access to the raw materials and skills necessary to create advantage through either low costs or differentiation. The close proximity of related industries can ensure a quicker response to market trends and changes, and facilitate rapid innovation. At the same time suppliers should not be locked in irrevocably and exclusively to manufacturers, and producers should be free to resource abroad if necessary or appropriate.

Italian leather goods are an example of this. Manufacturers of different types of shoes (often specializing in a limited product range), producers of gloves and handbags, machinery suppliers and the leather manufacturers themselves are located in a closely linked cluster which is mutually advantageous and self-reinforcing.

4. **Firm strategy, structure and rivalry in the domestic market**. There is no one single universal management style which guarantees competitive success. Whilst the Italians have developed flexible networks which meet their need to compete in fast-moving fashion markets, the medium-sized German companies which dominate the European engineering industry, by contrast, succeed because of their well-defined management hierarchies and working practices which emphasize quality, precision and reliability.

Rivalry amongst domestic producers acts as a powerful competitive stimulus. Hoffman-La Roche, Ciba-Geigy and Sandoz, the three main Swiss pharmaceutical companies, are a case in point. In industries where the Japanese have achieved domination, there are often several rivals: Porter's research team identified 112 machine tool manufacturers, 34 in semiconductors, 25 in audio equipment and 15 in cameras. The more this rivalry is concentrated geographically, the greater the intensity of the effect. Italian jewellery, Swiss pharmaceuticals and Japanese motorcycles have all benefited from geographic concentration.

A COMMENTARY

Porter's central message in *The Competitive Advantage of Nations* is that competition is good for nations, and that anything which departs from or undermines competition is, by definition, bad. This could be inconsistent with arguments put forward by Porter in his earlier books. To be fair he has always stressed the value of 'good' competition which forces rivals to strive for ever-higher standards. But he also emphasizes the importance of assessing industry attractiveness before seeking to establish sustainable competitive advantage. Industry attractiveness is related to the ability to make above-average profits. An industry with intense rivalry between competitors, powerful suppliers and demanding buyers, and possibly with stagnant or declining sales, may offer only low profit potential to even the most effective and efficient business. Rationalization, and the exit of certain producers, will be required to make the industry more attractive.

Porter believes that the source of competitiveness is the national home base. However, for many companies operating in Europe the home base has already become too small. Electrolux derives competitive advantage from a European base rather than its home base of Sweden. See Case 17.5.

Consistent with other work on the relative success of diversification and acquisition strategies in America (see Chapter 18) Porter argues 'companies should be narrowing their focus to build international strength in core businesses'. This may well be true in a number of cases, but some diversification may be inevitable for companies whose core products are experiencing long-term, even terminal, decline. Diversification may be tricky to implement successfully and be a high-risk strategy, but it may be the only realistic alternative to prevent decline.

Writing in *The Economist* (1990) Porter invokes European companies 'to compete and not collaborate' with too many cross-border mergers or strategic alliances. The benefits of the 1992 single market are most likely to be gained 'if competition is encouraged and collusive behaviour curtailed'. The trend towards alliances and cross-border mergers will not make firms more competitive: 'dominant firms, or ones caught in a web of links with rivals, will not innovate and

Continued overleaf

upgrade. Supposed efficiencies from mergers will prove elusive in practice. Companies depending on collaborative activity will become mired in problems of co-ordination.'

Porter may be correct to point out the dangers of cross-national mergers, such as those in the European airline industry, stifling competition. His arguments about the difficulties involved in implementing alliances, similar to those involved in making acquisitions work effectively, are also well-founded. Other researchers have reached similar conclusions. But alternative evidence clearly supports the contention that economies of scale do exist in industries like telecommunications, aircraft manufacture and semiconductors which have expanded beyond national borders. Equally the European car industry, where six manufacturers each enjoy market shares between 10 and 15%, is unlikely to be sustainable in its existing form when national barriers are removed. Some cross-national mergers, and/or a strengthening of existing alliances, seems inevitable. Indeed, the leading German and Japanese companies have already embarked on a series of alliances, and Ford of America has joined them.

Based on: Porter, M E (1990) *The Competitive Advantage of Nations*, Free Press; and a summary of the conclusions in *The Economist* (1990), 9–15 June, p. 23–6. A useful critique can be found in *Management Update*, **2** (1), Autumn 1990.

New windows of competitive opportunity are always opening.

☐ Products and services can be improved to open up new markets and segments, as was the case with organizers which competed for the market pioneered by Filofax.
☐ New technologies change behaviour and demand, e.g. personal computers, personal cassette players such as the Sony Walkman, and hole-in-the-wall cash dispensers.
☐ Changes in attitude. Concern for the environment created the opportunity for unleaded petrol; acceptance of fast foods led to the growth of McDonald's and Pizza Hut; and a new willingness to wear inexpensive fashionable jewellery was exploited by Ratners. Ratners' strategy was very dependent upon substantial sales over the Christmas period. Price discounting during December 1991 failed to stimulate sales during the retail recession, and the strategy appeared fragile.

Competitive strategies depend upon successful and effective functional strategies, and consequently it is important that we study how the various functions of the business might be managed in the context of creating competitive advantage (Chapters 10–14). Before we do this we shall look first at why organizations fail and go out of business (Chapter 8) and, second, at other environmental issues of importance (Chapter 9). This part of the book is then concluded by considering in greater detail how an organization might measure where it is currently incurring and saving costs and where it is creating differentiation (Chapter 15).

SUMMARY

In this chapter we have explored the issues behind competitive strategy, concentrating on the nature and structure of the industry and the position of the firm in the industry. Specifically we have

☐ emphasized the importance of timing in competitive strategy – there are push forces for change from competitor actions, and pull forces from the market; the organization must respond to these by recognizing that strategies have life cycles and that at times they need replacing

☐ considered the structure of industry in the UK – the meaning of monopoly power has been explored in relation to the experience curve and economies of scale; concentration ratios have been defined and examples of industries exhibiting high concentration have been analysed

☐ described the policy of the UK government towards competition in terms of structure, conduct and performance; and considered how this might affect strategic decision making – in particular the roles of the Office of Fair Trading, the Restrictive Practices Court and the Monopolies and Mergers Commission have been featured

☐ analysed the model proposed by Michael Porter which contends that an industry can be analysed in terms of five key forces: the threat of new entrants; the relative power of both suppliers and buyers; the threat of substitute products or services; and rivalry amongst the existing firms in the industry – these forces determine industry profitability

☐ linked to the above model, defined product differentiation and explored the linkage between cost structures, breakeven and profits

☐ analysed a second Porter model of competitive advantage which argues that three generic competitive strategies of cost leadership, differentiation and focusing can be based on lower costs and differentiation

☐ reviewed Porter's work on international competitiveness.

CHECKLIST OF KEY TERMS AND CONCEPTS

You should feel confident that you understand the following terms and ideas:

☐ Monopoly power
☐ Concentration ratios
☐ Competition policy in the UK
☐ Economies of scale; the experience curve
☐ Porter's model of five forces which determine industry profitability
☐ Product differentiation
☐ The relationship between cost structures, breakeven and profits
☐ Porter's model of competitive advantage
☐ Cost leadership, differentiation and focus strategies
☐ The diamond of national advantage.

QUESTIONS AND RESEARCH ASSIGNMENTS

Text related

1. From your own experience, and from newspaper and other articles you have read or seen, list examples of where monopoly power and restrictive practices have been investigated, and where proposed mergers have been considered by the Monopolies and Mergers Commission. (If you wish to follow up any of these investigations, all the reports are published by HMSO.)

2. Study Figure 7.5 and consider where you would place other major car manufacturers and why. Where should Rover be categorized? Which companies appear to be 'struck in the middle' without a clear strategy for competitive advantage?

Library based

3. Case 7.5 describes the pricing strategy of Thomson Holidays in 1982, and shows that throughout the 1980s and early 1990s. Thomson and its rivals have been locked in price warfare. Trace how this competition has developed and how pricing

strategies have been changed in an attempt to outflank competition.

4. Take an industry of your choice, perhaps the one you work for, and assess it in terms of
   (a) concentration
   (b) Porter's model of five forces.

   From this analyse one or more of the major competitors in terms of their chosen competitive strategies.

   The following might prove useful sources of information:
   ☐ Business Monitors (PA and PQ series)
   ☐ Annual Report of the Director General of Fair Trading (as a source of ideas)
   ☐ Monopolies and Mergers Commission reports, which usually feature a comprehensive industry analysis
   ☐ McCarthy's Index (press cutting service for firms and industries).

5. How successful has Crown Advance (Case 7.9) been? Have the market shares of the major competitors changed significantly? Has ICI responded?

   (Williams Holdings sold Crown Berger Paints after the launch of Advance.)

RECOMMENDED FURTHER READING

Ohmae (1982) provides a pithy and anecdotal introduction to competitiveness, and Michael Porter's two books (1980 and 1985) are valuable works of reference on industry structure and competitive advantage.

It would also prove fruitful to read at least one report of the Monopolies and Mergers Commission which analyses competition in a particular industry.

REFERENCES

Devine, P J, Lee, N, Jones, R M and Tyson W J (1979) An *Introduction to Industrial Economics*, 3rd edn, George Allen and Unwin.

HMSO (1978) *A Review of Monopolies and Mergers Policy*, Command 7198.

Ohmae, K (1982) *The Mind of the Strategist*, McGraw-Hill.

Porter, M E (1980) *Competitive Strategy: Techniques for Analysing Industries and Competitors*, Free Press.

Porter, M E (1985) *Competitive Advantage: Creating and Sustaining Superior Performance*, Free Press.

Prowse, M (1986) Competition policy: how the UK got left behind, *Financial Times*, 11 June.

WHAT CAUSES A COMPANY TO FAIL?

8

LEARNING OBJECTIVES

After studying this chapter you should be able to

☐ explain what is meant by corporate decline and failure;
☐ identify the main symptoms of decline;
☐ describe the most likely causes of decline;
☐ calculate a Z-score, a possible predictor of potential failure.

This chapter describes the main causes of decline and failure. These are usually financial and competitive weaknesses. Recovery strategies for companies in trouble are developed later in the book (Chapter 19).

INTRODUCTION

This very short chapter is outside the main framework for the book which was outlined in Chapter 2. However, it is instructive to consider how one might assess whether a company is doing badly and heading for failure.

We have discussed objectives and the importance of stakeholders, and looked at how one might measure success. Although it is common to use financial ratios to measure relative success, the key issue concerns whether the organization is meeting the objectives set for it by its stakeholders. The crucial role played by the strategic leader has been discussed and the importance of creating and sustaining competitive advantage has been raised. In this chapter we shall see that poor strategic leadership, insufficient control of the essential aspects of financial management and the failure to be competitive are the key issues behind corporate failure.

In broad terms it could be argued that a company is unsuccessful if it fails to meet the objectives set for it by its stakeholders, or if it produces outputs which are considered undesirable by those associated with it. A company which polluted or harmed the natural environment in some way would be classified as unsuccessful by certain stakeholders but it would not necessarily fail financially and go out of business. Companies sometimes develop and launch new products which fail because very few people buy them – the Ford Edsel car and Strand cigarettes are well-quoted examples. In this respect the companies are unsuccessful with particular competitive strategies, but again they may not necessarily experience corporate failure as a result.

Corporate failure and the lack of success should not be seen as synonymous terms. A private sector, profit-seeking, organization would be classified as a failure if it ended up in liquidation and was closed down with its assets sold off piecemeal. A similar company might be unsuccessful and in decline, but able to avoid failure. Appropriate strategic action which addresses the causes of the decline may generate recovery. For example the major shareholders might insist upon the appointment of a new strategic leader, or the financial or competitive weaknesses might be acted upon. Such a company might also be acquired by another, and this may be because the shareholders are happy to sell their shares or because the company has been placed in receivership and the receiver has arranged the sale of the business as a going concern. Receivership occurs when a business is unable to pay its creditors, for example its suppliers or bank loan interest. The receiver is normally a professional accountant and he is charged with saving the business if it is possible to do so. In a similar way a non-profit-seeking organization could be closed down or provided with new leadership and direction on the insistence of its major financial stakeholders or trustees.

A company might be relatively unsuccessful compared with its competitors for a prolonged period of time if the key stakeholders allow it. For example a small private company whose shares are not quoted on the stock exchange might be making only very limited profits and growing at a rate slower than its industry, but its owners may be happy for it to stay in existence whilst it is solvent. In the English football league a large number of clubs, particularly outside the Premier League, fail to make any profit on their footballing activities because their crowds are too low, but other commercial activities, sponsorship, sales of players and benevolent directors keep them in business. However, such a lack of success consistently will weaken the company, cause it to exhibit symptoms of decline (discussed below) and may ultimately lead to failure.

In this chapter we look at what factors typically lead to corporate failure and at how managers might realize that their company is heading for failure unless remedial action is taken. Turnaround strategies for companies in trouble will be considered in detail in Chapter 19.

SYMPTOMS OF DECLINE

Symptoms of decline are not the causes of failure but indicators that a company might be heading for failure. They will show when a company is performing unsuccessfully relative to what might be expected by an objective outsider or analyst. As mentioned above they will indicate the outcome of poor strategic leadership, inadequate financial management or a lack of competitiveness. Slatter (1984), building on the earlier work of Argenti (1976), has analysed 40 UK companies in decline situations which have either been turned around or have failed. He concludes that there are ten major symptoms. In the same way that relative success can be evaluated from financial analysis, a number of these symptoms of decline are finance based:

☐ falling profitability
☐ reduced dividends, because the firm is re-investing a greater percentage of profits
☐ falling sales, measured by volume or revenue after accounting for inflation
☐ increasing debt
☐ decreasing liquidity
☐ delays in publishing financial results, a typical indicator that something is wrong

☐ declining market share

☐ high turnover of managers

☐ top management fear, such that essential tasks and pressing problems are ignored

☐ lack of planning or strategic thinking, reflecting a lack of clear direction.

If any of these symptoms are perceived it will be necessary to identify the underlying causes before any remedial action might be attempted. Slatter concluded that a number of causal factors recurred on several occasions in the companies he studied, and these are summarized below, but categorized in terms of issues of leadership, finance and competitiveness.

CAUSES OF DECLINE

Inadequate strategic leadership

Poor management

Ineffective management concerning key strategic issues can be manifested in a number of ways. The company could be controlled or dominated by one person whose pursuit of particular personal objectives or style of leadership might create problems or lead to inadequate performance. The organization might fail to develop new corporate or competitive strategies such that previous levels of performance and success are not maintained when particular products, services or strategies go into decline.

This issue can be compounded or alleviated by weak or strong managers respectively supporting the strategic leader, and by the quality of non-executive directors on the Board. Poor strategic leadership in terms of building an appropriate organization might mean that key issues or key success factors are ignored or are not given the attention they deserve. A company that is dominated by accountants or engineers might, for example, fail to pay sufficient attention to chang-

ing customer requirements and competition. Equally a company without adequate financial management might ignore aspects of cost and cash flow management – a factor which will be explored later in this chapter. Similarly a company which is undergoing rapid change and possibly diversification might concentrate its resources in the areas of development and neglect the core businesses which should be providing strong foundations for the growth.

Acquisitions which fail to match expectations

This particular point will be explored in detail in Chapter 18, but the significance is worthy of mention here. Companies seeking growth or diversification may take over other companies or merge with them. Research, which will be discussed later, suggests that in many cases the profits and successes anticipated from the acquisition fail to materialize. This can be the result of a poor choice by the strategic leader who over-estimates the potential or an inability to manage the larger organization effectively because the problems are under-estimated.

It is not unusual for companies which fail to have sought fast growth, often following strategies involving major acquisitions. Examples include: Blue Arrow which acquired the American company Manpower to create the largest employment agency business in the world, funded by a major rights issue which over-stretched the company; Next, which failed to integrate a series of acquisitions effectively; Storehouse, formed when Habitat/Mothercare acquired British Home Stores; and leisure group Brent Walker, which borrowed heavily to fund the purchase of pubs, casinos and the William Hill chain of 1600 betting shops.

Mismanagement of big projects

This is related to the previous point, but incorporates a number of other possible strategic decisions. By big projects is meant any really new venture for an organization, including developing new and different products and entering new markets, possibly abroad. It is essential to forecast potential revenues without being unrealistically optimistic, and to control expenditures and costs, but this does not always happen. It seems that companies often

□ under-estimate the capital requirements, through poor planning, design changes once the project is underway, and inaccurate estimations of the development time that will be required;

□ experience unforeseen start-up difficulties, sometimes resulting from lack of foresight and sometimes from misfortune;

□ misjudge the costs of market entry because of customer hostility or hesitation, or the actions of competitors.

Companies should be careful not to stretch their financial and managerial resources with big projects as they can cause other healthier parts of the business to suffer.

Poor financial management

Poor financial control

This again can manifest itself in a number of ways. Particularly important are the failure to manage cash flow and the incidence of temporary illiquidity as a result of over-trading, which were discussed in Chapter 6. Inadequate costing systems can mean that companies are not properly aware of the costs of the different products and services they produce, and as a result they can move from profit to loss if the mix of products they produce and sell is changed. If an organization invests in expensive equipment for potentially lower costs or product differentiation, then it automatically increases its fixed costs or overheads. As we saw in Chapter 7, Figure 7.3, this will increase the breakeven point and consequently make the company

more volume sensitive. Investments of this nature should not be undertaken lightly and without a thorough and objective assessment of market potential; but some companies do invest without adequate analysis and create financial problems for themselves.

Finally some companies in decline situations appear not to budget properly. Budgets are short-term financial plans which forecast potential demand and sales revenue, the costs which will be incurred in meeting this demand, and the flow of cash in and out of the business. If budgeted targets are not being met it is essential to investigate why and take any steps necessary to improve the situation. Without proper budgeting companies cannot estimate profits and cash needs adequately and can therefore experience unexpected financial difficulties.

Cost disadvantages

In addition to the problem of breaking even and covering overheads, described above, companies can experience other cost disadvantages which result in decline. As we saw in Chapter 7, lower costs are a major source of competitive advantage.

Economies of scale and the experience curve were discussed in Chapter 7; companies without scale economies can be at a cost disadvantage relative to their competitors and suffer in terms of low profit or a failure to win orders because their prices are higher. Companies which are vertically integrated and able to exercise control over their supplies, or which are located in areas where labour or service costs are relatively low, can enjoy an absolute cost advantage over their rivals and thereby put pressure upon them.

Company structure can yield both cost advantages and cost disadvantages. Large multi-product companies can subsidize the cost of certain products and again put pressure on their rivals; or conversely they can find that their costs are higher than their smaller competitors because of the overhead costs of the organization structure, say through an expensive head office.

Finally poor operating management can mean low productivity and higher costs than ought to be incurred, and thereby cause decline. These cost problems all affect competitiveness and they are therefore linked to the additional competition factors discussed below.

Other issues

It was mentioned in Chapter 6 that the debt ratio should be controlled so that companies did not risk embarrassment through not being able to pay interest charges because of low profits. Companies which rely on loan capital may find that in years of low profits they are unable to invest sufficiently and this may lead to decline. Conversely other companies may decline because they have not invested as a result of conservatism rather than financial inability. This reflects another weakness of strategic leadership.

Tizer, featured briefly in Chapter 7, Case 7.1, is an example of this. Although at the end of the 1960s Tizer's product, distribution network and production systems were all in need of investment and modernization, Tizer had reserves of cash and no loans. They had simply chosen not to borrow and invest.

Competitive forces

Porter's model of the forces which determine industry profitability was discussed in Chapter 7. Whilst all these forces can be managed to create competitive advantage, each of them could cause a weak competitor to be in a decline situation.

The effect of competitive changes

Primarily companies can find themselves in decline situations if their products or services

cease to be competitive. Their effective life and attractiveness to customers might be ending; or their competitors might have improved their product or introduced something new, thereby strengthening their product differentiation and competitive edge and inevitably causing demand for other products to fall. In other words decline can result from a loss of clear differentiation and in turn a failure to maintain competitive advantage. Tizer is again an excellent example.

If costs increase, say because of increased labour costs which competitors manage to avoid, then pressure will be put on prices or profit margins, and it may no longer be worth while manufacturing the product or service.

Resource problems

It was mentioned above that increased labour costs can render a company uncompetitive; other resources controlled by strong suppliers can have a similar effect. In addition a company can experience cost problems as a result of currency fluctuations if it fails to buy forward appropriately to offset any risk and with property rents if leases expire and need renegotiating in a period of inflation.

Inadequate or badly directed marketing

This factor relates to issues of rivalry between competitors. It was emphasized in Chapter 7 that companies whose competitive strategies rely on differentiation must ensure that customers recognize and value the source of the differentiation. This requires creative and effective advertising and promotion targeted to the appropriate segments and can be very expensive, especially if the industry is characterized by high advertising budgets. Companies who fail to market their products or services effectively may decline because they are failing to achieve adequate sales.

Case 8.1
LAKER AIRWAYS

Freddie Laker, who became Sir Freddie in 1978, was an entrepreneur and a pioneer in the competitive international air transport industry. He was a well-quoted self publicist whose commercial exploits brought him fame and recognition. He introduced cheap transatlantic air travel, providing travel opportunities for many people who previously had not been able to afford the fares; but his business collapsed in the early 1980s.

In the 1960s Laker Airways was a small independent company 'operated on a shoestring' which offered a number of inclusive package holidays and provided charter flights for organizations who could book all the seats on a plane and flights for tour companies who did not own their own airline. Laker's stated intention was to stay small: 'If we get any bigger than six planes you can kick my arse.'

In the 1970s his ambitions changed and he became determined to 'try a new market and offer transport to a lot more people'. At this time the only cheap air fares across the Atlantic were charter flights, whereby travellers had to be a member of some sponsoring organization for at least six months before flying. The international carriers operated a price-fixing cartel organized by the International Air Transport Association (IATA) with the connivance of all governments concerned. Charter flight regulations tended to be abused, and consequently the major carriers fought for stricter monitoring which brought about a decline. Laker conceived Skytrain, a 'no booking, no frills' operation with prices significantly below those offered by the major airlines, who naturally opposed his idea.

Laker applied to the Civil Aviation Authority (CAA) for a licence first in 1971 and was refused. In late 1972 he was given permission as long as he flew out of Stansted, although his base was at Gatwick. Delaying tactics involving British and American airlines, the UK Labour government, the American government and the American equivalent of the CAA meant that the first flight did not take place until September 1977 when Skytrain was launched with enormous publicity, this time from Gatwick. In this period oil prices had increased dramatically and Skytrain, although still under £100 for a single fare, was double the price estimated in 1971. In turn the Skytrain fare was well under half the cost of the cheapest fare offered by IATA carriers who subsequently had to reduce their fares in the face of this new competition.

Skytrain made £2 million profits in its first year of operation, but difficulties experienced when it was extended to Los Angeles in 1978 effectively wiped out the profitability. In 1979 Laker became a fully licensed transatlantic carrier and for the first time was able to pre-sell reserved seats. Laker's confidence grew, and anticipating that he would be given permission to fly more routes around the world he ordered ten Airbus A-300s and five McDonnell Douglas DC10s at a total cost of £300 million. Eventually this was to bring his downfall. Laker was already using DC10s for Skytrain and when the US government grounded all DC10s for checks in 1979 Laker lost £13 million in revenue. In 1980 he failed to win licences to fly Skytrain in Europe and to Hong Kong, although he did begin services from Prestwick and Manchester and to Miami.

Profits of £2.2 million were reported for 1980–1, but significantly three-quarters of this came from favourable currency movements. By 1981 the pound was falling against the dollar, demand was declining, revenue was down, but the debt interest payments, mostly in dollars, were rising. There were, in effect, too many planes and not enough passengers flying the Atlantic. The major airlines wanted fares to rise, but Skytrain remained the force which kept them low.

Laker did manage to renegotiate some interest payments and a cash injection from McDonnell Douglas, but he also had to increase fares and sell his Airbuses. He was left with a breakeven level of virtually all the seats on every Skytrain, but was able to fill only one-third of them. When the receiver was called in (February 1982) Laker had debts of some £270 million.

Laker had pioneered cheap transatlantic airfares, which have stayed in different guises since his collapse, but he made the mistake of becoming over-confident. The man who originally intended to stay small went for growth. At the same time he was determined to retain total control of his company and therefore raised loan capital against very limited assets rather than seeking outside equity funding. The interest payments brought him down, particularly as he raised most of the money in dollars without adequate cover against currency fluctuations. Finally, as something of a buccaneering character described by one airline executive as a man who 'a few hundred years ago would have brass earrings, a beard and a cutlass', he underestimated the power of the vested interests who opposed him. Had their opposition not delayed the introduction of Skytrain by six years maybe things would have turned out differently.

Source: Monkton, C and Fallon, I (1982) *The Laker Story*, Christensen Press and Sunday Telegraph, 1982.

Case 8.1, Laker Airways, illustrates a number of the above points. Freddie Laker, when he launched his Skytrain, undercut the prices of the major airlines and appealed to a distinct sector of the market, but he was over-confident and committed too many resources on his new venture and on possible growth which did not materialize. His financial arrangements constituted his downfall. The case also illustrates the importance of understanding and not under-estimating the environmental forces which influence the organization. This is the theme of Chapter 9.

In a decline situation a number of the factors above may be present and interlinked; and it may not be easy to distinguish between cause and effect. For example a company may be losing market share or sales and experiencing a decline in profits because its product or service is no longer competitive. It may have a cost disadvantage or its competitors may have more effective sources of differentiation. Is the cause of this situation poor management internally which has failed to contain costs or create and sustain competitive advantage, or the result of external competitive forces to some extent outside the control of the organization? If the company is to be turned around, then both the symptoms of decline and the underlying causes need to be acted upon.

In simple terms, when a company is in real trouble the strategic leader, who may be new and brought in specially, might be expected to perform one of a number of alternative roles. He or she may have to act as firstly an

---

Key Concept 8.1
Z-SCORES

The original Z-score of Altman (1968) is:

$$Z = 1.2 \times X^1 + 1.4 \times X^2 + 3.3 \times X^3 + 0.6 \times X^4 + 1.0 \times X^5$$

where

X^1 = is working capital divided by total assets

X^2 = is retained earnings divided by total assets

X^3 = is earnings before interest and tax divided by total assets

X^4 = is market value of equity divided by book value of total debt

X^5 = is sales divided by total assets

and

☐ working capital is current assets less current liabilities
☐ total assets is fixed assets plus all current assets
☐ retained earnings is accumulated profits in the business
☐ market value of equity is the number of ordinary shares × their current market price + the value of preference shares
☐ book value of total debt is long-, medium- and short-term debt, including overdraft

For US companies, Altman argued that if Z is less than 1.8 they are 'certain to go bust' and if it exceeds 3.0 they are 'almost certain not to'. Argenti suggests the appropriate UK figures are more of the order of 1.5 and 2.0 respectively.

Companies with a strong asset base will tend to have a high Z-score under the Altman formula, but such businesses do fail, generally then being sold as going concerns.

Taffler (1977) has devised an alternative formula which places greater emphasis on liquidity:

$$Z = 0.53 \times X^1 + 0.13 \times X^2 + 0.18 \times X^3 + 0.16 \times X^4,$$

where

X^1 = profit before tax divided by current liabilities (incorporating profitability)

X^2 = current assets divided by total debts (working capital)

X^3 = current liabilities divided by total assets (financial risk)

X^4 = the no credit interval (liquidity)

and the 'no credit interval' is defined as:

$$\frac{\text{Immediate assets} - \text{Current liabilities}}{\text{Operating costs} - \text{Depreciation}}$$

Using Taffler's formula a score in excess of 0.2, and certainly 0.3, indicates a company with good long-term prospects; below 0.2, and definitely below 0.0, is a score characteristic of companies which have failed in the past.

Sources: Altman, E I (1968) Financial ratios, discriminant analysis, and the prediction of corporate bankruptcy, *Journal of Finance*, **23** (4), September. Taffler, R J (1977), Going, going, gone, *Accountancy*, March.

---

undertaker and liquidate the company, secondly a pathologist, carrying out major surgery such as divesting poorly performing parts of the business or cutting their size, or thirdly a health clinic doctor, restoring the

company's fortunes. Prices might be increased to generate more revenue or improve the gross margin. Variable costs, and if possible fixed costs, might well be reduced, again to improve margins and also to reduce the need for working capital. Divestment is one way of reducing assets and generating revenue. Attempts are also likely to be made to improve stock and debtor turnover in order to improve the cash flow. The alternative strategies will be explored in detail in Chapter 19.

PREDICTING A FAILURE

Financial data bases, such as Datastream, typically provide an index known as a Z-score, which was devised by Edward Altman (1968) and which purports to predict potential corporate failure as a result of insolvency. Altman's research in America in the 1960s found the Z-score to be a good indicator of potential bankruptcy, but further research in the UK by Argenti (1976) and others suggests that the index should be used cautiously. The Z-score, which is explained in Key Concept 8.1, tends to be more appropriate in the last two years before bankruptcy when it could be argued that a good financial analyst should be able to see clearly that a company is experiencing difficulties and is in decline. Argenti argues that managers rarely look for symptoms of decline, and consequently the Z-score can be a useful indicator of when such an analysis might be appropriate. If a company appears to be in decline and the trend is identified soon enough, then recovery strategies can be initiated.

SUMMARY

In this chapter we have attempted to draw together a number of topics considered earlier in the book and discussed how they can affect corporate decline. Specifically these issues are strategic leadership, financial management and competition.

In addition the distinction between a lack of success and decline and failure has been explored, and a number of symptoms of decline have been listed.

The Z-score, an index of corporate well-being or decline, has been illustrated briefly.

QUESTIONS AND RESEARCH ASSIGNMENTS

Text related

1. Do the causes discussed in this chapter provide an adequate explanation for any corporate failure with which you are familiar?

Library based

2. In 1983 Z-scores provided by Datastream suggested that the following companies (amongst others) were in decline:
   □ Rover Group (then British Leyland)
   □ British Aluminium
   □ Renold (chainmakers)
   □ Acrow (cranemakers)
   □ Dunlop
   □ Lucas
   □ Tube Investments.

   A number of other companies (including those listed below) were considered vulnerable to acquisition because their share prices were low in comparison with the book value of their assets:

   □ Lonrho
   □ P & O
   □ House of Fraser
   □ Debenhams
   □ Tootal Group
   □ Coats Patons

☐ British Aerospace
☐ Vickers.

Having studied this chapter, and before reading Chapter 19 on turnaround strategies, ascertain what has happened to these companies since 1983.

RECOMMENDED FURTHER READING

Readers who want more information on company failure are referred to Slatter's book.

REFERENCES

Altman, E I (1968) Financial ratios, discriminant analysis and the prediction of corporate bankruptcy, *Journal of Finance*, **23** (4), September. The Z-score is explored further in Altman, E I (1971) *Corporate Bankruptcy in America*, Heath.

Argenti, J (1976) *Corporate Collapse*, McGraw-Hill.

Slatter, S (1984) *Corporate Recovery: Successful Turn-around Strategies and their Implementation*, Penguin.

Taffler, R J (1977) Going, going, gone, *Accountancy*, March.

PART THREE

SITUATION
ANALYSIS

INTRODUCTION TO ENVIRONMENTAL AND RESOURCE ANALYSIS

A SWOT (strengths, weaknesses, opportunities, threats) analysis is an examination of an organization's strengths and weaknesses (an evaluation of its resources) in relation to possible opportunities and threats (an assessment of the environment). The forthcoming chapters (9–15) develop the idea behind a SWOT analysis and explore in some depth the concept of matching the environment with resources and values-E–V–R congruence.

A SWOT analysis represents an evaluation of how well the resources of an organization match the needs of the environment in which the firm operates and competes. We have considered the role and influence of stakeholders generally and the need for the organization to understand the forces of competition as they affect it. These constitute what are known as environmental influences, and they will now be examined in greater detail. After this assessment of environmental forces (Chapter 9) the organizations's resources will be examined in terms of how they can contribute towards the creation and maintenance of competitive advantage and, in turn, strategic success.

All major resources (for example, marketing of products and services,

Today's profitable companies are finding that success depends more and more on providing a flexible response to rapidly changing customer demands. British companies must learn to adapt their resources, skills and knowledge to changing market environments. Part of the secret of doing this is to be constantly alert to what both competitors and customers – at home and abroad – are thinking and doing.

Eric Forth MP, previously Under Secretary of State for Industry and Consumer Affairs

operations (design, creation and manufacturing of the products and services), finance and human resources) make a strategic contribution, although their individual strategies are normally referred to as functional strategies. In Chapter 1 we said that functional strategies, together with competitive and corporate strategies, are constituent parts of strategic management. The strategic role of these functions is therefore considered sequentially in Chapters 10–13. However, it is also vital that the functions are co-ordinated because they are interdependent. Decisions taken for one function will affect other functions and other managers in the organization. The communication of decisions, and an understanding of what is happening throughout the organization, depend on information flows and information systems (the subject of Chapter 14). Chapter 15 considers how resources overall can be managed to create competitive advantage.

Just as individual functions must work in harmony, it is also necessary that the various parts of the business be co-ordinated. These parts could be represented by different products or various strategic business units. Depending on the degree of diversification the links between them may be relatively strong or relatively weak. What matters is that their efforts are co-ordinated in order to achieve synergy (Ansoff, 1968). Synergy is defined in Key Concept III.1. Ansoff describes synergy as the $2 + 2 = 5$ effect: the combination of the parts produces results of greater magnitude than would be the case if the parts operated independently. If functions, products or business units were not co-ordinated efforts may well be duplicated, or delays might be built into the organization system because of a lack of understanding. Where several products or services are produced some common experiences or activities might well be shared. Figures III.1 and III.2 illustrate the relationship between corporate, competitive and functional strategies. There are functional strategies for each management function in the business; and at the same time the competitive advantage enjoyed by a product or service will be created in one or more of the functions. It could be any one of them, as will be discussed later. Consequently the competitive strategy, based partly on the competitive advantage, is supported by functional strategies. The corporate strategy is the amalgamation of the competitive strategies. This part of the book analyses functional and competitive strategies and leads on to Part IV, where we consider changes in the corporate strategy. Implementation of changes in the corporate strategy (Part V) requires effective co-ordination of competitive and functional strategies.

Synergy is more likely to occur if all these strategies are linked in such a way that the organization as a whole is managed effectively, which Drucker (1973) has defined as 'doing the right things'. Individual business units and functions must themselves be managed efficiently or, as Drucker would say, they must

Key Concept III.1
SYNERGY

Synergy is concerned with the returns that are obtained from resources. The argument is that resources should be combined and managed in such a way that the benefits which accrue exceed those which would result if the parts were kept separate. In other words, if an organization manufactures and markets six different products, the organization should be structured to yield the benefits which might be possible from combining these different interests. For example, central purchasing for all products might yield economies of scale; factory rationalization might increase productivity or lower production costs; salesmen might be able to obtain more or larger orders if they are selling more than one product; each product might gain from name association with the others; and distributors might be more satisfied than if the company offered only a very limited range or a single product. Some of the benefits are clearly measurable; others are more subjective.

There are three basic synergy opportunities:

☐ **Functional** – sharing facilities and competences
☐ **Strategic** – complementary competitive strategies
☐ **Managerial** – compatible styles of management and values.

Where an organization is considering increasing its range of products and services, or merging with or acquiring another company, synergy is an important consideration. In the case of an acquisition the combination of the companies should produce greater returns than the two on their own. Adding new products or services should not affect existing products or services in any adverse way, unless they are intended to be replacements. When such strategic changes take place the deployment of resources should be re-evaluated to ensure that they are being utilized both efficiently and effectively.

In just the same way the existing deployment and management of resources, the way they are combined, and the structure and management systems within the organization should be such that synergy is being obtained; i.e. that opportunities for greater returns are not being ignored as a result of poor resource management.

This may well imply the sharing of knowledge and other resources between divisions or business units, possibly attempting to disseminate best practice. This is only feasible if resource efficiencies are measured and compared in order to identify which practices are best. Internal rivalries may prevent the attainment of the potential benefits from sharing.

Benefits might also be gained by offering important skills to other organizations. The logistics of distribution and product support are critical success factors for Caterpillar, the world's largest producer of construction equipment. Caterpillar formed a new service business to capitalize on the expertise they had developed, offering warehousing, transport management and other support services world wide. They now distribute products as diverse as bathroom fittings, air compressors, vehicle parts and sportswear.

It will be suggested later in the book that anticipated synergy from strategic changes is easily over-estimated and that it may not accrue. Potential benefits from adding new activities may be misjudged. In Box 2 in the Preface one diversification by the Lex Service Group in the 1970s was mentioned briefly. Lex were successful and profitable with essentially car distribution and felt that their resources and skills would be ideally suitable for transfer into hotel management. They anticipated synergy because of their management skills. Their level of success from the

Continued overleaf

change, however, was below their expectations and they withdrew from this industry.

A SEARCH FOR SYNERGY

A number of Japanese electronics companies (manufacturers of televisions, videos and hi-fi equipment) have sought links with the American makers of music and films, arguing that there is potential synergy from merging hardware and software. New products are technologically feasible – the manufacturers want to secure their commercial exploitation. Such developments include high-definition televisions, flat screen TVs (both large and small for mounting on walls [like a picture] and carrying around), personal video disc players the same size as personal cassette players, and miniaturized CDs and CD players. Films can also be the basis for computer games. The large film companies have huge film libraries for video and games exploitation, both growth markets at the end of the 1980s. The strategy is similar to that of the manufacturers of razors who have derived benefits and synergy from also manufacturing razor blades.

Sony acquired CBS Records in 1987 and Columbia Pictures from Coca Cola in 1989. Previously Coca Cola had anticipated synergy from linking soft drinks and entertainment, but it had not accrued. Matsushita acquired MCA (Universal Pictures, record labels and part-ownership of a network TV station) in 1990. Toshiba negotiated a joint venture with Time Warner. Earlier Rupert Murdoch had bought Twentieth Century Fox to exploit the film library on his cable and satellite TV networks worldwide.

The strategy has been defended with logical arguments. It has been suggested that if Sony had owned Columbia in the 1970s their Betamax video format would have proved more successful because more pre-recorded videos would have been available on this format rather than the successful VHS – developed by Matsushita who were more resourceful in striking agreements with video makers. Similarly, CBS would prove a useful vehicle for forcing the pace of the switch from records to compact discs.

Sceptics argue the synergy will not accrue, arguing that the typical Japanese company and Hollywood film makers have dramatically different cultures which may not prove compatible. Moreover, Japan itself is not noted for creativity in entertainment. Interestingly record companies have been reluctant to release music in the new high-technology DAT (digital audio tape) format. Whilst Sony have pioneered the hardware, CBS have chosen not to break industry ranks.

Sources: Friedman, A and Rodger, I (1990) New money comes to tinsel town, *Financial Times*, 10 December; Friedman, A (1991) High anxiety in the dream factory, *Financial Times*, 16 December; and Huey, J (1990) America's hottest export: pop culture, *Fortune*, 31 December.

be 'doing things right'. Resource efficiency considers how well resources are being utilized and the returns being obtained from them. Effectiveness incorporates an evaluation of whether the resources are being deployed in the most beneficial manner. In our analysis of resources we shall concentrate on looking at how the various functions might achieve competitive advantage and thereby contribute to organizational effectiveness. It is assumed that readers will already be familiar with a number of the issues and concepts discussed, but references for further reading are provided.

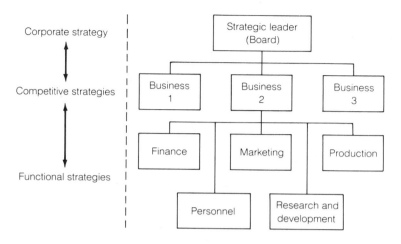

Figure III.1 Hierarchy of strategies: the contribution of functions.

Individual relationships can affect the whole organization indirectly. Customers for example normally meet marketing and sales management most frequently, and there is then a reliance on the communication system for ensuring that their needs are understood by operations management. The company's financial situation is best understood at any time by financial managers, but all parts of the organization are affected by it.

It is essential for managers throughout the organization, whatever function or business unit they might have responsibility for, firstly to understand the environment as it affects them and as it affects other parts of the organization, and secondly to appreciate how the various parts of the organization are interdependent.

There is energy in our strategy at several levels. In distribution, one of the secrets of our business is to control the channels of distribution, particularly the shops. When a new shopping centre is built in Hong Kong or Singapore we can obtain the best positions for shops because we are offering very prestigious brands like Dior, Celine, Vuitton, Givenchy and Christian Lacroix.

There is also synergy at the conceptual stage. We will shortly launch a Christian Lacroix perfume which is being developed by a subsidiary of Christian Dior perfumes. Not only are we using the creative genius of Christian Dior – the creators of Fahrenheit and Poison, which are very successful perfumes – but we will use the Dior worldwide sales network to market the product.

There are also synergies in advertising . . . you can use your negotiating strength to get the best prices.

Bernard Arnault, Group Chairman, LVMH, Moët Hennessy, Louis Vuitton.

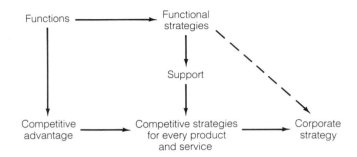

Figure III.2   The links between corporate, competitive and functional strategies.

The environment changes as events take place (for example a change in legislation or innovation by a competitor) and as the relative power and influence of the constituent parts changes (for example two key buyers merge and demand more preferential trading arrangements in line with their new buying power). The organization can influence events, and should seek to do so in order to achieve favourable results; but not everything can be influenced or forecast. Hence the organization must be flexible enough to adapt and change as necessary in the face of external changes. This is affected, as we have seen, by the culture and the role of strategic leadership.

The strategic leader may establish a broad strategic direction and delegate considerable responsibilities to business units and functions, to enable them to respond quickly to new opportunities and threats. These managers may work within reasonably tight policy guidelines or have greater individual freedom. Tighter objectives and more central control by the strategic leader is an alternative approach which is generally more suitable for stable environments and less diversified firms. Chapter 5 emphasized that it is necessary for the strategic leader to understand what is happening and what changes are taking place whatever the structure and culture of the organization. Changes can then be stimulated by reactions to external events, or a determination to influence events outside the organization. Many of these will be relatively small incremental changes; occasionally they will be major events. Acquisition of another company can be a determined major change of strategic direction, possibly involving considerable risks; acquisition by another company can be the result of previous failures to respond to environmental pressures, resulting in decline.

Some organizations and strategic leaders will seek to avoid taking high risk decisions and major changes of direction; most organizations will surely want to avoid having revolutionary changes forced on them by stronger external forces. The alternative in both cases is gradual evolutionary change by the organization which monitors the environment for new opportunities and takes those which are most desirable and appropriate. As indicated above this requires awareness throughout the organization of changes and trends in the environment, flexible resources which can be used to capitalize on the opportunities, and an ability to co-ordinate the resources in order to implement the desired changes effectively.

As will be seen later, when the management of change is discussed in Chapter 24, changes may often be resisted by people unless they clearly appreciate the reasons why the changes are necessary and share the objectives. This is again an issue of culture.

REFERENCES

Ansoff, H I (1968) *Corporate Strategy*, Penguin (originally published by McGraw-Hill in America in 1965).
Drucker, P F (1973) *Management*, Harper and Row.

WHERE ARE OUR OPPORTUNITIES AND THREATS?

9

LEARNING OBJECTIVES

After studying this chapter you should be able to

☐ explain issues of complexity, dynamism and uncertainty in relation to the organization's environment;
☐ identify how changes might be forecast;
☐ discuss the organization as an open system and assess the impact of a number of environmental forces;
☐ construct a focal zone diagram to illustrate the relative importance of the various stakeholders and other influences;
☐ describe certain changes taking place currently in the international and UK environments and consider the possible impact of the single European market in 1992;
☐ explain what is meant by a SWOT analysis and draw up a suitable framework to carry out such an analysis.

In this chapter we explore the relationship between the organization and its environment. Environmental opportunities and threats must be appreciated and evaluated for their potential impact on the organization. In addition, the organization's resources must be managed and developed in such a way that they match the needs of the environment.

INTRODUCTION

In this chapter we examine in detail the **environment** in which the organization operates and consider how the forces present in the environment pose both opportunities and threats. The topic of stakeholders, which was introduced in Chapter 5, is developed further as a number of the environmental forces which affect the organization clearly have a stake in the business. Competitors inevitably constitute a major influence on corporate, competitive and functional strategies and consequently, even though they were the subject of Chapter 7, they are an essential consideration in this topic.

If a firm is to control its growth, change and development it must seek to control the forces which provide the opportunities for growth and change, and those which pose threats and demand responses. Not only must managers be aware of environmental forces and environmental change, they must manage the organization's resources to take advantage of opportunities and counter threats. In turn the strategic leader should ensure that this happens and that the values and culture of the organization are appropriate for satisfying the key success factors. Quite simply, the environment delivers shocks to an organization, and the way in which resources are deployed and managed determines the ability to handle these shocks. This relates to E–V–R congruence.

UNDERSTANDING THE ENVIRONMENT

Although the constituent forces of the environment can be listed and assessed for opportunities and threats, and the forecasting of possible changes can be attempted, of most importance for managers is on-going insight and awareness. The important issues might well be listed as an essential part of the planning process and be used for developing and evaluating possible strategic changes. Managers, however, should always be attentive to changes and their decisions and actions should be both reactive and proactive

as appropriate. In other words their awareness should result from constant vigilance and attentiveness rather than from any isolated clinical analysis. This will in turn be dependent upon the information system within the organization, sources of external information and the uses made of it, and the ability of individual managers to evaluate the importance and potential significance of events they become aware of. Whilst environmental forces and influences clearly exist and change, what matters is the perception managers place upon their observations and experiences – i.e. the meaning they attribute to information. The information aspects are the subject of Chapter 14; manager capabilities are dependent upon experience and basic understanding of the overall strategic process. It is particularly useful if managers are able to take a strategic perspective rather than a functional one because then they may perceive opportunities and threats in areas outside their own particular specialisms. Case 9.1 considers why and how many farmers in the UK are looking at their farms as potentially diversified businesses and not simply farms.

Uncertainty, complexity and dynamism

Duncan (1972) argues that the environment is more uncertain the more complex it is or the more dynamic it is. An often used example of an organization facing a generally stable, non-dynamic and hence fairly certain environment is a small rural village post office. Whilst most organizations face far more uncertainty, their managers also enjoy more challenges.

The dynamic environment

Dynamism can be increased by a number of factors. Rapid technological change involving either products, processes or uses will mean that changes are likely to occur quickly and

---

Case 9.1
DIVERSIFICATION IN UK AGRICULTURE

Essentially the problem is one of over-capacity. Increasing surpluses of staple commodities such as grain, butter, milk and meat have developed as demand for many products has been static and the consumption of animal fats has declined. Prices have been forced down, costs have risen, and government and European Community support is being reduced. To remain viable many farmers must seek alternative uses for their resources, comprising land, labour and capital equipment.

There are limited opportunities for adding value to existing products and for producing alternative and unusual crops, but increasingly farmers are establishing non-farming enterprises to yield revenue, profit and employment. A number of opportunities exist, but many require skills which are different from those which are essential in farming. Farmers therefore need to be more strategically aware and take a wider view of the essential purpose of their enterprises.

The opportunities available include the following.

☐ Forestry: there is a large demand in the UK for wood and wood products, much of which is currently satisfied through imports
☐ Tourism: bed and breakfast accommodation, self-catering cottages, caravanning and camping facilities
☐ Retailing direct to the public through farm shops and garden centres
☐ Sport and recreation: ponds and gravel pits for fishing or growing fish to sell to angling clubs; shooting either game or clay pigeons, and possibly including gun hire; sailing facilities; equestrian opportunities including horses for trekking and hunting, and stabling; golf courses on surplus land; and using rough terrain and woodland for simulated war games
☐ Engineering, woodworking and craft workshops

---

that organizations must stay aware of the activities of their suppliers and potential suppliers, customers and competitors. Where competition is on a global scale the pace of change may vary in different markets, and competition may be harder to monitor. In such cases the future is likely to be uncertain. Risk taking and creative entrepreneurial leadership may well be required as strategies pursued in the past, or modifications of them, may no longer be appropriate.

The complex environment

An environment is complex where the forces and the changes involving them are difficult to understand. Quite often complexity and dynamism occur together. Technology-based industries are an excellent example of this. The structure of the organization, the degree of decentralization and the responsibility and authority delegated to managers throughout the organization, and information systems can render complexity more manageable.

One thing is clear. Even if you're on the right track you'll get run over if you just sit there!

Sir Allen Sheppard, Chairman
Grand Metropolitan plc

Managers will need to be open and responsive to the need for change and flexible in their approach if they are to handle complexity successfully.

Managerial awareness and the approach to the management of change are therefore key issues in uncertain environments. If managers are strategically aware, and flexible and responsive concerning change, then they will perceive the complex and dynamic conditions as manageable. Other less aware managers may find the conditions so uncertain that they are always responding to pressures placed on the organization rather than appearing to be in control and managing the environment. Hence a crucial aspect of strategic management is understanding and negotiating with the environment in order to influence and ideally to control events.

Case 9.2 looks at the UK footwear industry, which has experienced rapid change and uncertainty. Some manufacturers have handled the situation well; others have failed to survive.

Environmental influences

Systems thinking

Figure 9.1, which illustrates how the organization might usefully be seen as part of an open system, is really an elaboration of part of Chapter 1, Figure 1.1. Figure 1.1 looks at how the organization processes inputs into outputs within the constraints imposed by external environmental forces. Figure 9.1 looks at these forces in greater detail. The

---

Competitiveness across all our activities is the name of the game for continued corporate success in the '90s and beyond, allied to a proper regard for shareholders, employees and the community at large.

Sir Denys Henderson, Chairman, ICI plc

---

organization is shown as one of a number of competitors in an industry; and to a greater or lesser degree these competitors will be affected by the decisions, competitive strategies and innovation of the others. These interdependences are crucial and consequently strategic decisions should always involve some assessment of their impact on other companies, and their likely reaction. Equally a company should seek to be fully aware of what competitors are doing at any time.

Furthermore this industry will be linked to, and dependent on, other industries: industries from which it buys supplies, and industries to which it markets products and services. Essentially this relates to Porter's model of the forces which determine industry profitability that we considered in Chapter 7. The relationships between a firm and its buyers and suppliers are again crucial for a number of reasons. Suppliers might be performing badly and as a result future supplies might be threatened; equally they might be working on innovations which will impact on organizations they supply to. Buyers might be under pressure from competitors to switch suppliers. It is important to be strategically aware, and to seek to exert influence over organizations where there are dependences.

These industries and the firms which comprise them are additionally part of a wider environment. This environment is composed of forces which influence the organizations, and which in turn can be influenced by them. Particular forces will be more or less important for individual organizations and in certain circumstances. It is important that managers appreciate the existence of these forces, how they might influence the organization, and how they might be influenced. This relates to stakeholder theory. This systems approach, which considers the organization in relation to its environment, is useful for two main reasons. First, it can help managers to understand and explain the decisions and behaviour that can be observed throughout the organization. Individual

Case 9.2
THE UK FOOTWEAR INDUSTRY

Changes in the global industry environment have affected UK producers. As a result the number of producers has declined, as have the numbers employed in the industry. However, some producers have taken the new opportunities available.

Demand for non-leather casual shoes and trainers, produced with unskilled labour, has led to a growth in shoe production in such countries as Brazil, Taiwan and South Korea. At the same time Italian manufacturers, who produce both creative designs and well-made shoes, have become the most important producers of leather shoes in the world. Their success has been helped by membership of the European Community, the relative value of the lire as a currency, and investment in capital equipment.

In the UK production declined by one-third between 1972 and 1984; and during the same period the import penetration grew from 30% to 60% of the market. Fashion is important and the UK is acknowledged to be good at the design and production of court shoes for ladies and brogues for men. Demand for these has revived in the 1980s. Opportunities also exist for investment in sophisticated equipment for computer-aided design and computer-controlled machines for cutting and sewing.

Some large manufacturers have emerged through these opportunities. C & J Clark, with 8% of the UK retail shoe market, manufactures many of its own shoes. British Shoe Corporation, with some 20% of the retail market through such outlets as Saxone, Dolcis and Freeman Hardy Willis, built up a significant manufacturing business in the UK before selling their factories in a management buy-out in 1988. In the mid-1980s Clark's and BSC represented nearly one-third of UK shoe manufacturing. In addition many small companies still exist producing both hand made shoes and cheaper alternatives. Of 750 producers (mid-1980s) some 600 employed less than 50 people.

Exports and imports remain very important, and therefore the industry is heavily dependent on the value of the pound sterling in world markets.

managers may be aware of what is happening in their management area or business unit within the organization; it is also useful if they understand activities elsewhere in the corporation. Second, it enables greater insight into the changing equilibrium situation concerning the firm and its environment. As environmental forces change and as the organization adapts through incremental changes the equilibrium situation is in fact changing and managers should be aware of this.

Mintzberg (1987) has used the term 'crafting strategy' to explain how managers learn by experience and by doing and adapt strategies to environmental needs. He sees the process as being analogous to a potter moulding clay and creating a finished object. If an organization embarks upon a determined change of strategy certain aspects of implementation will be changed as it becomes increasingly clear with experience how best to manage the environmental forces. Equally managers adapt existing competitive and functional strategies as they see opportunities and threats and gradually change things. In each case the aim is to ensure that the organization's resources and values are matched with the changing environment.

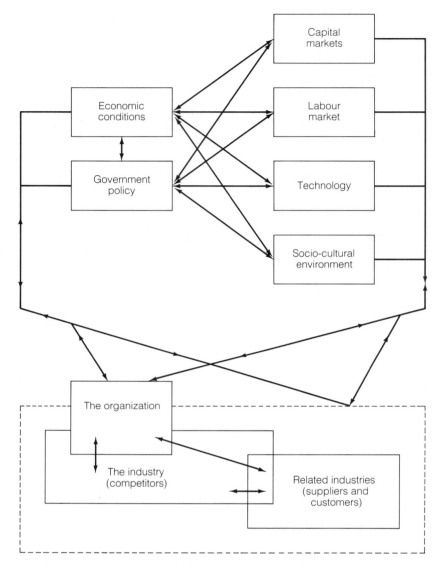

Figure 9.1 Environmental forces and influences. All arrows point both ways. Whilst the organization is influenced by the environment it must also seek to manage the environment.

External forces

Economic conditions affect how easy or how difficult it is to be successful and profitable at any time because they affect both capital availability and cost, and demand. If demand is buoyant, for example, and the cost of capital is low, it will be attractive for firms to invest and grow with expectations of being profitable. In opposite circumstances firms might find that profitability throughout the industry is low. The timing and relative success of particular strategies can be influenced by economic conditions. When the economy as a whole or certain sectors of the economy are growing, demand may exist for a product or service which would not be in demand in more depressed circumstances. Similarly the opportunity to exploit a particular strategy successfully may depend on demand which exists in growth conditions and does not in recession. Although a depressed economy will generally be a threat which results in a number of organizations going out of business, it can provide opportunities for some. When we consider turnaround strategies later in the book we shall consider appropriate strategies for depressed industries.

Economic conditions are influenced by **government policy**; equally they are a major influence affecting government decisions. There are numerous ways, however, that government decisions will affect organizations both directly and indirectly as they provide both opportunities and threats.

Whilst economic conditions and government policy are closely related, they both influence a number of other environmental forces which can affect organizations. **Capital markets** determine the conditions for alternative types of funding for organizations; they can be subject to government controls, and they will be guided by the prevailing economic conditions. The rate of interest charged for loans, for example, will be affected by inflation and by international economics, and will be government led. Government spending can increase the money supply and make capital markets more buoyant. The expectations of shareholders with regard to company performance, their willingness to provide more equity funding or their willingness to sell their shares will also be affected.

The **labour market** reflects the availability of particular skills at national and regional levels; this is affected by training, which is influenced by government and the TECs. Labour costs will be influenced by inflation and by general trends in other industries, and by the role and power of trade unions.

Technology in one respect is part of the organization and the industry half of the model as it is used for the creation of

competitive advantage. However, technology external to the industry can also be captured and used, and this again can be influenced by government support and encouragement. Technological breakthroughs can create new industries which might prove a threat to existing organizations whose products or services might be rendered redundant, and those firms which might be affected in this way should be alert to the possibility. Equally, new technology could provide a useful input, perhaps in manufacturing, but in turn its purchase will require funding and possibly employee training before it can be used.

The **sociocultural environment** encapsulates demand and tastes, which vary with fashion and disposable income, and general changes can again provide both opportunities and threats for particular firms. Organizations should be aware of demographic changes as the structure of the population by ages, affluence, regions, numbers working and so on can have an important bearing on demand as a whole and on demand for particular products and services. Threats to existing products might be increasing; opportunities for differentiation and market segmentation might be emerging.

The examples referred to here are only a sample of many, and individual managers should appreciate how these general forces affect their organization in particular ways. Table 9.1 provides a list of environmental influences and forces, but again it is general. Readers should use this outline framework to evaluate which forces influence their organization, how they exert influence, and how important relatively each of them is. This issue will be explored in greater detail later when we consider actual environmental changes in the early 1990s.

For any organization certain environmental influences will constitute powerful forces which affect decision making significantly. For some manufacturing and service businesses the most powerful force will be customers; for others it may be competition.

Table 9.1 Environmental influences

Influence	Examples of threats and opportunities
The economy	The strength of the economy influences the availability of credit and the willingness of people to borrow. This affects the level of demand Interest rates and currency fluctuations affect both the cost and demand of imports and exports
Capital markets	This includes shareholders, and their satisfaction with company success. Are they willing to buy more shares if offered them to increase equity funding? Would they willingly sell if someone bid for the organization? Also included is the banking system, the cost and availability of loan capital
Labour market	Changes in structure with an ageing population and more women seeking work. Availability of skills, possibly in particular regions. The influence of trade unions. The contribution of government training schemes
Technology	Robotics in manufacturing in such industries as car assembly. Computers for design and manufacturing. Information technology such as electronic point of sale in retailing
Sociocultural environment	Pressure groups affecting demand or industry location Changing tastes and values
Government	Regional aid policies Special industry initiatives, say where high technology is involved The legal environment is part of this, including the regulation of competition. Restraints on car exhaust emissions (pollution control) and labelling requirements would be other examples
Suppliers	The availability and cost of supplies, possibly involving vertical integration and decisions concerning whether to make or buy in essential components. In 1988, for example, Amstrad claimed they were having to limit their production of computers because of world shortages of particular memory chips
Customers	Changes in preferences and purchasing power Changes in the distribution system Tizer was referred to earlier; in 1987–8 W H Smith were affected by the decision of many daily newspaper publishers not to use their wholesale system any more
Competitors	Changes in competitive strategies Innovation
The media	The effect of good and bad publicity, drawing attention to companies, products and services

In some situations suppliers can be crucial. In the case of some small businesses external forces can dictate whether the business stays solvent or not. A major problem for many small businesses concerns the management of cash flow – being able to pay bills when they are due for payment and being strong enough to persuade customers to pay their invoices on time. A small subcontract metal working business which works mostly for the large car manufacturers and whose main supplier is British Steel will have little power of persuasion. Payments may be delayed, and the customers will be too large and important to be threatened in any meaningful way, such as by the refusal to do any more work for them; meanwhile the supplies will

have to be paid for or future deliveries are likely to be suspended. Whilst it is essential for all managers to have some insight into how their organization is affected by the environment, it is also desirable for them to consider how some of the environmental forces might be influenced and managed to gain benefits for the organization. This is less possible generally in the case of small businesses as they are relatively less powerful. However, small companies should examine their environment for opportunities and threats in order to establish where they can gain competitive advantage and where their resources might most usefully be concentrated. For many not-for-profit organizations such as London Zoo, the National Theatre and London's major museums the government constitutes a major environmental force because each of these organizations is dependent in different ways on government grants. The National Health Service is similarly very dependent upon government policies which affect all decision areas. Consultants' salaries, nurses' pay, new hospitals and wards, and new equipment are substantially determined by government decisions, which they will seek to influence.

Forecasting the environment

In analysing the environment managers should seek to do the following.

☐ Identify which forces are most important, and why they are critical. This will reflect opportunities and threats.
☐ Forecast how these forces might change in the future, using whatever methods are appropriate.
☐ Incorporate these expectations and predictions into decision making and management thinking. Fahey and King (1983) have emphasized the usefulness of including line managers from the whole organization in any teams which are specifically charged with environmental analysis, as this can lead to more effective dissemination of information to enable it to be used in decision making. Managers will be individually aware of many changes in the environment. Where strategic change takes place incrementally through managers with delegated authority, this information can be easily incorporated in decisions. But where major strategic change is being considered centrally by the strategic leader it is important to gather the relevant data together.
☐ Be honest and realistic when evaluating strengths and weaknesses relative to competitors, and when considering the organization's ability to respond to opportunities and threats. The environment should be managed wherever possible, and managers should seek to ensure that their resources are compatible with the organization's environment and the factors and forces that will influence and determine success.

This last factor implies that forecasts should be as realistic as possible; they should be used in decision making and for the determination of future strategy; and the implications of changes in the environment should be acted upon and not ignored.

Individual managers will develop their environmental and strategic awareness through experience and perception, and by thinking about their observations and experiences. It is particularly important to assess the significance of what happens and what can be observed to be happening. However, in considering future strategic changes there will be an additional need to forecast the changes which might take place in the environment concerning supplies, customers, competitors, demand, technology, government legislation and so on. Some of the future changes may be forecast through straightforward extrapolation of past events; many will not. Some of the environmental forces can be better quantified than others, and consequently some subjectivity will be involved. Hogarth and Makridakis (1981) have argued that the overall performance of organizations in predicting future changes is poor, and that the most sophisticated methods of forecasting are not necessarily the best. However, despite the difficulties, forecasting is important. Managers who are encouraged to think about future changes, to ask questions and to query assumptions will increase their insight and awareness and this should help decision making.

What, then, do managers need to forecast, and how might the forecasting be carried out?

The economy and the possible impact of economic changes can be assessed in a number of ways. Economic growth, inflation, government spending, interest rates, exchange rates, the money supply, investment and taxation may all be influential. The Treasury provides forecasts periodically, based on its own econometric model. A number of universities and business schools also publish predictions based on their econometric models. Sometimes they are in agreement, but often they are not. Analysts from City institutions are regularly quoted on television and radio news programmes, and again there is often disagreement. The problem lies in the number of interrelationships and interdependences amongst the economic variables and in imperfect understanding of all the cause and effect relationships. Additionally economic forces and changes around the world, such as changes in the exchange value of key currencies, inflation rates in major markets such as America and balances of payments in different countries can all affect the UK and organizations based in the UK, especially those with overseas interests. Although all the changes cannot be forecast with great accuracy, managers should be aware of what is happening at the moment and the implications of any trends that can be observed.

Demographic influences include some which can be forecast reasonably well and some which are more unpredictable. Changes in population structure can be readily forecast; changes in tastes and values are more difficult. Again it is essential to be able to appreciate the significance of observed events and changes. Predicting the impact on demand for various products and services of the emergence of a social group such as the yuppies is a case in point. Wax-covered country jackets are one example of products that have become popular. The government does provide statistics on social trends, which give some insight, but organizations need to be continually aware rather than rely on statistics which are a little dated when published.

Political influences relate to changes in governments and their priorities and legislation programmes. Opinion polls help in forecasting the former, and indications of the latter are readily available. However, planned legislation is not always passed for various reasons. One example of this which has affected a number of retailing organizations, and in turn their suppliers, is the failure to become law of the bill to legalize Sunday trading.

Developing from this is the need to forecast how certain laws and regulations might be implemented. Competition regulations have already been discussed. Organizations considering mergers or acquisitions have to try and predict whether a referral to the Monopolies and Mergers Commission is likely before mounting their bid. Contacts within the so-called corridors of power can be of great benefit.

Demographic and political forecasting often relies on expert opinion, which can be obtained through personal contacts, commissioned research or published information in journals and newspapers. Outside opinions may well be biased or prejudiced because of strong views on certain issues or because of political perspectives, and this must be taken into account. Wilson (1977) has shown how probability-diffusion matrices can be useful here. Where opinions concerning the likelihood or probability of certain events are being gathered it is useful to plot both the strength of feeling (high or low probability of occurrence) and the diffusion of opinion (consistency or dispersion) amongst the sources or experts.

Scenario planning is often used in strategic management to explore future possibilities. Possible happenings and events are considered by looking at potential outcomes from particular causes and seeking to explain why things might occur. The value is in increased awareness by exploring possibilities and asking and attempting to answer 'what if' questions. Although scenario planning can be predictive and can be used to plan strategic changes, it can also help decision making by providing managers with insight so that they can react better when things happen or change.

Technological forecasting covers changes in technology generally, and the possible impact of innovations which result from research and development by an organization, by its competitors, and by other firms with which it is involved in some way. Expert opinion through scenario planning and from technical journals can be useful. Technological changes can have an impact throughout an organization and consequently it is useful for managers in various functions to consider the possible effects on them.

Key success factors

Key success factors were introduced in Chapter 1, when it was pointed out that the environment dictates which factors an organization really needs to address if it is to secure long-term competitive advantage and strategic success. Figure 1.2, which illustrates the importance of congruency between environment, values and resources, stresses that congruency and in turn strategic success improves when the organization is able to manage its resources in such a way that the key success factors, determined by the environment, are met. In this chapter we shall consider the concept from three angles:

☐ industry-specific examples which consider the factors that all competitors in the industry must address
☐ individual company examples which illustrate where particular organizations have created competitive advantage by understanding their market and pursuing opportunities successfully
☐ the general keys to success in changing global environments.

Industry factors

Certain industries exhibit particular features which dictate which skills all competitors

must acquire if they are to prosper. It was mentioned in Chapter 1 that airlines experience high fixed costs through their investment in expensive aeroplanes and the inflexible routes and schedules which are allocated by the Civil Aviation Authority. As a result the load factor becomes critical, and strategies must concentrate on ensuring that planes fly with as many seats filled as possible.

In a similar way it is crucial for hotels to fill their bedrooms as often as possible. This need is evidenced in the high promotional activity of many hotels and their desire to acquire conference trade in non-tourist seasons. Restaurants and other services help acquire business and achieve repeat stays, but the rooms must be used if overheads are to be met. Both hotel rooms and airline seats are services which cannot be stored. In other words, if a plane flies with half its seats empty, or a hotel is only one-third full on a particular night, that lost revenue can never be recovered. This can be contrasted with products which can be stored. If, for example, a garage sells less than its target of new cars in a particular month and its stocks start to rise, an intensive selling effort might well recover lost ground, put the garage back on target and reduce stocks to the level they should be. The cars are simply held over for later sales. One key success factor for motor car manufacturers is in fact a good dealer network because the products are high value items with sales dispersed over a wide geographical area.

Building societies earn their revenue and surpluses essentially from mortgages. Competition for this market has been increasing as the banks are becoming more active. Mortgages can only be granted, however, when a society has money to lend, and consequently a key success factor is the ability to attract investors and deposits. High interest accounts, with returns improving as the amount deposited increases and where customers are willing to accept withdrawal restrictions, are a major competitive weapon.

If a grocery supermarket prices competitively and seeks only a limited profit margin on every item sold it becomes essential to generate a high and fast turnover of stocks. Consequently key success factors relate to making sure shelves are kept full, that customers can shop without being held up unduly and that check-out is fast and efficient. New electronic point-of-sale systems, which will be considered later when we look at information technology, are designed to speed up check-out and improve stock control.

Individual company examples

Some organizations manage their resources in an individual way in order to create a distinct or even unique competitive advantage. If this differentiation is valued by the market it becomes a key success factor for the organization in question. It is created by insight into the market and overall strategic awareness. Managers in the organization have spotted an opportunity in the environment and managed their resources in such a way as to exploit it.

An obvious example is the Body Shop chain which now operates in over 40 countries and which has exploited a desire for natural cosmetics. It is, of course, a point of debate about how much of the demand has been created by the existence of the products and how much the products were introduced to meet a demand that already existed.

W H Smith have pursued a number of strategies which they believe are key factors behind their success. On the one hand they have developed chains of small specialist stores such as Our Price Music in parallel with their major stores which sell a variety of different products, but including CDs and cassettes, arguing that the market is segmented and that different buyers are attracted by different types of store, atmosphere and stocking policy. At the same time they have invested considerably in design.

Store layout, shelf displays, uniforms and company house style have all been changed. The central theme in both examples relates to understanding how customers prefer to shop and providing that wherever possible.

The major skill possessed and marketed by Mary Quant is creativity and design. The Mary Quant name is attached to a whole variety of products, including cosmetics, dresses, tights, shoes, bed linen and carpets, which are all part of daily life. However, Mary Quant as an organization does not manufacture in any substantial way; instead products are produced under licence arrangements by other independent companies. The business has grown and become very successful because there is a genuine appreciation of customer tastes, and because the business has concentrated on exploiting the name and design skills effectively.

Success in a changing environment

Professor Roland Smith, Chairman of British Aerospace, has argued that, whatever the industry, success lies in the management and marketing of innovation and risk (Smith, 1987). Innovation, he contends, is at the heart of marketing, and without innovation businesses become sterile and decline. In today's increasingly global environment the need for innovation is becoming stronger, because the sources of innovation worldwide, and hence the sources of competition, are more widespread than was the case 20 years ago. Smith cites the Far East in particular as a source of innovation. If UK organizations are to compete and grow they will need to be more entrepreneurial or change oriented and more willing to take risks. The relationship between innovation and entrepreneurship was introduced in Chapter 3 and will be explored in greater detail in Chapter 11.

Strategic leadership, according to Smith, will need to balance technical expertise with strategic and marketing insights, as high quality research will need to complement an awareness of customer needs around the world. The speed of response to environmental changes, in particular to the actions of competitors, will be vital. There is already spare capacity in many industries, and hence no room to lag behind changes.

Sadler (1988) suggests that successful organizations in the 1990s must be able to:

☐ deliver high levels of service to customers – 'service' here means the total package of product and associated services;
☐ use information and information technology both to improve efficiencies and to obtain competitive advantage;
☐ motivate and develop a knowledgeable workforce – 'knowledge and talent are emerging as the only scarce resources'; and
☐ manage cultural change.

Kanter (1991) has concluded that the leading competitive nations have different priorities for achieving competitive success, and that these differences stem from national cultures. Her research indicated the following priorities:

Japan   1. Product development
            2. Management
            3. Product quality

USA   1. Customer service
            2. Product quality
            3. Technology

Germany   1. Workforce skills
            2. Problem solving
            3. Management

MANAGING THE ENVIRONMENT

If an organization is to manage its environment it will seek to be proactive rather than reactive. To achieve this managers must clearly appreciate the relative importance of the various stakeholders, and seek to influence them rather than be predominantly influenced by them. An organization will never be able to predict everything that might happen and avoid ever having to react to unexpected events, but some will be more in control of the situation than their rivals, who might find themselves always responding to changes instituted by others. (See Case 9.3.)

Aware organizations will seek to ensure that their interests are appreciated and supported by their local authority and that their local Member of Parliament is supporting them wherever government policy might affect them; they are active in the local community in a positive way; their employees are satisfied with wages and conditions of employment; industrial relations are more friendly than hostile; suppliers regard them as good reliable customers; and buyers regard them as competitive and reliable suppliers. In this situation it will be easier to implement changes when they become either desirable or necessary.

So far in this chapter we have considered the impact of environmental forces on the whole organization. In the case of organizations which are multi-product or multi-national the various forces may exert different influences upon particular business units and in different countries. Additionally individual functions within an organization will be affected by certain forces which have little impact on other areas of the business. It may well be necessary for the strategic leader to collate the information available concerning how the various stakeholders affect the various parts of the business in relation to the specific functions and business units, rather than in holistic or overall terms. Table 9.2 provides an example of how an appropriate framework might be built up to accomplish this. If, for example, a major supplier to the organization has been acquired recently by one of the firm's competitors, this will have an impact on the particular business units which buy from this supplier. However, this may well become a corporate issue if, say, the strategic leader feels that it would be worthwhile considering the establishment of a closer relationship with an alternative supplier,

Case 9.3
OPPORTUNITIES AND THREATS: MAN, BRITISH AEROSPACE, HAWKER SIDDELEY AND ICI

MAN Nutzfahrzeuge, the German truckmaker, has seized upon the unification of Germany as an opportunity for growth, despite recession and falling profits generally in the European truck industry. MAN's sales and profits both grew during 1991, whilst those of its main rivals, Daf, Volvo, Renault and Iveco (part of Fiat), all fell. During the 1980s MAN had looked to be a vulnerable competitor internationally because of its reliance on the German market, where it has a 20% share. This apparent weakness was turned into a strength with the acquisition of the Austrian manufacturer, Steyr (in 1991) and a heavy concentration on domestic sales – demand grew in Germany and fell everywhere else.

Volkswagen and General Motors (with its Opel subsidiary) have benefited similarly from increased German demand for cars.

The leading Western cigarette manufacturers have seen new market opportunities open up as trading arrangements with the Far East and Eastern Europe have been liberalized. A decade ago some 60% of the world market was effectively closed to them – China and Russia are the biggest markets.

British Aerospace were threatened in October 1991 when the level of shareholder acceptances for an important rights issue was just 5%.

Investors have delivered a resounding vote of no confidence in the strategy and management of Britain's largest manufacturer and defence contractor.

(Financial Times)

BAe had diversified into military and civil aircraft (the A146 passenger jet was 'the quietest airliner in the world'), defence systems, munitions, property and cars (Rover was bought from the government). Demand for aircraft was falling in the aftermath of the Gulf War and key institutional shareholders felt the company was too diverse.

Unwelcome take-over bids frequently provoke strategic changes, in particular the divestment of non-core businesses. The 1991 bid for **Hawker Siddeley** by BTR (which was successful) led to 'radical restructuring proposals'. Hawker Siddeley announced it would attempt to divest half its businesses and concentrate on three core areas of electrical motors, industrial batteries and aerospace, where it believed it could achieve international leadership.

Although Hanson never bid for **ICI** its acquisition of 2.8% of the shares (in 1991) provoked a similar response. ICI declared they would focus their efforts more clearly during the 1990s and concentrate on businesses where they could be in the top three in the world and exert some dominance in the market. These would certainly include paints, agro-chemicals and selected bulk chemicals. Existing fertilizer, soda-ash and polypropylene businesses may no longer be appropriate and would therefore be divested. (The detailed changes are described in Case 22.4.)

Table 9.2   Possible outline framework for environmental analysis

	Level of influence and strategy		
Stakeholder	*Organization* *Corporate strategy*	*Strategic business unit* *Competitive strategy*	*Marketing* *Functional strategy*
Customers		Preference change towards segment in which we are market leader	Opportunity to advertise and increase share of segment
Suppliers	Major supplier recently acquired by competitor		

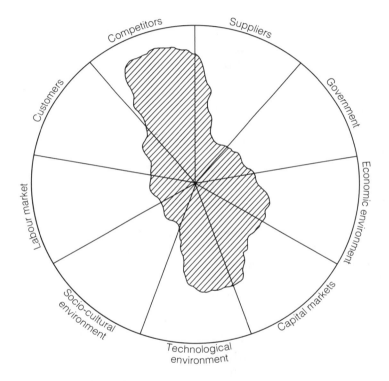

Figure 9.2   Environmental analysis: the focal zone. Adapted from Jauch, L R and Glueck, W F (1988) *Strategic Management and Business Policy*, 3rd edn, McGraw-Hill.

plier, perhaps through acquisition, merger or joint venture. If customer tastes for a particular product or service produced by the organization change favourably, perhaps because of innovation or the development of a new form of differentiation, or because of supply difficulties on the part of a competitor, the impact is most relevant for the compet-

itive strategy of the product or business unit in question. The contribution of this part of the business can be expected to increase. There is correspondingly an impact upon the marketing function, as opportunities to increase market share may be provided if a new advertising campaign is launched. The type of framework outlined in Table 9.2 could be used to summarize the ways in which environmental forces are affecting the organization, or the corporate, competitive and functional strategies of the organization in relation to the various stakeholders, or both.

It is important for managers to appreciate just where the greatest opportunities and threats lie at any time. Jauch and Glueck (1988) suggest that organizations might usefully examine the various forces along the lines of the map featured in Figure 9.2. The forces are each allocated a section of the circle and the extent to which the segment is shaded indicates the relative importance of the force at a particular time. The example represents a situation where the competitive sector is active and changing, with new entrants to the market and the need for strategic changes. There is greater focus on this sector than any other, indicated by the extent to which it is shaded. The cause lies mainly in new technologies which can be applied to the industry. The capital market is important because of the need for investment funding to utilize the technology. The supply situation is seen as stable, and the government is regarded as relatively unconcerned, perhaps because of the in-built competitiveness. This type of diagram is particularly useful for focusing attention on those areas which are currently affecting the organization and which require strategic attention.

Ideally changes in the environment will be seen more as opportunities for positive organizational change than as threats which force changes upon the organization which they were not ready for and which may be difficult to implement. Aware organizations will see changes as opportunities; others may see them as potential threats. Some companies may be unaware of environmental changes and be threatened to the extent that they are driven out of business. In 1987 legal practices were allowed to advertise in the UK for the first time. It was also made possible for them to use direct mail for promoting their services, to run seminars and to be present at exhibitions. Was this an oppor-

tunity or a threat? In addition independent conveyancers had been legalized, providing a new form of competition, particularly for those practices which rely heavily on property transactions. It has been suggested that the culture gap between the legal profession, which is essentially reactive, waiting for customers to bring business in, and marketing, which looks outwards and seeks both to create and to influence demand, could be a threat and an opportunity. Practices have responded differently, with some benefiting enormously and other less successful ones being acquired by more successful practices (Rock, 1987).

Case 9.4 illustrates the dramatic impact of a change in government policy on Thames Television.

Ansoff's model

Ansoff (1987) contends that 'to survive and succeed in an industry, the firm must match the aggressiveness of its operating and strategic behaviours to the changeability of demands and opportunities in the marketplace'. The extent to which the environment is changeable or turbulent depends on six factors:

☐ changeability of the market environment
☐ speed of change
☐ intensity of competition
☐ fertility of technology
☐ discrimination by customers
☐ pressures from governments and influence groups.

Ansoff suggests that the more turbulent the environment is, the more aggressive the firm must be in terms of competitive strategies and entrepreneurialism or change orientation if it is to succeed. The firms in an industry will be distributed such that a small number are insufficiently aggressive for the requirements of the industry, and as a result they are unprofitable or go out of business. Another small number will be above average in terms

---

Case 9.4
THAMES TELEVISION

During the 1980s the Conservative government introduced radical changes in the way commercial television franchises were to be allocated. Sealed bids would be invited for each designated region, with interested companies stating how much they would pay the government for the franchise for a given period of years. Advertising revenue and the sale of programmes to other television stations, both in the UK and abroad, are the main sources of income. The amount bid would therefore depend upon the projected revenue potential and the costs of providing both programming and broadcasting services. An independent commission would normally award the franchise to the highest bidder, selected from those companies whose proposals passed a quality test. A high bid might imply poor profits for the television companies and their shareholders; a low bid might not be successful.

Existing franchise holders were not guaranteed success, and many of them faced stiff competition when the new system operated for the first time in 1991. Some existing holders gambled on nobody significant competing against them, and bid low. The major companies to lose their franchises were Thames, TVam and Television South West.

Thames had previously produced a number of major networked programmes, including 'Minder', 'The Bill' and 'This Week', as well as broadcasting to the Greater London region on weekdays. There were 1400 employees. From 1 January 1993 Thames would no longer hold a broadcasting franchise.

Their challenge lay in deciding how to adapt to this change in circumstances. Revenue would fall dramatically, and clearly jobs would be lost, possibly as many as 1200. Drama programmes would still be made and hopefully sold to those companies owning franchises and the BBC. Another possible avenue for development might be satellite television.

In July 1992, in collaboration with a Canadian television entrepreneur, Thames was the only bidder for Channel 5, the proposed new commerical channel for the UK.

---

of success because they are best able to match the demands of the environment. Many will achieve results about average; and some others may also fail because they are too aggressive and try to change things too quickly again through lack of awareness.

Where an organization is multi-product or multi-national the various parts of the business are likely to experience some common environmental influences and some which are distinctive, which reinforces the need for managers who are closest to the market and to competitors to be able to change things.

Ansoff suggests that the environment should be analysed in terms of competition and entrepreneurship or change. By attributing scores to various factors the degree of competitive and entrepreneurial turbulence can be calculated. The competitive environment is affected by market structure and profitability; the intensity of competitive rivalry and the degree of differentiation; market growth; the stage in the life of the products or services in question and the frequency of new product launches; capital intensity; and economies of scale. Certain of these factors, namely market growth, the stage in the life of the product and profitability, also help to determine the extent to which the environment is entrepreneurial. Changes in structure and technology, social pressures and innovation are also influential.

The culture of the organization and managerial competences should then be examined to see whether they match and changed as appropriate if they do not. Again scores are attributed to various factors. Culture encompasses factors such as values, reaction and response to change and risk orientation. Problem-solving approaches, information systems, environmental forecasting and surveillance, and management systems are included in the competences. He is really arguing that the resources of the organization and the values must be congruent with the needs of the environment.

Systems thinking

Checkland (1981) suggests that when organizations are considered as human activity systems the key issues are structure, emergent properties, communication and control. Essentially the organization is a collection of components or subsystems and as such can be most readily analysed by looking at structures based on functions or business units. These component parts interact, and decisions made in one part of the organization have effects which are felt more widely. Consequently if decision makers are able and encouraged to take a holistic view such that the implications of their decisions on others are considered, then there is likely to be greater integration between the parts. This becomes increasingly important where the component parts are interdependent. Although certain business units in an organization might be substantially independent, functions rarely are. Marketing decisions often affect production management, for example. Financial decisions and decisions

concerning human resources may have widespread implications. To achieve the appropriate integration, communication and control systems are important. Emergent properties relate to behaviour that results from the way the component parts interact and behave and are 'properties which are only meaningful when attributed to the whole and not the parts'. Rivalries and co-operation result in particular decisions and behaviours which will differ from those which would emerge if departments or units were to consider themselves as being isolated. Ideally the emergent properties should result in synergy and therefore bring benefits to the organization.

The basic argument is that the organization is likely to be both reactive and proactive towards environmental forces in a more effective manner if resources internally are co-ordinated. This co-ordination requires awareness of the contribution of other departments and units and a commitment to helping them. A holistic or systemic organization-wide perspective rather than a narrower functional or divisional one is implied. Additionally a sense of common purpose is necessary rather than the pursuit of the personal objectives which were discussed in Chapter 5.

The relationship between environmental forces and internal resources is at the heart of Figure 9.3 which has been adapted from the Harvard Business School approach to strategy (Kelly and Kelly, 1987). The strategy statement framework included in Chapter 1 (Figure 1.4) showed resources and capabilities, products services and markets, and culture and values linked to corporate objectives and strategy. Figure 9.3 is essentially the same. The selected products, services and markets are environment driven and, here the competitive environment and stakeholders are shown with resources and values as four key strategic elements, again linked to corporate objectives. Resources should be viewed as strengths and weaknesses *relative* to those of competitors. These elements can

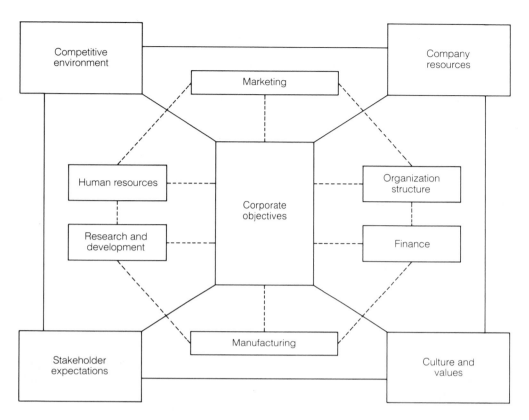

Figure 9.3 Matching the organization and the environment. Adapted from Kelly, F J and Kelly, H M (1987) *What They Really Teach You at the Harvard Business School*, Piatkus.

be changed, but in many cases not readily and not quickly, and consequently at any point in time they are reasonably fixed.

Six operating elements are also incorporated. **Marketing** relates to how the various products and services are positioned in relation to competitors, and how they are priced, advertised and distributed. **Manufacturing** involves the types of production process, location issues and technology utilization. **Finance** incorporates both performance targets and sources of funding. **Research and development** considers how much to spend on research and development and whether the perspective is short or long term. **Human resources** relates to the types of people utilized and how they are rewarded. The **organization structure** encompasses how

these functions are co-ordinated and controlled.

These operating elements determine whether or not the corporate objectives are achieved. It was mentioned earlier in this section that the different functions in the organization were affected to varying degrees by different stakeholders, and that certain stakeholders who have a significant impact on certain functions may have little direct importance for others. Equally the specific stakeholders may influence individual functions in quite different ways. Table 9.3 illustrates the influences and stakeholders that individual functions are most concerned with. Their impact upon the whole organization is therefore affected by the organization structure and relative power and influence

Table 9.3   Environmental influences and stakeholders with which individual functions are most concerned

Marketing and sales	*Manufacturing*
R & D	R & D
Manufacturing	Marketing (through them, customers)
Personnel	Personnel
Customers/consumers	Employees
Distributors	Trade unions
Competitors (strategies)	Competitors (quality; costs)
Advertising agents	Suppliers
Marketing research consultants	Government
Media	Pressure groups
Finance	*Personnel*
Organizational business units	Manufacturing
Manufacturing	Marketing
Private shareholders	Employees
Institutional investors	Trade unions
City analysts	Local community
Media	Job centres
Banks	Universities/colleges
Government (economy)	Media
Competition (investment expenditure)	Government (health and safety legislation, for example
	Competition (wage rates)

within the firm. This table also highlights the strategic value of functional managers taking a more holistic view of the organization and their role and contribution.

The behaviour of the operating elements, together with any emergent properties, also influences the objectives attained, as explained in Chapter 5, Figure 5.1. Policies for each of the functions, and control systems built into the structure, may be relatively rigid or relatively flexible. The greater the flexibility the more opportunity there is for managers to effect changes and ensure that

the organization responds to any perceived changes in environmental opportunities and threats. However, there is also more opportunity for managers to pursue personal objectives when policies are flexible. This reinforces the need for both strategic awareness and holistic or systemic thinking to ensure that there is some degree of commitment to a common purpose, the corporate objectives of the organization.

There is no doubt that the world is becoming one marketplace. Capital markets, products and services, management and manufacturing techniques have all become global in nature. As a result, companies increasingly find that they must compete all over the world – in the global marketplace.

Maurice Saatchi, Chairman, Saatchi and Saatchi Company plc

THE UK BUSINESS ENVIRONMENT

Now that we have considered the relationship between an organization and its environment in a conceptual way, it is appropriate to look at specific changes in the UK business environment.

The global environment

Ohmae (1985) has described a number of changes which have taken place as industries and competition have become increasingly global in nature. The point has already been made earlier that economies of scale, market shares and forms of differentiation must be considered in the light of the world market if competition stems from organizations based in different countries or from multi-national firms with plants in more than one country.

Where industries have become truly international, as is the case with cars, then organizations have developed interrelationships and joint ventures. The joint venture between Rover and Honda whereby Rover has manufactured an essentially Japanese car under licence is one example. Other examples include Seat of Spain making Fiat cars under licence, Porsche of Germany undertaking development work for the Russian Lada company and Peugeot diesel engines being supplied to Chrysler in America. This issue will be explored in greater detail as a strategic option in Chapter 18. The effect has been that different countries have concentrated their research efforts on specific aspects of car design and thereby have become expert in, say, fuel usage, electronics or ceramic engines. In a similar way different countries have concentrated their overall research and development expenditure on selected industries rather than attempting to cover everything. Ohmae suggests that Japan and Japanese businesses have concentrated on ceramics, automobiles and steel, plus electronics to a lesser extent; America on aerospace and electronics; West Germany on chemicals; and the UK on chemicals and aerospace. Defence electronics might also be added to the UK list. These concentrations have led to positions of power or dominance in the different industries. Ohmae specifically comments that the UK has not invested as heavily in automobiles and machine tools, both of which have undergone a relative decline. Where research expenditure is limited or specialized UK companies are likely to concentrate on specific market segments rather than maintaining a broad presence in world industries and markets.

Parallel with this has been a gradual switch from steel-based industries to electronics-based industries and the emergence of Japan as a major international competitor. Ohmae argues the existence of a business triad of America, Europe and Japan as interdependent developed commercial nations which must seek to work together. Other areas of the world, Latin America, Africa and Asia, are still developing industrially and are behind the triad. However, for this reason they often enjoy lower labour costs which pose a threat.

As countries become richer and per capita incomes increase, demand and tastes change. Also when countries are relatively wealthy the markets for certain products become saturated and demand is transferred to newer items. Consequently new products such as video recorders and compact disc players to supplement existing televisions and hi-fi units were initially successful in the richest countries. Over time, and especially when prices came down through the experience curve effect, they spread into other countries. At any time, therefore, the market for a product may be reaching saturation level in one country, growing in a less rich country and just taking off in a poorer country. This has implications for the way that products with potentially international demand are marketed world wide. Ohmae argues that the lag between the take-off times in different countries decreases continually, and therefore companies cannot simply aim to spread products around the world gradually and sequentially.

Whilst an international strategy of bringing the cheapest materials to the cheapest labour for manufacture before selling to the most expensive market seems to be logical, it may not happen. For one thing it can often be advantageous to be located close to markets; for another there may be benefits in capital intensity which uses few workers who are all very highly skilled and not available in certain developing countries.

Companies migrate over time, seeking

locations where costs are lower or which are nearer to markets, depending on the benefits they are seeking. Numerous American, European and Japanese companies have opened plants in countries with cheaper labour in order to reduce costs, partly to obtain higher profit margins. They have also opened subsidiaries near to international markets, even though there may not be cost savings. When Nissan started building cars on Tyneside it was to provide ready access to the British and European markets. It required government pressure to ensure that British-made components comprise a certain percentage of the total input value and that the plant is not simply assembling components imported from cheap labour countries.

A number of German companies have moved production from Germany to low-cost labour countries in order to remain competitive. Examples include Daimler Benz (diesel engines to South Korea), Bosch (car loudspeakers to Mexico and Malaysia) and Siemens (car-wiring systems to Turkey and Czechoslovakia). BASF has switched its fertilizer manufacturing to Belgium to reduce costs.

Proactive strategic changes of this nature transform the nature of competition in a country and force a reaction from existing competitors, who need to concentrate on their own competitive advantage and also ensure that government is sufficiently protective. British companies that are affected also need to try and persuade British consumers to buy British goods; and this in turn requires that they are genuinely competitive in terms of design, quality, price and availability.

Capital intensity requires significant investment and access to capital markets. Furthermore it creates barriers to entry, which were discussed in Chapter 7. Research and development expenditures, the cost of modern computer-controlled production facilities, the potential benefits from sophisticated informa-

tion technology, the need to maintain a strong sales network around the world, and the need to advertise heavily to establish brand identity and differentiation all create barriers to entry. At the same time they increase fixed costs and make firms volume sensitive, thereby emphasizing the need for global marketing.

In an earlier work Ohmae (1982) isolated five environmental factors which, he argued, affect strategy.

☐ Economic growth is relatively slow, consumers often have a wide choice, and therefore the margin for judgemental error by managers is reduced. It is important for managers to make effective strategic decisions and to create and sustain competitive advantage.

☐ The markets for several key industries are mature and therefore not growing in any substantial way. Companies which seek growth at a faster rate than the economy as a whole will therefore have to invest heavily to increase their market share, innovate or diversify.

☐ Strategic resources in terms of finance, raw materials and people are unevenly distributed around the world, and consequently global strategies need careful consideration.

☐ The complexity of international markets is increasing, with changes taking place around the world at varying speeds. Strategic adjustment for any business with international markets or competition becomes more and more difficult.

☐ Inflation seems irreversible, although the rate of inflation varies from country to country. This can reduce profits, increase the cost of capital and act as a disincentive to investment.

In the face of these changes in the international environment it is interesting to consider how well UK companies are doing.

British manufacturing industry in perspective

The Confederation of British Industry [CBI] (1991) says that 'contrary to popular opinion, Britain's manufacturing industries have made big strides throughout the 1980s, but, because they started so far behind their biggest competitors, they face another 10 year struggle – at least – to catch up'. Output rose 25% in ten years, and the UK's share of world exports began to rise after years of decline. Throughout the 1980s productivity rose faster than in any other country except Japan, partly because of an increased emphasis on quality, innovation and training. Nevertheless Britain's productivity still lags behind that of Germany, America and Japan; and the situation has been complicated by a world recession which resulted in over-capacity and reduced investment.

Dodsworth and Garnett (1987) comment that Britain's recovery from earlier recessions involved major problems and unusual opportunities, and argue that four crucial factors underlie the strategic changes which have taken place.

☐ Capacity has been reduced so much in certain industries that investment is not likely to take place on a scale which will return Britain's earlier market shares. Motor vehicles is one example of this.

In my experience, corporate life threatening problems in large manufacturing companies have developed over a long period. These problems should never have been permitted to grow so large, but they were allowed to do so by top management who were lethargic and self-satisfied, who engaged in self-delusion and congratulated themselves on their exalted status. In short, the managements were the problem.

Eugene Anderson, Chairman and Chief Executive, Ferranti International plc

---

☐ Companies in certain other industries are successful and profitable but concentrated only in specific sectors as a result of effective differentiation strategies. Textiles is an example, and as a result the country is a net importer of textiles.

☐ The UK has retained positions in declining industries more effectively than it has invested in new growth industries. The world economy has switched from steel-based to electronics-based industries but the UK has not been a leader.

☐ Internationally the UK does not have a reputation for being well organized in relation to markets and demand. Where this is the case organizations are more likely to be reactive to changes than proactive globally.

In considering the relative success of manufacturing companies in the UK it is important to distinguish between British companies and foreign-owned subsidiaries which compete in the same industries. Evidence suggests that, although improvements were taking place in British industry in the late 1980s, the lead was often coming from American and Japanese multi-nationals based here.

The changing environment in the United Kingdom

Rather than merely listing a number of environmental changes which have taken place in the UK, the following selective list has been applied to retailing to show something of the cause–effect relationship between environmental changes and organization strategies.

☐ **Consumers in the UK have had a generally increasing spending power over the last 25 years**. In other words, although there has been inflation, and sometimes very high inflation, incomes overall have stayed ahead of price increases. Between the mid-1960s and the mid-1970s retail expenditure essentially kept pace with total consumer spending, but it has since fallen back with the growth in expenditure on such things as home ownership and eating out, especially fast foods. Increasing home ownership in turn has generated opportunities for retailers of do-it-yourself (DIY) products, and this particular sector of the retail industry has become intensely competitive. Sainsbury (Homebase), Woolworth (B & Q) and W H Smith (Do It All) are all active alongside the specialist Texas Homecare. Product ranges are constantly extended (e.g., into kitchens and bathrooms), small independent companies have been taken over, large out-of-town developments are common, and price competition is important as supply exceeds demand.

☐ Such service businesses as Kwik Fit (car exhausts, tyres etc.) have also taken an increasing percentage of consumer expenditure because of **increasing car ownership**, which has had a number of effects. Grocery supermarkets have been developed with attached car-parking facilities and new out-of-town shopping centres have been built. Some of these have included non-retail activities such as entertainment and restaurants. In the 1990s location will increasingly become a source of competitive advantage with major retailers competing for new prime development sites. Early in 1992 Thorn–EMI announced that its Rumbelow's subsidiary would stop retailing electrical goods and focus instead on rentals – Thorn–EMI already owns Granada and DER. The reason was that specialist High Street electrical goods shops (most Rumbelow's shops were sited in towns) were losing ground to out-of-town stores.

☐ **Consumers have become increasingly knowledgeable and sophisticated in their tastes**. Foreign holidays have grown in popularity as they have become more affordable, and they have expanded people's horizons and changed certain tastes. At the same time the demand for

foreign holidays has created opportunities for travel agency services. Many small agencies have been opened on main streets throughout the country. As a result of both the education system and the information role of the media, people are more aware of their consumer rights and have higher expectations of service. Partly in response, and partly to create differentiation proactively, retailers have provided toilets, parking, and better shop displays and fittings, and have sought to create distinctive in-store environments. They have also extended opening hours. In addition, changes in consumer tastes have led to the successful development of the specialist retailers who appeal to specific segments, such as Tie Rack, Body Shop and speciality bookshops.

☐ **Demographic changes:** in simple terms the percentage of the population who are retired and over 60 is increasing and the percentage in the 15–30 age group is declining. Between the mid-1960s and the mid-1980s the percentage represented by 15–25 year olds fell from 15% to 11%, and it is still falling. In the early 1990s significantly fewer young people will reach the age of 18 in any one year, with obvious implications for entry into higher education and for employers seeking to recruit new staff. These changes have meant that retail demand patterns have changed and both manufacturers and retailers have had to respond. In the record business the number of singles sold has declined but new opportunities have arisen for selling compact discs to people over 30. Additionally cassette sales have increased as new stereo and portable cassette players have changed young people's listening habits. In clothing Next has been successful by concentrating on the 30–45 age range, who tend to buy at higher quality levels and less frequently.

☐ **The impact of technology:** the impact of electronic point-of-sale systems (see Chapter 14) has been dramatic, with both retailers and customers able to benefit from improved stock management. However, electronic point-of-sale systems increase the power and role of head offices in relation to individual branches. In addition, in-store videos are increasingly being used for product demonstrations and promotions.

The overall effects of these environmental forces and changes on retailing include the following:

☐ more competition
☐ more capital investment in new bigger stores, fixtures and fittings
☐ more merger activity, not all of which has succeeded (Asda merged with MFI for instance, but MFI was later bought back by its managers)
☐ increased concentration
☐ innovation, such as Body Shop and Sock Shop sometimes linked to
☐ segmentation and specialization
☐ greater diversification of product ranges
☐ diversification overseas by such majors as Marks & Spencer and W H Smith (after 1992 this can be expected to increase, and at the same time more foreign retailers are likely to enter the UK market), following the successful example of such companies as Benetton
☐ more professional management
☐ higher occupation costs (increased overheads) as a result of competition for prime sites
☐ increasing percentage of products with retailers' own brand names, as retailers have become increasingly powerful relative to their suppliers.

In the 1990s customer care and high levels of service will be increasingly important in the search for competitive advantage. This service is primarily delivered at branch level. The roles of branch managers and staff, which changed during the 1980s with the growth of information technology and centralized buying, will change again. The major challenge for many large retailers lies in finding the right ways to empower, motivate and reward their branch staff, allowing them to use their initiative for improving service, without losing the efficiency benefits of the centralized systems.

The impact of 1992

It was agreed in 1987 that by the end of December 1992 European Community members would implement legislation to create a barrier-free internal market. This means, ultimately, the removal of all physical (border controls), fiscal (VAT and excise duty harmonization) and technical (standards) barriers. The notice period allowed decision makers some five years to consider the effect on their particular business and design any appropriate new strategies for capitalizing on the opportunities and avoiding the potential threats. Companies will be free to enter new markets, and there should be equal treatment for all competitors. Competiton should increase within the EC, with both costs and entry barriers reduced. This could beneficially improve the competitiveness of European companies in world markets. Case 9.5 considers the impact on the European car industry.

Companies of all sizes in both manufacturing and service businesses are likely to be affected in various ways, some more than others. A market leader in an industry in the UK must see opportunities for growth abroad and threats from large European competitors attracted by the UK market. An EC Study (1988) predicted that companies will become larger and more specialized as they develop a new perspective on European markets and seek increased economies of scale, and that demand overall will be stimulated. Small companies with essentially a local market may not be affected commercially in quite the same way, but new sources of aid and grants might be provided. (However administrative difficulties might prove a deterrent.)

Case 9.5
CHALLENGES FOR THE EUROPEAN CAR INDUSTRY

☐ In aggregate terms there is over-capacity (early 1990s), although there are inconsistencies. Whilst Fiat, Renault, Peugeot and Ford have idle plants, both Volkswagen and General Motors (Opel) have benefited from a growth in demand in Germany since reunification.

☐ Interdependencies are increasing as a result of strategic alliances such as the one between Volvo and Renault (see Chapter 18).

☐ The Japanese car manufacturers are becoming more prominent. Throughout the 1980s France, Italy, Spain and Portugal, as well as the UK, were, to different degrees, successful in containing the volume of imports from Japan. In 1990, for example, Japanese makes took a 12% European market share compared with 30% in America. However, the combined impact of 1992 and the opening up of manufacturing plants by Nissan, Honda and Toyota, primarily in the UK, is increasing the uncertainty. The European car makers will have to become increasingly competitive in terms of product development and quality.

☐ There is a need for greater price harmonization and clearer policies on discounting to counter falling sales.

☐ There are pending distribution changes. The existing 'block exemption', which protects the exclusive franchise system, runs out in 1995. Some manufacturers, notably VW, Fiat, Toyota and Nissan, are attempting to gain greater control over car wholesaling in order to rationalize their marketing, pricing and advertising.

☐ Environmental regulations and pressures are increasingly significant.

Fiat, which owns Alfa Romeo and Lancia, is arguably the most vulnerable of the major producers. Historically Italy has accounted for some 60% of Fiat's sales, but their share of the market has fallen as Ford have increasingly targeted the Italian market. Japanese imports have been deliberately restricted to very small volumes. Fiat has no production plants outside Italy, but is continuing to invest heavily in new model development.

For some industries the existing policy differences are likely to prove difficult to reconcile. Road haulage, for example, has traditionally been highly regulated with quotas enforced to protect both railways and domestic hauliers. Some restrictions have been lifted since the creation of the EC, but many others remained at the end of the 1980s. Lorry standards (height, weight, noise level and exhaust emissions) have been harmonized, and a UK haulier has been able to take a load out from the UK to Germany and return with a load from Germany or elsewhere, possibly driving *through* France. He has not been free to take a German load *into* France. Road taxes and the extent of rail subsidies have varied markedly.

Marketing

There are obviously going to be new marketing opportunities for organizations with ambitions to sell more products or services around the world, and competition for market share in many markets is likely to intensify. Hence market structures and the significance of certain competitive forces are likely to change. It was mentioned earlier that even the largest UK companies with a significant share of the domestic British market are often small in comparison with their American and Japanese competitors. In 1992 the effective domestic market increased in size dramatically, and it became necessary to regard Europe, rather than the UK, as the home market. On the one hand companies who can demonstrate competitive advantage will be faced with growth opportunities; on the other hand companies from other countries in Europe will be looking to penetrate the UK market more aggressively. Consumers may have more choices, and the successful market penetration of imported manufactured goods since World War II demonstrates that UK buyers are happy to buy non-British goods where they offer competitive advantage.

However, it does not follow that because any visible barriers to trade are dropped a product which sells well in the UK will sell equally well in France or Germany. Tastes differ and few products are global in the sense that with very little differentiation for different markets they sell successfully world wide. It will continue to be necessary for many manufacturers to produce differentiated products to satisfy preferences in different countries and regions. Some companies will seek to trade more widely throughout Europe because they see it as an opportunity; others may feel constrained to do so as the UK market is likely to become increasingly competitive. Whatever the motive it will be necessary to invest time and effort to ensure that there is an understanding of differing needs and tastes.

Berghaus is a British producer of outdoor clothing and equipment for walkers and climbers. Their products are marketed throughout Europe, but with distinct differences for different markets. Waterproof jackets need to be more protective for the British market because of the extra rain and this has implications for design. The style and position of the pockets, for example, are affected. In the case of rucksacks there are different basic styles and sizes to meet particular preferences. Scandinavians appear to want very large rucksacks, British backpackers prefer them slightly smaller, and most of the rest of Europe buy ones which are smaller still. There are also distinct preferences concerning the number of compartments in the rucksacks. In addition the retail systems for distributing these products tend to vary from country to country. In some cases there might be a small number of chain buyers with several outlets, and in others large numbers of small independent retailers. A single range cannot be designed to cover the whole of Europe; alternative designs must be tailored to suit regional preferences. This requires awareness of demand, and a commitment to marketing over a wide geographical area.

In washing machines French customers want top loaders, whilst UK housewives prefer front loaders to fit in with their kitchen designs. Italians select low-powered machines and rely to a great extent on the sun for drying; Germans choose high power to spin out the maximum dampness. Nestlé market 20 different instant coffees under the Nescafé label to satisfy a variety of tastes. Such preferences and differences will change only slowly.

Pricing

There are similarly some noticeable discrepancies in comparative prices. Cars, glassware and tableware have typically been priced higher in the UK than in other European countries; chocolate and confectionery have been cheaper. There are often logical explanations for the differences, although in the case of cars the Monopolies and Mergers Commission investigated the differences during 1991–2. Mars Bars, for example, are cheaper in the UK because they contain less chocolate than their continental equivalent; and Coca Cola is expensive in Denmark because it has to be sold in more costly returnable containers. Nescafé is expensive in Italy because the market for instant coffee is small. Heinz have often reduced prices in countries where they are not market leader, whereas Levi Strauss 501 jeans are priced deliberately high in Spain to fit their perceived image of fashionable, rather than everyday, clothing.

Research and development

Increased harmonization could affect R & D strategies in a variety of ways. Many large pharmaceutical companies have established research facilities in each important national market to ease the problems involved in dealing with regulatory authorities. This may now be far less necessary. Case 9.6 discusses strategic changes in the European drug industry. For industries where development costs are huge, such as telecommunications switching equipment, there will be more opportunities for joint ventures.

Legislation

New Community-wide commercial legislation will affect British companies, and an awareness of the implications is necessary. One benefit might be that standards between different countries are regularized, although some requirements might well be different from existing UK legislation. Many products have historically been governed by quite

different regulations and standards in various European countries, which has meant that a product produced for the UK market may not have met certain continental requirements.

Financial implications

Companies may wish to raise money and see their shares traded across the Community in order to cement closer links with the new markets that they are seeking to penetrate. This could open up new opportunities but make certain aspects of financial management more complex. Both the users of capital and the providers will be affected.

Corporate strategies

A number of strategic issues will be affected by the single European market, and decisions will have to take account of the changed environment (see Box 9.1). Merger activity and new strategic alliances between European companies have increased, which goes against the trend of past merger activity by British companies. For example, in 1987 British companies invested £7 billion abroad, but little more than 10% was spent on European acquisitions. Investment in America has historically been more popular. One of the key factors underpinning this is the fact that legal restrictions and patterns of ownership have tended to make acquisitions in America more feasible and straightforward.

In recruiting and appointing key staff, it is essential to recognize not only the needs of the organization as it is today, but to try to identify what its needs will be in the future and the skills which will take it there.

David Collischon, previously Chairman, Filofax plc

Case 9.6
THE EUROPEAN DRUG INDUSTRY IN 1990

☐ The price of branded drugs varied by as much as ten times between different EC countries.

☐ The same brand names are not used internationally. Glaxo's Zantac (Case 7.4) is known as Zantic in Germany and Azantac in France.

☐ Government systems and procedures for regulating new drugs are not standardized.

☐ Social security and national health systems, which cover all or part of the cost of prescription drugs, again vary.

Standardization will, therefore, require new EC regulations governing advertising, licensing, patents and prices. Theoretically drug companies could apply to just one regulatory authority representing the whole of the EC.

In no other area are we seeing slower progress.
(Kenneth Clarke, Secretary of State for Health, 1990)

One problem concerns the relative power and record of the drug companies. Glaxo and SmithKline Beecham (UK), Hoechst and Bayer (Germany) and Ciba-Geigy (Switzerland) comprise five of the world's top ten drug companies, and they have a sound and valuable record of research, product development and export successes. Most of the companies would prefer to maintain the status quo as a competitive barrier against the large American companies.

In addition, needs vary considerably between countries. Liver medicines, for example, well used in Italy, are much less important in the UK and Denmark.

Past, and inevitable, government interest and involvement makes drugs a politically sensitive industry. Individual consumers have relatively little influence on the choice of a particular drug, which is prescribed by doctors who are often working under constraints or limitations imposed by their respective governments. This affects the marketing strengths of the drug manufacturers. Governments across Europe have frequently agreed favourable prices with international companies who locate and invest in their countries. This has led to the establishment of more plants than are really needed and some loss of production efficiencies. Individual governments believe their healthcare programmes to be superior and may well be resistant to European centralization.

There is little doubt that the medicines industry in Europe will remain for the most part a complex, fragmented, affair.

(Marsh, P (1990) A suitable case for treatment, Financial Times, 22 August)

Box 9.1
STRATEGIES FOR EUROPE

☐ Some organizations and industries will not be affected markedly by 1992. Examples include the providers of **local** services to a limited market and certain national monopolies. The privatization of such monopolies will, however, change the competitive situation. Since the UK water industry was privatized, for example, French water companies, such as Compagnie Générale des Eaux and Groupe Lyonnaise des Eaux, have acquired small British private water companies and bought blocks of shares in the large regional businesses.

☐ Other organizations will focus, crossing frontiers but concentrating on a particular region. This strategy may just be a first step.

One example is Dalgety, who manufacture foods (Golden Wonder, bought from Hanson after the Imperial Group acquisition), pet foods and agricultural products. Dalgety is strongest in the US and UK, but has selectively acquired businesses – on a limited scale – in Holland and France since 1988.

☐ Euro-wide companies will seek a presence throughout the EC. This may well involve strategic alliances rather than wholesale acquisition; and the challenge lies in developing an effective, integrated strategy for the whole of Europe. Key issues include competitive strategies, bearing in mind that Europe is segmented, rather than a single market with homogeneous tastes, and distribution – again, European countries have differing preferences.

Examples: **BSN Groupe** (France), one of Europe's largest food companies with plants in several countries. Products include HP Sauce, Nabisco biscuits, Kronenbourg beer and Evian mineral water. **Electrolux**, Europe's leading electrical appliance company. Headquarters are in Sweden, outside the EC, but several EC-based businesses, including Zanussi of Italy, have been acquired.

☐ Global companies may already be multinational and less dependent on Europe than other parts of the world. The issue for such organizations concerns whether an integrated Europe now offers fresh opportunities, implying a change in investment strategies.

Developed from Lynch, R (1990) *European Business Strategies*, Kogan Page.

Joint ventures and strategic alliances, of course, are a way of by-passing restrictions on acquisitions and achieving the benefits of synergy through co-operation. When growth strategies are explored in Chapter 18 we shall find that a major problem area in managing an organization after an acquisition relates to the fusion of two different cultures and sets of values. British companies are likely for all sorts of reasons to be different from their European competitors in a variety of ways; increased merger activity throughout Europe after 1992 will emphasize the significant strategic importance of organizational culture. Moreover, there is likely to be an increase in the mobility of managers throughout Europe, both within their existing organizations and between companies.

Location decisions for new plant will need to take account of the proximity of new market opportunities. Case 9.7 features a dilemma for Pilkington in 1988 followed by a review in 1991. Pilkington is not alone in realizing that a presence in northern Europe is important for obtaining orders and providing high levels of service in this prosperous region.

The changes that do take place, however, will be influenced by any new European competition legislation which might restrict particular proposals. The EC Study (1988) on the European economy suggests that reduced barriers to trade will have a greater effect on technology-related sectors such as electronics, where internationally the Community has performed less well than Japan and America, and less effect on the more traditional industries, where 'international barriers appear not to have imposed a severe competitive handicap'. In other words domestic markets have been sufficiently large to enable companies to grow, create compet-

---

Case 9.7
PILKINGTON'S LOCATION DILEMMA

THE DECISION IN 1988

Pilkington are the world's largest glass maker, and the company's main base has been in the north of England, at St Helens on Merseyside since the company was founded in 1826. Whilst the company has a 50% share of the UK market the major growth area is the southeast. In 1988 Pilkington decided to invest some tens of millions of pounds in a new float glass plant but was unsure as to where the plant should be located. Should it be in the southeast, or in St Helens?

In terms of distance there were seven competitor plants in northern France and Belgium which were nearer to London than St Helens. When European trade barriers are reduced and the Channel Tunnel is open this may prove a threat to Pilkington's market share. Equally a southern location would bring Pilkington closer to European customers.

However, a plant in the south would cost of the order of £60 to £80 million rather than the £40 to £50 million on Merseyside. When the last float glass plant was built in 1975 it was designed with a batch plant for assembling materials considerably in excess of current requirements. The capacity was such that it would feed two glass tanks (only one was constructed in 1975), thereby making future expansion on the site perfectly feasible. Consequently only a glass tank would be needed in St Helens, but both a tank and a batch plant for assembling materials would be necessary on a greenfield site in the south.

The local council, the two St Helens' Labour MPs and Pilkington's trade unions all campaigned for an expansion on the current site, arguing that the proximity issue could be overcome with a warehouse in the south. Moreover the opening of a spur to the M62 in 1992 would make road travel from St Helens to the southeast quicker.

In the event the decision was in favour of St Helens, and the plant was built in 1989.

Continued overleaf

THE FOLLOW-UP IN 1991

In 1980, as part of its strategy of acquiring glass companies in America and Europe, Pilkington had bought a majority shareholding in a German competitor, Flachglass. Minority shareholders prevented the proper integration of the two businesses until Pilkington bought them out in 1989.

In 1991 Pilkington was manufacturing float glass in four plants at St Helens, four in Germany, one in Sweden and one in Finland. In October that year Pilkington announced that they intended to move the headquarters for float glass (their core business) to Brussels. About 750 jobs would be lost in St Helens, where one float glass plant would close. The Group headquarters, where corporate strategy is formulated, would remain on Merseyside.

Pilkington justified the decision on the grounds that Brussels would provide a stronger base for attacking the automotive and construction markets of northern Europe, and better allow integration of all its float glass manufacturing. There would also be some production rationalization and switching to improve efficiencies in the face of market recession and industry over-capacity.

Sources: Hamilton Fazey, I (1988) Two way choice for Pilkington, *Financial Times*, 13 September; and Leadbeater, C (1991) Pilkington integrates European operations, *Financial Times*, 9 October.

---

itive advantage and compete internationally. Such is not the case for the new technology industries where the experience curve effect has proved significant and trade barriers have constrained international expansion to take advantage of scale economies. Different industries will be affected in various ways because of differences in demand and consumption patterns, and because a variety of trading barriers have emerged over the years.

The EC Study also suggested that in the long term there will be benefits from 'restructuring by industries to secure improved economies of scale and the eradication of inefficiency due to over-manning and excess inventories and overheads'. Companies might also be 'stimulated to exploit comparative advantage more effectively and to innovate faster'.

In essence 1992 will cause changes to the environmental map of most organizations, i.e., in terms of Figure 9.2, the focal zone will be changed. Companies must be alert for the implications, and wherever possible take the appropriate opportunities and avoid the most dangerous threats. Resources must be harnessed and managed with this in mind.

In a global company such as ours it is essential to have managers who think and operate internationally. International experience is a 'sine qua non' for anyone aspiring to top managerial posts. This is one of the key principles of our international guidelines on human resource policy.

International experience helps managers both professionally and personally as they work in a totally different business and cultural environment, use their skills at the 'sharp end' and adapt to unfamiliar circumstances. Facing the challenge of working abroad, learning new languages, living in unfamiliar societies – these mould character and are enriching experiences.

Hermann J. Strenger, Chairman of the Board of Management, Bayer AG, Leverkusen

DO OUR RESOURCES MATCH UP WELL?

Throughout this chapter the environment has been referred to in terms of opportunities and threats. In reality the opportunities are only potential opportunities unless the organization can utilize resources to take advantage of them and until the strategic leader decides it is appropriate to pursue the opportunity. It is therefore important to evaluate environmental opportunities in relation to the strengths and weaknesses of the organization's resources, and in relation to the organizational culture. Real opportunities exist when there is a close fit between environment, values and resources. Similarly the resources and culture will determine the extent to which any potential threat becomes a real threat. This is E–V–R congruence.

All the resources at the disposal of the organization can be deployed strategically, including strategic leadership. It is therefore useful to consider the resources in terms of where they are strong and where they are weak as this will provide an indication of their strategic value. However, this should not be seen as a list of absolute strengths and weaknesses seen from an internal perspective; rather, the evaluation should consider the strengths and weaknesses in relation to the needs of the environment and in relation to competition. The views of external stakeholders may differ from those of internal managers (who in turn may disagree amongst themselves) when evaluating the relative strength of a particular product, resource or skill. Resources should be evaluated for their relative strengths and weaknesses in the light of key success factors.

Even though an organization may be strong or weak in a particular function, the corresponding position of its major competitors must also be taken into account. For example, it might have sophisticated computer-controlled machine tools in its factory, but if its competitors have the same or even better equipment, the plant should not be seen as a relative strength. This issue refers to distinctive competences – relative strengths which can be used to create competitive advantage. As any resource can be deployed strategically, competitive advantage can be gained from any area of the total business. This idea will be developed further in Chapter 15 when the concept of the value chain for examining potential sources of advantage is examined.

SWOT analysis

An evaluation of an organization's strengths and weaknesses in relation to environmental opportunities and threats is generally referred to as a SWOT analysis. Figure 2.2 in Chapter 2 suggests that a SWOT analysis involves answering two questions:

☐ Where are our opportunities and threats?
☐ How can we capitalize on our strengths and reduce our weaknesses?

The first question relates to the environment, the second to resources. As mentioned above, a mere list of absolute factors is of little use. The opportunities which matter are those which can be capitalized on because they fit the organization's values and resources; the threats which matter are those that the organization must deal with and which it is not well equipped to deal with; the key strengths are those where the organization enjoys a relatively strong competitive position and which relate to key success factors; the key weaknesses are those which prevent the organization from attaining competitive advantage.

This short introduction to the concept of SWOT does not explain how the strategic importance of the various resources might be evaluated. That is one role of the remaining chapters in this part of the book.

Again, to be useful the lists of factors should be limited to those which matter the most, so that attention can be concentrated on them. In arriving at such a summary

Organizational resources / Environmental issues and significance score	Industry capacity (supply – demand relationship) – Industry X –	Power of suppliers	Demographic changes	Expectation and likelihood of innovation
	+8	−2	+5	−6
Products Range				
Segmentation				
Diversification				
Research and development				3

Figure 9.4   A possible framework for analysing strengths, weaknesses, opportunities and threats.

SWOT statement it can therefore be useful to start by drawing up a large grid and using it for assessing relative importances. Figure 9.4 illustrates a possible framework. Variations of this can easily be designed to suit particular purposes and preferences. The one illustrated features the environmental issues which affect the organization listed at the top of a set of columns together with a score for their relative importance. One typical issue might be the current relationship between demand and supply in the industries in which the firm competes. If demand exceeded supply, providing growth opportunities, this would justify a positive score; but if supply exceeded demand, suggesting intense competition, the score might well be negative. The larger the scores, both positive and negative, the more significant the issue. Other issues could be the power of suppliers, the power of distributors, population changes and innovation.

The organization's resources, which might be categorized in various ways, are listed down the left-hand side. Their relative strength or weakness in relation to the environmental issues can similarly be entered on to the grid as numbers, with high scores implying an ability to deal with potential threats and capitalize on potential opportunities, and low scores (all positive figures in this case) indicating vulnerability to threats and only limited opportunity for pursuing potential opportunities. For example if the organization was strong in a particular market segment and this segment was being affected positively by population changes, the firm would be well placed to deal with supply and demand issues. If total supply in the industry exceeded demand the firm would be to some extent protected; if demand already exceeded supply there would be real growth opportunities. Other resources such as investment capital and spare capacity would then need to be considered. Similarly research and development could be assessed in relation to innovation in the environment. Figure 9.4 with a score of −6 for the environmental issue might indicate a situation in which a competitor is expected to introduce a new product in the near future, making the environment more uncertain. The figure 3 against the organization's research and development resource would correspondingly indicate that the organization did not have a similar new product

Table 9.4   Chrysalis and Virgin: a comparison of capabilities and values during the 1980s

---

Distinctive capabilities (selection only)

Chrysalis	Virgin
☐ Artiste and repertoire development (i.e. acquisition of new artists and music)	☐ Artiste and repertoire development (relatively stronger than Chrysalis)
☐ Technical production skills	☐ Innovation
☐ Marketing	☐ Image
☐ Management of acquisitions	

Corporate values

☐ Cautious	☐ Adventurous
☐ Executive teamwork	☐ Individual
☐ Relatively democratic	☐ Relatively autocratic
☐ Professional management	☐ Informal management
	☐ High profile

---

ready. Consequently innovation would be seen as a threat, and research and development a relative weakness at the moment.

Drawing up the grid is one way of focusing attention on the key issues and allowing a summary statement of key strengths, weaknesses, opportunities and threats to emerge. This in turn would highlight possible directions for future strategic change.

Using SWOT analysis

The framework for a strategy statement introduced in Chapter 1, Figure 1.4, illustrated the relationship between resources and capabilities, values and culture, and products, services and markets, which in turn are very much dependent upon the competitive environment. SWOT analyses can be used in relation to this theme. The essential questions are the following.

☐ How well does the organization fit with its environment at the moment?
☐ How well do the resources and values match the changes we would like to see and the changes that we are forecasting?
☐ Is the organizational culture blending our resources and environmental issues effectively?

On the one hand the organization's distinc-tive capabilities and corporate values could be set down clearly and related to those of one or more major competitors. Table 9.4 compares Chrysalis and Virgin, competitors in the popular music and entertainment industries in the 1980s. Box 9.2 shows how this can be done diagrammatically. From here the question can be asked: what markets and market segments really appreciate these capabilities and values? In other words there is a search for new opportunities together with an assessment of current products, services and markets. Virgin is a more inno-vative organization than Chrysalis, and has diversified when attractive opportunities have been spotted. Virgin's culture is more one of opportunism than tight management control. It was perhaps not unexpected when Virgin sold a number of record stores to W H Smith because 'retail is detail' in the current competitive environment.

An alternative approach is to start with the products and markets where the organization already competes, and to evaluate these in terms of opportunities, threats and key success factors. The questions to be asked then are: Are our resources appropriate and adequate for us to be an effective competitor? Are our values appropriate? Table 9.5 features some of the key success factors which affect Chrysalis in four business areas, and summarizes very briefly their relative

Box 9.2
COMPETITIVE GAP ANALYSIS

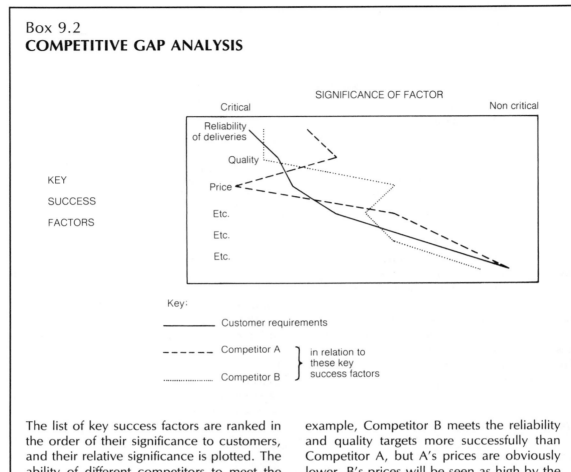

The list of key success factors are ranked in the order of their significance to customers, and their relative significance is plotted. The ability of different competitors to meet the key success factors can be illustrated by drawing comparison lines. In the above example, Competitor B meets the reliability and quality targets more successfully than Competitor A, but A's prices are obviously lower. B's prices will be seen as high by the market.

position in the late 1980s before the acquisition of Chrysalis records by Thorn–EMI.

Synergy is an important consideration in each of the above cases.

Ohmae (1982) contends that it can also be useful to consider resource capabilities and environmental influences in relation to specific strategic issues. Figure 9.5 develops this idea. If an organization has an objective of increasing the profitability of a particular product or service by a target amount in a

given period, it must evaluate how this might be accomplished. Sales might be increased in existing market segments if marketing opportunities exist; new market opportunities might be created, particularly if more value could be added to the product. Alternatively a cost reduction would also increase profitability, and this would involve manufacturing or operations management. The diagram breaks the decision alternatives down in a tree form with each box relating to how

Table 9.5 Chrysalis Group: key success factors and situation analysis in four business sectors

Activity	Key success factors	Situation analysis
Music	Artists	Small roster
	Repertoire/music	Few awards in later 1980s; previously more successful
	Promotion	Poor performance in USA
Facilities (production facilities for music, videos etc.)	Latest technology	Heavy investment in latest technology
	Technical skills	Highly skilled and innovative
	Location	International
		Complementary to main activity of music, but very competitive and there is over-capacity
Machines	*Juke boxes*	
	Site and content	UK market leader
	Fruit machines	
	Site and novelty	No. 3 in market
		Very profitable, but subject to rapid changes
Property development	Saleable acquisitions	Joint venture with builder (successful)
		Profitable
		Good for cash utilization

resources might be utilized to achieve certain ends. Alongside all these alternatives the relevant environmental issues must be evaluated. In this particular case, anticipated demand, competitor activity, current advertising expenditures, and opportunities for buying cheaper materials or improving productivity would relate to the boxes already completed.

SUMMARY

In this chapter we emphasized the importance of analysing the environment in terms of opportunities and threats and the need for managers in organizations to seek to manage their environment as well as understand how the organization is influenced. This requires matching the organization's resources and values with the environment.

Specifically we have

☐ considered the complex, dynamic and uncertain aspects of the environment, and how changes might be forecast

☐ introduced the concept of the organization as part of an open system whereby environmental forces impact upon the organization and in turn the organization can seek to influence or manage the environment, with functions within the organization seen as interdependent subsystems whose interrelationships create emergent properties

☐ developed the concept of key success factors, and looked at those factors which affect all competitors in an industry, those which can lead to the achievement of competitive advantage for individual companies and those which could be important for a variety of industries in the future

☐ considered the need to evaluate the relative power of different stakeholders in terms of managing the environment, and used the idea of the focal zone diagram for this

☐ briefly described Ansoff's model which aims to match resources with the dynamics of the environment

☐ emphasized that the various influences

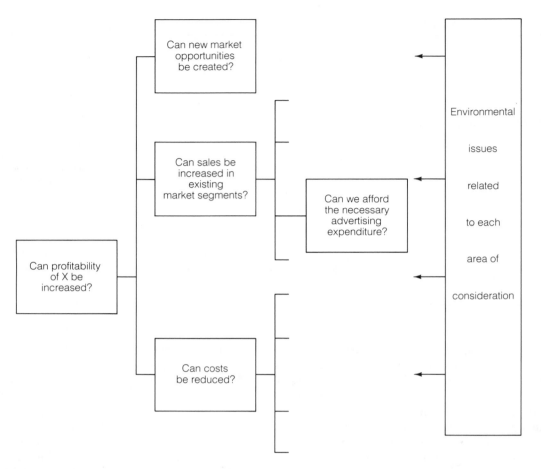

Figure 9.5   Analysis of issues. Adapted from Ohmae, K (1982) *The Mind of the Strategist*, McGraw-Hill.

and stakeholders may not affect every business unit or function in the organization in quite the same way, making it important for managers to take a holistic view of the whole firm

☐ considered current changes taking place in the international and UK environment, and looked at the impact of 1992

☐ discussed possible uses and the value of SWOT analyses, pointing out that opportunities are only real opportunities if resources and values can be matched with them

☐ provided a possible framework for drawing up a SWOT summary.

CHECKLIST OF KEY TERMS AND CONCEPTS

You should feel confident that you understand the following terms and ideas:

☐ The organization as part of an open system

□ Key success factors
□ SWOT analysis
□ Competitive gap analysis.

QUESTIONS AND RESEARCH ASSIGNMENTS

Text related

1. Draw a diagram incorporating the environmental influences and stakeholders for one of the pubs featured in the Bruce's Brewery case (Chapter 3, Case 3.5). Do the same for London Zoo (Chapter 5, Case 5.2).
2. Using Table 9.1 as a framework, evaluate the threats and opportunities faced by any organization with which you are familiar.
3. From this evaluation, develop a SWOT analysis and consider the strategic implications. You may wish to use the framework offered in Figure 9.4 or develop one of your own.

Library based

4. Consider the impact of 1992 on any one industry. In particular look at the specific regulations which have governed the industry in different European countries, and attempt to assess the impact of their removal.
5. Research the recent progress and changes at Chrysalis and Virgin. Which of the two companies, do you feel, has been better at managing its environment? Why?

RECOMMENDED FURTHER READING

Environmental analysis usually constitutes one topic in every text on strategic management, and few books concentrate exclusively on this subject area. However, Freeman, R E (1984) *Strategic Management*, Pitman, provides a useful analysis of strategic decisions from the point of view of stakeholders.

In addition Taylor, B and Sparkes, J (eds) (1977) *Corporate Strategy and Planning*, Heinemann, contains a number of relevant chapters.

Lynch, R (1990), *European Business Strategies*, Kogan Page, describes the development of several large European companies.

REFERENCES

Ansoff, H I (1987) *Corporate Strategy*, Penguin.

Checkland, P B (1981) *Systems Thinking, Systems Practice*, Wiley.

Confederation of British Industry (1991) *Competing with the World's Best*, CBI.

Dodsworth, T and Garnett, N (1987) British manufacturing: a wealth of contradictions, *Financial Times*, 23 November.

Duncan, R (1972) Characteristics of organizational environments and perceived environmental uncertainty, *Administrative Science Quarterly*, pp. 313–27.

EC Study (1988) *The Economics of 1992: European Economy, No. 35*, Office des Publications Officielles des Communautés Européennes, Luxembourg.

Fahey, L and King, R (1983) Environmental scanning for corporate planning. In *Business Policy and Strategy: Concepts and Readings*, 3rd edn, (eds D J McCarthy *et al.*), Irwin.

Hogarth, R M and Makridakis, S (1981) Forecasting and planning: an evaluation, *Management Science*, **27**, 115–38.

Jauch, L R and Glueck, W F (1988) *Strategic Management and Business Policy*, 3rd edn, McGraw-Hill.

Kanter, R M (1991) Transcending business boundaries: 12 000 world managers view change, *Harvard Business Review*, May–June.

Kelly, F J and Kelly, H M (1987) *What They Really Teach You at the Harvard Business School*, Piatkus.

Mintzberg, H (1987) Crafting strategy, *Harvard Business Review*, July–August.

Ohmae, K (1982) *The Mind Of The Strategist*, McGraw-Hill.

Ohmae, K (1985) *Triad Power: The Coming Shape of Global Competition*, Free Press.

PA Consulting Group and the Confederation of British Industry (1988) *UK Productivity – Closing the Gap*, PA Consulting Group, London, September.

Rock, S (1987) The law learns to solicit for business, *The Director*, November.

Sadler, P (1988) *Managerial Leadership in the Post Industrial Society*, Gower.

Smith, R (1987) The marketing challenge, *First*, **1** (2).

Wilson, I H (1977) Forecasting social and political trends. In *Corporate Strategy and Planning* (eds B Taylor and J Sparkes), Heinemann.

RESOURCES AND COMPETITIVE ADVANTAGE: AN OVERVIEW OF CHAPTERS 10–14

Chapters 10–14 are concerned with the management of resources. They concentrate on functional and competitive strategies.

In a SWOT analysis the strengths and weaknesses of resources must be considered in relative and not absolute terms. It is important to consider whether they are being managed effectively as well as efficiently. Resources, therefore, are not strong or weak purely because they exist or do not exist. Rather, their value depends upon how they are being managed, controlled and used.

In auditing resources we consider the functional areas of the business, as this is where the human, financial and physical resources are deployed. These areas might include finance, production, marketing, research and development, procurement, personnel and administration. However, it is also important to consider how they are related together in the organization's structure and control systems. A brilliant and successful marketing manager, for example, might seem to represent a strength; however, if there is no adequate cover for him and he leaves or falls ill, it is arguable that the firm has a marketing weakness.

Control systems, such as production and

Table 1   Aspects of the resource audit

Resource/function	Key considerations

Marketing	Products and services
	  range
	  brand names
	  stage in life cycle
	Patents
	Strength of salesforce
	Distribution channels

Operations	Location and plant Capital equipment Planning and manufacturing systems Quality control Supplies
Research and development	Annual budget Technology support Quality of researchers Record of success and reputation
Finance	Capital structure Working capital Cash flow Costing systems and variances Nature of shareholders Relations with bankers
Human resources	Numbers and qualifications Skills and experience Age profile Labour turnover and absenteeism Flexibility Development and training record and policies Motivation and culture

	Areas of strength	Areas of weakness	Significance of strength	Significance of weakness
Resource/ function				
Marketing				
Operations				
etc.				

financial control, and the ways in which managers co-operate within the organization influence how well resources are managed for efficiency and effectiveness. Table 1, which is not meant to be fully comprehensive, provides a sample of key resource considerations. In completing such an audit the various resources should be evaluated: their existence, the ways that they are deployed and utilized, and the control systems that are used to manage them.

Using Table 1 as an example, efficiency measures of the salesforce might include sales per person or sales per region, but the effectiveness of the salesforce relates to their ability to sell the most profitable products or those products or services which the organization is keen to promote at a particular time, perhaps to reduce a high level of stocks. The efficiency of individual distribution outlets can be measured by sales revenue in a similar way. But the effectiveness of the distribution activity relates to exactly which products are being sold and to whom, whether they are available where customers expect them, and how much investment in stock is required to maintain the outlets. The efficiency of plant and equipment is linked to percentage utilization. The effectiveness involves an assessment of which products are being manufactured in relation to orders and delivery requirements, to what quality and with what rejection levels.

It is also important to assess the relative strengths and weaknesses in relation to competition. Thus each of the designated areas of consideration included in Table 1 might be analysed with the chart above.

The theme of these chapters on the organization's resources is that managers must be aware of and must address strategic issues if the resources are to be used for creating and sustaining competitive advantage. Marketing can be looked at from the point of view of managing the activities which comprise the marketing function. Product design and pricing, advertising, selling and distribution would be included here. But if an organization is marketing oriented there is an implication that employees throughout the organization are aware of consumers and customers, their needs, and how they might be satisfied effectively whilst enabling the organization to achieve its objectives. Consumer concern becomes part of the culture and values. Consumers and customers are mentioned separately because for many organizations, particularly the manufacturers of products for consumer markets, their customers are distributors and their ultimate consumers are customers of the retailers they supply.

Innovation and quality can be seen as aspects of production or operations management. Again it is helpful if these factors become part of the culture. An innovatory organization is ready for change, and looking to make positive changes, in order to get ahead and stay ahead of competition. A concern for quality in all activities will affect both costs and consumer satisfaction.

In human resources management values are communicated and spread throughout the organization.

Financial management includes the control of costs so that profit is achieved and value is added to products and services primarily in areas which matter to consumers. This should provide differentiation and competitive advantage.

Lower costs and differentiation are the basic sources of competitive advantage. These relate to both an awareness of consumer needs and the management of resources to satisfy these needs effectively and, where relevant, profitably. Marketing orientation and the effective management of production and operations, people and finance are all essential aspects of the creation and maintenance of competitive advantage.

Whilst these chapters on functional and competitive strategies are important for an understanding of strategic management in all types of organization, they are especially important for a large proportion of small businesses and many not-for-profit organizations. Corporate strategic changes such as major diversification and acquisition, divestment of business units which are under-performing or international expansion may not be relevant for small firms with a limited range of products or services and a primarily local market, or for not-for-profit organizations with very specific missions. However, these organizations must compete effectively, operate efficiently and provide their customers and clients with products and services which satisfy their needs. Competitive and functional strategies are therefore the relevant issue.

MARKETING AS A STRATEGIC RESOURCE

10

LEARNING OBJECTIVES

After studying this chapter you should be able to

☐ differentiate between the concept of marketing as an aspect of culture and the marketing mix activities in relation to competitive and functional strategies;
☐ explain the strategic significance of market segmentation, positioning and targeting;
☐ draw a product life cycle diagram and relate it to a simple growth share matrix;
☐ evaluate the potential for a proposed new product;
☐ assess the strategic impact of distribution, advertising and pricing strategies;
☐ discuss marketing for service, not-for-profit and small businesses.

This chapter is about marketing – getting to know and satisfy consumer needs – and about the activities which must be managed effectively to achieve this. Good marketing strategies for any product and service are concerned with ensuring that the benefits of competitive advantage are enjoyed by the organization.

INTRODUCTION

In this chapter we look at the strategic importance and contribution of marketing for an organization. Marketing will be shown to be both a concept which should be part of the culture and values of an organization and a set of activities which must be managed.

It is assumed that readers will already have some understanding of marketing, and this chapter, as well as the next four chapters, do not cover the subject in depth. Instead we concentrate on those aspects which have key strategic implications. However, a comprehensive additional reading list is provided at the end of the chapter for readers who might wish to study marketing in greater detail.

The hierarchy of corporate, competitive and functional strategies was introduced in the introduction to SWOT analysis (see introduction to Part III). Competitive strategies concern the overall management of particular products and services produced by the organization. The decision to produce certain products or services in the first place, the current market opportunities for them, their positioning in the market in relation to competition, and the relevant pricing, distribution and promotion strategies are key aspects of the functional marketing strategy. For this reason they will all be considered in this chapter. In addition some consideration of the development of new products and services is included together with some comment on marketing for small companies and for not-for-profit organizations.

In Key Reading 10.1 we consider the need for marketing orientation to become a perceived value of the organization. Unfortunately this may not be the case in many companies.

The marketplace decides the extent of our success. Hoechst sets its sights on a partnership with customers based on a spirit of mutual interest. We aim to recognize our customers' needs swiftly, and satisfy them promptly in a cost-effective manner.
We respect the power of the marketplace.

Professor Wolfgang Hilger, Chairman
Hoechst AG

UNDERSTANDING MARKETING

Awareness of consumer needs

Marketing is not a specialized activity at all. It encompasses the entire business. It is the whole business seen from the point of view of its final result, that is from the customer's point of view. Concern and responsibility for marketing must therefore permeate all areas of enterprise.   (Peter Drucker, 1954)

Thus marketing is a concept, and as such it is an important aspect of organizational culture. Marketing links selling organizations with buyers. Selling, however, is concerned with converting finished products and services into cash; marketing involves decisions about what that product should be, how it should be promoted, and where and how it should be made available.

If an organization is marketing oriented, then decisions about products and services will clearly relate to the needs of the market. Product design, specification, quality and packaging will be designed to customer and consumer preferences. Prices will be influenced by competition and consumer perceptions of quality relative to alternative products or services, as well as by costs. Advertising and promotion will seek to show how the product or service meets consumer needs and will target the product to specific segments of the market; and the product will be made available where customers would expect to find it. These four decision areas (product, price, promotion and place) comprise what is known as the **marketing mix**, and the management of them lies within the marketing function. However, there is also an implicit need for production, financial and other managers in the organization to regard consumers as vital stakeholders in the business because if their needs are not met they may well buy from the company's competitors. Customers buy products and services because they believe that they will satisfy particular needs and wants, not simply

Key Reading 10.1
MARKETING IN PERSPECTIVE

Theodore Levitt (1960) introduced the term 'marketing myopia' which implied that many organizations failed to give sufficient attention to the needs and importance of their consumers. Instead they were more concerned with producing the products they chose and then attempting to sell them. Marketing orientation requires much more consideration of the market and consumer needs, but not at the expense of profit.

A truly marketing-minded firm tries to create value-satisfying goods and services that consumers will want to buy. Most important, what it offers for sale is determined not by the seller, but by the buyer.

(Theodore Levitt)

In the mid-1980s many companies producing consumer goods, particularly consumer convenience goods, have become marketing oriented, but many suppliers of consumer durable goods, capital goods and services still remain production and sales oriented. Exceptions exist, including Adidas and Moulinex (consumer durables), IBM (capital goods) and McDonald's and Club Méditerranée (services).

With the exception of packaged goods makers and retailers most European companies have not even defined what markets they are in or who their competitors are.

(Senior marketing specialist, McKinsey and Co.)

'We've been talking about marketing for 25 years, but very few companies really do it' (Philip Kotler, leading American marketing author, commenting on American companies). Kotler argues that Japanese companies are more marketing-aware and that this has been an essential element in their penetration of markets around the world.

One of the major reasons why marketing has not been adopted more widely is the fact that it depends heavily upon strategic leadership as it needs to become part of the organization's culture.

The entire corporation must be viewed as a customer-creating and customer-satisfying organism. Management must think of itself not as producing products, but as providing customer-creating satisfactions. It must push this idea (and everything it means and requires) into every nook and cranny of the organization. It has to do this continuously and with the kind of flair that excites and stimulates the people in it.

(Levitt, 1960)

In summary there are twelve specific reasons why companies in Europe and America have failed to become truly marketing oriented.

☐ **Organizational barriers**: marketing as a concept has failed to become part of the organizational culture; marketing is seen instead as a function which carries out certain activities such as distribution and promotion.

☐ **Structural failings**: the organization is not structured around products and services in the form of business units, and consequently managers not directly involved in marketing have little contact with customers or appreciation of their needs.

☐ **Hostile corporate cultures**: technical, sales or financial cultures, rather than marketing, prevail. These tend towards seeing the market as a mass market rather than a composite of segments with individual preferences.

☐ **Myopic marketers**: marketing managers themselves fail to communicate effectively within the organization, seeing marketing as a function rather than a concept.

□ **Confusion with sales**: this is partly because marketing is conceptually more difficult to encompass than the need for sales and revenue, and can be compounded by promoting sales managers into marketing management.

□ **Confusion with customer service**: airlines and banks are cited as service businesses which see customers as people who should be treated pleasantly but who often fail to take marketing much further.

□ **Confusion with market research and dominance by it**: research is used as a decision substitute rather than decision support, and as a result marketing becomes quantitative rather than behavioural. Marketing is as much about insight and consumer empathy as it is about market analysis and the statistics of market growth.

□ **The strategic planning barrier**: emphasis on planning techniques compounds the last-mentioned problem.

□ **Short-term horizons**: concentration on short-term targets draws attention away from the longer-term need to develop and sustain competitive advantage in line with market preferences.

□ **The 'theory gap'**: many of the theories associated with marketing concentrate on analysis rather than the implementation aspects of marketing decisions, again reinforcing the problem of confusion with market research and dominance by it.

□ **The 'competition gap'**: for many years marketing was taught as a discipline based on consumer satisfaction; the parallel need to consider competition was ignored until Michael Porter highlighted its importance.

□ **Degeneration**: there is a tendency in some organizations to stay with past successes rather than to respond fully to changing market forces and needs.

Summarized from Lorenz, C (1985) Marketing: an insidious disease, *Financial Times*, 1 April, and The complexities that often lead to failure, *Financial Times*, 17 April.

The reference for Levitt's article is Levitt, T (1960) Marketing myopia, *Harvard Business Review*, July–August.

---

because they are available. Acceptance of the marketing concept means that all the functions within the business work together to sense, serve and satisfy customers. Within the organization marketing might be expected to perform something of a co-ordinating role. Marketing managers are the ones who are closest to the market, and they should be the most aware of customer needs and of opportunities, threats and changing preferences. It is encumbent upon them to ensure that other managers are also made aware.

Customers, together with competitors who are also attempting to satisfy customers' needs more effectively, are therefore major influences, and many decisions within the organization must take some account of their needs. However, the requirements of other stakeholders, and the need for the organization's products and services to be profitable, cannot be ignored.

Key Reading 10.1 argues that the marketing concept in its true sense is not widely practised by organizations, especially those outside the consumer non-durable goods sector, and offers a number of reasons as to why this might be the case.

In summary the marketing concept suggests that products and services should not be created, produced and offered to the market without some clear appreciation of customer and consumer tastes and preferences. Activities within the organization should be co-ordinated to ensure that these market needs are satisfied as effectively as possible. Marketing management is responsible for decisions concerning what products and services to produce and their promotion, pricing and distribution. Depending upon the structure, sales may be separate from marketing but linked to it, or a part of it. Marketing management should also ensure that other managers throughout the organization are aware of changes in the market environment and of new opportunities and threats concerning customers and competitors.

Marketing must relate closely to innovation, which will be considered in greater detail in the next chapter. New products or services may result from a search to find better ways of satisfying needs; equally they may result from technical developments which create something new and different. In both cases there will be a need to persuade the market to change behaviour, in the first case by highlighting exactly how needs can be better satisfied, and in the second possibly by attempting to change needs and tastes. Some organizations will be more innovative than their competitors and willing to take greater risks. Davidson (1972) used the expression offensive marketing to 'describe a set of attitudes and techniques designed to exploit the marketing approach fully'. Companies, he argues, should innovate and respond to competition by counterattack and not by imitation. Offensive marketing companies are

□ **profitable**: they achieve an appropriate balance between the firm's and the consumers' needs
□ **offensive**: they seek to lead the market and make competitors followers
□ **integrated**: the marketing concept permeates throughout the organization
□ **strategic**: the marketing effort is directed towards long-term competitive advantage
□ **effective at implementing the strategy**.

Marketing strategy

The marketing strategy for each product and service must be linked to objectives and to the other functional strategies which together comprise the competitive strategy. It must address three things:

□ how to meet customer needs more effectively than competitors
□ how to compete with other manufacturers
□ what use to make of the various marketing mix elements.

Box 10.1 features four alternative marketing strategies which Reis and Trout (1986) argue will 'outwit; outflank and outfight competitors'.

In considering the decision areas above, marketing managers should be aware of

□ what might be realistically expected from a particular market or industry in terms of revenue and profit. This is related to market growth, why people buy the product or service, any significant demographic changes in the market and the stage that the product is at in its life cycle.
□ how the market might be segmented. Opportunities to benefit by concentrating on particular market niches may exist.
□ opportunities for differentiating the product, adding value and creating competitive advantage.
□ how best to position the product in relation to competitors. This requires some consideration of both the existing situation and how things might change if, for example, any new products are introduced.
□ strategic opportunities for pricing, promotion and distribution in relation to competition.

These factor are explored in the following sections.

Box 10.1
FOUR WAYS TO FIGHT THE MARKETING WAR

DEFENSIVE MARKETING

This is a strategy for the marketing leader and concerns attacking oneself. By introducing new products and services which make existing ones obsolete the leadership position can be strengthened, and competitors may be left always struggling to catch up. Gillette is an example with their introduction of a series of innovations including the bonded blade, the optimum shaving angle, the double-sided razor and the disposable razor.

OFFENSIVE MARKETING

Companies who are strong in a market but not leaders might use this to create competitive advantage and steal market share from the leader. It concerns attacking a perceived weakness in the leader's strategy which may well be a weakness which results from a strength. Hertz are world market leader for car hire, and this has presented Avis with competitive opportunities. The 'We may be Number 2 but we try harder' advertising campaign was very effective as was the argument 'Rent from Avis; our queue at the counter is shorter'. The latter is an example of a strength becoming a weakness; Hertz's position of leadership and popularity with customers led to queues.

FLANKING MARKETING

This strategy concerns marketing positioning and the search for new innovatory opportunities which create competitive advantage. The aim is to find a new market position ahead of competition. Personal desk-top computers would be one example; Timex opening up the market for watches several years ago by distributing them through a far wider range of outlets than the traditional jewellery and department stores is another.

GUERRILLA MARKETING

This is the appropriate strategy for small companies, and requires that they concentrate on just one segment of the market. 'A guerrilla reduces the size of the battleground to achieve superiority of force.'

Summarized from Reis, A and Trout, J (1986) *Marketing Warfare*, McGraw-Hill.

UNDERSTANDING PRODUCT AND SERVICE MANAGEMENT

Given that the four essential aspects of the marketing mix are the product (or service), price, promotion and place, it can be said that the objective of marketing is to ensure that the 'right' product is in the 'right' place at the 'right' time, with the 'right' price and promoted in the 'right' way. To achieve this the product must be more attractive to customers than competing alternatives are; and to be 'right' for the company it must also be profitable. At any time it is quite likely that a successful company which offers a number of different products will have some which have been in production for several years and which really have had their best days, others which are doing well and growing in strength at the moment, and some which are relatively new and upon which hopes for the future are based. These have been termed yesterday's, today's and tomorrow's products.

Products are sources of satisfaction to customers and consumers, and this is the way that they should be seen within the organization. Wide acceptance of this throughout the firm implies that the company is marketing oriented, as we have seen earlier. Examples of this in practice would include British Rail seeing itself as an organization which moves people, mail and other goods to suit the needs of customers, but at the same time profitably, not simply as a firm which runs a network of trains. A producer of photocopying machines is helping customers to increase the efficiency of their administration rather than manufacturing machinery; and similarly a fertilizer manufacturer is helping farmers increase their yield and productivity. Thinking along these lines should ensure that value is added in areas where customers value it and consequently will pay for it.

Thinking of the business in terms of broad need satisfaction will encourage an orientation towards the market, but there is a danger that it can encourage diversification into areas where the organization does not have appropriate skills and resources to compete. *Business Week* (1980) quotes the example of Holiday Inns Inc., the world's largest hotel chain, diversifying by acquiring a bus and a shipping company on the grounds that it was essentially a part of the travel industry rather than a hotel company. These acquisitions have been divested and Holiday Inns concen-

trates on providing food and accommodation for a wide range of customers. Hotels differ in various ways to appeal to different segments of the market with distinctive preferences. Some Crowne Plaza hotels, for example, are high rise rather than three or four storeys and offer above-average facilities; other hotels incorporate Holidomes, which are indoor recreation centres. Holiday Inn also have Garden Court hotels (high service levels, but few frills such as the moderately expensive restaurants found in standard Holiday Inns), and Express hotels and motels (budget prices and no restaurants). The French group, Accor, similarly differentiate their various hotels – Sofitel (city centre luxury); Novotel (four-star, but located near motorway junctions and at airports); Ibis (two-star family hotels); and Formula One (very basic properties where credit cards are needed because there is no traditional reception desk).

Products and services should therefore be analysed in terms of the way they are perceived by consumers in relation to competitive offerings and exactly why customers buy one product rather than another, and this will help define the appropriate differentiation and segmentation strategies. They must also be evaluated in terms of their ability to contribute both revenue and profits now and in the future. If the range of products currently being marketed does not offer growth potential it will be necessary to develop and introduce new products if the company is not to decline. A number of techniques are available to assist in these analyses, and some are considered in this chapter. One technique, portfolio analysis, is introduced here but expanded in greater detail in Chapter 16 when we look at planning systems.

I am convinced that well-balanced, well-managed companies who are alive to their customers' needs and able to take action efficiently and quickly to meet them, will move ahead of others.

Geoffrey Mulcahy, Chairman and Chief Executive, Kingfisher Plc

---

Product differentiation

Product differentiation, together with market segmentation, was introduced in Chapter 7, Key Concept 7.2. In relation to differentiation and competitive strategies Levitt (1980) argues that products and services can usefully be thought of from four viewpoints: as a generic product; as the expected product; as the augmented product; and as the potential product.

The **generic product or service** is the basic product, in terms of what it actually is. A steel plate is a piece of steel rolled to a particular size and shape; a retail outlet is a store with goods for sale in it. The idea of the **expected product** relates to the minimum purchase conditions, the essential requirements that customers have and that must be met if the alternative in question is to have any chance of being selected. These requirements may concern the specification (the steel plate must have particular strength and tensile properties, for example), price or availability. This could be related to Porter's lowest cost competitive strategy which was considered in Chapter 7, whereby a manufacturer is seeking to provide a basic product at a competitive price and be profitable by producing it at a lower cost than his or her competitors.

The **augmented product** gives customers not only what they expect and require, but more. Products are thus differentiated, but again, as seen in Chapter 7, to be an effective competitive strategy the value must be added in areas that customers perceive to be important. Differentiation could be in the performance, the design or the packaging; it could be provided through the provision of advice on usage, or delivery and installation services. Thinking about the **potential product** and what it might be in the future encourages managers to search for newer, different or better ways of achieving differentiation.

Product differentiation is linked closely with branding, which is explained in Key Concept 10.1.

Market analysis and segmentation

It is important for managers in an organization to understand how large in aggregate terms the market or markets in which they compete are, and how quickly they are growing. It is also vital that they appreciate how the market is segmented, and how it might be segmented.

In simple terms, not every customer seeks exactly the same specification, levels of performance, looks or availability from a product or service. Some will be more concerned with price than others; some will be loyal to particular brands whilst others will readily substitute. In other words they seek different satisfactions. Where these differences can be identified, and customers can be grouped and reached through specially targeted advertising and promotion, products can be tailored to suit particular needs; and this concentration on the special needs of a segment can make a product particularly attractive to certain customers.

Segmentation and preference might be based on geographical location, age, size and type of family, income, socioeconomic group, life-style, tastes, education, religion, race or nationality, personality and ambition, occasion of use, particular benefits sought, usage rate, status of user (new to the product, frequent user etc.), loyalty or availability and buying requirements.

The clear identification of segment opportunities can assist in the company's corporate, competitive and marketing strategies. Figure 10.1A is a very simple illustration. The company in question might be deciding whether to produce one or more products from a range of televisions, video recorders and hi-fi systems, and where to distribute them. The distribution choices are independent retailers, electrical chain stores and department stores. On the one hand the company might seek wide availability, although limited availability might support a more exclusive image; on the other hand the greater the number of outlets the greater is the investment in stock to support them. The stock issue also affects the product range decision. Obviously much depends on total demand and customer purchasing preferences

Key Concept 10.1
BRANDING

Many differentiated products, and some services, are identified by brand names. These brand names, and/or the identity of the companies which own them, convey an image to customers. Advertising is often used to create and reinforce this image. Successful branding generates customer loyalty and repeat purchases, enables higher prices and margins, and provides a springboard for additional products and services. Customers expect to find the leading brand names widely available in distribution outlets. In the case of groceries, branding has enabled leading manufacturers to contain the growing power of supermarket chains like Sainsbury and Tesco, which typically sell a wide range of own-brand items alongside the major branded products.

EXAMPLES

Persil and *Pampers:* brand names not used in conjunction with the manufacturer's name – they are produced by Unilever and Procter and Gamble respectively.
Coca-Cola: manufacturer's name attributed to a product.
Cadbury's Dairy Milk and *Leeds Permanent Solid Gold Savings Account:* combinations of company and product names.
St Michael: the personalized brand name used on all products sold by Marks & Spencer.

A number of large organizations have, through strategic acquisitions and investments in brands, established themselves as global corporations. Examples include:

Unilever: now own a variety of food (Bird's Eye, Batchelors, Walls, John West, Boursin, Blue Band, Flora), household goods (Shield soap, Persil, Lux and Surf detergents) and cosmetics (Fabergé, Calvin Klein and Elizabeth Arden brands).
Philip Morris: American tobacco company which has acquired General Foods (US; Maxwell House coffee) and Jacobs Suchard (Switzerland; confectionery and coffee).
Nestlé: including Chambourcy (France), Rowntree (UK) and Buitoni (Italy).
LVMH: discussed earlier, in the introduction to Part III.

These companies can afford substantial investments in research and development to innovate and:

☐ strengthen the brand, say by extending the range of products carrying the name;
☐ develop new opportunities, e.g. Mars Bars Ice Cream, launched simultaneously in 15 European countries (1988) and priced at a premium over normal ice cream bars;
☐ transform competition in the market; Pampers disposable nappies have been developed into a very successful range of segmented products selling throughout America and Europe.

Brand names are an asset for an organization. There is a so far unresolved debate concerning how these assets might be properly valued in a company balance sheet.

The American magazine, *Financial Week*, has postulated that the world's most valuable brand name is Marlboro (owned by Philip Morris), and that it is worth over $30 million. In terms of value Coca-Cola is second at some $25 million. The most valuable European company brand is Nestlé's Nescafé; and the three leading British-owned brands are Johnnie Walker Red Label whisky (owned by Guinness), Guinness itself and Smirnoff Vodka (Grand Metropolitan). Where the most recognized brand names are tied to high market share and above-average margins they are valued at over twice their annual revenues.

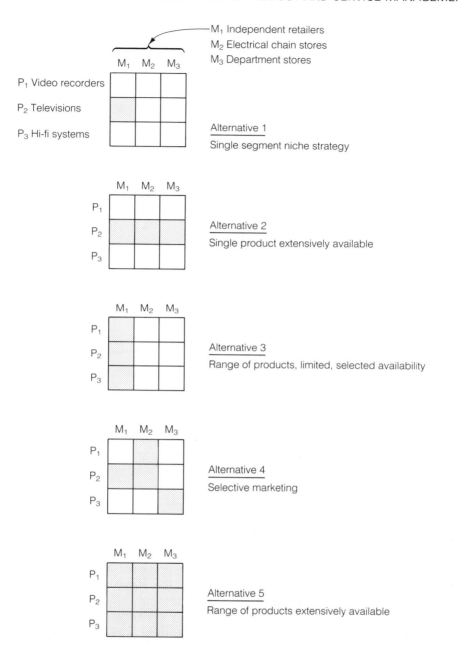

Figure 10.1A Alternative patterns of market coverage. Adapted from Abell, D F (1980) *Defining the Business – the Starting Point of Strategic Planning*, Prentice Hall; and Kotler, P (1984) *Marketing Management Analysis, Planning and Control*, 5th edn, Prentice Hall.

for the particular products. Five alternative strategies are illustrated in the figure.

Alternative 1, the niche strategy, might be very attractive to a small company who might

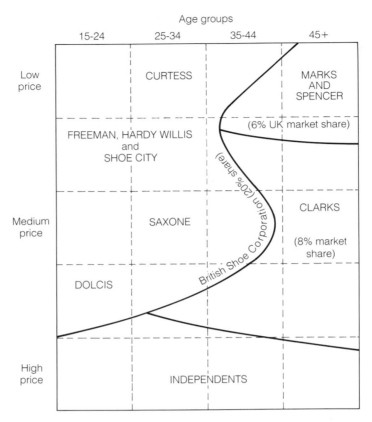

Figure 10.1B   An example of segment domination – shoe retailing in the UK, late 1980s, before strategic changes by British Shoe Corporation. (*Source*: Presentation by Ian Croft of British Shoe Corporation – Huddersfield Polytechnic, 17 January 1990. Reproduced with permission.)

seek a solid share of just one segment. Whilst Figure 10.1A illustrates an important idea, it is over-simplistic. For each of the products in question decisions will also have to be made concerning the range of sizes, specifications and qualities. However, this type of analysis forces managers to focus on competitive opportunities and alternatives. Hence a similar analysis might be done for alternative models for each of the products in question in relation to different types of buyer or buyer preferences.

In analysing the segmentation of a market it is important to consider whether the constitution of the various segments is changing, and how, in relation to where the company is strong and weak. Market

changes of this nature can open up new opportunities and pose potential threats. Although total market share is important as it affects such things as overall visibility, advertising presence and influence over distributors, the share of individual segments can also be very important. Market shares are relative, however, and the shares of major competitors must also be considered.

Figure 10.1B illustrates this point. British Shoe Corporation (BSC), with a number of branded retail outlets including Curtess, Freeman Hardy Willis, Saxone, Dolcis and Shoe City (a warehouse-type operation in out-of-town shopping centres) in the late 1980s, was the market leader. Clarks was second, and Marks & Spencer third. Each

---

Case 10.1
COURTAULDS TEXTILES

The diversified Courtaulds group was split into two companies in 1990 – Courtaulds (the engineering businesses) and Courtaulds Textiles, which would focus on price/quality niches, such as car seat fabrics, where performance and design were more important than low prices. This was aimed at countering competition from cheaper labour countries in the Far East.

Authority was devolved to discrete business units who were encouraged to search for, and develop, new market opportunities. These changes led to the revitalization of a product which had been effectively dormant for 40 years.

Ventile is a 100% waterproof and windproof breathable cotton fabric. It was first used in World War II for uniforms. Whilst production has continued in small quantities (mainly for firemen's uniforms), Ventile was never developed. In the 1980s Gore Tex opened up the market for coated fabrics and leisurewear, and wax coats also succeeded in this market. Ventile is now being used in high-quality, expensive, leisure clothing and production facilities have been extended considerably. Interest has been generated in several European countries.

This case again illustrates E–V–R congruence: *Environment* – new market opportunities in leisurewear; *Resources* – core competence in high-value-added products; *Values* – devolution which led to the identification and exploitation of the opportunity.

---

was dominant in particular sections of the market. BSC remains predominant for lower to medium prices and younger buyers. As Figure 10.1B shows the various brand names and retail stores have been positioned to appeal to different customer groups. Dolcis, for example, specializes in good quality, medium-priced stylish shoes for fashion-conscious youngsters. Trends in the market, such as stability (following real growth during the early and mid-1980s), intensifying competition from imports of cheaper shoes, changing customer tastes, and particularly the declining numbers of buyers in the youngest age grouping, meant that both Clarks and Marks & Spencer were better placed for the future than was BSC. As a result BSC has aimed to spread further into the area currently dominated by Clarks and rationalize at the lower price end.

Their strategy involved:

☐ a conscious re-positioning of their Manfield outlets. This required new store layouts and fittings, different ranges of shoes and a higher level of customer service. BSC, in 1990, developed 30 new Manfield outlets to support their 850 concessions in department and fashion stores which also trade as Manfield.

☐ the closure of some stores and the dropping of the Curtess name. BSC's Trueform brand has also been dropped. It is intended that in future Freeman Hardy Willis and Shoe City will cater for previous Curtess customers, and that over a two- to three-year period a new self-service operation, branded Shoe Express, will also be developed to appeal to customers seeking convenience at value-for-money prices.

Case 10.1 (Courtaulds Textiles) and the

launch of three new boxed chocolate products by Cadbury's in Autumn 1989 provides another useful illustration of segmentation. Cadbury's, who already marketed a number of boxes of chocolates including the popular and well-promoted Milk Tray, targeted three distinct segments, two of which were new to them. The three new brands were

☐ Heritage, a high-priced upmarket continental collection, designed to compete with imported chocolates and Thornton's – a new segment for Cadbury's
☐ Inspiration, marketed as a gift for women from women
☐ Tribute – an innovatory idea of chocolates specifically for men.

Whilst some companies will seek to develop a range of products which between them cover most of the preferences exhibited by the market, others will find it a valuable strategy to concentrate their appeal. By selecting one segment, or a small group of related segments, rather than attempting to cover the whole market, smaller companies can seek to achieve a significant market share in the chosen segment by a clear differentiation strategy.

Analysis of a market by individual segments will additionally focus attention on exactly what potential customers are looking for and the key success factors for the product in relation to different groups of customers, as well as for the market as a whole. In the case of Coca-Cola and Pepsi-Cola, for instance, it seems that wide availability and the general image created by advertising are likely to be more important issues than an analysis of differences between customer groups. However, for motor vehicles, although image and availability are both important, the design of the cars and the range of alternative specifications for each model are very dependent upon specific customer preferences. Added value in the form of a sunroof or quadraphonic stereo might appeal to certain customer groups, whilst others would not be willing to pay the necessary premium. The number of doors and the seating comfort will be influenced by family size and by physical differences between people. Additionally this market can be partially segmented by fleet and individual buyers.

Competitor analysis

Analysing the market in terms of customer preferences and segments can reveal new opportunities for creating competitive advantage, but organizations may not be able to take advantage of every opportunity they spot. The decision to try and take advantage of an opportunity should be related to the particular strengths of the organization and the closeness of fit between these and the preferences of the market. An organization should seek to define any distinctive competences it may have which will enable it to add value in particular ways and thus differentiate a product or service such that it is not easily copied by competitors. The distinctive competence could relate to product or service design or quality, distribution coverage, advertising and image or price.

In a competitive environment a firm will want its product or service to be clearly differentiated, attractive to the customers it is targeting and relatively more profitable than its competitors. This is the price–quality relationship. Where a number of products or brands compete with each other and where the market perceives them as substitutes, profitability is determined by both costs and market perceptions. The attractiveness of an individual product or brand to buyers will depend upon how it is priced relative to the alternatives and the perception of its relative quality. Customers will expect the alternative they perceive as being the best quality to be priced higher than the perceived lower quality alternatives. Conversely a manufacturer of a product or service which the market perceives as being inferior to competition, regardless of whether it is actually inferior,

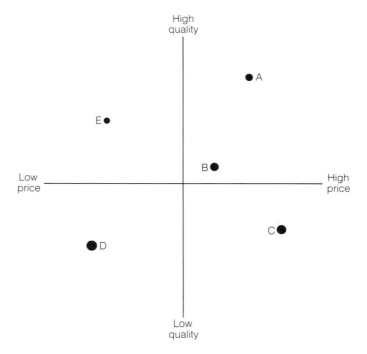

Figure 10.2 An example of a simple product positioning map. This simple example uses price and quality for the two axes. This analysis for a product or service should be reviewed periodically to accommodate changes in consumer values, tastes and preferences which might indicate that re-positioning and a new image could prove beneficial.

must price below those alternatives that the market perceives as being superior if it is to achieve any significant sales. A manufacturer in this position might well seek to add value in some new way in order to improve the perceived quality or seek to ensure that the costs attributable to the product are below those incurred by competitors.

In searching for new competitive opportunities it can be useful to place all the competing products on the type of positioning map illustrated in Figure 10.2. This simple example uses perceived quality and price for the axes. A and B are both products which exhibit above-average quality and sustain above-average prices. D reflects lower quality and a lower price. C would be unlikely to sell in any quantity as it is priced high but has low perceived quality. E has high quality but is priced low, and although it

may sell very well it is likely that it could be more profitable if it was re-positioned. Such maps as this are useful for relating products and services to each other, and by experimenting with different axes new competitive opportunities might well be seen.

United Distillers (owned by Guinness) used this type of analysis to evaluate and reposition a number of their Scotch whisky brands. The chosen parameters were price (three bands: de luxe, premium and standard) and 'social dimension' which featured extrovert 'show-off' brands at one extreme and traditional brands at the other. Johnnie Walker Black Label, perceived as representing an elegant, luxurious life-style, is priced de luxe to compete directly with Seagram's Chivas Regal. Johnnie Walker Red Label is promoted as an extrovert and masculine whisky with a premium price. White

> ### Case 10.2
> ### HORLICKS
>
> In the mid-1980s Horlicks had approximately a 45% market share of the malted food drink market, which is worth of the order of £30 million per year. Ovaltine represents about one-third of the market and Cadbury's Bournvita with some 10–12% is the only other major branded product.
>
> Horlicks was first marketed in America in 1883, and when Beecham bought the brand in 1969 it no longer had any presence in America. Sales in the UK were stagnant until the late 1970s, when they amounted to £6.5 million and a 30% market share for Horlicks.
>
> At this time Horlicks was still perceived primarily as a bedtime drink, and much of its popularity, particularly for young people, had been lost. Because of central heating a warm drink late at night was regarded as less important, and late night television was also changing habits. Beecham therefore used advertising to re-position Horlicks as an anytime drink, with such slogans as 'Don't wait until bedtime to enjoy it'.
>
> An additional problem was that people who were not familiar with Horlicks did not make it properly, often disregarding the instructions on the package. Milk needed to be heated, and quite often the resultant product was lumpy – hence the expression 'Making a Horlicks of it' meaning making a mess. In January 1982 a new instant version, requiring only hot water, was launched successfully.
>
> The result is a doubling of sales revenue, an increase in market share, and profitability.
>
> *Source*: Rapoport, C (1983) How bedtime drinks are losing their sleepy image, *Financial Times,* 27 October.

Horse, Haig, Vat 69 and Black & White have been traditional products at standard prices, but Black & White has been re-launched with a premium price and targeted at extrovert, young drinkers throughout Europe.

Case 10.2 shows how Horlicks was re-positioned as an anytime instant hot drink rather than a bedtime drink, with a resulting increase in sales and profits.

The product life cycle

Competitive and functional strategies for a product vary according to the stage that it is at in its life cycle. The idea of the life cycle is illustrated in Figure 10.3. Sales of a product or service follow a pattern – they grow slowly, then more quickly, peak and then decline. The time scale for different products can vary markedly, some staying in existence for over 100 years and others appearing and disappearing in just 1 year. The life cycle illustrated could represent a successful product in aggregate terms or individual competing brands of the same product or service. Conceptually the pattern is the same. However, the time scale, the steepness of the growth and decline, and the maximum sales achieved will vary between competing brands, with some being launched after others and some disappearing before their competitors.

In the **introduction** or development stage

Case 10.3
SHERRY – MARKET SATURATION AND
REEBOK – PRODUCT LIFE-CYCLE EXTENSION

SHERRY

At the end of the 1980s the world market for sherry appeared to be static, although sales had doubled since 1960. Sales had fallen in the UK throughout the 1980s, but they were rising in Germany, Spain and Belgium. Over this period in the UK, Harvey's and Gonzalez Byass (Tio Pepe) had seen sales fall whilst the popularity of Croft sherries had risen. The marketing challenge concerns how to change the poor image of sherry held by the significant 18–45-year-old segments.

REEBOK

Reebok launched 'The Pump', an inflatable sports shoe, in November 1989. Owners can pump in a small quantity of air after putting on the shoes in order to provide better support, protection and a customized fit.

The first application was in a basketball shoe, followed by variants for athletics (April 1990), tennis and walking (April 1991) and golf and aerobics (June 1991). In addition, extended ranges of basketball and athletics shoes have been introduced. This distinctive product, which emphasizes the importance of innovative design in marketing strategy, has proved to be popular internationally.

Reebok is also involved in another example of product life-cycle extension through a joint venture with Mattel. Mattel have successfully marketed their Barbie doll for over 30 years with the regular addition of new outfits and accessories. In 1991 a range of miniature Reebok sports shoes was introduced, along with a selection of Benetton outfits. The products are all available 'life size' so that youngsters can dress identically to their Barbie doll.

there are few competitors and relatively few buyers; the product or service is new and being tried by early adopters. In reality a number of products will never pass this stage, simply being withdrawn from the market. If the product is properly accepted by the market it will move into a growth phase when demand expands much more quickly. Manufacturers must persuade consumers to try the product by promoting awareness. Availability is likely to be selective.

During the **growth** phase demand develops and the product becomes more widely available, profit opportunities are spotted and new competitors enter the market. Competing products are increasingly differentiated and there is a search for new segment opportunities. Competitors invest in advertising and distribution which stress differentiation and segmentation in order to build market shares.

Once the **maturity** stage is reached the product is well established, but growth is slower, and competitors are more anxious to protect their market shares than increase them. Advertising is aimed at both retaining existing customer loyalty and persuading people to switch away from a competitor.

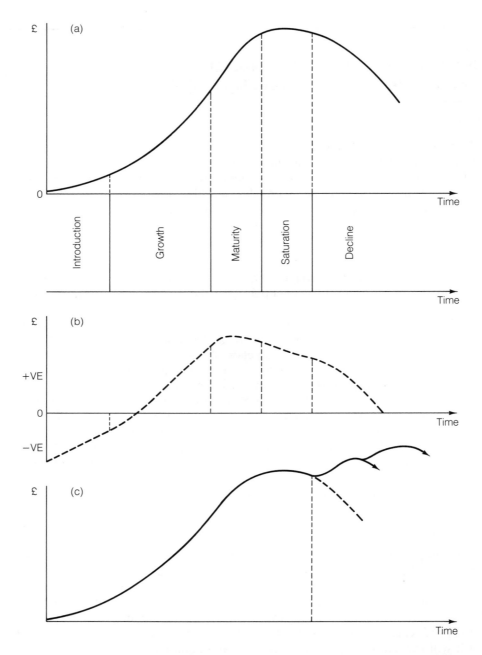

Figure 10.3   The product life cycle (a) Sales volume/revenue, (b) Profitability and (c) Extending the life cycle.

In the **saturation** stage no new buyers are likely to appear, and consequently there is a tendency for price competition to retain share in a static market or one that is beginning to decline.

The **decline** stage is characterized by further price competition as competitors strive to remain in the market profitably as others disappear. Lower cost companies reduce their prices to force others out of the market in order that they can increase their share of a declining market.

Figure 10.3(b) shows that the product or service is not profitable until the growth stage, and that it is most profitable during the maturity and saturation stages. Profits peak before sales revenue is maximized, and then fall away to zero during the decline phase. Strategies for retaining profitability in declining industries will be discussed in greater detail in Chapter 19, and Box 10.2 summarizes product strategies which are appropriate and necessary at different stages in the life cycle.

Once products start declining it becomes increasingly necessary for companies to replace them with something else if they are to remain viable. However, as featured in Figure 10.3(c), it is possible to extend the life cycle by continually finding new users or new uses for the product once the existing situation reaches saturation point. Nylon is an example which is often quoted to illustrate a product that has continually been applied to new uses. Radios is another. Originally radios were essentially non-portable and exclusively mains operated. Over the years portable versions have been developed, followed by battery-operated transistor radios, and more recently radio cassette players, stereo radio cassette players, car radios, ultra-thin radios, 'Walkman's' with radios and clock radios. Throughout these developments which have made listening easier and more convenient, there has been an increase in the number of stations which can be obtained and better reception. As a result owners of one type of radio have replaced them with the newer better models, and in many cases have increased their ownership to more than one radio per household. Personal organizers, launched by Filofax, became popular during the 1980s, many years after their introduction, since when they have faced competition from several other brands, many of them cheaper. The initial concept was developed around loose-leaf diary and time management systems, but the life cycle was boosted

and extended by encouraging owners to use their organizer wallets for more things. Special packages for gardening, wine and cookery have appeared along with maps and novels which readers, typically commuters, can separate into small sections and carry just a few pages every day. Case 10.3 provides further examples of these points.

It is important, therefore, that companies are aware of the stage in the product life cycle that their various products and services are at: first, because this provides an indication of the most appropriate competitive and marketing strategies; second, because it is an important determinant of profitability; and, third, because it helps highlight the need for new products or services if the company is to grow, or at least not decline. The product life cycle is not predictive in the sense that companies can easily forecast when the product will move from one stage to another, but a clear appreciation of the current situation is helpful. It increases awareness and at times indicates the need for change.

It was mentioned earlier that certain products and brands are able to enjoy extended life cycles with appropriate modifications. Such products as Bovril and Palmolive soap have been available for many many years. Other fashion-dependent products can disappear very quickly. Ohmae (1982) points out that the length of the product life cycle is decreasing for an increasing number of products, particularly those affected by microelectronics. Primarily there are three reasons:

☐ technological changes in materials and processes
☐ changing tastes of customers
☐ competitive activity aimed at increasing market share in order to gain greater benefit from the experience effect.

Particular models of electronic calculators, watches, stereo products and computer peripherals are examples of products whose life cycles have shortened. At the same time the development costs and times of the newer versions have increased, requiring companies

Box 10.2
PRODUCT STRATEGIES AND THE PRODUCT LIFE CYCLE

INTRODUCTION STRATEGIES

Pioneering

Organizations who pioneer new products need some form of defence against competition. This could be a patent, a real cost advantage, or differentiation which is difficult to replicate.

Pioneers have to choose whether to price relatively high or relatively low, and how much to spend on advertising. Low prices supported by extensive promotion can stimulate demand but result in low profit margins. A quieter entry with high prices will have only limited appeal but could be profitable if there are barriers to the entry of competitors. Visible profits, of course, attract competition.

Imitation

Large numbers of new products and new product ideas fail in the development and test stages. Consequently imitation, stepping in after a competitor has stimulated early demand, can prove more successful than pioneering, as long as the imitator times his or her entry correctly and is not prevented by entry barriers. This approach requires constant awareness of developments and changes and a research programme so that new products are available when required. Imitators must seek competitive advantage which separates them from the pioneer.

GROWTH STRATEGIES

Growth strategies require that new users and new uses are found for the product, or that existing users are persuaded to increase their consumption. These strategies are necessary during the growth phase and for extending the life cycle once growth slows down.

Competitive advantage is again an issue as companies compete for market share and market leadership.

SATURATION STRATEGIES

Once demand for a product has reached saturation stage the appropriate strategy is to milk it by reducing expenditure on development and promotion and using the profits obtained to fund the development of replacements.

STRATEGIES FOR THE FUTURE

Expenditure on research and development should be aimed at having new and replacement products available at the appropriate time. This again requires constant awareness of competitor activity and changes in consumer tastes, and insight into the new technological opportunities which might be available.

Developed from Onkvisit, S and Shaw, J J (1986) Competition and product management: can the product life cycle help? *Business Horizons*, July–August.

to make early decisions concerning the commitment of time and resources for research and development, which itself must be applied and consumer oriented.

Companies with a range of different products and services may seek to have them at different stages in the life cycle at any time. Relatively new products in the introduction stage may offer future profitability and growth; those in the competitive growth stage will contribute revenue and again offer future profits although not being especially profitable at the moment; mature products provide the profits which can be re-invested in supporting the others in the range; and those at the later stages in the life cycle may be retained as long as they can be profitable. This type of portfolio analysis is discussed further in the next section.

The Boston Consulting Group growth–share matrix

The Boston Consulting Group (BCG) growth–share matrix, typically referred to as the Boston matrix, is simpler and more straightforward than certain matrices used in strategic planning. The premises behind it, its uses and limitations, and its linkages with the product life cycle are discussed in this chapter. More complex matrices will be developed in Chapter 16 when strategic planning and changes in corporate strategy are explored. The Boston matrix, like other more sophisticated matrices, is used to evaluate the significance of each individual product or service produced by an organization in relation to all the others, in order to establish future priorities and needs (see Chapter 16). However, it can also be used to evaluate the current position and future potential opportunities for a product or service within the particular market or industry in order to establish the appropriate marketing strategy. It is for this reason that it is introduced in this chapter.

Basic premises

Bruce Henderson (1970) of BCG has suggested firstly that the margins earned by a product, and the cash generated by it, are a function of market share. The higher the market share is, relative to competitors, the greater is the earnings potential; high margins and market share are correlated. A second premise is that sales and revenue growth requires investment. Sales of a product will only increase if there is appropriate expenditure on advertising, distribution and development; and the rate of market growth determines the required investment. Third, high market share must be earned or bought, which requires additional investment. Finally no business can grow indefinitely. As a result products will at times not be profitable because the amount of money being spent to develop them exceeds their earnings potential; at other times, and particularly where the company has a high relative market share, earnings exceed expenditure and products are profitable.

Profitability is therefore affected by market growth, market share, and the stage in the product life cycle. A company with a number of products might expect to have some which are profitable and some which are not. Generally mature products, where growth has slowed down and the required investment has decreased, are the most profitable, and the profits they earn should not be re-invested in them but used instead to finance growth products which offer future earnings potential.

The matrix

The matrix is illustrated in Figure 10.4. Chart (a) shows the composition of the axes and the names given to products or business units which fall in each of the four quadrants; chart (b) features 15 products or business units in a hypothetical company portfolio. The sterling-volume size of each product or business is

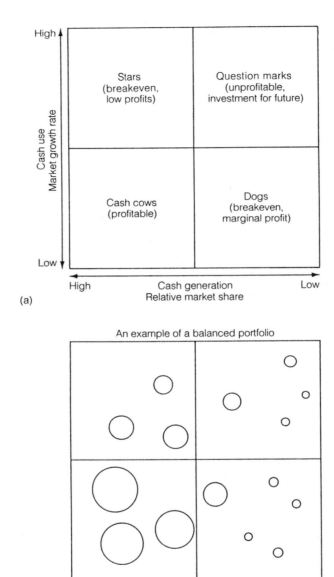

Figure 10.4   The Boston Consulting Group growth–share matrix.

proportional to the areas of the circles, and the positioning of each one is determined by its market growth rate and relative market share.

The **market growth rate** on the vertical axis is the annual growth rate of the market in which the company competes, and really any range starting with zero could be used. The problem is where to draw the horizontal dividing line which separates high growth from low growth markets. A figure of 10% is often used, but it is also feasible to use an index related to the growth of gross national product (GNP). In this case the dividing line would be 1.0, so that growth higher than GNP was in the top half of the matrix and growth lower than GNP was in the bottom half.

The **relative market share** on the horizontal axis indicates market share in relation to the largest competitor in the market. A relative market share of 0.25 would indicate a market share one-quarter of that of the market leader; a figure of 2.5 would represent a market leader with a market share that is 2.5 times as big as that of the nearest rival. The vertical dividing line is normally 1.0, so that market leadership is found to the left-hand side of the divider. It is important to consider market segmentation when deciding upon the market share figure to use, rather than using the share of the total market.

The growth–share matrix is thus divided into four cells or quadrants, each representing a particular type of business.

☐ **Question marks** are products or businesses which compete in high growth markets but where market share is relatively low. A new product launched into a high growth market and with an existing market leader would normally constitute a question mark. High expenditure is required to develop and launch the product, and consequently it is unlikely to be profitable and may instead require subsidy from more profitable products. Once the product is established, further investment will be required if the company attempts to claim market leadership.

☐ Successful question marks become **stars**, market leaders in growth markets. However, investment is still required to maintain the rate of growth and to defend the leadership position. Stars are marginally profitable only, but as they reach a more mature market position as growth slows down they will become increasingly profitable.

☐ **Cash cows** are therefore mature products which are well-established market leaders. As market growth slows down there is less need for high investment, and hence they are the most profitable products in

the portfolio. This is boosted by any economies of scale resulting from the position of market leadership. Cash cows are used to fund the businesses in the other three quadrants.

☐ **Dogs** describe businesses which have low market shares in slower growth markets. They may well be previous cash cows, which still enjoy some loyal market support although they have been replaced as market leader by a newer rival. They should be marginally profitable, and should be withdrawn when they become loss makers if not before. The opportunity cost of the resources they tie up is an important issue in this decision.

A successful product will move from the question mark quadrant to become sequentially a star, a cash cow and finally a dog. Less successful products which never become market leaders will always stay in the right-hand half, moving straight from a question to a dog.

Uses and limitations

The four cells can loosely be related to the product life cycle, with question marks representing the introduction stage, stars the growth stage, cash cows maturity, and dogs saturation and decline.

Figure 10.4(b) features a balanced portfolio whereby the company has products or businesses in each of the four quadrants, yesterday's, today's and tomorrow's products all providing and using cash in different ways. Importantly the cash cows are illustrated as the highest volume products, thus providing funds for re-investment in the business. However, for many companies a substantial proportion of their products are likely to be dogs, not market leaders and in lower growth markets. Given this they may be profitable but not highly profitable.

The Boston matrix can be useful for evaluating the products and services of organizations other than manufacturers. Consider, for example, a department store located in a recently opened shopping mall. Consumer spending in the mall as a whole might be increasing by some 20% per year, and this might be expected to continue as the mall becomes increasingly popular. However, sales of the different products sold in the department store will not all be growing at the same rate. Also, as new small specialist stores open up in the mall, the department store's market share, measured by its share of total sales in the mall for the different products, may be changing. Where competition is strong the margins on the different products will vary. Hence the Boston matrix might be useful for assessing the range of products that the store should be selling. Similarly one might postulate the case of a local authority arts and leisure department which faces private sector competition of some form for most of the services it provides.

The current and projected future positioning of the various products can be used for strategic decisions concerning investment, marketing expenditure and withdrawal, and this will be taken up later in Chapter 16. However, if the matrix is used for decision making it is essential that products or businesses are positioned properly. It was pointed out above that there is a problem in deciding what growth rate is appropriate for separating high and low growth markets. The choice can determine whether a product is categorized as a question or a dog, or as a star or a cash cow. Similarly relative market share should be the share of the relevant market segment, but this may not always be easily quantified. The matrix can be useful for analysing the current and future potential of the product portfolio and for increasing awareness, but where it is used as a basis for decision making other factors than the matrix position must be considered.

Finally it is important to point out that market share alone will not generate low costs and therefore high margins. The com-

petitor who is cost leader need not be the largest company, particularly if there are few economies of scale; and a really effective differentiation strategy which is difficult to replicate and which sustains competitive advantage can be the source of high profits through high margins. Hence one of the basic premises of the matrix may not always hold true.

Product strategy decisions

The concepts and considerations discussed above provide a useful base for exploring the key decision areas in the overall product strategy.

Product management

A competitive strategy for each product or business unit is required, and this decision can be assisted by considering the position of the product in relation to competing products, the current stage in its life cycle, and

---

No business, however modest its aspirations, can safely assume that the way it serves its customers today will be sufficient for tomorrow. New competitors are always on the horizon, potentially offering a better deal. Customers' tastes change, and so do the means of satisfying them, be it through advances in product and process technology or new ideas on the organization and motivation of the workforce, whose own aspirations and aptitudes in turn are rapidly altering.

In such a climate, mere survival demands at least a response to change; competitive success requires that change is anticipated, exploited, and at best originated.

John Banham, previously Director-General,
Confederation of British Industry

Case 10.4
SALOMON

The French company Salomon manufacture sports goods and aim for world leadership with all their products. At the end of the 1980s they were prominent with ski bindings (50% of the world market), ski boots (again world leader for both cross-country and slalom) and golf clubs – Salomon own the American company, Taylor Made.

In October 1990, after a year's trial by experts, Salomon launched a revolutionary new ski and targeted it initially at 'wealthy opinion makers' around the world. The ski had taken six years to develop (at a cost of FFr 300 million) and was both highly innovative and premium priced. The ski is distinctive in a number of ways:

- it is a monocoque, produced in a single mould – traditionally skis comprise several sandwiched layers
- it is streamlined (using computer-aided design) to yield better turning properties
- it is manufactured from a composite material to reduce weight, and
- reliable mass production techniques are feasible.

The initial reaction from distributors was that Salomon 'had reinvented the ski'. Future plans include tennis rackets and golf balls.

---

its position on a simple portfolio matrix. Decisions concerning positioning and differentiation, advertising, pricing and distribution can then be taken. The last three are considered below in the section on the marketing mix.

Pilditch (1987) contends that it is an important aspect of organizational culture for strategic leaders to express their pride in the company's products. Examples quoted include the chief executive of Sony of Japan, who always carries the company's latest electronic gadgets with him so that he can show them off, and Victor Kiam, who bought out Remington and then used television advertising to tell the world he bought the company because he liked the products. Sir Christopher Hogg, the Chairman of Courtaulds, is reported to always ask to see the products produced by a factory before he looks around it, arguing that 'a company exists only by reason of its ability to satisfy customers and markets'.

The mix and range of products

The expression 'product mix' is used to describe the assortment of different product types that a company produces and markets; the product line is the number of brands or related products in each product type. Procter and Gamble, for example, have four major product types in their mix: detergents, toothpaste, soaps and deodorants. For each one they market a number of different brands (Daz, Ariel and Bold detergents; Crest toothpaste; Camay and Fairy soaps; and Sure deodorant are all included) and the number of different brands represents the length of the product line for each product type.

Decisions concerning the mix and line relate to the number of segments that can be identified, and the number that the company feels constitute profitable opportunities and wishes to cover. In some cases economies of scale can result from adding products and sharing certain costs; it might also prove desirable to develop the mix or range in order to provide a more comprehensive package to distributors or customers.

New product development

Hamel and Prahalad (1991) claim that the most profitable companies in the 1990s will be those that create and dominate new markets, looking for opportunities to further exploit key skills and competencies. They will take measured risks, innovate and launch new products and services, some of which may fail. Such companies will learn from their experiences. See Case 10.4, Salomon.

New products are also needed to replace existing ones at appropriate stages in the life cycle and as additional products to foster growth. The latter would include additions to both the product lines and the product mix. Where new products are additional to those the company already markets, rather than replacements, there should be an analysis of where synergy might be obtained. New products will be aimed at generating new revenue, and they may boost the sales of existing products if they strengthen the overall line or mix, but they will also generate additional costs. Synergy can be obtained where such costs are not entirely new ones but where certain of them can be shared amongst an increasing number of products. Too diverse a range of unrelated products could lead to organizational problems because of the different skills required in manufacturing and marketing and key success factors which are different for each business area. Case 10.5 illustrates this point with regard to Kellogg and their decision to concentrate on breakfast cereals rather than diversify.

Organizations will often evaluate new product proposals quantitatively against several criteria, looking for ideas to achieve a minimum score. If funding is restricted the scoring framework may also be used to help prioritize the alternatives. The major issues are likely to reflect:

☐ growth potential
☐ profit potential
☐ market opportunities – global branding, segmentation potential
☐ implications for the rest of the business – issues of synergy and opportunity-cost
☐ technological, financial and production requirements and implications
☐ [where relevant] the opportunity and cost of acquiring a new business.

Cooper (1987), whose research work has concentrated on industrial products, argues that new innovatory products have a far greater chance of market success than 'me too' variants of existing competitive products, and that without realized competitive advantage the likelihood of success with new products is reduced. Innovation is dealt with in greater depth in Chapter 11, but Cooper contends that the most important determinants of new product success, in order of importance, are as follows.

☐ The product is superior to competing products in meeting customers' needs.
☐ The product has unique features for the customer.
☐ The product is of a higher quality than competing products.
☐ The product performs a unique task for customers.
☐ The product is highly innovative, new to the market.
☐ The product reduces customers' costs.

The emphasis in these factors is perceived competitive advantage.

Global products

Conventional marketing wisdom suggests that individual countries exhibit different needs and that the same product cannot be sold throughout the world. Modifications of varying degrees must be made to suit indivi-

Case 10.5
KELLOGG'S CEREALS

At the end of the 1970s and into the early 1980s Kellogg was the clear market leader for breakfast cereals throughout the world, but with a declining market share in America. Between 1979 and 1983 share fell from 42% to 38% in a market which was growing at only 2% per year, compared with 7% a decade earlier. One issue was public pressure against foods with a high sugar content.

It was anticipated that Kellog, like their main rivals in the cereals market, would diversify into other foods. Kellogg has diversified on a relatively small scale, but essentially has chosen to concentrate on grain-based products, in particular cereals, 'which it knows best'.

New products have been developed and launched on a regular basis, some featuring artificial sweeteners. Additionally, because of the declining birth rate, new products have been aimed at adults as well as children. Fibre content has been seen as important for this. Kellogg are careful not to target products too narrowly on the grounds that once they are in a house any member of the family is likely to eat them. There have been a number of successes, and some failures.

As a result Kellogg's market share of 42% was restored in 1985, and generally they have out-performed their main rivals who have not been too successful with their diversification strategies.

BREAKFAST CEREALS IN EUROPE

Kellogg is again market leader with a 50% market share and six out of the ten best-selling brands. British consumers eat more cereal per head than any other country, including America, but other European countries, which have tended to prefer breads, meats and cheeses for breakfast, provide a real opportunity as people are becoming more health conscious.

Kellogg has faced a challenge from a joint venture between Nestlé and General Mills of America, who are seeking a 20% market share. General Mills has provided the brands – particularly Cheerio's, an oat cereal which helps reduce cholesterol, and Golden Grahams, which compete with (and preceded) Kellogg's Golden Crackles – and Nestlé the distribution network. GM have also reformulated an existing Nestlé cereal called Chocapic, and after a relaunch it is selling more successfully. Moreover, Nestlé have won the exclusive Euro Disneyland food franchise which allows them to use Walt Disney characters for promotions in Europe and the Middle East.

Sources: Lorenz, C (1985) New breakfast menus from Battle Creek, *Financial Times*, 30 September; and Knowlton, C (1991) Europe cooks up a cereal brawl, *Fortune*, 3 June.

dual tastes. Specifically the marketing mix will be unique for each separate market. Levitt (1984) has argued that these differ- ences are narrowing and that opportunities for products to be more global in their market coverage are increasing. He emphasizes that although the same product may be sold in a variety of countries it does not follow that the branding, positioning, promotion and selling need be the same, although in certain instances they are. As a result manufacturers should examine both the similarities and differences in needs and tastes in their target markets. Globalization does not imply that tastes will become homogeneous throughout the world, but that market segments will expand across frontiers.

Manufacturers will benefit considerably in terms of cost savings if they can make their products global and market them in a similar way throughout the world; and a number of products have illustrated that this is possible. Coca-Cola, Levi jeans, Marlboro cigarettes, Kodak film, McDonald's and many electrical and electronic products are examples. See also Case 10.6, Benetton.

Ohmae (1985) suggests four reasons behind this trend:

☐ the growing capital intensity of certain industries. This offers substantial economies of scale and has encouraged manufacturers to try and market their products globally.
☐ the accelerating tempo of technologies and increasing development costs. In the past companies launched new products in one country initially, and then developed customized variations as they expanded sequentially in different countries and markets. It is now increasingly necessary to launch new products in certain industries in America, Europe and Japan almost simultaneously. Aero engines, computers, consumer electronics and certain cars are quoted as examples.
☐ changing tastes around the world, and an increasing willingness to purchase a universal product. Communications is a factor behind this trend.
☐ increasing covert protectionism, which encourages multi-national organizations to locate production in the countries in

which they sell but centralize their research and development.

Kotler (1988), however, argues that less than 10% of the world's products will lend themselves to global branding, and that many new life-styles are emerging that lead to the opening up of many new differentiated markets.

Branding, positioning, differentiation and segmentation are important aspects of competitive strategy. Functional marketing strategies, and the management of the other components of the marketing mix, are important in the implementation of the competitive strategies, and hence they are considered next. Following this the similarities and differences in marketing products and services is considered, together with the role of marketing in small businesses and not-for-profit organizations.

THE MARKETING MIX

Branding, positioning, differentiation and segmentation can all be used to create and sustain competitive advantage. If competitive advantage is to be gained and sustained, however, then consumers must recognize and appreciate the differentiation and the benefits offered by the product or service. Additionally they must be willing to pay the price being charged; and the product or service must be available where they expect to buy it. The management of the various marketing mix activities is concerned with ensuring that this happens. Competitive advantage, though, can be created by utilizing these other aspects of marketing instead of the product itself. Avon cosmetics, for example, have created competitive advantage by not distributing through traditional retail outlets but by selling direct to customers in their homes.

Distribution management

The distribution system for a product can be relatively straightforward or very complex.

Case 10.6
BENETTON

Benetton was founded in Italy in 1965 by a brother and sister to distribute home-made sweaters to retailers. Luciano Benetton had wholesaling experience, and his sister, Guiliana, design skills. Two other brothers joined later. The first Benetton store was opened in 1968. By 1978 there were 1000, and by 1988 5000, franchised outlets world wide. After 1978 more and more manufacturing was subcontracted. Benetton has also diversified into related goods like shirts, jeans, gloves, shoes and perfume.

Europe is seen as the home market, with production and marketing in both the West and East. However, Benetton is well established in America and Canada, and growing in Japan and the Pacific rim.

In 1972 Benetton started dyeing assembled garments rather than just the yarn; and this has enabled them to develop competitive advantage through a speedier response to fashion changes. Sophisticated information systems identify changes in demand and production schedules are then amended. Outlets are replenished with popular items very quickly. Production costs are increased by dyeing finished goods, but stock management overall (raw materials, semi-finished and finished items) is efficient.

'Much has changed in the world since Benetton was started in 1965, but not our mission: to satisfy people's needs with young, colourful, comfortable and easy-to-wear products. This has been our route to world leadership in the design, production and distribution of clothing, accessories and footwear for men, women and children. Our range has been constantly enriched over time by intensive research into new materials and designs – and further additions will follow.'

Benetton is an international company with a global brand image, which has been built around the theme 'The United Colours of Benetton'. This international image is boosted by a strong association with Formula 1 motor racing.

'Colour makes Benetton unique. The secret lies in presenting a broad spectrum of shades, creatively mixed and matched – new and different every time. The study of colour is our greatest research commitment as we constantly seek out new tones.'

Advertising features the same central message and choice of media throughout the world, although the actual themes of the advertisements vary. This is based on the premise that customers in different countries use clothing and accessories to express personal life-style preferences, with a tendency to demand increasingly higher quality goods. Advertising campaigns 'feature simplified, unambiguous images that convey meaning to the largest possible number of people and cultures throughout the world'.

(Quotations extracted from Benetton Annual Reports.)

Some manufacturers, particularly of industrial products, sell directly to their customers. In the case of consumer goods, some retail customers have their own warehousing and distribution systems and can buy in bulk from manufacturers. In other cases the product reaches the final consumer through a channel of wholesaler and retailer. The actual customer for a manufacturer's products may or may not be the final consumer; both require understanding. The product is designed, differentiated and manufactured to satisfy consumer needs; distributors who finally sell it to them have different needs, most probably concerned with sales volume and margins on the transaction. Where sales are not direct from manufacturer to final consumer, the retailer or distributor determines the actual selling price that the consumer pays for most products, although the manufacturer can influence this in various ways. Manufacturers are therefore very dependent upon their distributors and should regard them as key stakeholders.

The appropriate distribution of the product or service to final consumers is essential if any perceived competitive advantage is to result in sales, revenue and profits. The product should ideally be available wherever and whenever consumers might wish to buy it. However, investment in the provision of such high service levels can incur significant costs in the form of stock and in transporting that stock. Some manufacturers therefore choose to concentrate on a selected range of outlets and use advertising to inform their consumers exactly where the product is available. Good-quality carpets and furniture are examples of this. This restrictive availability may be essential for products which are aimed at selected segments or niches with distinctive buying preferences.

An alternative strategy is to use some distributors who stock a complete range of a manufacturer's products and others who stock only a part of the total range. The decision must be reached in conjunction with the distributors as it is important to ensure that there is a commitment on their part to push and promote the products. This may well require appropriate incentives. Where competitive advantage through cost leadership is sought, distribution costs must be carefully analysed.

The basic questions to address in an assessment of distribution effectiveness include the following. How does each product reach each segment of the market? What is the profit margin and importance of the product for everyone in the distribution channel? How much incentive does each individual have to promote the product? How does the system compare with competition? Is the system the most appropriate? How could it be improved?

Advertising and promotion strategy

Advertising can be used by a manufacturer to increase the size of the overall market, to increase his or her market share, to sell products, to promote the company itself, and as a competitive weapon against rivals. The need to spend money advertising and promoting a particular product depends upon competition and whether they are advertising, the importance of differentiation and whether the market perceives competing brands as easily substituted, the extent of any brand loyalty, and the importance of the product for both producer and consumer. Advertising may be a key determinant of the effectiveness of the competitive strategy; equally some products may be successful with very little advertising.

Advertising may be the only real communication between a manufacturer and the consumers of a product, especially if the product is sold through independent distributors. Consequently a manufacturer will use it to inform consumers about product differences, changes and availability, to persuade them to purchase his or her product rather than a competing one, to remind infrequent purchasers about the product and to reinforce previous messages. Where competitive advantage is being sought through differentiation resulting from essentially intangible benefits, rather than obvious and visible differences, advertising is important in creating the differentiation.

The management of advertising effectively requires that the needs of the market segment and target audience are understood clearly. The appropriate medium and message, plus the timing and frequency of advertisements, are dependent upon this awareness. It is also important to consider competitor advertising. The message should seek to create or reinforce the differentiation, and the strategy should aim to ensure that the advertisements stand out against competition. If competitors are spending heavily in one particular medium, a limited budget might be better allocated to a completely different approach rather than to competing directly but with an in-built disadvantage. Being different or noticeable without enormous expenditure, or with a budget which is below competitor spending, is a crucial challenge for many manufacturers.

Finally, advertising is a cost, and it should be seen as such. There should be a careful assessment of what is necessary to support the competitive strategy, in conjunction with an assessment of how much can be incorporated into the price without harming profitability.

Pricing strategies

Profit is basically the difference between the total costs of manufacturing and marketing a product and its selling price. In normal circumstances therefore the minimum acceptable price must be the total costs incurred in manufacturing and marketing, although some products may sometimes be sold at a loss for particular strategic reasons. Products though must be priced in relation to their perceived value to customers and consumers and in relation to competitor prices. Hence manufacturers must be aware of market perceptions. The competing alternative which is regarded by the market as having superior properties can carry the highest price; products regarded as being below the best must be priced accordingly if they are to sell. Pricing can be used to try and reap the benefits of superior properties and perceived differentiation, or as a weapon against competition. In the latter case profits may be forgone in the fight for market share.

The skill is not to price too low, or potential profits are being sacrificed, or too high, as this will result in a short-term or long-term failure to sell. A product which is regarded as superior can carry a high price, but how much higher than competitors is appropriate? If the price is too high, sales might be below their potential, and longer term the product might have diminishing appeal.

Compact discs, new in the 1980s, are perceived to have superior properties, but their production costs are only marginally higher than those for vinyl records. CDs are smaller, easier to handle, more robust than cassette tapes, and they give a higher quality sound reproduction. They have always been priced at a substantial premium and consumers have bought them in increasing quantities. In 1992 CDs and cassettes sold in roughly equal numbers and ahead of LP records.

In many decision situations data about alternative pricing strategies are available for analysis, but they will not lead to a clear single answer. Take as an example a valve manufacturer who supplies to the world oil industry and who has beaten competition with a new valve with special properties. The valve costs, say, £1000 to manufacture, but depending upon the oil field location can result in savings of between £10 000 and £50 000 over its estimated 5-year life as a result of greater reliability which causes fewer shut-downs in drilling. The manufacturer estimates that it will be some 12 months before there is an alterative valve with similar properties. Would a high price severely limit sales, or is the differentiation really significant? Should the strategy concentrate on maximizing benefits in the next 12 months or be seen as just one part of longer-term objectives?

In situations where price flexibility is constrained by market and competitive forces, profitability is very dependent upon managing costs. Value should be added to the product only where it is important for consumers and not where it cannot be rewarded in the form of higher prices.

MARKETING IN SERVICE, NOT-FOR-PROFIT AND SMALL BUSINESSES

Marketing is most commonly, but not exclusively, associated with manufacturers of products who are able to afford marketing research and advertising and whose products are widely available. However, the marketing concept and certain elements of the marketing mix are essential aspects of the strategic management of other types of organization.

It is crucial to recognize how critical in a service business is the performance and attitude of the very large numbers of relatively junior staff who are the ones that have contact with the customer. The care that all these staff show in dealing with customers will exactly match the care shown by their management in dealing with them. Not only must they be well trained and know what is expected of them, but they need to be supervised, coached and counselled effectively. They need to be listened to, their concerns addressed and their motivation sustained in their jobs, many of which are repetitive. Management achieve the quality of customer care they deserve.

Ultimately the achievement of quality is in the mind of the customer.

David A Quarmby, Joint Managing Director,
J Sainsbury plc

[These issues are discussed further in Chapters 12 and 23.]

Most businesses, whatever their type, are after all concerned with the satisfaction of consumer needs.

Marketing and service businesses

A number of service businesses such as airlines, hotels, insurance, banking and building societies are already very active and visible in their use of marketing. They target and segment their markets, they differentiate their products and they advertise heavily. However, a number of others have not yet applied marketing with the same enthusiasm, some because they are very small businesses, such as hairdressers, plumbers and jobbing builders who rely on word of mouth more than advertising and who may or may not specialize; others, such as the education sector have not felt it necessary as demand for their services has been obtained readily, and such professional practices as solicitors and accountants have regarded advertising and promotion as unprofessional.

But as these sectors have grown increasingly competitive, and as labour costs have risen (services are typically labour intensive) such service businesses have begun to take marketing more seriously. Kotler (1988) suggests that for service businesses there is a fifth 'p' in the marketing mix: people. As a result it is essential to train and develop staff if customer needs are to be satisfied effectively, because staff are in constant contact with the customers. McDonald's (Chapter 1, Case 1.3) emphasizes the importance of staff in this very successful service business. Pope (1979) argues that a major reason behind the success of Walt Disney Enterprises is an emphasis on 'positive customer attitudes' amongst all their staff.

Disney practise a number of policies to achieve this.

☐ New staff are properly welcomed to the corporation, and they undertake an induction programme with other new recruits.

☐ They are fully briefed, using high-quality audiovisual presentations, concerning the Disney philosophy and all the operations, and are introduced to the excellent staff facilities.

☐ There is on-the-job training, with emphasis on how to handle customer questions and queries.

☐ Managers spend one week per year in non-managerial 'front-line' jobs, to ensure that they stay in touch with customers.

☐ There is significant use of staff newspapers and feedback questionnaires.

As a result, attentiveness to customers and their needs has pervaded the culture and values of the company and this has resulted in excellent word-of-mouth recommendations, repeat visits to Disney theme parks and a worldwide reputation for excellence.

Not-for-profit organizations

Most not-for-profit organizations are services, and in addition they are often highly visible as far as the public is concerned. Consequently the points discussed above concerning the importance of people and customer orientation apply again. But the situation is perhaps more complex. When the objectives of not-for-profit organizations were considered in Chapter 5, the importance of a variety of different stakeholders that resulted in multiple and potentially conflicting objectives was emphasized. Consequently, in addition to appreciating and satisfying the needs of customers, the needs of other stakeholders, particularly providers of funds, must also be satisfied. Marketing in this case concerns an appreciation of the needs of all key stakeholders, and the management of all the resources to satisfy these needs as effectively as possible. The image of the organization, influenced by any advertising and publicity, can be particularly important, and it should be managed.

Small businesses

Small companies exist in both manufacturing and service industries, and whilst an appreciation of the marketing concept is as important as it is for any large business, the implementation of the marketing mix activities must inevitably be different.

Small companies have only limited resources. As a result their distribution might be restricted because of the cost of transport and the necessary investment in stock for large-scale availability; and advertising expenditure is likely to be severely constrained. However, they should use market analysis to search for strategic opportunities. Small segments with particular needs might be identified and targeted, and these might well be concentrated geographically. With such an approach a small business can create loyal customers through effective differentiation related to needs. Advertising must again be closely targeted, and it could be the case that direct mail is a viable alternative to media advertising; it might also be worth while to concentrate more on direct selling to emphasize a personal touch.

Despite the restrictions it is very important for small businesses to develop established relationships with both suppliers and customers, based on an appreciation of needs and preferences.

In this chapter we have concentrated on marketing as a source of competitive advantage. The way in which a product or service is positioned and promoted in relation to competition and defined market segments is a major aspect of its competitive strategy. However, the satisfaction of consumer needs is also affected to a significant extent by the operational aspects of the business. Product or service quality, delivery on time and to specification, product improvements and innovation, and so on are important for consumers and are potential sources of competitive advantage. They are discussed further in Chapter 11.

Data for Question 2:

SBU	Sales (£ million)	Number of competitors	Sales of top three companies (£ million)	Market growth rate (%)
A	0.4	6	0.8, 0.7, 0.4	16
B	1.8	20	1.8, 1.8, 1.2	18
C	1.7	16	1.7, 1.3, 0.9	8
D	3.5	3	3.5, 1.0, 0.8	5
E	0.6	8	2.8, 2.0, 1.5	2

SUMMARY

In this chapter we have considered the importance of the marketing concept and consumer orientation for a variety of businesses, not only manufacturing, and highlighted how marketing activities, notably product management, distribution, advertising and pricing, can be used to create and sustain competitive advantage.

Specifically we have

☐ defined the marketing concept in relation to culture and values, and the marketing mix in relation to competitive and functional strategies;
☐ discussed product differentiation branding, market segmentation and the usefulness of positioning analysis and targeting;
☐ considered the concept of the product life cycle and how the appropriate marketing strategies vary between the different stages in the cycle;
☐ introduced portfolio analysis and the Boston Consulting Group growth – share matrix, pointing out its uses and limitations;
☐ looked at the importance and management of new products, emphasizing the value of synergy;
☐ considered the global issue with regard to product management;
☐ briefly discussed distribution, advertising and pricing strategies;
☐ considered the role of marketing for service, not-for-profit and small businesses.

CHECKLIST OF KEY TERMS AND CONCEPTS

You should feel confident that you understand the following terms and ideas:

☐ Synergy (discussed in the introduction to SWOT)
☐ The marketing concept
☐ Branding
☐ Market segmentation and product positioning
☐ The product life cycle
☐ The Boston Consulting Group growth–share matrix.

QUESTIONS AND RESEARCH ASSIGNMENTS

Text related

1. Draw a brand positioning chart for motor vehicles. You might wish to use the following as axes:
   ☐ lowest price → highest price
   ☐ British made → foreign made
   or you could select any criteria that you feel are important.
2. A manufacturer of industrial products is structured around five separate strategic business units (SBUs). Use the data at the top of the page to construct a Boston matrix and assess how balanced the portfolio seems. Where are the strengths? Weaknesses?

Library and assignment based

3. In 1991 Trusthouse Forte (THF) changed the company name to Forte and re-grouped their various hotels into five brands:

   ☐ Forte Travelodges
   ☐ Forte Posthouses
   ☐ Forte Crest
   ☐ Forte Heritage
   ☐ Forte Grand.

Determine the target markets for each of these brands and comment upon Forte's segmentation strategy.

4. It has been argued that during the 1980s the market for blue denim jeans has moved into the decline phase of the product life cycle. Given this, what strategies are open to manufacturers of jeans, and what strategies have been pursued by the major manufacturers such as Levi Strauss?

5. By visiting one or more supermarkets and looking at breakfast cereals on the shelves, consider the product and segmentation strategies of Kellogg. How does their apparent product strategy compare with that of their main rivals?

6. Take a product of your choice and answer the following questions:

   (a) How many competing brands of the product are there, who manufactures them, and what are the major market shares?

   (b) Where is the product in terms of the product life cycle? Position each major competing brand in relation to this.

   (c) What are the differentiation and segmentation strategies of the leading competitors?

   (d) How is advertising used?

(Some marketing research data can be obtained from Mintel reports and similar analyses; advertising expenditures are available in Meal reports.)

RECOMMENDED FURTHER READING

Introductory texts

Baker, M J (1985) *Marketing: An Introductory Text*, 4th edn, Macmillan.
Christopher, M and McDonald, M (1991) *Marketing: An Introduction*, 2nd edn, Pan.
Kotler, P and Armstrong, G (1987) *Marketing: An Introduction*, Prentice Hall.

Comprehensive basic texts

Baker, M J (ed.) (1987) *The Marketing Book*, Heinemann.
Dibb, S, Simkin, L, Pride, W M and Ferrell, O C (1991) *Marketing: Concepts and Strategies* (European Edition), Houghton Mifflin.
Kotler, P (1991) *Marketing Management. Analysis, Planning and Control*, 7th edn, Prentice Hall.

Strategic marketing

Abell, D F and Hammond, J S (1979) *Strategic Market Planning*, Prentice Hall.
Weitz, B A and Wensley, R (1984) *Strategic Marketing – Planning, Implementation and Control*, PWS-Kent.

The marketing of services

Cowell, D W (1984) *The Marketing of Services*, Heinemann.

Marketing planning

McDonald, M H B (1989) *Marketing Plans. How to Prepare Them. How to Use Them*, 2nd end, Heinemann.

International marketing

Terpstra, V (1989) *International Dimensions of Marketing*, 2nd edn, PWS-Kent.

REFERENCES

Business Week (1980) Holiday Inns: refining its focus to Food, Lodging – and more Casinos, 21 July.

Cooper, R G (1987) *Winning at New Products*, Gage Educational Publishing, Toronto.

Davidson, J H (1972) *Offensive Marketing*, Cassell.

Drucker, P F (1954) *The Practice of Management*, Harper and Row.

Hamel, G and Prahalad, G K (1991) Corporate imagination and expeditionary marketing, *Harvard Business Review*, July–August.

Henderson, B D (1970) *The Product Portfolio*, Boston Consulting Group.

Kotler, P (1988) *Marketing Management. Analysis, Planning and Control*, 6th edn, Prentice Hall.

Levitt, T (1960) Marketing myopia, *Harvard Business Review*, July–August.

Levitt, T (1980) Marketing success through differentiation – of anything, *Harvard Business Review*, January–February.

Levitt, T (1984) *The Marketing Imagination*, Free Press.

Ohmae, K (1982) *The Mind of the Strategist*, McGraw-Hill.

Ohmae, K (1985) *Triad Power. The Coming Shape of Global Competition*, Free Press.

Onkvisit, S and Shaw, J J (1986) Competition and product management – can the product life cycle help?, *Business Horizons*, July–August.

Pilditch, J (1987) *Winning Ways*, Harper and Row.

Pope, N W (1979) Mickey Mouse marketing, *American Banker*, 25 July, and More Mickey Mouse marketing, *American Banker*, 12 September.

Reis, A and Trout, J (1986) *Marketing Warfare*, McGraw-Hill.

OPERATIONS AS A STRATEGIC RESOURCE

11

LEARNING OBJECTIVES

After studying this chapter you should be able to

☐ explain the links between research and development, design, production, marketing and costs;

☐ assess the contribution of operations strategy in satisfying customer needs profitably;

☐ describe a number of important manufacturing systems and techniques, such as JIT (just-in-time);

☐ explain the role of operations strategy and management in service businesses;

☐ define total quality management and assess its significance as an aspect of organization culture;

☐ discuss how innovation might be fostered in an organization.

Operations and marketing are directed to satisfying consumers' needs. Operations relate to the direct costs of running the business (labour, materials etc. used in producing the product or creating the service). These costs must be controlled. In this chapter we explore the strategic contribution of operations, research and development, innovation and total quality.

INTRODUCTION

Operations management is concerned with the design, planning and control of the production function, and the decisions which relate to the use of materials, people and machines.

In Chapter 10 we said that marketing decisions must satisfy demand in three ways:

☐ The correct products and services must be produced, and their market positioning and differentiation must be correctly chosen.

☐ The right markets and market segments must be served.

☐ Advertising, promotion and distribution must be correctly done in the right place at the right time.

Manufacturing or operations management is concerned with having the right product or service ready at the right time, produced to the right quality, but also at the right cost to ensure that profits are earned. Competitive advantage can be achieved by low costs and by differentiation (which normally adds on costs). Profits are the difference between selling prices and costs. There is an obvious need to control costs, which is a key objective of operations management. But it is also essential to build quality into the product or service, and this is another key objective of operations.

Thus operations management can deliver competitive advantage in a number of ways: product design, production to specification, and production and delivery on time and to the appropriate levels of quality. Thus the consumer is provided with what he or she wants profitably. Consumer and customer satisfaction are measures of effectiveness. Cost-effective production is a measure of efficiency.

At the same time innovation is required to ensure that the organization does not lose ground to its competitors. Innovation is clearly related to investment in, and strategies for, research and development, but it is also a function of an on-going search by every manager and employee for better ways of doing things. In this respect it is an aspect of organizational culture.

We shall consider in detail the management of operations to achieve competitive advantage. Firstly, there is an important link between marketing and operations. Consumer needs must be understood if quality

and timing is to be right, and costs should be added only where necessary and where the differentiation is important to the market. Second, manufacturing processes and technology must be managed to achieve control of costs and differentiation. Specific topics are capacity and flow, make or buy decisions, vertical integration, focused manufacturing, just-in-time systems and stock control, and the application of computer-based systems. Additionally the particular characteristics of operations management in service businesses are discussed. Innovation and quality management are discussed at the end of the chapter.

THE STRATEGIC IMPORTANCE OF OPERATIONS

According to Skinner (1978) operations management has become a central aspect of strategic thinking and is no longer an essentially supportive function, for a number of reasons.

☐ Competition, especially on a global basis, has increased in many industries, resulting in over-capacity or a surplus of supply over demand at any time. Manufacturers must therefore deliver satisfaction to customers and consumers or the customers will switch to alternative suppliers. The operations function must be able to achieve high quality and fast and reliable delivery at a cost which is still profitable for the firm.

☐ Product life cycles are shortening in many industries, requiring flexibility and readiness for change in the operations function.

☐ Sophisticated production systems, automation and technology at lower costs are increasingly available, but this may mean that costs become fixed rather than variable. Where this happens the breakeven point changes.

☐ High technology and automation have changed the nature of many production jobs. Shopfloor workers include graduate-level engineers who supervise machinery alongside relatively unskilled support workers. New training to deal with new technologies will be needed.

☐ Automation frequently requires major investment. This should result from clear market and financial forecasting and analysis. Operations and financial management are therefore linked.

MARKETING AND OPERATIONS MANAGEMENT

The link between marketing and operations

In this section we look at the relationship between marketing and operations and the need for the two functional strategies to be co-ordinated. Marketing and demand generate opportunities and expectations for the production and operations function; at the same time operational limitations can constrain marketing.

Hill (1991) contends that operations management can contribute to the achievement of competitive and corporate objectives in a number of ways, and these are detailed below. The significance of each factor for any organization will depend upon the key success factors.

The driving force in all the world's markets is competition. And the most aggressive drivers are the Japanese. Their competitive strength and ambitions are apparent around the world.

Ultimately the only way to succeed is to be fully competitive in the marketplace. Fundamentally this means offering products with utility, style and value that the buyers want, making them with world-class productivity and quality, and serving the customers better than anyone else.

John F Smith Jr, Vice Chairman (International Operations), General Motors Corporation

---

organization will depend upon the key success factors.

☐ **Capacity and capability:** Can the organization produce and provide the goods or services demanded? We must consider dependability and quality. Dependability is the ability to meet delivery and cost targets and promises, and as a result of just-in-time (JIT) systems (discussed later in the chapter) it is becoming increasingly important. Quality issues include the ability to maintain a reliable and consistent product quality, the quality of customer service both before and after sale, and the speed of delivery offered and achieved. It is important to understand which quality issues and measures customers and consumers regard as most crucial and to achieve these.

Organizations must identify and distinguish between **order qualifiers** (things they have to be able to do to compete in a market) and **order winners** (distinctive skills and activities which create competitive advantage). When one competitor opens up a competitive gap, say with an innovation, and this is attractive to customers, it becomes an order qualifier for rivals. The lead competitor must then search for a new competitive advantage to sustain its lead.

☐ **Efficiency:** The effectiveness of the production process, essentially costs, is determined by such measures as cost per unit produced and profit or turnover per employee.

☐ **Adaptability:** We must consider the flexibility in the short term to respond to changes in demand, and strategies for investing in the future through innovation and research and development. In some industries, as mentioned in the previous chapter, product life cycles are shortening, and this emphasizes the need for adaptability and a willingness and readiness to change in line with demand.

Wild (1984) contends that manufacturing

decisions should lead automatically from marketing decisions concerning the products or services to be offered, the markets to be served, and the form and level of service which is required or desirable.

In the 1980s Ford re-designed a number of their cars to fit in with consumer preferences. Wheels were moved closer to the corners to improve road holding; and the designers' preference for streamlined rear ends (to enhance the aerodynamic performance) was constrained in order to provide adequate storage space.

These marketing decisions affect, first, the choice of the appropriate operating system and production process. Manufacturing plants can be designed to produce products individually; to produce in batches whereby a range of different products are produced on the same equipment, although not necessarily following the same process route; to produce on assembly lines, which are designed to handle large volumes of the same product, utilizing either labour or robots to assemble parts; or to produce continuously, whereby a capital-intensive plant produces large volumes, again of one product, with labour used to supervise the equipment rather than to do the work. The choice of process is determined by the nature and volume of demand – how many and how similar – and the need for flexibility. In turn the process selected affects both costs and delivery lead times. Continuous plants tend to be the lowest cost and offer the shortest lead times, with individual production at the opposite end of the scale, but they require very large volumes to be viable and they can be very inflexible as far as changing the product is concerned.

Second, the market factors determine the objectives for the operating system. The objectives will concern the service required by customers (differentiation opportunities) and targets for resource utilization (which affects costs). Third, the operating strategies concerning the capacity of the plant or operation, the scheduling of production and

inventory (or stock) to be held in the system are involved. As a simple illustration of different objectives and strategies one might compare a department store, a supermarket and a mail order company. They all buy goods in, stock them, and then sell them on to customers, but the nature of the service they offer, customer expectations and the key success factors all differ. Consequently the operating systems, objectives and strategies will also differ. Department stores offer a wide range of goods which customers can see and handle, which means high stocks, and generally they are not low priced. Staff offer personal service. Supermarkets offer a more limited choice, and staff concentrate on maintaining full shelves and checking people out quickly. For some, low prices may be part of their strategy. A mail order company may offer the same goods as a department store and be able to control their stocks much more efficiently as they are all held in one place rather than in several stores. But the products cannot be seen or tried, and as a result returns may be high.

Holding stock at various parts of the production system can ensure that there is little likelihood of the organization running out. Raw material stocks can be useful to ensure that production can start if an order is received. Semi-finished goods might offer flexibility if they can be used in more than one final product, with the final choice depending again upon orders received. Finished goods stock can mean quick deliveries. But all these stocks are a cost, and generally there will be financial pressure to reduce stocks as much as possible. Stocks should really be considered from a strategic point of view. The amount of investment in stocks throughout the production system should relate to the importance of their possible contribution to the organization's marketing effort and needs.

Case 11.1 describes how Braun products are based upon seven strategic principles which embrace both marketing and manufacturing.

However, whilst demand and market

Case 11.1
BRAUN

Braun (Germany) manufacture consumer electrical goods which they market world wide. Products are designed, produced and marketed in the light of seven strategic principles:

1. Every Braun product is Braun designed; and marketing, technology and cost aspects are considered jointly.
2. The basic strategy is based on small electrical appliances for global markets. Braun target the mainstream market rather than specialist niches.
3. There is a concentration on known production technologies in plastics, metal working and electronics, and a reluctance to diversify away from these.
4. Braun looks to design innovative products with innovative features, and not imitate competitors. Products are constantly improved wherever they can be 'made more useful' for consumers. Half of Braun's products are under three years old.
5. Product quality standards exceed both the industry average and those that marketing stipulate.
6. Braun invests in manufacturing technology and automation to obtain better control and higher returns than are typical of low labour cost countries.
7. Braun looks for high vertical integration, sourcing strategic parts in-house.

The aim of these principles is to build in competitive advantage which other competitors find hard to replicate.

THE PRINCIPLES APPLIED

Braun manufacture toasters for which there is a huge market world wide. Some 10 million per year are bought in America alone. The toasters incorporate heating elements which are also used in their hair dryers and coffee makers, and an innovative infra-red sensor (which is a bought-in component contrary to Principle 7).

Braun alarm clocks again sell in a large international market. They are all black and flatter than most rival products. Braun have developed the ability to manufacture the clock workings, and they have introduced innovatory voice-control and infra-red hand movement mechanisms for switching off the alarm.

Both products are based on known technologies supported by high investment and automation.

Source: Presentation by Bernhard Wild, 'Practical manufacturing strategy: The neglected competitive weapon' conference, Strategic Planning Society, London, 26 November 1990.

---

opportunities will influence the appropriate operating system and strategies, operational aspects may constrain the marketing strategy. Case 11.2, which considers the marketing-operations link for McDonald's, illustrates that the appropriate level of service

Case 11.2
McDONALD'S: THE MARKETING AND OPERATIONS LINK

ASPECTS OF THE MARKETING STRATEGY

The product	A variety of fast foods, soft drinks and coffee for eating in and taking away
	Inexpensive relative to restaurants
Markets	Families with young children
	Teenagers
	Shoppers
	Office workers (at lunchtime)
	Children's parties
Service required	Rapid service; no waiting
	Busy and clean image
	Rapid turnover of customers, to maximize use of limited seating space

ASPECTS OF THE OPERATIONS STRATEGY

The operating system

The operating system is a joint kitchen and counter service system, with co-ordinated staffing, designed to have products cooked and ready for use when they are demanded. Popular products are always cooked ready for immediate sale; for others there is a limited waiting time. The aim is to minimize both waiting time and waste – cooked products not sold after a certain time are thrown away. All cooking and serving operations are consistent in every McDonald's, and training in the systems is extensive. This controls costs, service, quality and reliability.

Objectives

Customer service	Reliable and consistent quality
	Low cost/price
	Rapid service and little waiting
Resource utilization	High for low cost
	This imposes a constraint – minimum waiting means food is ready or prepared ready to cook which can only be achieved with a limited product range

Strategies

☐ **Capacity** must be linked to fluctuating demand (peaks and troughs throughout the day) and therefore part-time employees are utilized extensively.

☐ **Scheduling** depends upon demand forecasts for individual products, when to produce how many of which, in anticipation of demand.

☐ **Inventories**: because the product is food, and to save space (and costs), stocks will be maintained as low as possible but not so low as to risk running out of particular items.

    The significance of this is sharpened by the fact that suppliers are strictly controlled and food can only be obtained from certain sources.

For more detail see Love, J F (1986) *McDonald's: Behind the Arches*, Bantam.

---

from the chosen system can only be met if the product range, and consumer choice, is limited. Without this low prices and fast service would not be possible. Manufacturing strategy involves a number of trade-offs of this nature, and decisions should consider both customer and company needs.

The product range and variety reduction

No two consumers have identical needs, and market segmentation and product differentiation opportunities arise from this. However, the more a manufacturer tries to cater for all the different needs expressed by the market, the more his or her production costs will rise. Similarly the more the product or product range is standardized and limited to contain costs, the less perceived differentiation is likely to exist as far as the consumer is concerned. The appropriate product design, and the appropriate product range, are those which balance the need to differentiate, create and sustain competitive advantage with the need to manage costs in order to earn profits.

    Companies which produce several different products, and a number of variants of each, are likely to find that over time the number of separate products has grown quite large, and that some sell in only very small volumes. Producing these small volume items may offer a service to selected and important customers, which they may well be willing to pay for. There may be important strategic reasons for continuing with them, but they will tie up resources. Occasionally it is important for manufacturers to assess the relative importance of all the items they produce and to consider dropping some. This is known as variety reduction. The analysis, known as a Pareto analysis, could look at the percentage of total profit or total revenue contributed by each product.

    A typical Pareto analysis is likely to show that 80% of total revenue is provided by just 20% of the products manufactured (the so-called 80–20 rule). The low contributors should be analysed in terms of

☐ how long they have been made;
☐ whether the performance in the last few years has been upwards, level or downwards;
☐ whether the costs might be reduced or the price increased;
☐ whether the company really needs them.

This last point needs a careful and honest appraisal. Some customers are especially important to a company and they may value certain products; on other occasions this argument may be used for the retention of certain products when it is not really true.

The advantages of variety reduction can be seen in longer production runs, less downtime (when the plant is changed over for a different product), reduced stocks, the consequent cost savings of these changes, easier operations planning and control, and the fact that resources may be freed for future developments.

Capacity and capability

Production capacity is designed to link supply and demand. Demand for a product or service may grow steadily, or growth may be less predictable and affected by seasonal or cyclical fluctuations. It may not be easy to alter supply potential in the same pattern. For example the demand for three-star hotel accommodation may be growing at 10% per year in a town where there are already three such hotels. Say these are occupied at nearly full capacity most weeks and as a result a fourth hotel is opened. Supply then exceeds demand as, depending on the size of the new hotel, the number of rooms available has increased by perhaps a third overall. The new hotel may find it difficult to obtain business if the competing hotels enjoy customer loyalty; conversely, if it is better equipped the existing hotels may find themselves threatened. As a result marketing strategies might be expected to change.

Hence at any time demand and supply capability may be at odds. A manufacturer faced with this dilemma may have to choose between not investing and expanding, and thereby losing potential sales and market share, and investing in temporarily excess capacity which will increase total production costs. Where operating systems have some flexibility built in, say because they can produce different products which can be switched around, or because overtime working is a possibility, incremental changes up and down in line with market demand are possible. However, at other times major strategic decisions concerning investment will be required.

The last point is particularly important for new product development decisions. Proposed new products may fit into existing plants, possibly replacing other products which are declining or being withdrawn. However, they may require completely new capital equipment or new tooling which might amount to a considerable investment. Where large volumes, scale economies and the experience curve effect are being sought this is a crucial issue. In this situation a decision has to be made concerning when to invest in the equipment. New products, as we saw in the last chapter, may not succeed when they are launched. If considerable investment has taken place in anticipation of success which is not forthcoming, and the equipment in question is relatively inflexible, the trial could prove very expensive. However, if the investment is not made soon enough the trial launch of the new product may attract competition which challenges for market share before the new plant and equipment have been installed. Whilst there are no easy answers to this problem the need to link marketing and operations decisions is reinforced.

Declining products also present capacity problems. Where demand is falling the likely impact on manufacturing will be lower capacity utilization and increased production costs. Moreover there may be an opportunity to utilize the capacity in some alternative way. However, as was mentioned in the previous section on variety reduction, there may be key strategic reasons for continuing to produce a product even though it is in the decline stage of the product life cycle. Higher production costs may have to be accepted at the same time as price reductions – although there should be corresponding savings through less advertising and promotion expenditure.

Capability and resource allocation

In the section on product life cycles and the Boston matrix in Chapter 10 it was emphasized that products generate most cash at certain stages in their life cycle, and they require changing levels of financial support at different stages. Production and development resources in the form of plant capacity and research and development support must be allocated amongst the various products depending on their current situation.

Cash cows, which are the most profitable products, may not be especially demanding as far as resources are concerned, but it is essential to invest in any necessary product development to retain market share. This is particularly important where attempts are being made to extend the product life cycle. Stars, with high relative market share and high growth, are high priority items which will demand resources. Other products may have to be sacrificed to support them.

Questions are products which are still being developed and which absorb resources for this. If they are successful they will require further resourcing, essentially capacity, to support their growth. However, because they are relatively unpredictable – demand may be slow or may suddenly take off – they can create scheduling problems. Dogs should be the lowest priority items as they will require very little, if any, development work, and they should not be taking up substantial capacity. As they are declining in volume and may be subject to price reductions they are not particularly profitable, and ironically if they are scheduled around the higher priority items this is likely to increase their costs further.

In summary, marketing makes demands of manufacturing resources, whilst the operations function offers both opportunities and constraints for products and services in terms of costs and differentiation possibilities. Marketing personnel should understand the operational aspects of their products and services so that they do not make unrealistic demands on production. Equally production staff must appreciate the needs and requirements of customers if they are to satisfy demand effectively. Wheelwright (1978) suggests that there are six key elements of manufacturing strategy, and these are described in Box 11.1. The six elements are all interrelated and they should be linked to the needs and demands of consumers and to the key factors for success in the market.

MANUFACTURING MANAGEMENT AND STRATEGY

Technology and systems

Whilst it is essential for overall strategic success that manufacturing and marketing strategies are linked, manufacturing can be managed to create competitive advantage.

Caulkin (1988) argues that the manufacturing requirements for international competitiveness are changing. In the past it may have been adequate to argue that meeting and beating rivals on cost and product quality were the essential issues. Now, however, successful companies are also competing on two additional dimensions: variety and time. Variety is the ability to switch production quickly between numerous different items to meet the flexible needs of customers; time is the delivery lead time, which needs to be short despite the necessary flexibility. Satisfying these needs makes use of automated manufacturing technology (AMT) and just-in-time (JIT) production systems respectively. Both these terms are explained in Box 11.2.

Bolwijn and Kumpe (1990) emphasize the additional need for manufacturing to become more innovative and able to handle rapid design changes and product improvements.

New (1988) contends that if British companies are to become increasingly competitive in world terms costs must be reduced and quality improved. Specifically work in progress and stocks (money tied up) must be reduced; lead times must also be reduced; new products must be introduced faster,

Box 11.1
THE KEY ELEMENTS OF MANUFACTURING STRATEGY

Facilities: the number of plants, their locations and their sizes.

Processes: the capital equipment and laid-down production processes, which must match the relevant product characteristics and competitive pressures.

Aggregate capacity: the issue of whether supply capacity matches demand, and is ahead or behind it as it changes. Opportunities to expand or contract in the short term through flexible shifts or overtime working are also important.

Vertical integration: this includes decisions concerning whether to design and develop machinery and tooling in-house so that production needs are met exactly or to buy it in, and whether to make or assemble certain parts or to subcontract the work. YKK

(Chapter 4, Box 4.2), the world's largest zip manufacturer, design and build their own machinery very successfully, and it has helped them achieve cost leadership. Norman Aeroplane (Chapter 3, Case 3.3) use bought-in standard parts wherever it makes sense because they need the flexibility this gives them.

The manufacturing infrastructure: production planning and control, quality control and stock control systems. These influence both costs and delivery lead times and should be led by market forces.

Linkages with other functions

Source: Wheelwright, S C (1978) Reflecting corporate strategy in manufacturing decisions, *Business Horizons*, February.

---

particularly in certain industries where life cycles are shortening; and support labour must be reduced. Traditionally cost, product quality, flexibility and responsiveness to consumer demands have been seen as conflicting objectives, with trade-offs between themselves and with volume production. They must all be achieved in some significant measure now, because of world over-capacity in many industries, competition which is becoming increasingly global, and new standards of manufacturing efficiency, many of which are being set by Japan. This is not purely a question of automation. Bad practice can be automated. Caulkin argues that instead manufacturing must be viewed strategically and not as a support service to marketing and financial decisions. The factory is a source of competitive advantage and it must be viewed and managed in this light.

Manufacturing (too often) is seen as a reactive function supporting marketing. Instead it should be seen as supporting markets, and very evident in product/market decisions.

In turn this requires that the contribution of individual employees is encouraged and maximized. International competitiveness results from a process of continuous improvement in every aspect of a firm's activities, and this is now referred to as **total quality management**. This point will be developed later in this chapter in the section on quality and in Chapter 12.

Manufacturing systems

New (1988) argues that in a manufacturing plant value is added through cutting and

Box 11.2
MANUFACTURING SYSTEMS – THE TERMINOLOGY EXPLAINED

MRPI stands for **materials requirements planning**, and it is based upon computer software for resource scheduling in any fabrication-type business.

MRPII is a more recent concept of enhanced software for **manufacturing resource planning**. The important linkages between sales, manufacturing and purchasing can be incorporated into this integrated system. Additionally capacity, production planning and production control can all be linked.

Both the above systems can be very useful as long as managers who are using the system do not go outside it arbitrarily and, for example, reschedule work because someone is pressurizing them to make changes or improve a delivery.

Pioneered in Japan in the 1960s and 1970s **just-in-time** (JIT) systems are designed to improve overall productivity and eliminate waste by the cost-effective production and delivery of only the necessary quantity of parts at the right quality, at the right time and place, using a minimum amount of facilities, equipment, materials and human resources. Essentially bought-in parts and components are delivered several times a day or week, as appropriate, straight to the production point where they are required; stocks are eliminated. Where internally resourced parts are concerned, production is scheduled to manufacture only the amount needed at any time, and this implies a need for investment in flexible, fast-changeover machines and equipment.

As a result costs can be reduced and delivery times shortened. Additionally quality should improve in a number of ways.

To work JIT needs exact shift planning and controlled deliveries. The buyer–supplier relationship is extremely important; manufacturers are very dependent upon their suppliers meeting agreed commitments (see case 11.3). It is highly likely that an MRPII system would be used to underpin JIT.

Optimized production technology, an operating philosophy which has evolved from capacity scheduling, was devised by Eli Goldratt and is discussed in detail in an article by Haylett (1986). Goldratt argues that the goal of an organization is to earn money from throughput and sales, avoiding unnecessary operating expenses in the form of inventory. The key is to balance the **flows of goods** through the organization, rather than trying to balance demand and capacity at every stage of the total operation, and to make precisely what is needed to sustain immediate production programmes. At any time certain parts of the plant will be capable of producing in excess of what is required immediately; other operations may well be fully employed. Where demand for an operation at any time exceeds its capacity a bottleneck is created. Goldratt contends that in the case of operations where capacity exceeds immediate demand it is better to leave equipment standing idle than working to full capacity. If the latter happens the result must be increased stocks, tying up money and space, because there may be a bottleneck in the next operation required or no demand for the finished product in the short term. This constitutes overall effectiveness in operations but means low efficiency or utilization figures on particular activities. Consequently an important issue is the performance measures used. Efforts should be concentrated on improving the performance and throughput of the bottleneck areas.

The National Health Service provides a useful example of this. In December 1988 the House of Commons Public Accounts Committee criticized the low utilization of hospital operating theatres. In return the

Continued overleaf

British Medical Association argued that theatres would only achieve a higher utilization percentage when there were adequate wards, spare beds and nurses for post-operative care, and there are frequently other demands on these resources which result in shortages or potential bottlenecks.

Automated manufacturing technology (**AMT**) refers to any form of automation, including machines which can be programmed by a computer to set themselves and change their own tooling (so that an operative is not required to be in constant attendance and potential delays between jobs are avoided), robots, and automatically guided vehicles (AGVs) which again can be programmed to move materials automatically from where they are to where they are required next without delays.

Flexible manufacturing systems are a particular example of AMT, and relate to an **arrangement** of automated machinery in a configuration designed to maximize the benefits of continuous-flow production with very small batch quantities. Typically machines are arranged in cells. The objectives are to reduce lead times, lower costs (through higher productivity and freed-up space), increase flexibility and increase total

quality through less waste, faster deliveries, fewer customer complaints and less after-sales service.

They require substantial investment, however, and must therefore be part of a linked marketing and operations strategy. New (1988) argues that small incremental investments do not prove as effective, but that investment analyses of large-scale projects are often poorly carried out by British manufacturers. As a result potential costs and benefits may be misjudged.

Computer integrated manufacturing represents the ultimate system whereby customer orders arrive electronically and an integrated computer system runs everything from design through to final assembly. Although computers are frequently used for the various stages (computer-aided design, computer-aided manufacturing, or programmes which run the AMT, production planning and so on) fully integrated systems present a number of problems and are less popular.

New (1988) uses the term 'islands of technology' to illustrate that the independent constituent parts have to be brought together if there are to be maximum productivity gains. Software programs linking the parts are analogous to the use of tunnels or bridges or ferries to link a number of islands together.

machining, assembling, testing and manufacturing. Costs, not value, are added when items are moved around, counted, chased and searched for, stored, repacked, batched, inspected and recorded. These activities can constitute unnecessary waste. There are three rival methods for speeding the product flow from raw material to finished product: JIT; manufacturing resources planning; and optimized production technology. All three are explained in Box 11.2. Caulkin contends that JIT has been the most influential.

JIT is conceptually simple and aims to achieve no wasted time and no wasted quantity. Encouraging deliveries of the exact number of both bought-in components and items from elsewhere in the plant directly to the point where they are needed, exactly when they are required for production, removes buffer stocks from between work positions. This reduces costs and creates space which can be utilized productively. Moreover any obstacles to smooth work flows are quickly exposed and can be dealt

---

Case 11.3
TOYOTA

In 1989 Toyota began to select suppliers for a new production plant in Derbyshire, over three years in advance of the planned opening. The aim was to purchase 75% of the components required from 150 European suppliers. A typical European car company would buy directly from about 800 suppliers, but Toyota is looking to establish a network whereby it deals with only 150 components manufacturers, who in turn set up their own subcontracting deals. Some 2000 companies expressed interest in winning orders.

There are four main selection criteria:

☐ management capability and attitude
☐ production facilities and investment in technology
☐ quality control systems and philosophy, and
☐ research and development capability.

Toyota set all the standards for quality and delivery, putting pressure on interested suppliers, and placing firm orders only when both standards and costs are right.

Typical of a Japanese manufacturer, Toyota will look for their suppliers to:

☐ continually improve their quality standards;
☐ link in to Toyota's JIT production systems;
☐ deliver on time consistently; and
☐ reduce their costs incrementally, passing on to Toyota (and in turn their customers) the benefits of improved productivity.

A 1991 NEDO report highlights the challenge for interested UK companies. A typical UK supplier (at the end of the 1980s) rejected 1 component in 1000. This was the Japanese level some ten years earlier. By 1990 Japanese companies had improved to a rejection level of 1.2 in 10 000 and were aiming for 5 in 1 million before the mid-1990s. Western European companies were reported to be marginally ahead of the UK.

Reference: The Experience of Nissan Suppliers: Lessons for the UK Engineering Industry, NEDO, 1991.

---

with. Every work station can be seen as a receiver (or buyer) and supplier from and to other work stations, and the interdependences become obvious. Quality and quantity problems can be shared instantly and improvements sought. As a result productivity and quality should both improve. At the same time simpler layouts and systems are necessary so that managers can be more aware of what is happening at any time.

Manufacturing technology

Manufacturing resources planning, optimized production technology and JIT are all ways of using technology and automation. In addition there are a number of manufacturing technology systems which can be used alongside these concepts; Box 11.2 again explains the most important of these. Automation appears to be more effective when

---

Case 11.4
CATERPILLAR

Caterpillar, whose headquarters are in Illinois in America, are the world's biggest manufacturer of earthmoving and construction equipment. Profits declined in the early 1980s as a result of falling international demand, Japanese competition and the high relative value of the dollar. To maintain their world leadership Caterpillar embarked on one of the world's largest factory modernization programmes.

The change programme, started in 1987 and originally due for completion in 1993/4, involves 77 projects, 67 of which are designed to produce an aggregate drop of 18% in real production costs, and a more than one-fifth fall in inventory. Such changes as these require new skills in understanding workflows among factory planners, and higher numeracy skills among shopfloor workers.

The first projects have already been completed and the promised efficiencies and cost savings obtained – but the programme overall was a year behind schedule by 1990. Moreover, and not unexpectedly, the costs have been under-estimated. In addition, an initial aim to link up all production and related divisions through a fully integrated computer system has been abandoned as too ambitious.

As part of the implementation process Caterpillar have invested in training – production workers, for example, are spending 5% of their normal working time being trained. One major problem is the need to change attitudes. Manufacturing is now about 'problem solving, statistical process control and maintenance technology'. Operators have to be stopped from wanting to intervene. Another difficulty is persuading long-time shopfloor workers to change from a one man/one machine system to cell manufacturing where, say, two men control (but do not operate manually) six different computerized machines.

Source: Garnett, N (1990) Caterpillar gets dug into $2 billion factory modernization, *Financial Times*, 6 June.

---

systems are kept simple, but there are often problems of implementation. There are various levels of sophistication covering design, planning, control and manufacturing which can eliminate unnecessary costs and build in differentiation and competitive advantage, but the activities must be co-ordinated if productivity is to improve.

Case 11.4, Caterpillar, illustrates that implementing advanced manufacturing systems is very challenging, especially as major changes in working practices and culture are implied. World-famous organizations like Boeing have experienced real diffi-

culties in introducing flexible manufacturing systems, leading to long delays before the promised benefits are obtained.

Focused manufacturing

New (1985) contends that it is an idealistic hope that a manufacturer can 'deliver on time, on the shortest possible lead time, a superior quality product, making anything the customer asks for in any volume required at the lowest possible price, while not investing in any capital, and learning all one can about the market as one does it'. In other words competitive advantage cannot be achieved in every area; there must be selectivity and concentration on certain aspects.

Skinner (1974) makes the following statements.

☐ There are many ways an organization can compete; producing at low cost is only one. Quality and delivery may be just as important, possibly more important, than price.

☐ A factory cannot perform well on every yardstick. There is likely to be a trade-off between dependable delivery, short delivery, superior quality, reliable quality, flexibility in adjusting to volume changes, the ability to incorporate new products into a production schedule, low investment and low cost. Competitive advantage could be found in any one of these areas.

☐ Simplicity and repetition breed competence.

Whilst productivity is important, so too are consumer requirements, and the functional strategy for manufacturing should be derived from corporate and competitive strategies. However, a factory which focuses on a narrow product mix for a particular market niche will out-perform a plant with a broader mission as costs can be lowered and a stronger relationship with key customers can be built (Skinner).

Focusing therefore implies linking manufacturing facilities to the appropriate key factors for competitive success so that a company is able to sustain and develop competitive advantage. It has increased in significance as manufacturing technology has improved and product life cycles have shortened.

It may not be feasible, of course, to have one factory producing only one product for one market segment, in which case focusing implies concentrating on certain key aspects. Hayes and Wheelwright (1984) suggest three different approaches to focusing.

☐ Focusing on volume: high- and low-volume items demand different processes and infrastructures, and the plant should be segregated accordingly.

☐ Focusing on products and markets: market needs are central to the focusing decision, with manufacturing needs secondary.

☐ Focusing on processes: technologies are segregated and facilities are dedicated to specific products.

Much depends upon the range of different products involved, the volumes demanded, and the stages they are at in their life cycles. For example, product and market focusing can be important for new and declining products, but process focusing is probably better in the growth stage. A manufacturer who wishes to benefit from focusing must, argues Skinner,

☐ limit any process and technology differences, especially if they are new or unproven;

☐ be clear about which market demands need priority, and concentrate on achieving these;

☐ relate volumes to capacity;

☐ ensure that there is a clear, shared and appropriate commitment to quality throughout the organization.

In summary, different products and processes present different manufacturing problems. Different markets and consumers demand different added values. The key is to concentrate as much as possible and not mix too many product types, processes and forms of differentiation. Possibly linked to JIT systems, the decision to buy in more parts and components from suppliers or use subcontractors for specific requirements can enhance focusing by limiting the number of activities being undertaken in a factory. External sourcing is particularly useful if standard parts are required and where subcontractors can do a job at a lower cost (perhaps because they specialize, have more experience and the most appropriate technology). Whilst this is a manufacturing decision it can affect the overall corporate strategy if it affects in any significant way the extent to which the organization is vertically integrated. Vertical integration is mentioned as a key element of manufacturing strategy in Box 11.1 and it will be discussed in greater detail in Chapter 17. In simple terms it relates to the degree of control that a manufacturer has over the whole series of activities and processes which link raw material production, manufacturing, assembly and distribution.

Key Reading 11.1 considers how, in an ideal way, the competitive advantage which manufacturing can offer might be linked to the key success factors and market expectations. We have seen already that strategic changes can be both occasional major decisions and incremental gradual changes as changing market opportunities and threats are identified. Automation and technology for manufacturing require significant investment and they must be linked to proposed corporate objectives and strategies. However, incremental changes are still likely to be required, and therefore consideration should be given to the necessary flexibility to ensure that the organization will be able to respond to changing market needs and incorporate new products and innovations.

SERVICE BUSINESSES

It was pointed out in the introduction to this chapter that operations management relates to the management of the key resources of materials, people and machines (or facilities). Armistead (1985) suggests that service businesses have two essential characteristics. First, they are heavily dependent upon people. It was pointed out in Chapter 10 on marketing that in service businesses people actually become a fifth element in the marketing mix. Second, the service is often tran-

sient. Quite often it cannot be stored, as in the case of hotel bedrooms, airline seats, and time-slots at dentists and hairdressers. If a bedroom or aircraft seat is left empty for a particular night or flight the lost revenue can never be recovered. A dentist or hairdresser can recoup some financial losses by working longer hours than were otherwise intended, but the time has still been spent unproductively.

People

Invariably in service businesses close contacts are established between the providers and the users of the service. This contrasts with manufacturing where the people who actually make the product are far less likely to meet the consumers. In a service business something is done directly for the consumer (for example dental work or a hair cut) or indirectly, such as a taxi taking them from A to B, or a retailer selling them something manufactured elsewhere. Additionally services must normally be capable of dealing with a large number of customers whose particular needs are different in a variety of ways and who may be similar in only one respect – they want the basic service.

Understanding the various preferences and catering for individual needs is a major source of competitive advantage.

The more complex and customized the service (see Figure 11.1) the greater the opportunities for differentiation and adding value. In all cases the quality of customer service can be improved by appropriate training which concentrates on motivating staff to both satisfy and retain customers.

Transient services

Where services are transient or perishable and cannot be stored, matching demand and supply is absolutely crucial. If demand is misjudged and over-provided for, then

Key Reading 11.1
DETERMINING MANUFACTURING STRATEGY

There are four stages:

☐ Identify the pattern of **market expectations**.
☐ Determine the nature of the **optimum response**.
☐ Create the corresponding **manufacturing infrastructure**.
☐ Refine these to **maximize competitiveness**.

MARKET EXPECTATIONS

There are four elements, and a manufacturer must seek to provide a better balanced and more effective package than competitors. The importance of each factor will vary between different products and for different market segments. The four are as follows:

☐ fitness for purpose, which is essential in some products such as braking systems for cars
☐ prices – some undifferentiated products, such as domestic electric light bulbs, compete on price
☐ quality, which can manifest itself in a number of ways, e.g. one essential quality of an emergency battery is that it works immediately that it is called upon after standing unused for some length of time
☐ the level of service or speed of response.

Compromise is required: low prices conflict with high quality, for instance. The factors rarely carry equal importance, and the manufacturing system should deliver what is important to consumers, allocating priorities where appropriate.

THE OPTIMUM RESPONSE

This involves both external factors, developed from the market expectations, and internal constraints.

External factors

☐ Fitness for purpose demands high quality design and manufacturing facilities.
☐ Low prices require high productivity, low capital employed and minimal overheads if the organization is to be profitable.
☐ Quality is achieved by emphasizing quality in every aspect of the operation.
☐ Service is provided by short lead times, balanced stocks, and flexibility.

Problems are likely to be more significant if the factory is not focused and there is a variety of processes and systems in the same plant.

Internal factors

Two key constraints are **tanglers** and **manglers**.

☐ Tanglers are underlying complicators and include a wide product range, long production routes with several stages (and probable bottlenecks), a proliferation of common parts used in several products, many customers, and any operation which is multi-plant.
☐ Manglers, or dominant unpredictables, include a varying product mix or varying yields.

Manglers can be changed via methodology and technology, but tanglers cannot easily be eliminated. Manufacturers must learn to cope with them better than their competitors, perhaps using technology again.

Continued overleaf

THE MANUFACTURING INFRASTRUCTURE

When the above requirements, opportunities and constraints have been considered, the following should be analysed: material costs; direct labour costs; indirect labour costs; production overheads (such as maintenance); stock levels; lead times; and the anticipated cost and return from investment in new systems and technology.

Where appropriate:

☐ Products should be re-designed around preferred parts and systems.
☐ Processes should be re-designed.
☐ The organization of the operations function should be re-structured to cope with new processes, automation and changes to any of the tanglers.
☐ Finally, control systems should be designed after these other decisions have been taken.

MAXIMIZING COMPETITIVENESS

The best option is a compromise between

☐ achieving maximum competitiveness related to market expectations
☐ the perceived levels of confidence and risk in any alternative proposals
☐ the cost and availability of funds
☐ the most appropriate pattern and pace of change.

Changes might take place over an extended period, but what matters is a clear long-term strategy for the changes.

Summarized from Gray, J (1985) Manufacturing excellence, *Arthur Young Business View*, Spring.

---

additional costs will be incurred. This will be reflected in higher prices or lower profits.

At the time the transient nature of the service may be reflected in the competitive strategy, which might be aimed at boosting off-peak demand. Special weekend packages in hotels which normally cater for business people, or winter rates in summer resorts, are examples. British Rail's use of saver tickets and rail cards is another. There is need for care where price discrimination of this nature is involved, however. If existing customers of the service are able to switch their usage times so that they obtain the cheaper rates when they might otherwise pay higher

prices, lost revenue will result. Similarly if people who pay the highest prices, say on British Rail, cannot obtain a seat because the train is full of cheap-fare passengers, then customer goodwill is lost.

However, the key issues of linking marketing and operations strategies and seeking to create and sustain competitive advantage in the service itself mean that there are similarities between the operations management of manufacturing and service businesses. In both cases the needs to innovate and to ensure that quality is built into the operating system are paramount. These topics are discussed next.

SERVICE COMPLEXITY

	High	Low
Customized	Doctor Solicitor Garage	Hairdressing Landscape gardening Painting and decorating
Predominantly standardized	Cinema Museum Airline	Fast food Petrol station and car wash Dry cleaning

CUSTOMER REQUIREMENTS

Figure 11.1   Categorizing service businesses.

SERVICE AND TOTAL QUALITY MANAGEMENT

The **effective** satisfaction of the needs of the final consumer of a product or service involves everyone in the supply chain. Marketing must recognize opportunities for adding value; operations personnel must supply that value. This implies widespread awareness of consumer needs and expectations, and effective co-operation between

---

There is no conflict between good customer service and good returns to shareholders.

John J Wilson, Chairman, London Electricity plc

---

marketing and operations. However, if this is also to be achieved **efficiently** everyone in the supply chain must be committed to helping their personal customers. To accomplish this, manufacturing can learn from service businesses. External suppliers must be linked in to manufacturing; people at each stage of the manufacturing process should see the next stage as their customers and seek to provide them with quality and service. Manufacturers who do not sell directly to the final consumer must also work closely with their distributors. This systemic awareness comes from asking: 'Who is my customer, and who are my customer's customers?'

Consumer satisfaction can lead to loyalty and superior profits. If this profit is used in part to reward employees and to further improve quality and service, a cycle of improvement can be instigated.

It is hard to distinguish customer satisfaction from employee satisfaction. You can't have one without the other.

Winning companies compete by delivering a product that supplies superior value to customers rather than one that costs less. Most strategists have believed that business winners are those that capture commanding market share through lower costs and prices. The winning midsize companies compete on the value of their products and services and usually enjoy premium prices.

This contention from Peters and Austin (1985) reinforces the work of Michael Porter on competitive advantage, which was discussed in Chapter 7. Porter argues that low costs can create competitive advantage but that in a market there can be only one lowest cost competitor; differentiation provides the major opportunity for advantage for the other competitors. Quality is a key source of differentiation and competitive advantage. Customers value quality and are willing to pay a premium for it.

In this context quality implies more than the quality of the product itself although this obviously is important. It incorporates the organization's ability to meet the specific needs and requirements of customers, such as delivery on time of exactly the right quantity, packaged appropriately. This is an area of constant change as competing organizations strive to find new opportunities to create differentiation and to satisfy their customers' needs better. In turn this increases customer expectations, placing greater demands on supplying organizations.

Moreover, improving the quality of the way activities are managed and carried out in organizations invariably leads to lower costs through less waste and through 'getting it right first time', a central theme of total quality management.

Successful organizations will also strive to 'get it right every time'. Company reputations for good quality and service are quickly lost when customers start telling stories of their (possibly isolated) bad experience.

Clearly this impinges on the management of people, and will be discussed further in Chapter 12.

The expression 'total quality management' therefore relates to everything which happens in an organization and which can lead to lower costs and particularly the improvement of customer service. The speed of response to queries, the way in which telephone calls are dealt with, accurate delivery notes and invoices are all examples outside

---

We always travel with our teddy bears. When we got back to our room at the hotel we saw that the maid had arranged our bears very comfortably in a chair. The bears were holding hands.

I needed a few more minutes to decide on dinner. The waitress said: 'If you would read the menu and not the road map, you would know what you want to order.'

Binter, M J, Booms, B and Tetreault, M S (1990) The service encounter: diagnosing favourable and unfavourable incidents, *Journal of Marketing*, **54**, January.

Quality is not a label you can put on a product afterwards. Quality is a way of life that must apply to everything within the company and all its external relations. Quality is in essence a question of leadership. Only a minor part of errors are attributable to the shop floor. Quality is created by the attitude and action of management. It is something that must be part of corporate objectives and strategies.

Georg Karnsund, President, Saab-Scania AB

the direct production activity. They all reflect a concern for getting it right. All these activities should aim to provide customer satisfaction at a profit.

The background to total quality management

The strategic opportunity and value of total quality was really recognized by the Japanese in the 1960s. It happened when certain leading companies realized that policies they were following, designed to improve product quality, were also resulting in lower costs, and they looked for further ways of improving the overall quality of the service they offered their customers. American companies responded in the 1970s after a number of their key markets had been eroded by Japanese competitors. Britain and the rest of Europe has lagged behind, and it is only in the 1980s that total quality has become a major strategic issue.

Total quality management can usefully be viewed as a cycle, as featured in Figure 11.2 First of all customer needs must be identified and addressed. Their needs are basically what they say they are, not necessarily what a manufacturer would like them to be; and manufacturers should seek to provide their customers with exactly what they want, delivering the right number at the right time, neither early nor late. Suppliers should create a reputation for reliability.

In satisfying these needs manufacturers

People feel the best about their work when they do a high-quality job! Getting a job done quickly is satisfying. Getting a job done at low cost is rewarding. But getting a job done quickly, at low cost and with high quality is exciting!

Robert C Stempel, Chairman,
General Motors Corporation

---

should seek to improve the quality of their operations in terms of people, systems and technology. Improving people can be relatively inexpensive, but it requires that they are seen and treated as a key resource. Training is essential, and the ways in which employees might improve the quality of their individual contribution should be discussed with them. Most people know how they could perform more effectively, but quite often they are never asked. Systems should reflect clear policies and standards, and communication systems should keep people aware of how well or badly the company is doing at any time. Technology can improve quality through increased productivity and through eliminating human error, but it can be very expensive.

The organization needs to be recognized for the quality and value that it is building into its products and customer service if it is to benefit. Customer satisfaction and loyalty should be sought, resulting in a stronger market position. But then the process continues as organizations should strive to improve the quality of their products and services continually. Gradually costs should be reduced, and services and customer satisfaction should be improved as the quality improvements are sustained. Total quality becomes both a philosophy, which should be an essential value of the organization, and activities designed to deliver customer satisfaction profitably.

Total quality management therefore should start with the strategic leader who must emphasize a commitment to it, but it must spread throughout the company. Everybody in the organization is responsible for quality. The basic philosophy is that prevention (getting things right first time) is better than detection (finding out through expensive inspection systems or customer complaints). The underlying aim is continuous improvement. By focusing on quality, costs can be reduced and service improved.

Other employees within the organization should be seen as internal customers, and

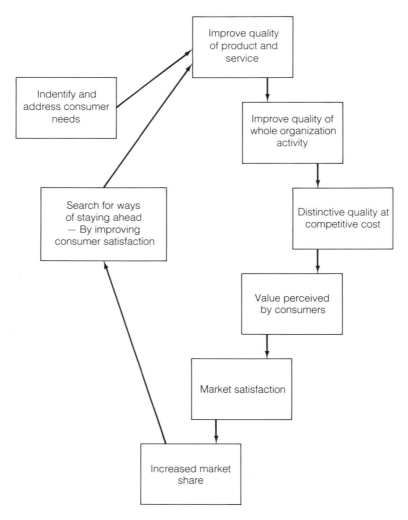

Figure 11.2 The quality cycle.

their needs should be recognized and satisfied. It was mentioned earlier that JIT systems similarly reinforce these interdependences. It is very likely that organizations who are quality minded, especially if they are operating JIT systems, will increase the pressure on their external suppliers to improve their quality. Garnett (1988) cites the example of manufacturers in America requiring that machinery suppliers meet increasingly tighter tolerances, grant substantial warranties, run training courses for users and carry out extensive pre-installation testing. As technology and automation become more complex and more expensive, total quality is becoming a more important issue.

The benefits of total quality management

PA Consultants (1987) contend that companies who have pursued total quality have been able to benefit in a number of ways. Specifically they have:

☐ improved the company image (British Airways, for example, believe that they have been able to increase their passenger volumes as a result of training all their employees to fulfil the interests of their customers, thereby improving their image and reputation);

☐ improved productivity;

☐ reduced costs;

☐ created greater certainty in their operations (by reducing conflicts within the operating system they have improved the speed of delivery and their flexibility in responding to changes in customer requirements);

☐ improved morale (employees have shown greater concern and commitment where they have seen that there is an emphasis on things being done well and that high standards have been encouraged, valued and rewarded);

☐ committed customers.

Organizational needs for total quality management

Peters (1988) argues that if an organization is committed to total quality management there are a number of issues which must be addressed.

First, the necessary commitment to getting things right first time must be encouraged and developed throughout the organization. Moreover, employees must be trained about how they can measure quality and quality improvements. Second, there must be a guiding system or ideology stemming from the strategic leader; continual quality improvements must be managed. To this end, and third, there need to be clear targets and measures of success. Numbers of rejects, repeats and returns from customers, and the cost of after-sales servicing are all examples. Results should be communicated. Fourth, quality improvements should be rewarded, as should new ideas for further improvement. This helps maintain a momentum.

Fifth, quality issues should be communicated laterally throughout the organization as problems can span several areas of the business. Finally, relationships with both buyers and suppliers should be developed. The organization is seeking to satisfy the needs and requirements of their customers; suppliers should be seeking to meet the requirements and needs of the organization. They are all linked in a chain of interdependences.

Research by consultants A T Kearney (1992) concludes that 80% of companies with TQM programmes do not encapsulate all these issues, and, as a result, fail to obtain any marked improvement in performance. Their research also showed that companies with the most successful programmes objectively 'benchmark' their competitors. Benchmarking is concerned with studying competitors to identify and understand 'best current practice' for adding and delivering value.

Peters also suggests that opportunities to improve will never dry up and that organizations who seek to innovate and find new and better ways of doing things are more likely to create differentiation and reduce their costs.

RESEARCH AND DEVELOPMENT AND INNOVATION

In some industries, such as pharmaceuticals (see Case 11.5) research and development, as well as investment in manufacturing technology, is essential for long-term survival and growth. However, Pearson (1988) argues that outstanding companies are consistently innovating in every area of the business, pursuing changes which create value for their customers and consumers. Their approach is to search for new opportunities and package or present them in such a way that they deliver consumer satisfaction. The meaning of innovation is explored in Key Concept 11.1.

Innovation may result from internal developments which arise from research and

---

Case 11.5
MÉRIEUX

After their acquisition in 1989 of Connaught BioSciences (Canada) the French company Mérieux, a subsidiary of Rhône Poulenc, became the world's leading manufacturer of vaccines. They had 32% of the world market when measured by volume rather than value. Some two-thirds of vaccines are bought by UNICEF (United Nations Children's Fund) for distribution in the Third World.

Manufacturers tender for UNICEF orders and prices are critical. For this reason Mérieux argue that any company with less than 20% world market share and the productivity benefits of the experience curve is uncompetitive. However, the leading American manufacturers such as Merck and Lederle tend to avoid such tenders and instead focus on domestic sales, which command dramatically higher prices. The American market represents – in value terms – 40% of world sales. Mérieux compete in America as well as relying on success with UNICEF orders.

Typical of the whole pharmaceutical industry, successful research and new product development is essential for survival and growth. Major benefits should accrue to companies who devise vaccines to counter the still unpreventable diseases such as malaria and particularly AIDS. Consequently, Mérieux spend huge sums (in relation to sales revenue) on R & D, and they have established links with a number of chemical companies in the search for new biotechnological products.

Source: Pavy, D (1991) Vaccine warriors, *Best of Business International*, Spring. Translated from an original article in Dynasteurs, May 1990.

---

development programmes, and from managers and other employees thinking about how activities might be carried out more efficiently or effectively. Innovation may also be driven by outside forces, such as changes in the nature of competition. Nayak (1991) argues that most good ideas do not come from marketing, sales or competitors, but from customers. It is therefore a function of research and development strategies and of the overall strategic awareness of people. In the latter respect it is cultural. In the case of large complex organizations comprising a number of divisions or business units, decisions have to be taken concerning whether research and development is primarily a centralized or a decentralized activity. At the same time, the extent to which authority and responsibility generally is decentralized affects the freedom and willingness of managers to be innovative.

Organizations need strategies for their research and development (R & D) activities because

☐ R & D constitutes an investment for which the appropriate level of funding must be found;

We believe that the continued excellence of our science base is the key to profitable organic growth, and we are prepared to spend significant sums of money on research and development, which is currently running at approximately £1000 per minute.

Sir Denys Henderson, Chairman, ICI plc

Key Concept 11.1
INNOVATION

Innovation takes place when an organization makes a technical change, e.g. produces a product or service which is new to it, or uses a method or input which is new and which is original.

If a direct competitor has already introduced the product or method then it is imitation, not innovation. However, introducing a practice from a different country or industry rather than a direct competitor would constitute innovation.

Innovation implies change and the introduction of something new. Creating the idea, or inventing something, is not innovation but a part of the total process. Whilst at one level it can relate to new or novel products, it may also be related to production processes, approaches to marketing a product or service, or the way jobs are carried out within the organization. The aim is to add value for the consumer or customer by reducing costs or differentiating the product or total service in some sustainable way. In other words, innovation relates to the creation of competitive advantage.

In summary there are four main forms of innovation:

☐ new products, which are either radically new or which extend the product life cycle
☐ process innovation leading to reduced production costs, and affected partially by the learning and experience effect
☐ innovations within the umbrella of marketing, which increase differentiation
☐ organizational changes which reduce costs or improve total quality.

☐ R & D efforts should be directed towards supporting other strategies concerning improvements in products, services and their manufacture and creation, or the development of new products and services to meet future needs.

It is significant that R & D generally in the UK has received lower priority status than is the case for most other major industrialized countries. Statistics show that whilst R & D spending (as a percentage of sales) by UK companies generally increased during the 1980s, it still lags behind comparable figures for America, Germany and Japan. The all-industry averages for 1991 were:

Germany	5.09%
USA	3.80%
Japan	3.71%
UK	1.69%

(*Source*: Company Reporting Ltd)

It is important to allocate R & D funds between *invention* (technical research) and *innovation* (applications in manufacturing and marketing). It has been argued that in many industries, such as electronics, both governments and companies in Europe have concentrated on technical research and failed to exploit the inventions. The more marketing-oriented Japanese companies have therefore been able to establish their strong market positions.

An innovatory firm might identify a segment, logically a substantial one, which they are not reaching and try to establish why those customers are not buying the firm's product or service. The reason might be the product itself or the total service package offered by the organization. From this it might be possible to develop an appropriate version for this segment. Competitive situations are rarely free from change. Proactive

---

Case 11.6
DAIMLER–BENZ

Daimler–Benz comprises four business activities:

☐ Mercedes–Benz (cars and trucks)
☐ AEG (electrical and electronic products)
☐ DASA (aerospace)
☐ DEBIS (financial and information services).

If the potential synergy from these related businesses is to be obtained, research and development skills must be exchanged and shared.

Daimler–Benz has created four separate research institutes for these activities, each with its own head. The concentration is on applications, and projects and targets are defined by R & D in conjunction with marketing and product development staff. This R & D is driven more by markets than by scientists. However, each institute head is also responsible for a 'global corporate task' which crosses all Daimler–Benz's interests. These cover:

☐ information technology
☐ environmental, traffic and energy technology
☐ materials and production technology research and
☐ technology assessment.

The focus here is medium to long term and researchers are working close to the frontiers of discovery. In addition:

☐ There has been an attempt to develop a new and informal culture of helping and sharing. Electronic speedometers, developed by AEG, have been modified for cars.
☐ If one institute has spare time or capacity it will do work for another.
☐ Researchers go on secondments to the operating units to enhance their awareness.
☐ Younger staff are being recruited and links with universities are being strengthened.
☐ Daimler–Benz are looking to establish new research centres in the USA (West coast) and Japan.

---

organizations will seek continually to improve their product and service and innovate ahead of competitors, but they may not always be first with new ideas.

Some companies will deliberately follow, but where this is the chosen strategy the leaders must not be allowed to open up a substantial gap. Successful leaders include G D Searle (NutraSweet), Du Pont (Teflon) and Pilkington with float glass. Significantly

float glass took 7 years to develop, involving 100 000 tonnes of scrapped glass, and 12 years to break even. Successful followers are IBM in personal computers, Seiko (quartz watches) and Matsushita (VHS format video recorders).

Innovation, as both an activity based on research and development and an important organizational value concerned with constantly searching for new opportunities and

Case 11.7
RESEARCH AND DEVELOPMENT IN THE EUROPEAN CHEMICAL INDUSTRY

The four largest chemical companies in Europe are Hoechst, Bayer, BASF and ICI. Hoechst and Bayer each spend some 6% of their sales revenue on R & D; BASF and ICI 4–5%. All four focus their R & D on specialist relatively high value areas, where competition is less strong and where products are sold because they can solve problems, not because they are low cost.

Additionally there is a drive to bring the research results to the finished product and market stage ever more quickly, and in turn this is requiring that research, marketing and operations are all closely linked. Twenty per cent of total research spending is allocated to new long-term developments, with the remaining 80% concentrated on short-term development work with existing products. Linked to this, the research work is frequently decentralized within the organization to ensure that it takes place in the countries where the finished or improved products will be sold. This again emphasizes the need to link research with operations and marketing. 'Research is about teamwork' (Dieter Schorning, Research Manager at Hoechst).

However, these links cause certain problems. Research chemists do not necessarily relate naturally with marketing specialists.

---

ways of doing things differently and better, is clearly linked very closely to total quality management.

The extent to which R & D should be decentralized, and the important linkages with operating divisions, are discussed in Cases 11.6 and 11.7.

Innovation and new products

Innovation can take place in any and every area of the business, but at times it will relate

---

We would rather be a conscious number two than number one by accident.

Bo Berggren, Chief Executive, Stora, Sweden

Either lead, follow or get out of the way.

Raymond G Viault, Chief Executive Officer, Jacobs Suchard, Switzerland

---

specifically to the introduction of a new product or service. New product innovations such as chilled prepared meals (Marks & Spencer), the compact disc (Philips) and the ABS braking system for cars (Bosch) took place in companies with established R & D strategies. As a set of activities major product changes and innovations involve idea generation; idea screening; concept definition; development; testing; trial; and launch. These activities are creative, developmental and analytical. Ideas can arise from talking to customers and researching their requirements, from searching internally for better ways of doing things, and by examining competitor activity. Developing a concept through to a stage of market acceptance is likely to be an incremental iterative process characterized by learning. Creativity is an essential requirement, together with entrepreneurial leadership within the organization to champion the changes involved. This need not be the strategic leader personally, as was pointed out in Chapter 3, but it will be important for the strategic leader to encourage entrepreneurship and provide innovatory managers with the necessary encouragement, support and freedom to implement changes.

Foy and Brady (1989) argue that successful innovation involves success in a least two of the following three elements:

☐ insight into consumer needs
☐ technological advantage
☐ business systems superiority.

Benetton, the Italian manufacturer and retailer of fashion clothing, is offered as an example of a company which

☐ understands consumer needs, especially in terms of colours and styles;
☐ uses technology in production in ways which cut lead times (for example they knit in grey wool and then post-dye the finished garment);
☐ feed back information about retail sales very quickly in order to allow adjustments in production.
(See also case 10.6)

A difficulty for many organizations stems from the fact that different skills are required for developing new businesses and managing major changes, and for running existing businesses with a view to increasing efficiency and effectiveness. When George Davies was sacked in December 1988 as Chairman and Chief Executive of the retailing group Next, an organization that he had created and built out of the Hepworth tailoring company, the argument was that his style of management was inappropriate. Whilst his autocratic style had been useful during the company's rapid growth and fast changes, it was less successful for managing the business that he had developed. Drucker (1985) quotes two examples of strategic leaders who implemented changes to give themselves new roles once their organizations were developed and successful. Edwin Land, who invented the Polaroid camera,

established a senior management team to run the organization, built himself a new laboratory and carried out research work. Ray Kroc, founder of McDonald's, similarly established a senior team and became himself the company's 'marketing conscience', visiting different restaurants all the time and monitoring service levels and customer reactions to both products and service levels.

Businesses which are being run well but not necessarily dynamically may experience the opposite situation. Change may be required as the environment changes, but the organizational culture may be change resistant.

Innovation and entrepreneurship

There is, then, a clear link between entrepreneurship, which was introduced in Chapter 3, and innovation. Drucker (1985) argues that innovation is the tool of entrepreneurs. Entrepreneurship can imply real change along the lines illustrated in Case 11.8, which postulates the change from steel to plastic car bodies; equally it can be a systematic im-

---

A successful business in the textile sector – which is dictated by fashion and therefore has ever shortening product life cycles – means that the Company as a whole has to remain flexible – and that implies almost constant change.

To manage this change successfully one needs a strong core team of specialist managers, who are continually striving for improvement – who aren't afraid of making mistakes, but who can quickly evaluate and refine ideas to accommodate changing external circumstances.

Essential to this are two factors: good inter- and intra-management communication and an almost constant training process.

Lowry Maclean, Chairman and Chief Executive,
Tomkinsons plc

Case 11.8
PLASTIC CAR BODIES

It has been argued that cars with plastic bodies could be in showrooms by the mid-1990s if opportunities which are available are grasped. Assuming that this happens, it will be a clear illustration of strategy changes resulting from innovation.

It has been estimated that plastic bodies would offer cost advantages over pressed steel at volumes over 250 000 units per year. As well as lower tooling costs there would be an added advantage of greater flexibility and the opportunity to offer a great variety of models — clear opportunities for competitive advantage.

The biggest hurdle, which has now been overcome, was the problem of how to dispose of millions of non-biodegradable panels when cars reached the scrapping stage. New thermoplastics, developed by General Electric in America, can be melted down and are fully recyclable. However, as the properties vary with every melting down, the plastic would subsequently have to be put to different uses than cars.

Moreover, substantial research work remains to be done on the behaviour of plastic bodies in crash situations and into long-term resistance to vibration. In summary long-term cost savings are being predicted, but the safety issue cannot be ignored.

Summarized from Griffiths, J (1988) First revs for the volume plastic car, *Financial Times*, 21 August.

---

provement of the way things are done, concentrating on improving total quality and adding new values. On the latter theme Drucker argues that McDonald's and Marks & Spencer have both been successful. The expression entrepreneurship is being used here to describe a culture oriented towards improvement and change, but the term intrapreneurship, introduced in Chapter 3, could be used instead. One advantage of using the word intrapreneurship is that it allows a distinction between the notion of an entrepreneurial culture and the entrepreneurial mode of strategy creation (Mintzberg, 1973) which postulates that strategy creation is very dependent on the contribution of the strategic leader. Intrapreneurship can be an aspect of the adaptive mode of strategic change (Mintzberg, 1973) which concentrates on incremental changes.

Changes in the service provided to customers and the development of new products and services imply changes in operating systems and in the work of employees, and some of the proposed changes may well be the result of ideas generated internally. But, as featured in Box 11.3, many of the ideas for innovations come from outside the organization, from changes in the environment. This emphasizes the crucial importance of linking together marketing and operations and harnessing the contribution of people (Chapter 12). Moreover innovation and change is an investment, and consequently the financial implications, developed in Chapter 13, are also an essential consideration.

To summarize this section, the theme of entrepreneurship is that change is normal but need not involve high risk. Entrepreneurs thrive on uncertainty and are involved in the search for innovatory changes in the ways things are done. Successful entrepreneurs are clear decision makers who take calculated risks rather than high risks. Entrepreneurial

Box 11.3
SOURCES OF INNOVATION

THE UNEXPECTED SOURCE

This could be an unexpected success, failure or outside event. New market segments could emerge, linked perhaps to life-styles, and demand different products. The demand by children for computer games introduced computers into the home, and this pulled the development of home computers.

INCONGRUOUS EVENTS

A perceived difference between what is felt should be happening and what is happening in practice can lead to innovations designed to close the gap. There is an argument that private hospitals grew to fill the gap which existed because patients felt the National Health Service waiting times for minor operations were too long.

INNOVATIONS BASED ON PROCESSES

Colour film was developed to supplement black-and-white, for example. Such innovations are clearly demand-led in that the existing product highlights a need for improvement.

CHANGES IN INDUSTRY AND MARKET STRUCTURES

Self-service supermarkets developed as a result of the abolition of resale price maintenance. Private pension plans are similarly a response to legislation, supported by increased awareness of the realities of retirement.

DEMOGRAPHIC CHANGES

Club Méditerranée capitalized on changing age groups and needs.

CHANGES IN PERCEPTION, MOOD AND MEANING

Pineapple Dance and similar studios were a response to a greater concern with health and fitness. Fast foods and microwaves are linked to changes in eating habits, but in these cases it is harder to discern cause and effect.

NEW KNOWLEDGE; SCIENTIFIC AND NON-SCIENTIFIC

Often thought of as the most likely source – incorrectly – this is invention related, and rarely are inventors the people who succeed with the development of the idea in the marketplace.

THE BRIGHT IDEA

Zips and ballpoint pens are examples of 'bright ideas' – not essential but extremely useful. In a different way the Japanese saw a potential for very small screen black-and-white television sets for kitchen and outdoor use when many regarded black-and-white technology as having been replaced by colour and had written it off.

Developed from Drucker, P F (1985) *Innovation and Entrepreneurship*, Heinemann.

innovative organizations perceive change as an opportunity, not a threat; expectation of change and improvement is part of the culture; employees expect changes and are supportive; and the financial implications are also properly thought through.

If the culture is change resistant rather than change oriented then proposed changes in systems, technology and ways of doing things may be resisted. In this case it will be necessary either to fit the approach to innovation into the existing culture or to seek to change the culture – ideally the latter.

SUMMARY

In this chapter we have considered the important strategic contribution of operations in ensuring that the right product is available at the right time in the right place, produced to the right quality to meet consumer needs satisfactorily, and at a cost that ensures that the organization can earn profits. Operations strategies must be derived from marketing strategies; but in turn operational considerations may constrain marketing.

Specifically we have

☐ emphasized the links between research and development, design, marketing, production and costs
☐ considered the importance of capacity (the relationship between demand and supply at any time), capability (the ability to meet customer and consumer needs and key success factors) and adaptability (flexibility to change)
☐ highlighted the usefulness of variety reduction and analyses of the product range in order to balance customer needs and costs
☐ shown that resource allocation decisions might be linked to product portfolio analysis

☐ emphasized the important contribution of the latest systems and technologies, and mentioned some of the implementation issues
☐ discussed the value of focused manufacturing
☐ looked at service businesses from the point of view of their dependence on people and the problems caused by the transience of many services
☐ emphasized that total quality management is a key organizational value which can contribute significantly towards the achievement of consumer satisfaction and lower costs – the importance of getting things right first time
☐ considered how innovation, linked to quality and entrepreneurship, can be another key value.

CHECKLIST OF KEY TERMS AND CONCEPTS

You should feel confident that you understand the following terms and ideas:

☐ The significance of capacity
☐ Variety reduction and the product range
☐ Just-in-time (JIT) systems
☐ Focused manufacturing
☐ Total quality management.

QUESTIONS AND RESEARCH ASSIGNMENTS

Text related

1. Using Case 11.2 (McDonald's) as a framework, derive the possible marketing and operations strategies for a specialist high quality restaurant located in the country.

2. An airport hotel was built originally to cater for international travellers and airline staff. Recently a decision was made to try and break into the very lucrative conference trade. What changes in the management of operations do you foresee?

   Do a similar analysis for a city general hospital which is introducing a specialist burns unit for the first time.

3. Place the following service businesses on the grid illustrated in Figure 11.1:
   - ☐ A dental practice
   - ☐ A plumber
   - ☐ A haute cuisine restaurant
   - ☐ A taxi service
   - ☐ A zoo
   - ☐ A private school
   - ☐ Refuse collection
   - ☐ A local bus service.

4. Take any product you have bought recently and consider exactly what constitutes quality as far as you as a consumer are concerned. What issues and difficulties will have been encountered in building in that quality?

Library based

5. Take a manufacturing organization of your choice, and determine the range of products produced. What do you feel might be the objectives and tasks of the operations manager (or whatever he or she might actually be called) in this organization? Where do you envisage the manager will encounter most problems? What difficulties might be involved in introducing new products into the organization?

RECOMMENDED FURTHER READING

Introductory text

Wild, R (1980) *Essentials of Production and Operations Management*, Holt, Rinehart and Winston.

Comprehensive basic texts

Hayes, R, Wheelwright, S and Clark, K (1988) *Dynamic Manufacturing*, Free Press.
Hill, T (1991) *Production and Operations Management*, 2nd edn, Prentice-Hall.
Wild, R (1984) *Production and Operations Management. Principles and Techniques*, 3rd edn, Holt, Rinehart and Winston.

Service businesses

Harris, D (1989) *Service Operations Management*, Cassell.
Voss, C, Armistead, C G, Johnston, B and Morris, B (eds) (1985) *Operations Management in the Service Industries and the Public Sector*, Wiley.

Quality

Oakland, J S (1989) *Total Quality Management*, Heinemann.
PA Consultants (1987) *How to Take Part in the Quality Revolution – A Management Guide*, Dr Steve Smith, PA Management Consultants.
Schonberger, R J (1982) *Japanese Manufacturing Techniques. Nine Hidden Lessons in Simplicity*, Free Press.

Innovation

Drucker, P F (1985) *Innovation and Entrepreneurship*, Heinemann.
In addition the following textbook written as a novel provides an excellent illustration of optimized production technology:
Goldratt, E M and Cox, J (1984) *The Goal. Beating the Competition*, Creative Output Books.

REFERENCES

Armistead, C G (1985) In *Operations Management in the Service Industries and the Public Sector* (eds C Voss, C G Armistead, B Johnston and B Morris), Wiley.

Bolwijn, P T and Kumpe, T (1990) Manufacturing in the 1990s – Productivity, flexibility and innovation, *Long Range Planning*, **23** (4), August.

Caulkin, S (1988) Manufacturing excellence. Britain's best factories, *Management Today*. September.

Drucker, P F (1985) *Innovation and Entrepreneurship*, Heinemann.

Foy, P and Brady, C J (1989) Innovation: the challenge for European business in the 1990s, *European Business Journal*, I (1).

Garnett, N (1988) The screw tightens on machine makers, *Financial Times*, 30 September.

Goldratt, E OPT is described in Haylett, R (1986).

Hayes, R H and Wheelwright, S C (1984) *Restoring Our Competitive Edge – Competing Through Manufacturing*, Wiley.

Haylett, R (1986) OPT – Production control with a difference, *Production Engineer*, May.

Hill, T (1991) *Production/Operations Management*, 2nd edn, Prentice Hall.

Kearney, A T (1992) Research findings, quoted in Taylor, P (1992) Such an elusive quality, *Financial Times*, 14 February.

Mintzberg, H (1973) Strategy Making in Three Modes, *California Management Review*, **16**(2), Winter.

Nayak, P R (1991) Technological change (Report), Arthur D Little.

New, C C (1985) Manufacturing in the 1980s. In *Manufacturing Systems. Context, Applications and Techniques* (eds V Bignell, M Dooner, J Hughes, C Pym and S Stone), Blackwell.

New, C C (1988) The strategic challenge for computer integrated manufacturing, Lecture at Huddersfield Polytechnic, 2 March.

PA Consultants (1987) *How to Take Part in the Quality Revolution – A Management Guide*, Dr Steve Smith, PA Management Consultants.

Pearson, E A (1988) Tough minded ways to get innovative, *Harvard Business Review*, May–June.

Peters, T J (1988) *Thriving on Chaos*, Knopf.

Peters, T J and Austin, N (1985) *A Passion for Excellence. The Leadership Difference*, Collins.

Skinner, W. (1974) The focused factory, *Harvard Business Review*, May–June.

Skinner, W (1978) *Manufacturing in the Corporate Strategy*, Wiley.

Wheelwright, S C (1978) Reflecting corporate strategy in manufacturing decisions, *Business Horizons*, February.

Wild, R (1984) *Production and Operations Management. Principles and Techniques*, 3rd edn, Holt, Rinehart and Winston.

PEOPLE AS A STRATEGIC RESOURCE

12

LEARNING OBJECTIVES

After reading this chapter you should be able to

☐ identify a number of important policy areas concerning the effective management of the flow of people into and out of an organization;
☐ describe the various contributions individuals might make to a team and assess the importance of management teams;
☐ explain management by objectives and performance management and discuss how they might be implemented effectively;
☐ evaluate the importance of leadership behaviour by managers;
☐ describe the leadership theory of John Adair.

People are a strategic resource. There is a need for clear strategies for developing managers and for allocating authority and responsibility to them. Management teams and leadership qualities are explored.

INTRODUCTION

Human resources – people – are an essential strategic resource. They are needed to implement strategies and to this end they must understand and share the objectives and values of the organization. They must be committed to the organization and they must work together well. If the organization is complex or decentralized, and operating in a turbulent environment, the strategic leader will rely on people to spot opportunities and threats and to adapt strategies.

It is useful to refer back now to customer orientation, innovation, entrepreneurship, flexibility to change, total quality management and getting things right first time. These were considered in previous chapters. People ultimately determine whether or not competitive advantage is created and sustained. They can be an opportunity and a source of competitive advantage, or they can act as a constraint.

Management should seek to develop people with appropriate skills who can work together effectively. People must be

☐ committed (commitment can be improved);
☐ competent (competences can be developed; and can bring improved product quality and productivity);
☐ cost-effective (ideally costs should be low and performance high, although this does not imply low rewards for success);
☐ in sympathy with the aims of the organization (are the values and expectations of all parties in agreement?).

We shall first consider the way that people are integrated and work together, in particular the flow of people through an organization (recruitment, development and appraisal). We shall also look at team building, motivation and management by objectives. Second, we shall examine leadership in organizations. Leadership will be shown to be a cultural issue affecting how well people are directed and how aware they are of the needs of the organization.

The executives and employees who go to make up a total work force are the most important assets of the company. They always have been and always will be. The real issue is how to maximize the value from those assets and that is why all senior executives irrespective of function have an obligation to contribute to people development at every level.

Unattributed quotation from a manufacturing company director. Taken from Coulson-Thomas, C and Brown, R. (1989) The Responsive Organisation. People Management: The Challenge of the 1990s, *British Institute of Management*

In times of discontinuity and accelerated change, survival depends on flexibility, on our ability to learn to adapt. Organizations which learn fast will survive. Management must take the lead. We must mobilize our greatest asset, our people, invest in their training and orchestrate their talents, skills and expertise. Their commitment, dedication, quality and care will build the competitive advantage of a winning team. Only they can provide our customers with the best product and service in the industry. The management of change takes tenacity, time, talent and training.

*J F A de Soet, President,
KLM Royal Dutch Airlines*

INTEGRATING PEOPLE

Management of the flow of people

It is important to manage the flow of people into, through and out of an organization in order to ensure that there are present, at the times they are needed, the necessary skills to carry out functions such as production, marketing and financial control. Flow management requires recruitment policies, training and development, performance appraisal, promotion policies, termination policies and reward systems. These determine the quality and quantity of the labour force, and strongly influence the interest that employees have in the organization and their commitment to it.

Strategic issues

There is a definite link between strategic change and people, because if the requisite skills are not present proposed changes to strategies may be constrained. Equally, particular skills may be a source of competitive advantage and strategic changes. Organizations which are growing quickly may find they are short of key people; firms who are experiencing decline in certain markets or with certain products must find alternative ways of using their people or make them redundant. Organizations experiencing stability may find it difficult to retain and reward people who want the challenge of change and growth. Acquisitions often bring problems, particularly as different cultures may be involved (this will be explored further in Chapter 18). Because strategic changes may be allowed or constrained by people it is important to ensure that people are developed to be ready for, and committed to, change.

The recruitment of new people into an organization should also be viewed strategically. Potential contributions in both the short term and the longer term should be assessed, and people who will fit into the organization and its values preferred. It is particularly useful to consider contributions to the organization as a whole rather than a particular area of expertise, and this issue will be explored further at the end of this chapter. The development needs of new employees should be assessed and dealt with if they are to make an effective strategic contribution.

In the 1990s the flow of people will become an increasingly significant issue for certain organizations, particularly those which rely on recruiting young people and school leavers on a regular basis. The decline in the UK birth rate between the early 1960s and the mid-1970s has resulted in a reduction in the numbers of young people aged 16–19. In the early 1980s there were 3.75 million people in this age group, but the figure falls to 3 million in 1990 and 2.5 million in 1994 before it starts rising again. Organizations like the National Health Service, the Civil Service, financial service organizations and retailers, all of whom have recruited young people in large numbers, are having to change their strategies and policies concerning recruitment. Older people, with different reward and development needs, will be relied upon more; and there will be increased opportunities for people, especially women, who break their careers to return to their previous jobs.

Understanding and developing managerial skills and competences

Skapinker (1989) highlights the importance for an organization of understanding the particular skills and competences that managers have. The argument is not that all managers should be good at everything but that the appropriate skills for the post held should be present. Where there are weaknesses, development and training should be utilized. To this end, according to Skapinker, Cadbury Schweppes appraise their managers in terms of 50 skills and competences, broken down into six groups: strategy, drive, influence, analysis, implementation, and personal factors.

Examples of the competences are as follows.

□ **Strategy**: the ability to think critically and to challenge conventional wisdom; environmental awareness, being well informed on the economic, social and political environment in which the business operates.
□ **Drive**: self-motivation.
□ **Influence**: the ability to communicate, both verbally and in writing; the ability to develop subordinates.
□ **Analysis**: being able to draw out information during meetings with colleagues; the ability to analyse, organize and present numerical data.
□ **Implementation**: the ability to understand

There is a simple rule for success in business: get the people you need in the right numbers with the right skills and competencies to do the job.

Sir Bob Reid, Chairman, British Railways Board

the impact of decisions on other parts of the organization.

☐ **Personal factors**: readiness to take unpopular or difficult decisions.

Performance appraisal

Tyson and York (1982) emphasize the need for regular and properly conducted performance appraisals as part of a programme of management development, in order to

☐ help determine the suitability of people for particular jobs and positions (this should include the present job and possible future posts);
☐ determine development needs;
☐ identify a readiness for promotion;
☐ contribute to the development of motivation and commitment by feeding back an evaluation of performance;
☐ provide a basis for the allocation of rewards.

If performance appraisals are to achieve the above objectives, and thereby contribute to the development of human resources in readiness for future changes, it is important that they are carried out conscientiously. It is easy not to do them well. The climate should be one of openness and honesty, with feelings expressed and explored; and the person being appraised should feel that the appraisal is fair. Future needs and preferences should be discussed and decisions concerning rewards, training and development followed through. Appraisals can be carried out by either line managers, a person's departmental or divisional head or personnel specialists.

Although performance appraisal, development and training will focus on individual managers, they should take place within the context of the current and future strategic needs of the organization. For example, in a diversified organization with a portfolio of distinct businesses, some of which may be mature cash generators and others invest-ment hungry future stars [see Chapters 10 and 16 for further details on portfolio analysis], the required managerial skills and contributions will vary between the businesses. Development programmes might well be based upon the strategic needs of the businesses rather than, say, general courses for different levels of manager in the organization, irrespective of the particular business area in which they work, or special courses for identified 'high flyers'. However, the parallel need to develop managers who can be flexible and change jobs within the organization (changing function, division or country) must not be overlooked – especially as firms become more European or global in scope.

Rewards

Rewards are an important motivator, but it is important to appreciate that an individual

---

Sooner or later you'll hear about someone who made a decision that you think was very good in terms of the company's strategy. When you do, make sure you give that person many strokes, and do it as officially as possible, so other people will learn from it. A positive example is the best way to create the right atmosphere.

Of course, if you think someone made a wrong decision, let him know, but tell him when you are alone – and don't let him view it as a punishment.

Over time you give people the security to take responsibility by measuring and rewarding performance. For a year or two you can motivate people through emotion and show biz, but, for the long run, people must know they will be measured in an accurate way in relation to the responsibility they have been given.

Jan Carlzon, President and Chief Executive Officer, Scandinavian Airlines System

---

may feel rewarded by things other than money or promotion. The demands and responsibilities of a job, and the freedom people are given to decide how to do things, can be rewarding. Additionally, working with a particular group of people, especially if they are seen to be successful, can be rewarding. If people feel that their efforts are being rewarded and that future efforts will also be rewarded, their quality of work is likely to improve. In this way total quality can be improved. Moreover where incremental strategic change is dependent upon individual managers seeing, and acting upon, opportunities and threats, the reward system must be appropriate and motivating. The issue of rewards is discussed again in Chapter 23.

Succession issues

Succession problems can concern both strategic leadership and managerial positions throughout the organization. Small firms whose growth and success have been dependent upon one person, most probably the founder, often experience problems when he or she retires, especially where there has been a failure to develop a successor in readiness. Some very large organizations also experience problems when particularly charismatic and influential strategic leaders resign or retire. Although they may be replaced by other strong leaders there may be changes to either or both the strategy or culture which do not prove successful. An example often quoted is Harold Geneen who developed ITT of America into one of the world's largest firms. When he retired profits fell and the company experienced a relative decline, and this resulted in comments that despite its size the success of ITT was very dependent upon one man.

However, succession problems can be seen with key people in any specialism and at any level of the organization. Firms need management in depth in order to cope with

growth and with people leaving or being promoted. This implies that people are being developed constantly in line with, and in readiness for, strategic change; and this relates back to appraisal and reward systems. ICI, for example, deliberately move managers between countries and product groups as part of their management planning. This, they claim, opens the company up to 'different ideas and outside perceptions'.

The management of the flow of people, and their development, relates to ensuring that people with the necessary skills are recruited, trained and available in relation to the managerial and other tasks which have to be carried out. However, it is also necessary that people are motivated and integrated if their performance is to be effective. One aspect of this is the issue of evaluating and building working teams, which is examined below. Management teams should be evaluated for their effectiveness and any weaknesses should be remedied, but team working can prove valuable everywhere in the organization. Case 12.1, Volvo's Kalmar Plant, which is presented later, illustrates this point.

Team-building

Both formal and informal teams exist within organizations. Formal teams comprise sections or departments of people who work directly together on a continuous basis and in pursuit of particular specified objectives, and teams of senior managers who meet on a regular basis with an agreed agenda. Informal teams can relate to managers from different departments, or even divisions, who agree informally to meet to discuss and deal with a particular issue, or who are charged with forming a temporary group to handle an organization-wide problem. In both cases relationships determine effectiveness. Ideally all members will contribute and support each other, and synergy will result from their interactions. Simply putting a group of people together in a meeting, however, does not ensure that they will necessarily work well together and form an effective and successful team.

A successful team needs:

☐ shared and agreed objectives;
☐ a working language, or effective communications;
☐ the ability to manage both the tasks and the relationships.

Cummings (1981) contends that individual contributions to the overall team effort are determined by personal growth needs (for achievement and personal development) and social needs – perceived benefits from working with others to complete tasks, rather than working alone.

Within any team, therefore, there will be a variety of skills, abilities and commitments. Some people will be natural hard workers who need little supervision or external motivation; others, who may be diligent and committed, may need all aspects of their task spelt out clearly; the major contribution of particular members might be in terms of their creativity and ideas. Meredith Belbin (1981) argues that a good team of people will have compensating strengths and weaknesses, and that as a group they will be able to perform a series of necessary and related tasks. Specifically they will

☐ create useful ideas;
☐ analyse problems effectively;
☐ get things done;
☐ communicate effectively;
☐ have leadership qualities;

Table 12.1 Team members – their skills and contributions

Team members	Their skills and contributions
Chairperson/team leader	The organizer of other members' efforts. Ideally he or she knows and uses their strengths. Not necessarily an ideas-person.
Shaper	Keen to find resolutions to problems and new ways of doing things – often developing and questioning other people's ideas. Naturally competitive, pragmatic, energetic and enthusiastic.
Plant	The intelligent and creative ideas person. Often better at concepts than detail. Inputs may be random and likely to involve changes of direction in the discussions.
Company worker	An organizer who is good at implementation. Unlikely to be creative or innovative.
Resource investigator	The sociable extrovert who is good at making and developing contacts and following up ideas.
Monitor evaluator	The solid and reliable analyst. Unlikely to contribute anything really original, but will evaluate the implications of alternative choices.
Team worker	The 'people-person', concerned with ensuring that the team works together cohesively and that members are involved. Will develop ideas and bring in quiet people to ensure that their potential contributions are not lost.
Finisher	The person who is good at detail and works well with systems. Contributes mostly to implementation and ensures that any necessary paperwork is properly completed. Disciplined and ordered and keen to prevent anything going wrong.
Specialist	The person who inputs technical or other expertise about products, services or systems. Dedicated and knowledgeable but likely to take a very narrow perspective.

Developed by the author from ideas contained in: Belbin, R M, *Management Teams – Why They Succeed or Fail*, Heinemann, 1981.

☐ evaluate problems and options logically;
☐ handle the technical aspects;
☐ control their work; and
☐ report back effectively either verbally or in writing.

Belbin has identified a number of characteristics or contributions which individuals make to teams. These are summarized in Table 12.1. They relate to the provision of ideas, leadership, the resolution of conflict, the gathering and analysing of data and information, carrying out certain detailed work which might be regarded as boring by certain members, organizing people to make their most useful contributions, and developing relationships within the group. Individuals will obviously contribute in a number of areas, not just one or two, but they will often be particularly strong in some and weak in others. A balance is required if the team is to work well together and complete the task satisfactorily.

Whoever is responsible for leading the team – it might be the strategic leader and his or her team of senior managers, or department managers – should consider the various strengths and weaknesses of people and seek to develop them into an effective and cohesive team. If any essential areas of contribution are missing this should be dealt with; and any potential conflicts of strong personalities, say if a number of shapers are present, should be determined early. If the team is effective, the individual members will respect each other for their different and particular contributions, and key values will be shared. Ideally these values will be synonymous with those that the organization considers to be strategically important.

In considering which managers might be appropriate for a particular informal team, an analysis along the lines of Belbin's classification can be useful for determining the appropriate balance. In addition the skills and competences listed earlier in the chapter might also prove valuable.

Involving and motivating people

If people are to be committed to the organization, and to the achievement of key objectives, they must be involved. Employees at the so-called grass roots level are likely to know the details of the business and what really happens better than their superiors and managers. If they are involved and encouraged to contribute their ideas for improvements, the result can be innovation or quality improvement.

Moreover, if managers and other employees are to make effective strategic contributions it is important that they feel motivated. Whilst money and position in the organization can motivate, there are other essential factors. Hertzberg (1968) emphasized the importance of the following:

☐ the potential to contribute and achieve through the job
☐ recognition for effort and success
☐ promotion opportunities
☐ interesting work
☐ responsibility.

Box 12.1 includes an extended list of ways in which managers can seek to motivate employees. In summary it is important to ensure that:

☐ jobs are interesting, challenging and demanding (Case 12.1, Volvo's Kalmar Plant, illustrates the benefits that can arise from jobs being made more interesting and employees being given wider responsibilities);
☐ people know what is expected of them and when they are meeting expectations;
☐ rewards and sanctions are clearly linked to effort and results.

David McClelland (McClelland and Winter, 1971) emphasizes the importance of knowing colleagues and subordinates and understanding what does in fact motivate them. He contends that people have three needs in varying proportions – achievement, power and affiliation – and individual profiles of

Box 12.1
MOTIVATING EMPLOYEES

A manager should

- ☐ know his or her staff individually, their strengths and weaknesses, and what is happening to them;
- ☐ know what interests them, outside work as well as at work;
- ☐ provide increasingly more challenging opportunities, possibly by delegating more and more, but be aware when people are stretched; employees should be encouraged to use their strengths, and their weaknesses should be covered;
- ☐ develop and train people in a variety of appropriate ways, particularly where they are weak;
- ☐ agree objectives and targets with people;
- ☐ recognize good performance immediately and during appraisal interviews;

- ☐ make sure their efforts are recognized throughout the organization;
- ☐ criticize poor performance immediately but in a positive manner; employees should feel sanctioned but encouraged to do better;
- ☐ ensure rewards are appropriate in relation to effort and performance;
- ☐ keep employees well informed and wherever appropriate involve them in decision making;
- ☐ invite people to discuss how they could improve their job and performance levels and encourage them to do this;
- ☐ make sure people are aware that they have a personal responsibility to be positive and to look for ways of improving both productivity and quality.

the balance between these needs vary. He argues that managers should attempt to understand how much their subordinates desire power, look for opportunities where they can achieve, and want close or friendly working relationships, manifested, say, by not working in isolation. If managers then seek to meet these needs, subordinates can and will be motivated.

Management by objectives

Hersey and Blanchard (1982) contend that organizational success and performance is

affected by the congruence between the objectives of managers and those of their subordinates. They argue that the organization can only accomplish its objectives if those of managers and subordinates are supportive of each other and of the organization. Moreover, McGregor (1960) has argued that people need objectives to direct their efforts, and that if objectives are not provided by the organization they will create their own. This may not necessarily be disadvantageous for the organization as Schein (1983) has suggested that managers are generally oriented towards economic goals and see profit as being important. But personal objectives, which were discussed in Chapter 5, are likely to be allowed more freedom if managers are not given clear objectives. Porter *et al.* (1975) contend that individual behaviour is affected by people's perceptions of what is expected of them; and hence it

---

Where people grow, profits grow.

Dr Alex Krauer, Chairman and Managing Director, Ciba-Geigy

Case 12.1
VOLVO'S KALMAR PLANT

In June 1974 Volvo opened a new and radically different car assembly plant at Kalmar in Sweden. Instead of the more traditional assembly system, whereby vehicles are assembled whilst they are moving along a production line and each employee performs the same task repetitively at a fixed position, Kalmar initially featured stationary work areas. Partially built cars were transported on computer-controlled pods along 'railway lines' to work stations, where groups of 15 to 20 workers (there are 30 teams in the factory) performed a number of tasks, agreeing amongst themselves who would do what. The employees could rest in specially designed rest areas whenever they wished, as long as certain agreed daily production targets were met. There were problems with this approach, particularly with missed deadlines and scheduling, and consequently it was revised so that the teams perform a series of tasks at a number of work stations but the cars keep moving all the time. Workers therefore enjoy greater responsibility and jobs can be rotated. The factory cost some 10% more than a traditional factory to build and the aim was to reduce the high labour turnover and absenteeism present in Volvo's other assembly plants.

The early years saw productivity levels roughly the same as in other plants, but with extra training required for employees. Quality was not as high as anticipated, but absenteeism and labour turnover were reduced.

Between 1977 and 1983 the production time per car fell by 40%, the number of quality defects was reduced by 39%, uptime was increased from 96% to 99% and stock turnover was increased from nine times per year to 21, thereby providing additional working capital. Labour turnover was reduced from 25% to 5%, but this was partly due to changing economic conditions, and absenteeism remained high by international standards. Volvo found they needed fewer supervisors and that production flexibility was much higher. As a result, a number of the lessons have been applied in their other plants.

As a result of the recession and a need for Volvo to rationalize production, the Kalmar plant was threatened with closure late in 1992.

Sources: 'The Volvo experiment ten years on', *Financial Times, 19 April 1985*; 'Letter from Kalmar', *Management Today*, June 1988.

---

could be argued that objectives pursued by managers will be dependent on

☐ personal motives;
☐ their understanding and perception of what the strategic leader and their colleagues expect them to contribute (expectations, although still subject to some interpretation, may or may not be made clear to managers);

☐ the culture of the organization.

Management by objectives (MBO) is one useful method of seeking individual manager commitment to the objectives of the organization and providing managers with clearly stated expectations. In simple terms managers are encouraged to agree individual objectives which can be seen to contribute to the attainment of departmental and functional objectives, which in turn can be shown as contributing towards competitive and corporate strategies.

In the early MBO systems (many of which were marketed as off-the-shelf packages) there was a tendency to see the organization as a set of discrete parts, and analyse their separate contributions, rather than take a more corporate and systemic perspective, and encapsulate issues of synergy and interdependence. Greater awareness of how individual efforts are making a corporate and strategic contribution allows people to place their jobs in a wider perspective, and consequently their decisions, particularly those which contribute to strategic changes, should take account of the implications for other parts and functions in the organization. Whilst MBO is fundamentally a system for breaking strategies down into achievable manageable parts and objectives, it also helps managers understand where the organization is aiming to go, and how it intends to get there.

Odiorne (1979) argues that MBO is a philosophy of management rather than simply a technique, and is valuable for developing competences and integrating the efforts of different managers in an open visible way. MBO:

□ defines objectives for individual managers, **which they agree**;
□ measures performance against these agreed objectives; and then
□ uses these measures to modify and redefine future objectives.

It is most likely that the formal review will be conducted on an annual basis, but performance should be monitored constantly and where necessary adjustments should be made. MBO can be linked into both reward systems and management development programmes.

Objectives are spread downwards from the strategic leader in a contributory vertical hierarchy throughout the organization, such that jobs and objectives are fed into a clear framework. Drucker (1974) emphasizes the value of also including contributions that managers should make to other managers horizontally throughout the organization, together with contributions that they can expect from their colleagues. In this way the functions can be integrated more effectively.

If MBO is to work effectively, Odiorne contends that the objectives and targets should be high enough to be challenging, but still attainable. They should be measurable so that performance can be assessed objectively, and they must be agreed with managers, not forced on them. If people appreciate their objectives together with those of their colleagues and bosses, they will have a clearer picture of the strategies of the organization. Under-performance and over-performance should be analysed thoroughly, and evaluated, before new targets are agreed.

However, there are drawbacks in the implementation of MBO, as Litterer (1973) and Golde (1976) point out. A number of the highest level objectives may be non-specific and therefore difficult to quantify, and hence difficulties can be encountered in being absolutely specific concerning the targets and objectives for individual managers. This can be especially difficult where several managers contribute towards the attainment of particular objectives. In some organizations certain targets may be set by managers who are

---

Purpose demands effective arrangements to fulfil it. But management without a firm sense of purpose is pointless. Structures are inanimate. By themselves they achieve nothing. Motivation is the key and motivation depends upon clear objectives. In the voluntary sector these are at least as much about values as they are about material goals. We are about the fight for a creative, caring, compassionate society – the fight back for civilization, no less.

Frank Judd, Director, Oxfam

distanced from the actual situation. Moreover it is likely that personal objectives, which were discussed in Chapter 5, will be excluded, and consequently MBO may not prove to be motivational. Finally a key premise of MBO is that objectives agreed with individual managers are all contributory stepping stones to the central organizational objectives, but managers may be tempted to see them as ends in themselves. This implies taking a narrow functional view of the organization rather than the desired corporate perspective.

In summary, although MBO has its limitations it can be very useful for increasing strategic awareness. However, as we have discussed earlier, strategic change may not necessarily be directed to specific objectives; instead both change and attained objectives can be the outcome of a response to a perceived threat or opportunity, with managers allowed the appropriate freedom to make these changes. In Chapter 3 the 'muddling through' theory of Lindblom (1959) and incrementalism, developed by James Quinn (1980), were discussed, and they both support this contention.

Finally Wrapp (1967) has claimed that skilful managers do not make policy decisions but rather 'wheel and deal without much attention to goals, strategies, performance measures and the like'. Wrapp suggests that MBO may be feasible at the lower levels of management but it becomes unworkable at the higher levels. Strategic leaders may feel it necessary on occasions to withhold certain objectives and strategies from other managers in the organization.

Later in this chapter the need for managers to exercise leadership is discussed. This links to the needs for innovation and entrepreneurship discussed in Chapter 11. Whilst MBO can generate greater awareness and understanding, which might allow managers to exercise greater entrepreneurship, innovation and leadership, the more specific the objectives they are given, the less freedom they may have to change things in the light of environmental opportunities and threats. The need of individual managers for clear objectives and direction must therefore be balanced with the organization's need for managers to exercise both flexibility and behaviour which is supportive of organizational objectives. Given this, MBO should be used and implemented with some caution. Performance appraisal and reward systems were discussed briefly earlier, and these can be very useful in support of MBO to achieve the appropriate link between individual and organizational needs.

Performance management

As a result of these various limitations the original packaged MBO systems have not been applied widely in organizations. The ideas behind MBO, however, are still important and they have been customized to suit individual companies. An alternative, and related, approach, performance management, is gaining in popularity.

Fowler (1990) stresses that performance management systems (PMS) share many common features with MBO, but start with a definition and clarification of the organization's mission, long-term objectives and corporate values, followed by the **strategic** contributions to be made by divisions and departments. Qualitative performance indicators, such as customer attitude and opinion surveys, are recognized alongside quantifiable targets and measures. In addition, there is an attempt to make performance measurement an on-going activity rather than an annual review.

Whilst it was generally envisaged that MBO would be linked to rewards and development programmes, these are integral within PMS. Discussions on results and performance are followed by:

☐ salary reviews;
☐ an assessment of individual strengths and areas for improvement;

☐ an agreed action plan for future development;

☐ on- and off-the-job training.

MANAGEMENT AND LEADERSHIP

We have referred to the ideal human resource
strategies which integrate people and help
develop organization-wide strategic awareness earlier in this chapter. Paul Marginson *et
al.* (1988) of Warwick University report that
'most large UK-owned companies have not
developed a strategic, integrated approach to
employee relations'. Of the companies in the
Warwick research programme that claimed to
have an employee relations strategy, Marginson *et al.* report, only half have a written
strategy and only a quarter inform employees
of the strategy.

As well as integrating managerial efforts it
is also important to consider what approach
managers take to their jobs and towards
innovation and opportunities for change and
improvement. Mintzberg (1975) contends
that managers do not spend a great deal of
their working time planning work. Rather,
they respond to situations and needs as they
arise. Time management is vital for them and
most tasks take only a limited amount of time
each. Although information is available and
mostly obtained informally, emphasizing the
value of close working relationships and
team development, judgement and intuition
are vital. It therefore follows that underlying
values and general strategic awareness are
likely to be vital considerations and significant influences on the decisions they reach.

Zaleznik (1977) develops this theme
further, suggesting that management is
basically about problem solving, producing
results, and controlling tasks in complex
organizations. Leadership, he argues, is
about managing the work other people do,
and involves organizing people and delegating tasks. Zaleznik contends that managers
should ideally exercise leadership qualities.

Managers who fail to exercise leadership will
aim to preserve the status quo and not
change things; managers who are leaders
are likely to be more effective in changing
behaviour patterns. It follows that constant
innovation, entrepreneurship and quality
improvement are more likely to happen
where managers, both at the strategic leader
level and throughout the organization, exercise leadership qualities. Kotter (1990)
expresses the distinction slightly differently,
arguing that management is concerned with
coping with complexity and achieving order
and consistency, whilst leadership is about
coping with change. Organizations need to
do both. Kotter says that ideally individual
managers will be able to achieve both, but
recognizes that only some are able to. This is
not material as long as the organization can
build an effective team with both managerial
and leadership skills. What, then, are leadership qualities, and how might they be manifested?

Selected theories of leadership

Trait theories

Early theories of leadership, dating from the
beginning of this century, concentrated on

A **real manager** has to be a good leader in the
sense that he has to embody an open-minded
attitude of leadership in himself, in his fellow
managers and even in the heads of each
employee of his organization. **Leadership**,
therefore, means to enable and help people
to act as individual entrepreneurs within the
frame of a commonly born vision of the
business. A **bad manager**, on the other hand,
is more an administrator who follows severe
rules and customs within a stiff bureaucrat-
ical hierarchy.

*Dr Hugo M Sekyra, CEO and Chairman,
Austrian Industries*

trying to determine whether leaders are born rather than made, and whether they have common personal characteristics. These were known as trait theories. Very few common factors have come to light, but Adair (1983) contends that trait theories are not moribund. Leaders need certain qualities such as charisma, integrity, enthusiasm, toughness, fairness and possibly a sense of humour (their value and importance depending on circumstances), even though these are not the qualities which make them a leader.

Situational theories

Situational theories argue that there is no such thing as a born leader; it all depends upon the situation. Quite simply a person may be a leader in one situation but not in another. Churchill, for example, was a far more successful leader in wartime than he was in peacetime.

Leadership requires three kinds of authority or sources of power: authority of position; authority of personality; and authority of knowledge. Some situational leadership theories concentrate on the last of these, playing down the importance of the other two, and this is regarded as a limiting factor in their usefulness. Some situational leaders who do rely heavily on knowledge may prove to be insufficiently flexible to change pressures.

Hersey and Blanchard (1982) argue that:

☐ the appropriate style of leadership depends upon the relative strengths and maturity of the 'followers';
☐ as followers become more experienced there should be increased participation and delegation;
☐ when this happens the leader will rely less on reward, coercive and legitimate power and more on personal, expert, information and connection power (see Chapters 3 and 24).

Action-centred leadership

As we have seen, the effective management of human resources involves

☐ looking after their interests and motives, allowing them to develop
☐ the accomplishment of the necessary tasks
☐ the building of management and other working teams so that jobs and expertise can be shared.

Task achievement is important for contributing to the attainment of strategic objectives, but it is also useful for developing morale. A sense of achievement and success can be valuable for motivating people and encouraging greater commitment. Where individuals feel that they have opportunities to achieve and develop and that they belong to organizations their contributions are likely to be more valuable strategically. Effective teams can generate synergy as individuals bring and share their different skills and expertise. Action-centred leadership, developed by John Adair (1983), is based on the premise that effective leadership requires a bonding of the task, team and individual needs. It is important to achieve tasks, build teams and develop individuals at every level of the organization if the company is to be flexible, reactive to environmental threats and opportunities, and at times proactive in innovating, improving quality and developing new competitive advantage. Without such leadership, Adair contends, there is a tendency for organizations to remain static. (See Figure 12.1.)

Developing leadership qualities

Peters and Austin (1985) have suggested that leadership involves vision, enthusiasm, passion and consistency, and that these qualities should be evident throughout the organiza-

Function	Task	Team	Individual
Set objectives	Identify resources and constraints and clarify tasks	Assemble and involve team in assigning responsibilities	Involve everyone in discussion
Plan	Consider options Establish priorities and time scales	Consult Encourage ideas Seek agreement	Involve and listen Assess contributions Agree targets and responsibilities
Organize	Brief the plan Establish control mechanisms	Structure, prepare and train	Check understanding Encourage
Control and support	Maintain standards Keep people informed of progress Adjust plan if necessary Lead by example	Co-ordinate Reconcile any conflicts	Recognize effort and success Counsel Encourage
Review and evaluate	Check results against objectives Consider future action	Recognize team's successes Learn from setbacks	Appraise individual performance Assess development needs

Figure 12.1   John Adair: action centred leadership. Developed from Adair, J (1983) *Effective Leadership: A Modern Guide to Developing Leadership Skills*, Pan. Originally published by Gower (1983). Copyright (1983), Gower. Reproduced by permission.

tion. Such leadership is accomplished and demonstrated through the following.

□ **Caring for customers and constant innovation**: Awareness of needs is increased by seeing and listening to customers and, where possible, consumers, and monitoring competitors. Innovation is the result of being constantly adaptive to these needs and competitive pressures.

□ **People**: Quality comes from employees; it is not a technique. Managers should talk to employees, solicit their ideas, listen to their contributions, encourage their greater involvement in decisions and their implementation, find out what motivates them, and counsel and generally encourage them.

Successful companies are often innovative

Box 12.2
HARD VERSUS SOFT HUMAN RESOURCE MANAGEMENT

Hard HRM assumes:

☐ people are viewed as a resource, and, like all resources, companies gain competitive advantage by using them efficiently and effectively;
☐ the deployment and development of employees – who are essentially there to implement corporate and competitive strategies – is delegated to line managers who are responsible for groups of people;
☐ scientific management principles and systems can be useful but should be used cautiously.

Soft HRM assumes:

☐ workers are most productive if they are committed to the company, informed about its mission, strategies and current levels of success; and

☐ involved in teams which collectively decide how things are to be done;
☐ employees have to be trusted to take the right decisions rather than be controlled at every stage by managers above them.

Soft HRM argues that people are different from other resources (and often more costly), but they can create added value and **sustainable** competitive advantage from the other resources. Therefore, soft HRM places greater emphasis on control through review and evaluation of outcomes, such that employees are led rather than managed.

The extent to which organizations take a hard or a soft approach will partially determine the involvement of people in strategy formulation. This is explored further in Chapter 16.

---

and deliver total quality by involving the whole workforce. Many such organizations, jobs and people have been made more flexible through decentralization. One critical issue concerns empowerment, and exactly where and how individual managers should be free to introduce changes. Major retailers, for example, now rely heavily on information technology to help determine the layout and detailed stock levels for each of their stores, and these decisions are substantially centralized rather than devolved to individual branch managers. However, branch managers can be given responsibility for the deployment and handling of the branch staff, and the staff as a whole can be trained intensively in customer service. In general terms, organizations must decide how hard or how soft their human resource strategies should be. See Box 12.2.

Peters and Austin (1985) use the expression 'management by wandering around (MBWA)' to emphasize the importance of keeping in touch with customers, people and opportunities to innovate.

Charles Handy (1989) argues that leadership must become endemic and fashionable, not exceptional, amongst managers. He defines a leader as someone 'who shapes and shares a vision which gives point to the work of others', and contends that:

☐ the vision must be different from what everyone else is doing;
☐ it must be clear, understandable, and capable of making a vivid impression;
☐ it must make sense to people, and relate to the work they do;
☐ the leader must 'live the vision' and be seen to believe in it;

☐ the leader must develop a team of people who share the vision and who are committed to its achievement.

Developing the contentions of Peters and Austin, Kotter, Charles Handy and John Adair, it becomes apparent that it is necessary for organizations, and strategic leaders in particular, to ensure that their managers are capable of being leaders. This involves:

☐ recruiting people with leadership potential;
☐ giving people challenges which involve taking measured risks, especially in the early stages of their managerial careers – success should be rewarded and failure should used as a basis for learning. This should contribute to the development of a change-oriented 'learning organization' which succeeds in keeping up with, or ahead of, changes in its environment;
☐ job switching between functions, divisions and countries to broaden people's perspectives. (The international aspects of human resources strategy are discussed in Chapter 17.)

Otherwise managers often tend to specialize in one particular area, say marketing, production, finance or information technology, and, helped by their functional training, they develop expertise. Adair argues that effective action-centred leadership requires that managers also develop skills and expertise in problem solving, decision making, creative thinking, listening and communicating. Organizations must address these needs if managers are to exercise leadership and thereby make more effective strategic contributions.

Tex Smiley (1988) of the International Management Institute of Geneva uses the expression 'blurred boundary management' to refer to the need for managers to be developed so that they can operate successfully across both functional and geographic boundaries, as well as within their natural specialisms. Smiley explains that this implies changes to both organization structures and cultures – thinking outside specialist areas should be seen as an important value.

SUMMARY

This chapter has been based on the premise that people are an essential strategic resource. Through quality, innovation, entrepreneurship and leadership they can create and sustain competitive advantage. Equally, a shortage of skills and expertise can constrain an organization strategically. Consequently the key issues of integrating and leading human resources have been considered.

Specifically we have

☐ looked at the strategic significance of the flow of people into, through and out of an organization, emphasizing the importance of appropriate recruitment, development, appraisal, reward and succession policies;
☐ considered the importance of effective management and working teams, and the characteristics and behaviour patterns of different team members;
☐ discussed the need for people to be motivated, and the potential contribution of management by objectives to the attainment of strategic objectives;
☐ highlighted the strategic value of managers exercising leadership characteristics and behaviour, and discussed what these might be and how they might be applied;
☐ considered the contribution of Adair (action-centred leadership) to an understanding of leadership behaviour;
☐ mentioned that leadership qualities must be developed in managers, and suggested that this is again an issue of organizational culture.

CHECKLIST OF KEY TERMS AND CONCEPTS

You should feel confident that you understand the following terms and ideas:

☐ Belbin's work on the characteristics of team members
☐ Management by objectives
☐ Performance management
☐ Action-centred leadership.

QUESTIONS AND ASSIGNMENTS

Text related

1. Consider how strategic changes in the retail sector, from an emphasis on hardware stores that specialize in personal service and expert advice to customers from all employees, to a predominance of do-it-yourself supermarkets, might have affected issues of staff motivation, personal development needs and appropriate reward systems.

2. Albeit by rule of thumb, take a team of people with whom you associate closely and evaluate their behaviour characteristics against Belbin's categories.
   Where is the team strong? Weak?
   Do you believe it is balanced?
   If not, what might be done to change things?

Activity based

3. Observe a discussion or decision situation involving a leader and a group of subordinates. This need not be in an organizational setting – it could involve a group of scouts or guides or something similar.

Evaluate the leader's behaviour in terms of task accomplishment, team involvement and the development of individuals.

RECOMMENDED FURTHER READING

Introductory text

Hunt, J (1979) *Managing People at Work*, McGraw-Hill (available in paperback, Pan, 1981).

Blanchard, K and Johnson, S (1983) *The One Minute Manager*, Collins, 1983 (the original US edition was published by Morrow, 1982, and a paperback edition was published by Fontana in 1983). In addition there are two companion volumes by Blanchard *et al.*: *Putting the One Minute Manager to Work* and *Leadership and the One Minute Manager*.

Comprehensive basic texts

Buchanan, D and Huczynski, A A (1991) *Organisational Behaviour: An Introductory Text*, 2nd edn, Prentice-Hall.

Kakabadse, A, Ludlow, R and Vinnicombe, S (1987) *Working in Organizations*, Gower.

Team building

Belbin, R M (1981) *Management Teams – Why They Succeed or Fail*, Heinemann.

Management by objectives

Odiorne, G (1979) *MBO 11*, Pitman.

Leadership

Adair, J (1983) *Effective Leadership: A Modern Guide to Developing Leadership Skills*, Pan. (Although this paperback is recommended, John Adair has written over 20 books on leadership.)

Fiedler, F (1967) *A Theory of Leadership Effectiveness*, McGraw-Hill.

Hersey, P and Blanchard, K (1982) *The Management of Organisational Behaviour*, 4th edn, Prentice Hall.

REFERENCES

Adair, J (1983) *Effective Leadership: A Modern Guide to Developing Leadership Skills*, Pan.

Belbin, R M (1981) *Management Terms: Why They Succeed or Fail*, Heinemann.

Cummings, T G (1981) Designing effective work groups. In *Handbook of Organisational Design* (eds P C Nystrom and W H Starbuck), Oxford University Press.

Drucker, P F (1974) *Management: Tasks, Responsibilities, Practices*, Harper and Row.

Fowler, A (1990) Performance management – the MBO of the '90s?, *Personnel Management*, July.

Golde, R A (1976) *Muddling Through: The Act of Properly Unbusinesslike Management*, Amacon.

Handy, C (1989) *The Age of Unreason*, Hutchinson.

Hersey, P and Blanchard, K (1982) *The Management of Organisational Behaviour*, 4th edn, Prentice Hall.

Hertzberg, F (1968) One more time how do you motivate employees?, *Harvard Business Review*, January–February.

Kotter, J P (1990) What leaders really do, *Harvard Business Review*, May–June.

Lindblom, CE (1959) *The Science of Muddling Through*. Reprinted in Pugh, D S (ed.) (1987) *Organization Theory*, 2nd edn, Penguin.

Litterer, J A (1973) *The Analysis of Organisations*, Wiley.

Marginson, P, Edwards, P K, Martin, R, Purcell, J and Sisson, K (1988) *Beyond the Workplace*, Blackwell.

McClelland, D and Winter, D (1971) *Motivating Economic Achievement*, Free Press.

McGregor, D M (1960) *The Human Side of Enterprise*, McGraw-Hill.

Mintzberg, H (1975) The manager's job – folklore and fact, *Harvard Business Review*, July–August.

Odiorne, G (1979) *MBO 11*, Pitman.

Peters, T and Austin, N (1985) *A Passion for Excellence*, Collins.

Porter, L W, Lawler, E E and Hackman, J R (1975) *Behaviour in Organisations*, McGraw-Hill.

Quinn, J B (1980) *Strategies for Change: Logical Incrementalism*, Richard D Irwin.

Schein, E H (1983) The role of the founder in creating organizational culture, *Organisational Dynamics*, Summer.

Skapinker, M (1989) Making the best of many moulds, *Financial Times*, 8 February.

Smiley, T (1988) Referred to in Skapinker, M Suddenly it's all becoming blurred, *Financial Times*, 18 November.

Tyson, S and York, A (1982) *Personnel Management Made Simple*, Heinemann.

Wrapp, H E (1967) Good managers don't make policy decisions, *Harvard Business Review*, September–October.

Zaleznik, A (1977) Managers and leaders: are they different?, *Harvard Business Review*, May–June.

FINANCE AS A STRATEGIC RESOURCE

13

LEARNING OBJECTIVES

After reading this chapter you should be able to

☐ assess the significance of financial objectives for organizations, and discuss examples of companies for whom these are of paramount importance;

☐ discuss the advantages and disadvantages of different sources of investment capital;

☐ apply a number of different investment appraisal techniques, and evaluate their contribution to investment decisions;

☐ calculate the optimal capital structure for a firm and its weighted average cost of capital;

☐ describe the capital asset pricing model;

☐ explain how a company might be valued, say for acquisition purposes;

☐ identify how financial strategies might yield competitive advantage.

Financial strategy is an important component of corporate strategy. Financial considerations can either provide opportunities for development or act as major constraints. The implications of giving financial objectives primary importance are also considered, using specific case examples.

INTRODUCTION

Financial measures of performance were introduced and discussed in Chapter 6, and in Chapter 8 the significance of poor financial management in corporate failure was shown. In this chapter we consider financial opportunities for and threats to growth and change. We consider, first, whether the organization is able to pursue the investment strategies that it would like to follow and needs to follow for survival.

Can it afford them? Is finance available? From where? Second, we discuss the risk and costs involved compared with potential returns. If an investment opportunity exists and the potential returns can be forecast, the lower the cost of borrowing money, the higher the profits that are available.

☐ Is the company profitable and able to pay its interest and dividend commitments? Is it performing well enough for its shares to have a valuation above the market average, providing some security from external predators and giving it strategic flexibility?
☐ How do shareholders, bankers and other investors and potential investors view the company's performance? Are they willing to lend more money for future growth and development, and at what cost to the company? What rate of return do they expect from their investment?
☐ How is the company financed in terms of debt and equity? Does this represent an opportunity or a threat?
☐ What investment opportunities are available, and how might they be evaluated?
☐ How can finance be a source of competitive advantage?

Texas Instruments, for instance, have pursued a strategy of being the lowest cost producer of certain electronics and components lines, but this has required substantial investment in capital, technology, people and research and development over an extended period. The success of the strategy has enabled Texas Instruments to raise the investment money needed relatively easily and more cheaply than many of their smaller American competitors. Competitive and financial strategies can and should be closely linked.

Financial strategy also relates to marketing, operations and human resources strategies. Marketing is a major determinant of the amount and consistency of revenues earned by the business; operations and human resources strategies determine the cost of producing goods and services. The difference is profit. However, financial resources, both long-term investment and short-term working capital, are required to carry out marketing, operations and human resources strategies.

We shall look at:

☐ financial strategy in general terms;
☐ sources and uses of corporate funds: debt, equity and leasing;
☐ capital structures and gearing;
☐ dividend policies;
☐ the cost of capital;
☐ investment appraisal and sensitivity analysis;
☐ company valuations;
☐ finance and competitive advantage.

FINANCIAL STRATEGY

Financial strategy involves:

☐ providing the firm with the appropriate financial structure and funds to achieve its overall objectives;
☐ examining the financial implications of various strategic alternatives such as acquisition, or investment in new products or new plants, and identifying the most lucrative ones (financial aspects may or may not be the only factor involved in the selection);
☐ providing competitive advantage through cheaper funding and a flexible ability to raise capital (Clarke, 1988).

Financial performance

The central objective of a strategic leader may be growth in profits. Relative success will be determined by how well assets and shareholders' funds are being used to earn profits and increase the value of the business. Such an orientation regards shareholders as the most important stakeholder in the organization, and is practised very successfully by, for example, Hanson plc. Hanson's approach is described later, but it is based on the acquisition of companies and their assets and the use of those assets in the most profitable manner, which usually involves quick sales of parts of the acquired businesses. In a different way it might be argued that GEC, which showed over £1 billion of investments in the balance sheet in the late 1980s, is choosing to earn money by careful specula-tion rather than investing to create jobs, and is thereby oriented towards its shareholders.

If other objectives such as growth are central, profitability is still an essential requirement. We saw in Chapter 12 that systems such as management by objectives rely on quantitative measures of perform-ance, and cost and revenue targets are used frequently.

Managers throughout the organization may be concerned with the survival of the organization as an independent entity in order to provide themselves with some personal security. Sound or above-average financial performance is likely to boost share prices. Long-term, consistent, above-average performance should keep the company's valuation relatively high, making it less vulnerable to a predator, and also making it easier for the company to raise money for further expansion. Financial performance objectives are therefore likely to be seen as important by managers. This theme is sup-ported by research by Schein (1983) which was mentioned in Chapter 12 and which suggests that managers are generally oriented towards economic goals and see profit as being important.

Fund raising

Finance is needed in order to maintain an adequate cash flow to keep the business operating and for development. For the latter the right amount is needed at the right time and at the right cost. Lesney (Matchbox) Toys was discussed briefly in Chapter 7, Case 7.1. During the 1960s Lesney was regarded as 'blue chip' as it experienced rapid growth and

high profits. The share price and earnings growth were above average. By the early 1970s, as a result of competition and a downturn in demand in America, profits had shown a fall. Lesney, which found it easy to raise money in the 1960s, was unable to raise finance to buy part of another toy company, Lines Brothers, which was in liquidation. A lack of finance constrained strategic develop-ment at that time.

Investments should yield more than the cost of the capital used to fund them. The profits earned should be greater than the money needed to finance a loan or increased equity funding. Similarly, from a financial perspective, if a company already has the funds and does not need to borrow, the returns from the investment should exceed the potential earnings from using the money for financial speculation.

Companies, then, should be able to raise money when they need it or potentially valuable strategic opportunities may be lost. The nature of the funding, equity or loan, which is discussed in the next section, should relate to both costs and risks. Loan funding requires regular and fixed interest payments, whilst equity offers more flexibility. How-ever, equity is generally more expensive. The decision therefore is influenced by the consistency of profits as inconsistency makes loan funding more risky. In addition the cost of the funding can lead to competitive ad-vantage through lower costs, and this point is taken up at the end of the chapter.

FINANCING THE BUSINESS

Sources of funds

Table 13.1 gives the sources of funds for UK companies, broken down into equity, borrowing and retained earnings, and the allocation of funds for fixed and current assets. The statistics indicate that most funds used by established organizations are gener-

Table 13.1 UK companies: sources and uses of funds

	1983	1984	1986	1989
Sources				
Capital issues	1	9	17	14
Borrowing	31	22	13	33
Retained earnings	66	62	69	52
Other sources				
(e.g. exchange differences)	2	7	1	1
Uses				
Payments out of income	31	24	30	21
Expenditure on fixed assets	42	45	49	53
Investment in current assets				
and investments	27	31	21	26

All figures are shown as a percentage of total sources and total uses. The data represents large UK companies. (*Source: Annual Abstract of Statistics*, HMSO, 1990 and 1992.)

Table 13.2 Advantages and disadvantages of equity and loan funding

	Advantages	*Disadvantages*
Share capital; equity	Dividends can be reduced or waived if profits low or there is a need to retain more money No fixed repayment date New equity increases creditworthiness	Can change shareholder register and voting rights Issue costs Dividends are not tax-deductible, interest is Can increase cost of capital
Borrowing; loan capital	Fixed cost; often lower than equity No dilution of equity Interest payments are tax-deductible	Increased risk for company, which can affect equity value Agreed repayment date Can be limited by willingness of people to lend

ated internally through retained profits, but from time to time it is necessary to raise funds externally. This conclusion applies to both the public and the private sectors. Generally loan capital or borrowing is used more extensively than equity, which might take the form of new equity issued openly or rights issues to existing shareholders.

Investment funding, then, is available through borrowing or increased equity, but assets can be increased without investing to the same extent. This is accomplished by leasing them rather than purchasing them. Table 13.2 summarizes the major advantages and disadvantages of equity and loan capital, and all three sources are discussed below.

Equity capital

Generally equity capital would be increased by a rights issue of ordinary shares to existing shareholders. As an example, holders of ordinary shares might be offered one new share for every two or three they already own, at a price equal to or below the current market price. At a higher price people would be unlikely to purchase. If all shareholders take up the offer then the percentage breakdown of the shareholders' register will remain the same; if they are not taken up by existing shareholders they will be offered to the market by the institutional underwriters, and the share register profile may change.

Blocks of shares could be built up quite readily, and at a price below the current market price; and depending upon who was buying them threats to the organization from powerful shareholders could emerge.

Potential take-over threats might also emerge, but these would normally be within the strictly enforced City Code of Practice on Takeovers. Any holding of 4.9% of ordinary shares must be declared. Once a holding of 14.9% has been obtained a buyer must wait at least a week before buying any more to allow both the company and other shareholders to assess the changing position. When a potential bidder acquires 30% of the shares he must automatically offer to buy the rest at a price not less than the highest price paid in the market over the previous 12 months.

Rights issues will not be successful without the support of institutional shareholders. We saw in Case 9.3 (British Aerospace) that this requires investor confidence in the company's strategy and strategic leadership.

Although many shareholders buy and retain shares with a view to a long-term capital gain, resulting from their sale at a price higher than the one they were bought at, dividend policy is important. Dividends represent a rate of return on shareholders' investments and they are discussed in greater detail below. Although dividends are not fixed and can theoretically be raised or lowered freely and in relation to increases or decreases in profits, and to any changing need for retained earnings for investment, companies generally seek stability.

Loan capital

There are various forms of loan capital, but they all have one essential characteristic. They do not carry ownership which ordinary shares do. Loans might well be for a definite period of time, after which they are repayable, and with a fixed rate of interest for each year of the loan. Hence interest payments come out of profits, but they cannot be reduced if profits decline through unfavourable trading conditions. Overdrafts provide flexible short-term funding up to an agreed limit, and their cost will vary both up and down as the prevailing market rate of interest changes. Loans are invariably secured against assets, which reduces the risk for the lender. If interest payments are not met, the bank, or whoever has loaned the money, is free to appoint a receiver and effectively take over day-to-day control of the company. Interest is paid out of profits before they are assessed for taxation, and they can thereby reduce the company's tax burden; dividends for ordinary shareholders are paid after tax.

Generalizing, the cost of borrowing can be expected to rise as the degree of risk for the lender increases. Lenders will expect higher returns from higher risk investments. Government securities are considered very safe, for example, and consequently the anticipated rate of return will typically be lower than for other investments. Secured loans are safer than ordinary shares, as mentioned above, and therefore borrowing should normally prove cheaper than equity.

The ability to obtain either – and the cost – are likely to be dependent upon how well the company has been performing, and how well it has been perceived by the market to have been performing. Opportunity, ability and cost are therefore essential criteria in deciding upon a preference between equity and loan funding, but this decision should be related to the decision concerning whether to invest at all. Investments, which are discussed later in the chapter, should be analysed by comparing their returns, discounted for the period they are earned, with the cost of financing them, or the opportunity cost of the money being used. The viability of an investment is therefore dependent upon the cost of the capital used. The cheaper the cost of capital, the more likely it is that an investment is viable and profitable. Hence if the cost of obtaining investment funding is high, opportunities might be lost.

Moreover, as we shall see in the next section on gearing, the capital structure of the company determines the impact of profit fluctuations on the money available after tax for paying dividends and for re-investment. Large loans and high interest payments absorb profits, and this can be crucial if profits fluctuate significantly for any reason. The more that is paid out in dividends, the less that is available for re-investing, and vice versa. In turn dividend payments are likely to affect the view that shareholders and the market have of the company's performance, and this will affect their willingness to lend more.

Leasing

In many cases organizations are more concerned with using assets than actually owning them. Leasing assets is one way of acquiring them without paying their full price at any one time, and as Table 13.3 illustrates the popularity of leasing has grown throughout the late 1970s and 1980s. The table also illustrates that leasing is popular for a wide variety of different types of asset.

When an asset is leased there will normally be an agreed annual charge for a fixed number of years, and possibly there will an arrangement whereby the company obtains ownership of the asset for a residual price at the end of the period of the lease. In aggregate terms leasing is unlikely to be cheap, but it can have a significant effect on cash flow. Additionally there have been advantageous tax regulations, including for a period the ability to offset against tax the full cost of the asset during the first year of the lease. This allowance was reduced in the mid-1980s. Leasing is generally low risk for the lessor, who retains legal ownership of the asset and can reclaim it if the lease payments are not met.

Leasing has offered strategic opportunities,

Table 13.3 Leasing

Leasing of equipment as a percentage of all UK investment in equipment (excluding property)

Year	Without purchase option (%)	With purchase option[a] (%)
1977	5.2	
1980	11.1	
1985	18.5	
1987	16.9	
1988	18.0	26.3
1989	20.0	28.6
1990	20.3	28.5

Types of asset leased as a percentage of total assets leased, 1987 and 1990

Asset	1987 (%)	1990 (%)
Plant and machinery	26	23
Computers and office equipment	27	18
Cars	21	35
Commercial vehicles	13	11
Aircraft and ships	8	4
Buildings	2	6
Other	3	3
	100	100

[a] Figures for 1977–1987 are not available.
Source: Equipment Leasing Association Annual Reports.

as well as financial benefits, for certain organizations. Some companies have chosen to sell and lease back property they owned, for example, finding willing partners in property companies and institutional investors. The funds released have then been available for other investments.

Funding and capital structure

The opportunity to raise equity and loan capital, and the cost of each, affects the organization's ability to invest and pursue certain strategies. However, a change in the relative percentages of equity and loan capital affects the overall capital structure of the organization.

The relationship between the relative percentages of debt and equity financing is known as **gearing**. The debt ratio, which was discussed in Chapter 6, is related to gearing. It measures long-term debts as a percentage of total capital employed. Gearing is debt as a percentage of total shareholders' funds. Hence if debts amounted to £1 million and shareholders' funds were also £1 million, the debt ratio would be 50% and gearing would be exactly 100%. Gearing therefore increases as the proportion of debt to equity increases.

The significance of gearing is its impact on profitability and changes in earnings. It becomes increasingly significant when profits fluctuate rather than exhibit relative stability. The following example illustrates this.

Let us assume that a firm has recorded the following profits before interest and tax, in constant pounds, over 5 years:

Year	1	2	3	4	5
Profit (£)	60 000	80 000	70 000	50 000	70 000
Percentage change over previous year		+33.3	−12.5	−28.6	+40.0

The fluctuations are assumed to be dependent on uncertain trading conditions and strong competition. Let us now assume that the company has a long-term loan of £125 000, on which it pays interest of £15 000 (12%) every year. For this example let us assume that tax is paid at a rate of 30% of earnings after interest is deducted. The above figures can be extrapolated as follows:

Year	1	2	3	4	5
Profit (£)	60 000	80 000	70 000	50 000	70 000
Profit after interest (£)	45 000	65 000	55 000	35 000	55 000
Profit after interest and tax at 30% (£)	31 500	45 000	38 500	24 500	38 500
Percentage change of profit before interest and tax over previous year		+33.3	−12.5	−28.6	+40.0
Percentage change of profit after interest and tax (available for shareholders) over previous year		+44.4	−15.4	−36.4	+57.1

The presence of debt with fixed annual interest payments increases the profit fluctuations as far as the amount available for shareholders (from which dividends are paid) is concerned. The greater the amount of interest in relation to profits, the greater the impact on funds available for shareholders. Let us finally assume that during the first year of our example an additional loan is taken out such that interest payments now amount to £20 000 every year:

Year	1	2	3	4	5
Profit (£)	60 000	80 000	70 000	50 000	70 000
Profit after interest (£)	40 000	60 000	50 000	30 000	50 000
Profit after interest and tax (£)	28 000	42 000	35 000	21 000	35 000
Percentage change in profit after interest and tax over previous year		+50.0	−16.7	−40.0	+66.6

If dividends are maintained, then retained earnings for re-investment will also vary by substantial amounts, leading to inconsistency in on-going investments unless new external funding is obtained. Depending upon the type – equity or loan – this problem could be eased or exacerbated.

Hence debt capital or loan funding must be considered in the light of profit trends, their relative stability or instability, and the company's dividend policy. This is the subject of the next section.

During the 1980s there has been a significant increase in the number of management buy-outs, whereby whole organizations or business units are bought from the existing owners by their managers, generally as a strategic divestment by the existing owners. This is explored in greater depth in Chapter 20. In addition there have been instances of buy-outs where chief executives who have previously floated their companies on the Stock Exchange, but retained a majority shareholding have borrowed money to buy back the shares and make the company private again. Examples include Virgin and the Really Useful Group (the company which markets the music of Andrew Lloyd Webber), and the reasons have related to different perceptions of the value of the companies by the strategic leaders and the market. However, one aspect of this trend has been the development of what are called leveraged buy-outs, popular in America, where the percentage of loan capital is very high. This has been paralleled by an increase in gearing generally. Some concerns have been expressed at these trends, but the Bank of England has argued in their favour on the grounds that management buy-outs have often been a useful source of new energy and new direction for companies.

Dividends

Dividends are the part of profits (after interest and tax) which are paid out to shareholders. The rest is retained and re-invested in the business. Retained earnings are the major source of investment funds for UK companies. Dividend policy therefore influences the extent to which these retained funds must be supplemented with external capital.

Gitman (1982) contends that in deciding upon their dividend policy companies should consider two interrelated objectives: first, the need to maximize owners' wealth in the long term and, second, the need for continued investment funding. In reality firms generally pursue an essentially stable dividend policy despite fluctuating profits, and increases are expected to take account of inflation. Figure 13.1 illustrates a stable dividend policy by Thorn–EMI plc during the 1980s despite substantial changes in the earnings per share.

Stable dividends – even during a recession, when they may not be covered fully by earnings – are justified as a reward to shareholders for their loyalty. Moreover, in relation to total reserves, the amount involved is often quite small. Unstable dividends are frequently perceived to represent inconsistency by the Board of Directors and a lack of Board confidence in the future.

Although some large companies have reduced their dividends in the recession of the early 1990s many have resisted, such that the average dividend cover for companies quoted in the *Financial Times* has fallen below 2 times. In 1980 the average dividend cover was nearly 3 times. When earnings rise more steeply after the recession it is unlikely that dividends will track them upwards, and instead, like Thorn–EMI in the 1980s, continue to increase gradually.

Weston and Brigham (1979) argue that stable dividends tend to lead to higher share prices because investors are more favourably disposed towards companies whose shares provide dividends 'they are sure of receiving' than they are towards less reliable companies who are regarded as more risky. The logic is that some shareholders rely on dividend income and are therefore willing to pay a premium for those shares they consider to carry least risk. Higher share prices are also

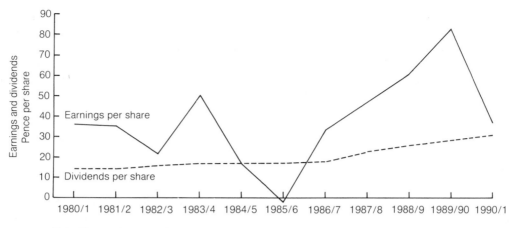

Note: The earnings per share are after extraordinary charges.

Figure 13.1   Thorn–EMI plc: earnings and dividends 1980–1991.

to some extent a defence against acquisition as they make the company more expensive to buy, and consequently they are very significant to managers as employees.

Stable dividends and variable earnings must mean either that the company is unable to pursue a consistent investment policy or that in some years it has to raise additional capital through the issue of new equity or through borrowing. Both earnings and dividends will affect the willingness of shareholders to provide increased equity funding. It is very important that shareholders understand why companies are following a particular dividend policy in order that they can react objectively. The onus is on companies to explain their decisions. This is particularly important if capital is required for future investments which should increase the shareholders' wealth in the long term. If dividends are not being increased at the same rate as earnings, this is one way of funding the investment.

Shares in Spring Ram, the successful kitchens and bathrooms group (featured in Chapter 15), have a very low dividend yield of 0.2% (1992). A more typical yield of 5% would be 'equivalent to the cost of building

two new factories'. Shareholders are aware of the company's investment programme and support the dividend policy – the share price is buoyant. Spring Ram has seen sales and profits rise rather than fall during the recession.

Thus, loans and equity both offer advantages and disadvantages in providing additional investment funding. One key point is that debt capital is usually cheaper as it carries less risk for the lender. Moreover, as debt capital increases, the company's cash value to its owners (shareholders) increases as the interest payments are tax deductible. But a company with high gearing may not be able to afford low profit years because of the risk of receivership and the impact upon dividends and retained earnings. Increased debt capital adjusts the capital structure in such a way that any fluctuations in earnings before interest and tax are exacerbated, affecting the money available for dividends and retentions. Retained earnings are the major source of investment capital for UK companies. Dividends affect the perceptions of shareholders and in turn both the potential to raise more equity and the overall share value of the company. If profits are declining this issue can present a dilemma. Maintaining dividends in the face of reduced profit means lower retained earnings and possibly a greater need for external financing. Increased loan capital for future investment can make the problem worse.

Companies in particular industries might usefully be analysed to check whether their capital structure and the percentage of debt reflects their overall stability. One would expect companies in stable industries to have a higher percentage of debt than those in more unstable dynamic industries.

Having looked at different types of funding and their implications for the business we shall next consider the cost of capital and how this might affect investment decisions.

The cost of capital

The optimal capital structure

In theory there is an optimal capital structure (OCS) in terms of debt and equity for any firm, and it will depend on:

☐ the amount of risk in the industry;
☐ the riskiness of the company's corporate and competitive strategies, and their potential impact on profits;
☐ the typical capital structure for the industry, and what competitors are doing – the cost of funding can provide competitive advantage as we shall examine later;
☐ management's ability to pay interest without too serious an impact on dividends and future investment;
☐ both the owners' and the strategic leader's preference for risk, or aversion to it.

The weighted average cost of capital

In considering, or attempting to decide, the optimal capital structure it is important to evaluate the **weighted average cost of capital**

(WACC). The WACC, again in theory, is the average rate of return that investors expect the company to earn. In practice it is the average cost of raising additional investment funding. If a company used only loan funding the WACC would be the after-tax cost of borrowing more. But most organizations have a complex structure of debt and equity, each of which carries a different cost.

The WACC is therefore an attempt to approximate what more funding would cost if it were raised proportionately to the percentages of debt and equity in the optimal capital structure. In practice it will relate to the current capital structure.

Determining the weighted average cost of capital

The formula is

WACC = (Percentage of long-term debt in the OCS × After-tax cost of debt)
plus
(Percentage of ordinary shares in the OCS × After-tax cost of equity)

As mentioned above, the WACC will normally be calculated in terms of the firm's current capital structure rather than the theoretical OCS.

The **cost of long-term debt** is the weighted average of the various interest rates incurred on existing loans – after accounting for tax. Hence for a company which pays 10% interest on 40% of its loans, 12% on the other 60% and tax at an effective rate of 30%, the cost of long-term debt is

$$((10\% \times 40) + (12\% \times 60)) \times (1 - 0.3)$$
$$= 7.84\%$$

The **cost of equity** is more difficult to calculate. One popular model for estimating it is the capital asset pricing model (CAPM), which is described here only in outline. Franks and Broyles (1979) provide a much more detailed explanation.

The capital asset pricing model

In theory the cost of equity for an individual company should equal the rate of return that shareholders expect to gain from investing in that company. This is based on their perception of the amount of risk involved. The CAPM attempts to capture this. The formula is

$$R = F + beta(M - F)$$

R is the expected earnings or return on a particular share and F represents the risk-free rate of return expected from the most secure investments such as government securities, where the likelihood of default is considered negligible. The expected risk-free rate is determined by the current interest rate on these securities and expected inflation. M is the average rate of return expected from all securities traded in the market and beta is a measure of risk based on the volatility of an individual company's shares compared with the market as a whole. A beta of 1.6 (empirically high) means that a company's share price fluctuates by 1.6 times the market average. In other words, if the market average rises or falls by 10%, the company's share price increases or decreases by 16%. A low beta might be 0.3. Low beta shares in a portfolio reduce risk, but in general high beta shares do little to reduce risk.

As an example, assume the risk-free rate is 10%, the market as a whole is returning 18%, and a company's beta is 1.2.

$$R = 10 + 1.2(18 - 10)$$
$$= 19.6\%$$

In other words the market would be expecting the company to achieve 19.6% earnings on shareholders' funds. As explained in Chapter 6 this is earnings after interest and tax divided by total shareholders' funds, including reserves.

By contrast, if a company's beta was 0.5,

$$R = 10 + 0.5(18 - 10)$$
$$= 14\%$$

The CAPM is useful for estimating the cost of equity but there are certain problems in implementing it. Primarily all the data will be adjusted and extrapolated historical data, when really it is realistic forecasts of future earnings and returns that matter. F and M theoretically represent expected future returns, and beta should be based on expected future fluctuations, but normally historical data will be used in the model on the assumption that trends continue. The prevailing and predicted rates of interest in the economy will be used to increase or decrease past return figures.

The WACC can now be calculated. Assume that a company has £1.2 million equity funding and £800 000 in long-term debt, and that the relative costs of each are 16% and 8% respectively.

Source of funding	Total (£ million)	Percentage of total	Cost (%)	Weighted cost (%)
Equity	1.2	60	16	9.6
Loans	0.8	40	8	3.2

Thus WACC = 12.8%.

Of course, retained earnings which can be re-invested in the company could alternatively be paid out as dividends, which shareholders could themselves invest wherever they chose. Consequently the return on such re-investments in the company should be at least the same as that which investors expect from their existing shares. Given that all shareholders' funds are incorporated in the CAPM, this is taken into account.

Gearing and the cost of capital

It has been argued that in general terms equity is normally more expensive than debt capital. Consequently one might expect that as the proportion of debt increases relative to equity the weighted average cost of capital will decrease. However, there are drawbacks

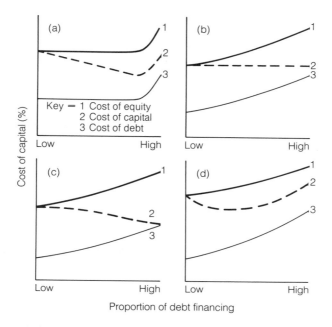

Figure 13.2 Gearing and the cost of capital – various theories: (a) traditional model; (b) Modigliani and Miller – without tax; (c) Modigliani and Miller – with tax; (d) compromise model.

with high debt financing, as mentioned earlier, and consequently firms can be expected to seek to limit the amount of debt in their OCS. At some stage, and influenced by profit stability, the proportion of debt capital constitutes a higher risk to lenders and this can increase the cost.

This traditional view, illustrated in model (a) of Figure 13.2, has been contested by Modigliani and Miller (1958) who argue that the cost of capital is constant if no taxes are paid but is constantly reduced when corporation tax is considered. Their arguments are illustrated in models (b) and (c) of Figure 13.2, but their justification is too complex and algebraic to be described in this text. The Modigliani and Miller theory has been criticized for a number of assumptions it uses, and consequently a compromise model is often favoured to explain the cost of capital. This is model (d) in Figure 13.2 and it illustrates that as the proportion of debt increases the overall cost of capital falls initially and then begins to increase as the proportion of debt rises above

a certain level. Although there is a theoretical OCS (the minimum point of the cost of capital curve shown as the broken line), the curve is seen as relatively shallow. Hence the penalty for not being at the OCS is not enormous. This gives firms some flexibility in selecting between various forms of finance.

In summary, this whole area is extremely complex, but nevertheless the cost of capital is an important consideration alongside availability. The cost of capital can affect the viability of a proposed investment, and it can affect the overall costs of producing a product or service and thereby influence competitive advantage. Investments, and how they might be evaluated, are the subject of the next section.

INVESTMENTS AND CAPITAL BUDGETING

Decisions concerning where a company's financial resources should be allocated are known as investment or capital budgeting decisions. The decision might concern the purchase of a new piece of equipment, the acquisition of another company, or financing the development and launch of a new product. The ability to raise money, and the cost involved, are key influences, and should be considered alongside two other strategic issues:

☐ Does the proposed investment make sense strategically, given present objectives and strategies?
☐ Will the investment provide an adequate financial return?

The latter question is partly answered by the company's cost of capital and is explored in this section. Strategic fit is a broad issue and is addressed at various points in the book.

In simple terms, an investment represents the commitment of money now for gains or returns in the future. The financial returns are therefore measured over an appropriate period of time. Estimating these returns relies substantially on forecasts of demand in terms of both amount and timing; and generating the returns further relies upon the ability of managers to manage resources in such a way that the forecasts are met. Uncertainty is therefore an issue.

Generally any investment should be evaluated financially on at least the following two criteria:

☐ Individually, is it worth proceeding with?
☐ Is it the best alternative from the options the company has, or if money is reasonably freely available to the company, how does the proposal rank alongside other possibilities?

In the financial evaluation of a proposed investment which produces a cash flow over a period of time, it is necessary to incorporate some qualification for the fact that inflation and other factors generally ensure that a 'pound tomorrow' is worth less than its current value. This is achieved by discounting the cash flow, which is discussed below and illustrated in Box 13.1.

Evaluating proposed investments

If an organization wishes to be thorough and objective investments could usefully be analysed against the six criteria listed below. The first three of these are essentially quantitative; the second three incorporate qualitative issues. Sometimes the strategic importance of a particular proposal may mean that, first, the most financially rewarding option is not selected or that, second, an investment is not necessarily timed for when the cost of capital would be lowest. As an example of the first point consider a firm in a growing industry which feels that it has to invest in order not to lose market share, although the current cost of capital may mean that the returns from the investment are less than it would wish for or that it could earn with a strategically less important option. An example of the second point would be a firm whose industry is in recession but predicted to grow, and where investment in capital in readiness for the upturn might result in future competitive advantage. At the moment the cost of capital might be relatively high, but the strategic significance of the investment might outweigh this.

The six criteria for evaluating a proposed investment are as follows:

☐ the discounted present value of all returns through the productive life of the investment
☐ the expected rate of return, which should exceed both the cost of capital (the cost of financing the investment) and the opportunity cost for the money (returns that might otherwise be earned with an alternative proposal)
☐ payback – the payout period and the investment's expected productive life –

which is a popular measure as it is relatively easily calculated
- ☐ the risk involved in not making the investment or deferring it
- ☐ the cost and risk if it fails
- ☐ the opportunity cost – specifically, the potential gains from alternative uses of the money.

The three quantitative measures (the first three measures) are explained in Box 13.1.

Discounting techniques are theoretically attractive and used in many organizations, though more in America than Europe, and particularly where the proposal is capital intensive. But the technique must involve uncertainty if the cash flows cannot be

---

Box 13.1
ANALYSING PROPOSED INVESTMENTS

DISCOUNTED CASH FLOWS

Background explanation

If the prevailing rate of interest on bank deposit or building society accounts is 10% an individual or organization with money to invest could save and earn compound interest with relatively little risk. If the rate stayed constant £100 today would be worth £110 next year and £121 the year after if the interest was not withdrawn annually. To calculate future values simply multiply by 1 + r each year, where r is the rate of interest. Therefore in ten years' time £100 is worth £100$(1 + r)^{10}$.

Reversing the process enables a consideration of what money earned in the future is worth in today's terms. In other words, if a company invests now, at today's value of the pound, it is important to analyse the returns from the investment also in today's terms, although most if not all the returns from the investment will be earned in the future when the value of the pound has fallen. This is known as **discounting future values**. So £100 earned next year is worth £100/$(1 + r)$ today, i.e. £90.9.

Similarly £100 earned ten years hence would be worth in today's terms £100/$(1 + r)^{10}$. This is known as **net present value**.

In discounting cash flows and calculating net present value discount tables are used for simplicity.

An example

Assume that a company invests £1 million today and in return earns £250 000 each year for five years, starting next year. Earnings in total amount to £1.25 million, but they are spread over five years. The company's estimated cost of capital is 10%.

Year	Cash flow receipts (£ thousand)	Discount factor at 10%	Net present value (£ thousand)
1	250	0.909	227
2	250	0.826	206
3	250	0.751	188
4	250	0.683	171
5	250	0.621	153
			945

Hence £1 million is invested to earn £945 000 in today's terms – a loss of £55 000. Logically a positive figure is sought; and if the investment is required to show a return which is higher than the cost of capital, this target return rather than the cost

Continued overleaf

of capital should be used as the discount rate and a positive net present value should be sought at this level.

Financially this investment would only be viable with a lower cost of capital. Logically all projects look increasingly viable with lower capital costs.

The calculation below is of the cost of capital at which this particular project becomes viable.

THE INTERNAL RATE OF RETURN

The next step would be to discount at a lower rate, say 5%.

Year	Cash flow receipts (£ thousand)	Discount factor at 5%	Net present value (£ thousand)
1	250	0.952	238
2	250	0.907	227
3	250	0.864	216
4	250	0.823	206
5	250	0.784	196
			1083

This time a positive net present value of £83 000 is obtained.

The following formula is used to calculate the internal rate of return:

$$\frac{83\,000}{138\,000} \times \frac{5}{100} = 3\%$$

(£83 000 is the positive net present value at a 5% cost of capital, £138 000 is the difference in net present value between the 5% and 10% rates, and the 5/100 represents the percentage difference between the 5 and 10.)

This 3% is added to the 5% to give 8%, which is the yield or internal rate of return from this investment.

Check:

Year	Cash flow receipts (£ thousand)	Discount factor at 8%	Net present value (£ thousand)
1	250	0.926	232
2	250	0.857	214
3	250	0.794	198
4	250	0.735	184
5	250	0.681	170
			998

In other words this investment gives a yield of 8%. This is also known as the internal rate of return, the discount rate which makes the net present value of the receipts exactly equal to the cost of the investment. In the same way that one might look for a positive net present value, one would be looking for an internal rate of return that exceeded the cost of capital.

PAYBACK

Payback is simply the length of time it takes to earn back the outlay; and obviously one can look at either absolute or discounted cash flows, normally the former. In the example above the payback is four years exactly. The outlay was £1 million, and the receipts amounted to £250 000 each year.

Payback is quite useful. For one thing it is relatively simple. For another it does take some account of the timing of returns, for returns can be re-invested in some way as soon as they are to hand.

forecast accurately, as is often the case. Additionally the net present value is dependent on the discount rate used, and this should relate to the weighted average cost of capital, which again may be uncertain. Research by Richard Pike (1982) concludes that payback is the technique used most widely because of its simplicity in both calculation and comprehension. The expected rate of return and the net present value are used less frequently as they are more complicated and of arguably less value if payback periods are relatively short. In his research Pike also determined that most respondents used a discount rate of 15% rather than a weighted average cost of capital specific to them.

There will always therefore be some important element of managerial judgement, and one might argue that this managerial intuition will be preferred in some smaller firms which place less emphasis on planning than do larger firms and in those companies that are more entrepreneurial and risk oriented. However, if the decision maker really understands the market and the strategic implications of the proposed investment, this may not be detrimental.

Large organizations evaluating possible investments for different divisions or business units should consider the estimated rate of return from each proposal, the current returns being obtained in each division and the company's average cost of capital – as well as any strategic issues. Take the following two possibilities:

	Division A	Division B
Rate of return on proposal	20%	13%
Current returns	25%	9%

Division A's proposal could seem unattractive as it offers a lower return than existing projects, whilst B's investment offers an improvement to current returns. If the company's cost of capital is 15%, A's proposal is profitable and B's proposal is not.

Sensitivity analysis

We saw earlier that the evaluation of a proposed investment depends on forecasts of the revenue which might be generated and the ability of managers to ensure that the anticipated earnings do accrue. Risk and uncertainty are therefore important issues. Sensitivity analysis is one way of incorporating a consideration of risk into investment decisions. Another way would be to increase the discount rate, implying that the cost of capital might realistically be higher than the value being used. A higher discount rate, as illustrated in Box 13.1, will effectively reduce the present value of future earnings and make an investment seem less attractive than it would at a lower discount rate. However, research in both America and the UK by Donaldson and Lorsch (1983) and Pike (1982) respectively suggests that many managers do not specifically include risk in their investment decisions.

In simple terms sensitivity analysis involves changing certain parameters and assessing their implications. For example an investment might be forecast to yield cash flows over six years as follows: £500 000; £750 000; £1.2 million; £1.4 million; £1.5 million; and £1 million in Year 6, to give a total of £6.35 million in absolute terms. If the cost of the investment is £4 million, payback comes very early in the fifth year.

The effect of extending the payback period by slowing down the build-up but without reducing the overall total might be evaluated by comparing the two net present values. An appropriate absolute flow might be £400 000; £600 000; £800 000; £1 million; £1.2 million; and £2.35 million in Year 6. Payback this time takes five years and more of the revenues are earned in later years when they will be discounted more heavily. This second flow will not only take longer to pay back, but the net present value and the internal rate of return will also both be lower.

Finally the sensitivity of a reduced overall cash flow might be evaluated: £500 000; £750 000; £1.1 million; £1.3 million; £1.4 million; and £800,000 in Year 6. Payback again is early in Year 5, but the absolute cash flow and in turn the net present value are lower.

These flow changes could result from changing the parameters of market growth rate, market share achieved, prices or costs incurred. Sensitivity analysis tests the robustness of proposed investments to any changes in the essential component variables.

An example of sensitivity analysis

A specific example was provided in the offer for sale of shares in Euro Disneyland SCA (France) in October 1989. Euro Disneyland is the introduction into Europe (near Paris) of the highly successful theme parks and resort concepts, including hotels, developed by The Walt Disney Company firstly in America and subsequently in Japan.

The basic assumptions concerning customers, incomes and costs in the calculations of expected investment returns generated a projected internal rate of return of 13.3% for the 25 years between 1992 and 2017. Alternative calculations were made by varying the basic assumptions. The changes in the assumptions are listed opposite, together with their effect on the internal rate of return (IRR) projections.

From these figures, and some consideration of risk and the likelihood of the revised assumptions actually happening, one can derive a greater insight into the potential profitability of the venture.

Valuing a company

Acquisition of another company constitutes an investment, and similarly one major strategic objective might be to avoid being taken

Assumption	IRR (%)
(i) Reduced attendances	12.7
(ii) Increased attendances	13.8
(iii) Reduced per capita spending	12.3
(iv) Increased per capita spending	14.1
(v) 6 months delay in opening	12.8
(vi) Increased construction costs	13.2
(vii) Reduced resort and property development income	13.0
(viii) Increased resort and property development income	13.5
(ix) Increased inflation	15.3
(x) Lower inflation	11.2
(xi) Higher real interest payments	13.2
(xii) Lower real interest payments	13.3
(xiii) Higher residual value	13.4
(xiv) Lower residual value	13.1

over by another firm. In both cases the current value of an organization is important. A company can be acquired by buying an appropriate percentage of its shares, and the likely purchase price of these in a bidding situation will be influenced substantially by their current market price in trading. However, the market price at any time may or may not reflect the value of the organization.

The balance sheet valuation

The balance sheet value of a company is normally taken from the value of the net assets. Divided by the number of ordinary shares issued this yields the asset value behind every ordinary share, and it can therefore be useful in assessing what an appropriate bid price for the ordinary shares might be. However, caution is needed because the balance sheet traditionally records historic costs rather than present values, and this can be misleading in the case of property. In addition, although some companies do account for this, the value of such intangible assets as brand names is rarely reflected in the balance sheet.

The market valuation

The market valuation of a company is the number of ordinary shares issued multiplied by their present price. This will reflect the likely lowest cost to a buyer, as any bid for shares at a price below their existing price is unlikely to succeed. In reality the price of shares is likely to increase during the period between when current shareholders realize that a bid is likely, or when one is announced, and when control is finally achieved by the bidder.

The current share price and the asset value of shares should be looked at together.

Earnings potential

Allen (1988) contends that it is future earnings potential that determines how valuable a company is, not historical results. An analysis of past and current performance is therefore limited in its usefulness. In isolation a high return on capital employed, for example, can hide the reality of an asset base which is declining in real terms. Therefore one should estimate the future cash flows which the company is capable of generating and discount these by the cost of capital. The current value of the company is determined by this net present value calculation.

The decision to acquire a company, however, will not be based solely on the discounted future earnings, nor the purchase price, but both these are very important. Acquisition strategies will be explored in greater depth in Chapter 18, but here it is important to stress the need to consider both strategic and financial issues. Future earnings potential for both the acquiring and the acquired companies could be improved with a merger if valuable synergy of some form is derived, and for this potential a premium price might be justified.

Financial objectives and strategies

Acquisitive companies like Hanson seek to acquire companies whose potential is high but whose overheads and other indirect costs such as interest payments are also high. Such companies will show a high gross margin, which indicates that the market is willing to pay a price much higher than the direct labour and materials costs of producing the product or service, and relatively low profitability, or even losses, when overheads, interest and tax are deducted. Profits should be improved by appropriate rationalization and cost cutting. Quite often the acquirer is able to reduce the cost of loan capital, which also increases profits. Additionally the purchase price can be offset by the sale of parts of the company which do not fit the strategic objectives of the acquirer. Case 13.1 details the sale by Hanson of parts of Imperial Group after the company was acquired in a hostile and competitive take-over in 1986. Hanson's strategy is summarized as part of the case. More recently, in 1989, Hanson acquired Consolidated Goldfields with a carefully timed bid after an earlier hostile bid from Minorco failed. Hanson started to divest parts of the business almost immediately. In 1991 Hanson bought Beazer, a UK building company. Beazer already owned America's second largest aggregates business – a cyclical industry. Hanson were counting on a growth in infrastructure spending after the recession.

In such take-overs financial objectives and issues are often predominant, and a key objective for the companies is the increase in the value of the company for the shareholders. The constant need for achievement in financial performance measures will be an essential feature of the organization culture. Senior executives, often known as tracking teams, are likely to devote time and energy looking for strategic acquisition opportunities which can be used for financial gain through the input of more effective management and appropriate divestment. However, whilst such acquisitions can provide real growth opportunities the ability to finance them can prove to be a constraint, and once the acquisition activity and growth slows down the companies look vulnerable. See Case 13.2, FKI–Babcock.

Case 13.1
THE ACQUISITION OF IMPERIAL GROUP BY HANSON

In 1986 Hanson won control of Imperial Group for £2.8 billion. The bid was unwelcome to the Imperial Directors who supported a rival bid from United Biscuits.

In the financial year which ended in October 1985 Imperial Group sales were £4.92 billion with pre-tax profits of £235.7 million. Approximately half of the sales and half of the profits arose from the tobacco interests, but Imperial was diversified as follows:

Tobacco	Players, Embassy, Golden Virginia, St Bruno
Foods	Ross Frozen Foods, Youngs Seafoods, Golden Wonder Crisps, HP and Lea and Perrin Sauces
Brewing	Courage (incl. John Smith and Harp Lager)
Hotels	Anchor Hotels (in 1985 Imperial had sold the Howard Johnson chain of American hotels)
Restaurants	Happy Eater Roadhouses, Welcome Break Motorway service areas
Shops	Finlays Newsagents.

Divestments

In 1986 the hotels and restaurants were sold to Trusthouse Forte for £186 million. The sale was subject to approval by the Monopolies and Mergers Commission which investigated the effect of linking the Happy Eater chain and Welcome Break services with THF's Little Chef group.

Also in 1986 Courage was sold to Elders IXL (Australia) for £1.4 billion. Since this sale Elders has sold Courage's public houses for £1 billion, retaining the breweries.

Golden Wonder was sold to Dalgety for £87 million in 1986.

1.7 billion pounds out of a buying price of £2.8 billion was thus recouped in the year of purchase.

In 1988 HP and Lea and Perrins were sold to BSN (France) for £199 million and Ross Frozen Foods and Young Seafoods were sold for a further £335 million.

After two years Hanson had recouped over £2 billion and still retained the tobacco interests, which, as mentioned above, constituted some 50% of Imperial turnover and profits.

This success was matched in America – where Hanson also has substantial interests – with the acquisition of SCM, again in 1986. After paying $1 billion to buy SCM, disposals recouped $1.3 billion and Hanson still retained Smith-Corona typewriters and a profitable chemical business.

Rationalization

Imperial Tobacco was rationalized by reducing the number of factories from five to two and cutting both the workforce and the number of brands. Productivity and profits improved. Significantly Hanson treated Imperial Tobacco as one business and looked for synergies – before the acquisition the old Players and Wills companies, despite being merged, had operated with separate headquarters in Nottingham and Bristol.

This approach was similar to Hanson's management of Ever Ready batteries which it had acquired in 1981. Profits, poor at the time of the acquisition, were again improved by rationalization and concentration in the UK – factories overseas were closed. In addition expenditure on research and development was cut back such that Ever Ready has been perceived to be less innovative than its main rival, Duracell. Ever Ready has, however, developed and introduced Gold Seal batteries to compete successfully with Duracell. Ever Ready was sold in April 1992 'to help finance further acquisitions'.

The Hanson strategy

The strategy is based on three essential principles:

☐ The key objective is to maximize shareholder value.
☐ Many companies do not do this and are therefore run badly.
☐ Such companies are good buys because their assets can be made to create more value for shareholders.

The strategy can be applied successfully in any industry, and Hanson has diversified into a number of unrelated areas including construction, bricks, textiles, animal foods and meat processing, pulp, coal, gold and chemicals. Hanson has not always stayed in the industry, but divested companies and business units when appropriate for its strategy.

In the main businesses in competitive industries, and which require investment, are sold, and mature, slow-growth companies retained. Cyclical businesses are also attractive targets for Hanson. In the early 1990s some 90% of Hanson's profits were from mature industries. Despite the lack of growth potential in these businesses the Hanson re-structuring strategies have generated a high and consistent growth in group profits.

Earnings per share are maximized when business units achieve the highest possible sustainable return on capital employed. Earnings per share can be improved by increasing returns from existing capital or by reducing capital and maintaining earnings. The latter theme encapsulates divestments.

Although it does not always happen it could be argued that in an organization such as this, which is not primarily concerned with staying in particular industries, business units should be sold when their earnings cannot be increased further and should be replaced by others with greater potential.

Shareholders who support such organizations expect the increased returns to be generated quickly, and consequently Hanson is not thought to be interested in companies which cannot be improved within three to four years.

Although earnings per share can be improved by investing and using debt financing rather than equity, Hanson are basically risk averse and seek to constrain their gearing.

Business units are decentralized and given strict targets to achieve, but all capital investments are carefully scrutinized at Board level. Within these financial constraints businesses can adapt their competitive and functional strategies.

BTR and Williams Holdings are similar acquisitive diversifiers, and in 1991 both were looking for new take-over opportunities, partly to satisfy shareholder expectations. BTR was diversified into control systems, electrical products, construction (Tilcon and Graham Builders' Merchants), transportation and consumer goods (Pretty Polly tights, Dunlop Slazenger). In 1991 the first two of these were supporting the other three. Historically BTR had tended not to sell off parts of acquisitions in any major way, but a new chief executive, Alan Jackson, stated that in future BTR would be more like Hanson. BTR sought to divest some of its existing businesses, and also bid for the under-performing Hawker Siddeley, which it hoped to turn around with more efficient management. The contested bid proved successful, and immediately BTR set about re-structuring Hawker, which was to be focused on three or four core divisions where the company could gain a global presence through further acquisition – to be financed by selling the rest.

Williams had built upon a base in foundries, and acquired Rawlplug, Dupont, Fairey Engineering, Kidde Aerospace, Crown Paints, Polycell, Yale and Valor. Crown and Polycell were later sold. Several Williams companies marketed products with well-known brand names. Williams' management style is based around a 'hit squad' approach – a small corporate team investigates recent acquisitions for their potential, sets demand-

---

Case 13.2
FKI–BABCOCK

FKI's strategy was to 'buy loss making companies, chop their costs and make them profitable' (*Financial Times*, 21 September 1988). FKI was the result of a management buy-out in 1974 led by the 1988 chief executive, Tony Gartland. In 14 years FKI acquired 26 electronics and engineering companies, only two of them profitable at the time of take-over. One of these two was Babcock International, the boilermakers and engineers, which FKI acquired in 1987. In terms of turnover Babcock was five times the size of FKI but in need of drastic rationalization which it was unable to fund. Babcock was already highly geared, which prohibited debt financing, and they could not launch a successful rights issue to raise equity.

The rationalization programme for Babcock involved reducing the workforce by 4000 to 34 000 and closing 25 manufacturing sites, approximately one in five. In relation to a turnover of £1.2 billion, £50 million in costs was saved. The decisions were based on FKI's key requirements of full factories and correct manning levels.

As a result of the Babcock acquisition, group turnover was trebled, and in December 1988 FKI–Babcock announced interim six month profits (April to September 1988) of £50.7 million in comparison with £48 million for the whole of the financial year 1987–8, and £13.3 million for the first half of that year. Earnings per share for the half year rose from 5p to 9p. However the share price of 122p reflected a price-to-earnings ratio of only 6. Tony Gartland was quoted in the *Financial Times* of 9 December 1988: 'High interest rates [now] make it very difficult to make large earnings-enhancing acquisitions, although the balance sheet is strong with gearing of just 10%. Issuing shares is out of the question given a poor market rating and an overhang of stock following the 1987 rights issue, which ended up in the hands of underwriters.'

The *Financial Times* commented that some analysts felt that FKI–Babcock was under-valued with a price-to-earnings ratio of 6, given its record of growth, but others felt that such rapid growth could not be maintained. As a small company FKI acquired to grow and to increase earnings; as a much larger company it would find it more difficult to find acquisitions of a sufficiently large size to make any real impact upon earnings.

Having grown through acquisition FKI–Babcock put in motion, in 1989, a demerger process. A decision was made to split the company into three parts: power engineering (the core Babcock business) to be known as Babcock International; electrical products (comprising some Babcock mining and engineering interests together with 25 FKI companies bought between 1973 and 1987) which was to be split off with an unlisted securities market (USM) listing; and the US interests which were to be sold. The stated objectives for the re-structuring were to maximize the value for the shareholders and to provide increased opportunities for managers. On 20 July 1989 the *Financial Times* quoted Tony Gartland as saying that the stock market had failed to value the company adequately and that the parts would be worth more than the whole.

In the event the proposed sale in the US failed with the collapse of the leveraged buy-out market, and these interests were retained in the newly floated FKI. In Spring 1991 Tony Gartland severed his remaining involvement with FKI – he had been the non-executive chairman. During the 1989–91 period FKI 'disappointed' and profits fell. At the same time Babcock International had grown stronger in a buoyant energy industry.

ing (financial) targets, rewards success, and sacks managers who fail. In 1991 a hostile bid for Racal failed – Williams would have to look elsewhere for future growth.

Occasionally financial consortia will be formed specifically to acquire diversified conglomerate businesses which could be 'unbundled' for financial gain. Piecemeal sales like this assume that the separated parts are worth more than the whole. Even when such bids fail the outcome frequently involves divestment of at least part of the business. See Case 13.3.

It has been suggested earlier that the search for sustainable competitive advantage is an essential requirement if a company is to be financially and strategically successful. Investments, whether they are in the form of acquisitions, additional capital equipment or the development of new products or services, should not be undertaken without some consideration of competitive advantage. The contribution of financial strategies to competitive advantage is summarized next.

FINANCE AND COMPETITIVE ADVANTAGE

Michael Porter (1985), whose work was discussed in Chapter 7, argues that companies achieve competitive advantage through lower costs and differentiation. Low cost finance (a cost of capital lower than one's competitors), cost-effective production and high quality through low wastage can all lower costs. Investments which can create new differentiation opportunities are also

Case 13.3
THE HOYLAKE BID FOR BRITISH AMERICAN TOBACCO (BAT)

BAT is a leading tobacco company, based in the UK, but dependent upon sales in the US and internationally rather than in Britain. BAT brands include Kent, 555, State Express and Kool. All the leading tobacco companies diversified in a search for growth opportunities outside an industry which was increasingly being constrained by government restrictions and public opinion in certain parts of the world. Most chose consumer goods; BAT pursued a different strategy.

BAT's diversification programme

1965	Cosmetics	Lentheric, followed later by Morny, Yardley, Carven and Gres amongst others. All sold to Beecham in 1984
1970	Paper	Wiggins Teape, and later, Appleton
1972	Supermarkets	International Stores (UK) – sold 1984
		Others in US: Marshall Field (1982)
1973	Department stores	Saks Fifth Avenue (US)
1979	Retailing	Argos
1984	Financial services	Eagle Star (1984)
		Allied Dunbar (1985)
		Canada Trust (1986)
		Farmers Group, US (1988)

Results for Year Ending 31 December 1989

	Turnover (% of total)	Profits (% of total)
Financial services	38	45
Tobacco	54	52
Other interests	8	3
North America	32	55
Europe	42	27
Rest of World	26	18

The Hoylake bid

Hoylake was a financial consortium formed by Sir James Goldsmith (General Occidental Investments), Kerry Packer (Consolidated Press, Australia) and Jacob Rothschild (merchant banker). Their bid in July 1989 was leveraged against the BAT assets and they argued that BAT had not diversified sensibly and that there was a lack of synergy. The parts would be worth more if they were separated. Hoylake intended 'to liberate the company for the benefit of its shareholders'. BAT opposed the bid but proposed a number of divestments as part of their defence strategy. BAT argued that whilst shareholders might well benefit some 40% of any increase in value would go to the owners of Hoylake.

The bid was abandoned in April 1990 as a result of some financial difficulties but mostly because of legal requirements in America. Hoylake needed to obtain proper approval to run an insurance business in every State in America where BAT had a financial presence. The estimated cost to Hoylake was £40 million, roughly half of which was covered by potential profits on the sale of the BAT shares it had bought. The BAT defence was projected to cost £100 million.

BAT divestments

During 1990 both Argos and Wiggins Teape Appleton were floated off as separate companies. BAT shareholders were simply given shares in the new businesses. The paper company has subsequently merged with the French paper manufacturer Arjo. Saks Fifth Avenue and Marshall Fields were put up for sale. BAT intended to retain its other businesses, using the profits from tobacco to invest in financial services, which offered higher growth potential. Both were marketing businesses with a strong emphasis on brands – synergy was possible. It was argued that this implied no fundamental change in the strategy, just less diversification.

Table 13.4   Comparative costs of capital – end 1980s
Ranking: 1 = lowest cost of capital; 4 = highest cost.

	USA	Japan	Germany	UK
Research and development (10-year payback)	3	1	2	4
Equipment and machinery (20-year life)	4	2	1	3
Expensed items (3-year life)	4	2	1	3

Source: Federal Reserve Bank of New York.
Whilst banking systems are different, the key is the success of respective governments in containing inflation.

influenced by the company's financial strength – the ability to raise the necessary funding from appropriate sources and the cost. The cost of raising the money influences the prospects for the investment. Proposed investments by companies in the UK have often had to appear more profitable than similar proposals elsewhere because the cost of capital has been higher. Table 13.4 shows that at the end of the 1980s lower investment costs in Germany and Japan provided opportunities for competitive advantage. Differentiation strategies are designed to add value which matters to consumers and for which they will pay a premium price. The lower the cost of adding the value, the greater is the profit opportunity.

Clarke (1988) argues that companies can also achieve competitive advantage through 'strategic mobility' which involves such factors as

☐ knowing clearly the current and future value of all parts of the business, so as to know whether they are worth keeping or whether any offers for any part might be worth accepting

□ knowing which companies are available for purchase and what the costs and values are

□ being able to raise the money to acquire them.

Strategic mobility of this nature is obviously a more relevant benefit for some companies than others. It is particularly applicable for companies with several business units, and those whose willingness to consider buying and selling businesses is derived from strong financial objectives.

Working capital and competitive advantage

Pass and Pike (1987) emphasize the value of managing working capital effectively as a way of reducing costs and contributing to competitive advantage. Working capital is measured as the difference between current assets and current liabilities.

Current assets include stock (raw materials, work in progress and finished goods), debtors (unpaid bills for goods and services supplied to customers), cash in hand, and short-term investments.

Current liabilities include monies owed to trade creditors (for raw materials etc.), bank overdraft and other short-term loans, and outstanding tax, dividend and interest obligations.

As a **flow of money** working capital is related to the movement of funds in, through and out of the business. If there is better management of stock levels, debtors (days of credit given) and creditors (days of credit taken) then overdrafts can be reduced or cash available increased. Given this there is either a saving of interest payments, which corresponds to a reduction in costs, or potential earnings from short-term investments.

Astute multi-national companies will seek to minimize their tax payments by moving profits and funds between countries and businesses and making use of tax havens. This will lead to higher after-tax profits which enable higher dividend payments to shareholders, higher retentions and lower cost investments. Hanson, for example, have recently paid taxes equivalent to 22% of pre-tax profits, well below the prevailing corporation tax rates for the UK and US – 35% and 34% respectively.

SUMMARY

In this chapter we have considered financial strategy in terms of the cost and availability of capital and the implications for the firm of different types of funding. These issues have been shown to influence the ability of the company to pursue certain strategies and the opportunity to gain competitive advantage through effective financial management. Additionally the financial evaluation of proposed investments has been examined, but it has been pointed out that other strategic issues are also important in deciding whether or not to pursue an investment.

Specifically we have

□ considered the significance of financial objectives for organizations;

□ discussed the advantages and disadvantages of equity and loan capital, and the impact of high debt funding or high gearing especially when profits are prone to fluctuate;

□ looked at the importance of dividend policy and the typical policies pursued by UK companies;

□ summarized the techniques for calculating the optimal capital structure and the weighted average cost of capital and discussed the thinking behind the capital asset pricing model;

□ considered how investments might be evaluated both in terms of strategic fit and financially, and described three quantitative techniques, namely net present

value, the internal rate of return and payback;
☐ highlighted the potential value of carrying out a sensitivity analysis;
☐ discussed how a company might be valued, say for acquisition purposes;
☐ looked briefly at strategies pursued by companies for whom financial objectives are arguably central;
☐ evaluated how financial strategies might yield competitive advantage.

CHECKLIST OF KEY TERMS AND CONCEPTS

You should feel confident that you understand the following terms and ideas:

☐ Gearing
☐ The optimal capital structure
☐ The weighted average cost of capital
☐ The capital asset pricing model (in each case a conceptual understanding primarily)
☐ Investment appraisal
☐ Sensitivity analysis
☐ Company valuations.

QUESTIONS AND RESEARCH ASSIGNMENTS

Text related

1. Calculate the weighted average cost of capital given the following information:

   Optimal capital structure   50:50
   Debt funding: half is at 10% interest, half at 12%
   Effective tax rate   30%

Risk-free rate   8%
Return expected in the stock market 12%
Company's beta   1.2

2. A firm has two investment opportunities, each costing £100 000 and each having the expected net cash flows shown in the table. Whilst the cost of each project is certain, the cash flow projections for project B are more uncertain than those for A because of additional inherent risks. Those shown in both cases can be assumed to be maxima. It has therefore been suggested that whilst the company's cost of capital is of the order of 10%, B might usefully be discounted at 15%.
   (a) For each alternative calculate the net present value, the internal rate of return and the payback.
   (b) On the data available what would you advise the firm to do?
   (c) How limited do you feel this analysis is?

| | Expected cash flows | |
	Project A (£)	Project B (£)
Year 1	50 000	20 000
Year 2	40 000	40 000
Year 3	30 000	50 000
Year 4	10 000	60 000

Library based

3. Obtain the accounts for a number of competitors in the same industry (using the annual reports, Extel or Datastream). Evaluate the capital structure and dividend policy of each company. How have recent investments been funded: retained earnings, debt, equity or leasing? Consider why the differences you have found might have arisen. Considering the capital

structure and profit trends of each company, which of the competitors do you feel best matches the risk and uncertainty of the industry?

4. Take a small company and a large company in an industry you consider to be relatively low risk and in one you consider much higher risk. Compare and evaluate the respective capital structures and the implications. Do the figures confirm your expectations of how the companies might be expected to be funded?

5. Evaluate the 1989 bid for BAT by Hoylake and BAT's reaction and defence. Was BAT vulnerable because it had failed to look after the interests of its shareholders as effectively as it might? Do you feel the shareholders have benefited from the outcome?

6. Examine the progress of Williams Holdings since the abortive bid for Racal. Have Williams bid for any other companies? What has been the reaction of the stock market?

RECOMMENDED FURTHER READING

British texts

Drury, C (1992) *Management and Cost Accounting*, 3rd edn, Chapman and Hall (particularly for capital budgeting).

Franks, J R, and Broyles, J E (1979) *Modern Managerial Finance*, Wiley.

Franks, J R, Broyles, J C and Carleton, W T (1985) *Corporate Finance: Concepts and Applications*, Kent.

American texts

Gitman, L J (1982) *Principles of Managerial Finance*, 3rd edn, Harper and Row.

Weston, J F and Brigham, E F (1979) *Managerial Finance*, 6th edn, Holt, Rinehart and Winston.

REFERENCES

Allen, D (1988) *Long Term Financial Health – A Structure for Strategic Financial Management*, Institute of Management Accountants.

Clarke, C J (1988) Using finance for competitive advantage, *Long Range Planning*, **21**(2).

Donaldson, G and Lorsch, J W (1983) *Decision Making At The Top*, Basic Books.

Franks, J R and Broyles, J E (1979) *Modern Managerial Finance*, Wiley.

Gitman, L J (1982) *Principles of Managerial Finance*, 3rd edn, Harper and Row.

Modigliani, F and Miller, M H (1958) The cost of capital, corporation finance and the theory of investment, *American Economic Review*, June.

Pass, C and Pike, R H (1987) Management of working capital: a neglected subject, *Management Decision*, **25**(1).

Pike, R H (1982) *Capital Budgeting in the 1980s*, Institute of Cost and Management Accountants Occasional Paper.

Porter, M E (1985) *Competitive Advantage: Creating and Sustaining Superior Performance*, Free Press.

Schein, E H (1983) The role of the founder in creating organizational culture, *Organisational Dynamics*, Summer.

Weston, J F and Brigham, E F (1979) *Managerial Finance*, 6th edn, Holt, Rinehart and Winston.

INFORMATION AS A STRATEGIC RESOURCE

14

LEARNING OBJECTIVES

After studying this chapter you should be able to

☐ identify the importance of information for strategic awareness and for decisions relating to strategic change;
☐ explain how misinterpretation can lead to what is known as counter-intuitive behaviour;
☐ define information technology and management information systems;
☐ assess the impact of information needs and processing difficulties on organization structure;
☐ describe a number of cases where information technology has been used to create competitive advantage.

In this chapter we consider the vital role of information in strategic decision making at all levels, and some of the difficulties involved in ensuring that decision makers have the information which they need at the time decisions need to be made. The increasing contribution of information technology is discussed.

INTRODUCTION

Information is needed for, and used in, decision making. Information, information systems and information technology are all aids to decision making. The more information managers and other employees have about what is happening in the organization, the more strategically aware they are likely to be. Information about other functional areas and business units can be particularly helpful in this respect.

However, decisions and decision making involve both facts and people. Whilst the right information available at the right time can be extremely useful, the real value of information relates to how it is used by decision makers, particularly for generating and evaluating alternative possible courses of action. In designing and introducing information technology and management information systems into organizations it is necessary to consider the likely reaction of people as well as the potential benefits which can accrue from having more up-to-date and accurate information available. Information gathering should never become an end in itself, for the expertise and experience in people's heads can be more useful than facts on paper.

Moreover it is important to evaluate who actually needs the information, rather than who might find it useful for increasing awareness, and to ensure that those people receive it. Hence the structure and culture of the organization should ensure that managers who need information receive it, and at the right time. Information can lead to more effective decision making, but it is a manifestation of power within the organization, and this aspect needs monitoring. If information which could prove useful is withheld from decision makers, negligently or deliberately by political managers pursuing personal objectives, the effectiveness of decision making is reduced. This theme will be developed in greater depth when we consider strategy implementation towards the end of the book.

Information is used through a filter of experience and judgement in decision making, and its relative value varies between one decision maker and another. In certain instances the available information will be accurate, reliable and up to date. In other circumstances the information provided may already be biased because it is the result of the interpretation of a situation by someone who may have introduced subjectivity. Some managers, perhaps those who are less experienced, will rely more heavily on specific information than others, for whom experience, general awareness and insight into the situation are more important.

In this chapter information and information technology will be examined in relation to organization structure, decision making, planning, control and people. Although information technology and information systems can be expensive to introduce, those organizations which receive information, analyse and distribute it to the appropriate decision makers faster than their competitors can achieve a competitive edge, particularly in a turbulent environment.

INFORMATION, INFORMATION SYSTEMS AND INFORMATION TECHNOLOGY

Information

Information has been defined as 'some tangible or intangible entity that reduces uncertainty about a state or event' (Lucas, 1976), which is a way of saying that information increases knowledge in a particular situation. When information is received, some degree of order can be imposed on a previously less well-ordered situation. Davis and Olsen (1985) define information more rigidly as 'data that has been processed into a form that is meaningful to the recipient, and is of real perceived value in current or prospective decisions'. Information, then, must be received by those who need it, although the channels through which it flows can be either formal or informal. Computer analyses, written and oral reports, telephone conversations and lunchtime chats can all provide information. The grapevine or word of mouth in an organization can be extremely important. Bias might be introduced at any stage where interpretation of data is an issue, and some sources may in fact be unreliable. Data can be misinterpreted quite innocently and cause misunderstanding, and decision makers can handle only so much information. Hence the availability of information does not mean that it will lead to more effective decisions. Information technology and systems should contribute towards making the provision of information more useful for decision makers.

Decision making and interpretation of information

Spear (1980) argues that when information systems and the provision of information for managers are being considered it is important to bear in mind how people make decisions, interpret data and information, and give meaning to them. In decision making managers sometimes behave in a stereotyped way and follow past courses of action; sometimes they are relatively unconcerned with the particular decision and may behave inconsistently. In each case they may ignore information which is available and which if used objectively would lead to a different conclusion and decision. At other times information is used selectively and ignored if it conflicts with strongly held beliefs or views about certain things. In other words information may be either misused or not used effectively.

Moreover when considering a problem situation managers have to interpret the events they are able to observe and draw certain conclusions about what they believe is happening. The question is: do managers perceive reality? The following example will explain the point. Worker directors have

---

Swift, accurate and relevant information will be ever more at a premium in the years ahead, and the sources will proliferate. But information is not knowledge, and there will be an even greater premium on knowledge: informed comment, new ideas, fresh perceptions about facts.

Jason McManus, Time Warner Inc. Quoted in Fortune, 26 March 1990, p. 86.

---

always been a controversial issue amongst managers and trade union officials in the UK, with some of them supportive and others, in reality a majority, strongly opposed to their introduction. Managers who oppose them argue that they will reduce managerial power to run an organization; union opponents argue they would increase managerial power because the directors would be carefully selected or co-opted to include mainly those who were antagonistic to many of the aims of the union. These views represent meaning systems. The idea of worker directors, and what they are, is definite and agreed; their meaning and the implications of using them are subjective and interpretive.

A parallel situation would concern the interpretation of economic data. If, say, interest rates are rising, share prices are falling or the value of the pound is strengthening, would a supporter of monetarist economics draw the same conclusions about the possible future impact on his or her business as would someone who opposed monetarism in favour of demand management?

Information needs are also related to meaning systems. A prison, for example, is concerned with both punishing and rehabilitating offenders, and different interested parties will have conflicting views on which of the two is more important. The measurement of the success of the strategies derived from these objectives can be related to the behaviour of prisoners both during their period in prison and afterwards. Information collection should relate to this, and then it is subject to interpretation. At the same time prison officers may be most concerned with making sure that potential trouble is contained and possible protests against, say, over-crowding are avoided. Their information needs relate to intelligence about potential trouble.

In large complex firms it is useful if managers understand what is happening elsewhere in the organization at any time. The importance of this always applies to managers in the various functions of a business unit, and an appreciation of progress and performance in other business units increases in value if the business units are interdependent in some way. However, unless the information systems, both formal and informal, are successful in providing an objective picture, meaning systems are likely to play a significant role. Given this, there may well be misunderstandings about other parts of the firm.

One problem for decision makers is how to react to information received from a source which is viewed sceptically and not trusted. People who design new information systems need to take some account of the way the information might be received, interpreted and used if decision-making effectiveness is to be improved.

Counter-intuitive behaviour

A failure to think through the implications of certain decisions on other managers, departments or business units can have effects that are unwelcome. The same can happen if there is an inability to appreciate the consequences because of a lack of information, or if there is a misunderstanding resulting from the wrong interpretation of information. This relates to meaning systems, which were described above. Such an event is known as counter-intuitive behaviour, and it often creates a new set of problems which may be more serious than those which existed originally.

Jay Forrester, in his book *Urban Dynamics* (1969), discusses how a strategy of building low cost housing by the American equivalent of a local authority in order to improve living conditions for low income earners in inner city areas has done more harm than good. The new houses draw in more low income people who need jobs, but at the same time they make the area less attractive for those employers who might create employment. General social conditions decline. The area

becomes even more destitute, creating again more pressure for low cost housing. 'The consequence is a downward spiral that draws in the low-income population, depresses their condition, prevents escape and reduces hope. All of this done with the best of intentions.'

Related problems occur with misinterpretation of information. Consider the example of an independent retailer who finds that he or she is selling more of a particular item than normal and more than he expected to sell. Deliveries from his wholesaler or other suppliers require a waiting period. Does he simply replace his stock, or increase his stockholding levels? How does he forecast or interpret future demand? When he starts ordering and buying more, or buying more frequently, how do his suppliers, and ultimately the manufacturer, respond? On what do they base their stockholding and production decisions, given that there will be penalties for misunderstanding the situation? Such problems are made worse by time lags or delays. The use of information technology by major retail organizations lessens the impact of this dilemma.

Summarizing, the fact that information is available does not necessarily mean that more effective decisions will result.

Information technology

The literature on technology is inconsistent concerning whether one is referring only to the machinery or hardware involved or to the organization of work around the hardware. Winner (1977) contends that the term is now used to describe 'tools, instruments, machines, organizations, methods, techniques, systems, and the totality of these'. Adapting the above definitions of information, information technology (IT) can therefore be regarded as 'the application of hardware (machinery) and software (systems and techniques) to methods of processing and presenting data into a meaningful form which helps reduce uncertainty and is of real perceived value in current or future decisions'.

An OECD Report (1989) suggests that the real impact of IT has yet to be realized. The report contends that IT has so far failed to produce the major spur to economic growth normally associated with major technological change, but suggests it will happen in the 1990s. The report draws a parallel with the development of electricity and transmission systems between 1860 and 1900, pointing out that it was in the early twentieth century that manufacturers properly realized and benefited from its potential for increasing productivity. This required changes in machine tooling, plant design and attitudes. If organizations are to benefit from the potential of IT work practices and organization cultures will again have to change; the potential is not achieved simply by investing in computers.

Management information systems

Whilst computers and IT might be an essential feature of a management information system (MIS), the basic ideas behind an information system have little concern with computers. A management information system collects, processes and distributes the information which is required for managers to make decisions. It should be designed to be cost effective, in that the additional revenue or profits generated by more effective decisions exceed the cost of designing, introducing and running the system, or that the value of management time saved is greater than the cost of the system. Additionally the information provided should be valid, reliable and up to date for the decisions concerned.

Ackoff (1967) suggested that management information systems can easily be based on erroneous assumptions.

☐ Managers are short of information. In many cases managers have too much irrelevant information.

☐ Managers know the information they require for a decision. However, when asked what information they might need, managers play safe and ask for everything which might be relevant, and thereby contribute to the over-abundance of irrelevant information.

☐ If a manager is provided with the information required for a decision he or she will have no further problem in using it effectively. How information is used depends upon perceptions of the issues involved. Moreover, if any additional quantitative analysis or interpretation is required, many managers are weak in these skills.

As a result management information systems may fail to fulfil their promises and not prove beneficial in terms of generating more effective decisions. Information systems **serve** decision makers, and really should not be designed and introduced without a clear and objective appreciation of the information needs of the decision makers. However, the potential of IT and information systems to create competitive advantage should not be overlooked.

THE IMPACT OF INFORMATION SYSTEMS AND INFORMATION TECHNOLOGY ON ORGANIZATIONS

Information, information technology and decision making

It was noted above that a number of researchers, including Ackoff, contend that many formalized information systems fail to meet expectations. This applies to those which are particularly dependent upon the application of computers and IT. Lorsch and Allen (1973) have suggested that this is because when information systems become

Table 14.1   The information processing mix

	Routine	Non-routine
Official	Formal MIS Budgeting and financial systems Production planning and control	Occasional task groups (special problems) Liaison roles
Unofficial	Political activity	Organization grapevine Lunchtime discussions

Developed from Earl, M J and Hopwood, A G (1980) From management information to information management. In *The Information Systems Environment* (eds Lucas, Land, Lincoln and Supper), North-Holland.

increasingly complex they facilitate upward but not downward information flows. This might result in increased information and strategic awareness for the strategic leader and senior executives but not for those who manage competitive and functional strategies lower down the organization and who adapt strategic changes in the light of environmental trends. In contrast Mintzberg (1972) argues that it results from top managers selecting and preferring personal contact and informal information processing in much of their work and decision making.

Earl and Hopwood (1980) point out that there is a tendency for the potential of IT to lead to an increasingly technological perspective on the way information is processed by managers. This leads to increasingly formal systems and bureaucratic procedures which 'neither fit nor suit the realities of organizational activity'. They advocate distinguishing between routine and non-routine, official and unofficial modes of information processing as illustrated in Table 14.1. Some decision situations are routine whilst others are non-routine and in response to particular problems or opportunities. Often these require special co-operation and information exchange between managers from different functions or business units. Sometimes informally exchanged information between managers who trust and respect each other is extremely important; and in some organizations political activity and power is important in certain decisions. Given an appreciation of these different situations and dependences,

the role of formal information systems for official and routine decisions is clear and can lead to a higher level of exploitation of the possibilities offered by IT. Without this appreciation there may be a tendency to constrain the spontaneity, flexibility and informality upon which the effectiveness of much decision making depends. In other words, information systems and IT do not, and cannot, enable universally better decision making. They need putting into perspective, and a consideration of where they can be most useful. In the next section different types of decision are considered in this context.

Information and types of decision

Anthony (1965) has provided a useful taxonomy of planning and control decisions, which is often presented in the form of a triangle, as illustrated in Figure 14.1. Decisions at the base of the triangle are essentially concerned with the control of operations. A considerable amount of data are generated within the organization and need processing and analysing. The data are summarized into information as they move up the triangle and up the organization; and for strategic decisions there is a need for externally sourced information in addition to that provided internally. Information systems and technology can be valuable for analysing control data and translating them into information which can be useful for

Figure 14.1   The management triangle. Developed from Anthony, R N (1965) *Planning and Control Systems: A Framework for Analysis*, Harvard University Press.

higher level decisions, and for transmitting strategies and decisions reached at the top throughout the organization. Typically this would be in the form of implementation policies and procedures, and systems for controlling operations. However, the contribution of information systems and IT to strategy creation and to certain tactical decisions is less straightforward and considered below.

Operational decisions

Operational decisions relate to the basic and routine aspects of jobs, such as scheduling instructions. Production control systems, stock control systems and wage payments would all be included, and these are ideal for computerization and the application of IT for more effective decision making. As a result costs might be saved and the total quality of the service provided improved. However, in designing the applications it is important to consider the people who will use the technology and the systems.

Tactical and management control decisions

These decisions concern policies both for implementing strategic decisions and for measuring performance. Involved are

☐ the design of organization structures
☐ the selection and motivation of people for particular jobs
☐ the establishment of policies and procedures
☐ budgeting.

In many instances IT can prove useful, as illustrated in Case 14.1 on Huddersfield Royal Infirmary. Better tactical decisions can result in more effective control and in turn contribute to more effective strategic decisions. But there are limitations concerning its applicability for certain decisions. In evaluating staff performance, for example, data may be available but in need of interpretation, when meaning systems become an issue. Data on absenteeism, an important factor in evaluating morale and motivation, may not be reliable. Supervisors and managers may not keep accurate records especially if they regard minor infringements as being unimportant.

Decisions concerning strategic change

Whether the decisions are taken as part of a formal planning process, more randomly by the strategic leader, or periodically by managers throughout the organization in the

---

Case 14.1
HUDDERSFIELD ROYAL INFIRMARY

Huddersfield Royal Infirmary was one of a number of hospitals selected to take part in a National Health Service (NHS) initiative in the late 1980s concerned with improving information for more effective resource management. This initiative was a precursor for changes in the NHS announced early in 1989.

The objective of the initiative was to 'provide an internal, computerized MIS [management information system] for hospitals which identifies product ranges, resource inputs, costs, outputs and quality measures'. As mentioned earlier (Chapter 5), the outputs of not-for-profit organizations are often not measured in this way. It was commented that for the first time there will be real knowledge available concerning success rates and whether patients are getting better. Doctors will be able to compare the costs for an operation at different hospitals; patient treatment costs will be measurable against average or expected costs and variances can be analysed. This system will enable more efficient resource management and will lead to greater effectiveness when the customers of the hospitals (general practitioners who refer their patients) can choose where to send their patients using the data generated from the information system. These changes are now in place.

Essentially IT has been harnessed to allow the NHS to carry out the analyses and measures of effective performance that are commonplace in many manufacturing firms. There is an effect on hospital strategies, because hospitals have needed to become more customer oriented when there is greater customer choice.

---

form of incremental changes, there is a need to interpret data and information from both inside and outside the firm. Case 14.2 on popular records highlights the need for up-to-date and accurate information if the competitive strategy for individual records is to be managed effectively. However, in addition, the company's current performance must be evaluated, and whilst information systems can assist with financial analyses, there are other aspects relating to the satisfaction of customers and other stakeholders. Trends and changes in the external environment must be evaluated; but appreciating the significance of particular events often requires judgement. Future opportunities and threats must be considered; and again, whilst IT can project past data forward and collate and summarize data concerning economic trends, market shares and competitor activities, judgement will be required in assessing their significance.

Judgement is discussed at greater length in Chapter 21.

Hence as one moves up the management triangle the contribution of IT and information systems to decision making changes. At the bottom the systems once established, can make the decisions and drive the operations. In measuring performance, the system can again often make a valuable contribution and highlight when things are going wrong. However, for strategic decisions, IT is primarily an aid to decision making. The system cannot realistically make the decisions, and consequently interpretation and meaning systems become increasingly significant. For such decisions the systems should be designed to provide information in a form which is useful to decision makers.

Case 14.2
INFORMATION TECHNOLOGY AND THE MARKETING OF POPULAR RECORDS

In the popular record industry there can be up to 150 new products in any week, in the form of new single and album (LP, cassette and CD) releases. The typical lifespan of a single might be effectively six weeks. At any time some 80 000 items (different singles and albums) are being retailed throughout the UK, and the record companies collectively need up-to-date and accurate information on these. Individual stores can stock only so many titles and so many copies of each, but they need to be assured of speedy replenishment when titles sell well. Additionally production costs make it worth while for record companies to press only so many copies of singles and albums at any time, quickly producing more when demand justifies it. In this way they are less likely to be left with surplus stock. However, such decisions can only be effective if the information needed is accurate and up to date.

The Gallup organization gathers information daily from 850 stores. When records, cassettes and CDs are sold the bar codes are read by the tills and the information is stored on disc and then transmitted to Gallup through modems. Record companies buy this information rather than seek to collect their own individually. In addition to production decisions, marketing decisions are also more informed as the data are regional. In this way local radio and television promotions can be adjusted to take account of sales trends.

At the same time information technology can improve and speed up re-ordering and re-stocking. A few years ago record shops used to ring up record companies with their orders at least weekly and most frequently on Monday mornings after a weekend rush. Now in-store terminals can be linked directly to record companies' computers.

Information, information technology and organization structure

According to Jay Galbraith (1974), if the organization is to benefit from information systems and technology it must be structured in such a way as to allow effective information processing. He argues that the need for information processing relates primarily to the extent of the uncertainty faced by the organization, together with the degree of differentiation and interdependence between activities and business units. These in turn are related to the size of the organization, the tasks and technologies involved, and the nature of the environment. In general, the greater the uncertainty, the greater the

co-ordination and control problems. It follows that as these problems and difficulties increase, the need for information processing and the opportunities for IT become stronger. More information must be processed in order to achieve results, and less can be planned because of the uncertainty. Paton (1980) has summarized this contention in the diagram overleaf.

The overall tasks of the organization are more likely to be accomplished effectively if subtasks are performed with the whole in mind, in other words, if functional and competitive decision makers take account of the implications for the whole organization. If they are to do this they must be strategically aware, and it is one role of the structure to ensure that managers are provided with

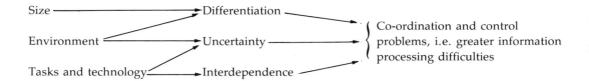

the relevant information. This is accomplished by co-ordination, which Galbraith argues can be by policies or rules concerning the way things should be done, by the managerial hierarchy in the sense that important decisions are referred upwards, or by establishing appropriate objectives for managers throughout the organization. The potential value of objectives increases as complexity increases, but it is important to consider the limitations of management by objectives systems which were discussed in Chapter 12.

As information processing requirements increase, the organization has a choice of four strategies, each of which affects the structure in different ways.

☐ First, slack resources can be created. Deadlines can be extended to relieve pressures and make decisions less essential. This inevitably incurs costs, and may be at the expense of quality of service for customers.

☐ Second, there can be greater decentralization and divisionalization to enable more delegation of responsibility to managers throughout the organization. This will encourage more incremental adaptive changes as opportunities are spotted and threats responded to. The effectiveness will depend upon the policies which provide guidelines for managers, their strategic awareness, and the ability of the strategic leader to monitor and interpret the overall picture.

In general, both of these alternatives reduce the need for information processing. The third and fourth options below are concerned with increasing the capacity of the organization to process information.

☐ Third, there can be an investment in vertical information systems. These are found in centralized decision making. A sophisticated management information system gathers internal and external data, and the system spreads information and decisions downwards. This can sometimes reduce flexibility to changes in the environment, and consequently may be less useful as turbulence increases. See Case 14.3.

☐ Fourth, lateral relationships can be created or extended. In other words there is an attempt to design integration between functions and business units into the structure, so that key decisions involve a number of people from involved parts of the organization. There are a number of ways of accomplishing this, and they will be examined in greater detail when we look at structures in depth in Chapter 22.

One conclusion from Galbraith's work is that if the organization seeks to utilize IT and sophisticated management information systems for strategic decision making through centralization and planning, there is a potential loss of flexibility in terms of the organization's ability to respond to changes in the environment. If there is a move towards decentralization and managers are encouraged to accept responsibility for business units, products and functions, and to make necessary changes, the appropriate application of IT is also likely to be decentralized. There will be no organization-wide management information system. Hence the choice of IT should take account of the way strategic decisions are taken within the organization.

Case 14.3
MRS FIELDS' COOKIES

Mrs Fields' Cookies has used IT to gain the control benefits of centralization whilst maintaining a decentralized organization structure. The company operates soft cookie stores in most states in America and in selected countries world wide. In America they are typically located in busy shopping areas but in the UK they are most likely to be seen at main railway stations and airports. A wide range of cookies are baked in the store and sold either individually or in small quantities.

IT is used for control and to instruct individual store managers direct from Utah in America. Whilst there is a regional sales network, Mrs Fields' has relatively few middle managers. See also Key Reading 14.1.

Each store has a computer built into the sales till. The computer analyses the latest sales patterns and provides an hourly baking schedule for cookies, which are baked throughout the day and only sold fresh. Sales data are also fed back to Mrs Fields' head office in Utah, where they are again analysed and projections revised. One argument for this system is that it allows staff more time to concentrate on customer service – interestingly the in-store computer also flags when sales are below estimated targets and instructs staff to introduce special promotions or hand out free samples. The company motto is 'Good Enough Never Is' and employees are encouraged to feed back their ideas for improving the business. The founder and Chief Executive, Mrs Debbi Fields, attempts to maintain some form of personal contact with every store, even if it is only pre-recorded messages.

Information technology and managers

A number of researchers have looked into the impact of IT on managers, and their conclusions are not altogether consistent. Hofer (1970) suggests that managers will be forced to work under greater constraints, but that the impact of this is most likely at the operational level. Stewart (1971), however, contends that a richer data base, and the possibilities for manipulating information, allow managers to explore decision areas more deeply and consider more options. Given the diversity of organizations, and the variety of tasks to be performed, both these contentions might be true under different circumstances. Eason (1980) indicates that the strongest impact of IT has been felt within departments in an organization rather than between them. This is because IT is particu-larly useful where there are strong task interdependences, and these are most common inside departments.

The Amdahl Executive Institute (1989) argues that British managers are less well equipped than many of their European counterparts to take advantage of the potential of IT because they are less aware of the potential, and less confident in their ability to use it. This suggests the need for cultural changes within organizations if IT is to be harnessed more effectively; this point is also addressed by Schein (1985) and by Drucker (1988) in his article which considers organizations of the future. Drucker contends that as a result of IT organizations will move away from what he calls command-and-control structures to ones based on information, and the result will be organizations composed largely of specialists, with fewer than half the

Key Reading 14.1
THE FUTURE ORGANIZATION

Large businesses, 20 years hence, will typically have half the levels of management compared with organizations in the late 1980s and about one-third of the managers. The structure will be based essentially on knowledge and will be composed of specialists who will enjoy considerable independence and will discipline their performance through organized feedback from colleagues. These changes will result from the greater need for innovation and entrepreneurship, and from the implications of IT. The amount of data available will increase, and IT will need to be utilized increasingly to analyse it. IT, though, must not be seen merely as an opportunity to process data or crunch numbers faster than can be done manually.

Currently a number of management posts exist primarily to relay data around the organization; the managers concerned are neither decision makers nor leaders. Applied properly, IT will allow more effective data processing to generate better information. In other words, and bearing in mind comments made earlier in this chapter, developments in IT will enable managers to enjoy greater strategic awareness and to contribute more reliable information concerning strategic change decisions. Managers can then be responsible for business units or functions in the organization and manage them as independent units, much in line with the web structure and power culture (Handy, 1978) which was discussed in Chapter 4. Competitive and functional strategies will therefore continually be adapted as circumstances change.

Strategic developments which affect a number of parts of the organization will stem from special project groups and task forces composed of seconded members of business units and functional departments.

The strategic leader will have access to more information, provided in an appropriate form and quickly, and will therefore be able to direct the whole organization with fewer managers to relay information to and from the business units and functions. In this respect Drucker compares the organization with a symphony orchestra, where over 100 specialist musicians all respond to one leader. The conductor can control the whole orchestra without assistance as he can see and hear everyone and be seen by the musicians. IT will simulate this effect.

As another example, Drucker praises the way in which, from the middle of the eighteenth century, the British Government administered the whole of the Indian subcontinent with just 1000 civil servants. Many of these lived in isolated outposts and operated as individuals, with four clearly delineated tasks to perform. In total there were nine provinces, each with a political secretary, and some 100 people reporting directly to him. The system worked, despite limited communications, because it was designed to enable people to have the information they needed to do their job. Each of the 1000 district officers wrote a comprehensive monthly report detailing what he had expected would happen in the previous month, what had happened and, if there were discrepancies, why. This was followed by comments on what he expected to happen in the next month, together with perceived opportunities, threats and needs. In return he received a comprehensive reply from the political secretary.

Drucker argues that in information-based organizations it will be necessary that

☐ there are clear, simple and few common objectives that translate into particular actions;
☐ managers are allowed the freedom to operate, rather than being told in detail how to do things, but are given expected targets and measures;

☐ all managers accept responsibility for information.

In other words, managers will appreciate who they depend on, and for what, and who depends on them. In addition a manager will understand clearly the information needed for a particular decision and the information needs of other managers if they are to perform effectively. This implies a break-through from the notion that the more data there are available, the better it is for decision makers. When this happens IT can begin to be really useful. However, it does imply major change, including a change in culture, to switch from a situation where managers do not appreciate precisely the information they need to make decisions. This was first highlighted by Ackoff (1967) and com-mented upon earlier in the chapter.

Drucker contends that the information-based organization will have four critical problem areas to deal with:

☐ developing rewards, recognition and career opportunities for specialist
☐ creating a unified vision where every manager is a specialists
☐ devising an effective structure to encompass the task forces (this relates to the problems encountered with matrix organizations, which are discussed later in Chapter 22)
☐ ensuring the development of managers for strategic leadership.

Whilst the problems can be identified, the solutions are less obvious. Hence, Drucker concludes, the information-based organ-ization is the managerial challenge of the future.

Based on Drucker, P F (1988) The coming of the new organization, *Harvard Business Review*, January–February.

---

levels of management today and no more than a third of the managers. Drucker's forecast is explored further in Key Reading 14.1.

Generally managers are resistant to change if it threatens their existing stability, and Schein (1985) suggests that greater accept-ance of technological change requires a change in culture. Practices and values, he contends, are built around the underlying technology; and where managers and organ-izations are successful because of their mast-ery of a particular technology, their self-image is built around it. One of the strongest elements of organization culture is the status system attached to this traditional technology and the possession by individuals of key items of information or critical skills. If IT is introduced without due regard to its impact upon power realignments, there can be unfortunate results such as subordinates now

knowing more than their bosses. Fearing such a loss of power, people are often resistant to pressures to change. Further resistance relates to the uncertainty and anxiety associated with the changes, but this can be overcome, according to Schein, by involving lower management in the design and implementation phases and changing things gradually.

INFORMATION TECHNOLOGY AND COMPETITIVE ADVANTAGE

It has already been shown that IT offers many potential strategic opportunities which go beyond the notion of faster data processing, but that harnessing these opportunities will involve changes of attitude and culture amongst managers. PA Management Consultants (1985) have suggested that many chief executives in the UK are indecisive with regard to IT, sensing that it is leading to the reshaping of markets and to changes in the way that businesses are managed but feeling unsure about how to use it for the benefit of their own organization. Specifically PA conclude from their survey that

☐ IT is seen more as a support function than a competitive weapon;
☐ executives are unsure about how IT might be used as a competitive weapon;
☐ most of the companies involved in the survey view IT from a technical rather than a business approach. In other words most of their expectations relate to productivity improvements rather than competitive advantage.

McFarlan (1984) claims that IT strategies should relate to two criteria:

☐ How dependent is the organization on IT systems which are reliable 24 hours a day, 7 days a week? International banks and stock and currency dealers who trade around the clock, and who use IT to monitor price movements and record their transactions, need their systems to be wholly reliable.
☐ Is IT crucial if the organization is to meet key success factors? If it is, there is an implication that companies can benefit from harnessing the latest technological developments. An obvious example is the airline industry. Case 14.4 looks at IT in British Airways, but in fairness it reflects developments by all the leading airlines.

Case 14.4
BRITISH AIRWAYS

British Airways invests in excess of 3% of its gross revenue in IT, and expects this to rise to 5% by the end of the 1990s. IT was first utilized over 30 years ago to streamline the reservations systems. Subsequently it was used for aircraft scheduling and spares control and for crew rostering. Improved efficiencies in these areas are critical as cargo and passenger volumes grow, and continue to grow.

Increasingly, IT has also been used to add value and to improve BA's overall service and effectiveness in a very competitive industry. A number of the applications are described below.

Computerized reservation systems now link travel agencies directly with the airlines and provide instantaneous information on availability followed by reservations and tickets. There are a number of systems but the market is dominated by two, which carry up-to-date information on hundreds of airlines and their flight schedules. Sabre (owned by American Airlines) covers some 5–10% of European flights and 45% of the US market; Galileo/Apollo (two merged systems, owned by United Airlines and BA together with nine other airlines) covers 40% of Europe and 30% of America. These systems allow airlines to change prices and pricing policies frequently in their attempt to maximize their yield. In other words, fares for a particular flight can be adjusted in line with demand, and ticket prices can be discounted to try to fill the aeroplane if there are spare seats. The airlines want to sell seats at the highest prices they can obtain, but an empty seat means lost and irrecoverable revenue. This is complex as there are 30 different fares available on a typical transatlantic flight on a Boeing 747.

Travel agents, with access to substantial information, will often shop around for the lowest fares. Additionally, computer reservation systems allow passengers to be allocated specific seats well in advance of their flight rather than when they check in at the airport. Clearly both the airline and the passenger can benefit. The airlines further argue that these systems give them better control over their deliberate over-booking policies. An airline is often willing to sell more seats than they have available on a flight, assuming that some passengers with tickets will not travel, and balancing the cost of compensation and lost goodwill against the lost revenue from empty seats.

New ticketing machines at airports enable passengers on domestic shuttle flights to buy their ticket and obtain their printed boarding card in 40 seconds. The technology also exists for machines to scan a passenger's thumb print (assuming it has been previously verified), issue a ticket and debit that person's bank account. This is seen as more secure than the existing machines, which respond to credit and debit cards, and more likely to generate customer loyalty. Hand-held computers are available to speed up checking-in and reduce queuing.

ACARS (Aircraft Communications Addressing and Reporting System) allows fast transfer of information by radio waves between computers on the ground and computers on board aircraft. Data transmitted during a flight can help plan routine and extra ground maintenance and boarding delays can be reduced. Some of the ground time between flights is spent analysing and responding to information on load and balance.

Personal video players, which are typically standard in first class, can be adapted to enable passengers to book hotels and cars during their flights and possibly use their credit cards for mail-order shopping. (Hertz already have touch-panel machines with visual prompt screens at airports to enable passengers reserve cars at their destination just before they fly. A printed confirmation takes 6 seconds.)

Major car manufacturers have similarly become increasingly dependent in IT which is used for:

☐ computer-aided design and engineering to speed up product development;
☐ robotics on the assembly lines to reduce costs and increase productivity;
☐ databases for gathering marketing intelligence and targeting promotional campaigns. As markets become increasingly segmented IT can help establish a database of potential customers who meet very specific criteria. Direct mail campaigns can then be targeted more effectively.

Michael Porter (1985) further suggests that technological change, and in particular IT, is amongst the most prominent forces that can alter the rules of competition. This is because most activities in an organization create and use information. Porter and Millar (1985) contend that IT is affecting competition in three ways:

☐ IT can change the structure of an industry, and in so doing alter the rules of competition;
☐ IT can be used to create sustainable competitive advantage and provide companies with new competitive weapons;
☐ as a result of IT new businesses can be developed from within a company's existing activities.

These three themes are examined in greater detail below.

Industry structure

According to Porter (1980), the structure of an industry can be analysed in terms of five competitive forces: the threat of new entrants; the bargaining power of suppliers; the bargaining power of buyers; the threat of substitute products and services; and rivalry amongst existing competitors. These forces were discussed in detail in Chapter 7.

Porter and Millar (1985) suggest that IT can influence the nature of these forces, and thereby change the attractiveness and profitability of an industry. This is particularly applicable where the industry has a high information content, such as airlines, and financial and distribution services. In distribution, for example, the automation of order processing and invoicing may lead to an increase in fixed costs, and as a result encourage greater rivalry between competitors for additional business. Moreover, firms which are either slow or reluctant to introduce IT may be driven out of the industry, because they will be unable to offer a competitive service. Where the cost of the necessary IT, both hardware and software systems, is high it can increase the barriers to entry for potential new firms.

Case 14.5, Thomson Holidays, explains how package holiday tour companies have made use of IT to lower costs and allow them to compete more aggressively on pricing. The result of all the competitive activity has been an increase in concentration, with the largest companies gaining market share at the expense of smaller rivals, many of whom have left the industry.

Porter and Millar show that IT can both improve and reduce the attractiveness and profitability of an industry, and that as a consequence manufacturers should analyse the potential implications of change very carefully.

IT has transformed such financial services as banking, enabling customers to carry out many of their financial transactions without needing to queue for a cashier. However,

there is the disadvantage that aspects of banking are being made more impersonal, and the personal service aspect is being reduced.

The creation of competitive advantage

Porter (1985) argues that competitive advantage results from lower costs or differentiation, and that these strategies can be applied with either a broad or a narrow market focus. This was discussed fully in Chapter 7.

Lower costs

If costs are reduced to a level below competitors' costs and this advantage is maintained, above-average profits and an increased market share can result. Porter and Millar suggest that whilst the impact of IT on lower costs has historically been confined to activities where repetitive information processing has been important, such restraints no longer apply. IT can lead to lower labour costs by reducing the need for certain production and clerical staff. As a result there should be both lower direct production costs and reduced overheads. IT applied to production systems can improve scheduling, thereby increasing the utilization of assets and reducing stocks, and in turn lowering production costs.

Case 14.6 on the application of IT at W H Smith illustrates the potential for improving stock turnover and increasing profitability with electronic point-of-sale (EPOS) systems.

Major supermarkets like Sainsbury use hand-held computers which allow staff to record the current stock levels each evening. Shelves can then be replenished overnight or the next day from regional warehouses. Sales representatives from say food manufacturers who sell extensively to small outlets can use similar hand-held computers for entering their orders. The computer can price the order immediately and a confirmation can be

Case 14.5
THOMSON HOLIDAYS

Case 7.5 earlier examined competition between rivals in the package holidays industry and argued that price competition has been a feature throughout the 1980s, especially competition between Thomson and Intasun, part of International Leisure Group. Colin Palmer of Thomson Holidays has argued that Thomson was able to keep prices at 1985 levels in 1988 as a result of savings accumulated through the utilization of IT. This pricing strategy stimulated demand, but the booking system was in place to cope with it. Thomson argue that they have achieved competitive advantage from their pioneering development of IT in holiday booking systems.

In general it is difficult to create and sustain competitive advantage in this industry. Package tour companies hire beds and airline seats, put them together, and by adding fringe services market them as a package holiday. Offering better service at airports or a wider range of tours in the various resorts can easily be copied by rivals, and so any competitive edge is quickly eroded.

Thomson first introduced computers in ten regional offices in 1976, allowing easier access for travel agents. Previously agents had to telephone one location; now they had access to ten linked centres. The computer generated management information and invoices as well as providing availability data for agents, but the agents still relied on the telephone, backed up by paperwork for confirming bookings.

Thomson recognized that what was needed was a terminal in every travel agent's office, but appreciated that if the system were exclusively Thomson it might be less popular than one which also allowed access to rival organizations. In 1979 they began experimenting with Prestel, and in 1982 introduced TOP or the Thomson Open-line Programme.

Through TOP travel agents enjoy instant access to Thomson holiday information on their terminal screens, but their terminals also access rival, but less sophisticated, systems. The problem of customers having to wait whilst telephone calls to check availability ring unanswered because the system is congested has been largely eliminated. This has proved particularly valuable on busy Saturdays and has enabled Thomson to save on staff costs. The computer can handle both options and confirmed bookings, and customers are encouraged to book because more and better information can be made available to them. The system has been continually improved, and the effect has been reduced booking costs for both Thomson and the travel agents. In addition the role of the agent has been changed more towards selling than administration. Other operators have followed, but the time lag has proved beneficial to Thomson.

Thomson have also been able to obtain more control and planning information for future capacity planning; and the gradual introduction of terminals linked to the UK in their offices abroad has improved the total service in other ways. Electronic funds transfer is regarded as an ideal extension of the system, because if holidays can be paid for without using cheques there will be further cost savings for both Thomson and the agents and some of this saving can be passed on to customers.

Source: Palmer, C (1988) Using IT for competitive advantage at Thomson Holidays, *Long Range Planning*, **21** (6).

printed out. The stored information can be easily transferred to streamline the delivery.

Cost saving is also possible where computer systems can be networked. If, for example, a manufacturer can establish a computer link with either his or her suppliers or buyers, there is considerable scope for both lowering costs and improving service. This would be particularly useful for supporting a just-in-time manufacturing system.

Similarly, Tesco has sought to establish closer linkages with their suppliers. Orders for immediate delivery are transmitted electronically, although projections based on the latest sales analyses will have been provided some weeks earlier. If supplier delivery notes are sent ahead of the actual delivery these can then be used to check the accuracy of the shipment and a confirmation returned. This represents a promissory note to pay by an

---

Case 14.6
INFORMATION TECHNOLOGY AND W H SMITH

W H Smith (WHS) have applied IT to their retailing activities in two major ways. Firstly they began introducing electronic point of sale (EPOS) in the mid-1980s, and more recently they have applied computer-aided design (CAD) to store layouts. Amongst the retail leaders in both areas, they have the additional objective of linking the two applications 'to create a marketing advantage other retailers may find hard to match'.

EPOS improves profitability by speeding up replenishment times and by allowing better stock control in individual stores. Previously stock checking and re-ordering was normally on a three week manual cycle. Since a large WHS branch would have 60 000 lines, three times the number in a large Sainsbury's, it was difficult for the head office to understand what was selling well at any particular time, and consequently branch managers and staff were responsible for stock management within availability constraints.

The objectives for EPOS were:

☐ increased profits through better sales and margins
☐ better staff utilization – stock counting is hardly challenging
☐ improved stock turn.

The relatively expensive system chosen by WHS links every store to a central computer, and hence stock is now controlled from the centre. The decision involved risk, as the equipment is American and the price is subject to currency fluctuations because the equipment is being purchased over several years as branches are converted systematically. The expense was felt to be justified as the discounted benefits indicated a 2% increase in gross profits.

The system also required co-operation from suppliers, as much of the potential benefits are lost if items are not bar-coded at source to enable the light pen to read them at the point of sale.

Many of the tills used for operating this system are also able to read credit and debit cards and print out the sales vouchers. This reduces the time required to serve those customers who prefer not to pay with cash, and also speeds up the money transfer from the customers' banks to WHS.

The computer-aided design link

Using information generated through EPOS, CAD enables the space and layout of stores to be adjusted to capitalize on the products which are selling well, particularly those with superior margins. High-value-added items can be placed in the most beneficial shelf spaces and bins. This will improve, and ideally maximize, sales per square foot, a key success factor for retailers. These developments were originally linked to a strategy of re-designing 20 stores every year, and commissioning 20 new ones. These targets have been reduced in the current recession.

WHS need flexibility as the demand for their various lines can fluctuate significantly. Moreover new lines need different display stands, an excellent example in recent years being compact discs.

A number of individual examples demonstrate the potential benefits for both customers and the company:

☐ One branch saw an unrealized demand for children's books.
☐ WHS were able to organize a special reprint of a book when they saw the sales opportunity quickly enough.
☐ One high-value-added toy was kept in production by its manufacturer beyond the planned time because demand was closely monitored.

---

agreed date, and no further invoicing is required.

Enhancing differentiation

Differentiation can be created in a number of ways including quality, design features, availability and special services that offer added value to the end consumer. McFarlan *et al.* (1983) contend that IT offers scope for differentiation where

☐ IT is a significant cost component in the provision of the product or service, as in banking, insurance and credit card operations;
☐ IT is able to affect substantially the lead time for developing, producing or delivering the product (CAD/CAM systems play an important role in this);
☐ IT allows products or services to be specially customized to appeal to customers individually;
☐ IT enables a visibly higher level of service

to customers, say through regular and accurate progress and delivery information, which might be charged for;
☐ more and better product information can be provided to consumers.

Most insurance companies quote rates for insuring property and cars partially based upon specified postcode districts. To achieve this they need accurate information on the risks involved in different areas and how these are changing. This in turn requires close liaison and information exchanges with brokers. The insurers, brokers and ultimately customers can all benefit as premiums more accurately reflect risks.

The scope of competitive advantage in relation to a broad or narrow focus can also be affected by IT, which can be used to identify and satisfy the needs of specialized market niches. The technology is used to analyse company and industry databases to highlight unusual trends or developments. Porter and Millar suggest that large companies which differentiate their range of products or services to appeal to a broad group of segments can use IT to target niches more effectively and segment individual products in ways that previously were only feasible for smaller more focused companies.

New competitive opportunities

It appears that information technology is resulting in the creation of new businesses in three distinct ways.

☐ New businesses are made technologically feasible. Telecommunications technology, for example, has led to the development of facsimile services and organizations that provide fax services. In a similar way microelectronics developments have made personal computing possible.
☐ IT can create demand for new products such as high-speed data communications networks that were unavailable before IT caused the demand.
☐ New businesses can be created within established ones. A number of organizations have diversified into software provision stemming from the development of packages for their own use.

Peters (1989) quotes the example of an airport kiosk business that provides instant customized children's books. Customers answer a series of questions concerning their interests and preferences, a computer selects an appropriate story, and a desk-top publishing system linked to a laser printer quickly produces a bound version.

Box 14.1 lists further examples of where information technology has yielded competitive advantage.

Implementing information technology for competitive advantage

Porter and Millar suggest a number of steps which might be taken in order to gain advantage from the opportunities offered by information technology.

First, it is important to assess the information intensity of the company's products and services. In some cases the intensity will be relatively low, offering few opportunities; in other cases the possibilities will be much greater. A newspaper like the *Financial Times*, for example, has been able to benefit from computerized typesetting and production systems, and from IT supporting all the share price and other information it includes every day.

Second, it is useful to consider how IT might affect the structure of an industry, and whether the changes will make it more or less attractive and profitable. There may be opportunities to benefit; equally there may be a case for lowering any dependence on a particular industry.

Third, it is appropriate to search for ways in which competitive advantage might be enhanced. Opportunities might exist for lowering production costs, for using IT to improve performance, and for using IT to locate new and potentially profitable segments.

Fourth, consider whether new business opportunities are available which might lead to profitable diversification.

Finally, develop a strategy for taking advantage of IT.

In summary, implementing IT for competitive advantage requires:

☐ an awareness of customer and consumer needs, changing needs, and how IT can improve the product's performance or create new services;
☐ an awareness of operational opportunities to reduce costs and improve quality through IT;
☐ an appreciation of how the organization could be more effective with improved information provision, and how any changes might be implemented. The impact upon people is very significant.

The argument is that competitive advantage can stem from any area of the organization

Box 14.1
EXAMPLES OF COMPETITIVE ADVANTAGE RESULTING FROM INFORMATION TECHNOLOGY

CHANGES IN INDUSTRY STRUCTURE

☐ Electromechanical and electronic typewriters: their ease of use, new facilities and higher quality output have made manual typewriters essentially obsolete.

☐ Newspapers: IT allows typesetting direct from the journalist's input at a terminal. Prior to this compositing took place separately after the article was written. The benefits of this technology for national newspapers was first obtained with the launch of *Today* by Eddie Shah. Unfortunately cash flow and circulation difficulties led Shah to sell his interests in the paper. Other national dailies have since followed and used the technology.

☐ Debit cards, such as Barclay's Connect: these cards, physically identical to credit cards, replace cheques and allow money to be debited immediately from the holder's current account.

RELATIONS WITH BUYERS AND SUPPLIERS

☐ JIT systems, which link manufacturers more closely with their suppliers.

☐ McKesson, who supply over-the-counter pharmaceuticals to retail chemists, used their sales force to record on a computer the counter layouts of their customers. This allowed them to pack orders in such a way that customers could unpack them and display them quickly and sequentially.

THE EFFECT ON ENTRY BARRIERS

☐ Microwave ovens, developed in Japan, feature large-scale production of the basic microwave-radiation-generating component and highly automated production of the ovens.

PRODUCT DEVELOPMENT

☐ Variable interest accounts: the use of computers to store and process information has enabled the clearing banks and the building societies to offer rates of interest which increase and decrease as the size of customers' deposits changes.

Source: Jackson, C (1989) Building a competitive advantage through information technology, *Long Range Planning*, **22** (4).

and that IT can offer scope for improvement and benefit in all these areas. What is required is a framework for analysing the activities of the organization and assessing their significance and scope for improvement. The concept of the value chain can provide such a framework and consequently it is the subject of the next chapter.

INFORMATION IN CONTEXT

To conclude this chapter, it is useful to refer back to Figure 2.4, the model around which this book is structured. The question 'How good is our information?' is shown to link the awareness and change parts. Information is needed for decision making about changes in the corporate strategy. Incremental changes to competitive and functional strategies will happen when managers respond to opportunities and threats that they perceive – again information is needed. On-going strategic awareness by managers is dependent upon information. In all cases both formal and informal sources and systems will prove important. In turn the incidence and impact of formal and informal channels is affected by the organization structure and the styles of management within the structure as well as any specifically designed management information system. Many management information systems, however, will be designed primarily to provide information for monitoring and control purposes.

In the event, what really matters is that decision makers have the important information they need about what is happening both inside and outside the organization at the appropriate time for them to be able to use it effectively. Strategic information, therefore, involves far more than quantitative and financial data that provide analyses of performance, important though these are. Because of the nature of much of the information, and the sources used, strategic information cannot be wholly systematized.

appropriate decision makers has been highlighted, as has the significance of managers' interpreting data and information. It has been suggested that managers can be more effective if they are aware strategically; and the contribution of IT to achieving this has been discussed. Finally, there has been consideration of how information and IT might create a competitive advantage.

Specifically we have

☐ considered how managers interpret information and give meaning to it and how this might affect decisions, and following on from this shown that incorrect interpretation can lead to counter-intuitive behaviour;
☐ defined information technology and management information systems;
☐ argued that IT has obvious applications for operational and control decisions but that for decisions concerning broad strategic issues and change, whilst IT can contribute, there still remains a significant element of managerial judgement;
☐ looked at the relationship between information needs and organization structure, and summarized the work of Jay Galbraith on this theme;
☐ considered the impact of IT on managers – arguing that greater utilization of IT is a cultural issue – and Peter Drucker's arguments concerning the future impact of IT on managers and organizations;
☐ featured how IT can create and sustain competitive advantage by affecting the structure of an industry, reducing costs, enhancing differentiation and leading to the establishment of new businesses, products and services.

SUMMARY

This chapter has been based upon the contention that strategic decision making and decision makers require information. The importance of the information reaching the

CHECKLIST OF KEY TERMS AND CONCEPTS

You should feel confident that you understand the following terms and ideas:

☐ Meaning systems and counter-intuitive behaviour

☐ Decision making at the operational, control and strategic change levels.

QUESTIONS AND RESEARCH ASSIGNMENTS

Text related

1. For an organization with which you are familiar identify an operational system which is heavily dependent on IT and assess its strategic impact.

    ☐ In what ways does the system contribute towards competitive advantage?

    ☐ How might this contribution be increased?

2. Consider how the increasing utilization of information technology in retailing has affected you as a customer. Do you feel that the major retail organizations who have introduced and benefited from the greater utilization of IT have attempted to ensure that the customer has also benefited and not suffered?

3. Consider why it is argued that the increasing utilization of IT by organizations is a cultural issue. How might managers be encouraged to make greater use of the technology which is available?

Library and assignment based

4. For an organization of your choice ascertain the range of products and services offered.

    ☐ What are essential information needs from outside the organization (the environment) for managing these products and services both now and in the future?

    ☐ Where are the limitations in availability?

    ☐ What role might IT play in improving availability?

5. By visiting and talking to staff at an appropriate level, in both a travel agency and a retail store using an EPOS system, ascertain the effect that IT has had on their decision making. Do you feel the staff are more aware strategically? If so, has this proved valuable?

RECOMMENDED FURTHER READING

Text

Jackson, I F (1986) *Corporate Information Management*, Prentice Hall.

Journal articles

Drucker, P F (1988) The coming of the new organization, *Harvard Business Review*, January–February.
Porter, M E and Millar, V E (1985) How information gives you a competitive advantage, *Harvard Business Review*, July–August.

REFERENCES

Ackoff, R L (1967) Management misinformation systems, *Management Science* (14), December.
Amdahl Executive Institute (1989) *Clues to Success: IT Strategies for Tomorrow*.
Anthony, R N (1965) *Planning and Control Systems: A Framework for Analysis*, Harvard University Press.
Davis, G B and Olsen, M (1985) *Management Information Systems: Conceptual Foundations, Structure and Development*, 2nd edn, McGraw-Hill.
Drucker, P F (1988) The coming of the new organization, *Harvard Business Review*, January–February.
Earl, M J and Hopwood, A G (1980) From management information to information management. In *The Information Systems Environment*

(eds H C Lucas, F F Land, J J Lincoln and K Supper), North-Holland.

Eason, K D (1980) Computer information systems and managerial tasks. In *The Human Side of Information Processing* (ed. N Bjorn-Andersen), North-Holland.

Forrester, J (1969) *Urban Dynamics*, MIT Press.

Galbraith, J R (1974) Organization design: an information processing view, *Interfaces*, May.

Handy, C (1978) *Gods of Management*, Souvenir Press.

Hofer, C W (1970) Emerging EDP pattern, *Harvard Business Review*, March–April.

Lorsch, J and Allen, S (1973) *Managing Diversity and Independence*, Harvard University Press.

Lucas, H (1976) *The Analysis, Design and Implementation of Information Systems*, McGraw-Hill.

McFarlan, F W (1984) Information technology changes the way you compete, *Harvard Business Review*, May–June.

McFarlan, F W, McKenney, J L and Pyburn, P (1983) The information archipelago – plotting a course, *Harvard Business Review*, January–February.

Mintzberg, H (1972) The myth of MIS, *California Management Review*, Fall.

OECD (1989) *New Technology in the 1990s – A Socioeconomic Strategy*, OECD.

PA Management Consultants (1985) *Survey of Chief Executives and their Perceptions of Office Automation*. Quoted in Why Britain's bosses are in the dark, *Business Computing and Communications*, November.

Paton, R (1980) *Systems Organization: The Management of Complexity*, Unit 7, *Organization Structures*, The Open University T243.

Peters, T (1989) Tomorrow's companies, *The Economist*, 4 March.

Porter, M E (1980) *Competitive Strategy: Techniques for Analysing Industries and Competition*, Free Press.

Porter, M E (1985) *Competitive Advantage: Creating and Sustaining Superior Performance*, Free Press.

Porter, M E and Millar, V E (1985) How information gives you a competitive advantage, *Harvard Business Review*, July–August.

Schein, E H (1985) *Organizational Culture and Leadership*, Jossey Bass.

Spear, R (1980) *Systems Organization: The Management of Complexity*, Unit 8, *Information*, The Open University T243.

Stewart, R (1971) *How Computers Affect Management*, Macmillan.

Winner, L (1977) *Autonomous Technology: Technics-out-of-control as a Theme in Political Thought*, MIT Press.

WHERE IS OUR COMPETITIVE ADVANTAGE?

15

LEARNING OBJECTIVES

After studying this chapter you should be able to

☐ demonstrate how competitive advantage might be created in any functional area of the business;

☐ describe the value chain and explain how it might be used for evaluating competitive advantage;

☐ identify typical linkages in the value chain and explain their significance;

☐ apply the value chain concept to specific examples;

☐ appreciate why speed is an important aspect of competition in the 1990s.

This chapter looks at the sources of competitive advantage stemming from the functions discussed in the preceding chapters. A possible framework for evaluating competitive advantage is developed.

INTRODUCTION

Environment, values and resources have been linked in this section of the book. In Chapter 9 the need to understand environmental forces in terms of opportunities and threats was explored, and in subsequent chapters some of the functional resources were examined individually. The strategic role of marketing, operations, human resources and finance and the contribution of these functions were discussed, and the ways in which the resources can create competitive advantage were considered. Changes to these functions often involves changing the culture and values of the organization, and in Chapter 14 we saw the need for the functions and business units which comprise the organization to operate in harmony rather than conflict. The value of managers being strategically aware and appreciating the implications of decisions in their area for other parts of the business were also discussed.

Thus, competitive advantage can be derived from any part of the business. Arthur Young, the management consultants, have suggested that distinctiveness consists of the way that people achieve low costs and create differentiation, and good timing. This includes the ability to spot opportunities and act quickly to exploit them. It is important for the strategic leader and other managers to appreciate where, at any time, the organization must be successful if it is to be an effective competitor, and where it might develop and sustain a distinctive competitive advantage. What are the key success factors, and which functions of the business are most significant? The following list of examples illustrates that distinctive competitive advantage can result from different activities and functions:

Company	Source of distinctive competitive advantage
Ford Motors	Product technology
3M	Innovation
Benetton	Ability to respond to changes in fashion
IBM	Customer service
Avon Cosmetics	Distribution
Rolls Royce	Quality and image
Swissair	Service and reliability

Whilst all activities can contribute towards competitive advantage, and should be managed with this in mind, certain areas may be more significant than others, although the priorities can change over time. The need to concentrate effort on these essential areas is likely to be tied to the culture. For example, from the mid-1960s to the late 1970s, developments in the car industry were relatively limited. There was little real technological change. Competition was based on producing models which appealed to customers

with lower production costs than competitors; and consequently the significance of the finance function grew. In the 1980s there has been a growing concern with fuel economy and environmental pollution, and hence there has been a shift of emphasis towards research and design.

When industries become very competitive the opportunities for adding value to the product itself are likely to reduce. Consequently there will be increased emphasis upon the total service – delivery on time, packaging, after-sale support etc. Lawler (1992) extends the debate, pointing out that it is management style within the organization which determines the ability to innovate and deliver service. He argues that empowerment and flatter structures (discussed in detail in Chapters 22 and 24) lead to 'high involvement organizations' and that these will become increasingly important for competitive success. Successful structures are difficult to copy; products are easier.

To assess the significance and relative contribution of the various resources employed by the organization the aspects of the resource audit introduced earlier could be extended. Functions could be evaluated as a

---

A manager's ability to initiate and manage change will be critical in determining the success of his business. He must monitor the competitive environment constantly and be prepared to react quickly to changes in market conditions. More importantly, though, he must also be seeking to take the initiative by building up and using competitive advantage through innovation; not just through new products but through pursuing an innovative approach to production, marketing, personnel policies, control systems and every other aspect of the business. Efficient management is essential, but it is innovative management that is the real key to success.

Patrick Sheehy, Chairman, BAT Industries plc

series of activities and each activity assessed in terms of relative importance both in the past and in the future. The idea will be to check that efforts have been concentrated most appropriately, and to ascertain where efforts should be concentrated in the future.

Porter (1985), however, contends that an examination of the value chain provides an ideal framework for analysing the activities of the business. Firstly it is useful for assessing the ability of the various functions to contribute towards competitive advantage, and secondly the allocation or distribution of costs incurred in running the business can be evaluated. The value chain which Porter uses has been developed from the business system concept, devised originally by McKinsey and Company which basically describes the essential activities that add value to the product or service:

☐ research and design
☐ development
☐ production
☐ marketing and sales
☐ distribution.

In addition there are important support services.

The main subject of this chapter is the role of the value chain in diagnosing competitive advantage by

☐ generating an understanding of the behaviour of costs and the implications for strategy;
☐ identifying a firm's actual and potential sources of differentiation.

However, as Ohmae (1988) argues, it is important to remember that competitive advantage is being sought for one major purpose – to serve customers' real needs. It is not simply to beat competition, although clearly an organization is seeking to be more effective, competitively, than its rivals.

In addition to ensuring that resources are concentrated on creating and sustaining core competences which meet today's key success factors, there must be some investment in the future. Hamel and Prahalad (1989) cite the Japanese approach of 'strategic intent' – strategies concerned with changing the competitive environment and using customer-oriented innovations to weaken those competitors who are currently strong and, at the same time, develop new key success factors.

One critical aspect of this is design. Design translates customer needs into products and services, adds value and creates distinctiveness. Design can sometimes reduce costs by focusing attention on the most critical activities. The design and development of compact cameras which are self-focusing and automatic exposure has changed demand dramatically. Many casual photographers are comfortable with their simplicity. Experienced photographers use them in addition to more expensive cameras with interchangeable lenses because there is a significant saving of weight and bulk for little loss of quality. However, some radical design changes are not popular with consumers. Dunlop, for example, have failed with innovatory 'run-flat' tyres which prevent major blow-outs after a puncture. Michelin have successfully tested (in motor sport) puncture-proof tyres which are filled with a mousse instead of air, and these may prove more successful if they can be produced in volume at an acceptable cost.

THE VALUE CHAIN

Whilst strategic success depends upon the way the organization as a whole behaves, and the ways managers and functions are integrated, competitive advantage stems from the individual and discrete activities that a firm performs. A cost advantage can arise from low cost distribution, efficient production or an excellent salesforce who succeed in winning the most appropriate orders. Differentiation can be the result of having an excellent design team or being able to source high quality materials or high quality production. Value chain analysis is a systematic way of studying the direct and support activities undertaken by a firm. From this analysis should arise greater awareness concerning costs and the potential for lower costs and for differentiation. Quite simply, argues Porter, competitive advantage is created and sustained when a firm performs the most critical functions either more cheaply or better than its competitors. But what are the most critical factors? Why? How and where might costs be reduced? How and where might differentiation be created?

The value system

Developing his earlier work on industry structure (Porter, 1980), where he highlights the significance of the relative power of buyers and suppliers, Porter (1985) argues that in the search for competitive advantage a firm must be considered as part of a wider system:

suppliers → firm → distributors → consumers

As well as seeking improvements in its own activities, a firm should assess the opportunities and potential benefits from improving its links with other organizations. A firm is linked to the marketing and selling activities of its suppliers, and to the purchasing and materials handling activities of its distributors or customers. As an example just-in-time (JIT) manufacturing systems require clear links and shared understanding if both the firm and its suppliers are to gain the potential benefits. Similarly a company might package and deliver its products in a way that is ideal for its distributors – this might well arise from an awareness of how the distributor operates and what his needs are.

Matsushita of Japan assemble television sets in south Wales. When they were interested in incorporating Invar mask technology (which gives high-quality picture definition but historically has been too expensive for domestic sets) they approached and subsequently collaborated successfully with Philips Components, a UK subsidiary of the Dutch electricals company. Philips have been able to reduce the costs of the technology, but not at the expense of quality – Matsushita require their products to be 100% defect-free when they reach the consumer. The outcome has been constant discussions and exchange visits, interdependency and loyalty. This linkage is typical of those Marks & Spencer establishes with its suppliers.

Activities in the value chain

The value chain developed by Michael Porter is illustrated in Figure 15.1. There are five primary activities, namely inbound logistics, operations, outbound logistics, marketing and sales, and service. In the diagram they are illustrated as a chain moving from left to right, and they represent activities of physically creating the product or service and transferring it to the buyer, together with any necessary after-sale service. They are linked to four support activities: procurement, technology development, human resource man-

---

Ours is a business which is judged by the quality of service, attention to detail and a consistent level of personal commitment by all those engaged in it. This can only be achieved by dedication, training and perceptive management. The good manager endeavours to solve problems before they arise and to anticipate the needs of guests. He must think today what he does tomorrow and learn from the lessons of yesterday. As a result, the level and status of management in Britain has risen dramatically in the past few decades – and continues to rise – putting us among the leaders internationally of the hotel and catering industry.

Lord Forte of Ripley, Chairman, Forte plc

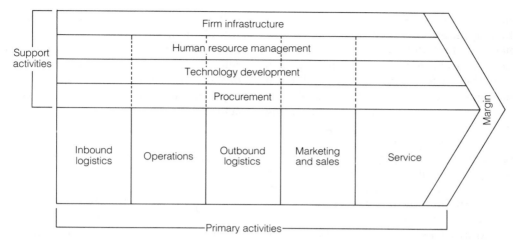

Figure 15.1 The value chain. (*Source*: Porter, M E (1985) *Competitive Advantage: Creating and Sustaining Superior Performance*, Free Press.) Copyright Michael E Porter, © 1985. Adapted with permission of the Free Press.

agement, and the firm's infrastructure. The support activities are drawn laterally as they can affect any one or more of the primary activities, although the firm's infrastructure generally supports the whole value chain. Every one of the primary and support activities incurs costs and should add value to the product or service in excess of these costs. It is important always to look for ways of reducing costs sensibly; cost reductions should not be at the expense of lost quality in areas which matter to customers and consumers. Equally costs can be added justifiably if they add qualities which the customer values and is willing to pay for. The difference between the total costs and the selling price is the margin. The margin is increased by widening the gap between costs and price. The activities are described in greater depth below.

Primary activities

☐ **Inbound logistics** are activities relating to receiving, storing and distributing internally the inputs to the product or service.

They include warehousing, stock control and internal transportation systems.

☐ **Operations** are activities relating to the transformation of inputs into finished products and services. Operations was the subject of Chapter 11 and includes machining, assembly and packaging.

☐ **Outbound logistics** are activities relating to the distribution of finished goods and services to customers.

☐ **Marketing and sales**: as discussed in Chapter 10, the marketing mix includes such activities as advertising and promotion, pricing, and salesforce activity.

☐ **Service** relates to the provision of any necessary service with a product, such as installation, repair, extended warranty or training in how to use it.

Each of these might be crucial for competitive advantage. The nature of the industry will determine which factors are the most significant.

Support activities

☐ **Procurement** refers to the function or process of purchasing any inputs used in the value chain, as distinct from issues of their application. Procurement may take place within defined policies or procedures, and it might be evidenced within a number of functional areas. Production managers and engineers, for example, are very important in many purchasing decisions to ensure that the specification and quality is appropriate.

☐ **Technology development**: technology is defined here in its broadest sense to include know-how, research and development, product design and process improvement. It encapsulates issues discussed in Chapter 11 on operations management and in Chapter 14 on information technology.

☐ **Human resource management** involves all activities relating to recruiting, training, developing and rewarding people throughout the organization, issues discussed in Chapter 12.

☐ **The firm's infrastructure** includes the structure of the organization, planning, financial controls and quality management designed to support the whole of the value chain. Financial aspects and quality management are discussed in Chapters 13 and 11 respectively.

Again, each of these support activities can be very important in creating and sustaining competitive advantage.

Sub-activities

Porter argues that it can often be valuable to subdivide the primary and support activities into their component parts when analysing costs and opportunities for differentiation. For example it is less meaningful to argue that an organization provides good service than to explain it in terms of installation, repair or training. The competitive advantage is likely to result from a sub-activity specifically. Similarly, as was discussed in Chapter 10, the marketing mix comprises a set of

linked activities which should be managed to complement each other. However, competitive advantage can arise from just one activity in the mix, possibly the product design, its price or advertising, technical support literature, or from the skills and activities of the salesforce.

Linkages within the value chain

Although competitive advantage arises from one or more sub-activities within the primary and support activities comprising the value chain, it is important not to think of the chain merely as a set of independent activities. Rather it is a system of interdependent activities. Linkages in the value chain, which are relationships between the activities, are very important. Behaviour in one part of the organization can affect the costs and performance of other business units and functions, and this quite frequently involves trade-off decisions. For example, more expensive materials and more stringent inspection will increase costs in the inbound logistics and operations activities, but the savings in service costs resulting from these strategies may be greater. The choice of functional strategies and where to concentrate efforts will relate to the organization's competitive and corporate strategies concerning competitive advantage.

Similarly a number of activities and sub-activities depend upon each other. The extent to which operations, outbound logistics and installation are co-ordinated can be a source of competitive advantage through lower costs (reduced stock holding) or differentiation (high quality, customer-oriented service). This last example uses linkages between primary activities, but there are also clear linkages between primary and support activities. Product design affects manufacturing costs; purchasing policies affect operations and production costs; and so on.

In addition the firm can benefit from establishing linkages between activities in its value chain and the value chains of both its suppliers and its customers, as was mentioned earlier.

Linkages, argues Porter, must be understood and managed if the firm is to succeed in creating and sustaining competitive advantage. Whilst some of the links are obvious, others are more obscure and may go unnoticed without a proper search for them, which can be a further opportunity for utilizing information technology effectively.

In this section we have argued that looking at all the activities and sub-activities in the value chain systematically will highlight how well the various functions and business units within the organization are being managed and co-ordinated. If they are managed effectively, and linkage opportunities are seized, then costs can be controlled better. Equally, thinking about the purpose of each activity and sub-activity, and considering the possible linkages in the light of the needs and preferences of customers, can generate differentiation.

Competitive scope and the value chain

Porter's model of competitive advantage (Porter, 1985) was developed in Chapter 7 and illustrated in Figure 7.4. The competitive strategies of cost leadership, differentiation, cost focus and differentiation focus depend upon whether the organization is looking to be the lowest cost producer or to differentiate on either a broad or a narrow scope.

A firm's competitive scope has four dimensions:

☐ Segment scope   product or service varieties; and buyers targeted

☐ Vertical scope   the extent to which activities are performed within the organization rather than subcontracted or bought-in

☐ Geographic scope   regions covered with a co-ordinated strategy

☐ Industry scope   the range of related industries in which the firm competes with a co-ordinated strategy.

Each of these factors affects both the value chain and competitive advantage. Each product/market, service/market or business unit will have a separate value chain; and where the scope is narrow and the strategy focused, the activities should be assessed specifically in terms of the particular market niche targeted. This should be carried out with a view to achieving competitive advantage through close linkage with the market. Where the scope is broader – several linked segments, regions or industries, for example – each product, service or business unit should be evaluated independently, but in addition the opportunities for more effective linking should be assessed. Examples of opportunities might be a shared salesforce, shared distribution, common brand names or shared technology and systems. Where these can be capitalized upon, they can result in lower costs or enhanced differentiation, which in reality result from achieved synergy.

Organization culture

Cultural differences between business units, however, can make it difficult to link value chains and gain the potential synergy. There may be different perceptions of the ways things should be done.

Alliances and joint ventures between independent organizations, which will be considered in greater detail in Chapter 18, are an attempt to gain the potential benefits of broad scope or linkages between organizations without a full merger of the two firms. This can be particularly useful in the case of two multi-product firms where the linkages in question relate to individual products or business units only, and no realistic case could be made for a merger. In addition some of the cultural problems involved in take-overs and mergers, which are also discussed in Chapter 18, can be avoided.

We have introduced and discussed the concept of the value chain and it is now important to consider how it might be applied in the evaluation of costs and differentiation opportunities.

THE VALUE CHAIN AND COMPETITIVE ADVANTAGE

Cost leadership and differentiation strategies

Cost leadership

We discussed in Chapter 7 the argument of Porter (1985) that the lowest cost producer in either a broad or narrow competitive scope

☐ delivers acceptable quality but produces the product or service with lower costs than competitors;
☐ sustains this cost gap;
☐ achieves above-average profits from industry-average prices.

This cost advantage will be achieved by the effective management of the key determinants of costs. The cost leadership strategy of Spring Ram is outlined in Case 15.1.

The differentiation strategy

Similarly Porter argues that the successful application of a differentiation strategy involves

☐ the selection of one or more key character-istics which are widely valued by buyers (there are any number of opportunities relating to different needs and market segments);

☐ adding costs selectively in the areas per-ceived to be important to buyers, and charging a premium price in excess of the added costs.

The success of this strategy lies in finding opportunities for differentiation which can-not be matched easily by competitors, and being clear about the costs involved and the price potential. Costs in areas not perceived to be significant to buyers must be controlled, and in line with competitor costs, for other-wise above-average profits will not be achieved.

The successful implementation of both these strategies therefore requires an under-standing of where costs are incurred throughout the organization. Understanding costs and the search for appropriate cost reductions involves an appreciation of how costs should be attributed to the various discrete activities which comprise the value chain. Table 15.1 compares a possible cost breakdown for a manufacturing firm with that for a firm of professional accountants. If an analysis of the value chain is to be meaningful, it is important that the costs are genuinely attributed to the activities which generate them – and not simply apportioned in some convenient way – however difficult this might prove in practice. Given the figures in Table 15.1 one might question whether the manufacturing firm is spending enough on human resources management and marketing, and the accountancy practice too much.

Cost drivers

It is important to appreciate which cost drivers are the most significant. The follow-ing cost drivers can all influence the value chain.

☐ Economies of scale and potential experi-ence and learning curve benefits.
☐ Capacity utilization, linked to production control and the existence of bottlenecks.

Case 15.1
SPRING RAM'S COST LEADERSHIP STRATEGY

Spring Ram is a Yorkshire-based producer of kitchen and bathroom suites. The company was started in 1980, since when it has achieved (in 1990) a 20% share of the bathrooms market (second to Armitage Shanks) and 12% of kitchens, where it is out-performing its main rivals, MFI–Hygena and Magnet, both of whom have financial difficulties. Pre-tax profit growth has averaged 50%. In 1991, when most companies were experiencing falling profits in the recession, Spring Ram's profits rose by 25%. In 1990 the company won the CBI Business Enterprise Award.

There are a number of reasons for the success:

- ☐ Spring Ram produce market-led products of guaranteed quality at lower, unchanging prices.
- ☐ Delivery times are short (48 hours).
- ☐ New plants, heavily automated with the most advanced technology, have been built on land owned by Spring Ram and financed internally.
- ☐ Supply costs are kept down by ordering well ahead and accurate forecasting.
- ☐ Spring Ram takes 70 days credit and gives 28.
- ☐ Low dividends (see Chapter 13) have enabled Spring Ram to build up their reserves to earn interest as well as fund capital investments.
- ☐ Waste products are recycled. Spring Ram recycle both excesses and broken pieces in their ceramics factory, and sawdust is used as fuel in the heaters.

Interestingly each subsidiary maintains an independent salesforce, despite common distribution outlets. Spring Ram contends this allows them to be more dedicated.

Further growth should be provided by the development of new products for different parts of the house, the targeting of new niches (upmarket kitchens were introduced in 1991), and extending distribution. Spring Ram originally relied on independent retailers, but as they have grown they have penetrated both DIY superstores and builders' merchants.

Sources: Fuller, J, Three categories for success, *Financial Times*, 2 January 1991; Fuller, J, Breeding success from a budding generation, *Financial Times*, 23 March 1992.

- ☐ Linkages. Time spent liaising with other departments can incur costs, but at the same time create savings and differentiation through interrelationships and shared activities.
- ☐ Interrelationships and shared activities. Shared activities, possibly a shared salesforce, shared advertising or shared plant, can generate savings. Close links between activities or departments can increase quality and ensure that the needs of customers are matched more effectively.
- ☐ Integration. This incorporates the extent to which the organization is vertically integrated, say manufacturing its own component parts instead of simply assembling bought-in components, or even designing and manufacturing its own machinery. This again can influence costs and differentiation, and is an important

Table 15.1 Indicative cost breakdown of a manufacturing and a service business

	Manufacturing firm (% of total)	Professional firm of accountants (% of total)	
Primary activities			
Inbound logistics	4	8	(data collection for audits)
Operations	64	26	(actual auditing)
Outbound logistics	1	5	(report writing and presentations)
Marketing and sales	7	21	(getting new business)
Service	1	3	(general client liaison)
	77	63	
Support activities			
Procurement	1	1	
Technology development	10	8	(IT development)
Human resources management	2	16	
Firm's infrastructure	10	12	
	100	100	

These figures are only indicative, and should not be seen as targets for any particular firm.

element of the strategy of YKK which is featured as an example later in this chapter.

☐ Timing – buying and selling at the appropriate time. It is important to invest in stocks to ensure deliveries when customers want them, but at the same time stockholding costs must be monitored and controlled.

☐ Policies. Policy standards for procurement or production may be wrong. If they are set too low, quality may be lost and prove detrimental. If they are too high in relation to the actual needs of the market, costs are incurred unnecessarily.

☐ Location issues. This includes wage costs, which can vary between different regions, and the costs of supporting a particular organization structure.

☐ Institutional factors. Specific regulations concerning materials content or usage would be an example.

Porter argues that sustained competitive advantage requires effective control of the cost drivers, and that scale economies, learning, linkages, interrelationships and timing provide the key opportunities for creating advantage.

In the case of a low cost leadership strategy, the cost advantage is relative to the costs of competitors, and over time these could change if competitors concentrate on their cost drivers. Consequently it is useful to attempt to monitor and predict how competitor costs might change in the future linked to any changes in their competitive and functional strategies.

Common problems in cost control through the value chain

It was mentioned above that it can prove difficult to assign costs to activities properly, and this is one of the difficulties which are likely to be encountered in using value chain analysis as a basis for more effective cost management. Porter contends that there are several common pitfalls in managing costs for competitive advantage:

☐ Misunderstanding of actual costs and misperceptions of the key cost drivers.

☐ Concentrating on manufacturing when cost savings are required. Quite frequently it is not the area to cut if quality is to be maintained, especially once a certain level of manufacturing efficiency has been achieved.

- ☐ Failing to take advantage of the potential gains from linkages.
- ☐ Ignoring competitor behaviour.
- ☐ Relying on small incremental cost savings when needs arise rather than introducing a long-term permanently installed cost management programme.

Differentiation opportunities

It has been mentioned on a number of occasions that competitive advantage through differentiation can arise from any and every area of the business. In relation to the component parts of the value chain, the following are examples of where differentiation might originate.

Primary activities

- ☐ **Inbound logistics**: careful and thoughtful handling to ensure that incoming materials are not damaged and are easily accessed when necessary, and the linking of purchases to production requirements, especially important in the case of just-in-time (JIT) manufacturing systems.
- ☐ **Operations**: high quality; high-output levels and few rejections; and delivery on time.
- ☐ **Outbound logistics**: rapid delivery when and where customers need the product or service.
- ☐ **Marketing and sales**: advertising closely tied to defined market segments; a well-trained, knowledgeable and motivated salesforce; and good technical literature, especially for industrial products.
- ☐ **Service**: rapid installation; speedy after-sales service and repair; and immediate availability of spare parts.

Support activities

- ☐ **Procurement**: purchasing high-quality materials (to assist operations); regional

warehousing of finished products (to enable speedy delivery to customers).

- ☐ **Technology development**: the development of unique features, and new products and services; the use of information technology to manage inbound and outbound logistics most effectively; and sophisticated market analyses to enable segmentation, targeting and positioning for differentiation.
- ☐ **Human resources management**: high-quality training and development; recruitment of the right people; and appropriate reward systems which help motivate people.
- ☐ **Firm's infrastructure**: support from senior executives in customer relations; investment in suitable physical facilities to improve working conditions; and investment in carefully designed information technology systems.

It will be appreciated that these factors are really a summary of the issues discussed in Chapters 10–14. In searching for the most appropriate means of differentiating for competitive advantage it is important to look at which activities are the most essential as far as consumers and customers are concerned, and to isolate the key success factors. It is a search for opportunities to be different from competitors in ways which matter, and through this the creation of a superior competitive position. The Japanese zip manufacturer YKK, the world market leader, enjoys a superior competitive position, and the company's strategy is analysed against the value chain in the next section. The underlying philosophy of YKK, the cycle of goodness, was illustrated in Chapter 4, Box 4.2.

An application of the value chain

YKK have arguably succeeded in creating both cost leadership and substantial differentiation with their corporate, competitive and functional strategies, and these have resulted in effective barriers to entry into the industry and close relationships with customers. The idea might be illustrated as follows:

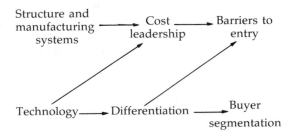

The essential components of the strategy, summarized below, are illustrated in Figure 15.2, which places them in the context of the value chain and highlights the linkages.

YKK is structured as a multi-plant multinational company with both wholly owned subsidiary companies and joint ventures throughout the world. The latter organizations are primarily the result of local politics, particularly in low cost labour countries in the Far East. Whilst the subsidiaries are decentralized and enjoy some local autonomy, they are invariably managed at the top by Japanese executives on a period of secondment. Consequently there is substantial influence from the Japanese parent.

YKK invests a significant percentage of after tax profits back in the business, and as a result is heavily automated and able to enjoy the benefits of the experience/learning curve. Moreover YKK prices its finished products very competitively both to generate customer satisfaction and to create barriers to entry. The company is vertically integrated, designing and manufacturing its own production machinery, and this gives it a unique competitive edge. It is also particularly innovative as far as both machinery and finished products are concerned.

Coils of semi-finished zips are produced in the Far East, particularly Japan, and exported to such countries as the UK, where they are cut to size and finished in response to customer orders. This results in both cost advantages and speedy deliveries from semi-finished stocks. A wide range of colours and sizes is kept ready for finishing. In the UK the key garment manufacturers and the retail outlets they serve are targeted by YKK and are given special service.

The cycle of goodness philosophy has not been exported in its complete form, but employee relations are an important aspect of the human resources strategy. Participation and involvement are essential features, and total quality management is a key feature.

Conceptually the value chain is a useful way of analysing resources and functions within the organization in the context of how they might individually contribute to competitive advantage. At the same time the linkages between them should be assessed, because it is from these interrelationships and linkages that synergy in the form of additional cost savings or differentiation is created. To apply the value chain properly it is important also to allocate costs to activities and to evaluate whether costs could be saved in various areas or whether additional spending on certain activities might yield additional benefits by adding value in ways which are important to consumers. In practice it can be difficult to assign costs accurately. In this respect the actual application, rather than the

---

Corporate restructuring to improve international competitiveness is a vital priority for British and European businesses in the 1990s. However, such restructuring must be a continual process of change and revitalisation if we are to consistently satisfy the consumer's need for the highest quality products and services at the most competitive cost. The leadership of this process is the primary role of management in the modern company.

Ian G McAllister, Chairman and Managing Director, Ford Motor Company Limited, UK

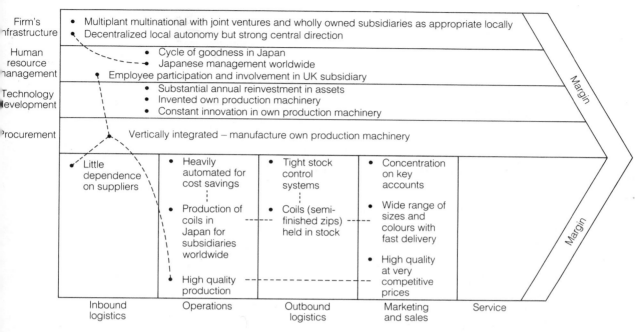

Figure 15.2   YKK's competitive advantage and the value chain. Developed from Channon, D F and Mayeda, K, *Yoshida Kogyo KK 'A' and 'B' Case Studies.* Available from The European Case Clearing House and Ireland. The dotted lines (---) illustrate the linkages.

concept, of the value chain is more applicable for managers than for students of this subject.

In my experience, applications of the value chain do pose difficulties for managers, primarily because the management accounting systems in many organizations do not readily provide the data in the form required. Developing this theme, Johnson and Kaplan (1987) contend that certain costs are extremely difficult to allocate to certain individual products, but they are the costs of activities which are very significant in relation to total quality and in turn competitive advantage. Machine failures are one example, and they affect a number of products and can mean that deliveries are late and possibly priorities are changed. But how should the costs be allocated? As production systems become increasingly sophisticated, overheads, as a proportion of total costs, increase relative to the direct costs of labour and materials.

Genuinely allocating these production overheads is difficult.

Nevertheless the value chain can provide an extremely useful framework for considering the activities involved in producing products and services and considering their significance for customers.

SPEED AND COMPETITIVE ADVANTAGE

Companies, however successful they might be, are likely to be knocked over by innovative competitors if they stand still and ignore a changing environment. They must adapt and improve if they are to retain their position. To sustain any competitive advantage and grow they must innovate more quickly than their rivals. Consequently, speed is becoming an increasingly important

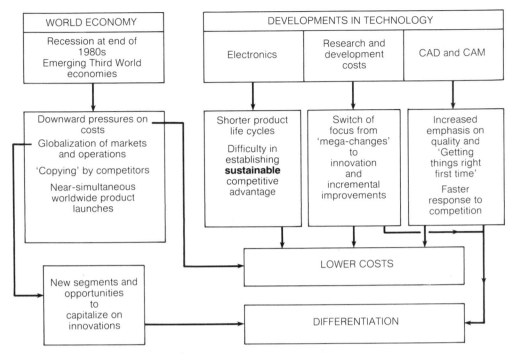

Figure 15.3 Speed and competitive advantage. Developed from: Lorenz, C (1991) Competition intensified in the fast track, *Financial Times*, 28 June.

factor in the search for competitive advantage. There are a number of reasons for this and they are illustrated in Figure 15.3. Significantly the issue of speed does not contradict Porter's work on cost leadership and differentiation; rather it complements it.

The world recession at the end of the 1980s, coupled with the continued economic progress of such Third World countries as Taiwan and Korea, is increasing worldwide competition. The results are greater cost pressures, new global marketing and production opportunities, the tendency for competitors to copy each other's innovations, and the launching of new products almost simultaneously throughout the world – previously launches tended to be staged over a number of months or even years.

Technological developments in electronics are leading to shorter life cycles for many products and growing difficulties in estab-

lishing **sustainable** competitive advantage. Increasing research and development costs are focusing attention on the strategic value of innovation and incremental change – the constant search for gradual improvements. This is enhanced by the possibilities of computer-aided design and manufacturing, and, in turn, just-in-time systems.

The emergence of global markets and competition is opening up new segmentation opportunities. Companies who can capitalize on these through innovation and product and market development – strategies which are explored more fully in Chapter 17 – are often able to differentiate their products and services.

Shorter product development times, just-in-time manufacturing, together with the benefits of learning and incremental improvements, can all lead to lower costs. Hence cost leadership and differentiation remain key

Case 15.2
SPEED AND COMPETITIVE ADVANTAGE:
BENETTON AND DOMINO PIZZA

BENETTON

Benetton clothes are available from some 5000 stores in 60 countries world wide, many of them franchised operations. The business is run from a headquarters in Italy. If an item is selling unexpectedly well in one particular shop, and additional stocks are wanted, Benetton aims to provide the additional stocks faster than its competitors could. Requests are relayed through terminals to Benetton's mainframe computer, which also carries comprehensive product details and production requirements – the benefit of using CAD and CAM extensively. Production requirements can therefore be fed quickly into the manufacturing system, even though a lot of work is subcontracted. This process is aided by Benetton's ability to dye finish garments rather than yarn. Finished products are stored in one central warehouse, run by robots and just a handful of people. A quarter of a million items can be handled daily. Benetton aims to replenish their shops with popular items in one week ex-stock, four weeks including production.

DOMINO PIZZA

At the end of the 1980s Domino Pizza was the second largest pizza chain in America – Pizza Hut is the market leader. Speed is very much part of the culture of the business, and is manifested in several ways.

Customers are offered a generous discount on any home delivery which takes longer than 30 minutes. Delivery staff are required to wear trainers, to run between their delivery trucks and customers' houses, and to run up stairs rather than use lifts. The business is run on a regional basis with competitions between the regions for the best pizzas and the fastest deliveries. Winning chefs are filmed and the videos circulated for training purposes. It is perhaps not unexpected that the Chief Executive also owns the Detroit Tigers baseball team.

Source: Dumaine, B, Business speeds up, *Fortune*, 13 February 1989.

sources of competitive advantage – speed can enhance their potential.

Speed can, therefore, be manifested in a number of ways. Product development times can be reduced; deliveries from suppliers can be speeded up through just-in-time; and, by utilizing information technology, distributor and retail stocks can be replenished faster. Speed can relate to the whole of the value chain. However, obtaining the competitive benefits of speed is likely to involve more than improved efficiencies through cutting the time taken to do things. A change of attitude towards providing faster, better and customized service is also required. All activities in the value chain need reviewing in an attempt to improve effectiveness.

Case 15.2 illustrates these points – the

Benetton example amplifies points introduced in Case 10.6. To reinforce the importance of changing attitudes, Chrysler President Lee Iacocca is reported to have asked an engineer for a prototype sports car for a road test when he felt the market for convertibles might be re-emerging. He was promised one in nine months. His response was to tell the engineer to take a car out of stock and just saw the roof off.

Implications

Competitive advantage through speed will only be feasible if the organization structure facilitates the changes implied, rather than constrains them. Ideas and information must be able to permeate quickly through the organization; and managers at the operational level must be empowered to make decisions. This implies decentralization and possibly fewer levels of management in the hierarchy, issues discussed in Chapter 22.

Successful organizations will become fast learners, ideally finding out about changing customer preferences and expectations ahead of their competitors. They will also need to be able to respond quickly to changes in competitor strategies. This again emphasizes the importance of decentralization.

When speed was less important it was quite normal for products to be developed and tested in advance of any investment in the new plant which would eventually be required to produce them in volume. These must now be seen as parallel, not sequential, activities. This necessitates close co-operation between the various functional areas of the business, perhaps using special project teams. As we shall see in Chapter 22, such changes can prove difficult to implement.

Finally, the notion of speed must be considered very carefully in certain industries. The design and development of new drugs and new aeroplanes, for example,

should not be hurried if safety and reliability could be compromised.

SUMMARY

This chapter has concluded the section on resource analysis, and in it the theme of how the various sources of competitive advantage might be evaluated and developed has been extended. The previous five chapters looked at the strategic contributions of marketing, operations, human resources, finance and information management, and at how each of these functions and activities can generate competitive advantage. Referring back to Figure III.1 at the beginning of the section, the emphasis has been on understanding how functional strategies can create competitive advantage and thereby help determine competitive strategies.

Porter's value chain analysis has been introduced and considered as a framework for evaluating the activities of the business in the context of competitive advantage.

Specifically we have

☐ introduced the notion of the value chain and described its component primary and support activities;

☐ discussed the importance of linkages between the activities, highlighting that they can be a major source of synergy;

☐ looked at how the four dimensions of competitive scope, namely segment, vertical, geographic and industry, affect competitive advantage;

☐ recapped on the essential aspects of cost leadership and differentiation strategies;

☐ highlighted the need to attribute costs to activities if the value chain is to be useful for decision making, emphasizing that this may not be straightforward;

☐ discussed the various cost drivers and some common problems in controlling costs as a result of value chain analysis;

☐ summarized how differentiation might be created anywhere within the organization;

☐ used the Japanese zip manufacturer, YKK, as an illustration of the value chain;

☐ looked at the increasing importance of speed as a competitive weapon.

Strategic awareness has been the main theme of the book so far: understanding how strategic changes come about; appreciating the significant contribution of the strategic leader and the culture of the organization; considering how the relative success of the organization might be measured; realizing the need to match the skills and resources of the organization with the environment; and considering how each of the functions affects competitive strategy and how important it is that managers in each of the functions appreciate the wider strategic implications of the decisions they make.

The following chapters again address important questions in strategic management and there are subtitled questions concerning strategic change. In this respect they refer more directly to decisions concerning the overall **corporate strategy** of the organization – how the strategy might be created and selected, and the requirements for effective implementation. Awareness of the possibilities and implications of various strategic choices is emphasized throughout, but in addition there is consideration of **how** the decisions might be made and implemented.

CHECKLIST OF KEY TERMS AND CONCEPTS

You should feel confident that you understand the following terms and ideas:

☐ The value chain
☐ Primary and support activities
☐ Linkages
☐ Cost drivers
☐ Sources of differentiation.

QUESTIONS AND RESEARCH ASSIGNMENTS

Text related

1. Given the following information about Ratners, the High Street jewellers, draw up a value chain summarizing their strategy similar to that for YKK included in the text.

Gerald Ratner took over as chief executive (and later chairman) of his family-controlled company in 1984, when Ratners had a market share of 2.5% of retail jewellery. Five years later, and following a series of strategic acquisitions, Ratners had over 1000 outlets, trading under the following names: Ratners, H. Samuel, Ernest Jones, Terrys, Zales and Watches of Switzerland. Salisbury's, the luggage, bags and related products retailers, are also part of the chain. Market share had risen to 25%. The next largest retail competitor is Argos who have Elizabeth Duke outlets in their stores. The rest of the market is composed of smaller chains and independent outlets.

Ratners' strategy was based on the following:

☐ cheap competitive prices
☐ aggressive visible marketing with colourful window displays and prices clearly featured
☐ giving jewellery a fashionable but affordable image – customers are offered what they can afford to buy rather than quality they cannot afford
☐ common merchandising and window displays in all stores – pad and window layouts are thoroughly researched and tested and then photographs are sent to store managers for them to follow
☐ tight central control of buying and stocks – unsold stock is returned to manufacturers
☐ sophisticated information technology systems in the warehouses to ensure fast replenishment

☐ incentives for sales staff
☐ product developments in conjunction with manufacturers.

[The cost of more recent acquisitions in America, and falling sales in the UK (during the recession) have caused profits to collapse. These difficulties, together with adverse publicity after Gerald Ratner described his company's products as 'crap' at an Institute of Directors' Conference, led to his resignation as Chairman (1991) and later (1992) as Chief Executive. He disagreed with the new chairman's strategy of switching over to higher margin products.]

Library based

2. Take an organization of your choice, research its strategy and again draw up a value chain.

   If you are able to gain access to the costs of the firm, allocate them to the value chain following the principles incorporated in Table 15.1.

REFERENCES

The content of this chapter is based substantially upon ideas contained in
Porter, M E (1980) *Competitive Strategy: Techniques for Analysing Industries and Competitors*, Free Press.
Porter, M E (1985) *Competitive Advantage: Creating and Sustaining Superior Performance*, Free Press.

Other references

Hamel, G and Prahalad, C K (1989) Strategic intent, *Harvard Business Review*, May–June.
Johnson, H T and Kaplan, R S (1987) *Relevance Lost: The Rise and Fall of Management Accounting*, Harvard Business School Press.
Lawler, E E III (1992) *The Ultimate Advantage. Creating the High Involvement Organization*, Maxwell Macmillan.
Ohmae, K (1988) Getting back to strategy, *Harvard Business Review*, November–December.

Readers interested in design and competitiveness are referred to: *Benefits and Costs of Investment in Design*, the Open University (Design Innovation Group), 1991.

INTERLUDE
STRATEGIC
CHANGE

INTRODUCTION TO STRATEGIC CHANGE

In Chapter 1 the notion of E-V-R (environment, values, resources) congruence was introduced. Effective strategic management requires that the skills and capabilities of the organization are matched with the key success factors of the environment. Figure IV.1, developed from Chapter 1, Figure 1.2, and material covered in the first part of the book, explains this.

The organization's resources constitute its skills and capabilities, and although these can all be developed, at any time managers should be looking for new opportunities where these skills can be deployed most effectively. The opportunities, together with possible threats, are environmental issues. Managers should consider the skills required to meet key success factors, capitalize on potential opportunities and handle possible threats that they have spotted. If they are not the skills and capabilities that the organization has at the moment, the potential for developing them should be evaluated in the light of the perceived significance of the opportunities and threats. Matching resources with environmental needs effectively requires sound management. Quite possibly change will be required and the

ability to accomplish it successfully will depend on the values and culture of the organization.

The environment, particularly customers, consumers and competition, dictates the potential for certain sources of competitive advantage; the organization's resources should be developed, deployed and co-ordinated to create and sustain competitive advantage. Competitive advantage will be reflected in the functional and competitive strategies, and these all contribute towards the overall corporate strategy.

Managers should therefore be aware of

☐ objectives and strategies being pursued;
☐ sources of competitive advantage;
☐ how well these current strategies constitute congruence;
☐ how successful the strategies being pursued are for profit, growth and stakeholder satisfaction.

It is important to think ahead, considering where managers, and in particular the strategic leader, want the organization to go (growth, profit etc.). At the same time they must assess where the organization is going with present strategies. If the organization

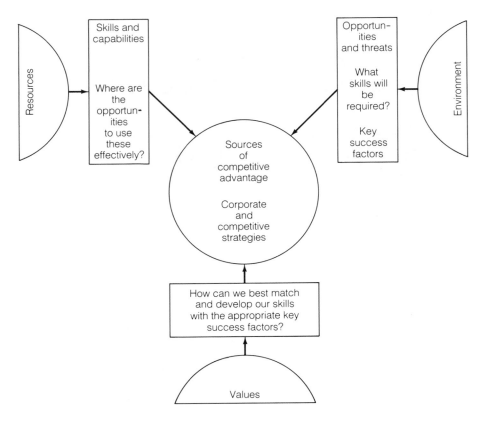

Figure IV.1 E–V–R congruence.

continues with essentially the same strategies, modifying them wherever necessary, is it likely to meet the expectations of management? If expectations and likely results do not match, then corporate strategic changes should be planned and implemented. After assessing alternative opportunities and courses of action for feasibility and desirability it may be necessary to restate the objectives.

The two relevant questions are:

☐ Where do we want to go?
☐ Where can we go realistically?

These are reconciled by asking:

Chapter 16

☐ How do we go about finding the alter-

native courses of action, and evaluating them? (the overall process)
☐ What techniques might assist?

Chapters 17–19 on strategic alternatives, growth, recovery, recession and divestment strategies

☐ How can we get to where we would like to be?
☐ What options are available?
☐ What lessons should we pay attention to?

Chapter 21

☐ What really makes sense?
☐ What constitutes a good choice?

How well the questions are addressed and answered will determine the quality of the strategy selected, which then needs implementing.

It is then necessary to consider:

Chapter 22

☐ How appropriate is the current organization structure?
☐ What changes might we consider?

Chapter 23

☐ How well are we managing our **resources** in the context of future needs?

Chapter 24

☐ How are we going to manage the changes?
☐ To what extent do we need changes in culture and values?

The extent to which the latter questions are addressed properly will influence how well the strategy is understood throughout the organization and the commitment that managers have towards it.

Addressing these questions systematically constitutes *strategic planning*. In addition, it is important

☐ always to be thinking about the issues raised by these questions and

☐ to realize that systematic planning is not the only way in which strategies are created. (This particular point is explored further in Chapter 16.)

It is important to appreciate that *strategic change* always involves

analysis   choice   implementation

but that the way in which these activities are carried out, and the emphasis given to each, varies with the mode of strategy creation.

The chapters in the final two parts of this book actually vary this terminology slightly and consider strategic change in terms of:

objectives/planning   alternatives
(instead of analysis)

choice   implementation

Specifically they address:

☐ strategic planning, and the form of planning used;
☐ the possible strategic alternatives that follow from this;
☐ the realistic options;
☐ the choice from the options;
☐ implementation.

PART FOUR

CHANGES IN CORPORATE STRATEGY

WHERE DO WE WANT TO GO?

16

LEARNING OBJECTIVES

After studying this chapter you should be able to

☐ distinguish between planning as a cerebral activity carried out by all managers and systematic corporate planning;
☐ describe a number of approaches to corporate planning and in relation to these discuss who should be involved in planning;
☐ explain the concept of the planning gap;
☐ assess the contribution of a number of planning techniques, including directional policy matrices and PIMS;
☐ discuss how corporate planning might be applied to local government and not-for-profit organizations;
☐ evaluate the potential contribution of systems ideas to corporate planning and the role of formal planning in strategy formulation;
☐ prepare a strategy statement.

This chapter is about strategy formulation, planning and strategic planning systems. Planning is a cerebral activity: managers think about where the organization should be going, why and how. It can also be an established system which collects and evaluates data before future courses of action are determined. A number of strategic planning techniques are discussed.

INTRODUCTION

In this chapter we look at how decisions about future strategic change and areas for development are made. We examine the role of planning systems, and the contribution of planning techniques to the broad issue of which direction the organization should take in the future.

The planning era, if one may call it that, occurred some time ago, and has been discredited as we have moved on to the greater belief in the development of common values in the organization, and are rediscovering again today the necessity to be close to the market.

(Sir John Harvey-Jones,
Past Chairman ICI, 1987)

Planning is one of the most complex and difficult intellectual activities in which man can engage. Not to do it well is not a sin; but to settle for doing it less than well is.

(Russell Ackoff, 1970)

Planning the future – thinking about the most appropriate strategies, and changes of strategic direction – is essential for organizations, particularly those experiencing turbulent environments. The above quotations and Key Reading 16.1 by Michael Porter remind us of the need for strategic thinking. Rigid systematic planning is no longer fashionable, nor is it the only way in which strategic change decisions are made. There are dangers if organizations become reliant upon professional planning and the only outcome is a plan. This may not allow for effective strategic thinking, and may not result in a clear direction for the future.

There are also dangers in thinking that all strategic changes can be planned systematically. Whether it is the result of formal and systematic planning, or much more informal and *ad hoc* management, an organization will have strategies and processes whereby these strategies are changed. The processes need to be understood, and in many cases improved.

Key Reading 16.1
THE STATE OF STRATEGIC THINKING

Strategic planning, popular in the 1960s and 1970s, deservedly fell out of fashion. In most companies planning had not contributed to **strategic thinking**; but, because strategic thinking is essential, a new role should be found for planning.

Strategic planning became fashionable for two basic reasons.

☐ Short-term budgeting to control operations developed after World War II, and because many of the implications of current decisions have a long-term significance these essentially financial plans were stretched into longer-term plans.
☐ As firms grew increasingly complex it was recognized that the various functions and business units needed to be integrated. Strategic planning seemed an ideal way of setting corporate strategies systematically rather than intuitively.

The outcome for many organizations was formal planning systems, heavily reliant on financial data, and supported by thick planning manuals.

On the positive side planning can encourage managers to think about the need and opportunities for change, and to communicate strategy to those who must implement it. This was particularly important in the 1960s and early 1970s when there was an abundance of investment opportunities and a dearth of capital and key priorities needed to be established. In complex multi-activity organizations, decisions have to be made concerning where to concentrate investment capital in relation to future earnings potential, and this has generated a number of portfolio analysis techniques such as the Boston growth–share matrix. Rather than use these techniques for gaining greater awareness and insight, for which they are well suited, managers sought to use them prescriptively to determine future plans. (Techniques are limited in this respect; this issue is discussed in the main text.)

Planning had become unfashionable by the 1980s for a number of reasons.

☐ Planning was often carried out by planners, rather than the managers who would be affected by the resultant plans.
☐ As a result, the outcome of planning was often a plan which in reality had little impact on actual management decisions, and therefore was not implemented.
☐ The planning techniques used were criticized primarily because of the way in which they were used.
☐ The important elements of culture and total quality management were usually left out.

However, many industries have experienced turbulent environments caused by such factors as slower economic growth, globalization and technological change, and consequently strategic thinking is extremely important. The following questions must be addressed.

☐ What is the future direction of competition?
☐ What are the future needs of customers?
☐ How are competitors likely to behave?
☐ How might competitive advantage be gained and sustained?

Strategic planning should be rethought so that these questions are constantly addressed rather than addressed occasionally as part of an annual cycle. Line managers who implement plans must be involved throughout the process. 'Every executive needs to understand how to think strategically.' Rigorous frameworks and planning manuals are not necessary as long as the proper thinking takes place.

There should be a strategic plan for each business unit in a complex organization, i.e. clear competitive strategies built around an understanding of the nature of the industry in which the business competes, and sources of competitive advantage. Chosen strategies must have action plans for implementing them, including an assessment of the needs for finance and for staff training and development. This is generally less difficult than formulating a corporate strategy for the whole organization.

Corporate strategies relate to the nature and diversity of the businesses which comprise the organization. Business units should benefit individually from being part of the whole organization, and together they should generate synergy. This happens all too rarely because of a number of recurring issues and misconceptions.

☐ **Re-structuring**, rationalizing, cutting costs, closing factories, is more a way of dealing with the failures of past strategies than a strategy in itself. If an organization is to be successful in the long term, it must build.
☐ **Buying competitors**, rather than beating them, often brings short-term gains but rarely adds real competitive advantage for the benefit of consumers.
☐ **Corporate alliances/joint ventures** again are more effective in the short term.
☐ **Imitation is often preferred to innovation**.
☐ **Diversification** which provides growth but not added value does not create synergy.

(These issues will be explored in later chapters.)

Summarized from Porter, M E (1987) The state of strategic thinking, *The Economist*, 23 May.

It is important to assess where and how the organization should change and develop in the light of market opportunities and competitive threats, but there are lessons to be learnt about their appropriateness to certain strategic opportunities. Managers should say clearly where the organization is, and where it might sensibly go, and start making appropriate changes. They should then monitor progress and be aware of changes in the environment; in this way they can be flexible and responsive.

Robinson (1986) argues that the role of the planner should not be to plan but to enable good managers to plan. It is not the task of the planner to state the objectives; rather he or she should elicit and clarify them. Planning should concentrate on **understanding the future,** which is, of course, uncertain and unpredictable, and helping managers to make decisions about strategic changes. Thus the aim of planning should be to force people to think and examine, not to produce a rigid plan.

We shall look at how organizations and managers might seek to address future issues. First, we consider what is meant by the term planning, and what is involved in the systematic planning cycle approach to the management of strategic change. The contribution of a number of planning techniques will be evaluated, and possible pitfalls and human issues in planning will be pinpointed. Planning, entrepreneurial and adaptive modes of strategic change, introduced in Chapter 4, will be developed further and examined. A soft systems approach to planning will be adopted, and finally the strategy statement framework (Chapter 1, Figure 1.3) will be extended to consider which specific questions need to be addressed within the broad issue of where the organization wants to go.

PLANNING AND PLANNING SYSTEMS

What do we mean by planning?

All managers plan. They plan how they might achieve objectives. However, a clear distinction needs to be made between the cerebral activity of informal planning and formalized planning systems.

A visionary strategic leader, aware of strategic opportunities and convinced that they can be capitalized upon, may decide by himself where the organization should go and how the strategies are to be implemented. Very little needs to be recorded formally. Conversations between managers may result in plans which again exist only in individual managers' heads or in the form of scribbled notes. Equally, time, money and other resources may be invested by the organization in the production of elaborate and formally documented plans.

In all cases planning is part of an on-going continuous activity which addresses where the organization as a whole, or individual parts of it, should be going. At one level a plan may simply describe the activities and tasks which must be carried out in the next day or week in order to meet specific targets. At a much higher level the plan may seek to define the mission and objectives, and establish guidelines, strategies and policies which will enable the organization to adapt to, and to shape and exploit, its environment over a period of years. In both cases, if events turn out to be different from those which were forecast, the plans will need to be changed.

The value of strategic planning

When managers and organizations plan strategies they are seeking to

---

I have a saying 'Every plan made is an opportunity lost' because I feel that if you try to plan the way your business will go, down to the last detail, you are no longer open to seize any opportunity that may arise unexpectedly.

Debbie Moore, Chairman, Pineapple Ltd

□ be clearer about the business(es) that the organization is in, and should be in;

□ increase awareness about strengths and weaknesses;

□ be able to recognize and capitalize on opportunities, and to defend against threats;

□ be more effective in the allocation and use of resources.

Irrespective of the quality or format of the actual plans, engaging in the planning process can be valuable. It helps individual managers to establish priorities and address problems; it can bring managers together so that they can share their problems and perspectives. Ideally the result will be improved communication, co-ordination and commitment. Hence there can be real benefit from planning or thinking about the future. What form should the thinking and planning take? Should it be part of a formalized system making use of strategic planning techniques?

Corporate and functional plans

Corporate and strategic plans concern the number and variety of product markets and service markets that the organization will compete in, together with the development of the necessary resources (people, capacity, finance, research and so on) required to support the competitive strategies. Strategic plans, therefore, relate to the whole organization, cover several years and are generally not highly detailed. They are concerned with future needs and how to obtain and develop the desired businesses, products, services and resources. The actual time-scale involved will be affected by the nature of the industry and the number of years ahead that investments must be planned if growth and change is to be brought about.

Functional plans are derived from corporate strategy and strategic plans, and they relate to the implementation of functional strategies. They cover specific areas of the business; there can be plans relating to product development, production control and cash budgeting, for example. Functional plans will usually have shorter time horizons than is the case for strategic plans, and invariably they will incorporate greater detail. However, they will be reviewed and up-dated, and they may very well become on-going rolling plans. Whilst strategic plans are used to direct the whole organization, functional plans are used for the short-term management of parts of the organization.

Competitive strategies and functional strategies and plans are essential if products and services are to be managed effectively, but they should be flexible and capable of being changed if managers responsible for their implementation feel it necessary.

Ohmae (1982) emphasizes that individual products must be seen as part of wider systems or product groups/business units, and that although short-term plans must be drawn up for the effective management of individual products, it is important to ensure that thinking about the future is done at the appropriate level. As an example a particular brand or type of shampoo targeted at a specific market segment would constitute a product market. The company's range of shampoos should be produced and marketed in a co-ordinated way, and consequently they might constitute a strategic planning unit. The relevant strategic business unit might incorporate all the company's cosmetics products and there should be a competitive strategy which ensures that the various products are co-ordinated and support each other. In terms of strategic thinking Ohmae suggests that it is more important to consider listening devices as a whole than radios specifically, and that this type of thinking resulted in the Sony Walkman and similar products. In just the same way the Japanese realized a new opportunity for black and white television receivers in the form of small portable sets, when other manufacturers had switched all their attention to the development of colour sets. If the level of thinking is appropriate, resources are likely to be allocated more effectively.

The strategic issues involved in the various functions and the theme of competitive advantage have been the subject of Chapters 10–15, and this chapter really concentrates on corporate strategy and decisions concerning changes in corporate strategy. These changes must be thought about, evaluated and planned in some way, but the planning need not be rigorous, formal and systematic to be effective.

Alternative approaches to planning

Taylor and Hussey (1982) feature seven different approaches to planning which are detailed briefly below.

☐ **Informal planning** takes place in someone's head, and the decisions reached may not be written down in any extensive form. It is often practised by managers with real entrepreneurial flair, and it can be highly successful. It is less likely to be effective if used by managers who lack flair and creativity.

☐ **Extended budgeting** is rarely used as it is only feasible if the environment is stable and predictable. Extended budgeting is primarily financial planning based on the extrapolation of past trends.

☐ **Top-down planning** relates to decisions taken at the top of the organization and passed down to other managers for implementation. These managers will have had little or no input into the planning process. Major change decisions reached informally may be incorporated here, and then a great deal depends upon the strength and personality of the strategic leader in persuading other managers to accept the changes. At the other extreme, top-down plans may emanate from professional planners using planning techniques extensively and reporting directly to the strategic leader. These are the type of plans that Porter (1987) in Key Reading 16.1, suggests may not be implemented.

☐ **Strategic analysis/policy options** again uses planning techniques, and involves the creation and analytical evaluation of alternative options. Where future possible scenarios are explored for their implications, and possible courses of action are tested for sensitivity, this form of planning can be valuable for strategic thinking. It is an appropriate use of planning techniques, but it is important to consider the potential impact on people.

☐ **Bottom-up planning** involves managers throughout the organization, and therefore ensures that people who will be involved in implementing plans are consulted. Specifically functional and business unit managers are charged with evaluating the future potential for their areas of responsibility and are invited to make a case for future resources. All the detail is analysed and the future allocation of resources is decided. In an extreme form thick planning manuals will be involved, and the process may be slow and rigid. Necessary changes may be inhibited if managerial freedom to act outside the plan is constrained. A formal system of this nature is likely to involve an annual planning cycle, such as is shown in Table 16.1.

☐ **Behavioural approaches** can take several forms, but essentially the behavioural approach requires that managers spend time discussing the future opportunities and threats and areas in which the organization might develop. The idea is that if managers are encouraged to discuss their problems and objectives for the business freely, and if they are able to reach agreement concerning future priorities and developments, then they will be committed to implementing the changes. However, it is quite likely that all the

Table 16.1 An example of a planning cycle

Month	Corporate headquarters	Business units
January February	Organization-wide SWOT analysis (or similar), and statement of major strategic concerns	
March April May		SWOT analysis and development plans, including request for resources
June July August	Review of business unit plans and requests; resource allocation to current and future activities	
September October		Functional, operating plans based on resources available; budgeting
November December	Review of budgets	

conflicts concerning resource allocation and priorities will not be resolved.

☐ The **strategic review** was developed to take the best features of the other six approaches and blend them together into a systematic and comprehensive planning system. A typical system is discussed in detail in the next section.

All of these approaches have individual advantages and disadvantages, and they are not mutually exclusive. The approach adopted will depend upon the style and preferences of the strategic leader, who must, as we saw in Chapter 3:

☐ clarify the mission and corporate objectives and establish the extent and nature of changes to the corporate perspective;

☐ approve competitive and functional strategies and plans for each part of the business, however they might be created; and

☐ establish appropriate control mechanisms, which may or may not involve substantial decentralization.

It has been established that planning may be either informal or formal. Informal planning, as such, cannot be taught; but formal planning systems can. These are the subject of the next section.

A systematic approach to planning

The planning gap

A number of essentially similar models of systematic planning have been developed by such authors as Argenti (1980), Hussey (1976), Cohen and Cyert (1973) and Glueck and Jauch (1984) whose models of the process of formulating, implementing and monitoring corporate strategy are considered below. All these models utilize the concept of gap analysis, which is extremely useful for strategic thinking purposes and which is featured as Key Concept 16.1.

The concept of the planning gap relates very closely to issues which were raised in Chapter 5 on objectives. It addresses the questions:

☐ Where do we want to go?
☐ Where can we go realistically?

When considering where and how an organization might develop in the future, both the desired and realistic objectives are essential considerations. Desired objectives relate to where the strategic leader and other decision makers would like to take the organization if it is possible to do so. Realistic objectives incorporate the influence of the various stakeholders in the business, and their expec-

Key Concept 16.1
THE PLANNING GAP

The planning gap should be seen as an idea which can be adapted to suit particular circumstances, although gap analysis could be regarded as a planning technique.

An example of the planning gap is illustrated in Figure 16.1. The horizontal axis represents the planning time horizon, stretching forward from the present day; either sales volume or revenue, or profits, could be used on the vertical axis as a measure of anticipated performance. The lowest full line on the graph indicates expected sales or profits if the organization continues with present corporate, competitive and functional strategies; the top broken line represents ideal objectives, which imply growth and which may or may not ultimately be realized. The difference between these two lines is the gap. Quite simply the gap is the difference between the results which the organization can expect to achieve from present strategies continued forward and the results that the strategic leader would like to attain.

The example illustrated in Figure 16.1 shows the gap filled in by a series of alternative courses of strategic action, ordered in an ascending hierarchy of risk.

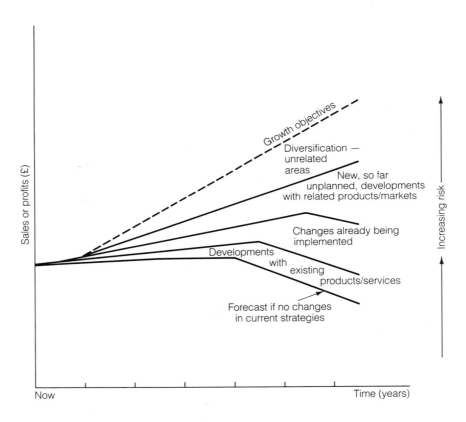

Figure 16.1 An example of the planning gap.

	Product	
Market	Present	New
Present	Market penetration	Product development
New	Market development	Diversification

Figure 16.2 Ansoff's growth vector. (*Source*: Ansoff, H I (1987) *Corporate Strategy*, revised edition, Penguin.)

Risk is constituted by the extent to which future products and markets are related to existing ones; and this idea of increased risk and strategic alternatives is developed further in Figures 16.2 and 16.3.

The least risk alternative is to seek to manage present products and services more effectively, aiming to sell more of them and to reduce their costs in order to generate increased sales and profits. This is termed market penetration in the simple growth vector developed by H Igor Ansoff and illustrated in Figure 16.2. It can be extended to strategies of market and product development, which imply respectively

□ new customers or even new market segments for existing products, which might be modified in some way to provide increased differentiation; and
□ new products, ideally using related technology and skills, for sale to existing markets.

(In this context 'new' implies new to the firm rather than something which is necessarily completely new and innovative, although it could well be this.) Figure 16.1 distinguishes between market and product development strategies which are already under way and those which have yet to be started.

The highest risk alternative is diversification because this involves both new products and new markets. Figure 16.3 develops these simple themes further and distinguishes between the following:

□ replacement products and product line extensions which are based on existing technologies and skills and which represent improved products for existing customers
□ new products, based on new or unrelated technologies and skills, which constitute concentric diversification (these may be sold to either existing or new customers)
□ completely new and unrelated products for sale to new customers. This is known as conglomerate diversification and is regarded as a high-risk strategic alternative.

USING THE PLANNING GAP

Thinking about the extent of the initial gap between present strategies and ideal objectives enables managers to consider how much change and how much risk would be involved in closing the gap and achieving the target objectives. Some of the strategies considered might be neither feasible nor desirable, and consequently the gap might be too wide to close. Similarly the degree of risk, especially if a number of changes are involved, might be greater than the strategic

Continued overleaf

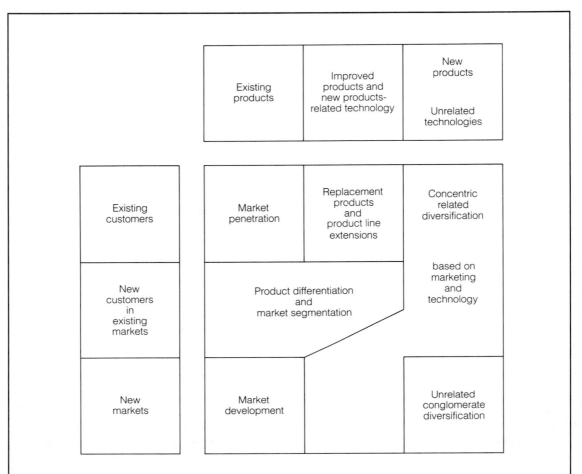

Figure 16.3   An extended growth vector.

leader is willing to accept. In these cases it will be necessary to revise the desired objectives downwards so that they finally represent realistic targets which should be achieved by strategic changes that are acceptable and achievable.

This type of thinking, of course, is related to specific objectives concerning growth and profitability. It does not follow, as was discussed in Chapter 5, that either growth or profitability maximization will be the major priority of the organization, or that the personal objectives of individual managers will not be an issue.

tations; the existence of suitable opportunities; and the availability of the necessary resources. The issue of the risk involved in the alternative courses of action which might be considered is crucial. The discussion of the planning gap in Key Concept 16.1 draws attention to the increasing risk which is typically associated with certain strategic alternatives, in particular diversification, which is often implemented through acquisition. Failure rates with diversification are high, as will be discussed in Chapter 18. However, diversification may be the only feasible route to the achievement of high-growth targets or the maintenance of present rates of growth in profits and sales revenues. The strategic leader, perhaps under significant pressure from City investors, shareholders and analysts who expect growth rates to be at least maintained, may be forced to pursue high-risk strategies.

(We do not discuss again in this chapter the types of objective – profit, growth, security, stakeholder satisfaction and so on – which the organization might set. Readers may wish to refer back to Chapter 5.)

Steps in systematic planning

Cohen and Cyert contend that there are nine sequential steps in systematic planning:

1. *The formulation of goals* Corporate goals or objectives must be decided upon, and they will represent an amalgam of the goals of the key stakeholders: owners, consumers, employees and the general public. They are likely to deal with such issues as growth, size, diversity, product and service availability and any international aspirations; and initially they are expressed qualitatively.

2. *Analysis of the environment* Because the organization and its environment are in a state of dynamic equilibrium, such that when the organization does something there is an environmental reaction, and vice versa, the key relationships must be understood clearly. The analysis should include both the industry and the wider environment, which were discussed in Chapter 9.

3. *The establishment of quantitative targets or 'milestones'* Wherever possible, and following the environmental analysis, quantitat-

ive targets should next be ascribed to the qualitative goals established in 1 above. These may be expressed as percentage growth rates or absolute values. Given the latter, the dates for achievement are essential. The quantitative targets might be stated in terms of total sales revenue in year X, percentage sales growth, return on capital employed of ZZ % or a total net profit figure for year X. Instead of sales or profits, the value of assets owned by the organization might be used, or the number of people employed, or sales per employee. The targets will relate to the whole organization and certain targets are likely to be seen as having high priorities; from them target expectations might be given to every business unit in the organization.

4. *Strategy formulation* Where specific targets are given, each business unit will be asked to formulate its own strategic plan, based on a SWOT analysis, highlighting the resource support which will be required if the plan is approved. If specific targets are not provided, the business units might be asked to state a number of possible levels of achievement in terms of market share, sales and profits together with the likelihood of success and the resources required to support each alternative.

5. *Aggregation* These business unit plans are then aggregated into a corporate plan, which should be assessed in terms of, first, the organization's ability to support it, and, second, the level of achievement it represents. This can be used as part of a gap analysis which identifies the extent to which the organization will have to develop, change and diversify if the overall target goals are to be attained.

6. *Strategic search* The plan developed from the existing business units, together with the gap analysis, lead to a search for new strategies. These might be pricing strategies, cost reduction strategies, innovation and acquisition strategies.

7. *Selection of the strategic action portfolio*

Alternative action plans should be evaluated for possible synergy and strategic fit within the organization. If in particular the actions being considered involve a change in the organization's domain, the opportunity to create and sustain competitive advantage in the new businesses should be carefully analysed.

At this stage it could prove beneficial to re-evaluate the targets established in 3 above and consider target achievements for any new developments proposed.

Planning techniques, especially portfolio analysis, could prove extremely useful as part of 5, 6 and 7 above.

8. *Implementation of the strategic programme* The resource requirements of the selected action plans should be looked at in detail. Ideally all resources will be considered, rather than just finance, because although budgeting is very important it is quite likely that development programmes for other resources will be required. It is also possible that changes to the organization structure might be appropriate, depending on the degree of change implied by the decisions reached in 7 above.

9. *Measurement, feedback and control* The quantitative targets which have finally been established will serve as control parameters. However, simply measuring performance against targets may be inadequate as managers wanting to appear successful within the organization may attempt to massage figures and present results in such a way that they hide any aspects of potential concern. Variances should be analysed and explanations sought before decisions are taken concerning alterations to the plan.

This last stage is vital because in a turbulent dynamic environment planning is difficult. It is impossible to forecast all events which might take place, and therefore plans must have inbuilt flexibility.

The model suggested by Glueck and Jauch (1984) is similar, but does not separate out the contribution of individual business units. There are eight stages as follows:

1. Set objectives.
2. Determine present and potential threats and opportunities in the environment.
3. Determine comparative advantages by considering the size, distribution, strengths and weaknesses of resources.
4. Consider strategic alternatives.
5. Choose the strategy or strategies which are most appropriate for the objectives.
6. Develop the organization structure and climate to match structure with the strategy.
7. Develop short- and medium-term policies, plans and programmes and assign resources as required by the strategy chosen.
8. Evaluate the strategy to ensure that it will achieve the objectives. If not, the objectives should be revised.

Progress against target objectives should also be assessed when the strategy is implemented.

It has already been emphasized that systematic planning along these lines will rarely explain how all strategic change decisions are reached. The adaptive and entrepreneurial modes are discussed in detail later, but it is possible for both of them to operate within or alongside a planning system. Planning may be used to establish priorities and directions for growth and development but with managers given freedom to adapt competitive and functional strategies in order to achieve their agreed targets. Equally, planning may be used to ensure that interdependent short-term plans fit into an organization-wide framework and that managers appreciate the interdependences, but the overall framework may be extended and re-thought if an appropriate opportunity is spotted and followed.

The idea behind these comments is that the questions involved in systematic planning should not necessarily be addressed sequentially, or at only one time in the year. Rather,

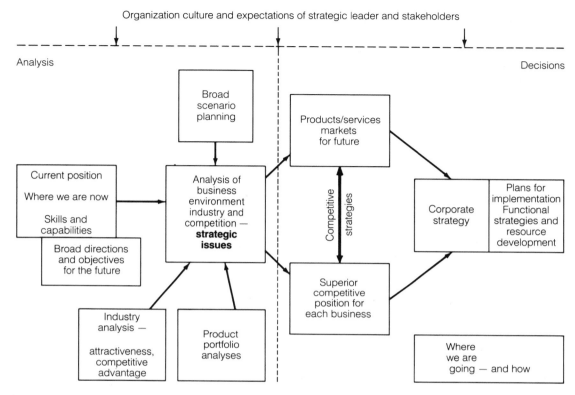

Figure 16.4   A contemporary approach to strategic planning.

they should be considered all the time, and new opportunities and threats spotted early and in time for the organization to act positively. In this way managers can seek to become and stay strategically aware. Planning systems have a valuable role to play in strategic management, but their contribution should not inhibit the organization's ability to respond quickly and decisively to changes in the environment.

A contemporary approach to strategic planning

In order to ensure that planning does not become an end in itself, and that planners do facilitate management thinking, many large companies have evolved more contemporary

planning mechanisms from the above systematic models. Figure 16.4 is an illustration of the type of planning system which is becoming increasingly popular and which appears to be a composite of many of the types of planning discussed earlier in this section. We attempt to harness the most beneficial ideas from earlier models and relate them to the most up-to-date thinking about strategic management. The influence of Michael Porter's thinking can be seen in this contemporary approach.

The organization's culture and the expectations of the strategic leader and the key stakeholders influence the whole process of analysis and decision making. The thinking starts with an assessment of the current position of the organization, its skills and resources, and an evaluation of whether there is a clear understanding of the 'mission', the broad objectives and directions for the future.

Then we analyse the business environment thoroughly, concentrating on the industries in which the organization currently competes and those in which it might apply its skills and resources. Feeding into this analysis are three other analyses:

☐ broad scenario planning – conceptualizing a range of different futures which the organization might have to deal with, to ensure that the less likely possibilities, threats and opportunities are not over-looked, and to encourage a high level of flair and creativity in strategic thinking
☐ product portfolio analyses, which are dis-cussed in greater detail in the next section; contingency and possible crisis planning considerations can be incorporated in this
☐ industry analyses, following the Porter criteria for judging attractiveness and opportunities for competitive advantage (discussed earlier).

This environmental analysis should focus on any **strategic issues** – current or forthcoming developments, inside or outside the organ-ization, which will impact upon the ability of the organization to pursue its mission and meet its objectives. Ideally these would be opportunities related to organizational strengths. Wherever possible any unwel-come, but significant, potential threats should be turned into competitive opportun-ities.

From these analyses competitive strategy decisions must be reached concerning

☐ the reinforcement or establishment of a superior competitive position, or compet-itive advantage, for each business within the existing portfolio of products and services;
☐ product markets and service markets for future development, and the appropriate functional strategies for establishing a superior competitive position.

Amalgamated, these functional and compet-itive strategies constitute the corporate strat-egy for the future, which in turn needs to be broken down into resource development plans and any decisions relating to changes in the structure of the organization, i.e. decisions which reflect where the organiza-tion is going and how the inherent changes are to be managed.

It is important that new strategic issues are spotted and dealt with continuously, and the organization structure must enable this to happen, either by decentralization and empowerment or by effective communica-tions.(See Chapter 22.)

An organization might choose any one of the planning approaches described above, or develop its own personalized system. What-ever the system, there are certain key issues and lessons concerning who should be involved, potential planning traps, and the impact upon managers throughout the organization which should be considered. These are discussed next.

Strategic planning issues

Who should plan?

Amongst the various authors on corporate planning who have been referred to earlier in this chapter, there is a consensus of opinion that strategic planning should not be under-taken by the chief executive alone, planning specialists divorced from operating man-agers, marketing executives or finance departments. An individual or specialist department may be biased and fail to produce a balanced plan. Instead it is import-ant to involve, in some way, all managers who will be affected by the plan, and who will be charged with implementing it. How-ever, all these managers together cannot constitute an effective working team, and therefore a small team which represents the whole organization should be constituted, and other managers consulted. This will require a schedule for the planning activities and a formalized system for carrying out the tasks. As discussed above, it is important that planning systems do not inhibit on-going strategic thinking by managers throughout the organization. Threats must still be spotted early and potential opportunities must not be lost.

Planning traps

Ringbakk (1971) and Steiner (1972) have documented several reasons why formal planning might fail and have discussed the potential traps to avoid. Amongst their conclusions are the following:

☐ Planning should not be left exclusively to planners who might see their job as being the production of a plan and who might also concentrate on procedures and detail at the expense of wide strategic thinking.
☐ Planning should be seen as a support activity in strategic decision making and not a once-a-year ritual.
☐ There must be a commitment and an allocation of time from the strategic leader. Without this managers lower down the organization might not feel that planning matters within the firm.
☐ Planning is not likely to prove effective unless the broad directional objectives for the firm are agreed and communicated widely.
☐ Implementors must be involved, both in drawing up the plan (or essential information might be missed) and afterwards. The plan should be communicated throughout the organization, and efforts should be made to ensure that managers appreciate what is expected of them.
☐ Targets, once established, should be used as a measure of performance and variances should be analysed properly. However, there can be a danger in over-concentrating on targets and financial data at the expense of more creative strategic thinking.

☐ The organizational climate must be appropriate for the planning system adopted, and consequently structural and cultural issues have an important role to play.
☐ Inflexibility in drawing up and using the plan can be a trap. Inflexibility in drawing up the plan might be reflected in tunnel vision, a lack of flair and creativity, and in assuming that past trends can be extrapolated forwards.
☐ If planning is seen as an exercise rather than a support to strategy creation, it is quite possible the plan will be ignored and not implemented.

The impact of planning on managers

Unless the above traps are avoided and the human aspects of planning are considered, the planning activity is unlikely to prove effective. Abell and Hammond (1979) and Mills (1985) highlight the following important people considerations.

☐ Ensure the support of senior executives.
☐ Ensure that every manager who is involved understands what is expected of him or her and that any required training in planning techniques is provided.
☐ Use specialist planners carefully.
☐ Keep planning simple, and ensure that techniques never become a doctrine.
☐ Particularly where detailed planning is involved, ensure that the time horizon is appropriate. It is harder to forecast and plan detail the further into the future one looks.
☐ Never plan for the sake of planning.
☐ Link managerial rewards and sanctions to any targets for achievement which are established.
☐ Allow managers of business units and functions some freedom to develop their own planning systems rather than impose rigid ones, especially if they produce the desired results.

In summary, planning activities can take a

number of forms, and organizations should seek to develop systems which provide the results they want. Ideally these should encapsulate both strategic thinking and the establishment of realistic objectives and expectations and the strategies to achieve them. Planning techniques can be used supportively, and their potential contribution is evaluated in the next section. Systematic corporate planning, though, should not be seen as the only way in which strategic changes are formulated.

STRATEGIC PLANNING TECHNIQUES

It has already been shown in Chapter 1 that different strategists and authors of strategy texts adopt different stances on the significance of vision, culture and strategic planning techniques in effective strategic planning.

In this book we take the view that the role of the strategic leader, styles of corporate decision making and organization culture are key driving forces in strategy creation and implementation. However, we accept that strategic planning techniques, which rely heavily on the collection and analysis of quantitative data, do have an important contribution to make. They help increase awareness, and thereby reduce the risk involved in certain decisions. They can indicate the incidence of potential threats and limitations which might reduce the future value and contribution of individual products and services. They can help in establishing priorities in large complex multi-product multi-national organizations. They can provide appropriate frameworks for evaluating the relative importance of very different businesses in a portfolio.

However, their value is dependent upon the validity and reliability of the information fed into them. Where comparisons with competitors are involved, the data for other companies may well involve guesstimation.

In my opinion strategic planning techniques should be used to help and facilitate decision makers. They should not be used to make decisions without any necessary qualifications to the data and assumptions.

Portfolio analysis

The Boston Consulting Group growth–share matrix was introduced in Chapter 10. This type of portfolio analysis can be very useful for positioning products in relation to their stage in the product life cycle as long as one is both careful and honest in the use of data. It can provide insight into the likely cash needs and the potential for earnings generation. However, whilst a particular matrix position indicates potential needs and prospects it should not be seen as prescriptive for future strategy. In certain respects, all competitive positions are unique, and it is very important to consider the actual industry involved and the nature and behaviour of competitors. Business unit and product managers are likely to be able to do this with greater insight than specialist planners as they are in a better position to appreciate the peculiarities of the market.

The product portfolio suggests the following strategies for products or business units falling into certain categories:

☐ Cash cow   milk and redeploy the cash flow
☐ Dog   liquidate or divest and redeploy the freed resources or proceeds
☐ Star   strengthen competitive position in growth industry
☐ Question   invest as appropriate to secure and improve competitive position.

Given that a dog represents a product or service in a relatively low growth industry sector, one which does not enjoy market segment leadership, it follows that many companies will have a number of dogs in their portfolios. Liquidation or divestment will not always be justified. Products which have a strong market position, even though they are not the market leader, and which have a distinctive competitive advantage can have a healthy cash flow and profitability. Such products are sometimes referred to as cash dogs. Divestment is most appropriate when the market position is weak and when there is no real opportunity to create sustainable competitive advantage – as long as a buyer can be found. Turnaround strategies for products which are performing very poorly are examined further in Chapter 19.

According to Hamermesch (1986) many businesses which are classified as cash cows should be managed for innovation and growth, especially if the industry is dynamic or volatile, or can be made so. In other words, strategies which succeed in extending the product life cycle can move it from a state of maturity into further growth. One example quoted is coffee. This market experienced renewed growth when the success of automatic coffee makers increased demand for new varieties of fresh ground coffee.

At one time in the ballpoint pen market Bic was the clear market leader and a cash cow when the market reached a stage of maturity. However, the introduction of roller ball pens and erasable biros generated new growth and marketing opportunities for other competitors.

When 'milking' products care also has to be taken not to reduce capacity if there is a chance that demand and growth opportunities might return as a result of scarcities or changes in taste. When restrictions on the import of Scotch whisky into Japan were eased in the late 1980s, the product enjoyed star status even though it was seen as a cash cow in the UK.

Strategic decisions based on portfolio positions may also ignore crucial issues of interdependence and synergy. Business units may be treated as separate independent businesses for the purposes of planning, and this can increase the likelihood of the more qualitative contributions to other business units, and to the organization as a whole, being overlooked when decisions are made about possible liquidation or divestment.

Directional policy matrices

The best known directional policy matrices were developed in the 1970s by Shell and General Electric and the management consultants McKinsey. They are broadly similar and aim to assist large complex multi-activity enterprises with decisions concerning investment and divestment priorities. A version of the Shell matrix is illustrated in Figure 16.5; further details can be found in Robinson, Hitchens and Wade (1978).

In using such a matrix there is an assumption that resources are scarce, and that there never will be, or should be, enough financial and other resources for the implementation of all the project ideas and opportunities which can be conceived in a successful, creative and innovative organization. Choices will always have to be made about investment priorities. The development of an effective corporate strategy therefore involves an evaluation of the potential for existing businesses together with new possibilities in order to determine the priorities.

The matrix is constructed within two axes: the horizontal axis represents industry attractiveness, or the prospects for profitable operation in the sector concerned; the vertical axis indicates the company's existing competitive position in relation to other companies in the industry. New possibilities can be evaluated initially along the vertical axis by considering their likely prospects for establishing competitive advantage. It will be appreciated that Michael Porter's work links closely to this.

In placing individual products in the matrix the factors shown in Table 16.2 are typical of those which might be used.

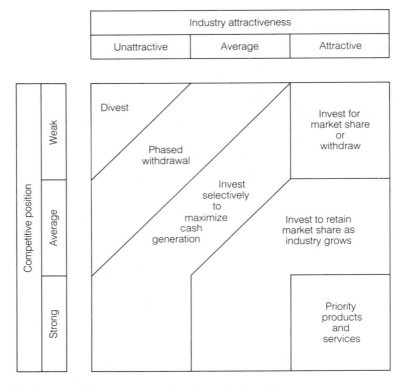

Figure 16.5 The directional policy matrix developed by Shell.

Table 16.2 Factors in the directional policy matrix

Industry attractiveness	Market growth
	Market quality, or the ability for new products to achieve higher or more stable profitability than other sectors
	Supplier pressure
	Customer pressure
	Substitute products
	Government action
	Entry barriers
	Competitive pressure
Competitive position and relative strength	Competition
	Relative market shares
	Competitive postures and opportunities
	Production capability
	Research and development record and strengths
	Success rate to date, measured in terms of market share and financial success (earnings in excess of the cost of capital)

Each factor would be given a weighting relative to its perceived importance, and each product being evaluated would be given a score for every factor. The aggregate weighted scores for both axes determine the final position in the matrix.

Using the matrix

Figure 16.5 illustrates that the overall attractiveness of products diminishes as one moves diagonally from the bottom right-hand corner of the matrix to the top left. Priority products, in the bottom right-hand corner, are those which score highly on both axes. As a result they should receive priority for development, and the resources necessary for this should be allocated to them.

Products bordering on the priority box should receive the appropriate level of investment to ensure that at the very least market share is retained as the industry grows.

Products currently with a weak competitive position in an attractive industry are placed in the top right-hand corner of the matrix. They should be evaluated in respect of the potential to establish and sustain real competitive advantage. If the prospects seem good, then carefully targeted investment should be considered seriously. If the prospects are poor it is appropriate to withdraw from the market. A weak position in an attractive industry might be remedied by the acquisition of an appropriate competitor.

Products across the middle diagonal should receive custodial treatment. It is argued that a good proportion of products are likely to fall into this strategic category, which implies attempting to maximize cash generation with only a limited commitment of additional resources.

Currently profitable products with little future potential should be withdrawn gradually, but retained as long as they are profitable and the resources committed to them cannot be allocated more effectively elsewhere.

Products for divestment are likely already to be losing money if all their costs are properly assigned.

The directional policy matrix, like other matrices, is only a technique which assists in determining which industry and product sectors are most worthy of additional investment capital. Issues of synergy and overall strategic fit require further managerial judgement before final decisions are reached.

LVMH, Moët Hennessy. Louis Vuitton, is a diversified French conglomerate whose luxury products include Dom Perignon and Moët & Chandon champagnes, Hennessy cognac, Christian Dior and Christian Lacroix fashion clothing and cosmetics and Louis Vuitton luggage. The products are sold throughout the world.

LVMH must keep its present shape. On the one hand, wines and spirits with their regular, stable growth. On the other hand, luxury products which are more sensitive to fashion and thus to economic conditions. The 'centre of gravity' of our business lies somewhere between these two extremes.

In practice we must combine the stability of the first with the opportunities for growth of the second. In other words, the income from a great Champagne allows us to launch a perfume. My company is like a passenger liner which moves forward slowly and is safe in storms; overhead flies a fighter plane which is sensitive to pressure changes, but which is capable of exceptional performance.

Bernard Arnault, Group Chairman, LVMH

SPACE (Strategic Position and Action Evaluation)

Rowe *et al.* (1989) have developed a model based on four important variables:

☐ the relative stability/turbulence of the environment
☐ industry attractiveness
☐ the extent of any competitive advantage
☐ the company's financial strengths – incorporating profitability, liquidity and current exposure to risk.

Scores are awarded for each factor, and then diagrammed – see Box 16.1. This particular

Box 16.1
SPACE: STRATEGIC POSITION AND ACTION EVALUATION

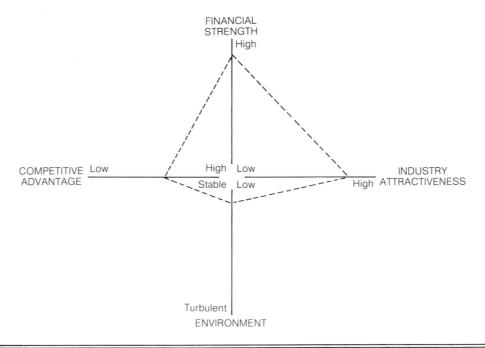

Strategic thrust:	Aggressive	Competitive	Conservative	Defensive
Features:				
Environment	Stable	Unstable	Stable	Unstable
Industry	Attractive	Attractive	Unattractive	Unattractive
Competitiveness	Strong	Strong	Weak	Weak
Financial strength	High	Weak	High	Weak
Appropriate strategies	Growth — possibly by acquisition Capitalize on opportunities Innovate to sustain competitive advantage	Cost reduction, productivity improvement, raising more capital — to follow opportunities and strengthen competitiveness Possibly merge with a less competitive but cash-rich company	Cost reduction and product/service rationalization Invest in search for new products, services and competitive opportunities	Rationalization Divestment as appropriate

Source: Rowe, A J, Mason, R O, Dickel, K E and Snyder, N H (1989)
Strategic Management: A Methodological Approach, 3rd Edn, Addison Wesley.

illustration features a financially strong company (or division or product) enjoying competitive advantage in an attractive industry with a relatively stable environment. The appropriate strategy is an aggressive one. The table shows the appropriate strategies for four clearly delineated positions, and judgement has to be applied when the situation is less clear cut.

This technique usefully incorporates finance, which will affect the feasibility of particular strategic alternatives and the ability of a company to implement them. It has similar limitations to directional policy matrices.

PIMS (Profit Impact of Market Strategy)

According to Buzzell and Gale (1987) the profit impact of market strategy (PIMS) approach is similar to portfolio analysis in that industry characteristics and strategic position are seen as important determinants of strategy and strategic success. However, PIMS was designed to explore the impact of a wide variety of strategic and environmental issues on business performance, and to provide principles that will help managers to understand how market conditions and particular strategic choices might affect business performance.

PIMS was invented by General Electric in the 1960s as an internal analysis technique to identify which strategic factors most influence cash flow and investment needs and success. Its scope was extended by the Harvard Business School and eventually in 1975 the Strategic Planning Institute (SPI) was established to develop PIMS for a variety of clients.

PIMS is a very sophisticated computer model and its database is information submitted by clients. They provide about a hundred pieces of information about the business environment and the competitive position of each product, production processes, research and development, sales and marketing activi-ties and financial performance. From an analysis of the data those elements which are most significant to the performance for each business are identified and the information is relayed to the client.

PIMS can be used for

☐ evaluating business performance relative to competitors and
☐ establishing targets for return on investment and cash flow.

The SPI claim that variables in the PIMS models are able to explain some 80% of the variations in performance of the businesses included.

Major findings

Amongst the most significant findings which have emerged from the PIMS models are the following.

☐ High investment intensity (investment as a percentage of sales) is associated with low profitability. Substantial investment creates additional production capacity which companies seek to use. Quite often this results in low prices and low margins for products. Japanese industry, in contrast, has been able to harness good management and labour practice with their high investment intensity, and this has resulted in high profitability. This links to the next conclusion from PIMS.
☐ High productivity (value added per employee) and high return on capital are associated. This appears to be an obvious conclusion, but the significance of the point is that, whilst the previous finding indicates that high investment in capital and the corresponding reduction in labour intensity do not create profits, improvements in working practices have a more positive impact on profitability.
☐ Additional investment in products and industries which are currently performing well is not guaranteed to bring increased profits.

☐ High relative market share has a strong influence on profitability but is not the only factor.

☐ High industry growth rates absorb cash, and can have a harmful effect on cash flow – this is made worse by high capital intensity.

☐ High relative product quality is related to high return on investment. An element of managerial judgement is involved in the data substantiating this. High relative quality is said to exist when managers in the organization believe that they have a superior competitive position.

☐ Product innovation and differentiation lead to profitability, especially in mature markets, but relative market share also has a considerable influence on this factor.

☐ Vertical integration is more likely to prove successful in stable industries than in unstable ones. Vertical integration tends to increase fixed costs, making the firm more vulnerable if there is intense competition or technological change.

☐ The conclusion of the experience curve is sound in that unit cost reductions over time prove profitable for companies with high market share.

Limitations of PIMS

It is important to appreciate that there are certain drawbacks which Constable (1980) amongst others have listed. These include the following.

☐ PIMS assumes that short-term profitability is the prime objective of the organization.

☐ The analysis is based on historical data and the model does not take account of future changes in the company's external environment.

☐ The model cannot take account of interdependences and potential synergy within organizations. Each business unit is analysed in isolation.

Planning techniques can be extremely useful, particularly as they force managers and organizations to ask themselves many relevant and searching questions and compile and analyse important information. But the techniques do not, and cannot, provide answers; they merely generate the questions. The danger is that some managers may perceive the output of a technique such as PIMS or a matrix analysis as answers to strategic issues.

Having looked in some detail at planning systems, and certain planning techniques which support them, we next consider the alternative modes of strategy creation and evaluate the most appropriate roles for planning in strategic management.

STRATEGY FORMULATION

Mintzberg (1989) argues that strategies either can be planned and deliberate or can emerge from a pattern of decisions taken over time. These two alternatives are not mutually exclusive, and most organizations are likely to pursue them simultaneously. As a result, strategies can be formulated in three different ways.

☐ They can be **planned** rationally and systematically. It could be argued, for example, that Hanson plan, as they track organizations which are suitable for acquisition for a lengthy period before deciding which ones to bid for, and when.

☐ They can be created **entrepreneurially** by a visionary strategic leader, who essentially conceives the strategy in his or her head by appreciating the current fit between the organization and its environment and suitable opportunities for change.

☐ They can emerge **incrementally** as managers throughout the organization adapt competitive and functional strategies to environmental changes.

Mintzberg and Waters (1985) and Bailey and Johnson (1992) have shown how this categorization might be extended, but the underlying implications remain unchanged.

The major characteristics of the three modes were listed in Chapters 3 and 4. The entrepreneurial and adaptive modes will, of course, involve planning at least as a cerebral activity, whilst the planning mode refers specifically to a type of formal planning system.

If all strategies were planned formally, then organizations would be able to look back and review the decisions that they had made over a period of time. At some stage in the past there would have been a clear recorded statement of intent which matched these events closely. In reality stated plans and actual events are unlikely to match closely. In addition to strategies which have emerged incrementally and been introduced entrepreneurially, there are likely to have been expectations and planned possible strategies which have not proved to be viable. However, broad directions can be established and planned and then detailed strategies allowed to emerge as part of an on-going learning experience within the organization.

Lowe (1986) illustrates how this has happened in McDonald's. The mission and broad appeal of McDonald's has remained largely unchanged whilst new products have been added and new market opportunities seized. The Big Mac, which was introduced nationally in America in 1968, was the idea of a Pittsburgh franchisee who had seen a similar product elsewhere. The aim was to broaden the customer base and make McDonald's more adult oriented. The company allowed the franchisee to try the product in his restaurant in 1967, although there was some initial resistance amongst executives who wished to retain a narrow product line, and it proved highly successful.

Egg McMuffins in the early 1970s were a response to a perceived opportunity – a breakfast menu and earlier opening times. Previously McDonald's restaurants opened at 11.00 am. Although the opportunity was appreciated the development of the product took place over four years, and the final launch version was created by a Santa Barbara franchisee who had to invent a new cooking utensil. When Chicken McNuggets were launched in 1982 it was the first time that small boneless pieces of chicken had been mass produced. The difficult development of the product was carried out in conjunction with a supplier and there was immediate competitive advantage. The product was not readily copied. From being essentially a hamburger chain McDonald's quickly became number two to Kentucky Fried for fast food chicken meals.

Strategic perspective and competitive position

It was pointed out in Chapter 1 that organizations have both **strategic perspectives** (their competitive scope; the range and diversity of activities) and **competitive positions** in each business area. Planning can be related to proposed changes in both perspective and positions. Entrepreneurial change is generally concerned with the strategic perspective, and adaptive change with the competitive positions.

Planning and strategy formulation

Mintzberg contends that the strategic leader should be the chief architect, in conjunction with planners, of corporate plans; the process should be explicit, conscious and controlled; and issues of implementation should be incorporated. Essentially analysis leads to choice, which leads on to implementation. The process is sequential:

$$ANALYSIS \rightarrow CHOICE \rightarrow IMPLEMENTATION$$

Certain organizations might claim that detailed long-term planning is essential for them. An airline, for example, must plan capacity several years ahead because of the long delivery lead times for new aeroplanes and the related need to manage cash flow and funding. In addition resources must be co-ordinated on an international scale. Whilst planes are utilized most days and fly as many hours in the day as possible, crews work only limited hours, and typically finish a flight or series of flights in a location which is different from their starting point.

However, Mintzberg argues that this is planning the implications and consequences of the strategic perspective, not necessarily the perspective itself. Detailed planning of this type should not inhibit creativity concerning the perspective.

The entrepreneurial mode

A visionary strategic leader who formulates strategic change in his or her mind may only be semi-conscious of the process involved. He or she will clearly understand the current and desired strategic perspective, and ideally the culture of the organization will be one where other managers are receptive of the changes in perspective. The personality and charisma of the leader, and his or her ability to sell his/her ideas, will be crucial issues, and as speed of action, timing and commitment are typical features the strategy can prove highly successful.

The entrepreneurial approach suggests that the strategic leader is very aware of the strengths, weaknesses and capabilities of the organization; the current matching with the environment; a wide range of possibly diverse opportunities for change; and the likely reaction of managers to certain changes. Similar to the 'bird approach' described in Chapter 1, Box 1.1, the selection is made somewhat arbitrarily without careful and detailed planning, and therefore an element of risk is involved. This informality in the process is important to allow for

creativity and flair. The strategic leader then sells the idea to other managers, and the strategy is implemented and adapted as experience is gained and learning takes place. In other words, the vision acts as an umbrella and within it specific decisions can be taken which lead to the emergence of more detailed strategies.

With this mode it is difficult to separate analysis and choice, so that

$$\left. \begin{array}{c} \text{ANALYSIS} \\ \text{(in the form of} \\ \text{on-going} \\ \text{awareness)} \\ \text{and} \\ \text{CHOICE} \end{array} \right\} \rightarrow \text{IMPLEMENTATION}$$

Dangers

The success of this mode in the long term depends upon the continued strategic awareness and insight of the strategic leader, particularly if the organization revolves around a visionary leader and becomes heavily dependent upon him or her. People may be visionary for only a certain length of time, and then they become blinkered by the success of current strategies and adopt tunnel vision, or they somehow lose the ability to spot good new opportunities. It might also be argued that, if luck is involved, their luck runs out. The problems occur if the strategic leader has failed to develop a strong organization with other visionaries who can take over.

On a current basis the strategy requires management as well as leadership. In other words, managers within the organization must be able to capitalize on the new opportunities and develop successful competitive positions within the revised strategic perspective. This might involve an element of planning; equally it might rely more on the adaptive approach described below.

The adaptive mode

Under the adaptive mode strategies are formed and evolve as managers throughout the organization learn from their experiences and adapt to changing circumstances. They perceive how tasks might be performed, and products and services managed, more effectively, and they make changes. They also respond to pressures and new strategic issues. There will again be elements of semi-consciousness and informality in the process. Some changes will be gradual, others spontaneous, and they will act collectively to alter and improve competitive positions. As individual decisions will often involve only limited change, little risk, and possibly the opportunity to change back, this is essentially the 'squirrel approach' described in Chapter 1, Box 1.1. Managers learn whether their choice is successful or unsuccessful through implementation.

Hence this mode implies limited analysis preceding choice and implementation, which are intertwined and difficult to separate. A proper analysis follows in the form of an evaluation of the relative success:

$$\text{Analysis (limited)} \rightarrow \left\{ \begin{array}{c} \text{CHOICE} \\ \text{AND} \\ \text{IMPLEMENTATION} \end{array} \right\} \rightarrow \text{ANALYSIS}$$

Adaptive strategic change requires decentralization and clear support from the strategic leader, who also seeks to stay aware of progress and link the changes into an integrated pattern. It is often based upon setting challenges for managers – challenging them to hit targets, improve competitiveness and

---

The key macro and micro variables of our business are so dynamic that poker becomes more predictable than planning and reactivity more profitable than rumination.

Dr John White, Managing Director, BBA Group (many of whose customers are involved in the motor vehicle industry).

---

stretch or exploit internal systems and policies to obtain the best possible returns. The greater the challenge, the more care needs to go into establishing a suitable reward system. When the structure enables effective adaptive change, then intrapreneurship can be fostered throughout the organization and individual managers can be allowed the necessary freedom. However, if adaptive changes are taking place in a highly centralized organization, and despite rigid policies, there is a problem which should be investigated. The major potential drawbacks concern the ability of the organization and the strategic leader to synthesize all the changes into a coherent pattern, and the willingness and ability of individual managers to take an organization-wide perspective. This latter point is examined later in the chapter.

Information technology provides opportunities for collecting and co-ordinating information and should be harnessed to support decentralization. In addition **team briefing** can prove useful. Here a strategic leader would regularly brief his or her senior executives, discussing progress, and any proposed changes to the corporate strategy and policies. On a cascading basis managers would quickly and systematically communicate this information downwards and throughout the organization by meeting with teams of people responsible to them. The secret lies in utilizing team briefing meetings to also communicate information upwards by reporting on new strategic issues and how they are being handled.

Figure 16.6 shows the three modes of strategy creation together. The diagram incorporates E–V–R (environment–values–resources) and extends Figure 3.1. Notably:

☐ Although it is not made explicit some strategies, especially those formulated by a visionary entrepreneur, attempt to shape and change the environment, rather than react to changing circumstances. In other cases the strategies might be forced on the organization by strong environment threats and pressures.

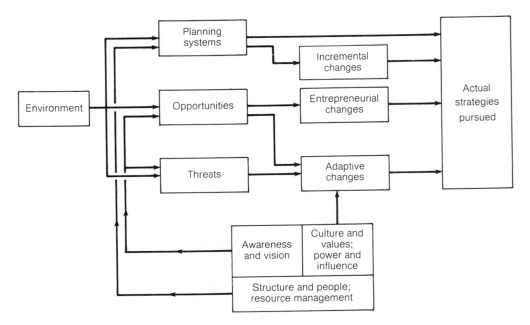

Figure 16.6 Strategy formulation.

□ The organization structure and the actual planning process will affect the nature of planned objectives and strategies. Wherever a group of managers are involved in planning, their personal values and relative power will be reflected. See Cyert and March's behavioural theory, Chapter 5.

□ Adaptive and incremental changes will also reflect the values, power and influence of managers.

□ I have deliberately separated the ideas of incremental and adaptive strategy, although their impact is effectively the same. Incremental changes are shown as amendments to structured, planned strategies as a result of learning during implementation. Adaptive changes reflect strategies pursued in a decentralized organization where the broad strategic direction may be clear, but with the detailed strategies emerging as managers adapt in a more dynamic environment. Whilst the ideas are distinct, in reality the *words* adaptive and incremental are interchangeable.

It is important to appreciate that the three modes described above are not mutually exclusive, that one mode frequently leads on from another, and that organizations as a whole are likely to be utilizing more than one mode at any one time. It is also essential that managers understand and support the processes. The mixed approach is both sensible and justifiable. In typical manufacturing industries the time taken from starting to plan a substantive innovatory change to peak profit performance can be ten years. This needs planning, although the concept may be visionary. Throughout the implementation there has to be incremental learning and change.

Where strategies are being adapted in a changing environment it is also useful, on occasions, to evaluate the current situation and assess the implications. This could well be part of an annual planning cycle. National Children's Homes opened schools and homes specifically to cater for children with educational learning difficulties. The impact of other providers and changing needs has caused a gradual drift towards caring for children with social as well as educational problems. The implication is a switch from 30 to 52 weeks a year care.

The following comments on strategy formulation in local government and in one not-for-profit organization, and Case 16.1 (Lex Service), develop the above points. The Lex case illustrates a visionary strategic change which was managed incrementally; the Natural History Museum features a mix of the planning and adaptive modes. The example of local government illustrates changes to a planning process which is based upon political bargaining. Historically plans have sought to build upon past efforts and successes; now objectives and priorities are reviewed more regularly.

Strategy and local government

A typical local authority is likely to perceive the aim of the activities it carries out as the provision of more, and ideally better, services for the local community. These services fall into three broad categories: front-line (housing, education and leisure); regulatory (environmental health, planning and building control) and promotional (economic development and tourism).

Consequently, many councils will want to increase spending wherever possible. In simple terms spending minus income (including grants from central government) equals the sum to be raised from householders and businesses, and generally more spending is likely to lead to higher local taxes. The freedom to increase these is constrained by central government. Borrowing is used primarily to fund capital programmes – for example, new council houses, the rent from which can help pay the interest on the loan – and for managing the cash flow on a temporary basis.

It is very difficult to measure quantitatively the benefits which accrue from certain services, such as parks and gardens for public recreation. Performance measures were discussed in Chapter 6. Information from the Audit Commission enables one authority to compare its costs and spending in total, and per head of the population, for individual services with those incurred by similar authorities in the UK. Where this is utilized it is basically a measure of efficiency, rather than an assessment of the overall effectiveness of the service provision.

In addition the growing incidence of competitive tendering is forcing a closer examination of the costs of providing particular services. Where services are put out for tender an authority will determine the specific level of service to be provided, and then seek quotations for this provision. Tendering organizations neither suggest nor influence the actual level of service. This power remains firmly with the local authority. As more and more services are compulsorily put out to tender local authorities will essentially become *purchasers* of services on behalf of the local community. Historically they have been the service providers, and it is quite feasible that this will continue if their employees win the contracts. Inevitably more attention will be focused on standards and community responsibilities. In the past such analyses of effectiveness have been rare.

Historically, in fixing a future budget a typical local authority is likely to have started with the existing service provision and extrapolated forward the costs of at least maintaining this service. To this will have been added the costs of providing new, additional services; and the selection of priorities amongst alternative options will have been heavily affected by the relative power and influence of certain councillors and sub-committees on what is typically called the Policy and Resources Committee. In addition, there may have been one-off, non-recurring items such as special refurbishments or maintenance programmes. It is likely that the process will have been incremental rather than the whole activity being viewed in a detached way, whereby specific objectives are evaluated and re-stated. It is unlikely that there will have been any initial

Case 16.1
LEX SERVICE GROUP

In 1968 Lex was a public company, most of whose turnover came from vehicle distribution and leasing – including Volvo, British Leyland and Rolls Royce cars. Trevor Chinn took over from his father as managing director and established the objective of diversifying to reduce the company's dependence on the vehicle industry. Lex's success was substantially dependent upon the strategies and relative success of the vehicle manufacturers.

Trevor Chinn believed that Lex had evolved a number of skills which could be transferred successfully to other service industries which met certain criteria, and his strategy was built on this. Hotels, travel and freight forwarding were targeted.

The hotel strategy emerged gradually during the 1970s as opportunities arose. Hotels are expensive to acquire or build, and this can affect the debt ratio. At the same time, suitable hotels are not always available for acquisition. Hotels can be owned as a property investment and not managed by the owner, owned and managed by the same company, or simply managed for another investor. In the UK hotels at Heathrow and Gatwick airports were built by a construction company which Lex acquired in 1970, together with the Hilton at Stratford-upon-Avon, which Lex owned but never managed. Originally the Heathrow was to be managed for Lex by Hyatt, but this agreement was rescinded and Lex managed both the Heathrow and Gatwick hotels when they opened. The Carlton Tower in Central London was bought in 1971, but the building was sold in 1977. Four more hotels were bought in North America, two of them at airports and two in city centres. All eight hotels were upmarket properties.

The relative profitability of each hotel was dependent on room occupancy, and generally Lex managed the UK properties quite profitably. They were less successful in America. All were managed as individual units with some central service provision. In terms of ownership or management of the hotel, or both, Lex never developed a consistent strategy, and overall they were never satisfied with their level of success. Finance and opportunity constrained Lex to only eight hotels, not, they believed, a large enough group to establish an effective presence even in a narrow market segment.

In the 1980s, and essentially on an individual basis, Lex have sold all their hotel interests except for the ownership of the Stratford Hilton, thereby generating revenue for alternative strategies. In recent years Lex has concentrated its diversification efforts on the distribution of electronic components, especially in America. At the end of the 1980s this represented one-third of the company's turnover. The activity was never as profitable as vehicle distribution, and in 1991 Lex divested these activities to concentrate again on automotive distribution and service.

Source: The original material for this case was obtained from a case study of the Lex hotel strategy by Constable, C J and Brewin, D (1978), available from the European Case Clearing House.

assessment of whether any existing services might be withdrawn, although this might have happened later.

Once a budget was established departments were able to amend the levels of service they provided with particular activities, and make changes as long as they operated within their spending limits. Unexpected needs for additional spending might be met from special contingency funds which were held back for this purpose.

Central government pressure is now forcing local authority executives to change their approach to corporate strategic management. Policies and service levels are evaluated and questioned, and priorities reviewed. Structures are being changed in a more serious attempt to co-ordinate the various services and achieve co-operation and synergy. In the past internal conflict has frequently been the norm.

Strategy creation in not-for-profit organizations

Planning can play a very useful role in determining future strategic priorities for not-for-profit organizations. Corporate planning at the Natural History Museum is used here as an example of this contention.

The objectives of the NHM relate to carrying out and publicizing scientific research, and providing a service to visitors. Research activities generally could absorb an unlimited budget, and spending limits need to be established to cover the cost of continuing existing programmes and introducing desirable new ones. Entertaining, interesting and educating visitors in natural history is accomplished through permanent exhibits and a series of special exhibitions which are changed periodically. The scope and diversity of these exhibitions is influenced and constrained by the space and money available.

Hence the executives of the museum must agree with the curators of the various activity areas the essential and desirable activities and services to be carried out, and their costs. Against this can be set the projected income given that no changes are made in either government funding (in real terms) or current operating practices. Assuming that a gap opens up, strategies for closing the gap can be evaluated. These strategies will relate to cost reductions and increases in revenue. Cost reductions may impinge upon the research activities and the services provided to visitors, and priorities will need to be reviewed and established. Eventually, and through an iterative process, spending targets for each area of activity and action plans for generating the necessary revenue should emerge.

On a current basis, and within the spending limits, curators would be able to change priorities and manage research activities, exhibits and exhibitions as they deem appropriate. If additional revenues are generated, in excess of the plans, then incremental improvements can be introduced.

The role of planning and planners

In the light of the comments above on strategy formulation I conclude this section by considering further the role of planning and planners. Planning and strategy creation are different in the sense that planners may or may not be strategists but strategists might be found anywhere in the organization. Mintzberg suggests that planning activities are likely to involve a series of different and very useful analyses, but it does not follow that these must be synthesized into a systematic planning system. Planners can make a valuable contribution to the organization and to strategic thinking by:

☐ programming strategies into finite detail to enable effective implementation (this will involve budgeting and ensuring that strategies are communicated properly, plus the establishment of monitoring and control processes);

□ formalizing on-going strategic awareness – carrying out SWOT analyses and establishing what strategic changes are emerging at any time;

□ using scenarios and planning techniques to stimulate and encourage thinking;

□ searching for new competitive opportunities and strategic alternatives, and scrutinizing and evaluating them.

In other words, all the activities incorporated in the planning systems discussed earlier in the chapter are seen to be making an important contribution, but they need not be component parts of a systematic model. Rather they are contributors towards strategic thinking, awareness and insight.

Johnson (1992) further points out that on occasions plans are documented in detail only because particular stakeholders, say institutional shareholders or bankers, expect to see them as justification for proposals. There is never any real intention that they should be implemented in full.

In the next section we explore strategic thinking in greater depth, drawing on the chapter so far and considering the contribution of soft systems ideas.

STRATEGIC CHANGE AND SYSTEMS THINKING

This section is a consideration of strategic change using ideas from systems thinking and Checkland's soft systems methodology (Checkland, 1981).

Soft systems thinking, introduced briefly in Chapter 9, led to the development by Peter Checkland of a methodology for dealing with complex problems. The ideas and the thinking behind the methodology are used in this section to

□ evaluate strategic change, related to the planning, entrepreneurial and adaptive modes;

□ consider the nature of strategic planning and strategic thinking at the corporate, business unit and individual manager levels.

Adaptive change

The notion of meaning systems was introduced in Chapter 14, and it was pointed out that these can be particularly important in the perception of problems by individual managers. At any time in organizations there are problem situations or things which are perceived to be wrong in some way: outcomes from present activities are not those that are desired; people's (individual) objectives are not being met. In simple terms, there is a difference between what is perceived to be happening and what managers feel should be happening.

However, managers often fail to agree on exactly what is wrong and what should be done about it. Their personal objectives and viewpoints differ. They have what Checkland terms individual and possibly conflicting *weltanschauungs*. There is no ideal English translation of this German word, but loosely it means world view. In other words managers have different underlying attitudes towards the problem situation, and this frequently results from their personal backgrounds, experiences and position within the organization.

Sir John Harvey-Jones (1990) examined Morgan Motor Company for a BBC 'Troubleshooter' programme. Morgan hand-build sports saloon cars in limited numbers, and because demand invariably exceeds capacity, there is normally a long waiting list. Taking a growth and profit perspective he concluded 'Morgan needs a major investment programme to increase efficiency, and this means introducing an element of automation'. He also recommended that prices should be increased. Harvey-Jones was at odds with the Morgan management (the company is family owned and controlled), and he described their perspective as 'providing cars at a certain price to a certain type of person whom they happen to like'. Managers and employees appear to regard the old-fashioned way in which the car is built, and the length of the waiting list, more as virtues to be preserved than as problems to be tackled. But individual managers and teams of managers are charged with making decisions. As far as on-going functional decisions are concerned, they are generally made within the constraint of different perceptions. However, it has already been argued earlier that the more strategically aware that managers are, the greater is the likelihood that they will take account of other managers' perceptions and needs. This is particularly important in the case of organizational learning and adaptive strategic change, where decisions are often made to try things out to see whether they work.

Where this happens, managers are seeking feasible resolutions to problem situations which are both efficient and effective in relation to their personal *weltanschauung*. Whilst their decisions may meet their own criteria, and be seen as generally efficient, they may not be effective in terms of the wider needs of the organization as a whole if they are based on a narrow perspective.

Strategic planning includes the setting of objectives, which can be used to monitor and measure performance and as a basis for deriving strategies, as an essential activity. Soft systems thinking and the Checkland methodology for addressing complex problems contend that in practice organizations do not have set, agreed and defined objectives, and that objectives and strategies emerge from organizational processes and management decisions. But the organization does have a purpose. It was emphasized in Chapter 5 that there is a distinction between long-term objectives which relate to the broad purpose and mission of the organization, and which managers may agree upon, and tighter more specific short-term objectives about which they are more likely to disagree. The broad objectives are infinite in

certain respects, and may never be wholly achieved. Where short-term targets are set, they are meant to be achieved and should be monitored as contributors to corporate strategies. However, it does not follow that established short-term objectives will explain all the decisions which are made, and the incremental changes which take place. The personal objectives of individual managers, and their perceptions of problem situations, influence these.

An organization is a group of business units or functions with managers whose decisions and interactions result in emergent properties. Ideally one is looking for synergy or effectiveness in the form of positive gains from these interactions. Communication and control systems within the organization are consequently key features of strategic management. Communication systems influence strategic awareness, learning and adaptive changes, and help determine the interactions between managers with different perceptions. Control systems should monitor whether the organization is behaving effectively and doing the right things as well as doing things well. Checkland (1989) argues that it is important to consider whether decisions and actions are feasible, efficient and effective. This is illustrated in Figure 16.7. The relative success of functional strategies should be assessed all the time to ensure that, in the light of environmental and competitive changes and any specific objectives set for them, they are both feasible and efficient. Where they are not, then control action should be taken to improve performance. At the same time it is important to assess functional strategies and contributions in the context of the needs of the overall organization to ensure that they are making an effective contribution. Whilst individual managers in charge of business units and functions can be charged with assessing both feasibility and efficiency, effectiveness should be addressed at the strategic leader level. Effectiveness is more likely to be evident if managers throughout the organization are

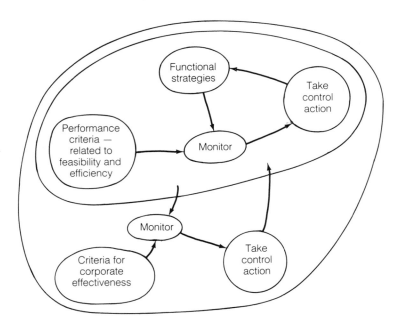

Figure 16.7   Monitoring strategic performance. Developed from work by Professor Peter Checkland at the University of Lancaster.

clearly aware of the mission and broad purposes, as well as the contribution which is expected from them. Where responsibilities are delegated, and managers are encouraged to make adaptive incremental changes, the strategic leader must ensure that he or she stays aware of what is happening within the organization.

Planning strategic change

These ideas relate to both the planning mode and entrepreneurial strategy creation.

Checkland's soft systems methodology is concerned with building what he calls purposeful conceptual models of human activity systems. Human activity systems are collections of activities which are structured in such a way that they can pursue a purpose. Purposeful implies that there is a clear sense of purpose which can be determined and influenced by key decision makers. Views on the way the purpose should be pursued will differ as a result of different perceptions and *weltanschauungs*.

Simplifying the methodology, one starts by examining the current problem situation and identifying any key **themes** – for example, a decision needs making but the information which is required, and which should be available, is not readily to hand; or there are concerns with product deliveries or quality, but a lack of clear information concerning customer requirements; or there is conflict in evidence between interdependent units. All these have strategic implications and result from organization-wide issues. They are perceived as problem areas becase they inhibit certain managers and the organization in the pursuit of its essential purpose.

From these problem themes are derived what Checkland calls root definitions of relevant systems and conceptual models. Root definitions state clearly the essential purpose of the system or activity concerned, and incorporate a consideration of the actual activity, its customers, the key people involved, the problem owner and his or her

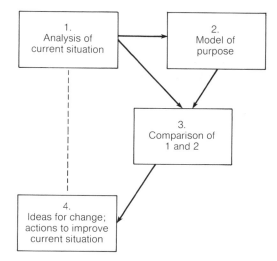

Figure 16.8 Checkland's methodology simplified.

weltanschauung, and any additional environmental constraints. Conceptual models are derived from these and represent a theoretical representation of how the system or activity might be organized and managed in order to achieve its purpose and satisfy the interests and needs of the people involved. Conceptual models are neither statements of ideals nor what any manager feels ought to be happening. Rather they are a model of a changed and effective system which clearly achieves its purpose and with which the current situation can be compared.

By comparing these conceptual models with current reality, examining the differences, and searching for actions which are both feasible and desirable, one can arrive at useful ways forward. See Figure 16.8. The conceptual model is likely to be visionary and elusive but, by iteration, one can explore what is possible and discover ways forward which improve the current situation.

The changes are likely to be in terms of

☐ **Structure**   organizational groupings, reporting structures, functional responsibilities

☐ **Procedures**   dynamic elements of process; the way things are done

☐ **Attitudes/ values**   intangible characteristics residing in both individual and collective managerial minds.

In strategic management terms, changes of strategic perspective and position would be encapsulated under structure. Policies would be part of procedures. Attitude changes relate to changes of culture.

These desirable feasible changes are not necessarily going to bring about the conceptual model, but they will be agreed ways of improving the problem situation. The methodology is extremely useful for structuring the thinking process involved in analysing problem areas and seeking ways of changing things. In this respect the ideas behind the methodology can be useful in strategic thinking, and in the search for suitable strategic changes relative to the current situation, desired improvements, the organization's skills and capabilities, and competitive, environment and cultural issues.

The methodology can be related to the visionary mode of strategy creation as an awareness of problem themes, say limitations of present strategies, and strategic opportunities can lie behind the strategic leader's vision for the future. Equally ways of fulfilling the vision must be sought, and this could well be an iterative process linking capabilities and skills with strategic opportunities.

The methodology also relates to planning as it is a way of looking ahead from where the organization is to where it might seek to go, linked to an exploration of constraints and options.

Both of these are illustrated in Figure 16.9. The top part of the diagram represents where the organization is at the moment, in terms of strategy, structure and performance. This, historically, will have been affected by strategic leadership and cultural issues, and by the influence of stakeholders. Under the

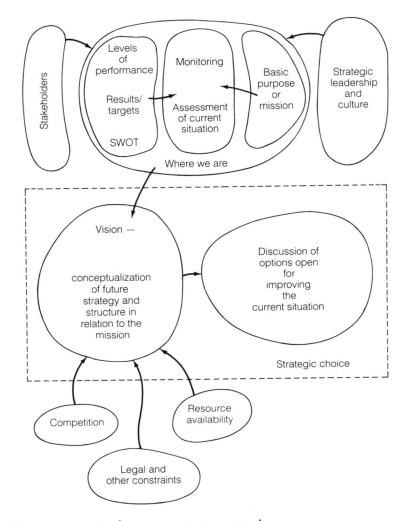

Figure 16.9   Planning strategic change: a systems approach.

planning mode this question would be addressed analytically and the results quantified; under the entrepreneurial mode, ongoing awareness and insight by the strategic leader is quite likely to provide the assessment and evaluation.

The entrepreneurial organization might be expected to be more visionary, dynamic and risk oriented in the selection of strategic options for changing the strategic perspective. The planning organization will establish objectives and targets for growth and change, linked obviously to the mission, and assess whether current strategies, and improvements in current strategies, will close the gap between where the organization is going and where it wants to go. If a gap still remains an iterative process of evaluating strategic alternatives, their implications and risks, can be used to assess whether the objectives should perhaps be revised downwards and which options should be pursued, and how. In effect there is an iterative examination of options until something plausible emerges from the discussion and deliberations amongst the managers who are asked to

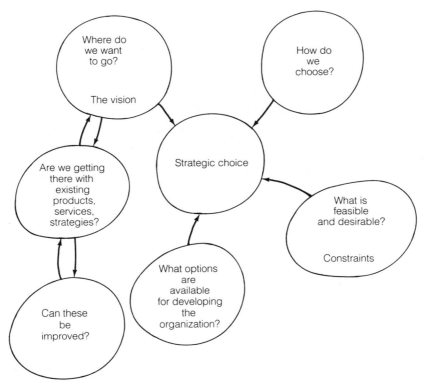

Figure 16.10 Strategic choice: questions and issues.

Box 16.2
STRATEGIC CHOICE DECISIONS: ISSUES FOR DISCUSSION

☐ Corporate objectives and ethos
☐ Forecasts, targets and gaps
☐ Organizational strengths and weaknesses
☐ Threats and opportunities
☐ Potential for existing products, services and strategies

☐ Alternative strategies
☐ Criteria for strategy selection
☐ Development and implementation requirements
☐ Action plans and budgets
☐ An appropriate monitoring system

contribute. Competition, resource availability and any legal or other constraints affect the choice. The issues affecting the choice of strategy are shown in greater detail in Figure 16.10, and Box 16.2 lists the key items for discussion.

Referring back to the illustration of the planning gap earlier in this chapter, it will be appreciated that the corporate objectives may be achievable either with existing competitive strategies or with improvements to current competitive strategies, and without changes in the overall strategic perspective. If it is necessary to change the perspective, then some form of diversification may add new products or business units to the organization. In other words there will have been a change in the corporate strategy rather than just in competitive and functional strategies. These issues and the alternative strategic options are discussed in greater detail in the next two chapters.

This general approach could be applied at the level of each business unit equally effectively in a search for competitive strategies.

Ackoff's planning model

Ackoff (1986) has suggested a planning model which is very similar to this approach and contains the following steps.

☐ Project the future based upon two essentially false assumptions:
  ☐ the organization maintains its present course;
  ☐ known environmental threats and opportunities will remain as they are.

☐ Establish an ideal future position for the organization, and assess the significance of the gap between these two positions.
☐ Establish the **means to close the gap**, considering possible actions, practices, projects and policies, and test these thoroughly for feasibility before deciding upon courses of action.

This implies a parallel consideration:

☐ Estimate **resource requirements**:
  ☐ people
  ☐ facilities and equipment
  ☐ materials, energy and services
  ☐ money
  ☐ information.

☐ Design an **implementation programme**.
☐ Design a **control programme**.

The emphasis in both Ackoff's planning model and the approach derived from

systems thinking, and illustrated in Figure 16.9, is on **strategic thinking**. The iterative process focuses attention on key issues, and requires that the decision makers, the planners and other managers involved in evaluating future development paths discuss and evaluate:

☐ the extent to which the organization should realistically seek to change and grow;
☐ the options available, and the extent to which they involve real changes in the organization;
☐ the desirability and feasibility of each of these options, particularly considering the risks;
☐ the implementation requirements – specifically changes of structure, management, culture and policies. Existing power bases and political activity need to be considered here.

At the end of the thinking and discussion managers will still retain their different perspectives to some degree, although if they have been fully involved they will appreciate the views and needs of other managers. Conflict will not be removed, but it might be better constrained. Throughout the process, Checkland argues, one is not seeking consensus amongst the various managers but is rather hoping for accommodation and an appreciation of the needs of other managers and the organization as a whole.

Criteria for strategy selection will be considered in greater detail in Chapter 21 after a discussion of the various strategic alternatives.

Having discussed a number of approaches for choosing strategies for the future, and before examining strategic alternatives in detail, in the last section of this chapter we develop further the notion of the strategy statement and consider how the proposed changes might usefully be documented. This will enable their widespread communication throughout the organization to managers who need to be informed.

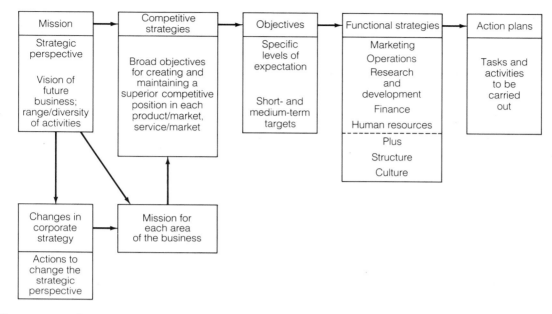

Figure 16.11 Strategy statements.

STRATEGY STATEMENTS

Strategy statements were introduced in Chapter 1, and a framework was illustrated in Figure 1.3. This represents a statement of current strategies, starting with long-term objectives and corporate strategies derived from the mission. Linked to this is a summary of key strategic issues: resources and capabilities; products, services and markets; and culture and values. Competitive strategies for individual product markets and service markets, and functional strategies for the various areas of the business, are stated in the form of short- and medium-term objectives and actions that are being undertaken to achieve them.

In this chapter we have moved on from the current position and addressed the issue of where the organization wants to develop in the future – whether current strategies are adequate to achieve future objectives, and, if not, what alternatives are most appropriate. Gap analysis highlights any difference between the expected results from a conti-nuation of current strategies and any desired results. Improvements in the way products, services and resources are managed can close a gap to some extent. Beyond this, new products or new markets will be required, possibly involving diversification and a radical change in the strategic perspective.

The strategy statement illustrated in Figure 16.11 could be regarded as a suitable output from the thinking and planning. It encapsulates the essential issues and decisions; and if it is communicated widely it will ensure that managers throughout the organization are aware of the contribution expected from various business units and functions.

The mission may or may not change over time; a great deal depends upon the extent to which its allows the organization to develop and change its strategic perspective. The thinking and planning may well result in changes in the strategic perspective and in corporate strategy, and actions such as acquisition to bring these about.

Each business unit or activity area should have its own mission, from which will be derived the competitive strategy for the business unit. This will encompass broad objectives for

☐ establishing competitive advantage and a superior competitive position;
☐ targeting selected market segments;
☐ resource development and deployment;
☐ the development and change of necessary values.

This leads on to the establishment of specific objectives and firm levels of expectation in terms of sales, profits, production and so on. Functional strategies will be developed to ensure that these targets are achieved and that the appropriate action plans, or tasks to be carried out, are defined. Although not explicit on the strategy statement there should be monitoring and control systems to assess performance against targets.

It has already been mentioned that circumstances may change and actions taken by competitors or other events outside the control of the organization may mean that planned actions are not implemented and have to be replaced by new more feasible ones. Equally, specific objectives or targets may not be met. The important issue is to be aware of what is happening and why things are changing as they are. This reality does not negate the value of the planning activity which establishes the competitive and functional strategies and the objectives and action plans. These are essential for providing clear direction and yardsticks for measuring performance so that the organization can be clear about where it is going, why and how.

A strategy statement example

The following hypothetical example was included in Chapter 5, Box 5.1 as a possible mission statement for the music business of the Virgin Group:

We aim to be recognized as the premier recorder and publisher of audio/visual mater-

ial by providing the very best in technology, facilities and service to our artists and employees in order to increase our shareholder wealth.

This mission statement can now be developed further.

Two aspects of the **competitive strategy** might be

☐ to ensure high quality output of recorded material and promotional videos from existing artists in order at least to consolidate the current position;
☐ to strengthen the roster of artists in specially targeted areas in order to provide growth and a more secure base for the future.

Specific **objectives** and expectations would relate to

☐ the number of chart successes for both singles and LPs (records, cassettes and

---

The management of change is both difficult and time-consuming, the more so if a company's leadership and strategies have been successful in the past. However, we have found at Grand Metropolitan that if time and resources are invested in developing a clear 'vision' – that is, in defining a company's ambition in terms of the role it will play, the geographic and market sectors in which it will compete, and the sustainable competitive advantage it has or can achieve, as well as the distinctive skills that will make it successful and resilient – then this creates a major integrating force which can help leadership overcome barriers to change, channels the energy of management to strive towards their highest aspirations, and positions the company to exploit strategic opportunities.

Sir Allen Sheppard, Chairman,
Grand Metropolitan plc

compact discs combined) from both existing and new artists; and from this

☐ the number of cassettes and CDs to be released at various times throughout the year.

Some of the **functional strategies and action plans** to bring this about would concern

☐ finding and contracting new artists;
☐ obtaining appropriate music for artists who do not write their own material, and recording the music;
☐ promoting both the artists and their music.

The issue of values would also have to be addressed. It would be important for Virgin to ensure that their image and reputation are attractive to the new artists they are seeking to contract.

This particular example is not meant to be fully comprehensive but indicative of the way the mission statement could be utilized to develop definite strategies and targets. As mentioned earlier, Virgin music is now part of Thorn–EMI.

SUMMARY

In this chapter we have considered the question of generally where the organization might go in the future, as a preamble to an evaluation of specific development paths. The role and contribution of planning and planning systems in relation to this decision have been discussed. The concept of gap analysis has been introduced and it has been emphasized that a variety of strategic alternatives can be assessed in terms of feasibility, desirability and risk as means of closing the gap – the difference between where managers expect the organization to reach if they continue with present strategies and where they would like to reach. Alternative approaches to planning have been considered, and it has been emphasized that strategies are not necessarily created through a planning process. They can be established entrepreneurially with vision playing a more significant role than systematic planning, and they can emerge with learning and incremental change.

Specifically we have

☐ considered the need for planning, and its relative importance in helping strategic thinking, given that rigid formal planning systems have become unfashionable;
☐ distinguished between planning at the corporate and functional levels;
☐ described seven basic approaches to planning, and an example of a comprehensive formal planning system;
☐ examined the concept of the planning gap and, in outline, ways of closing the gap;
☐ looked briefly at a more contemporary approach to planning;
☐ discussed who should plan, planning pitfalls and the impact of planning on managers;
☐ developed the theme of portfolio analysis first introduced in Chapter 10, considered directional policy matrices and SPACE, and in addition discussed the potential contribution of PIMS as a planning technique;
☐ recapped on the key features of the planning, adaptive and entrepreneurial modes of strategy creation, examining these in terms of (a) analysis, choice and implementation issues and (b) strategic perspective and competitive position;
☐ considered these modes in the light of strategic change in local government and one not-for-profit organization;
☐ discussed the contribution of systems ideas, and the thinking behind Checkland's methodology for tackling complex problems, to strategic thinking and strategic planning – especially in relation to the planning gap;
☐ developed further the idea of strategy statements, and considered the type of

statement which might usefully emerge from strategic thinking and planning.

CHECKLIST OF KEY TERMS AND CONCEPTS

You should feel confident that you understand the following terms and ideas:

☐ Strategic thinking and strategic planning
☐ Systematic planning models
☐ Strategic issues
☐ The planning gap
☐ Ansoff's growth vector
☐ Directional policy matrices and SPACE
☐ PIMS
☐ Strategic perspective and competitive position
☐ Planning, entrepreneurial and adaptive modes of strategy creation
☐ The ideas behind Checkland's soft systems methodology – in relation to strategic thinking and planning
☐ Strategy statements.

QUESTIONS AND RESEARCH ASSIGNMENTS

Text related

1. Mintzberg has distinguished between 'grass roots' strategies (which can take root anywhere in the organization but eventually proliferate once they become more widely adopted) and 'hothouse' strategies which are deliberately grown and cultured.
   What do you think he means?
2. Who should plan? What should they plan, how and when?

3. In the context of the Boston matrix, is the Big Mac a cash cow? What do you feel McDonald's competitive strategy for the Big Mac should be?

Library based

4. Analyse the corporate portfolio of the Virgin Group using any of the matrices included in this text or with which you are familiar.
5. For an organization of your choice, ideally one with which you are familiar:
   (a) ascertain how the planning, entrepreneurial and adaptive modes might apply currently to strategic change in the organization. Which mode is predominant? Why do you think it is the preferred mode? How successful is it?
   (b) What would be the opportunities and concerns from greater utilization of the other modes?
   (c) As far as you are able, draw up a directional policy matrix for the products and services of the organization. (Use your own judgement in assigning weights to the various factors for assessing industry attractiveness and competitive position.)
6. In 1975 the Boston Consulting Group wrote a report for the British government concerning the penetration of Honda motorcycles in the United States. They concluded that the success was the result of meticulous staff work and planning.

Pascale (1984) disagrees and argues that the success was entirely due to learning and persistence, and that it was Honda's learning experience concerning operating in the USA that eventually led to a more rationally planned approach.

Both arguments are documented in Pascale, R (1984) Perspectives on strategy – the real story behind Honda's success, *California*

Management Review, **26**(3). Read this article and assess the points Pascale makes.

RECOMMENDED FURTHER READING

Ansoff (1987) is a comprehensive but easy-to-read book on strategic decision making.

Readers interested in corporate planning are recommended to read one of the several books written by either John Argenti or David Hussey. Those included in the references are both ideal.

Mintzberg, H. (1989) *Mintzberg on Management*, Free Press, provides a thorough analysis of planning, adaptive and entrepreneurial strategy creation. Quinn, J B (1980) *Strategies for Change: Logical Incrementalism*, Richard D Irwin, is an excellent reference work on adaptive or incremental change.

Hofer, C and Schendel, D (1978) *Strategy Formulation: Analytical Concepts*, West, is a good introduction to techniques which are useful in strategic decision making.

Checkland (1981) provides a review of the history of systems thinking and describes a soft systems methodology which contributes a valuable framework for assessing future strategic changes.

REFERENCES

Abell, D F and Hammond, J S (1979) *Strategic Market Planning*, Prentice Hall.

Ackoff, R L (1970) *A Concept of Corporate Planning*, Wiley.

Ackoff, R L (1986) *Management in Small Doses*, Wiley.

Ansoff, H I (1987) *Corporate Strategy*, revised edition, Penguin.

Argenti, J (1980) *Practical Corporate Planning*, George Allen and Unwin.

Bailey, A and Johnson, G (1992) How Strategies Develop in Organizations. In *The Challenge of Strategic Management* (eds. G Johnson and D Faulkner), Kogan Page.

Buzzell, R D and Gale, B T (1987) *The PIMS Principles – Linking Strategy to Performance*, Free Press.

Checkland, P B (1981) *Systems Thinking, Systems Practice*, Wiley.

Checkland, P B (1989) Presentation to MBA students at Huddersfield Polytechnic, March.

Cohen, K J and Cyert, R M (1973) Strategy formulation, implementation and monitoring, *Journal of Business*. **46**(3), 349–67.

Constable, J (1980) Business strategy, Unpublished paper, Cranfield School of Management.

Glueck, W F and Jauch, L R (1984) *Business Policy and Strategic Management*, 4th edn, McGraw-Hill.

Hamermesch, R (1986) Making planning strategic, *Harvard Business Review*, July–August.

Harvey-Jones, J H (1987) In an introduction to Ansoff, H I *Corporate Strategy*, Penguin.

Harvey-Jones, with Mosey, A (1990) *Troubleshooter*, BBC Books.

Hussey, D (1976) *Corporate Planning – Theory and Practice*, Pergamon.

Johnson, G (1992) Strategic direction and strategic decisions, presented at 'Managing Strategically: Gateways and Barriers', Strategic Planning Society conference, 12 February.

Lowe, J F (1986) *McDonald's – Behind the Arches*, Bantam.

Mills, D Q (1985) Planning with people in mind, *Harvard Business Review*, July–August.

Mintzberg, H (1989) Presentation to the Strategic Planning Society, London, 2 February. (Further detail can be found in Mintzberg, H. (1973).)

Mintzberg, H (1973) Strategy making in three modes, *California Management Review*, **16**(2), Winter.

Mintzberg, H and Waters, J A (1985) Of strategy deliberate and emergent, *Strategic Management Journal*, **6**(3).

Ohmae, K (1982) *The Mind of the Strategist*, McGraw-Hill.

Porter, M E (1987) The state of strategic thinking, *The Economist*, 23 May.

Ringbakk, K A (1971) Why planning fails, *European Business*, Spring.

Robinson, J (1986) Paradoxes in planning, *Long Range Planning*, **19**(6).

Robinson, S J Q, Hitchens, R E and Wade, D P (1978) The directional policy matrix – tool for strategic planning, *Long Range Planning*, **21**, June.

Rowe, A J, Mason, R O, Dickel, K E and Snyder N H (1989) *Strategic Management: A Methodological Approach*, 3rd edn, Addison Wesley.

Steiner, G (1972) *Pitfalls in Comprehensive Long Range Planning*, Planning Executives Institute.

Taylor, B and Hussey, D E (1982) *The Realities of Planning*, Pergamon.

WHAT STRATEGIC ALTERNATIVES ARE AVAILABLE?

17

LEARNING OBJECTIVES

After studying this chapter you should be able to

☐ identify and describe a number of possible strategic alternatives;
☐ explain how selected strategies might be implemented through internal or external growth;
☐ discuss the important considerations involved in international strategies.

As a preamble to a more detailed treatment of growth, recovery and divestment strategies, and management buy-outs, in this chapter we describe the various strategic alternatives that exist. Only some of them will be appropriate for an organization at a particular time. The international dimensions of strategy are explored.

INTRODUCTION

In this chapter we outline the various stra- tegic alternatives that might be available to an organization in thinking and deciding where it wants to go, and for helping to close the planning gap. The attractiveness of particular alternatives will be affected by the objectives of the organization. Whilst a whole range of options are discussed in this chapter, it does not follow that they will all be available to an organization at the same time. Because of the costs or risks involved, particular alternatives might be quickly rejected. Chapters 18 and 19 consider certain of the strategies in greater depth. In particular, in Chapter 18 I discuss diversification, acquisition and joint ven- tures. Retrenchment and turnaround strat- egies are the subject of Chapter 19. The factors which determine the attractiveness and wisdom of particular alternatives are explored in Chapter 21. The appropriate strategy always matches the environment, values and resources congruently.

For many organizations the appropriate

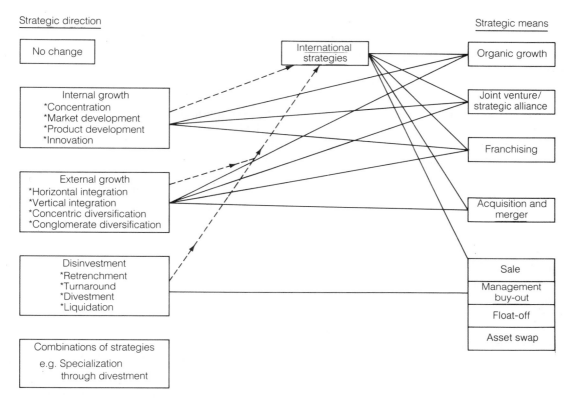

Strategic direction

Strategic means

Figure 17.1 Strategic alternatives. The dotted lines signify that internal growth, external growth and divestment may all have an international dimension.

strategies will have a global dimension, and consequently I have included a section on international issues in this chapter.

In their consideration of strategic alternatives, some organizations will be entrepreneurial and actively search for opportunities for change. Others will only consider change if circumstances dictate a need. Some organizations will already have sound and effective strategies which are producing results that they are satisfied with. Others may ignore the need to change. Some texts have quoted the example of the typewriter companies who knew instinctively that electric typewriters, let alone word processors, would never catch on.

The strategies considered range from the choice to do nothing, to alternatives which represent gradual and internal growth, to

those which involve substantial diversification and investment in acquisitions. The last involve different degrees of risk: new skills, new knowledge, courage and flexibility might be required. The choice must take into account the risk that the strategic leader considers acceptable given any particular circumstances, and the ability of the organization to deal with the risk elements. Some organizations will not select the most challenging and exciting opportunities because they are too risky.

Figure 17.1 illustrates the strategies considered in this chapter in terms of direction and means. The directional strategies are grouped into those which represent internal growth, those which imply external growth, and disinvestment strategies. External growth, often involving a change of strategic perspective, is likely to involve greater change and risk than internal development. This typically relates to the functional and competitive strategies discussed earlier. All these alternatives can have an international dimension, and this is considered separately because of the complexities involved. These options should not be thought of as being mutually exclusive – two or more may be combined into a composite strategy, and at any time a multi-product organization is likely to be pursuing several different competitive strategies.

Growth alternatives can be implemented through organic growth, investing money to develop the existing organization, merger or acquisition, joint ventures with other companies and franchising.

Disinvestment can involve closure, sale, asset swaps with another company or floating off a subsidiary as an independent business; and occasionally it may involve a management buy-out. Buy-outs are discussed in Chapter 20.

THE DO-NOTHING ALTERNATIVE

This do-nothing alternative is a continuation of the existing corporate and competitive strategies, whatever they might be, and however unsuccessful the company might be. The decision to do nothing might be highly appropriate and justified, and the result of very careful thought and evaluation. However, it can also be the result of managers lacking awareness, being lazy or complacent or deluding themselves into believing that things are going well when in fact the company is in difficulties. Doing nothing when change is required is a dangerous strategy.

A company might appear to an outsider to be doing nothing when in reality it is very active. Some companies, for example, prefer not to be the first to launch new product developments, especially if they know that

their competitors are innovating along similar lines. A product may be developed and ready to launch but be held back whilst another company introduces its version into the market. This allows the initial reaction of consumers to be monitored and evaluated and competitive and functional strategies reviewed before eventual launch. Timing is the key to success with this strategy. A company will want sufficient time to be sure that its approach is likely to prove successful; at the same time it must react sufficiently quickly that it is not perceived to be copying a competitor when that competitor has become firmly established.

In general the do-nothing alternative may be viable in the short term but is unlikely to prove beneficial or realistic in the long term as environmental factors change.

INTERNAL GROWTH STRATEGIES

Four internal growth strategies are discussed in this section. However, it should be appreciated that the strategies described are not fully discrete and independent of each other. The ideas behind them are closely linked, and it may be very difficult to classify a particular strategic change as one of these strategies rather than another. Consequently the important issue is the line of thought and the reasoning behind the strategy in question, and the objectives.

Concentration or specialization

This strategy implies what Peters and Waterman (1982) designate 'sticking to the knitting' in their book *In Search of Excellence*, which was discussed in Chapter 4. It involves concentrating on doing better what one is already doing well. Although it may seem similar to doing nothing, growth is an objective and there is an implicit search for ways of doing things more effectively. In this respect it overlaps with the ideas of market and product development described below.

Resources are directed towards the continued and profitable growth of a 'single' product in a 'single' market, using a 'single' technology. This is accomplished by attracting new users or consumers, increasing the consumption rate of existing users, and, wherever possible, stealing consumers and market share from competitors. The word 'single' needs careful interpretation, as companies like Kellogg (breakfast cereals) and Timex (watches) would be classified as organizations which have succeeded with specialization strategies. An extensive product line of differentiated brands designed to appeal to specific market segments would periodically have new additions and withdrawals.

The two main advantages are, first, that the strategy is based on known skills and capabilities and in this respect it is generally low risk. Second, because the organization's production and marketing skills are concentrated on specialized products and related consumers, and not diversified, these skills can be developed and improved to create competitive advantage. The company has the opportunity to be sensitive to consumer needs by being close to them, and may build a reputation for this.

There are three key limitations, however. Whilst concentration is a growth strategy, the long-term growth is likely to be gradual rather than explosive. This should not be seen as a disadvantage, because steady growth can be more straightforward in managerial terms. Any firm pursuing this strategy is susceptible to changes in the growth rate or attractiveness of the industry in which it competes, and therefore the strategy can become high risk if the industry goes into recession. There is also a constant need to monitor competitors and ensure that any innovations do not constitute a major threat.

This strategic alternative is particularly applicable to small businesses which concentrate their efforts on specific market niches.

Market development

Market development, together with product development which is considered next, is very closely related to a strategy of specialization. All these strategies build on existing strengths, skills and capabilities. Market development is generally another relatively low-risk strategy; and the idea behind it is to market present products, with possible modifications and range increases, to customers in related market areas. Changes in distribution and advertising will typically support this strategy.

One example of a market development strategy would be a firm who decided to modify its product in some minor way to make it attractive to selected export markets where tastes and preferences are different. This would be supported by advertising and require the opening of new channels of distribution. In the mid-1990s, as the numbers of 18-year-old students seeking higher education decline, universities may well design new courses or modify existing ones, and look at alternative teaching methods, in order to attract increasing numbers of more mature students.

Product development

Product development implies substantial modifications or additions to present products in order to increase their market penetration within existing customer groups. It is often linked to an attempt to extend or prolong the product life cycle, and typical examples would include the second and revised edition of a successful textbook, or the re-launch of a range of cosmetics with built-in improvements which add value. In 1989 Ford launched their new re-styled Fiesta, incorporating a new engine, new transmission system and specially designed components. The objective was to maintain

---

Case 17.1
LEGO

In a volatile and competitive environment we have concentrated and used our strength to go deeper into what we know about.   (Kjeld Kirk Kristiansen, President)

Lego, the brightly coloured plastic building bricks, were launched in 1949, and have always proved popular in an industry renowned for changing tastes and preferences and for innovation. Lego is Danish, family owned and secretive, hiding its actual sales and profit figures.

The basic strategy is one of product development, with Lego developing an enormous number of variations on its basic product theme. At any time some 300 different kits (at a wide range of prices) are available world wide. There are 1300 different parts, including bricks, shapes and miniature people, and children can use them to make almost anything from small cars to large, complex, working space stations with battery-operated space trains.

In a typical year Lego replaces one-third of its product range, with many items having only a short life span. New ideas are developed over a 2–3 year period and backed by international consumer research and test marketing. Lego concentrates on global tastes and buying habits. 'If you differentiate too much you start to make difficulties for yourself, especially in manufacturing.' Competition has forced Lego to act aggressively. One American company, Tyco, markets products which are almost indistinguishable from Lego. Lego has attempted unsuccessfully to sue for patent infringement and now views this competition as undesirable but stimulating.

Lego manufacture in Switzerland, Germany, Brazil, South Korea and America as well as Denmark, making their own tools for the plastic injection moulding machines. Tool making could easily be concentrated in one plant, but takes place in three to engender competition and to emphasize quality. Lego deliberately maintains strong links with its machinery suppliers. In this and other respects Lego sees itself as being closer culturally to a Japanese company than an American one.

Source: Marsh, P (1991) Family continuity holds the key to longevity in a one-product company, *Financial Times*, 20 June.

---

and improve the competitive position of the Fiesta by attracting customers who might currently own another small hatchback such as a Metro and by encouraging owners of existing Fiestas to replace them with the 1989 model. Similarly, the new Volkswagen Golf (1991) has an improved body and is promoted as stronger and more re-cyclable than its predecessor. Case 17.1, Lego, also looks at product development.

Innovation

Innovation is linked to the three strategies described above but involves more significant changes to the product or service. The strategy implies the replacement of existing products with ones which are really new, as opposed to modified, and which imply a new product life cycle. The line which differentiates a really new product from a modifica-

Case 17.2
PREMIER BRANDS

Premier Brands was formed in 1986 as a result of a management buy-out from Cadbury's. Cadbury's drinking chocolate, biscuits, Smash instant mashed potato, Marvel and Coffee Compliment, Chivers and Hartleys products and Typhoo tea were the main brands involved.

There has been little innovation with tea since the introduction of tea bags in the 1950s; and the product has declined in popularity relative to coffee. At the end of the 1960s six cups of tea were drunk for every cup of coffee; in 20 years the ratio decreased to 2:1.

Premier Brands sought to improve the position and profitability of Typhoo. Market research indicated that the product itself was perceived as perfectly satisfactory; advertising alone was unlikely to improve market share; and price competition was regarded as impractical as Typhoo held 21% of the market, Brooke Bond 30% and Lyons Tetley 18%. A typical oligopoly. Their research also indicated that 'freshness, convenience and quality' matter, and consequently in early 1989 Typhoo was marketed with improved packaging.

The product was made available in more rigid outer cartons, featuring a new logo, and each carton contains two sealed foil pouches with 40 tea bags in each. The improvement was supported by advertising.

Sales increased, but not sufficiently to offset the higher costs, and in 1991 Typhoo Extra Fresh was launched. These are again foil packed tea bags with tea processed in the normal way, but the tea is sealed away from air within 24 hours of being picked to prevent any loss of flavour. The product carries a premium price, and the challenge lies in persuading consumers that 'fresh tea' really is different.

Also in 1991 the leading tea manufacturers all launched freeze-dried granulated instant teas under their normal brand names.

Sources: Rawsthorne, P (1989) How Premier Brands is stirring up the tea market, *Financial Times*, 20 April; and Harris, C (1991) Premier seeks a premium with an innovative brew, *Financial Times*, 24 January.

---

tion is extremely difficult to quantify. In the case of the new Fiesta, for example, there are a number of very major changes. The car is very different from the existing model – but the name is the same.

Similarly, it is important to consider which product life cycle is being addressed. The Sony Walkman and similar personal cassette players have enjoyed their own successful life cycle; at the same time they have extended the product life cycle of cassette players generally.

It can be risky not to innovate in certain industries as a barrier against competition. Innovatory companies can stay ahead by introducing new products ahead of their rivals and concentrating on production and marketing to establish and consolidate a strong market position. All the time they will search for new opportunities to innovate and gain further advantage. A number of food manufacturers have utilized innovation to consolidate their market positions as the major food retail chains have increased in

---

Case 17.3
SWISS WATCHES

In the early 1980s the Swiss watch industry was in deep trouble. Many firms had closed and numerous jobs had been lost. Only the select companies manufacturing expensive and high-quality watches were secure from competition from the Far East, particularly the low-labour-cost countries, and their digital electronic watches. The Swiss watch industry had effectively missed out on the early growth of electronic watches, although the first one was actually produced in Switzerland.

By the mid-1980s the situation had been transformed as a result of the Swatch, and similar analogue electronic watches. They were low priced, plastic, reliable and fashion oriented. It has been estimated that in 1985 output from the Swiss watch industry accounted for 45% of world output in value terms from 10% of the volume. The corresponding figures for Japan were 35 : 35 and for the rest of Asia 14 : 50.

This required a change of culture in response to changes in consumer expectations. Although there are limited but highly profitable opportunities for expensive quality watches, in general watches are no longer expected to last a lifetime. They are now perceived as a fashion accessory, and consumers buy them more often and replace them periodically or when they go wrong. In the mid-1970s 274 watches were purchased for every 1000 Britons; ten years later the figure had risen to 370. In America the corresponding figures are 240 and 425.

Source: The Economist, 17 May 1986.

---

size and power. Not only were the retailers in an increasingly strong negotiating position concerning prices and trading arrangements, they were also beginning to market their own-brand alternatives at very competitive prices. Astute manufacturers have innovated and maintained a flow of new products to retain a competitive advantage by limiting the market potential for retailer own-brands.

Constant innovation is likely to prove expensive, and will require other products and strategies to be successful in order to provide the funding.

Cases 17.2 and 17.3 are examples of internal growth strategies. Premier Brands highlights the attempt to consolidate the market position of Typhoo tea relative to other brands of tea and coffee. The opportunities for change were limited as tea drinking is in long-term gradual decline relative to coffee, but at the same time consumers are perfectly happy with the existing product. The Swiss Watch industry case might also be considered as a turnaround strategy because in the early 1980s the industry was in difficulty. But innovation, and the appeal to new market segments through repositioning the products, have proved extremely successful. Elements of market and product development are included.

Combination strategies

A firm with a number of products or business units will typically pursue a number of different competitive strategies at any time.

Product development, market development and innovation may all be taking place.

The internal growth strategies discussed in this section are primarily concerned with improving competitive strategies for existing businesses. Such changes may not prove adequate for closing the planning gap, and consequently higher risk external growth strategies may also be considered. Such changes are likely to involve a new strategic perspective.

Case 17.4 looks at how Tube Investments changed from being a diversified company into one which specializes in engineering products for selected market segments. The change was implemented through the divestment of bicycles and domestic appliances, leaving a core of engineering businesses. External growth through the further acquisition of companies, particularly in America, which produce related engineering products has allowed Tube Investments to pursue strategies of product and market development in order to consolidate its position as a global competitor.

EXTERNAL GROWTH STRATEGIES

External growth strategies are frequently implemented through acquisition, merger or joint venture rather than organic growth. Franchising can provide another means of generating external growth, but it is only likely to be applicable for certain types of business.

External growth can involve the purchase of, or an arrangement with, firms which are behind or ahead of a business in the added value channel which spans raw material to ultimate consumption. Similarly it can involve firms or activities which are in directly related businesses or industries, those which are tangentially related through either technology or markets, and basically unrelated businesses. The key objectives are additional market share and the search for

opportunities which can generate synergy. The outcome from this will be larger size and increased power, and ideally improved profitability from the synergy. In reality, as will be explored in greater depth in Chapter 18, the outcome is more likely to be increased size and power than improved profitability. Synergy often proves to be elusive.

Proposed acquisitions of organizations which would result in substantial market share and possible domination may well be subject to reference to the Monopolies and Mergers Commission which, as was discussed in Chapter 7, may act as a restraint on proposed corporate development. Certain avenues for growth may in effect be closed to an organization.

Horizontal integration

Horizontal integration occurs when a firm acquires or merges with a major competitor, or at least another firm operating at the same stage in the added value chain. The two organizations may well appeal to different market segments rather than compete directly. Market share will increase, and pooled skills and capabilities should generate synergy. Numerous examples exist. Rover Cars, now part of British Aerospace and previously known as Austin Rover, and before that British Leyland, is the result of a series of amalgamations over many years. Such brand names as Austin, Morris, MG, Wolsley, Standard, Triumph and Rover, which were all originally independent car producers, are incorporated. Jaguar was also included until it was re-floated as an independent company in the mid-1980s. By contrast the more successful Ford Motor Company has grown more by internal investment and development than by acquisition.

In the financial services sector, the National Westminster Bank was created by the merger of the National Provincial Bank and Westminster Bank, and more recently a number of building society mergers have taken place.

Case 17.4
TUBE INVESTMENTS

Christopher Lewington was recruited in 1986 to become the new Chief Executive and he quickly decided that Tube Investments (TI) needed a clear vision and strategy, in contrast with previous acquisition strategies which had been relatively haphazard.

It was stated in early 1987 that 'TI's strategic thrust is to become an international engineering group concentrating on specialized engineering businesses and operating in selected niches (particularly automotives) on a global basis. Key businesses must be able to command positions of sustained technological and market share leadership.'

In 1986 Raleigh cycles and a number of varied domestic appliance products constituted 42% of TI sales revenue, 30% of pre-tax profits and 45% of capital employed. These were the areas for divestment. Cycles, with their low technology, had been affected by foreign competition which compounded the problems caused by falls in demand in parts of Western Europe. Because different markets required specific product differences, and because of the emergence of defined niches such as those for BMX and mountain bikes, Raleigh 'needed marketing which TI could not provide'. Domestic appliances was an international industry and multi-nationals such as Philips and Electrolux were very powerful competitors. TI was too small.

Lewington felt that TI had neither the financial resources nor the breadth of management to run a company diversified across specialist engineering and consumer products and markets. Specialist engineering was where TI could add most value and gain the greatest benefit.

In 1987–8 TI sold Raleigh to Derby International, a specially formed foreign-backed consortium who more recently acquired Royal Worcester pottery. Glow Worm and Parkray central heating systems were sold to Hepworth Ceramics; Creda and New World domestic appliances to GEC and Birmid Qualcast respectively; and Russell Hobbs kitchen equipment to Polly Peck. Machine tool interests and some welded tube products were also divested.

At the same time TI has acquired companies, especially in America, including Bundy, the largest US manufacturer of small diameter tube for use in cars and refrigerators, and John Crane, a manufacturer of mechanical seals.

TI now specializes in a range of engineering products including aircraft piston rings, industrial furnaces, and tubes for specific market segments. For the automotive industry, silencers, suspension systems, car seats and seat slide mechanisms are manufactured. Profitability has improved.

In 1992 TI launched a hostile bid for the Dowty Group. Approximately half of Dowty's turnover comes from aerospace and polymer engineering, businesses which fit closely with TI's current strategy. TI would keep these and look to sell the remaining Dowty businesses – information technology (modems and terminals) and electronic systems.

Case 17.5
ELECTROLUX

In 1970 Electrolux was a Swedish-based manufacturer of mainly vacuum cleaners, supported by refrigerators. A new chief executive introduced a strategy of horizontal integration and acquisition, and within 20 years Electrolux became the world's leading manufacturer of white goods — refrigerators, freezers, washing machines, tumble dryers and dishwashers. Electrolux's major acquisitions include:

1984   Zanussi (Italy)
1986   White Consolidated (third largest US producer)
1987   Tricity (UK, from Thorn–EMI)
1988   Corbero/Domar (Spain)
1991   Lehel (largest producer of white goods in Hungary — providing a base for expansion in Eastern Europe).

Electrolux bought 400 companies over 20 years, with unrelated businesses and surplus assets often being sold off to recoup part of the purchase price.

Production has been rationalized, with many parts standardized, in an attempt to reduce costs, but Electrolux remains a global manufacturer. Wherever possible the best practices from new acquisitions are shared across frontiers, and clearly Electrolux has faced a series of challenges in integrating the new businesses with their distinctive, national cultures. The integration strategy is based upon speed and the immediate input of a small task force to search for synergy and divestment opportunities.

The ultimate success will depend upon the ability of Electrolux to integrate its marketing, particularly in Europe, which accounts for some two-thirds of the sales. Product differentiation is possible, but the fact that competing white goods invariably look alike in many respects adds difficulties. In addition, tastes and preferences concerning particular features vary from country to country.

In 1991 products carrying the Electrolux brand name were re-launched as a pan-European upper mass market brand, with new design features and common advertising and promotion. A similar strategy, but with a more downmarket image, will follow for Zanussi-branded products. Local brands are also being retained, targeted at individual country preferences — for the UK this means Tricity and Bendix. This dualistic strategy differs from that of Whirlpool, the US company which acquired Philips' white goods business, and is Electrolux's main rival. Whirlpool is more reluctant to differentiate between countries.

In June 1992 Electrolux agreed a new joint venture with a smaller European competitor, AEG, a subsidiary of Daimler–Benz (see Case 18.3). Cross-shareholdings are involved. The two companies will continue to compete using their own identities and brand names but will collude on production and development. Eventually they will operate integrated plants for lower costs and increased efficiency.

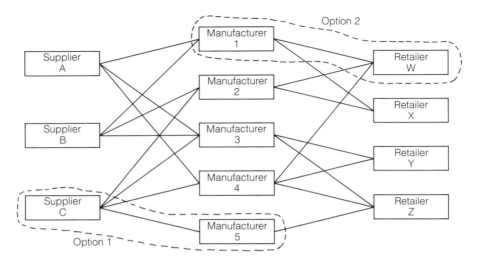

Figure 17.2 Vertical integration.

The Alliance and Leicester and Nationwide Anglia are typical examples.

In 1988 Elders, the Australian brewers of Foster's lager and owner of Courage in the UK, bid for Scottish and Newcastle Breweries. Courage and Scottish and Newcastle are approximately the same size, and together they would have a UK market share of 19%, only slightly smaller than the market leader, Bass. The bid was referred to the Monopolies and Mergers Commission, and in 1989 the Commission recommended that permission for the merger should be refused. Courage has since been allowed to acquire Grand Metropolitan's Breweries and become number two in the market.

Case 17.5, Electrolux, is an example of international horizontal integration.

Vertical integration

Vertical integration is the term used to describe the acquisition of a company which supplies a firm with inputs of raw materials or components, or serves as a customer for the firm's products or services (a distributor or assembler). If a shirt manufacturer acquired a cotton textile supplier this would be known as backward vertical integration; if the supplier bought the shirt manufacturer, its customer, this would constitute forward vertical integration.

At times firms will reduce the extent to which they are vertically integrated if they are failing to obtain the appropriate benefits and synergy from the fusion of two sets of skills and capabilities. Early in 1988, for example, the Burton Group sold the last of its suitmaking factories in order to concentrate on retailing. At one time Burton had been one of the leading clothing manufacturers in Europe, but that was before made-to-measure suits were substantially replaced in popularity by ready-made suits.

Backward vertical integration aims to secure supplies at a lower cost than competitors, but after the merger or acquisition it becomes crucial to keep pace with technological developments and innovation on the supply side, or competitive advantage may be lost. Forward vertical integration secures customers or outlets and guarantees product preference, and it can give a firm much greater control over its total marketing effort. At the consumer end of the chain, retailers generally are free to decide at what final price they sell particular products or services, and their views may not always accord with those of the manufacturer. However, greater control over distribution might mean complacency and a loss of competitive edge through less effective marketing overall. In addition, manufacturing and retailing, if these are the two activities involved, require separate and different skills, and for this reason synergy may again prove elusive.

With vertical integration there will always be uncertainty as the system of relationships amongst a group of suppliers and manufacturers, or a group of manufacturers and distributors, is changed. Generally it is argued that if there are only a few suppliers and several buyers vertical integration can have significant effects. Figure 17.2 features a system comprising three suppliers, five manufacturers and four retailers, all of whom are independent. The lines joining the boxes show the trading relationships. If supplier C acquired, or was acquired by, manufacturer 5 (option 1) then a number of issues have to be resolved. Currently manufacturer 5 relies exclusively on supplier C. Does it make sense for this to continue, or might it be useful to establish a trading relationship with another supplier (also now a competitor) to hedge against future possible difficulties such as technological change and innovation? At the moment, also, competing manufacturers 2, 3 and 4 all buy some of their supplies from supplier C. Will they continue to do so? If not, supplier C is likely to have substantial spare capacity. Similar issues would be raised by option 2, integration between manufacturer 1 and retailer W.

Many of the benefits of vertical integration can be achieved without merger or acquisition. Joint ventures, discussed later, are one option. In addition there may simply be agreements between companies who appreciate that there can be substantial gains from proper co-operation. Marks & Spencer provide an excellent example. Marks & Spencer benefit from long-term agreements with their suppliers with whom they work closely. Many suppliers of a wide variety of products sold by Marks & Spencer rely very

heavily upon them, as they are their major customer. At the same time Marks & Spencer set exacting standards for cost, quality and delivery and guarantee to buy only when these standards are met continuously; and there will always be competitors who would like them as a customer.

The effect of vertical integration can be created organically, without merger or acquisition, but this is likely to be more risky. New skills have to be developed from scratch. Examples of this would be a manufacturer deciding to make components rather than buying them from specialist suppliers, or starting to distribute independently rather than relying on external distributors.

Because new and different skills are involved, vertical integration really implies diversification, but normally these strategic change options are considered separately.

Concentric diversification

Any form of diversification involves a departure from existing products and markets. The new products or services involved may relate to existing products or services through either technology or marketing; where this is the case, the diversification is known as concentric rather than conglomerate. A specialist manufacturer of ski clothing who diversified into summer leisure wear to offset seasonal sales would be an example. Potential consumers may or may not be the same; distribution may or may not change; the existing production expertise should prove beneficial.

Similarly, when retailers such as Boots and W H Smith add new and different lines and products they are seeking to exploit their resources and their retailing skills and expertise (core competences) more effectively.

There is an assumption that synergy can be created from the two businesses or activities; and ideally the new, diversified, company enjoys strengths and opportunities which decrease its weaknesses and exposure to risks.

Any organization seeking concentric diversification will look for companies or opportunities where there are clearly related products or markets or distribution channels or technologies or resource requirements. The related benefits should be clear and genuinely capable of generating synergy. However, diversification might be adopted as a means of covering up weaknesses or previous poor decisions. Benefits will not be expected immediately, and the change involved may divert interest and attention away from existing problems or difficulties.

Conglomerate diversification

In the case of conglomerate diversification there is no discernible relationship between existing and new products, services and markets. The diversification is justified as a promising investment opportunity. Financial benefits and profits should be available from the new investment, and any costs incurred will be more than offset. Financial synergy might be obtained in the form of greater borrowing capacity or acquired tax credits.

The strategy is regarded as high risk because the new technologies, new skills and new markets involved constitute unknowns and uncertainties. Moreover, because the change is uncertain and challenging, it can be tempting to switch resources and efforts away from existing businesses and areas of strength; and this compounds the element of risk involved.

Conglomerate diversification is often linked to portfolio analysis, and the search for businesses which might remedy any perceived weaknesses. A company with reserves of cash to invest, because it has a number of cash cow businesses, might seek to buy businesses with growth potential in new industries. Some acquisitive and financially oriented companies diversify in this way with a view to rationalizing the businesses they buy. Parts will be retained if they feel they can add value and benefit accordingly; other parts will be divested. Some companies diversify to reduce the likelihood of being acquired themselves by an unwelcome outsider.

Diversification and acquisition strategies and tests to establish whether or not a proposed diversification seems worthwhile will be considered in Chapter 18.

After considering both internal and external growth strategies, in the next section we describe a number of consolidation and reductionist strategies, primarily for companies experiencing difficulties. Quite often the problems arise because previous growth, diversification and acquisition strategies have been either poorly conceived or poorly implemented.

DISINVESTMENT STRATEGIES

The term disinvestment strategies is used to represent strategic alternatives where money is not invested for growth purposes. However, the sale of assets or businesses may be involved and money raised from this may well be re-invested to develop or enhance competitive advantage and support those remaining areas of the business which are seen as essential. Where disinvestment strategies are successful, and businesses in difficulty are turned around, money may then be invested for future growth.

In 1990 ACT, UK manufacturers of Apricot computers, were in financial difficulties. The hardware business was sold to Mitsubishi and ACT focused on their remaining core competence: computer services. Some of the money from the sale was used to acquire a financial services software company. Rappaport and Halevi (1991) defend such a strategy, arguing that the best opportunities for adding value in computing in the 1990s lie in applications. Existing technology has created powerful machines whose potential consumers have yet to exploit.

Disinvestment strategies involve con-

Case 17.6
THE ASDA–MFI MERGER AND DE-MERGER

Asda's real growth into one of the UK's largest food retail chains began in the mid-1960s when it first recognized the potential for out-of-town sites with large car parks. Asda are concentrated in the north of England; the head office is in Leeds. By the early 1990s Asda owned some 200 food stores, having acquired 60 supermarkets from Gateway in 1989. Asda's other main retailing activity is carpets and furnishings. Asda had tried unsuccessfully to divest Allied Carpets in the mid-1980s and instead boosted it by buying two-thirds of Waring & Gillow (furniture shops) and forming Allied Maples – again in 1989. [See Case 21.3.] Asda's success has been attributed to low overheads, cost control, high sales per square foot and low-cost sites – but it is smaller and less profitable than its main rivals, Sainsbury and Tesco.

In 1985, with a welcome bid, Asda acquired MFI, the nationwide retailer of self-assembly furniture. This represented concentric diversification as, although the products were different, the customer base was essentially the same. Synergy was expected between the food superstores and MFI rather than through the furniture links, as both were professional edge-of-town retailers in complementary businesses. Both were innovators and their management teams could learn from each other. There was an additional hidden motive. The Chairman of Asda, Sir Noel Stockdale, was approaching retirement and there was no natural successor. Derek Hunt of MFI was thought to be an ideal replacement. Hunt became Chief Executive of Asda–MFI in 1986, but retained his working base in the south of England where MFI headquarters had been.

The expected benefits and synergy did not accrue. In 1984 the return on net assets of Asda was 43% and of MFI 38%. In the three years that the companies were merged the relevant figures for the group dropped from 40% in 1985 to 27% in 1987.

In 1987 MFI was sold in a management buy-out to a consortium led by Derek Hunt, but Asda retained a 25% interest. Since the de-merger MFI has acquired its main supplier of furniture packs, Hygena, and this backward vertical integration appears to have brought some tangible financial benefits.

However, in the recession at the end of the 1980s/early 1990s MFI traded at a loss. Interest costs arising out of the buy-back and a reputation for poor quality compounded their trading difficulties.

At Asda, John Hardman took over as Chairman in 1987, but he resigned in 1991 when Asda also started losing money. The losses continued in 1992. Asda had paid too much for the Gateway sites and still owned 25% of the debt-ridden MFI. The MFI shares have since been sold, but the Gateway stores are valued in the balance sheet at just two-thirds of their acquisition price. Moreover, Asda lacked an effective competitive identity and was perceived to be a less successful retailer than its main rivals, who were also proving more successful in obtaining the premium sites for new stores. Asda had centralized its distribution into a limited number of regional warehouses, but had been a follower rather than a leader in this key strategic

Continued overleaf

development. In 1990 Asda formed a joint venture with George Davies (ex-Next – see Case 21.2) in an attempt to revive its non-food activities with a range of designer clothes.

The new Chairman (Patrick Gillam) and Chief Executive (Archie Norman) embarked on a three-year programme which 'would not produce significant results in the immediate future'. Their aim is to turn back the clock and return to 'meeting the weekly shopping needs of ordinary working people and their families'. The market is being carefully segmented and prices made keener; productivity is being improved and service quality stressed; and there is an increased emphasis on fresh foods. There are also regional variations in stocking policy. Norman perceives the increasing success of the discount-price food retailers to be a threat as Asda has retained a number of small stores in less affluent areas. Asda decided to convert 65 such stores to a discount format and offer core food lines only. [This sector is already very competitive.] The remaining 140 stores would remain as multi-product supermarkets, but their layouts are to be re-designed. They will continue to stock a wide range of non-food items and thereby differ from Sainsbury, Tesco and Safeway. A number of the Allied Maples furnishings stores have been closed.

The *Financial Times* suggested that Asda's institutional investors 'would be persistently whispering thoughts of mortality into the ears of Asda's new emperors'.

(The actual logic behind the diversification is evaluated in a follow-up case in Chapter 18.)

solidation and re-positioning strategies as well as the sale or closure of one or more parts of a business. They are applicable in certain circumstances, including

- where a firm is over-extended in a particular market
- where it experiences an economic reversal because of competitor or other pressures
- when demand declines
- where the opportunity cost of resources being used is such that better returns could be earned elsewhere
- when the synergy expected from an acquisition proves elusive.

Case 17.6, which covers the de-merger of Asda and MFI in 1987, is an illustration of the last point. The two organizations merged in 1985 and used potential synergy as a justification. In the event the combined organizations were less successful than they had been individually before the merger. This case also illustrates the search (by Asda) for effective corporate and competitive strategies.

Disinvestment can be accomplished through retrenchment, turnaround, divestment or liquidation, and the choice from these particular alternatives determines whether the changes relate to functional, competitive or corporate strategies. Sometimes the term 'turnaround' is used to represent both the retrenchment and the turnaround strategies described in this section; and the expression 'recovery strategies' is also synonymous with both. Where part of a firm is sold to generate funds which can be channelled into areas or business units which are regarded as good future prospects, this too would be categorized as a recovery strategy.

The causes and symptoms of decline, which determine the need for such strategies, were discussed in Chapter 8; and whilst this chapter outlines the alternatives, recovery and divestment strategies are discussed further in Chapter 19. During the 1980s management buy-outs have increased in popularity, and they are generally related to disinvestment decisions. Chapter 20 looks at buy-outs in greater detail.

Retrenchment

Remedial action is required when a company experiences declining profits as a result of economic recession, production inefficiency or competitor innovation. In such circumstances efforts should be concentrated on those activities and areas in which the company has distinctive competence or a superior competitive position. The assumption would be that the firm can survive.

In order to improve efficiency three aspects are involved, either individually or in combination:

☐ **cost reduction** through redundancies, leasing rather than buying new assets, not replacing machinery or reducing expenditure on such things as maintenance or training – the danger lies in cutting spending in areas where competitive advantage might be generated
☐ **asset reduction**, selling anything which is not essential
☐ **revenue generation**, by working on the debtor and stock turnover ratios.

Essentially the aim is to reduce the scale of operations to a position where the company has a solid, consolidated and competitive base. The key issue concerns how much reduction is needed, whether it is minor or drastic, and how quickly the company must act. Where any changes are regarded as temporary, it is important to ensure that there is the necessary flexibility to allow for renewal and growth.

Turnaround strategies

Turnaround strategies involve the adoption of a new strategic position for a product or service, and typically lead on from retrenchment. Resources which are freed up are re-allocated from one strategic thrust to another; particularly significant here is the re-allocation of managerial talent which can lead to an input of fresh ideas. Revenue-generating strategies, such as product modifications, advertising or lower prices designed to generate sales, are often involved; and in addition products and services may well be re-focused into the niches which are thought to be most lucrative or defensible.

Divestment

Where retrenchment fails, or is not regarded as feasible, a part of the business is likely to be sold. Basically the organization is hoping to create a more effective and profitable portfolio of products and services. The key problem is finding a buyer if the business in question is in difficulties, and particularly a buyer who is willing to pay a premium price for the assets. This can happen where a prospective buyer feels that he or she has the appropriate skills to manage the business more effectively, or where there is potential synergy with the activities already managed by the acquirer. Management buy-outs relate to the first of these issues. Existing managers often feel they could manage their business more profitably if they were freed from any constraints imposed by the parent organization and were completely free to try out their ideas for change.

Divestment, then, is most likely when a company needs to raise money quickly, or when a business is seen as having a poor strategic fit with the rest of the portfolio and, as a result, is holding back the whole organization. Two special cases of divestment are

☐ the successful entrepreneur whose business has grown to a size where he or she has obtained all the benefits they sought and is seeking to sell out

☐ divestments of parts of the business following an acquisition. This strategy, usually designed to maximize the value of the business for shareholders, was discussed in Chapter 13.

Where a business is not contributing strategically to a parent organization, but there is no urgent need for cash, it may be floated off as an independent company rather than sold. Existing shareholders are simply given separate shares in the newly formed company, which needs to be strong enough to survive on its own. Organizations adopting this strategy hope to see the market value of their shares improve as the more concentrated business is perceived to be stronger.

Sometimes companies will swap assets with other organizations. In 1992 ICI swapped their fibres operations for the acrylics businesses of Du Pont, the US chemicals company. This is one aspect of ICI's current strategy of specializing in activities where it can achieve a strong global presence, and divesting others (see Case 9.3). Du Pont benefit by becoming the leading supplier of nylon in Europe, an area they had targeted for expansion; ICI moves from third place to world leadership in acrylics, which are used, for example, in windows and bathroom furniture.

Liquidation

Liquidation involves the sale of a complete business, either as a single going concern or piecemeal to different buyers, or sometimes by auctioning the assets. It is an unpopular choice as it represents an admission of failure by the present management team, but it may well be in the best long-term interests of the stakeholders as a whole.

THE INTERNATIONAL ALTERNATIVE

Internal growth, external growth and disinvestment strategies may all involve an inter-national dimension with special complexities. Countries differ economically (variable growth rates), culturally (behaviours, tastes and preferences) and politically. National politics can dictate the appropriate strategy – some markets cannot be penetrated effectively without joint ventures with local companies.

Internal growth might involve exporting to new markets overseas and the development of special varieties of a product or service in order to target it to the specific needs and requirements of overseas customers. External growth can range from the creation of distribution or assembly bases abroad, to joint ventures and licensing agreements with foreign companies, to the establishment of a comprehensive multi-national organization.

Kay (1990) recommends that organizations should seek to determine the smallest area within which they can be a viable competitor. Whilst a retail newsagent can still succeed by concentrating on a local catchment area, most car manufacturers, in common with many other industries, now see their relevant market as a global one. The short cases on Grand Metropolitan, Thorn–EMI (later in this chapter) and Trafalgar House (Chapter 18)

In the industries that have changed the world, from fertilizers to machinery to computers, the firms that make the big capital investment early are the ones that survive. The cost advantages are tremendous for those who have scope and scale – the ability to make many products out of the same set of materials. If we continue to do what we did in the 1980s – look to make money on the deal and sacrifice long-term investment for dividends or interest – then the people who buy our companies will be foreigners . . . You have to create a world-wide organization to compete, or you will be bought by someone.

Alfred D Chandler, Harvard Business School. Quoted in Fortune, *26 March 1990, p. 83* all illustrate companies which now seek to concentrate on products or services where they can be an internationally strong competitor. Such companies are hoping to create synergy by specializing on core skills and competencies and exploiting these as widely as possible.

Organizations which develop their corporate strategy internationally have to consider in particular:

☐ marketing and financial strategies
☐ the structure of the organization
☐ cultural and people issues.

Marketing

The question of how global products and services can be made, and the extent to which they have to be tailored to appeal to different markets, was introduced in Chapter 10. The challenge to design the 'world car', for example, remains unresolved. Honda initially hoped to achieve this when it began redesigning its Accord range in the mid-1980s, but realized that internationally performance needs, and in turn components, are irreconcilable. In Japan the Accord is seen as a status symbol car for congested roads where driving is restricted; in America it is a workaday vehicle for travelling long distances on open highways.

There is a follow-up issue concerning the appropriate range of products or services. The following framework could be a useful starting point for analysing both opportunities and competitor strategies:

	Product/service range	Geographic scope
1	Narrow	National
2	Broad	National
3	Narrow	Global
4	Broad	Global

Where organizations find it necessary to be located close to customers in order to provide the delivery and other services demanded, this can be achieved with strategic stockholding rather than manufacturing.

Finance

The management of currency transfers and exchange rates adds complexity. Floating exchange rates imply uncertainty, although companies can, and do, reduce their risk by buying ahead. The European Exchange Rate Mechanism is designed to minimize currency fluctuations, but, as happened to the pound sterling in 1992, economic pressures may still force a devaluation. Predictable or fixed rates benefit, for example, a car manufacturer which produces engines and transmission systems in one country, transfers them to assembly plants in a second and third country, each specializing in different cars, and then finally sells them throughout Europe. Costs and estimated profits must be based on predicted currency movements, and any incorrect forecasting could result in either extra or lost profits.

Where such an organization structure is created, transfer pricing arrangements are required. If managers of the various divisions or business units are motivated or measured by their profitability figures there will be some disagreement about transfer prices which affect their value-added figures. Equally, the organization may be seeking to manage transfer arrangements for tax purposes, seeking to show most profit where taxes are lowest.

Structure, culture and people

The two key questions are:

☐ Where to make the various products and services to obtain the necessary people and other resources required, to be as close as appropriate to each defined geographic market, and to manage costs efficiently.

☐ How best to structure the organization in order to control it effectively, but, at the same time, ensure it is sufficiently responsive to changing environments. The speed and nature of change pressures may be uneven. IT increasingly offers opportunities for more effective control of globally dispersed businesses.

The alternatives are:

☐ A globally centralized organization, remote from markets, and relying on exporting. This is likely to prove cost-efficient but possibly out-of-touch.

☐ Manufacturing plants located close to markets in order to satisfy local needs and preferences. This structure, known as both international and multi-domestic, could still be controlled centally, or substantially decentralized into fully autonomous units, in which case the plants may be independent or may co-operate in some way. This is a more expensive structure, but one that can offer higher levels of service. Unilever, which relies on localized manufacturing and marketing, is an example.

☐ Centralized manufacture of key components, possibly in a low-wage country, with final assembly or finishing nearer to markets. Caterpillar Tractor utilize this strategy.

☐ An integrated global structure with production locations chosen on resource or cost grounds. Finished goods will be transported to markets. In this structure the organization will have an international presence, but in, say, country X its sales could consist mainly of products imported from other locations, whilst most of country X's production is exported.

Marketing, production *control*, purchasing and research and development will all be co-ordinated globally if they are not centralized.

Centres of excellence may be established where cultural values and behaviours are most appropriate. Philips concentrate technology development in the Far East, where a long-term perspective is natural; IBM have established R & D facilities in Italy, which they regard as suitably intuitive and innovative. However, if national preferences and requirements are markedly different, there is an argument in favour of establishing dedicated R & D facilities in several countries. ICI has a technical centre in Japan for developing special chemicals and materials in collaboration with the major car and electronics manufacturers. The intention is to sell their products to Japanese plants throughout the world. 'Japanese companies prefer to collaborate with chemicals suppliers which have scientists and engineers in Japan, and a factory to produce material locally.'

This alternative has many strategic advantages, but it can be complex to control and costly in overheads. Typical companies are Sony (Case 17.7) and Coca-Cola. Coca-Cola, based in Atlanta, command 46% of the world's soft drinks market and 41% of the American domestic market. Their main competitor is Pepsi-Cola with 33% of the US market, but only a 15% global share. Non-American sales constitute 67% of Coke's output and 80% of earnings. The key success factor is obtaining distribution and access to markets, and because Coca-Cola is mostly water this is decentralized. Branding and marketing is global and centralized. The strategy is to sell concentrate or syrup to local bottlers, be they independent businesses or joint-venture partners. Pricing is based on what can be afforded locally, and a variety of support mechanisms are offered. Coke is frequently promoted with local endorsements, but marketing and advertising also features sponsorship of international events, such as the Olympic Games.

Whatever the structural format, a truly international business must develop a global mission and core values (such as consistent quality world wide), and achieve integration

---

Case 17.7
SONY

Sony is renowned as an innovative company within the consumer electronics industry, and its success has depended substantially on televisions, videos and hi-fi equipment. Through the Walkman Sony has 'changed the lifestyle of a generation'.

In recent years Sony has followed a strategy of globalization and diversification – arguably in related product areas. Sony manufactures computer work stations and floppy discs – it has 25% of the world market for 3½ inch discs. Sony also acquired CBS Records (1988) and Columbia Pictures (1989), arguing there was potential synergy from linking their existing hardware with records and pre-recorded videos.

The international strategy has been called global localization. Sony aims to be a global company presented locally, and this involves devolving authority away from Tokyo and expanding manufacturing and R & D around the world. In contrast, other major Japanese companies such as Toyota and Matsushita (Panasonic and Technics) have chosen to remain centralized. Sony have divided the world into four – Europe, America, Asia and Japan – and created four organizations which should be virtually self-sufficient, and ultimately locally financed independent businesses. Structurally Sony companies in the UK report to Sony Europe in Cologne, whose Chairman is Swiss.

Sony is looking to devolve investment decisions, R & D, product planning and marketing. Whilst it would be cheaper to produce everything in Southeast Asia and ship it out, Sony feels it would be too remote from its markets. In theory only corporate strategic issues should be referred back to Tokyo, but in practice managers occasionally attempt to shortcut the regional layers and contact Tokyo about operational matters.

Sony now manufactures in all leading European countries and has technology development centres in Germany and the UK. The locally sourced content of the products averages 60%. Sony manufacture televisions at Bridgend in south Wales, buying over 90% of the components locally, even though the plant was started in 1974 as a screwdriver operation to assemble imported parts. Seventy-five per cent of the output is exported, mostly to Europe.

Sources: Cope, N (1990) Walkmen's global stride, *Business*, March; and de Jonquieres, G and Dixon, H (1989) Sony goes European, *Financial Times*, 2 October.

---

through effective communications. The organization must be able to embrace the different national cultural traits and behaviours, and this presents an important managerial challenge. Decisions have to be made concerning the balance of local managers and mobile 'international' managers who are easily transferable between divisions and countries.

Bartlett and Ghoshal (1989) summarize the above points as three potentially conflicting issues which must be reconciled. These are:

☐ the need for efficiency through global centralization

☐ the need to respond locally through decentralization

☐ the need to innovate and transfer learning internationally.

More recently Bartlett and Ghoshal (1992) have concluded:

☐ There can be no such thing as a 'universal international manager'. Large global companies will need functional specialists (such as production experts) and national managers (committed to one country and most familiar with that culture) as well as those executives who are able to switch readily between divisions and countries. International managers are responsible for corporate and competitive strategies within the organization, whilst national managers ensure that the needs of local customers, host governments and employees are satisfied effectively. The organizational challenge in respect of functional managers is to ensure that best practices are learned and spread throughout the organization.

☐ The attempts to integrate all the global operations (products, plants and countries) should be concentrated towards the top of the organizational hierarchy. At lower levels managers should have clear, single-line, responsibilities and reporting relationships. [This structural issue is discussed further in Chapter 22.]

Globalization is now no longer an objective, but an imperative, as markets open and geographic barriers become increasingly blurred and even irrelevant. Corporate alliances, whether joint ventures or acquisitions, will increasingly be driven by competitive pressures and strategies rather than financial structuring.

John F Welch Jr, Chief Executive Officer, General Electric (US), quoted in Fortune, *26 March 1990, p.34*

One benefit of adopting these recommendations is a limited requirement for international managers, who, inevitably, are in short supply because of the qualities they are required to have. Some industrialists would argue that this supply constraint is the deciding force, and that a successful global matrix structure would be preferable. One such structure is described in Case 22.5, Asea Brown Boveri.

Contrasting views on international strategy

We saw in Key Reading 7.1 that Porter (1990) believes global strategies essentially supplement the competitive advantage created in the home market. Firms must retain their national strengths when they cross over borders. Ohmae (1990) disagrees and argues that global firms should shake off their origins. Managers must take on an international perspective, avoiding the near-sightedness which often characterizes companies with centralized and powerful global headquarters. Markets, he says, are driven by the needs and desires of customers around the world, and managers must act as if they are equidistant from all these customers, wherever they might be located.

Ohmae is perhaps presenting a futuristic vision of how he believes things will be as global forces strengthen. At the moment, whilst world leaders like IBM, Sony and Nestlé, are spread around the world, and substantially dependent on non-domestic customers, their underlying cultures and competitiveness remain rooted in America, Japan and Switzerland respectively.

Chandler (1990) stresses the continuing importance of economies of scale (cost advantages with large-scale production) and economies of scope (the use of common materials and processes to make a variety of different products profitably). This implies carefully targeted investment in large-scale operations and a search for international marketing opportunities.

STRATEGIC MEANS

The internal growth strategies described earlier in this chapter are most likely to be implemented through the re-investment of past profits, building on existing strengths and capabilities. This is generally known as organic growth, and it does not involve any formal arrangements with other organizations. However, certain forms of joint venture, together with franchise arrangements, can also be useful in bringing about market and product development.

The external growth strategies could also be achieved through organic growth, but for the reasons outlined below, they are more

---

It is necessary for a group like LVMH, which controls and exploits a range of high quality brand names, [Dom Perignon, Moët and Chandon, Christian Dior, Christian Lacroix, Louis Vuitton and Hennessy] to invest in order to consolidate the global position of these names.

We must maintain and develop our own brand names so that they are more and more sought after by those who, like the Japanese, seek a social status through these symbols.

We will undoubtedly grow by buying new businesses.

An industrialist today does not merely increase the profitability and productivity of a factory. He must also be able to buy other businesses, for there are crucial benefits of scale in trades like the wine and spirit business or the perfume and cosmetic industry.

Bernard Arnault, Group Chairman, LVMH, Moët Hennessy. Louis Vuitton

In 1989 LVMH and Guinness agreed a joint venture for the distribution of their various brands. In particular Gordon's gin and Johnnie Walker whisky are now distributed with Hennessy cognac and Moët champagnes.

---

likely to involve acquisition, merger or joint venture. These three strategic means are mentioned briefly in this section and given a more detailed treatment in Chapter 18.

Organic growth

Organic growth is an attractive option in that it can be controlled and the changes need not be sudden or traumatic as is typical of an acquisition or merger. In addition, there is no problem of different organizational cultures which have to be harmonized.

However, if organic growth is used to implement an external growth strategy, it may take considerable time; and whilst it is happening competitors may have more than enough opportunity to prepare their defences and possibly introduce strategies designed to create barriers to entry and thwart the potential success of the proposed changes. If diversification is involved, new skills and capabilities will be required, and these may be difficult to develop to a stage where there is competitive advantage. If existing management resources are allocated to the new development, there is an opportunity cost involved when they are removed from areas in which they are currently contributing. Finally it may be easier to raise money for an acquisition, as it happens more quickly and consequently the money invested starts to earn returns sooner.

Acquisition, merger and joint venture

An acquisition, merger or joint venture is likely to take place when an organization lacks a key success factor for a particular market. Joint ventures and strategic alliances are particularly useful where there are strong reasons against a full merger or acquisition. The justification and potential drawbacks of mergers and acquisitions are discussed in Chapter 18.

Joint ventures and strategic alliances, also discussed further in Chapter 18, can take a number of forms. When a group of oil companies collaborated in the development of the Alaskan pipeline to transport oil from the wells in the north of Alaska to the unfrozen ports in the south, it amounted to joint ownership. The strategy was logical; the pipeline was prohibitively expensive for one company alone, and the appropriate capacity was far in excess of the demand from any single company involved. Agreements could concern collaboration on design or rights to manufacture products designed by other companies. These types of joint venture are particularly popular with companies in different countries. Finally, if a manufacturer acquired a minority shareholding in a supplier, this would also constitute a form of joint venture aimed at achieving the advantages of vertical integration without a full merger and the need to fuse two cultures and sets of skills.

Joint ventures with local companies are essential for strategic development and growth in many Third World countries, who wish to limit foreign ownership, promote domestic employment and obtain some involvement in industries which operate multi-nationally.

Whatever the strategic means selected, there are likely to be problems in bringing together the interests, skills and managers of two companies and cultures. The managerial time required to make it work can compromise the value added and reduce profitability, and divert attention away from other important issues within existing businesses.

Franchising

Franchising again takes many forms, and it provides an opportunity for rapid growth for established businesses and a relatively low risk means of starting a small business. Service businesses are more common than manufacturing in franchising, and as the UK continues to switch from a manufacturing to a service economy they may become increasingly important. Tie Rack is one example of a retail organization which has concentrated on specific market segments and grown rapidly with franchising. Thornton's chocolate shops, Fastframe picture framing, Prontaprint printing and copying shops, Body Shop and the British School of Motoring are other examples. Although McDonald's is franchised throughout America, the restaurants in Britain are owned by the company. Kentucky Fried Chicken, Burger King and Spud-U-Like, however, are franchised.

A company which chooses franchising as a means of strategic growth enters into contractual arrangements with a number of small businesses, usually one in each selected geographical area. In return for a lump sum initial investment and on-going royalties the typical franchisor provides exclusive rights to supply a product or service under the franchisor's name in a designated area, know-how, equipment, materials, training, advice, and national support advertising. This allows the business in question to grow rapidly in a number of locations without the investment capital which would be required to fund organic growth of the same magnitude. Another advantage for the franchisor is the alleviation of some of the need for the development of the managers, skills and capabilities required to control a large, growing and dispersed organization. Instead efforts can be concentrated on expanding market share. It is essential, though, to establish effective monitoring and control systems to ensure that franchisees are providing the necessary level of quality and service.

The small business franchisee needs sufficient capital to buy into the franchise, but the risk is less than most independent starts because the business is already established. As a result a number of small independent businesses operate as part of a chain and can compete against larger organizations.

Case 17.8
GRAND METROPOLITAN

In 1992 Grand Metropolitan (GM) is the world's leading manufacturer and distributor of spirits, through its IDV subsidiary, and an important manufacturer of foods, particularly in America. GM own Pillsbury, the Jolly Green Giant foods company. The strategic perspective has changed dramatically in the last 25 years, influenced markedly by three strategic leaders. The changes are illustrated in Figure 17.3.

In the early 1960s, led by Sir Maxwell Joseph, GM, then known as Grand Metropolitan Hotels, was a leading hotel company and specialized. Through a series of acquisitions GM diversified into restaurants (Chef and Brewer, 1966 and Berni Inns, 1970), dairies and supermarkets (Express Dairies, including Eden Vale and Ski products, 1969), leisure activities (Mecca, 1970), brewing (Truman Hanbury Buxton, 1971 and Watney Mann, 1972) and spirits (IDV, 1973). Additional hotel chains were also acquired. This external growth activity slowed down in the 1970s because GM had become highly geared and was affected by the international oil crisis and high interest rates. When Joseph retired in 1980 three strategic problems could be identified:

☐ GM was over-reliant on the UK (90% of turnover).
☐ IDV were inadequately represented in America, a key market for spirits.
☐ Many hotels needed up-grading if they were to capitalize upon the increase in tourism, especially from America.

The new Chief Executive, Stanley Grinstead, sought mainly to consolidate and build, concentrating on America. GM acquired its American spirits distributor, Liggett and Myers, in 1980. Liggett also manufactured cigarettes but the tobacco interests were quickly sold off. GM bought Inter-Continental hotels from Pan American and adopted a strategy of re-positioning its hotels. Lower grade properties were divested. GM concentrated on exploiting its major brand names and also bought Pearle Health Products in America. By the mid-1980s hotels contributed 19% of turnover and 6% of profits. The breweries were suffering as lager became more popular at the expense of bitter beers.

Sir Allen Sheppard, who took over in 1986, chose to focus on those businesses where GM could obtain world market strength and divest everything else. The major acquisitions were Heublein (1987), owners of Smirnoff Vodka, the world's second largest spirits brand, and Pillsbury. Pillsbury's main brands are Green Giant, Burger King and Häagen Dazs ice cream. After divestments over half GM's revenue is now earned in America.

IDV boasts over ten of the leading spirits in the world and has approximately 10% of the world market. The brands include Smirnoff and Popov vodka, J & B whisky, Gilbey's Gin, Malibu, Croft and Bailey's Irish Cream, the result of a joint venture with Express Dairies. IDV also distribute wines, owning Piat d'Or, and retail wines and spirits through their Peter Dominic stores.

GM's structure is decentralized and it is traditional that managers are seen as transferable between companies in the group. Their success has always relied upon synergy and the sharing of skills and expertise. Whilst the strategy has changed dramatically the structure and culture has been more consistent.

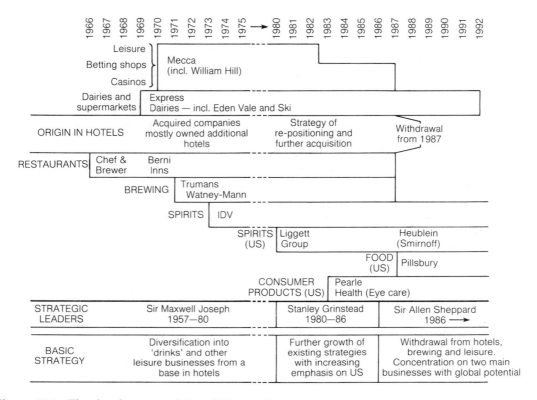

Figure 17.3 The development of Grand Metropolitan.

Case 17.9
THORN–EMI

Thorn–EMI was formed in 1979 when the two companies merged. The first Chairman, Richard Cave, sought to consolidate the merged group and make Thorn–EMI a leader in the diverse fields of information technology, industrial products, entertainment and leisure. In 1983 Cave was succeeded by Peter Laister, an internal appointment, and he chose to expand the strategy and take Thorn–EMI into a number of new areas, most notably semiconductors. Inmos, a joint UK–US manufacturer of sophisticated computer memory chips and backed with UK government capital, was bought. Growth became dependent mostly upon new acquisitions. By the mid-1980s the company was perceived as a 'lumbering giant'.

In 1983 Thorn–EMI had bought a software house called Software Sciences, whose founder, Colin Southgate, joined the company and rose to be Chief Executive by 1987 and more recently, Chairman. Southgate concluded Thorn–EMI faced two major strategic problems. First, the company was too diverse, with a consequent lack of focus on core businesses and, second, the company was not big enough in most of its markets to really benefit from economies of scale. He feared a loss of earnings and ultimately acquisition.

A major divestment programme was begun, and, over three years, some 60 companies worldwide were sold. These included property companies, telecommunications, television and video manufacture, and Inmos. More recently Kenwood (consumer appliances) has been divested, and gradually lighting products are also being sold. A small, focused, acquisition programme has sought to build in key product areas. Thorn–EMI was concentrating on products where it felt it could achieve an important world market share. These were:

☐ Rental and retail, including Granada, DER, Rumbelows and the HMV music shops in the UK plus interests in Europe and America.
☐ Technology – primarily software and security systems.
☐ Music, where it is vertically integrated. EMI Records developed through the acquisition of a series of major labels, and in the 1990s has been strengthened dramatically by the purchase of, first, Chrysalis Music, and, in 1992, Virgin Music. Thorn–EMI is clearly amongst the world leaders in the music industry, competing with Sony (CBS), Time-Warner (Warner-Elektra-Atlantic labels) and Polygram. Thorn–EMI is the world's leading music publisher, and is also one of the few manufacturers of compact discs.

Thorn has a controlling interest in Thames Television which it acquired more by chance than design.

Licensing

Licensing is an arrangement whereby a company is allowed to manufacture a product or service which has been designed by someone else and is protected by a patent. Companies in different countries are often involved. Pilkington, for example, patented float glass and then licensed its production throughout the world. Pilkington earned money from the arrangements and established world leadership; they would not have been able to afford to establish production plants around the world. In contrast Mary Quant, designer of cosmetics, tights, footwear, beds and bed linen, has never manufactured the products she designs. They are all licensed; and some are marketed under the Quant name and some under the manufacturer's name (Myers beds and Dorma bed linen). One argument in favour of this arrangement has been that production and labour relations problems are avoided, enabling the business to concentrate on the areas in which it has expertise and competitive advantage.

THE SELECTION OF A STRATEGY

The issue of what constitutes a good strategic choice is the subject of Chapter 21, but it is important here to emphasize that the strategic choices described above may not be real options for an organization at any given time. Theoretically they may exist as alternatives; realistically they could not be implemented. Equally, certain alternatives may be forced on organizations.

Whilst internal or external growth strategies might be preferred to fulfil objectives and fill the planning gap, disinvestment strategies may be required because of competitor or other environmental pressures. Strategies are only feasible if they can be implemented; a desire to grow through horizontal or vertical integration, concentric or conglomerate diversification, may require a suitable acquisition to be available at a price the company can afford to pay. An inability to raise money for any reason can act as a constraint on a particular choice. If management skills are not available to manage a merger or acquisition it may prove sensible to avoid or delay such a choice, however desirable it might be. Penrose's (1959) argument that growth is limited by the organization's spare resources, particularly management, was discussed in Chapter 5. The ability to succeed with product or market development will be dependent on the firm's relative strength and power in relation to competition; there may be competitive barriers to successful implementation.

Whichever strategy is selected issues of competitive advantage and implementation become paramount. Chances of success increase if there is an opportunity to create and sustain competitive advantage.

The influence and preference of the strategic leader will be a major determinant of the strategy selected. The strategic leader will also build the organization structure, and ideally the strategy and structure will mould together to generate synergy from the various activities. This in turn will depend upon the organization culture. Hence there is a relationship between strategy, structure, leadership and culture. When there is a change of leadership there may well be a change of strategy and in turn of structure and culture; when strategies fail to meet up to expectations, there may be a change of leadership. Cases 17.8, Grand Metropolitan, and 17.9, Thorn–EMI, are both examples of companies whose corporate strategies have undergone major changes of direction and focus. In both cases the developments can be linked to changes in strategic leader.

SUMMARY

In this chapter we have outlined the strategic alternatives which firms select to meet objectives and constraints, and the means by which they might be implemented. It has been mentioned that at any particular time all the options will not be realistically available to an organization. A firm in real difficulties is less likely to be considering major growth options than disinvestment strategies, for example. It has also been shown how individual strategies can be combined, and how strategies are changed over time and with changes of strategic leadership.

Specifically we have

☐ described briefly the no change, internal growth, external growth, disinvestment and combination strategies;
☐ considered some of the special problems involved when the strategic change has an international dimension;
☐ discussed how organic growth, acquisition, merger, joint venture, franchising and licensing can be used to implement the strategy;
☐ emphasized the linkage between strategy, strategic leadership, structure and culture.

CHECKLIST OF KEY TERMS AND CONCEPTS

You should refer back to Figure 17.1 and ensure that you understand conceptually all the strategic alternatives incorporated in the diagram.

QUESTIONS AND RESEARCH ASSIGNMENTS

Text related

1. For each of the following strategic alternatives, list why you think an organization might select this particular strategy, what they would expect to gain, and where the

problems and limitations are. If you can, think of an example of each one from your own experience.

- ☐ Do nothing; no change
- ☐ Concentration
- ☐ Market development
- ☐ Product development
- ☐ Innovation
- ☐ Horizontal integration
- ☐ Vertical integration
- ☐ Concentric diversification
- ☐ Conglomerate diversification
- ☐ Retrenchment
- ☐ Turnaround
- ☐ Divestment
- ☐ Liquidation

2. What are the relative advantages and disadvantages of organic growth as opposed to external growth strategies?

Library based

3. When MFI was bought back from Asda in 1987, considerable loan funding was involved. In the 1988–9 financial year operating profits were £92 million but net interest payments took £50 million of this. During 1989 consumer spending on the types of products that MFI sells fell. Moreover, interest rates have risen.

   As far as MFI are concerned, do you feel the merger with Asda was a strategic error?

   Having up-dated the situation, describe what strategic decisions have been taken by MFI to counter their decreasing profits.

4. What was the outcome of the bid by Tube Investments for Dowty? What impact has it had on TI as an aeroplane components supplier? Given the re-structuring which is taking pace in this industry, how significant do you believe the outcome was?

5. (a) What are the essential differences between an export, an international and a global organization?

   (b) What might be the most appropriate strategy for a sizeable UK-based company with international ambitions in the following industries? [Assume your choice could be implemented.]
      steel
      pharmaceuticals
      civil aircraft
      ladies' cosmetics.

6. For an organization of your choice, trace the changes of strategy and strategic direction over a period of time. Relate these changes to any changes of strategic leadership, structure and, wherever possible, culture.

7. In October 1988 Edinburgh Hibernian football club was floated successfully in the third market of the Stock Exchange. It was only the second professional football club in the UK to become a public company; Tottenham Hotspur was the first. One month later Hibernian acquired a pub/disco in Exeter, Devon, using funds generated by the flotation. In February 1989 Hibernian issued more shares to fund the purchase of Avon Inns, a property-based company also in the southwest of England. Avon owned 15 properties including hotels, pubs, wine bars and a DIY shop. Hibernian argued that these businesses would generate a cash flow to sustain the football interests. The company also has land adjacent to its stadium in Edinburgh which it could develop.

   In relation to the strategic alternatives outlined in the chapter, what was the Hibernian strategy?

   What further changes have been implemented since February 1989?

   How successful has the company been? In answering this question, consider what the appropriate measures of success should be.

REFERENCES

Bartlett, C and Ghoshal, S (1989) *Managing Across Borders: The Transnational Solution*, Harvard Business School Press.

Bartlett, C and Ghoshal, S (1992) What is a global manager? *Harvard Business Review*. September–October.

Chandler, A D (1990) The enduring logic of industrial success, *Harvard Business Review*, March–April.

Kay, J A (1990) Identifying the strategic market, *Business Strategy Review*, Spring.

Ohmae, K (1990) *The Borderless World*, Harper.

Penrose, E (1959) *The Theory of the Growth of the Firm*, Blackwell.

Peters, T J and Waterman, R H Jr (1982) *In Search of Excellence: Lessons from America's Best Run Companies*, Harper and Row.

Porter, M E (1990) *The Competitive Advantage of Nations*, Free Press.

Rappaport, A S and Halevi, S (1991) The computerless computer company, *Harvard Business Review*, July–August.

GROWTH STRATEGIES: DIVERSIFICATION, ACQUISITION AND JOINT VENTURE

18

LEARNING OBJECTIVES

After studying this chapter you should be able to

☐ identify the typical growth patterns of large companies;
☐ discuss the extent of diversification in the UK in relation to other countries;
☐ list why organizations might seek to diversify, often by acquisition;
☐ discuss the risk involved in this strategic alternative;
☐ explain why acquisitions often fail to bring the desired level of benefits;
☐ summarize the stages involved in designing an effective acquisition strategy;
☐ describe forms and examples of joint ventures and strategic alliances.

In this chapter we explore selected growth strategies: diversification, acquisition and joint ventures. The justifications for pursuing them are considered, together with research evidence about their relative success. In addition there is a section on effective acquisition strategies.

INTRODUCTION

In this chapter we look at selected aspects of growth strategies, namely diversification, mergers and acquisitions, strategic alliances (agreements between two or more companies) and joint ventures (alliances involving minority ownerships or the establishment of a new, jointly owned company). The advantages and potential drawbacks of external growth strategies are compared with internal (or organic) growth in Table 18.1. External growth strategies are popular alternatives for many companies, particularly larger ones, but research suggests that they often fail to

Table 18.1 Alternative growth strategies

	Advantages	Possible drawbacks
Organic growth	□ Lower risk □ Allows for on-going learning □ More control	□ Slow □ Lack of early knowledge – may be misjudgements
Acquisition	□ Fast □ Buys presence, market share and expertise	□ Premium price may have to be paid □ High risk if any misjudgement □ Preferred organization may not be available □ May be difficult to sell unwanted assets
Strategic alliance	□ Cheaper than take-over □ Access to market knowledge □ Useful if acquisition impractical	□ Possible lack of control □ Potential managerial differences and problems
Joint venture	As for joint venture plus □ greater incentive and closer contact □ can lock out other competitors better	As for strategic alliance

meet expectations. Growth strategies need careful, thorough and objective analysis before they are pursued, and care and attention in implementation.

Most diversification by UK companies since the 1960s has been through acquisition and merger rather than the internal creation of new activity. A merger of two organizations will always be agreed mutually, and in some cases acquisition of one firm by another is friendly and agreed. In other cases proposed acquisitions are opposed and fought bitterly by managers in the threatened firm who try to persuade their shareholders that the company would be better off remaining under their control. These are typically known as take-overs, and when the bid succeeds a premium price is often paid. Although not all acquisitions are aimed at bringing about diversification, the majority appear to represent some form of diversification.

However, many acquisitions and mergers lead to disappointing results – profitability is reduced; synergy does not emerge. It is difficult to predict success or failure in advance, as issues of both strategy creation and implementation are involved. Changes in corporate strategy are generally more unpredictable and risky than those which concentrate on improving competitive and functional strategies. However, growth opportunities for the present products and markets may be limited and insufficient to fill the planning gap. Few products and ideas cannot be copied and so a company must build and retain a superior competitive position. Experience, applied properly, is of great importance in this. Nevertheless, well-executed acquisitions and diversifications can be sound and very good strategic moves.

We shall explore diversification and acquisition strategies by UK companies, and consider the major reasons why a number are regarded as failures. In addition we shall consider how to manage these strategies effectively. At the end of the chapter joint ventures and strategic alliances, again strategies which are increasing in popularity but sometimes characterized by disappointing results, are evaluated.

Implementation is the subject of Chapters 22–24. However creative and imaginative strategies may be, they can only be regarded as effective if they can be implemented successfully.

Table 18.2 Diversification by UK and international companies

	United Kingdom				International comparisons			
	% of top 200 companies				France, % of top 100	Germany, % of top 100	USA, % of top 500	
	1950	1960	1970	1980	1970	1970	1970	1980
Single	35	20	11	8	16	22	10	0
Dominant	40	43	29	27	32	22	41	22
Related	20	28	49	48	42	38	36	54
Conglomerate/unrelated	5	9	11	17	10	18	13	24

Sources: Channon, D F (1983) *Strategy and Structure in British Industry*, Macmillan; Dyas, G P and Thanheiser, H T (1976) *The Emerging European Enterprise: Strategy and Structure in French and German Industry*, Macmillan.

DIVERSIFICATION AND ACQUISITION BY UK COMPANIES

The increasing tendency to diversify

Channon (1983) has analysed the extent to which the largest firms in the UK have become increasingly diversified since 1950. He used the Times Top 200 companies as his database and categorized them as follows:

☐ *Single product companies* Not less than 95% of sales derived from one basic business.
☐ *Dominant product companies* More than 70%, but less than 95%, of sales from one major business.
☐ *Related product companies* Companies whose sales are distributed amongst a series of **related** businesses, where no single business accounts for 70% of sales. This would include companies who had pursued strategies of vertical or horizontal integration or concentric diversification.
☐ *Conglomerate/unrelated product companies* Companies whose sales are distributed amongst a series of **unrelated** businesses, again where no single business accounts for 70% of sales.

Channon contends that typically a company will start life as a single product enterprise and then graduate through the dominant product stage to become a related business,

before finally emerging into a conglomerate. However, he emphasizes that companies do not have to follow this particular growth pattern. Some will miss one or more of the natural stages; others will choose to stay in one form and not change.

Table 18.2 illustrates the changes in the structure of the largest UK enterprises between 1950 and 1980, and compares the structural patterns with those of the largest 500 US companies in 1970 and 1980. Utilizing data from Dyas and Thanheiser (1976) some comparisons with French and German companies in 1970 are also provided.

In 1950 only 25% of the top 200 companies in the UK had become diversified to the related or unrelated stage, and of these only 5% were classified as conglomerates. By 1980 the respective percentages had increased steadily to 65% and 17% respectively. This compares with percentages of 78% and 24% for the largest 500 companies in America. Over the same period the number of concentrated single product companies had declined from 35% to 8%.

In contrast with 1970 UK figures of 60% (related and unrelated) and 11% (conglomerate/unrelated) the respective figures for France were 52% and 10%, and for Germany 56% and 18%.

During the late 1980s and early 1990s **conglomerate** diversification has decreased in popularity, and instead companies have sought to grow in related areas where skills and competences are more clearly transferable. Acquirers now typically seek to avoid diversifications that are unrelated to their basic businesses on more than one of the following dimensions: geography, technology, type of product/market or service/market, and the style of corporate parenting required (i.e. cultural and leadership issues).

As markets and industries become increasingly global a certain minimum size and market share is often thought to be necessary for competitive viability. This is known as **critical mass** and it is one explanation for the growing incidence of mergers and alliances between related and competing organizations. Critical mass is important to ensure that

□ there is sufficient investment in R & D to keep pace with the market leader;
□ the important cost benefits of the experience curve can be achieved;
□ marketing activities achieve visibility and a competitive presence. This might require a wide product range and good coverage globally.

Much of the growth and diversification by UK companies has been brought about by merger and acquisition. Some of this has been outside the UK, mostly in America.

Identify the strengths of your business and build on them. Do not diversify into unrelated areas. Find out what your managers can do and let them have a go.

It is a common fault of British companies to spend large amounts of money acquiring other companies, and remove from the budget those activities that increase costs and overheads in the short term, but which would build the existing business. Always find money to invest in the future by building on strengths.

Leslie Hill, Chairman and Chief Executive,Central Independent Television plc

---

Statistics from J P Mervis, London-based corporate finance advisers, suggest that, of acquisitions by UK companies in Europe and America in the late 1980s, over 90% of the spending was in the US. Recent acquisitions have involved some well-known companies and brand names. Grand Metropolitan, the leisure and hotels group, have taken over Pillsbury (the Jolly Green Giant foods group) after an acrimonious battle; and Marks & Spencer have bought Brooks Brothers, an upmarket menswear retailer. Marks & Spencer have experienced some early implementation difficulties with this acquisition.

In the 1990s links with European companies will inevitably grow in popularity. Because of both competitive requirements and regulatory and cultural issues it seems likely that many of these links will be between existing competitors and take the form of joint ventures and strategic alliances rather than mergers or acquisitions. On occasions there will be clear arguments in favour of linking two organizations, but pressure from shareholders, managers or governments may mean acquisition is not feasible.

Causes and effects of diversification activity

An exploration of the UK trend

Constable (1986) argues that the UK has experienced the highest rate of diversification amongst the leading industrial nations since 1950, and as a result now has the most concentrated economic structure. Industrial concentration was defined in Chapter 7.

The minimum scale for effective survival is always rising. A niche can easily become a tomb.

Lord Weinstock, Managing Director, GEC

Coincidentally this trend has been accompanied by a trend to the weakest small company sector.

The process of diversification has been achieved largely through acquisitions and mergers, which have taken place at a higher rate than that experienced in other countries, especially Japan where there are few large-scale acquisitions. Constable contends that Japan, America and Germany have concentrated more on product and market development and on adding value to current areas of activity, and that partly as a result of this they have enjoyed greater economic prosperity. Hilton (1987) has suggested that one reason behind this is that in Germany and Japan there is a greater emphasis on the banking system's providing funding, rather than shareholders, and this has influenced both the number of take-over bids and expectations of performance.

As a result of the diversification, merger and acquisition activity the UK has developed a number of large companies with sizeable asset bases and domestic market shares, but few which are dominant in their industries or sectors at a world or even a European level. Constable argues that the high level of strategic energy devoted to these strategies has created an illusion of real growth, with an emphasis on the shorter-term financial aspects of strategic expertise as opposed to the operational and market-based aspects which, long term, are of great significance. Arguably too much top management time and effort has been spent on seeking and implementing acquisitions, and avoiding being acquired.

Although the nature of investment funding and stock market expectations have been significant influences behind the diversification and acquisition activity in the UK, there are other explanations. If a company has growth objectives and there are finite limits to the potential in existing markets, as well as barriers to becoming more international in order to penetrate related markets abroad, diversification may be an attractive option. However, there may already be intense competition in domestic markets which the company considers entering, especially if the industries involved are attractive and profitable. The competition may be both UK producers and imported products and services and may be compounded by active rivalry for share and dominance. In such circumstances, direct entry may seem less appropriate than acquisition of an existing competitor.

As acquisitions and mergers increase industrial concentration and the power of certain large organizations, government policy on competition may act as a restraint on particular lines of development for certain companies. Large firms may be encouraged to diversify into unrelated businesses where there is little apparent threat to the interests of consumers, rather than attempting horizontal integration which might be prevented by the intervention of the Monopolies and Mergers Commission. Joint ventures offer a way round this constraint.

A contrasting argument suggests that a company which has grown large, successful and profitable in a particular industry is likely to seek diversification whilst it is strong and has the resources to move into new business areas effectively. The benefits of such a move are likely to seem more realizable by the acquisition of an existing organization than by the slower build-up of new internal activities. This type of growth requires finance, which generally has been available for successful companies.

When companies are acquired then both sales and absolute profits increase quickly, and sometimes markedly. But does profitability also increase? Are assets being utilized more effectively in the combined organization? Is synergy really being obtained? Or are the increased sales and profits merely an illusion of growth?

Finally, Constable offers two further arguments to explain the strategic activity in the UK. First, strategic leaders of large organizations are typically aggressive in nature, and acquisition is an expression of aggression. Second, there is a commonly held belief that the larger a company becomes the less likely it is itself to be a victim of a take-over bid. Hence, whilst diversification is essentially offensive and designed to bring about expansion and growth, it could be argued that on occasions it is a defensive strategy.

Reasons for diversification and acquisition

There are a number of sound and logical reasons why a firm might seek to diversify through acquisition. Some of these have been mentioned above; others are discussed below. Most are economic. The fact that diversification and acquisition strategies often prove less successful than the expectations for them is more likely to result from the choice of company to acquire and from issues and problems of implementation than the fact that the idea of diversification was misguided. This will be explored further later in the chapter.

Diversification may be chosen because the existing business is seen as being vulnerable in some way: growth potential may be limited; further investment in internal growth may not be justified; the business may be threatened by new technology. Some businesses are under-valued by the stock market, making them vulnerable to take-over if they do not diversify. Some products and businesses may currently be valuable cash generators, but with little prospect of future growth. In other words they may be cash cows generating funds which need to be re-invested elsewhere to build a future for the company. Leading on from this, the company may have growth objectives which stretch beyond the potential of existing businesses. Case 18.1 on Trafalgar House explores a strategy of diversification which stretches over a number of years and which has been based on a series of acquisitions. Trafalgar House's acquisitions have normally been in mature industries, and consequently

corporate growth has required more acquisitions because the companies they have bought have offered only limited internal growth potential.

Diversification may occur because a company has developed a particular strength or expertise and feels it could benefit from transferring this asset into other, possibly unrelated, businesses. The strength might be financial (high cash reserves or borrowing capacity), marketing, technical or managerial. If genuine synergy potential exists, both the existing and newly acquired businesses can benefit from a merger or acquisition.

A company which has become stale or sleepy, or which has succession problems at the strategic leader level, may see an acquisition as a way of obtaining fresh ideas and new management, and this may seem more important than the extent to which the businesses are related.

Some diversification and acquisition decisions are concerned with reducing risk and establishing or restoring an acceptable balance of yesterday's, today's and tomorrow's products in a complex portfolio. This will be especially attractive where a company is relying currently on yesterday's products.

Some strategic changes in this category will result from the ego or the ambitions of the strategic leader, who may feel that he or she can run any type of business successfully, regardless of the degree of unrelatedness. Some may be very keen to grow quickly, possibly to avoid take-over, and acquisitions may happen because a company is available for purchase rather than as the outcome of a careful and detailed analysis.

It will be suggested later that the major beneficiaries of an acquisition are often the existing shareholders of the company being acquired. Consequently it is sometimes argued that the self-interest of the City and large institutional shareholders might be behind certain mergers and acquisitions.

Case 18.2 looks at the diversification strategy of Yorkshire Water since privatization.

Case 18.1
TRAFALGAR HOUSE

In the 1970s Trafalgar House (TH) grew into a large, acquisitive, diversified conglomerate from a base in property and construction. Acquisitions included Cunard, best known for the QE2 cruise liner, The Ritz Hotel in London, and Beaverbrook Newspapers, publishers of the *Daily Express* and *Sunday Express*. Newspapers have since been divested. In the 1980s further acquisitions have concentrated on shipbuilding and marine construction linked to North Sea oil.

By 1991 Trafalgar House were diversified into five main areas: engineering; construction; cargo shipping; passenger shipping and hotels; and residential and commercial property. In July 1991 TH acquired Davy Corporation, which was in financial difficulty, and thus created the UK's largest engineering contractor and a globally competitive technology base. At the same time most of the cargo shipping interests were sold to P & O, and it is assumed that TH will sell its leisure interests at some time when the price is right, and thereby focus on property, construction and engineering. A joint venture with another shipping operator might be a suitable strategy for the cruise liners.

Trafalgar House have tended to concentrate on acquiring well-known names in declining or mature industries which involve only low or modest technology. Generally their targets have been under-performing and in some difficulties as a result of ineffective management and strategies and are capable of being turned around. Early acquisitions were bought with new shares; later ones were primarily for cash.

After acquiring a company Trafalgar concentrate their managerial changes at the top, normally removing some or all of the Board and promoting promising middle managers. Tight financial controls and systems are imposed. Where appropriate some parts of the businesses are sold off to enable Trafalgar to concentrate on selected market segments, but normally businesses are retained rather than sold once they have been turned around.

Whilst there has often been a quick turnaround and return to healthier profits, acquired companies in mature slow growth industries do not offer long-term growth potential through development and further investment. Corporate growth therefore requires further acquisition – assuming that the right companies can be found, at the right price, and that Trafalgar House can raise the necessary funds without compromising their gearing.

The acquisition of Davy increased TH's gearing substantially. This coincided with the serious impact of the economic recession on the majority of this businesses, especially property development, construction and upmarket leisure. Ironically the prestige brand names taken over and revived by Trafalgar have again lost much of their sparkle. The share price has fallen dramatically and TH may itself be vulnerable to take-over. Late in 1992, for example, Hongkong Land began to build up a shareholding.

Case 18.2
YORKSHIRE WATER

Since being privatized in 1989 most of the ten water companies in the UK have pursued diversification strategies. The core business activities are water supply and the management of waste water (i.e. sewerage). Prices and quality standards are closely regulated, and consequently the diversification is aimed at offsetting the perceived risks and constraints inherent in regulated businesses. The most popular activity has been waste management, the collection and disposal of industrial and domestic waste. For example, Severn Trent Water have acquired Biffa, and Wessex have formed a joint venture with Waste Management of the US, one of the world's largest companies in the industry.

Yorkshire Water has created two separate, but linked, businesses: YW Services to control the core businesses, and YW Enterprises for other commercial ventures. Their distinct missions are summarized in Box 5.1.
YW Enterprises is active in:

- □ *Waste management* – industrial effluents and clinical waste.
- □ *Engineering consultancy and support* – a joint venture with Babcock International. Since 1989 YW have been investing in treatment plants (mainly) and piping networks. By the mid-1990s piping will be more important, and this will free up engineering resources which the joint venture will seek to deploy and exploit.
- □ *'Pipeline Products'* – the sale of existing stores items to external customers. At present there are no plans to develop further into merchanting.
- □ *'Waterlink'* – a network of approved subcontractor plumbers. YW provide an arrangement service.
- □ *Laboratory services*
- □ *Management training* – primarily exploiting existing markets and competences.
- □ *Property development* – representing 'real' diversification.

The Director General of OFWAT, the industry regulator, has stated he is not going to ignore these strategic developments. 'Customers of core services must not be affected adversely.' For example, the water companies are likely to be prevented from selling services from the associated businesses to the core at contrived prices which benefit shareholders at the expense of captive water customers. Additionally, 'the required investment funds for the water supply services must not be put at risk'.

Yorkshire Water has stated that it does not intend to build and then manage a diversified corporation. Once the appropriate business has been constructed, with YW's resources deployed effectively, the layers will be peeled away systematically until only the core business remains. This will entail divesting certain activities into either wholly owned or independent subsidiaries (with appropriate contractual linkages) and more joint ventures.

The strategy aims to offset the risks inherent in a regulated industry.

RESEARCH INTO DIVERSIFICATION AND ACQUISITION

The relative success of diversification and acquisition

A number of research studies have been carried out in both Britain and America on the relative success of diversification and acquisition strategies. There are some general conclusions as well as specific findings, and the major ones are documented here. In the main most of the findings are consistent.

It is important to emphasize, however, that this is a particularly difficult area to research because of problems with data availability. If, for example, one is attempting to study the change in a company's performance before and after an acquisition, then one needs several years of data to ensure that longer-term effects are studied once any teething problems of early implementation are overcome. However, company W may have acquired company X in, say, 1985 and as a result been included in a research study which began the same year. Ideally the performance of the combined WX would be compared with the previous performance of W and X as independent companies. If company W is naturally acquisitive it may divest some unattractive businesses from X during 1986 in order to raise money to help finance the purchase of company Y in 1987 and company Z in 1989. An on-going programme of this nature means that it is impossible to compare the long-term effects of one particular acquisition on an organization. The original sample continually reduces. In the same way a comparison of the performance over a period of time of companies which might be classified as single, dominant, related and unrelated product will be affected by firms which change category as a result of the strategies they follow.

General conclusions from the research suggest that no more than 50% of diversification through acquisition strategies are successful. Quite simply, the synergies which were considered to exist prior to acquisition are frequently not realized. There is also agreement that shareholders in a company which is taken over or acquired benefit from selling their shares to the bidder, who often pays an unwarranted premium. Shareholders who accept shares in the acquiring company instead of cash, together with the existing shareholders in that company, tend to be rewarded less in the longer term in terms of share price appreciation. As mentioned earlier in the chapter, the research findings also support the contention that the profitability gains attributable to internal investments in companies are generally much greater than those accruing to acquisition investments.

Lorenz (1986) suggests that research in this field can be classified into four schools: accounting, economic, financial and managerial. The accounting school have concentrated on post-merger profitability in the 1970s, and their general conclusion, accepting sampling problems, is that few acquisitions resulted in increased profitability and for most the effect was neutral. Some had negative effects. Cowling, Stoneman and Cubbin (1979), members of the economic school, concluded that there has been an increase in market power but no increase in economic efficiency.

The financial school have analysed share price movements and concluded that bid premiums are often as high as 20–40%. Many take-overs in both the UK and the USA are hostile and opposed aggressively, and this often leads to the payment of high premiums. Five years after acquisition, half of the American acquirers had out-performed the stock market; the other half had performed below average. The success rate is thought to be lower in the UK. One issue in this type of research concerns whether or not stock market prices and performance accurately reflect economic performance.

Kitching (1973), categorized in the managerial school, has concluded that the less related an acquisition is, the more risky it is. Additionally it is more risky to move into new markets than into new technology, assuming that the two are not achieved together. Critics of this conclusion argue that related acquisitions are more likely to be in attractive industries, and consequently more likely to succeed for this reason.

Specific research findings

British research

Reed and Luffman (1986) analysed the performance of 349 of the largest 1000 companies in the UK between 1970 and 1980. These 349 were selected because their product base did not change during the decade. They concluded that the more diversified companies grew fastest in terms of sales and earnings, and the capital value of their shares declined by the lowest amount. The respective figures, after accounting for inflation, were 2.1% average annual growth in sales and 1.3% average annual growth in earnings before interest and tax. The capital value of their shares declined by 3.44% per year on average. Dominant product companies were the next most successful group against these measures, followed by related companies and finally single product companies.

However, the return on capital employed ratios were not consistent with the growth figures. Dominant product companies were the most profitable (19.1% on average), followed by single product companies (18.1%), related product companies (16.9%) and finally unrelated product companies (16.7%). Reed and Luffman conclude that this is a result of the complexities of the inherent changes rather than of the strategy itself.

These findings replicated US research by Rumelt at the Harvard Business School (1974), and they suggest that the contention by Peters and Waterman (1982) that successful companies 'stick to the knitting' is justified.

Meeks (1977) looked at post-merger profitability during the late 1960s and early 1970s. He started with a sample of 213 firms, reducing the sample size annually as the organizations concerned changed their strategies again in some significant way. In four years the sample halved; and after seven years there were only 21 companies left from the original 213. Meeks looked at the percentage of remaining firms each year and considered whether their profitability had increased or decreased. In the first year after the merger 34% of the firms exhibited lower combined profitability than they had enjoyed previously as independent companies. This percentage increased during the first four years to a high of 66%, with half the original sample left. At the end of seven years of research, 62% of the remaining 21 companies were showing reduced profitability.

Meeks concluded that mergers which involved related businesses increased market power, but this was not the case for conglomerate mergers. All types experienced lower profitability and reflected reduced efficiency as a result of the merger activity. Greater size primarily yields higher salaries for executives, a generally more stable corporate performance and increased immunity from takeover.

American research

Salter and Weinhold (1982) studied 36 widely diversified US companies between 1967 and 1977 and concluded that 'diversification strategies designed to raise performance actually brought return on equity down'. In 1967 the companies concerned were producing returns which were 20% above the Fortune 500 average, and consequently they could afford to diversify. In 1977 they were 18% below average.

Porter (1987) analysed the strategies and performance of 33 large American conglomerates during the 1970s, and based his general conclusions upon the pattern of later divestment of the acquisitions. Well over half his sample divested at least some of their acquisitions, and a typical retention period seemed to average five to six years. Companies which moved into related activities generally performed better than those which diversified into unrelated areas. From this research Porter suggested three tests for successful diversification, and these are discussed later in this chapter.

McKinsey, in research published in 1988, have documented the performance of 116 large UK and US companies since 1972. Sixty per cent had failed to earn back the cost of capital on the funds invested in acquisitions, and this figure rose to 86% for large unrelated acquisitions.

Nesbitt and King (1989) examined the progress of 1800 US companies between 1978 and 1988 and concluded that corporate performance is dependent upon strategy implementation rather than the strategy itself. The degree of diversification as opposed to specialization, taken in isolation, has little impact.

Burgman (1985) studied 600 US acquisitions which took place between 1974 and 1978 and concluded that:

☐ the higher the premium paid to acquire a company, the less likely it was to be successful;

☐ prospects for success were greater where the acquirer had a functional appreciation of the business being acquired;

☐ success depended upon the ability to retain key managers in the acquired company;

☐ larger acquisitions were often more successful, possibly because the sheer size and financial commitment necessitated a thorough appraisal beforehand.

These research programmes and papers by Biggadike (1979) and Kitching (1967) suggest a number of reasons why acquisitions fail, and these are considered below.

Why acquisitions fail

It has been mentioned previously that a key reason why acquisitions fail is that they do not generate the synergy which was anticipated or at least hoped for. This is particularly true for conglomerate rather than concentric diversification. Case 18.3 looks at the search for synergy by Daimler–Benz. In general it is easier to gain synergy from production and operations than it is from marketing. It is difficult to gain real additional benefit from selling more than one product or service into one market.

Linked to this issue is the reality that in many cases the real weaknesses of the acquired company are hidden until after the acquisition, and consequently are under-estimated. Also under-estimated are the cultural and managerial problems of merging two companies and then running them as one. As a result insufficient managerial resources are devoted to the process of merging, and hence the hoped-for synergy remains elusive.

This problem typically arises because the acquiring company concludes that the skills which were to be transferred to new acquisition in order to generate the synergy are in reality not available. They are already fully committed and in the end are not transferred.

Key managers who have been responsible for the past growth and success of the company being acquired may choose to leave rather than stay with the new conglomerate. Where this happens, and depending on the extent of the contribution of these managers, past successes may not be repeatable.

Further reasons concern the amount paid for the acquisition, and the extent of the premium. For a contested take-over in particular, the bidding company may become over-enthusiastic and optimistic about the prospects, over-stretch itself financially and

Case 18.3
DAIMLER–BENZ – A SEARCH FOR SYNERGY

Daimler–Benz is Europe's largest manufacturing group, and comprises:

		% Total sales
Mercedes–Benz	commercial vehicles	27
	passenger cars	40
AEG	electrical and electronic products	15
Dasa	aerospace	14
Debis	financial information services	4

The majority of the non-vehicle businesses were acquired systematically during the 1980s. Daimler–Benz's objectives were, first, to offset stagnating vehicle sales by expanding into high-technology growth markets and, second, to strengthen the automotive businesses by applying advanced technologies from the new acquisitions. Their challenge is to achieve this potential synergy. The time-scale to realize the benefits has been set at ten years, and the important institutional shareholders have pledged their support.

Initially vehicles have had to subsidize the new businesses; and critics have argued that the second of the two objectives did not require ownership and that in reality the synergy argument is being used as an afterthought to justify the diversification.

Daimler–Benz's strategic dilemma is that both AEG and Dasa require turning around at the same time vehicles are under threat. Japanese car manufacturers are becoming increasingly competitive in the more upmarket sectors, and Mercedes need new, competitive models to prevent being squeezed into too small a niche. AEG, which was rescued from near bankruptcy, was already diversified (including white goods, typewriters and traffic control systems) and was itself searching for synergies. Some business areas were losing money. Dasa (Deutsche Aerospace) comprised a number of separately acquired companies and there is some duplication of activities. Messerschmitt supplies the European Airbus project, but mostly with less sophisticated parts.

A series of strategic alliances has been mooted – with Mitsubishi (cars), Pratt and Whitney (aero engines) and the other members of the Airbus consortium (to develop commuter aircraft and helicopters); and in 1992 Daimler–Benz acquired the Dutch aerospace company, Fokker. Fokker manufacture military and commuter aircraft and contribute to the Airbus. The joint venture between AEG and Electrolux was featured in Case 17.5

Daimler–Benz is renowned for engineering excellence, product quality and marketing. It now needs new organizational and political skills if the diversification strategy is to succeed during the 1990s.

Source: de Jonquières, G and Fisher, A (1991) Sizeable challenge for the colossus, *Financial Times*, 15 March.

Case 18.4
QUAKER OATS – STRATEGY IMPLEMENTATION PROBLEMS

The American Quaker Oats Corporation is best known in the UK for porridge and breakfast cereals, but its largest US business is pet foods. This industry has become increasingly competitive as cats have replaced dogs in popularity (cats are more suitable for one-person households and where everyone is out all day) – and cats eat less food. Quaker Oats acquired a competitor, Gaines, in 1986 'to achieve critical mass and scale economies'. However, the expected benefits and synergy were over-estimated and not immediately forthcoming. The merged organizations possessed a wide range of products and some brand re-positioning was required; key managers left; and competition intensified.

Quaker Oats now had 15% of the market, still a long way behind the leader, Ralston Purina, who held 28%. Moreover, they were strong in different segments – Quaker Oats were most active with semi-moist products, Ralston Purina with dry. But Ralston had also sought to acquire Gaines! Ralston followed up by buying another semi-moist business, invested heavily in it, and slashed prices dramatically. Quaker's margins and profits were forced down. Smaller competitors were also affected, and their further aggression had a spiralling effect.

Quaker Oats also diversified with toys, and experienced further, but different, difficulties. Quaker had acquired Fisher-Price (pre-school toys) in 1969, but were threatened in the 1980s when Mattel licensed several Disney characters and launched a new, competing range. Quaker responded by moving into electronic toys, which it identified as an attractive growth market. But misjudgements and production difficulties caused retailers to start cancelling orders. Eventually Fisher-Price was floated off as an independent business.

Source: Saporito, B (1990) How Quaker Oats got rolled, *Fortune*, 8 October.

---

then not be able to afford the necessary investment to generate benefits and growth in the new company. When a premium is paid the acquirer is likely to set high targets initially for the new company in order to try and recover the premium quickly. When these targets are missed, because they are unrealistic, enthusiasm is lost and feelings of hostility may develop. It can be argued that if synergy really is available, price is less significant as an issue, and a premium may well be justifiable. On the other hand, if an acquisition is fundamentally misconceived a

low or a cheap price will not make it successful at the implementation stage.

Finally the reaction of competitors may be misjudged. See Case 18.4.

The difficulties apply in service businesses as well as manufacturing, as the following examples illustrate. General Accident acquired a related insurance business in New Zealand in 1988 and as part of the purchase inherited the NZI Bank. The loan book deteriorated in the worldwide recession, and, lacking the necessary turnaround skills, General Accident decided to close the bank.

The Prudential similarly chose to exit estate agencies after incurring huge losses. They had over-paid for their acquisitions and the anticipated learning and synergy was slow to materialize. Some would argue the strategy of linking insurance with estate agencies was misjudged; others that the problems were really those of implementation. In particular, the Prudential attempted to exercise central control over a disparate group of acquisitions.

In reality acquisition is an uncertain strategy. However sound the economic justification may appear to be, implementation or managerial issues ultimately determine success or failure. These issues are the subject of the next section.

Issues in diversification and acquisition

Where two companies choose to merge there is the opportunity for a reasonably comprehensive assessment of relative strengths and weaknesses, although it does not follow that one or both will not choose to hide certain significant weaknesses. In the case of a contested take-over only limited information will be available. Crucially the information which will affect the ease or difficulty of merging the two cultures and organizations, and implementing the changes, is less freely available than financial data. As a result financial analysis may be used to justify the acquisition, but it will not answer questions relating to implementation. Table 18.3 highlights the significant information which is unlikely to be available until after the acquisition.

The following list of questions and issues indicates the key considerations which should be addressed by a company before it acquires another:

☐ how the acquiring company should restructure itself in order to absorb the new purchase, and what implications this will have for existing businesses and people

Table 18.3 Information available before and after an acquisition

Before	After
Organization charts	Inner philosophy and culture
Data on salaries of top management	Real quality of staff in decision roles
Reasonably detailed information on board members and key executives – but only brief details on middle management	Salary and reward structures and systems
	Decision processes
	Interrelationships, power bases, hidden conflicts and organizational politics
Products	Individual objectives being pursued
Plants	
Corporate identity, image and reputation	
Past record, especially financial	

☐ what acceptable minimum and maximum sizes are for proposed diversifications in relation to present activities

☐ what degree of risk it is appropriate for the company to take

☐ how to value a proposed acquisition and how much to pay

☐ how to maintain good relationships with key managers during negotiations to try to ensure that they stay afterwards

☐ how to maintain momentum and interest in both companies after a successful offer

☐ how fast to move in merging organizational parts and sorting out problems

☐ reporting relationships and the degree of independence allowed to the acquired company, particularly where the business is unrelated

☐ whether and how to send in a new management team.

Some of these issues are considered in the next section where effective acquisition strategies are discussed, but many of them are taken up in later chapters which consider the implementation aspects of strategic change. Figure 18.1 illustrates that an effective strategy is one which is based upon good vision and sound implementation prospects. Vision is in relation to the organization's strengths

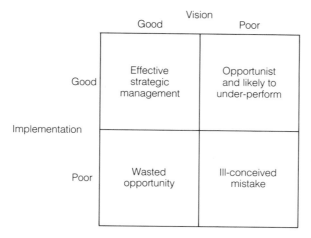

 shows a matrix with "Vision" along the top (Good, Poor) and "Implementation" along the left side (Good, Poor):

	Vision Good	Vision Poor
Implementation Good	Effective strategic management	Opportunist and likely to under-perform
Implementation Poor	Wasted opportunity	Ill-conceived mistake

Figure 18.1 Strategy creation and implementation. Based on a matrix devised by Booz, Allen and Hamilton.

and market opportunities, and an effective strategy will match these. In the context of diversification and acquisition, implementation relates to a consideration of how the two organizations will be merged together and the changes required to structures, cultures and systems in order to ensure that potential synergy is achieved. Poor vision and poor implementation will both cause strategic management to be less than effective. If the logic behind an acquisition is poor, then the merged corporation is likely to under-perform, however well the two companies might be managed as one corporate whole. If the vision is good but implementation is weak, under-performance is again likely because synergy will not be created.

If companies develop by a series of acquisitions it is quite typical for several banks to become involved. These could be spread world wide; their cultures and lending philosophies may differ; their levels of exposure will vary; the assets securing the loans will not be the same; and certain banks may see themselves as lenders to just one company rather than the whole organization. Problems are likely to arise if one of the banks gets into financial difficulties or if the company seeks to extend a loan or adjust the terms. The protracted re-structuring of Brent Walker in 1991/2 was a manifestation of this.

EFFECTIVE ACQUISITION STRATEGIES

A number of authors have suggested ways of improving the effectiveness of acquisition strategies.

Drucker (1982) argues that there are five rules for successful acquisitions.

☐ It is essential for the acquiring company to determine exactly what contribution it can make to the acquired company. It must be more than money.

☐ It is important to search for a company with a 'common core of unity', say in technology, markets or production processes.

☐ The acquiring company should value the products, services and customers of the company that it is taking over.

☐ Top management cover for the acquired company should be available in case key managers choose to leave after the acquisition.

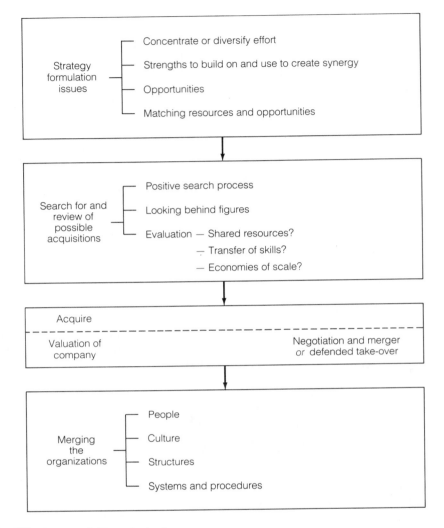

Figure 18.2   Effective acquisition strategies.

□ Within a year managers should have been promoted across company boundaries.

In a report entitled 'Making Acquisitions Work: Lessons from Companies' Successes and Mistakes', Business International (1988) offer the following guidelines.

□ **Plan first:** As a company, know exactly what you are going to do. Ascertain where the company being acquired has been, and maybe still is, successful, and ensure that it can be maintained – taking special

account of any dependence on key people. Appreciate also where it is weak. It is quite possible that it will have good products but overheads which are too high.

□ **Implement quickly:** People in the acquired company expect decisive action, and delay prolongs speculation. At the same time it is important not to act without thinking things through first.

□ **Communicate frankly:** Explain the acquisition or merger, the expected benefits and the changes which will be required. In addition it is useful to ensure that there is an understanding of the values and expectations of the acquiring company.

☐ **Act correctly,** particularly as far as redundancy is concerned.

Ramsay (1987) argues that effective acquisition strategies have four stages, which are illustrated in Figure 18.2:

☐ the need to formulate a clear strategy
☐ the search for possible acquisitions
☐ the acquisition
☐ the merger of the organizations following acquisition.

The formulation of a clear strategy

An effective, well thought through, diversification and acquisition can constitute real strategic growth by providing entry into a new market, a new opportunity to build on competitive strengths, an opportunity to create and benefit from synergy, and the possibility of removing some element of competition. This, however, implies more logic behind the acquisition than mere sales growth or the purchase of a profit stream. Hence there are a number of issues to consider in attempting to formulate an effective strategy for acquisition.

☐ First, the issue of how much to concentrate and how much to diversify must be examined. We mentioned earlier that research indicates that concentration is generally superior but that the opportunities available may not be sufficient to fill the planning gap. A major advantage of concentration, and a limit on diversification, is that experience is difficult to copy. Learning and experience can lead to superior competitive positions through an understanding of customers and how to satisfy their needs through production and service. Horizontal integration and concentric diversification can both provide

opportunities to capitalize on learning and experience.

☐ Second, a good strategy will build on existing strengths and develop synergy around them. This requires an opportunity to transfer skills and achieve economies of scale. This issue is discussed further below.

☐ Third, it is important to be able to spot an opportunity and act quickly and decisively to capitalize on it. It has been argued, for example, that, once legislation permitted it in the mid-1980s, the building societies which moved quickly into estate agencies benefited far more than those who lagged behind, because the cost per site increased with the acquisition activity. Such a strategic move would be classified as vertical integration because an estate agency is really a channel of distribution for mortgages.

☐ Fourth, resources (strengths) and opportunities need to be matched. The ability to do this effectively relates to the way the company is managed, and to the culture and values.

The search for, and review of, possible acquisitions

☐ There should be an active and positive search process. Acquisitions are difficult, diversification is risky, and the decisions can prove expensive if they are wrong. Strategic leaders should track and carefully analyse possible acquisitions rather than rely on opportunities which might arise.

☐ It is essential to be realistic. Where there is a friendly merger, or the acquisition of a company in difficulties, it is possible that certain key weaknesses may be hidden; and in the case of a hostile bid situation it is important not to become unrealistic through determination and, as a result, pay too much.

☐ Before acquiring it is crucial to assess just how resources are going to be shared, where and how skills are going to be transferred, and where and how economies of scale are going to be obtained. If such an analysis is left until after an acquisition, synergy is likely to prove more elusive.

The price paid to acquire a company relative to its earning potential, and the ability to generate synergy through shared activities or transferred skills, are the key determinants of likely success.

Porter (1987) contends that a portfolio of unrelated companies is only a logical corporate strategy if the aim is re-structuring. Restructuring is the strategy pursued by conglomerates like Hanson (discussed in Case 13.1), and it requires the identification of companies which are under-performing and which can be transformed with new management skills. Ideally they are valued below their real potential for acquisition. The new owner seeks to improve the competitive position of the organization and improve its profitability. Logically companies or business units are sold when they no longer have potential for increasing earnings further. The opportunity to pursue this strategy effectively lies in the ability to spot and acquire under-valued companies cheaply and to manage unfamiliar businesses better than the existing managers.

In any acquisition, Porter argues, three tests should be passed.

☐ The industry involved should be or could be made structurally attractive. In other words, the potential returns exceed the company's cost of capital.
☐ The entry cost should not be so high that future profit streams are compromised. As well as the purchase price, the cost must also take account of professional fees involved in the merger or acquisition. When the UK pharmaceutical company Beecham agreed to merge with American SmithKline Beckman in 1989 to create the world's second largest drug company, the professional fees were estimated at £70 million.
☐ One of the companies should be able to gain competitive advantage, and the newly acquired business should be better off in the new corporation than elsewhere. In other words the interrelationships, based on shared activities and transferred skills, must give added value which outweighs the costs incurred. These benefits are often not gained for two main reasons. The new, more diverse, more complex, organization is likely to be decentralized, but the business units may be independent in practice rather than interdependent. Managers may not be able to understand and implement the interrelationships.

Case 18.5 evaluates the Asda–MFI merger against these three tests and argues that it did not pass them all. It was mentioned in Case 17.6, which described the merger and de-merger, that the expected synergy was not achieved.

Hence companies which are seeking to grow through acquisition and the consolidation of the acquired and existing businesses should ensure either that skills can be transferred or that activities can be shared, i.e. clear interrelationships can be identified. These can relate to any part of the value chain. The aims are greater economies of scale, lower costs or enhanced differentiation through sharing activities, know-how or customers, or transferring skills and know-how. The research findings quoted earlier suggest that these opportunities are more likely to be found in industries which are in some way related. Tobacco companies in both the UK and the USA, for example, when faced with declining demand and hostile pressure groups realized that they would have to diversify if they were to avoid decline. They chose such industries as food, wine and brewing initially because they felt that they could transfer their skills and expertise in marketing consumer products. However,

Case 18.5
THE ASDA–MFI MERGER

The case considers whether the merger of Asda and MFI, described earlier in Case 17.6, met the criteria for successful diversification suggested by Porter.

The attractiveness of the kitchen furniture industry

Suppliers of kitchen furniture did not enjoy as strong a market profile as did MFI, and buyers individually had very little power. *En masse* they are influential. Any competitor wanting to enter the market on the MFI scale would require massive investment; substitute products were essentially units which were already assembled, such as those sold by Magnet Southern. Increases in disposable income might make these more attractive. There was intense rivalry for market share, however, as sales of kitchen furniture were flat in the 1980s.

On balance the industry was not unattractive, and MFI was a past 'winner'. Profits had grown 87% in real terms between 1980 and 1985.

The cost of entry

MFI cost Asda £570 million, which represented 5½ times net assets and 14 times 1984 pre-tax profits. It was a 31% premium on the current market capitalization, and it measured MFI on a price-to-earnings ratio of 22 rather than the 18 that it had been before the bid. Debt and equity funding were both involved; and Asda's gearing increased from little more than zero to 40%.

Both shareholders were supportive, but with hindsight it seems a high price.

Increased competitive advantage

There was no real benefit to be gained from common purchasing; no site sharing; and the two companies enjoyed different geographical concentrations. Asda was northern and MFI national.

After the merger the companies were run autonomously with few activities shared.

Prior to merging it had been argued that there would be intangible benefits from shared expertise. In the event there was little cross-flow of managers, product innovation, marketing or operations skills. The cultures remained separate; and Derek Hunt, who became Chief Executive, worked from London despite Asda's northern base.

Whilst Asda did compete with Sainsbury's, who have a chain of Homebase DIY stores, this was not seen as a threat which MFI would address, and in any case MFI was very narrowly focused within the DIY sector.

Whilst the industry was not unattractive the merger proved expensive for Asda, and the potential synergy used to justify the merger to shareholders seemed not to be there in reality.

Case 18.6
WOOLWORTH HOLDINGS

In 1984 F W Woolworth (UK) was acquired by a financial consortium which re-launched it. In 1982–3 Woolworth had a return on capital employed of 5%, with sales per square foot of retail space of £81 per annum. Marks & Spencer achieved £306 per square foot for the same period.

In 1988 the new Woolworth Holdings announced a five-year strategy concentrating on three areas:

☐ high street retail, essentially the Woolworth chain stores and the recently acquired drug stores
☐ out-of-town stores, essentially B & Q (DIY), Comet (electrical goods) and Charlie Browns (car parts)
☐ property sales and development.

Between 1983 and 1988 the number of variety chain stores was reduced. Some sites were sold; some were developed and then sold. The range of products was rationalized and focused, and efforts were made to improve the image of the stores and staff. At the same time the B & Q chain, which was already owned, was doubled. Comet was acquired in 1984 with a friendly bid, and provided further diversification.

In 1986 Dixon's, the electrical goods chain, attempted to take Woolworths over but was unsuccessful after an acrimonious battle.

In 1987 Woolworth diversified into car parts by acquiring Charlie Browns and drug stores. Drug stores sell toiletries, certain medicines and household goods at discount prices, but they are not pharmacies. Woolworth acquired sequentially the only three drug store groups to be quoted on the Stock Exchange: Superdrug (March 1987, an agreed bid yielding 297 stores); Share Drug (145 stores); and Tip Top Drug Stores (110 outlets). The number of stores has since been expanded rapidly. In November 1989 Woolworth, now known as Kingfisher Group, bought 86 Medicare drugstores from Gateway.

In October 1989 Woolworth having changed its name, acquired the Lasky's chain of 53 electrical goods stores to supplement the 308 Comet outlets. Lasky's was bought from Granada, who themselves had bought it from Ladbroke's in 1986. Lasky's was losing money. In February 1993 it was revealed that Kingfisher and Darty (French retailers of electrical goods) were discussing a possible merger.

---

managerial know-how can be a transferable skill between unrelated industries, as both Trafalgar House and Hanson have proved. General management skills in turning companies around are able to add value. Case 18.6 describes the strategy of Woolworth Holdings in the second half of the 1980s as they have diversified, looking for opportun-ities where they can apply their retailing skills. Company results suggest that these changes have proved successful. Woolworth Holdings, incidentally, was renamed 'King-fisher' in 1989.

Acquisitions are likely to prove disappoint-ing if the opportunity for such synergy is not evaluated objectively in advance, or if the companies convince themselves that synergy must be possible without establishing where and how.

Acquiring the company

The key issues involved in the acquisition itself have been discussed earlier. Valuations were considered in Chapter 13, and it was emphasized above that it is important to look for hidden weaknesses in friendly mergers and avoid paying too much in a contested take-over bid. It was mentioned earlier that if too high a premium is paid the acquisition is less likely to be successful (Burgman, 1985), and a vicious circle of disillusionment can easily be created. If the acquisition is over-valued or a substantial premium is paid, the expected early returns on the investment will be very high. An acquisition involves an investment which must be paid back by generating returns which exceed the cost of capital involved. If targets are missed the possible disillusionment and loss of confidence may mean that additional investment to develop the business, which really is needed, will not be forthcoming. Consequently, performance will deteriorate further and the business will run down. A likely outcome of this will be its sale at a discounted price, and the acquirer will have lost money from the acquisition. The payment of any premium should be related to the ability of the acquirer to add value by sharing activities or transferring skills.

Unwelcome bids

Organizations which find themselves the object of an unwelcome bid can defend themselves in a number of ways. A revised profit forecast, promising improvements, can prove effective – but subsequently the improvement must be delivered. This will sometimes be linked to a promise to restructure and divest parts of the business which are not core and not contributing synergy. An appeal to regulatory bodies may at least impose a delay; and finally, the company can seek a 'white knight', a preferred friendly bidder. Jenkinson and Mayer (1991) have shown, first, that white knight interventions normally succeed but, of course, the company's independence has still been lost, and, second that where there is no white knight cash bids are more difficult to defend against than equity bids.

Merging the two organizations

Merging two organizations involves decisions about the integration of strategic capabilities, in particular:

☐ operating resources – salesforces, production facilities
☐ functional skills – product development, R & D
☐ general management skills – strategy development, financial control, human resource strategies.

The speed and pattern of the integration will be dependent upon the desired interdependency of the businesses, and the opportunities for synergy. It is essential that there is a strategy for the implementation, and ideally this will be developed after the merger or acquisition when fuller details are available. Moreover, important issues concerning people, culture, structure systems and procedures must be thought through.

☐ **People:** It is accepted that many chief executives and other senior managers leave acquired companies either immediately or within 1–2 years after the acquisition, especially where the acquisition was contested. This may or may not be significant, depending on the strengths of the acquiring company. In some cases it will prove crucial, particularly where the managers have been the major source of competitive advantage. The managers in the two organizations being merged may well have different values, ethics and beliefs in quality and service, and these will somehow have to be reconciled.

☐ **Culture:** It is quite possible that the two organizations will have different cultures, which also must be reconciled. One may be a large company and the other small, with typical role and power cultures respectively. Managers will be used to different levels of responsibility. One may be much more formal and procedural than the other. One may be entrepreneurial and risk oriented, and the other cost conscious and risk averse.

These cultural issues should be considered when the post-acquisition structure is designed, and in the new systems and procedures.

☐ **Structure systems and procedures:** Whilst mentioned here, this is the subject of Chapter 22, and it concerns the degree of decentralization. As companies become larger and more complex they must be broken down into business units, and managers must be given some degree of independence – to motivate them and to ensure that functional and competitive strategies can be adapted in response to environmental changes. However, if activities are to be shared, or skills transferred, it is essential to ensure that independence does not inhibit, or even prohibit, the implementation of the necessary interdependences.

McLean (1985) contends that six factors determine whether the integration of two or more companies is a success or a failure:

☐ first, active leadership by the strategic leader of the acquiring company in conveying objectives and expectations, and in re-designing the structure of the organizations

☐ second, the conscious development of shared values and a transfer of the important aspects of the culture of the acquiring firm

☐ third, an appropriate interchange of managers between the firms, which can be one way of retaining valuable managers from the acquired company

☐ fourth, proceeding with caution (although some changes may have to be implemented quickly, say to reduce costs in certain areas, others will be less urgent; this provides an opportunity to learn about the underlying strengths of the new business which might be capitalized upon)

☐ fifth, relationships with customers must be protected until decisions about future products and market priorities are taken

☐ sixth, rigid new systems, which might be inappropriate for the new business, should not be imposed too ruthlessly or too quickly. Where there are differences in, in particular, culture, technology and marketing needs, managers in the acquired company should be allowed the necessary freedom to manage the competitive and functional strategies and respond to market pressures.

To summarize this section, it could be argued that:

☐ the price paid for an acquisition should reflect the ability of the acquirer to add value, share resources and transfer skills;

☐ the strategy for achieving this should be soundly based, and the potential synergy real rather than imagined;

☐ post-acquisition management should recognize that, whilst changes will have to be made in order to add value, two cultures have to be integrated if the strategy is to be implemented effectively.

In this chapter so far we have concentrated on diversification and acquisition strategies. Joint ventures and strategic alliances are an attempt to obtain the benefits of diversification and access to new competitive opportunities without the costs and implementation problems of acquisition or merger. They are not without problems of their own.

JOINT VENTURES AND STRATEGIC ALLIANCES

Whilst some form of partnership can be one of the quickest and cheapest ways to grow or develop a global strategy, it is also one of the toughest and most risky. Many alliances fail. The needs of both partners must be met, and consequently three important questions must be answered satisfactorily:

☐ **Why** use an alliance?
☐ **Who** to select as a partner?
☐ **How** to implement the agreement?

There is disagreement amongst authors concerning definitions of the terms 'joint venture' and 'strategic alliance'. I use strategic alliance to encapsulate all forms of agreement between partners, and joint venture for those agreements which involve either the establishment of a new, independent company owned jointly by the partners, or the minority ownership of the other party by one or both partners.

An alliance could involve direct competitors sharing a common skill, or related companies sharing different skills and competences. These organizations might well be linked in the same added value chain (e.g. a manufacturer and either a supplier or a distributor). Such an alliance should generate synergy through co-operation, innovation and lower costs whilst allowing each partner to concentrate on its core competences. The intention will be to increase competitive advantage without either merger or acquisition.

Reasons for joint ventures and strategic alliances

☐ The cost of acquisition may be too high.
☐ Legislation may prevent acquisition, but the larger size is required for critical mass.
☐ Political or cultural differences could mean an alliance is more likely to facilitate integration than would a merger or acquisition.
☐ The increasing significance of a total customer service package suggests linkages through the added value chain – to secure supplies, customize distribution and control costs. At the same time individual organizations may prefer to specialize in those areas where they are most competent. An alliance provides a solution to this dilemma.
☐ The threat from Japanese competition has driven many competitors into closer collaboration – but they may not wish to merge.
☐ Covert protectionism in certain markets necessitates a joint venture with a local company.

Forms and examples of joint ventures and strategic alliances

Joint ventures and strategic alliances can take a number of forms. The six categories which follow should not be seen as mutually

---

Everywhere in Europe companies are giving up sovereignty because of the costs involved in research and development. The extent and speed of technological changes are such that no one thinks he is capable of doing it all on his own.

Lord Weinstock, Managing Director, GEC

exclusive; some joint ventures will cover more than one.

☐ Component parts of two or more businesses might be merged.

Case 18.7, GEC, Alsthom and Siemens, illussrates the difficulties in cross-border European alliances of this nature.

☐ Companies might agree to join forces to develop a new project.

Club Méditerranée and Carnival Cruise Lines (US) have joined forces to provide cruise-based holiday packages for Europe and Asia. Philips and Nintendo are developing a new generation of video games together. These will be on compact discs rather than cartridges and compatible with Philips' CD-Is – compact disc-interactive players which link up to high-definition televisions. Philips are already allied with Motorola (US) for chips for their CD-Is. Airbus Industrie was formed because no partner alone could afford the development costs of large passenger aircraft, and because of pressure from European governments who wanted to reduce the predominance of the large American companies.

☐ Companies might agree to develop a new business jointly.

Sony of Japan and Apple (computers) of the US formed a new multi-media company in 1991. The aim is to produce a 'palm-size, wire-less personal communication device with digital audio and visual functions'.

☐ There might be specific agreements between manufacturers and their suppliers.

Jaguar Cars and GKN reached an agreement in 1988 whereby GKN would become the sole supplier of car bodies to Jaguar. Since the privatization of Jaguar in the mid-1980s its bodies had been supplied by the Rover Group, its previous parent company, which was vertically integrated in this respect. Jaguar and GKN formed a new company, owned 50 : 50, and the aim to build a new

plant and have it operative by 1991 was accomplished successfully.

☐ A company might make a strategic investment in another firm.

Volvo of Sweden and Renault of France have taken minority shareholdings in each other and are now co-operating in several areas. They have a single purchasing unit for commonly used components for both trucks and cars (such as tyres); they have exchanged engines and engine technology; they are jointly developing a commuter bus; there is some joint marketing and a joint research centre for advanced materials.

☐ Companies might form international trading partnerships.

Fujitsu of Japan now owns 80% of ICL, the UK computer manufacturer, but runs it as an independent subsidiary. However, they are allied in the form of joint retailing and servicing in North America and Australia.

Developing from these forms of joint venture and strategic alliance, Connell (1988) contends that companies collaborate strategically for primarily three reasons:

☐ First, to gain access to new markets and technologies as markets become increasingly international.

In 1989 Pilkington, the UK float glass manufacturer and world market leader, sold 20% of its American vehicle glass subsidiary to Nippon Sheet Glass of Japan. Pilkington had 17% of the world market for *vehicle glass*, Asahi of Japan 19%. Nippon already had 9% and manufactured float glass under licence from Pilkington. Nippon gained access to the American market; Pilkington were looking to build a customer base in Japan, arguing that as car manufacture becomes increasingly global they needed a presence in all major markets. Pilkington already supplied the Toyota plant in America.

☐ Second, to share the costs and risks of

Case 18.7
GEC, ALSTHOM AND SIEMENS

'Not all of our alliances have been successful' (Lord Weinstock, Managing Director of GEC) – but this has not stopped GEC searching for more. The strategy is to forge protective joint ventures around key interests in order to compete more effectively both in Europe and globally. The alliances have addressed areas of strategic weakness and strengthened GEC against possible unwelcome take-over bids.

In 1988 GEC and Siemens joined forces to acquire Plessey – a hostile take-over of a competitor. Had GEC attempted this alone it would probably have been stopped by the Monopolies and Mergers Commission. GEC owned 40% and Siemens 60% of the new company. Although the stated intention was to run Plessey as a joint venture, only one subsidiary, CGT (the telecommunications business) is now jointly owned, and this 60% by GEC. Within two years all the other businesses had either been split up between GEC and Siemens or sold. Some commentators suggest the two companies always intended to do this, others that they could not work together effectively. Siemens is bureaucratic, has an engineering culture, and is committed to long-term research and development projects. Most research at Siemens is centralized, whilst at GEC it is decentralized. GEC has a very distinctive financial culture, with divisions controlled by targets and results.

Also in 1988 GEC Alsthom was established as a 50 : 50 joint venture company when the power systems divisions of GEC were merged with the Alsthom subsidiary of France's CGE, creating the largest manufacturer of generating equipment and other power systems in the European Community. The objective was to rival Asea Brown Boveri (ABB), the Swedish/Swiss multi-national formed in 1987 and the world's biggest electrical engineering group. ABB is said to be 'willing to buy any power station equipment manufacturer that comes on the market'.

Synergy potential was identified. Both companies had different geographical power bases – GEC in the UK, China and the Far East, Alsthom in France, North Africa and the Middle East. Alsthom were strongest in large and small transformers, GEC in mid-size. In the UK electricity privatization created demand for power stations driven by gas turbines – GEC does not make gas turbines for power stations. At the same time there was some overlap in turbines and generators, both core products, and potential overcapacity in certain weak markets. The alliance would also strengthen Alsthom against German competition, especially from Siemens. The challenge, therefore, was to achieve the synergy and merge the interests effectively. This requires the fusion of two different cultures.

However, the headquarters of GEC Alsthom are in Paris, the chief executive is French, and initially the British members of the Board did not speak French. Alsthom have typically invested 3–4% of sales revenue in R & D, GEC only 1–2%. French engineers are said to be more theoretical than their pragmatic British counterparts. Alsthom have been strong on management development and human resource strategy, and arguably were sales oriented. GEC's financial strategies are profit oriented. Prior to the joint venture Alsthom produced six-monthly financial summaries – now there are more detailed monthly reports.

Continued overleaf

In summer 1992 GEC–Alsthom won orders worth over £500 million from European railway companies for 27 high-speed trains, beating off competition from Siemens. A few months earlier British Rail had preferred Brel (which is affiliated to Asea Brown Boveri) for a smaller order for commuter trains.

GEC also has alliances with the American General Electric (GE) and Matra. GEC's and GE's household appliances are marketed jointly in Europe; GE components are now used in GEC's Hotpoint and Creda appliances; and GEC has access to GE's superior research and development. GEC's Marconi space interests are allied with those of Matra, the French defence and electronics group.

Financially GEC's joint ventures make sense and should yield profits. Dispersed activities have been made more manageable. But GEC's management may become distanced from those assets and businesses which are generating an increasing proportion of its profits.

increasingly expensive research and development.

The alliance between Rover and Honda is an example of this. The agreement was started with an initiative from Sir Michael Edwardes in 1978 when he was Chief Executive of the Rover Group, then called British Leyland (BL). Edwardes considered that the new models being developed by BL were inadequate, particularly in the middle car range. He chose Honda because they were not too big to be interested in a deal with BL and because their technology was regarded as being very good. The Triumph Acclaim was the first car to emerge from the collaboration. BL enjoyed exclusive production and marketing rights to a Honda design and bought the necessary tooling from Honda. The first Rover 200 series was also developed jointly, with the 213 model having a Japanese engine. More recently the agreement has included the assembly of each other's related models – specifically the Rover 800 series and the Honda Legend.

During 1989 further progress was made. In July, having been acquired from the UK government by British Aerospace, Rover bought 20% of Honda (UK), which was to build a manufacturing plant in Swindon,

Wiltshire. In return Honda acquired 20% of the Rover shares. In October Honda agreed that Rover's Longbridge plant in Birmingham would be the sole European source of its new model, the Concerto. The up-dated Rover 200 series is a comparable car.

More recently Honda has agreed to help Rover raise its efficiency and productivity to world class levels during the 1990s. Honda will also buy most of the body panels required for its European factories from Rover, but develop its new Swindon plant to produce more than one car. Rover will then cease to assemble for Honda.

☐ Third, to manage innovation more effectively. This is important because of high research and development costs and greater globalization, which together often ensure that any competitive advantage gained from technology is relatively short-lived. Both the opportunities and threats require that companies are able to be flexible and change quickly.

There is arguably a fourth reason – an attempt to regain lost competitiveness in a marketplace. This is thought to be the cause of a series of agreements amongst European electronics manufacturers, and links between them and Japanese and American competitors.

Whilst there are a number of reasons and justifications for such strategic alliances, they can again be difficult strategies to implement effectively.

Key issues in joint ventures and strategic alliances

Ohmae (1989) argues that the following issues are significant and help to determine whether the agreement is likely to prove effective.

☐ Successful collaboration requires commitment on both sides. Without sufficient management time, trust and respect the agreement is likely to fail.

In reality, all the required resources must be committed. Either for managing linkages, or for managing a new joint venture company, capable managers must be transferred or seconded. The outcome of the alliance will depend upon both the commitment of the partners and the emergent power and influence they exert.

☐ There must be mutual benefits, the attainment of which may well involve sacrifices on both sides. Both partners should appreciate clearly what the other party wants from the agreement, and their objectives.

If the commitment of each ally is uneven, the keener partner or the faster learner is likely to assume control. This might mean that the interests of the weaker partner are either bought out or simply taken over.

☐ If circumstances change during the period of the alliance, flexibility may be required as the objectives and priorities of either or both partners may change.
☐ Cultural differences, which might be either geographic or corporate in origin, will have to be reconciled.

Where companies enter an alliance through weakness rather than strength, it is vital that they use the partnership for learning and development.

In 1991 Ford formed an alliance with Yamaha to develop a new engine for the Fiesta and Escort ranges. Whilst such high-

---

There are large, and in part contradictory, movements afoot in the marketplace. The trend towards globalization is blurring the borderlines between national markets. The drive towards a unified European market in 1992 is part of this trend. The unification of standards . . . will make it possible to produce in greater unit volume and hence enjoy the cost saving of scale. On the other hand, there is increasing demand in many countries for greater local content in the microelectronics industry. This means continuing to build local manufacturing facilities, procure materials from local vendors, and employ trained local personnel for installation and maintenance.

As a result of these trends, we are forced to examine whether our corporate structures are in tune with the new demands, and whether new strategies and new alliances may not be necessary in order to share the cost burdens of development, achieve larger sales volumes and economies of scale, provide local content and access through co-operation with indigenous firms, promote the wider use of microelectronics by means of partnerships between electronics manufacturers and users, and facilitate the creation of a total, integrated solution.

Dr Karlheinz Kaske, President and Chief Executive Officer, Siemens AG

In 1990 Siemens entered into a joint venture with IBM to develop and produce sophisticated dynamic random access memory chips. Their aim was to compete more effectively with Japanese producers.

performance engines as the Ford–Cosworth are the outcome of past joint ventures, this was the first incidence of an alliance for mainstream car engines. Analysts have commented that Ford needed an agreement because they had become weak in a rapidly changing industry, stimulated by new materials, higher fuel consumption expectations and tighter emission standards. 'Ford must learn from the deal, and not subcontract their engine technology for the long term'.

It was mentioned earlier that acquisitions should be evaluated in terms of their ability to generate synergy. Joint ventures and strategic alliances should be regarded in the same light. Devlin and Bleackley (1988) argue that the key issues are the strategic wisdom behind the decision to form an alliance in the first place, the choice of partner, and the management of the alliance once it has been agreed. The position of both parties to the agreement should be improved from the alliance. If there is a real opportunity for synergy, joint benefits and mutual trust and commitment by both parties, joint ventures can be an effective means of implementing strategic change. However, although some of the inherent difficulties of acquisition are avoided by this type of agreement, there will still be implementation issues. Unless these are tackled properly, the joint venture is likely to prove expensive and tie up resources which might be deployed more effectively.

SUMMARY

This chapter has concentrated on the specific growth strategies of diversification and acquisition, and we have also considered joint ventures. The emphases have been on why organizations might select such strategies, how they might be managed effectively and the key considerations and issues. It was emphasized that diversification and acquisition were being discussed together as diversification in the UK is more likely to be implemented through acquisition than through internal growth, and most acquisitions involve some degree of diversification. The issues and difficulties involved therefore relate to both.

Specifically we have

☐ considered the typical growth pattern of large companies, and the extent of diversification by the largest firms in the UK, USA, France and Germany;
☐ looked at the reasons behind the increasing diversification and industrial concentration in the UK, the effects and implications;
☐ considered more generally why organizations might choose a strategy of diversification and acquisition, emphasizing the issues of growth and economic reasoning;
☐ discussed a selection of research findings which conclude that diversification and acquisition strategies often fail to bring about the benefits which were forecast, and are therefore relatively high risk;
☐ summarized the findings on why acquisitions fail, emphasizing that money and people are key aspects;
☐ listed the major considerations and issues concerning diversification and acquisition;
☐ discussed the components of an effective acquisition strategy, namely the logic under-pinning the formulation of the strategy; the search for, and review of, possible acquisitions; the acquisition itself; and implementation aspects of merging the two organizations;
☐ considered forms and examples of joint ventures and strategic alliances;
☐ discussed briefly the key issues in formulating and implementing this strategy effectively.

CHECKLIST OF KEY TERMS AND CONCEPTS

You should feel confident that you understand the following terms and ideas:

☐ The distinction between single product, dominant product, related product, and unrelated product/conglomerate companies
☐ The conclusions from the research by Reed and Luffman, Meeks, Salter and Weinhold, Porter, Nesbitt and King and Burgman
☐ The key financial and people issues in diversification and acquisition
☐ The key aspects of an effective acquisition strategy
☐ Joint ventures and strategic alliances.

QUESTIONS AND RESEARCH ASSIGNMENTS

Text related

1. From the various points and issues discussed in this chapter list the possible advantages and disadvantages of (a) diversification and acquisition strategies and (b) joint ventures and strategic alliances.

   From your experience list one successful and one unsuccessful example of each strategy. Why have you selected these particular cases?

2. In March 1982 Coca-Cola acquired Columbia Pictures – but sold it seven years later to Sony of Japan. The anticipated synergy had not materialized.

   What synergy might a globally oriented soft drinks company like Coca-Cola have expected from a movie company? Might the increasing demand for home videos have been significant?

Library based

3. Obtain statistics on either a selection of large companies which interest you, or, the largest 20 companies in the UK, and
   (a) ascertain the extent to which they are diversified and classify them as either single, dominant, related or conglomerate product companies;

   (b) determine their relative size in relation to their competitors in the USA, Japan and Europe.

4. Develop a summary of the diversification and acquisition strategies of Trafalgar House plc. (A useful early summary can be found in Barber, L (1986) Bruised Trafalgar struggles to regain its political touch, *Financial Times*, 19 May.)
   (a) Trafalgar bid for the P & O shipping line in 1983, but it was referred to the Monopolies and Mergers Commission. Although approval was granted, Trafalgar allowed the bid to lapse. Given they already owned Cunard, was this an appropriate strategic move?
   (b) Trafalgar acquired the Scott Lithgow (1984) and John Brown (1986) shipyards from British Shipbuilders. Where do you think they might have been able to add value in this declining industry?
   (c) Did the acquisition of Davy consolidate this move and offer real potential synergy?
   (d) Trafalgar bid unsuccessfully against Eurotunnel for the Channel tunnel, proposing a linked bridge and tunnel scheme. They were successful in a bid to build a bridge across the Thames at Dartford to relieve congestion in the existing Dartford tunnel. Trafalgar built the bridge with private investment money which will be recouped by tolls on traffic. Do you believe these developments could be justified strategically? Why? Why not?
   (e) Should Trafalgar House divest its interests in passenger shipping and hotels?
   (f) What has happened since Hongkong Land acquired a minority shareholding early in October 1992?

5. Why did Woolworth Holdings change their name to Kingfisher in 1989? What

was the reaction of the City to this proposal?

How successful has Woolworth/Kingfisher been? Has their diversification been successful?

RECOMMENDED FURTHER READING

Channon (1983) provides a useful background to this chapter, and the articles by Constable (1986) and Reed and Luffman (1986) illustrate the problems of diversification and acquisition very effectively.

Ohmae's paper on strategic alliances (1989) is a valuable summary of the issues in this increasingly popular strategic alternative. Also useful is Lyons, M P (1991) Joint ventures as strategic choice – a literature survey, *Long Range Planning*, **24** (4).

REFERENCES

Biggadike, R (1979) The risky business of diversification, *Harvard Business Review*, May–June.

Burgman, R, Research findings quoted in McLean, R J (1985) How to make acquisitions work, *Chief Executive*, April.

Business International (1988) *Making Acquisitions Work: Lessons from Companies' Successes and Mistakes*, Report published by Business International, Geneva.

Channon, D F (1983) *Strategy and Structure in British Industry*, Macmillan.

Connell, D C (1988) Strategic partnering and competitive advantage, Presented at the 8th Annual Strategic Management Society Conference, Amsterdam, October.

Constable, C J (1986) Diversification as a factor in UK industrial strategy, *Long Range Planning*, **19** (1).

Cowling, K, Stoneman, P and Cubbin, J (eds) (1979) *Mergers and Economic Performance*, Cambridge University Press.

Devlin, G and Bleackley, M (1988) Strategic alliances – guidelines for success, *Long Range Planning*, **21** (5), October.

Drucker, P F (1982) Quoted in Drucker: The dangers of spoonfeeding, *Financial Times*, 15 October.

Dyas, G P and Thanheiser, H T (1976) *The Emerging European Enterprise: Strategy and Structure in French and German Industry*, Macmillan.

Hilton, A (1987) Presented at 'Growing Through Acquisition', conference organized by Arthur Young, London, 31 March.

Jenkinson, T and Mayer, C (1991) *Takeover Defence Strategies*, Oxford Economic Research Associates.

Kitching, J (1967) Why do mergers miscarry?, *Harvard Business Review*, November–December.

Kitching, J (1973) *Acquisitions in Europe: Causes of Corporate Successes and Failures*, Report published by Business International, Geneva.

Lorenz, C (1986) Takeovers. At best an each way bet, *Financial Times*, 6 January.

McLean, R J (1985) How to make acquisitions work, *Chief Executive*, April.

Meeks, J (1977) *Disappointing Marriage: A Study of the Gains from Merger*, Cambridge University Press.

Nesbitt, S L and King, R R (1989) Business diversification – has it taken a bad rap? *Mergers and Acquisitions*, November–December.

Ohmae, K (1989) The global logic of strategic alliances, *Harvard Business Review*, March–April.

Peters, T J and Waterman, R H Jr (1982) *In Search of Excellence: Lessons from America's Best Run Companies*, Harper and Row.

Porter, M E (1987) From competitive advantage to corporate strategy, *Harvard Business Review*, May–June.

Ramsay, J (1987) The strategic focus: deciding your acquisition strategy, Paper presented at 'Growing Through Acquisition', conference organized by Arthur Young, London, 31 March.

Reed, R and Luffman, G (1986) Diversification: the growing confusion, *Strategic Management Journal*. 7 (1), 29–35.

Rumelt, R P (1974) *Strategy, Structure and Economic Performance*, Division of Research, Harvard Business School.

Salter, M S and Weinhold, W A (1982) *Merger Trends and Prospects for the 1980s*, Division of Research, Harvard Business School; quoted in Thackray, J (1982) The American takeover war, *Management Today*, September.

RECOVERY, RECESSION AND DIVESTMENT STRATEGIES

19

LEARNING OBJECTIVES

After studying this chapter you should be able to

☐ identify the four possible outcomes of strategic change when companies are in difficulties;
☐ describe a number of retrenchment and turnaround strategies;
☐ discuss the thinking behind divestment strategies and the implementation issues involved;
☐ explain which strategies are important during a recession;
☐ summarize the possible strategies for individual competitors in declining industries.

The causes and symptoms of decline were discussed in Chapter 8. In this chapter we examine the potential for recovery and alternative strategies that might be considered. We also look at strategies appropriate for a recession.

INTRODUCTION

At any given time certain industries will provide attractive growth prospects for those companies who already compete in them, and for potential newcomers. At the same time, however, other industries will be in terminal decline. This might be taking place slowly or rapidly. In the case of slow decline, profitable opportunities may still exist for those companies which can relate best to changing market needs. Where decline is rapid, prospects are likely to be very limited. A third group of industries might be undergoing significant change, and the companies which can adapt effectively will be able to survive and grow.

The motor cycle industry in the UK is an example of an industry which has collapsed. In 1950 Britain made 80% of the world's motor cycles. In the early 1990s it makes less than 1%. Inefficient production, poor marketing and inadequate product development in the face of Japanese competition are the causes. By contrast certain shipbuilders in the UK and Europe have survived competition from the developing countries and Japan by adapting to changes in demand and adding value. Sophisticated engineering components, such as automated steering systems, have been added. The UK shipbuilding industry overall, though, has declined dramatically. In Chapter 20, on management buy-outs, the example of Hornby is discussed. The toy industry is another example of an industry which has both declined and changed radically for those competitors who have survived. The name Hornby is associated with model trains, and there is still a market for model electric trains, but it is not as substantial as it once was. Hornby has had to diversify to survive.

The causes and symptoms of decline were discussed in Chapter 8. The most obvious **symptoms** are slower growth figures for sales or profits and a deterioration in the various financial measures of performance. The major **causes** are poor management and leadership, acquisitions which fail to provide synergy and meet expectations, the lack of effective financial controls, cost disadvantages, poor marketing, and a general inability to compete.

Any recovery from a difficult situation will be related to:

☐ improving marketing effectiveness and competitiveness, and hence increasing revenue;
☐ managing the organization more efficiently, and thereby reducing costs.

Where these changes in functional and competitive strategies prove inadequate, something more drastic will be required. In the outline summary of strategic alternatives in Chapter 17, four disinvestment strategies were introduced:

☐ Retrenchment strategies aim to increase revenue and reduce costs by concentrating and consolidating. These involve changes in functional strategies.
☐ Turnaround strategies relate to changes in competitive strategies and frequently feature re-positioning for competitive advantage.

Retrenchment and turnaround strategies are often collectively called recovery strategies.

☐ Divestment.
☐ Liquidation.

These result in changes to the company's corporate strategy.

In this chapter we explore recovery and divestment strategies in greater detail, considering first the overall feasibility of recovery and different recovery situations. These issues are of primary concern to companies that are already experiencing difficulties and showing symptoms of decline. In the last section we look at strategic alternatives for declining industries, which is relevant for companies that may be currently successful or unsuccessful in a situation of change.

Chapter 20 builds on this chapter, and we discuss management buy-outs, which are increasing in popularity and are one way of managing a divestment situation.

THE FEASIBILITY OF RECOVERY

When sales or profits are declining because a company is uncompetitive or because an industry is in decline, recovery may or may not be possible. If a company is a single product firm, or heavily reliant on the industry in question, then it may be in real difficulties and in danger of liquidation unless it can diversify successfully. If profits are declining, such a strategy may be difficult to fund. Where the situation applies to one business unit in an already diversified company, the company as a whole may be less

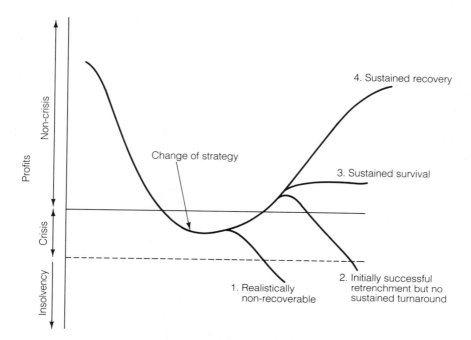

Figure 19.1 The feasibility of recovery. Adapted from Slatter, S (1984) *Corporate Recovery*, Penguin.

threatened. However, a change of strategy will be required, and the issue concerns whether or not a successful recovery can be brought about and sustained.

The likelihood of a possible recovery improves where

☐ the causes of the decline in the firm's sales and profits can be tackled and the problems overcome – this depends upon how serious and deep-rooted they are;
☐ the industry as a whole, or particular segments of the industry which might be targeted, remains attractive;
☐ there is potential for creating or enhancing competitive advantage.

Recovery situations

Slatter (1984) has postulated that there are essentially four types of recovery situation, and these are illustrated in Figure 19.1. Once the profits of the firm or business unit have

declined to a crisis stage, then a change in strategy is essential. However, the industry and competitive factors might be such that recovery simply is not feasible. Insolvency is

---

We weren't making money at SAS (Scandinavian Airlines System) when I came here. We were in a desperate situation, and that's the worst time to focus on preventing mistakes and controlling costs. First, we had to increase revenues. We had to decide what business we were going to do – before you can start managing effectively you must know who is your customer and what is your product – and go to work on the revenue side. Then we could think about cutting costs, because only then would we know which costs could be cut without losing competitiveness.

Jan Carlzon, President and Chief Executive Officer, Scandinavian Airlines System

---

inevitable, whatever alternative strategies might be tried. Successful retrenchment strategies might be implemented and profits improved to a non-crisis level again. However, unless the industry remains in some way attractive and potentially profitable, or the firm retains its competitive advantage, the retrenchment might subsequently fail. A third alternative is a successful turnaround but no real growth and sustained recovery. Possibly in a low-profit industry insufficient funds are generated to finance investment for further growth and diversification. A sustained recovery implies real growth, and possibly further changes in functional, competitive and corporate strategies.

Non-recoverable situations

Slatter argues that in situations where there is little chance of survival and the likelihood

that both retrenchment and turnaround strategies will fail, a number of characteristics are likely to be present.

☐ The company is not competitive and the potential for improvement is low. This might be the result of a cost disadvantage which cannot be remedied. Certain businesses and industries which have declined in the face of foreign competition, especially from countries with low wage costs, are testament to this.
☐ The company is not diversified and lacks both the resources and access to resources to remedy this weakness.
☐ Demand for the basic product or service involved is in terminal decline.

Temporary recovery

Where a retrenchment strategy is implemented successfully it may or may not be sustained. If new forms of competitive

---

Case 19.1
THE BURTON GROUP

The Burton Group is now primarily a retailer of fashionable clothing for men and women through a number of branded outlets.

The company was started as a single shop in 1901 by Montague Burton, who had built the company into a vertically integrated organization of factories and some 600 stores when he died in 1952. The main product area had been made-to-measure suits for men.

In the late 1960s the company had problems of management succession and it was basically stagnant with under-utilized assets. Burton was also experiencing a number of specific problems.

☐ The menswear market was switching in preference from made-to-measure to ready-made suits.
☐ The company had a large manufacturing base in relation to the falling demand for its products. Moreover the factories were inefficient and insufficiently capital intensive.
☐ There was growing competition from such stores as Marks & Spencer.
☐ The company had an old-fashioned image, made worse by stores which were not designed or fitted for the growing market for ready-made clothes.

A new management team was appointed and their strategy was one of diversification. In the early 1970s Burton acquired five new businesses:

☐ Evans – outsize fashions for women with fuller figures
☐ Ryman's – office supplies
☐ St Remy – clothing stores in France
☐ Green's – cameras and hi-fi equipment
☐ Trumps – an employment agency.

Burton also opened a chain of womenswear shops with the Top Shop brand name.

The diversification strategy failed in overall terms, although parts did prove successful, and divestment began in the mid-1970s.

In addition:

☐ Branches were modernized, and some were enlarged. The aim was to make Burton stores more appealing to younger buyers. Some stores, though, were closed.
☐ A new chain of Top Man stores was opened to complement Top Shop.
☐ There was greater emphasis on the womenswear market, with more Top Shops and the acquisition of Dorothy Perkins.
☐ The Principles chain was developed.
☐ Manufacturing was pruned; and the final factory was disposed of in 1988.

Between 1976 and 1979 the number of employees was reduced from 21 400 to 11 000.

These changes were led by Ralph Halpern, who became Chief Executive in 1977 (and Executive Chairman in 1981), and the result was revitalization, new growth and profitability. The Burton Group built up a 12½% share of the UK clothing market, second only to Marks & Spencer. Halpern was feted as a retailer of genius, and rewarded with a million pound salary, a knighthood and celebrity status. However, when this expansion required consolidation in the 1980s, a number of strategic misjudgements were made.

☐ In 1985 Burton took over Debenhams after a fierce battle. The new department stores required expensive revamping and the payback was slower than anticipated. Moreover, different retailing skills were involved.
☐ Burton diversified into shopping centre development, and was financially exposed when property prices fell.
☐ The growth led to over-expansion and the acquisition of new sites with very high rent and lease charges. These proved too expensive in the retail recession of the late 1980s.

Profits and the share price collapsed and Halpern departed in November 1990, to be replaced as Chief Executive by his deputy, Lawrence Cooklin. In mid-1991 Burton sought to raise money in a 'desperate rights issue', imposed a pay freeze and looked to rationalize by reducing both the number of stores and head office administration.

The flagship, Harvey Nichols department store, was sold in August 1991. Analysts commented that Burton was still searching for a retail format suitable for the 1990s. Cooklin was replaced in February 1992 by John Hoerner from Debenhams.

advantage are found and sustained, or the product or service is effectively re-positioned, subsequent insolvency may be avoided. However, if costs are reduced or additional revenues are generated in an essentially unattractive and declining industry, the effect will be limited. In such cases it will become important for the company to invest the cash generated from the retrenchment to diversify if that is possible.

Case 19.1 illustrates a temporarily successful turnaround by the Burton Group which was not sustained. Further retrenchment has been required.

Sustained survival

Sustained survival implies that a turnaround is achieved but there is little further growth. The industry may be in slow decline, or generally competitive and unprofitable. Survival potential and limited profit opportunities continue to exist, but little more. Sustained survival would also apply where a company failed to use its increased earnings effectively and did not diversify into new more profitable opportunities which could provide growth prospects.

Sustained recovery

A sustained recovery is likely to involve a genuine and successful turnaround – possibly new product development or market re-positioning. In addition the turnaround may well be followed by a growth strategy, perhaps acquisition and diversification.

The recovery is helped if the industry is strong and attractive and the company's decline has been caused by poor management rather than because the industry itself is in a decline.

Both a sustained survival and a sustained recovery may involve divestment of assets or part of the business to enable the company to concentrate on selected market segments or products.

Slatter (1984) studied a number of successful and unsuccessful attempts at turnaround, and concluded that there are three main features of a sustained recovery.

☐ Asset reduction is invariably required in order to generate cash. Quite frequently this will be achieved by divestment of part of the business.
☐ A new strategic leader is usually necessary. The new strategic leader will typically be associated with a re-structuring of the organization, the introduction of new strategies and a re-definition of roles and policies.
☐ Better financial control systems are also a normal feature.

Whilst retrenchment and initial survival can be achieved by concentrating on improving *efficiencies*, sustained survival and recovery will invariably require more *effective* competitive and corporate strategies.

To summarize this section, the opportunities for sustained recovery, or at least survival, improve where:

☐ there are fewer causes of the decline;
☐ the crisis is not deep-rooted, perhaps because the decline is the result of poor management rather than an unattractive declining industry;
☐ there is support from key stakeholders for the changes required (this may involve understanding by financiers and the commitment of managers and other employees to the necessary changes);
☐ strategic opportunities to differentiate, re-focus and create competitive advantage exist;
☐ the company has the ability to reduce costs.

Having considered the background feasibility of recovery, we now examine the actual recovery strategies in greater detail.

RETRENCHMENT STRATEGIES

In this section organizational and financial changes, cost and asset reduction, and strategies aimed at generating revenue are considered. Retrenchment strategies are essentially functional, rather than competitive or corporate, and are aimed at making the company more productive and profitable whilst retaining essentially the same products and services, although there might be some rationalization. By concentrating on financial issues, they often address major causes of the company's decline.

Organizational changes

It was emphasized above that a change in strategic leadership is frequently involved in recovery strategies. In addition there might be a need to strengthen the management team in other areas. The fact that there are personnel changes is not the important issue. The subsequent changes to strategies, structure and policies, and the effect on the existing staff and their motivation, are what matter. Re-organizations are likely to take place, involving new definitions of roles and responsibilities. Policies and management and control systems may also be changed to give managers new opportunities to achieve, and to convince them that recovery prospects are real.

Financial changes

Poor financial control systems, say a badly managed cash flow, are often a feature of companies in difficulties. In addition overheads may have been allowed to become too high in relation to direct production costs, and the company may not know the actual costs of producing particular products and services or be able to explain all expenditures. The establishment of an effective costing system, and greater control over the cash flow, can improve profitability and generate revenue.

Another retrenchment strategy is the restructuring of debt to reduce the financial burden of the company. Possibly repayment dates can be extended, or loan capital converted into preference shares or equity, thereby allowing the company more freedom through less pressure to pay interest.

Cost reduction strategies

When the acquisition strategies of such companies as Hanson were discussed, it was emphasized that they looked for companies with high gross margins and relatively low after-tax profitability. These are indications of overheads which have been allowed to grow too much, thereby providing opportunities for improving profits by reducing organizational slack and waste. Companies could address the overheads issue for themselves, without being acquired, if they recognized the extent of the problem and were determined to reduce their costs in order to improve their competitiveness and profitability.

In terms of reducing costs, the normal starting place is labour costs. In many cases opportunities will exist to reduce labour costs and improve productivity, but if the reductions are too harsh there can be a real threat to the quality of both the product and the overall service offered to customers. One opportunity is to examine working patterns and attempt to manage overtime, part-time arrangements and extra shifts both to meet demand and to contain costs. Companies can slip easily into situations where overtime and weekend working are creating costs which cannot be recovered in competitive prices.

Redundancies may be required to reduce costs and bring capacity more into line with demand. Again this can be implemented well or poorly. In most cases the issue is not losing particular numbers of people and thereby saving on wages, but losing non-essential staff or those who fail to make an effective contribution. There is always the danger in a voluntary redundancy programme that good people will choose to leave or take early retirement.

Costs can be reduced anywhere and everywhere in the value chain. Better supply arrangements and terms can reduce costs; products can be re-designed to cost less without any loss in areas significant to customers; and certain activities, such as public relations, training, advertising, and research and development might be cut. The argument here is that these activities are non-essential, and this might be perfectly plausible in the short term. It may not be the case for the longer term, and therefore they would need to be re-instated when extra revenues had been regenerated.

Asset reduction strategies

Divestment of a business unit, or part of the business, is an asset reduction strategy but is considered in greater detail later. It is really more of a corporate than a functional strategy, and the decision should not be made on financial grounds alone. Whilst the sale of a business can raise money, this gain may be more than offset if there is existing synergy with other parts of the company which suffer in some way from the divestment.

Internal divestment or rationalization can take a number of forms. Plants might be closed and production concentrated in fewer places; production might be re-scheduled to generate increased economies of scale. The idea is both to reduce overheads and reduce direct costs.

Assets might be sold and leased back. As far as the balance sheet is concerned, assets have been reduced and in turn cash has been generated. The scope and capacity of the business may be unaffected; the changes are exclusively financial.

Revenue-generating strategies

The marketing strategies considered in the next section on turnarounds are essentially revenue-generating strategies, and they frequently involve changes in competitive strategies. However, revenue can also be generated by improving certain management control systems. If stocks are reduced by better stock management or by a review of the whole production system and a move towards just-in-time, cash is freed. In just the same way, if debtors can be persuaded to settle accounts more speedily, cash flow can be improved.

TURNAROUND STRATEGIES

Retrenchment strategies will usually have short time horizons and they will be designed to yield immediate results. Turnaround strategies are likely to address those areas which must be developed if there is to be a sustained recovery. They involve changes in the overall marketing effort, including the re-positioning or re-focusing of existing products and services, together with the development of new ones. They are designed to bring quick results and at the same time contribute towards longer-term growth. They overlap with the internal growth strategies outlined in Chapter 17, and they may also be a stepping stone to growth through diversification.

Retrenchment strategies do not affect customers directly but the following turnaround strategies are designed to improve the effectiveness of the company's marketing. Consequently they are addressing customers and consumers directly, and for this reason some degree of caution is required in implementing the changes involved.

Changing prices

Prices can be changed at very short notice, and price increases or decreases can result in increased revenue. Price rises can increase revenue as long as the elasticity of demand ensures that sales do not decline unacceptably with the price increase. Price decreases can improve demand and hence revenue – again depending on the elasticity of demand. Hence it is important to have an insight into the demand elasticity for individual products and services although forecasting the effect of · price changes will be subject to some uncertainty. In general the opportunity to increase prices is related to the extent of existing differentiation, and the opportunity to differentiate further and create new competitive advantage.

It is important to remember that unless particular products and services are regarded as underpriced by customers in relation to their competition, a price rise should be accompanied by advertising support and possibly minor changes and improvements in the product or packaging. The price change must be justified.

It is also important to consider the likely reaction of competitors, which in turn will be influenced by the structure of the industry and the degree and type of competitive rivalry. Oligopoly markets, an essential feature of the UK industrial structure, were introduced in Chapter 5, when it was emphasized that oligopoly competitors tend to follow price decreases but not price rises.

In relation to the concept of price changes, discount structures might be altered to favour certain groups of customers at the expense of others. Such a strategic move can both raise revenue and improve the attractiveness of a company to certain market segments. Any negative effect on other customer groups should be monitored carefully.

Re-focusing

The idea behind re-focusing is to concentrate effort on specific customers and specific products, relating the two closely together. The strategy requires careful thought and attention in relation to why people buy and opportunities for differentiation, segmentation and competitive advantage. The selection of particular product/market and service/market niches for concentrating effort will depend upon revenue and growth potential, gross margins, the extent and type of competition for the segment or niche, and the potential to create a response to marketing activity, such as advertising.

In the short term products or services which sell quickly and generate cash quickly may be attractive opportunities even if their gross margin is small; and there may well be a group of customers for whom an appropriate package can be created.

New product development

The replacement of existing products with new ones, discussed earlier in the book, may be required to effect a turnaround if a company has been losing competitiveness in an attractive industry by falling behind competitors in terms of innovation and product improvement. Equally product improvements, designed to prolong the product life cycle, can be extremely useful in low growth or declining industries. They can be used to help a company concentrate on the particular segments of the market which are remaining relatively strong.

Rationalizing the product line

Variety reduction, which was discussed in Chapter 11, can similarly be useful for concentrating efforts on the stronger market segments and opportunities, particularly where the industry overall is losing attractiveness. Such a strategy needs a proper understanding of costs, and which individual products and services are most and least profitable. In a multi-product organization, with interdependences between the business units, for example, transfer price arrangements can distort profitabilities. It has already been mentioned earlier that certain products and services can be vital contributors to overall synergy, but individually not very profitable, and care needs to be taken with these.

Emphasis on selling and advertising

An emphasis on selling and advertising might take the form of selected additional expenditure in order to generate greater revenue, or the examination of all current marketing expenditure in order to try and ascertain the best potential returns from the spending.

Expenditure on advertising, below-the-line promotions and the salesforce is used to promote products and services in order to generate sales revenue. However, all these activities are investments, and their potential returns should be considered. The increased revenue expected from any increased spending should certainly exceed the additional

---

Case 19.2
LAURA ASHLEY AND PENGUIN BOOKS

LAURA ASHLEY

Laura Ashley was started in the 1950s by the late Laura Ashley and her husband, Bernard. The company was very successful with an instinctive approach to designs for fashions and fabrics. Laura Ashley designed, manufactured and retailed mostly clothes and furnishings. The company later diversified with a chain of perfume stores, leather goods stores and a knitwear business in Scotland. The company fared badly in the recession, and by 1991 was losing money.

An American, Jim Maxmin, was brought in as Chief Executive. His short-term challenge was to improve the balance sheet, which he achieved by disposing of the peripheral businesses, closing seven factories (and instead sourcing goods from commercially attractive suppliers), and selling a 15% stake to Aeon of Japan. At the same time Laura Ashley invested in better control systems based on information technology.

To stimulate growth Maxmin sought to change Laura Ashley from 'being product-led to consumer-led', placing great emphasis on marketing supported by proper research.

You have to find out what your customers want, give it to them, and just love 'em to death.
(Maxmin)

Marketing research determined that 25–34-year-old women should be the key target market, that 'style, cut and fit' could all be improved, and that female office workers constituted a new opportunity. Laura Ashley developed a more international focus, and re-designed store layouts based around colour ranges rather than product lines.

Laura Ashley is a *brand* – management's task is to unleash the intrinsic strength of that fantastic brand.
(Maxmin)

PENGUIN BOOKS

In the early 1970s Penguin Books was losing market share in paperback books, and as a result debts and overheads were increasing. It was generally accepted that there were marketing weaknesses, and Penguin had something of an old-fashioned image.

A new chief executive was appointed in 1978, and the results of the changes he made have been clearly visible during the 1980s as the company has survived and grown:

☐ Editorial, design, production and marketing functions have been integrated more.
☐ The list of titles was rationalized and then increased again as the company experienced renewed growth.
☐ Books were promoted more aggressively and more carefully targeted to market segments.
☐ The availability of books has been increased by using outlets other than bookshops, such as newsagents and hotel foyers – ideal for inexpensive paperbacks.
☐ There has been vertical integration into retail outlets, but only very selectively.

costs incurred, and there is an argument that the opportunity cost of the investment funds should also be assessed.

Whilst five alternative approaches to improving marketing effectiveness have been considered in this section, a number of them may be used in conjunction at any time. Moreover these turnaround strategies may also be combined with the retrenchment strategies discussed earlier, the aim being both to reduce costs and to improve revenue at the same time.

Case 19.2 looks, first at how Laura Ashley has both rationalized and strengthened its marketing in an attempt to recover from a loss-making situation and, second, at how Penguin Books was successfully turned around, again by concentrating on marketing. Case 19.3 describes attempts by three organizations in very different industries to recover from positions of strategic weakness.

It has already been explained that the divestment of products or business units can be useful for reducing assets in retrenchment strategies. Divestments can also be used to rationalize the product line, as discussed

above. They are the subject of the next section.

DIVESTMENT STRATEGIES

Divestment can be essentially **internal**, the closure of a plant as part of a rationalization programme, or **external**, the sale of part of the business. The justification will be similar for each, and any resources saved or generated should be re-allocated.

Davis (1974) argues that divestments are often sudden decisions rather than decisions reached as part of a continual evaluation process which reviews all the products and services in the firm's portfolio periodically. Companies who utilize portfolio analysis as part of their planning will be in a position to identify which parts of the business are the poorest performers and possible candidates for divestment (see Case 19.4). However, Devlin (1989) contends that effective divestment is a skill which few strategic leaders actually possess. This, he suggests, is a critical strategic issue, given that many acquisitions fail to achieve their expected returns. Divestment, though, suggests an admission of failure.

There will be an obvious reluctance to sell a business unit to another company, especially a competitor, who might succeed and

---

Case 19.3
USINOR-SACILOR, LEEDS PERMANENT AND GENERAL MOTORS

USINOR-SACILOR

Usinor-Sacilor, the French steel company formed by merger in 1986, is the second largest steel business in the world. At the time of the merger the company was uncompetitive, over-manned and substantially dependent on government subsidies. Usinor-Sacilor has followed a mix of retrenchment and growth strategies.

There has been selective investment in new capital to increase productivity and a reduction in the workforce – modelled on the successful British Steel approach. Training has been improved and attempts made to increase job flexibility and to persuade staff that profit is more important than output. Usinor-Sacilor has concentrated on flat products, which it regarded as more recession-proof, and made acquisitions in special steels (high added value) and merchanting (downstream vertical integration). Profits have improved, but the company is now very highly geared.

LEEDS PERMANENT BUILDING SOCIETY

In the mid-1980s the Leeds had, like all building societies, been affected by the growth in bank mortgages. Whilst the Leeds had branches throughout the country it was considerably smaller than the two market leaders, Halifax and Abbey National. Its asset reserve ratio (a key measure) was 'the lowest in the industry' and its management was seen to be relatively weak but high cost.

In 1988 a new Chief Executive, Mike Blackburn, was recruited from Access, the credit card company. There was speedy rationalization. Independent investment agencies, which supplemented the Leeds' own branch network, were reduced by 75%; and later some branches and estate agencies were closed.

Blackburn introduced a new vision. The Leeds would not follow Abbey National and become a plc (see Case 4.6), and, unlike most rival large societies, it would not move into transactional retail banking and current accounts. Instead the Leeds would concentrate on its traditional core businesses (mortgages and savings accounts) and closely related activities. The organization has been re-structured (a layer of regional management has been stripped out), branches have been re-designed and the company has introduced a visa credit card and invested heavily in marketing, especially television advertising and direct mail.

Market share and profits have improved, but is the Leeds now strong enough to survive the 1990s when financial services analysts believe many 'middle ground building societies will be swept away'?

GENERAL MOTORS

GM is the world's largest car producer, but not the most profitable. GM's share of the US market fell from 46 to 35% between 1979 and 1989, since when it has been steady, but in 1991/2 GM traded at a loss. Faced with intense competition from Ford and Chrysler, as well as the Japanese, GM has selected new strategies to try to restore profitability followed by improved market share.

☐ GM has invested in safety aspects and fuel economy, partially forced by legislation, although this can put upward pressure on both costs and prices.
☐ There has been considerable emphasis on productivity and on reducing the number of man-hours required to make a car.
☐ Attempts have been made to foster co-operation between the various GM marques and plants, instead of internal competition.
☐ The number of models has been reduced from 85 to 65, but new models are still launched every year.
☐ The Saturn project has led to the development of a new small car, which GM aims to produce at comparable cost to imported Japanese rivals. Saturn features innovatory design and production methods, and involves team working, advanced technology and supplier interdependency. Nevertheless, in 1992, both Ford and Chrysler, together with the Japanese, were still able to produce cars with lower direct costs.

Case 19.4
ALLIED TEXTILES

Allied Textiles, based in Huddersfield, pursue an acquisition and strategic divestment strategy. AT manufacture, process and distribute textile products, and operate at various stages of an integrated added value chain. Their philosophy is that at any time some activities will be enjoying better trading conditions than others.

AT attempt to specialize in high value-added products with growth prospects — effective competition in 'average value products' is difficult because of manufacturers in the Far East. Currently these include coatings, specifically waterproof and breathable fabrics, parachutes, hot air balloons and fire-resistant fabrics for aircraft. AT looks for opportunities where it can enjoy competitive advantage against its Far Eastern and European rivals, although this is unlikely to be sustainable long term. Japan and Germany are two of AT's most important markets.

Activities or businesses are divested when the prospects for earning satisfactory returns disappear, say because of cheaper copies. Worsted spinning and knitwear have recently been perceived to be under threat. Individual businesses are automatically reviewed on a three-year cycle.

AT is also diversified into property, leasing and financial services.

transform the business into an effective performer. This will be particularly important if such success could pose a future threat to business units which have been retained. For these reasons divestments are often associated with a change of strategic leader as an outsider is less likely to feel any loyalty to past decisions.

Issues in selecting a divestment candidate

There are a number of possible considerations which might be relevant in selecting a product, service or business unit for divestment. Both financial and strategic aspects are important:

☐ the current position in the product life cycle, and the likely future potential for further growth and profitability
☐ the current market position, and opportunities for competitive advantage
☐ taking these two points further and considering portfolio analyses, the future potential for cash generation and future investment requirements in order to remain competitive (linked to this is the opportunity cost of the resources being utilized)
☐ identified alternative uses for the resources which could be freed up, and in certain cases the extent of the need to free up resources for relocation
☐ the ability to find a suitable buyer willing to pay an acceptable price
☐ in addition to these points, the strategic potential to divest some business or activity which is profitable in order to raise money to invest in something which is likely to be even more profitable (implicit in this might be a desire to limit the strategic perspective and scope of diversification, or a desire to contain borrowing)
☐ the issue of whether it is cheaper to close a business or plant or keep it running despite low returns, i.e. exit costs and barriers
☐ the contribution to existing synergy, and the overall value to the organization (certain businesses may be making a loss

but be valuable to the organization because of their contribution to other activities, their past reputation, their significance to certain customers who are important to the organization and their general value as a competitive weapon)
☐ the opportunity to satisfy existing customers, which the organization would wish to retain, with alternative products and services
☐ the tangible and intangible benefits from specializing and reducing the extent to which the organization is diversified. In this context Tube Investments was discussed in Chapter 17, Case 17.4. Case 18.2 described how Yorkshire Water intend to divest non-core businesses but maintain important linkages in the form of a strategic network. Such specialization strategies are increasing in popularity and they are not necessarily related to recovery situations. See also Case 19.5.

Issues in the divestment

Once the decision to divest has been taken, there are a number of further considerations.

First, there is the issue of how active and how secretive the search for a buyer should be. It can be argued that there should be an active search for an acceptable buyer who is willing to pay an appropriate premium, on the grounds that it is all too easy to sell a business cheaply. A low price might be expected where the sale is hurried, perhaps because there is a pressing need to raise money or where a first offer is accepted without an exploration of other options. There is also an argument in favour of secrecy and speed as opposed to prolonged and publicized negotiations. Employees may leave if they feel their company is no longer wanted by its existing parent; relationships with important suppliers and customers may also be affected.

In addition, simply offering a business for sale may not be productive. Sales must be negotiated and potential buyers must be

---

Case 19.5
PHILIPS

Philips, the Dutch electricals and electronics group, has invented such everyday products as the cassette recorder, video recorder and compact disc, but invariably has failed to be the major beneficiary from their development. Late in the 1980s Philips was under-performing and in need of revised strategies and re-structuring. There were 'too many managers and not enough management'. Arguably Philips was too diversified and involved in businesses where it had neither critical mass nor the resources to grow to the required size. Semiconductors was one example.

Systematically Philips divested its interests in defence electronics and telecom-munications, and in 1989 sold 53% of its domestic appliance division (refrigerators, cookers etc.) to Whirlpool of the US, the world's leading manufacturer. Whirlpool purchased the remaining 47% in 1991. At this time Philips was losing money and the sale helped reduce debts.

Strategically Philips could now concentrate on consumer electronics and lighting products. Although it is managed on a hands-off basis, Philips owns 80% of Polygram, one of the major competitors in the global recorded music business, and this supports its interests in consumer music products. In 1992 Philips was preparing to launch its new DCC (digital compact cassette) system to compete with Sony's new mini compact discs and players. Both of these systems offer high-quality recordings and reproduc-tion in a reduced size format. Some experts were suggesting that Philips would have the advantage because the new DCC players would also play existing tape cassettes — mini-disc players are not compatible with any other system. Other commentators suggest the opposite result because the mini-disc will replace the Walkman.

In 1991 Philips launched a new light bulb, based on the principle of induction, and without either filaments or electrodes. The new bulb, although expensive, has an exceptionally long life of some 15 years and is very efficient. It is seen as ideal for certain uses such as tunnel lighting.

---

vetted. The terms of the sale should be financially acceptable; and the buyer should not be an organization who can use the newly acquired business to create a compet-itive threat to retained activities.

Devlin (1989) suggests that, in general, speed is of the essence. Long delays are likely to mean lost confidence. But some businesses may be difficult to sell.

Second, buyers can be categorized into different types, and the potential of the business for them needs careful consider-ation during negotiations.

☐ There are **sphere-of-influence buyers**, who might expect immediate synergy from the acquisition. These would include competitors for whom it would be hori-zontal integration, and buyers and sup-pliers for whom it would imply vertical integration. These are the buyers who are most likely to pose future threats unless the divestment removes any involvement in the industry in question.

☐ There are **related industry companies** who might not be current competitors but for whom it might be possible to share activ-ities and transfer skills.

☐ There are **unconnected conglomerate acquirers**.

☐ There are **management buy-outs**.

Third, there is an argument that the cash raised from the sale should be deployed effectively and without undue delay. If a company is decreasing in size, building up reserves of cash, and can find no suitable investment opportunities, it might become vulnerable to acquisition. Ideally a use for the cash will be determined before the sale, but implementation of a combined sale and investment may prove difficult. Devlin argues that where these changes can be managed effectively, divestment can provide a source of new competitive advantage.

Having explored retrenchment, turnaround and divestment strategies, we now look at these strategies specifically in the context of an economic recession, and then conclude the chapter by considering alternative strategies for declining industries and how the most appropriate strategy might be selected.

MANAGING IN A RECESSION

The second edition of this book is being written as Britain remains in a stubborn and very deep economic recession. The recession has been global and has affected most countries, industries and businesses, regardless of size or sector. In a recession retrenchment strategies are frequently required as demand falls and costs need containing; at the same time, there is a need, wherever practical, to invest and prepare the organization to benefit from the recovery when it comes.

Recession alone will not necessarily put a company into a crisis or turnaround situation; rather it highlights existing weaknesses either created in, or hidden in, boom conditions. The organizations which are best prepared to cope with a recession are those with relatively low borrowings. Highly geared companies may be forced to divest assets in order to raise cash to cover their interest and repayment needs. Case 19.6 illustrates how TNT overcame difficulties resulting from rapid expansion.

Clifford (1977) has suggested that com-

panies which survive a recession most successfully are characterized by superior management which emphasizes the protection of margins, the efficient use of capital, and a concentration on markets or segments where distinctive competitive advantage is possible. Such competitive advantage will result from more effective cost control, innovative differentiation, a focus on service and quality and speedy reaction and change in a dynamic environment. Airtours, Case 19.7, is an opportunistic company which reacted quickly when a major competitor collapsed. The recession of the late 1980s/early 1990s has forced organizations to be creative in their search for cost reductions – earlier productivity drives have eliminated many inefficiencies. Information technology has provided some valuable opportunities. Cost savings must then be controlled to ensure that they do not creep up again. The focus of the cost cutting is critical. Training and research and development, for example, should not be sacrificed unnecessarily because new ideas and service quality are increasingly important for adding value, helping customers find new competitive opportunitites themselves and persuading consumers to buy when their spending power is limited. R & D, then, should be managed better rather than cut, and directed more towards short-term improvements. However, the long-term needs should not be wholly ignored. In particular the development time for new products and services should be speeded up.

Dividend payments and investment funding may have to be traded off against each other. Some organizations will reduce dividends when profits fall to conserve their resources; others will maintain them to appease shareholders. See Chapter 13.

Moreover, increasing global competition has forced companies to target markets and niches more effectively, and, in many cases, increase their marketing rather than cut expenditure. The emphasis has typically focused on efficiencies and savings rather than luxury – consumers with less dis-

Case 19.6
TNT

TNT, the Australian transport and distribution group, has interests in shipping, aviation and trucking around the world. Throughout the 1970s and 1980s TNT pursued high-risk growth strategies aimed at creating a global transport giant which could carry anything from an urgent letter to a crate of machinery in a range of time-scales appropriate for different customers. This has been achieved fully in Australia and substantially in Europe, but the growth has been dependent upon high borrowings to buy market share. Generally TNT has operated efficiently and this has helped offset the debt burden. TNT has linkages with Rupert Murdoch's News International Group and helped distribute his newspapers when strikes and picketing followed the move from central London to Wapping.

TNT achieved large size and high market share, but with low margins, limited profitability and high debt. When the company was threatened by the world recession the share price and investor confidence fell. Strategic change was demanded.

TNT sold its holdings in non-core businesses such as brewing and mining to focus on its core distribution activities. Whilst a US trucking business was floated off as an independent company, TNT acquired a French express carrier to consolidate its position in Western Europe. In addition TNT entered a subcontract deal with Federal Express, a leading competitor, whereby TNT handled deliveries in Europe for Federal Express.

The most important move, in July 1991, was a joint venture with the state-owned post offices of Germany, France, Holland, Sweden and Canada. TNT owned 50% of a new, independent company (the network of post offices, which could be increased in number, owned the other 50%) which would provide an overnight delivery of packages and letters world wide. Not only did this increase the utilization of TNT's infrastructure, in particular its aircraft, it also involved a cash injection by the post offices which substantially reduced TNT's debt.

cretionary purchasing power have been more selective.

Whittingham (1991) reinforces points made earlier in the book and contends that innovation and product and service improvement is a more effective use of scarce resources in a recession than is diversification, and that cutting back too much leaves companies exposed and under capacity for the recovery. Ideally organizations will consult and involve employees, looking to, say, negotiate pay freezes and reduce hours rather than make staff redundant. This provides greater flexibility to grow. Nevertheless, many firms will not have sufficient resources to pursue their preferred option.

When companies do emerge from a recession and attempt to satisfy increasing demand there is a fresh challenge – the need to control events, monitor the cash flow and guard against over-trading.

STRATEGIES FOR DECLINING INDUSTRIES

Harrigan (1980) draws upon the themes outlined when portfolio analysis was dis-

Case 19.7
AIRTOURS

In 1990 Airtours was a relatively small but fast-growing package tour operator. Based in Lancashire it offered low-price holidays in cheaper resorts and for a while had a reputation for carrying rowdy youngsters. Most of its customers were based in the north, and Airtours benefited competitively when the impact of the recession was felt first in the south. When bookings fell dramatically before and during the Gulf War (in Airtours' case, by 40%), the company pulled out of selected markets, slowed down its planned move to new premises and froze capital expenditure on new information technology. Airtours was, however, building an airline, and was committed to taking delivery of five McDonnell Douglas aircraft (on lease) which would operate from Manchester (three planes), Birmingham and Stansted.

Airtours successfully predicted the collapse of International Leisure Group, which included Intasun, the second largest package tour operator. When ILG ceased trading in March 1991 Airtours had agents in place in targeted resorts (the Balearic and Canary Islands, Portugal and Greece) who were ready to buy up all the released Intasun beds. Striking early, and with the Gulf War still an issue, Airtours obtained good price deals. Within just one week Airtours booked 90,000 new holidays and quickly became the third largest package tour operator. The company had no debt. In 1992 Airtours bought Pickfords, the third largest travel agency in the UK with 333 branches, using its own cash reserves; and early in 1993 Airtours launched a hostile bid for Owners Abroad, the UK's second largest tour operator.

---

cussed in Chapter 16 and considers whether retrenchment, turnaround or divestment is the most appropriate strategy for an individual competitor in a declining industry. Strategies of leadership and niche marketing (turnaround), exploiting or harvesting (retrenchment) and divestment are considered in the light of the overall attractiveness of the industry whilst it is declining and the opportunities for an individual competitor to create and sustain competitive advantage. These are illustrated and defined in Figure 19.2.

Harrigan contends that the most appropriate strategy is dependent on four factors:

☐ The nature of the decline, and the causes – the speed at which decline is taking place, and whether specific segments are still surviving and offering differentiation and niche marketing opportunities for companies who can create and sustain competitive advantage. These factors affect the attractiveness of the industry.

☐ The ability of a company to target these market segments effectively and create consumer preference. This is affected by company strengths and weaknesses.

☐ The **exit costs** for all competitors. Exit costs influence the degree of urgency that companies feel towards finding a way of remaining competitive rather than simply withdrawing. Exit costs relate to

☐ the inability to find a buyer for the business, and the cost of closure;

☐ the strategic significance for the company as a whole, particularly if vertical integration strategies are affected;

☐ the possible effect upon key stakeholders, such as shareholders, man-

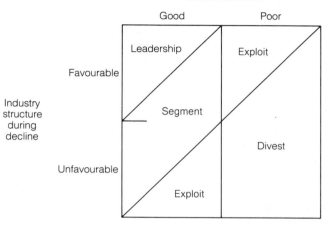

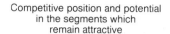

Leadership	Selective investment*; turnaround
	Invest as appropriate to give real competitive advantage
	Idea: Become one of the strongest competitors in the declining industry with either the lowest costs or clear differentiation
Segment or niche	Selective investment*; turnaround
	Identify one or more attractive segments, those with greatest potential for longer-term survival or short-term returns, and seek a strong position whilst divesting in other segments
Exploit or harvest	Phased withdrawal*; retrenchment
	Controlled disinvestment, reducing product alternatives, advertising and so on in order to cut costs
	Problem: losing the confidence of suppliers and buyers as they witness the obvious reduction of commitment
	Must lead eventually to divestment or liquidation
Quick divestment	Immediate sale or liquidation

Figure 19.2 Strategies for declining industries. The asterisks indicate the terms that are used in the directional policy matrix discussed in Chapter 16 (Figure 16.5). Developed from Harrigan, K R (1980) *Strategies for Declining Businesses*, Heath; Harrigan, K R and Porter, M E (1983) End-game strategies for declining industries, *Harvard Business Review*, July–August.

agers and the strategic leader, especially if they have had a long-term commitment to the product, service or business unit.

☐ Linked to all these, the opportunities or threats which exist as a result of competitor activity, what they choose to do and why. If the product or industry is strategically significant, certain competitors may choose not to withdraw, accepting very low profits or even no profits, and thereby making it more difficult for others.

Figure 19.2 encapsulates the first two points above; the decision will also involve the last two points.

Competitive advantage is likely to be attained by those companies who are aware early of the decline, and the opportunities present during the decline, and who seek to create the most advantageous positions ahead of their competitors. Companies who react when things have started to go wrong are less likely to succeed in creating an effective strategy.

IMPLEMENTING RECOVERY STRATEGIES

In the previous chapter we stressed that organizational issues and difficulties often result in failure of the diversification and acquisition strategies to yield the desired results. Organizational issues will again be important in the case of recovery strategies. Time is likely to be limited, and proposed changes will have to be implemented quickly. The support and co-operation of managers and other employees will be essential, particularly where redundancies, changes in organization structures or changes in working practices are required. Quite possibly changes in attitudes – an issue of organiza-

tional culture – will be involved. Although the gravity of the situation may be visible, and the dangers of failing to change clearly understood, the changes will need managing properly if they are to prove effective. The issues involved in managing change are discussed in Chapter 24.

Organization development is a process that must deal with more than just structure, but with attitudes and relationships. It needs to be planned and continuous, but most importantly it needs managing. The successful turnround in the fortunes of BR has been achieved because we were determined

- [ ] to convince our workforce that their future depended on satisfying the customer;
- [ ] to convince our managers that they were held accountable for achieving the targets set them;
- [ ] to convince our customers that we were giving them value for money;
- [ ] and to convince Government that we were well managed and able to meet agreed objectives.

Sir Robert Reid, retired Chairman,
British Railways Board

SUMMARY

At any time certain industries will be declining and others will be relatively unattractive as far as particular companies are concerned because of intense competition. Individual companies might be performing poorly and in need of either a recovery strategy or an appropriate divestment. These strategies have been discussed in this chapter, which has built on Chapter 8 where the symptoms and causes of decline were discussed.

Specifically we have

- [ ] considered the feasibility of recovery in a particular situation, and the four possible outcomes of a change in strategy: a failure to recover, temporary recovery, sustained survival and sustained recovery;
- [ ] discussed the retrenchment strategies of organization and financial change, cost and asset reduction, and revenue generation;
- [ ] examined how a number of strategies aimed at improving marketing effectiveness might bring about a turnaround;
- [ ] looked at divestment strategies, in terms of the divestment decision itself, and the financial and strategic justifications, and the issues involved in implementing the strategy;
- [ ] considered strategic management in a recession;
- [ ] briefly considered declining industries and the possible strategies for individual competitors.

CHECKLIST OF KEY TERMS AND CONCEPTS

You should feel confident that you understand the following terms and ideas:

☐ The four possible recovery situations illustrated in Figure 19.1: non-recoverable, temporary, sustained survival and sustained recovery
☐ Retrenchment strategies
☐ Turnaround strategies
☐ Divestment strategies
☐ Leadership, segment, exploit and divestment strategies in the context of a declining industry.

QUESTIONS AND RESEARCH ASSIGNMENTS

Text related

1. Why might a company wish to remain a competitor in an industry despite low or declining profitability?

    Classify your reasons as objective or subjective. Can the subjective reasons be justified?

Library based

2. How successful have Usinor-Sacilor, Leeds Permanent and General Motors been recently? Where do you believe they all are in relation to the recovery strategies illustrated in Figure 19.1?

3. Reed International's origins are not in publishing, where they now concentrate, but in paper and packaging. They became a force in publishing when they acquired IPC (International Printers Ltd) in the early 1970s.

    ☐ Why has Reed chosen to divest all non-publishing activities in recent years?
    ☐ What is Reed's current position in the publishing industry? How strong are they?
    ☐ What growth strategies in publishing do you feel would be appropriate?

RECOMMENDED FURTHER READING

Slatter (1984) is a very comprehensive study of turnaround strategies, but Harrigan (1980) provides useful insight into declining businesses. Harrigan, K R and Porter, M E (1983) End-game strategies for declining industries, *Harvard Business Review*, July–August, combines Harrigan's research into declining businesses with Porter's work on competitive advantage.

Nelson, R and Clutterbuck, D (1988) *How Twenty Well-Known Companies Came Back From The Brink*, Allen, contains a number of interesting case studies.

REFERENCES

Clifford, D K (1977) Thriving in a recession, *Harvard Business Review*, July–August.
Davis, J V (1974) The strategic divestment decision, *Long Range Planning*, February.
Devlin, G (1989) Selling off not out, *Management Today*, April.
Harrigan, K R (1980) *Strategies for Declining Businesses*, Heath.
Slatter, S (1984) *Corporate Recovery: Successful Turnaround Strategies and Their Implementation*, Penguin.
Whittingham, R (1991) Recession strategies and top management change, *Journal of General Management*, **16** (3), Spring.

MANAGEMENT BUY-OUTS

20

LEARNING OBJECTIVES

After studying this chapter you should be able to

☐ explain the growing incidence of management buy-outs in the UK in recent years;
☐ identify the main parties involved and assess their objectives and expectations;
☐ discuss the issues behind success and failure;
☐ construct the financial profile of a typical buy-out;
☐ describe the similarities and differences between buy-outs and management buy-ins.

Management buy-outs became increasingly popular in the UK in the 1980s, and for many organizations they are an ideal way of implementing a divestment strategy. The reasons for management buy-outs and the objectives of the parties involved, together with relative success rates, are considered in this chapter.

INTRODUCTION

Management buy-outs (MBOs) have been imported from America, although the typical format has been modified. They have so far proved more popular in the UK than in the rest of Europe, but they are steadily growing in popularity throughout the European Community. They have been assisted by governments who have made the conditions for them increasingly favourable through legislative and tax changes designed to encourage enterprise. They have also received a boost by the increasing tendency of many conglomerates, particularly American corporations, to reduce the extent of their diversification and concentrate more on core activities. In Europe concentrated organizations which might benefit from the opportunities presented by the single market in 1992 are in vogue.

We have already mentioned a number of management buy-outs. Case 1.4 was about the buy-out of the Virgin organization by its founder Richard Branson after its flotation as a public company proved to be an unhappy experience. Case 17.2 featured Premier

Brands, which was created through a buy-out of selected brands from Cadbury's, and in Case 17.6 we discussed the buy-out of MFI after the merger of Asda and MFI failed to generate the forecast synergy. The privatization of National Bus was accomplished through a series of sales to existing company managers.

These examples are amongst the largest management buy-outs in the UK. The Asda–MFI de-merger involved £720 million, Virgin was valued at some £250 million when it was bought back, and Premier Brands cost £100 million. Wright, Coyne and Robbie (1987) contend that before 1982 there were about 200 identifiable buy-outs whose average value was about £1 million, and that since then there have been upwards of 200 per year, with an average value in 1987 of £12 million.

The highest number was 500 in 1990, since when there has been a reduction. The average value rose to £14 million in 1989, but the vast majority still involve less than £5 million. Whilst the recent economic recession has increased the number of opportunities, particularly in certain industrial sectors, high interest rates and lower customer demand for the products and services render many possible buy-outs non-viable.

The number of 'large' buy-outs, defined as involving £10 million and over, has followed a similar trend. The figures below have been published in the *Financial Times*:

Year	Number of buy-outs over £10 million
1986	28
1987	35
1988	54
1989	71
1990	61
1991	44
1992 (Jan.–Nov.)	43

Management buy-outs generally involve three parties: managers (and on occasions other employees who may become equity holders); vendors; and external financiers, who provide both equity and loan capital. All have objectives and expectations. **Managers** acquire control of their own business, often with a substantial equity stake whilst investing only a small proportion of the total funding involved. This reverses the trend to divorce ownership and control, which was discussed in Chapter 5, and clearly influences the organizational culture and objectives. **Vendors** divest businesses which may be performing poorly or failing to create synergy with their other activities, and they frequently accomplish this amicably and profitably. **Financiers** are attracted to management buy-outs because they offer the potential to earn higher financial returns than investing in large companies and lower failure rates than traditional start-up businesses.

There are also **management buy-ins** whereby a group of outside managers are brought in to run a company which is sold to them and their backers rather than to existing managers. The disadvantage is the loss of continuity and the lack of insight and experience in the particular company; a possible advantage in certain circumstances is the influx of fresh ideas.

The term **leveraged buy-out**, which originated in the USA, is often used where the lead financiers take the lead role in large buy-outs (and buy-ins). The name refers to the high level of borrowing which the company takes on, using the assets being purchased as leverage.

The general conclusion from research over a number of years by the Centre of Management Buy-Out Research at the University of Nottingham is that buy-out teams improve the performance of businesses and that, after an initial drop in employee numbers, they create jobs.

In this chapter the background causes of management buy-outs are explored, together with the interests, expectations and objectives of the parties involved. The advantages for the various interested parties are considered along with the key issues of exit facilities and overall success. A worked example of a hypothetical buy-out is featured to illustrate a typical financial package; and the chapter concludes with a brief consideration of management buy-ins.

MANAGEMENT BUY-OUTS IN THE UNITED KINGDOM

Management buy-outs, described simply, involve the purchase of a business from its existing owners by the current managers in conjunction with one or more financial institutions.

Buy-outs first became significant in America in the 1970s, but prior to the early 1980s legislation in the UK restricted their potential. Until 1981 it was illegal for a company to finance the purchase of its own shares. Batchelor (1988) contends that the growth in popularity of management buy-outs in the UK has been founded on a different model to that popularized in America. In the UK the proposal to purchase a business from its existing owners has typically come from the managers; in America, where the investment banks play a more aggressive role, the idea has often originated with the financial institutions. In America the sales have often been associated with a need to reduce borrowing; in the UK this has been less of a necessity. Sales have been aimed at generating greater concentration and divesting businesses which are not producing acceptable financial returns or generating synergy. One motive for this has been to reduce the prospect of a hostile take-over bid resulting from poor overall performance. Some buy-outs occur because family owners have no organized succession and a sale to the existing managers is seen as more desirable than sale to an unknown outsider who has no personal involvement in the company. In addition

some businesses have been bought from the receivers after the original owners had got into difficulties, and some have been bought from the government as part of their privatization programme.

Research by Coopers and Lybrand (1989) has yielded the following breakdown of causes of buy-outs in 1986. The percentages are in relation to the total number of buy-outs analysed and not the money or assets involved.

Divestment	85%
No family succession	10%
Receivership	3%
Privatization	2%

Whilst divestment and sales of family companies remain dominant, there has been an increasing number of purchases from receivership in recent years. Such buy-outs are frequently at attractive prices, but often require speedy decisions with little time to analyse and plan the venture thoroughly.

Objectives and key success factors

Whilst there are important issues of managers wanting to own their own businesses, and possibly preserve their jobs when their company is in difficulties, management buy-outs are characterized by important financial objectives and constraints. Buy-outs typically have unusual financial structures and high gearing, as will be illustrated later, and the financial institutions which back them have financial targets and expectations. Consequently management buy-outs are expected to prove to be profitable for their shareholders and other backers by earning out the debt assumed when the company is bought out and by improving the company's performance in comparison with the results achieved by the previous owners.

In order to meet these expectations, and in addition to the essential key success factors for the business and the industry, it is important that managers are able to make the business more competitive and overcome the constraints imposed by the high debt burden. In addition they must be able to generate a positive cash flow. Eustace (1988) suggests that this is easier where the technology involved is relatively stable and where the products or services are not affected significantly by seasonal demand.

The managers and employees involved in a buy-out are likely to have a number of objectives, as highlighted above. Where they have invested in the company, they will be seeking a return on that investment, and it is in this area that their objectives are closely related to their financial backers. However, the expectations of the institutional investors who have provided equity capital and the banks who have lent money on fixed interest terms may differ. Coopers and Lybrand suggest that banks are likely to regard buy-outs as a better alternative than many other lending opportunities: they will pay a higher rate of interest than large established companies are willing to pay; they are more likely to succeed than traditional start-ups; and they are generally safer than lending to the Third World. The banks will normally agree to a higher percentage of debt in relation to equity (gearing) or in relation to total capital employed (the debt ratio) than is conventional, and will look for a cash flow which can both pay the interest and repay the debt after an agreed number of years. Despite the flexibility of the banks, borrowers should be cautious about the debt burden they accept. The MFI buy-out from Asda, described earlier, is a useful example of the need for caution. The buy-out was highly geared and the downturn in demand for MFI products in 1989 made the interest payments increasingly problematical. Because the deteriorating results were seen as temporary rather than long term, the financial institutions were willing to exercise flexibility, and hence a possible crisis was averted.

Their confidence and flexibility was justified when MFI, after two difficult years (1990 and 1991) when interest payments turned respectable trading profits into pre-tax losses, was profitable again in 1992. Predicting further growth and success MFI sought to re-float the company late in 1992. The business, which was valued at £670 million, some £50 million less than the 1987 buy-back value, was a 'very different animal from the one it was in 1987'. Using information technology to link their shops with their warehouses and factories MFI had slashed stocks. Many products are now delivered direct to customers rather than everything being theoretically available for instant collection.

Institutions are frequently concerned about long-term growth prospects and the ultimate flotation of the company, but this is not always the ideal outcome. Some floated companies are later re-privatized.

Management buy-backs

There are normally four benefits when a business is floated. The company's profile becomes more visible. Capital is generated, and there are opportunities for further borrowing through either equity or debt. Acquisitions using equity rather than cash are possible; and employees can become shareholders.

There are, however, perceived penalties. The owner loses effective control, and some entrepreneurs find it difficult to come to terms with this. Moreover, regular meetings with City institutions add to the frustration of the more intuitive managers. The increased visibility attracts comments from journalists and analysts and sensitive information can be made available to competitors. Institutional investors also have expectations of short-term success and profitability whilst some strategic leaders would prefer to concentrate on longer-term strategies. As a result, some floated companies are subsequently bought back by their managers, but this can result in a new set of issues and problems.

Virgin (Case 1.4) was re-privatized in 1988 after being floated in 1986. The informal management style of Richard Branson had not fitted in with City expectations. Branson complained that the institutions did not understand the volatility of the music industry; the City argued that Virgin did not have a long-term strategy. The buy-back was followed by a series of joint ventures with minority partners in order to raise money, and ultimately the sale of Virgin Music to Thorn–EMI to help fund the growth of Virgin's airline. Sir Andrew Lloyd Webber's Really Useful Group (RUG) was similarly bought back in 1990 after a flotation in 1986. RUG primarily exploits Lloyd Webber's music, which includes the scores for such shows as Phantom of the Opera, Evita, Cats and Aspects of Love. There was a clash of interests. Lloyd Webber wanted to be free to pursue personal music projects, including serious and classical works; the institutions felt the focus should be on the most commercial opportunities. Later 30% of RUG was sold to Polygram. International Leisure Group (ILG), which owned Air Europe and Intasun, the second largest package tour operator in the UK, was bought back by Harry Goodman in 1987. Goodman had felt constrained in his desire to build a larger European airline and offer scheduled as well as charter flights. This investment proved damaging in the recession and the Gulf War. Revenues fell; ILG was short of money and collapsed in 1991.

The expectations of the parties involved are explored in greater detail in the next section.

Advantages and issues

The advantages to the vendor and to the managers buying out the business are featured in Box 20.1, and these relate to the objectives of both parties. The issues included also relate to the objectives and motives of the managers and the company selling the business. Issue 2 suggests that there might well be a conflict of interest as far as the vendor is concerned. It is important for the vendor to negotiate a good financial deal in selling the business, particularly as far as existing shareholders are concerned, but at the same time other motives may be important. The company may want to deal with the business once it has been bought out, and would trust the managers already involved; or the sale may be because of financial pressures and the strategic leader or owner of the parent might be concerned to ensure that managers and employees who have been loyal in the past are provided with a secure future. A sale to them rather than an outsider might seem a better guarantee of this. Consequently there might be a clear **preference** to sell to the managers rather than invite a number of bids and select the highest. It has been suggested that some companies would prefer not to sell the business to its existing managers and then see them succeed where previously the business has failed to meet expectations, but this is not thought to be generally a significant issue.

It has already been mentioned that financial institutions who provide equity and loan funding will have financial targets, and they will be reluctant to support a business which is not thought capable of meeting their specific financial expectations. This is the first issue detailed in Box 20.1. A vendor may be willing to sell a business at a particular price, and the business may be commercially viable with a product or service which can be produced and sold profitably. However, if the financial returns are expected to be too low to meet the financiers' requirements, the transaction is unlikely to go ahead.

Success and failure

From points made earlier in this section, it is clear that a successful buy-out is likely to

Box 20.1
MANAGEMENT BUY-OUTS: ADVANTAGES AND ISSUES

ADVANTAGES TO THE VENDOR

☐ The cash is from a willing buyer who has knowledge of the business. If the price is acceptable, the cash is neither better nor worse than cash from elsewhere, but such a sale is good for the corporate image.
☐ It can reduce borrowings, divest a loss-making activity, or enable specialization and concentration.
☐ Because of the existing knowledge of the buyers, the negotiations will concentrate on the financial package rather than any possible hidden truths about the business.
☐ If there are any interrelationships or interdependences with activities which are being retained, continuity should be maintained.

ADVANTAGES TO THE MANAGERS

☐ There is continuity of employment, and also continuity of both management and trading relationships for suppliers and customers.
☐ There is commitment to the business because of personal financial involvement, providing real incentives to succeed. This is often used to justify the high gearing allowed by financiers.

☐ They know the problems, and probably how to improve productivity and reduce overheads. The latter is often crucial for transforming a marginal business into a profitable operation.
☐ It could lead to real substantial long-term gains if a flotation results.

ISSUES AND DRAWBACKS

☐ A company or business unit which a vendor is willing to sell at a particular price may be seen as incapable of being turned round sufficiently to meet the needs of potential financiers.
☐ The vendor has the problem of ensuring that he or she obtains a good deal, if not the best deal, for existing shareholders, and at the same time takes appropriate account of other stakeholders. The managers may not be the only bidders.
☐ A company is possibly unwilling to sell a business to its existing managers and then watch them improve performance, thereby exposing the previous failings. This is regarded as less of an issue than it used to be.
☐ There may be a negative effect on the motivation of managers who are not equity holders in the buy-out.
☐ There may be a negative effect on manager motivation again if the buy-out fails and the company is sold to another external buyer.

involve the purchase of predictable cash flows at an economical price. Coopers and Lybrand (1989) argue that for investors the ideal company would be one in a mature market, with established market share, low speculative research and development and a predictable cash flow. In reality the buy-out is more likely to involve a poorly performing business or division with an under-utilized asset base, which is seen as a non-core activity by its existing parent company.

The success rate, however, tends to be high. Batchelor (1988) contends that 3i (Investors in Industry), the financial institution most involved in buy-outs, have an overall failure rate of 12½%, with 14% of buy-outs involving less than £500 000 failing, and only 4% of those exceeding £500 000 failing. Failure implies that the institution does not receive the financial returns it forecast, and not that the business collapses and goes into receivership or liquidation. In contrast 3i expect a failure rate of one in three of the start-ups they support.

More recently 3i have argued that MBO companies typically perform better than their industry average in the medium term, but this claim has not been substantiated in research by the Centre for Management Buy-Out Research (CMBOR) and Warwick Business School (Lander, 1990). They conclude that MBOs succeed in improving performance for three years, and then their results often deteriorate to below the industry average.

At the same time the CMBOR argue that 7% of buy-outs ultimately achieve a stock market flotation, typically on the unlisted securities market (USM). The number of buy-out teams stating their intention to float is substantially higher than 7%, but of course there can be a lengthy time-lag before it is achieved.

Eustace (1988), again quoting data from the CMBOR, points out that 70% of bought-out companies exhibit improved profits, and 60% improved turnover, compared with pre-buy-out figures. 50% prove more profitable than their plans, and 45% turn over more than their expectations. There is, of course, no way of knowing how a company would have fared if the buy-out had not taken place. Although the defined failure rate is low, about one-third of bought-out companies experience cash flow problems and need to cut costs and overheads more than they

anticipated. Case 20.1 discusses the buy-out of Hornby Hobbies in 1982. Hornby was in the toy industry, which was affected by declining demand for certain products and by imports; the company needed to follow retrenchment strategies to cut costs before it could pursue growth and diversification opportunities. It took a number of years to turn the company round, but it did succeed with a USM flotation in 1986. The case highlights the need to be wary of the debt burden taken on at the time of purchase.

Having considered a number of general factors concerning buy-outs in the UK, the next section looks at the parties involved in greater detail, and their possibly conflicting expectations.

THE PARTIES INVOLVED AND THEIR EXPECTATIONS

A management buy-out normally involves a vendor, a management team which may include employees amongst the equity holders, institutional providers of most of the equity capital, and banks and other institutions who loan money to the business. In this section we concentrate on the role and expectations of the managers and the financial institutions. The objectives and motives of the vendor were discussed in the last section.

The management team

Coopers and Lybrand contend that the financial backers will expect the management group involved in the buy-out to be a team. They will expect them to be competent in all the functional areas of the business and to have skills in those areas which are essential for competitive success. In the case of the purchase of a business unit from a large company, it is important to consider which functions were previously performed by the vendor's head office rather than by the managers involved in the buy-out, and how this will be dealt with. The appointment of a non-executive chairman from outside the company might prove valuable in the provision of new strategic ideas. The team of senior managers should be cohesive; and the level of management below them, those without an equity holding, should be motivated and committed to the new organization. The company may seem less secure to them, and consequently they might be tempted to consider leaving.

Case 20.1
HORNBY HOBBIES

Hornby was founded in the 1920s by the same family which manufactured Meccano, the construction kits which eventually lost popularity with the growth of Lego. The best-known Hornby product was model electric railways, although the first models produced by Hornby were larger clockwork trains. In 1964 Hornby was acquired by Lines Brothers, then the largest UK toy manufacturer. Lines already owned Rovex, the company which manufactured Tri-ang railways, Hornby's main competitor. In addition Rovex also made Scalextric, the slot car racing system. Lines went into liquidation in 1971 and was acquired by Dunbee-Combex-Marx (DCM), another toy company which itself collapsed in 1981. The receivers of DCM transferred the Hornby, Tri-ang and Scalextric activities into a new company called Hornby Hobbies, based in Margate, Kent, which was bought out by its managers in 1982. The buy-out cost £5.5 million but took some 12 months to arrange because prospective institutional backers were reluctant to commit their funds to an industry in trouble. Managers and employees acquired 20% of the equity.

In 1982 the demand for traditional toys and games was hit by the growing popularity of electronic toys and home computers. Hornby's turnover fell from £13 million in 1981 to under £10 million in 1982, and subsequently to £7.6 million in 1984; the company was forced to follow a **retrenchment** strategy designed to cut costs and reduce overheads. When DCM went into receivership in 1981, 1300 people were employed at Margate; within 18 months this had been reduced to 320.

Hornby also decided to follow a strategy of **diversification** which began in 1983 in order to lessen its dependence on the traditional lines which continued to experience declining demand. Hornby introduced products with relatively short lives in addition to those which are basically collectable ranges. Their new products have included Flower Fairies (toy dolls and accessories), Pound Puppies (soft toys), Boo Boos Care (a baby doll), Gro-Toys and Tendertoys (pre-school toys) and LA Gear (a range of aerobic exercise toys for girls). Some products, particularly soft toys, are manufactured by subcontractors in Hong Kong. In addition, in 1985 Hornby launched Thomas the Tank Engine and Friends, a range of clockwork and electric train systems based on the Reverend W H Awdry characters and manufactured alongside the existing Hornby models to the same quality standards. By 1986 40% of turnover was contributed by the new products, and this percentage has continued to grow.

Continued overleaf

In 1991 Hornby launched a new product range, plastic American wrestler figures, in the autumn – traditionally new toys are introduced in spring, when retailers begin thinking about Christmas. In 1992, after lengthy development, Hornby launched Cassy, a fashion doll, which, at 7 inches tall, was 5 inches shorter than the two well-known market leaders, Sindy and Barbie. Various accessories are available, including a country house with a set of audio cassettes to set the atmosphere for each room.

Diversification outside the toy industry had taken place in 1988 with the acquisition of Fletcher sports boats, the UK market leader.

After losing money in 1982 the company has been consistently profitable. However, 1985 was the first year that a profit after interest and tax was recorded, because of the high interest charges resulting from the buy-out.

In December 1986 the company sought a flotation on the Unlisted Securities Market, offering 61% of the equity at a price which represented over 11 times current earnings per share. Hornby was wanting to raise £5 million in order to reduce its debts, which amounted to some £6 million. The flotation was successful. Turnover rose steadily to £40 million in 1990 with pre-tax profits of £3.8 million. Earnings per share of 30 pence were treble those of 1986. However, the recession caught up with Hornby in 1991 and turnover fell to £32 million and profits to £2 million. Within the context of the troubled toy industry Hornby has been relatively successful, growing around a strong base – demand for electric trains and Scalextric has held up.

It is important that the management team, whatever their personal motives and expectations, appreciate the performance expectations of their backers and are willing to make the necessary changes to reduce costs and reposition the company's products as appropriate. Managers may conflict initially rather than agree on the future objectives for the company. Those who are most committed to existing products, services and practices may be less willing to support change than others who have less loyalty to the past. Certain managers, possibly any who are near to retirement, might be most concerned with security, and therefore look to minimize risks; others may be more growth and risk oriented. Such differences must be reconciled to agree future direction. The changes which are required may involve changes of culture as well as of products and services, particularly where growth and diversification into new areas is considered desirable.

Financial institutions

In putting together a proposed buy-out package it is important to seek a fit between the expectations of potential backers and the ability of the business to meet these expectations. Certain institutions might prefer a steady and regular return over a number of years; others might seek rapid growth and an early flotation, and as a result accept a higher level of risk with their investment. Coopers and Lybrand suggest that banks typically look for a rate of interest of 2% above base rate on loans secured against assets; and an interest cover (profit before interest and tax divided by interest payments) of at least a factor of 2. Batchelor (1988) suggests that the rate charged to very large companies would be perhaps 1% above base rate. Because of the need for assets and security it may be more difficult for a service business to organize a buy-out than a manufacturing company. Institutional providers of equity seek a mini-

Table 20.1 Exit from buy-outs

Form of exit	Investors leaving			Comments
	Management	Employees	Financiers	
Liquidation	X	X	X	Ideally all investments recovered in full
Sale to another organization	X	X	X	Again, all investments repaid, ideally
				Managers and employees may remain with the new owners
Earn out – managers use profits to buy out financiers			X	Financiers cease to be owners
Managers use own money (or borrow) to purchase financiers' shares			X	As above
Private sale of shares by financiers			X	Financiers replaced by other financiers
Managers, employees trade shares amongst themselves	X	X		Individuals able to exit; newcomers may become owners
Stock market flotation	X	X	X	Full or partial exit by financiers; partial exit by managers, employees

mum rate of return on their investment of 40%, the actual expectation being influenced by the level of risk. This 40% could be made up of interest or dividends together with any repayments and the growth in the value of their capital investment in the business. This in turn depends upon the percentage of the issued ordinary shares owned by them. Research by KPMG Peat Marwick (1991) shows that the average annual rate of return to institutions providing equity capital is 54%.

Exit routes

One important consideration for all parties investing in a buy-out is their ability to withdraw their money at any time. Exit routes are particularly important for financiers, who are likely to want some flexibility. Table 20.1 features seven different exit routes and shows which investors benefit from each alternative.

In summary, the important issue is the closeness of fit between the expectations of all the parties involved and the potential of the business to achieve certain targets. If the requirements of the parties, especially the investors, are not met, they are likely to seek an exit route. Case 20.2 describes the successful buy-out of the pen company Parker from its American parent and subsequent disagreements between the stakeholders involved.

FINANCING A BUY-OUT

It has already been mentioned that management buy-outs are funded by a mixture of investment capital provided by managers

Case 20.2
PARKER PENS

Parker, the pen company, became a £41 million buy-out early in 1986. It was sold by its parent company, Manpower, because it was losing money and because Manpower decided to follow a strategy of concentration on its core business as an employment agency. The buy-out was led by the head of Parker's UK operation, Jacques Margry.

At the time of the buy-out Parker was losing money in America but was profitable in Europe, which also constituted its major market. Sales internationally were approximately as follows.

Europe	49% of total
North America	18%
South America	13%
Asia and Pacific	13%
Middle East and Africa	7%

Not unexpectedly the new corporate headquarters were based in Newhaven, Sussex.

A retrenchment strategy was undertaken to reduce stock levels and employee numbers, both of which were judged to be too high. In the USA a turnaround was needed to improve differentiation and re-position the pens upmarket – their image and reputation had been damaged by attempts to compete with cheaper lower quality Japanese imports and by direct price competition with Shaeffer. Parker also chose to target the segment for expensive gift items. In addition research was begun into the feasibility of a global pen, which could be finished in a variety of ways to accord with different cultures and preferences around the world. Plastic finishes are popular in Japan, for example, and gold in Asia and Latin America.

Although the bought-out company was financially successful and profitable, friction grew between the management and the external financiers because of differing interests and expectations. Equity was distributed as follows:

Management	25%
Pkr Associates (the Parker family)	15%
Schroder Ventures	30%
Electra Investment Trust	10%
Chemical Ventures (US)	10%
Bankers Trust (US)	10%

These differences came to a head in June 1988 when a proposed stock market flotation was abandoned. The financiers and their City advisers disagreed on the valuation of the company and the price of the shares. The financiers were seeking £155 million; the advisers felt £139 million was more realistic in the current market environment. Schroder Ventures and Electra then proposed that Parker should be offered for sale to a corporate buyer, and persuaded other investors to agree.

The first company to show a real interest was Pentland Industries, a UK industrial conglomerate with a substantial interest in Reebok sports shoes and outfits. Margry agreed with the Pentland chairman that there was no product synergy between the companies, but they shared a common attitude towards branding and market positioning. In addition both marketed their products internationally. It was both an advantage and a disadvantage that individually they were most successful in different countries. Pentland were to pay £170 million for 85% of Parker's equity — the management team would retain a share. However, the deal fell through in December 1988 because agreement on terms and conditions could not be reached. At this stage the *Financial Times* quoted Jacques Margry as saying that he did not want any more offers and that he intended to recapitalize the company with the help of the existing shareholders and continue operations as an independent company.

By the early 1990s the company, still independent, had been turned around and successfully re-positioned. Whilst 'upmarket' the pens were not promoted as designer accessories but as fountain pens. Profits had grown since 1987 and Parker had a 53% share of the UK market. Parker's main rivals all had around 5–7% each.

In early 1992 it was reported that Jacques Margry and his management team now wished to leave the company and Parker Pen would be auctioned, hopefully raising around £300 million. Bids were invited from around the world.

In September 1992 Gillette, the US company best known for its shaving products and toiletries, offered £285 million. Gillette already owned Paper Mate (bought in 1955) and Waterman (bought in 1987). Whilst some 60% of Parker's sales are now in Europe, Paper Mate is strongest in North and Latin America. Waterman is strong in the expensive fountain pen segment, which is not the major target for Parker. Nevertheless, the bid was referred to the Monopolies and Mergers Commission.

In February 1993 the MMC agreed that the bid could proceed.

(and possibly other employees) and institutional shareholders and by loans. The equity holdings can be composed of ordinary shares, preference shares and preferred ordinary shares with enhanced rights. The preference shares will carry a fixed annual dividend which might increase in amount annually unless the shares are redeemed by a certain date. The nature of the equity provision will be linked to the risk, the anticipated returns, and the ability of the investor to withdraw without financial loss.

The equity stake of the managers might vary through what is known as a **ratchet mechanism**. Where this applies the number of ordinary shares issued to managers increases if certain performance criteria (say profit or revenue targets, or a flotation by a certain date) are met. The aim is to provide an incentive for managers, particularly if their initial shareholding is only a very small percentage of the total because of the magnitude of the funding involved. One difficulty of ratchet mechanisms relates to the establishment of targets which are acceptable to all parties involved, and in addition there is the possibility that they will encourage the pursuit of short-term targets in preference to the longer-term interests of the business.

Loans are occasionally separated into mezzanine finance and senior debt. Mezzanine loans, usually unsecured, rank after senior (secured) debt but before equity in the event of a company failing. To compensate for the

Table 20.2   A worked example of a successful buy-out

Capitalization

Ordinary shares	*£ thousands*	*Ownership*
Management	50	(20%)
Investors	200	(80%)
	250	

Preference shares		
Investors	1000	

Debt		
Secured bank loan	1750	
	3000	

Profit and loss account		
Turnover	12000	
Less: Cost of sales	9500	
Equals: Gross profit	2500	
Less: Overheads	1600	
Equals: Profit before interest and taxation	900	
Less: Interest	300	
Tax	250	
Preference dividend	150	
Equals: Profit available for ordinary shareholders	200	
Less: Dividends	100	
Retained in the business	100	

greater risk they typically carry interest one to three percentage points above secured loans.

A worked example

The buy-out illustrated in Table 20.2 is hypothetical but the figures and percentages are based on real examples.

The first decision would concern the amount of money required to capitalize and establish a viable business. The assumption is a figure of £3 million. The maximum amount of debt which could be secured against the assets of the business is illustrated as £1 750 000. The profit and loss calculation is based on a rate of interest of 17% per annum on this loan, which might be representative of 70% of the company's existing trade debtors, 60% of the property value, and 40% of plant and machinery and stocks. Hence £1 250 000 is required in equity. The institu-

tional shareholders might accept an 80 : 20 preference : ordinary split, and the example illustrates preference shares yielding 15% per annum, a favourable rate for the company. The ordinary shares are again split 80 : 20, with the managers being required to invest a total of £50 000 for their 20%. Figure 20.1 illustrates the relative percentages of the total funding provided by the managers, institutional investors and the banks, who are likely to be the major source of the loan capital. This type of breakdown, with a debt ratio of nearly 60%, is very typical for a small buy-out. The percentage of loan funding is higher than would normally be found in a more conventional situation.

The profit and loss account shows a profit before interest and tax of £900 000, interest of £300 000 (17% of the £1 750 000 loan), tax estimated at £250 000 and preference dividends of £150 000. The loan interest cover is a factor of 3. £200 000 is therefore available for ordinary shareholders, and, if £100 000 is paid in dividends (a 40% return), £100 000 is

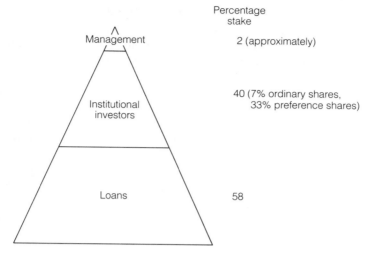

Figure 20.1   A typical management buy-out capitalization.

available to re-invest in the business. It could be that the managers would re-invest their dividends as well. Whilst this might seem successful, it would have to be improved as the business developed if the preference shares were to be redeemed and the bank loan paid off.

In conclusion, the following list summarizes the key factors and issues which are likely to determine the relative success of a buy-out:

☐ the ability to raise a significant amount of debt in relation to the assets and other sources of funding
☐ the strengths and abilities of the managers involved
☐ the ability of the business to generate a cash flow which is strong enough to pay the interest burden and subsequently pay off the loans
☐ the price negotiated with the vendor
☐ the exit opportunities for the investors.

MANAGEMENT BUY-INS

Management buy-ins occur where an organization is established to buy-out a company.

Examples quoted earlier are the consortium created to buy out F W Woolworth in 1982 (Case 18.6), and Derby International, the foreign-backed organization which acquired Raleigh Bicycles from Tube Investments. Buy-ins typically start with the financiers who spot the opportunity and then create a management team to exploit the potential.

There are certain features which are similar to management buy-outs. There are again investors who provide the bulk of the investment, and a management team who take an equity stake in the business. But this time the managers are not internal to the business and fully aware of the strengths and weaknesses. Consequently their management skills and their ability to manage a new unfamiliar situation are crucial issues.

De Quervain, quoted in Batchelor (1987), argues that there are three essential characteristics of a successful buy-in.

☐ The management team are successful and experienced, ideally in the same or a similar industry, and they are familiar with the problems associated with independent companies. In other words their experience is not solely with subsidiaries of large conglomerates where head office performs a number of key strategic roles. It is particularly useful if they have previous experience of a buy-out or buy-in.

☐ The investors are willing to accept risks which are higher than those associated with buy-outs. The failure rate is likely to be higher, and consequently the investors must place considerable trust in the management team.

☐ The target company, which may already be independent or a subsidiary of a larger organization, is known to be underperforming and is capable of being turned around.

Issues of culture and change are particularly important where a new management team has ideas which are significantly different from those of existing managers. An example might be a relatively stable, possibly sleepy, family company which is taken over by professional managers who wish to introduce new systems, improve efficiencies and cut overheads. Some existing managers will feel threatened and seek to leave; others will not be required. Uncertainty will surround the changes. In relation to these issues, Batchelor suggests that agreed and fully supported deals are more likely to succeed than those

---

Case 20.3
DAVID BROWN

In January 1990 David Brown, based in Huddersfield, was bought from its 87-year-old family owner, Sir David Brown, by two businessmen, Chris Brown (no family ties) and Chris Cook. The company had been owned by generations of the Brown family since it was founded in 1860, but in recent years it had declined and become unprofitable. Sir David was resident in the south of France and reliant on a management team. There was perceived to be a lack of drive and control. Brown and Cook had worked together previously and both had backgrounds in large engineering companies. They had joined forces to look for a suitable buy-in opportunity and they had support from Bankers Trust who organized the financing from banks and venture capitalists.

Essentially David Brown is an engineering business, with an international reputation for its gears. Earlier it had also been renowned for tractors – which it no longer produces. At one point during World War II Brown was the only available source of gears for the engines of Spitfires and Hurricanes. In 1947 David Brown acquired Aston Martin and Lagonda (later divested) and manufactured high-performance cars for some years. The company also diversified into manufacturing machine tools, particularly for producing gears, and fast ships – Vosper Thorneycroft was acquired. The company became increasingly dependent upon defence business but was slow to adapt as demand changed and fell. David Brown was bought for £46 million and financed as follows:

	£ million
Ordinary shares	2.0
Preference shares	5.8
TOTAL EQUITY	7.8
Mezzanine debt	9.2
Senior loans	29.0

The company has been re-structured since the buy-in. The existing head office staff has been reduced dramatically, and new managers brought in. The workforce has also been cut. Shopfloor practices have been changed and productivity has risen. There are new products and new information and financial control systems. The business has been made financially viable.

The company is separated into four discrete divisions, arguably to enable a strong focus on markets, customers and service. These are:

☐ standard gearboxes for electric motors
☐ customized, special gearboxes and machine tools
☐ vehicle transmissions, especially for tanks and trains
☐ pumps – for the oil and petrochemical industries.

Despite the recession David Brown has been profitable and the debt has been reduced.

Nothing we did was particularly clever or unusual. It was just about managing a business properly – and buying the right one. (Chris Brown, Joint Managing Director)

The original capital structure was due for review in January 1993 when the supporting institutions were free to take out their equity (75% of the total) if they wished. Were this to have happened, Brown and Cook would have had four options:

(1) reverse into an already listed company
(2) increase borrowings again to buy out the investors
(3) sell out
(4) float.

However, David Brown's strong cash flow had enabled the managers to repay a £16 million loan five years ahead of schedule, invest £10 million on capital expenditure since 1990, and spend a further £3.5 million acquiring related businesses. The institutions were supportive and the decision was made to float the David Brown Group with a market value of £70 million.

which involve an external management team making a hostile bid. Particularly difficult are those situations where the existing managers make an unsuccessful counter-bid to buy out their company.

Management buy-ins have fallen in popularity during the early 1990s because of their relatively low success rate, and also because of the difficulties in matching keen and suitable managers with appropriate acquisitions. The failure rate is greatest in the case of small companies bought from private ownership. Case 20.3, David Brown, illustrates the successful acquisition and turnaround of a private company by two managers actively searching for a suitable buy-in opportunity.

Robbie, Wright and Chiplin (1991) highlight three main problems with management buy-ins:

☐ Unknown difficulties which typically come to light after the buy-in. Often these are the result of poor control systems and are not fully appreciated by the vendor.
☐ Many buy-in managers have a large company background and consequently less appreciation of small companies and their particular problems.
☐ Where the buy-in is of a company in difficulty there may be problems with key stakeholders. Important suppliers may be owed money and see this as an opportunity to press for payment; despite redundancies employees may be hoping

for pay rises to compensate for sacrifices during the decline.

To reduce the risk, some buy-in teams may try to negotiate staged payments based upon their relative success.

SUMMARY

Management buy-outs are one means by which owners can sell their companies or organizations can divest a subsidiary that they no longer want. Sale to the existing management offers several attractions to both vendor and buyers and raises a number of interesting issues. The incidence of buy-outs has grown in the UK through the 1980s and has often involved financial packages which differ from those which might be considered more conventional. Management buy-ins are similar in many respects, but they feature external managers rather than those who already work for the company concerned. In this chapter we have explored the issues involved in the growth and popularity of this particular strategic option.

Specifically we have

☐ considered the growing incidence of buy-outs in the UK, and why they have become increasingly popular;
☐ discussed the objectives and expectations of all the interested parties: vendor, managers, employees, and providers of both loan and equity funding;
☐ Shown that some company flotations lead to a management buy-back;
☐ explored the advantages for the various parties and the issues raised;
☐ looked at success and failure rates, and the ability of investors to exit from the buy-out;
☐ presented a worked example of a typical buy-out, highlighting the financial aspects;
☐ briefly considered buy-ins, and the similarities and differences.

CHECKLIST OF KEY TERMS AND CONCEPTS

You should feel confident that you understand the following terms and ideas:

☐ Management buy-outs
  ☐ Why they happen
  ☐ What they offer the parties involved
  ☐ The unusual funding arrangements

☐ Management buy-ins.

QUESTIONS AND RESEARCH ASSIGNMENTS

Text related

1. What factors do you feel would be most significant to all parties involved in a proposed buy-out during the negotiations? Where are the major areas of potential conflict?
2. Were the institutions supporting David Brown (Case 20.3) to have taken the unusual step of removing their equity, how would you rank the four options available to the buy-in team?

   If they had decided to reverse into an already listed company (option 1) what selection criteria would you use in searching for a suitable partner?

Library based

3. In the mid-1980s the Lex Service Group, whose hotel strategy was discussed in Case 16.1, was diversified into three areas: motor vehicle distribution, transport in the UK, and the distribution of electronic components, mainly in the USA. Lex chose to divest itself of its transport businesses.

   Lex Wilkinson and Lex Systemline subsidiaries were sold to an American buyer;

Bees Transport and Carpet Express were both management buy-outs in June and July 1986. Bees involved £2.5 million and Carpet Express £4.6 million. Carpet Express was capitalized as follows:

	£
Five senior managers	137 500
Five depot managers	12 500
Managers' total equity	150 000
Preferred ordinary shares, institutional buyers	225 000
Total equity	375 000
Preference shares (redeemable)	1 775 000
Loan capital	2 450 000

Research the relative success of Carpet Express since the buy-out, and consider whether all the parties involved have benefited.

RECOMMENDED FURTHER READING

The most substantial publications in the area of management buy outs are by Wright and Coyne at the Centre for Management Buy-Out Research at Nottingham University.

Parker, H (1986) How to buy out, *Management Today*, January, provides a useful summary and discussion. However, the *Financial Times* publishes a special supplement on this topic every few months, and these supplements contain both up-to-date statistics and case studies.

REFERENCES

Batchelor, C (1987) Revival of the fittest, *Financial Times*, 24 March.

Batchelor, C (1988) Where Britain leads the field, *Financial Times*, 12 July.

Coopers and Lybrand (1989) Presentation at Huddersfield Polytechnic, 21 February.

Eustace, P (1988) Britain's buyout boom. *The Engineer*, 4 February.

KPMG Peat Marwick (1991) Quoted in *Financial Times Management Buy-Out Survey*, 1 October.

Lander, R (1990) Research by Centre for Management Buy-Out Research and Warwick Business School quoted in Difficulties of measuring the success of a buy-out, *The Independent*, 26 October.

Robbie, K, Wright, M and Chiplin, B (1991) *Management Buy-Ins: An Analysis of Initial Characteristics and Performance*, Centre for Management Buy-Out Research.

Wright, M, Coyne, J and Robbie, K (1987) *Trends in UK Buy-Outs*, Venture Economics/Centre for Management Buy-Out Research.

WHAT CONSTITUTES A GOOD CHOICE?

21

LEARNING OBJECTIVES

After studying this chapter you should be able to

☐ define the key criteria for evaluating the appropriateness, feasibility and desirability of a particular strategic alternative;
☐ discuss why there may be a trade-off between these factors;
☐ explain the contribution to this evaluation of ten techniques described earlier in the book;
☐ list eight key strategic principles;
☐ argue the importance of strategy implementation;
☐ explain the role of judgement in strategic choice.

In this chapter we summarize the criteria which might be used to assess whether or not existing strategies are effective, and to evaluate proposed future changes in strategy. Useful techniques described earlier in the book are recalled.

INTRODUCTION

There is no single evaluation technique or framework as such that will provide a definite answer to which strategy or strategies a company should select or follow at any given time. Particular techniques will prove helpful in particular circumstances. A number of frameworks and techniques which are often classified as means of evaluating strategy have been discussed in earlier chapters; they are reviewed here.

There are certain essential criteria, however, which should be considered in assessing the merits and viability of existing strategies and alternatives for future change. This chapter considers how one might assess whether or not a corporate, competitive or functional strategy is effective or likely to be effective. The issues concern **appropriateness**, **feasibility** and **desirability**. Some of the considerations are likely to conflict with each other, and consequently an element of judgement is required in making a choice. The most appropriate or feasible option for the firm may not be the one that its managers regard as most desirable, for example.

Two manufacturers of small aircraft, Norman Aeroplane and Optica, were mentioned in Chapter 3. Desmond Norman's first company, Britten–Norman, set up extensive subcontracting arrangements when demand for its Islander aeroplane exceeded the company's ability to supply. This arrangement proved inflexible and costly when demand fell to a level where supply capability exceeded demand. The choice had been appropriate and feasible for Britten–Norman; it may not have been the most desirable as it led to severe cash flow problems. In contrast Optica invested in a very sophisticated production capability before any firm orders were received, arguing that this was needed to guarantee quality. It was desirable to the strategic leader, but, as orders were very slow to be placed and the company ended up in receivership, it could not be seen as either appropriate or truly feasible.

In many respects the key aspects of any proposed changes concern the **strategic logic**, basically the subject of this book so far, and the **ability to implement**. Implementation and change are the subject of the final chapters.

Strategic logic relates to:

☐ the relationship and fit between the strategies and the mission of the organization; and the current appropriateness of the mission, objectives and the strategies being pursued (synergy is an important concept in this);
☐ the ability of the organization to match and influence changes in the environment;
☐ the availability of the necessary resources.

Implementation concerns the management of the resources to satisfy the needs of the organization's stakeholders. Implicit in this is the ability to satisfy customers better than competitors are able to do. Matching resources and environmental needs involves the culture and values of the organization; and decisions about future changes involve

an assessment of risk. Relevant to both implementation and strategic logic is the role and preference of the strategic leader and other key decision makers in the organization.

In this chapter, by recapping on the evaluation techniques and frameworks discussed previously and by exploring the issues behind effective strategies, we address the following questions: What constitutes a good strategic choice? What can the organization do and what can it not do? What should the organization seek to do and what should it not seek to do?

STRATEGY EVALUATION

Corporate strategy evaluation

Rumelt (1980) argues that corporate strategy evaluation at the widest level involves seeking answers to three questions:

☐ Are the current objectives of the organization appropriate?
☐ Are the strategies created previously, and which are currently being implemented to achieve these objectives, still appropriate?
☐ Do current results confirm or refute previous assumptions about the feasibility of achieving the objectives and the ability of the chosen strategies to achieve the desired results?

It is therefore important to look back and evaluate the outcomes and relative success of previous decisions, and also to look ahead at future opportunities and threats. In both cases strategies should be evaluated in relation to the objectives they are designed to achieve. A quantitative chart along the lines of Table 21.1 could be devised to facilitate this. In order to evaluate current and possible future strategies, and to help select alternatives for the future, the objectives are listed at the top of a series of columns. It will be appreciated from the examples provided that some of the objectives can have clear and

Table 21.1 Evaluating strategies in terms of objectives

	Objectives[a]					
Strategic alternative	*Ability to achieve specific revenue or growth targets*	*Ability to return specific profitability targets*	*Ability to create and sustain competitive advantage*	*Synergy potential – relationship with other activities*	*Ability to utilize existing (spare) resources and skills*	*Etc.*
Existing competitive strategies for products, services, business units	Score out of say 10					
and	or					
Possible changes to corporate and competitive strategies	rank in order of preference					

[a] For evaluation purposes, each objective could be given a relative weighting.

objective measurement criteria and others are more subjective in nature. The alternatives, listed down the left-hand side, could be ranked in order of first to last preference in each column, or given a numerical score. In making a final decision based on the rankings or aggregate marks it may well prove appropriate to weight the objectives in the light of their relative importance.

In terms of assessing the suitability of strategic alternatives in particular circumstances Thompson and Strickland (1980) suggest that market growth and competitive position are important elements. Table 21.2 summarizes their argument. Concentration, for example, is seen as an appropriate strategy where market growth is high and the existing competitive position is strong. By contrast, where market growth is slow and the competitive position is weak, retrenchment is likely to be the most suitable strategy for the organization. Where 'not material' is listed in a column, the contention is that the strategy is appropriate for either high or low growth or strong or weak competitive positions.

Evaluation techniques

Evaluation techniques can be helpful in assessing whether a particular strategic

Table 21.2 Strategic alternatives: their appropriateness in terms of market growth and competitive position

Strategy	Market growth	Competitive position
Concentration	High	Strong
Horizontal integration	High	Weak
Vertical integration	High	Strong
Concentric diversification	Not material	Not material
Conglomerate diversification	Low	Not material
Joint ventures into new areas	Low	Not material
Retrenchment	Low	Weak
Turnaround	High	Weak
Divestment	Not material	Weak
Liquidation	Not material	Weak

Developed from ideas in Thompson, A A and Strickland, A J (1980) *Strategy Formulation and Implementation*, Irwin.

option is appropriate, feasible and desirable. A number of them have been discussed in earlier chapters of this book, and these are summarized in Table 21.3. It should be emphasized that techniques and frameworks of this nature can be helpful for analysing data, structuring thoughts and increasing managers' strategic awareness, but alone they cannot provide a definitive answer. Subjective issues and judgement are also involved.

Table 21.3 A summary of strategy evaluation techniques

Evaluation technique	Discussed in Chapter
SWOT analysis	9
Planning gap analysis	16
Porter's industry analysis and competitive advantage frameworks	7
Investment appraisal techniques using discounted cash flows	13
Net present value	
Internal rate of return	
Payback	
Plus cost–benefit analysis for public sector	
Cash flow implications	6
Breakeven analysis	7
Sensitivity analysis	13
Portfolio analyses	10 and 16
Scenario modelling	9 and 16
Simulations of future possibilities using PIMS	16

SWOT analysis is useful at corporate, competitive and functional strategy level as it addresses the current fit between the organization and its environment, and considers the potential impact of environmental change. Decisions taken in the light of a sound and thorough SWOT analysis can be informed to the extent that the organization becomes proactive and seeks to manage the environment, rather than reactive, responding to changes which managers had failed to foresee.

Planning gap analysis focuses attention on forecasted revenue and profit returns from the continuation of existing strategies, without major changes, and compares these with desired levels of achievement. Corporate and competitive strategies to close the gap between the expected and desired levels can be evaluated in terms of their appropriateness, feasibility and desirability. If satisfactory options cannot be found the desired objectives and levels of achievement can be revised downwards in an iterative process.

Michael Porter contends that **industry attractiveness and competitive advantage** should be key determinants of strategy, and

he has devised frameworks which enable an analysis of these factors. Whilst these themes are conceptually very rich, the elements cannot all be quantified. Nevertheless the thinking involved in considering the attractiveness and potential profitability of a particular industry, and searching for opportunities to create and sustain competitive advantage, focuses attention on crucial issues.

All strategic changes at functional, competitive and corporate level which involve financial outlays designed to yield higher returns are **investments which need appraising** in terms of financial benefits as well as strategic logic. Individual companies might well establish their own specific criteria for attainment in this type of evaluation. For example, in screening possible acquisitions, a company might look for a return on the capital invested of 25% or, re-stated, payback in 4 years. In addition they may look for companies which have sound products with competitive strengths. The measure might well be a gross margin (revenue in excess of direct costs) of 40%, regardless of profitability after accounting for overheads, interest and tax. From this they may assume that their policies and systems can contain overheads to 25% maximum, leaving a 15% profit margin.

In the public sector, cost–benefit analysis follows similar lines to investment appraisal. Judgement is required to impute financial values to all the anticipated benefits society and the community should receive from particular projects, and the figures obtained can be compared with the costs involved. Ideally the figures are discounted. Projects can be evaluated against each other for the purpose of allocating limited funds; and some account should be taken of the opportunity cost of not investing in particular projects.

Cash flow analysis is linked to investment appraisal, but concentrates on the ability of the organization to manage and implement the proposed change in terms of the financial resources which will be required. **Breakeven**

analysis considers the sales volume required to cover all fixed and indirect costs associated with a product or service, and the profit sensitivity around the breakeven point. If demand is difficult to forecast, or unpredictable, it allows a firm to consider the financial risk inherent in a particular option. It can also be used in **sensitivity analysis** for considering the potential impact of different prices and cost structures, which in turn might be related to different production or operations systems.

Portfolio analyses can be useful in a number of ways. The Boston Consulting Group growth–share matrix, linked to the concept of the product life cycle, can highlight future investment needs and revenue generating ability of individual products and services, and this can be helpful in reviewing competitive strategies. In addition possible future weaknesses in the company's overall portfolio might be pinpointed. More sophisticated matrices can be used to consider which products and services should receive priority of funding and other resources, and how to deal with the overall portfolio of businesses. The analysis and the interpretation should be seen as company-specific. One organization, for example, might draw up a portfolio analysis of its products and conclude that all are worthy of some investment as all offer future potential but choose not to develop any product which fails to obtain particular scores on both axes of the matrix. Another company might conclude that its best product scores less than the ones the first company is not developing but opt to give it priority.

Scenario modelling focuses attention on future changes in the environment. Companies can assess the impact of pursuing, and not pursuing, certain alternatives. This type of analysis is extremely useful for developing proactive strategies, and for considering the effect of possible changes on competitors and their likely reactions. An algorithm of how competitor decisions and activities might be dealt with could be developed from this.

Subscribers to **PIMS** can also use the model and the data for testing the likely results and robustness of possible changes in strategy.

All these techniques and frameworks relate to the issues of appropriateness, feasibility and desirability which are the subject of the next section. These issues are considered separately because they affect or determine the effectiveness of current strategies and the potential of possible changes; the techniques and frameworks help in the evaluation process, but they are not determinants.

CRITERIA FOR EFFECTIVE STRATEGIES

When assessing current strategies, and evaluating possible changes, it is important to emphasize that there is no such thing as a right or wrong strategy or choice in absolute terms. However, certain factors will influence the effectiveness of strategies and the wisdom of following certain courses of action. These factors are considered in this chapter in three sections: **appropriateness**; **feasibility**; **desirability**. This categorization has been selected for convenience, and it will be appreciated that there is some overlap between the sections.

Key strategic principles

Before we discuss these factors, it is useful to summarize a number of key strategic principles that have been referred to earlier in the book. Where these principles are evident, and particularly where they are strong and powerful forces, the likelihood of strategic success and effectiveness is enhanced. The principles can be applied at corporate, competitive and functional strategy levels.

Principles of strategy

☐ Market orientation
☐ Distinctiveness – relating to differentiation and competitive advantage

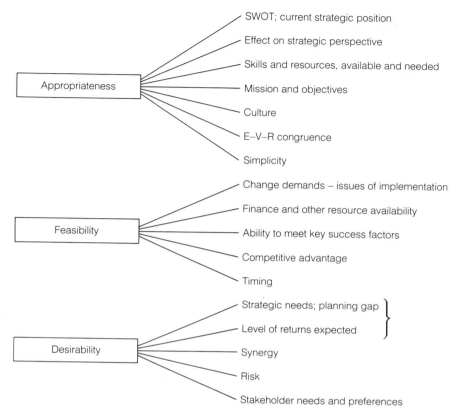

Figure 21.1 Criteria for effective strategies.

□ Timeliness (appropriate for the current situation) and
□ Flexibility (capable of change)
□ Efficiency – relating to cost control and cost efficiency, particularly in production and operations
□ Building on strengths
□ Concentration and co-ordination of resources (rather than spreading them too widely) to achieve synergy
□ Harmonization of strategy creation and implementation
□ Understanding – if a strategy is to be supported by employees who are motivated and enthusiastic it must be communicated and understood.

Effective strategies

A number of authors, including Tilles (1963) and Hofer and Schendel (1978), have discussed the factors which determine the current and future possible effectiveness of particular strategies. The major issues are summarized in Figure 21.1 and are discussed below.

Appropriateness

In reviewing current strategies, assessing the impact of adaptive incremental changes that have taken place and considering strategic alternatives for the future it is important to check that strategies are consistent with the needs of the environment, the resources and values of the organization, and its current mission. These general points are elaborated below. For the rest of this section the term 'the strategy' is used to refer to each particular strategy being considered, be it a current one or a proposed change or addition.

SWOT; current strategic position

Is the strategy appropriate for the current economic and competitive environment?

Is the strategy able to capitalize and build on current strengths and opportunities, and avoid weaknesses and potential threats?

To what extent is the strategy able to take advantage of emerging trends in the environment, the market and the industry?

Effect on the strategic perspective

Does it have the potential for improving the strategic perspective and general competitive position of the organization?

The company, then, must be responsive to changes in the environment and it may wish to be proactive and influence its market and industry. All the time it should seek to become and remain an effective competitor.

Skills and resources: available and needed

Are the strategies being pursued and considered sufficiently consistent that skills and resources are not spread or stretched in any disadvantageous way?

Mission and objectives

Does the strategy fit the current mission and objectives of the organization? Is it acceptable to the strategic leader and other influential stakeholders? (This issue is developed further in the desirability section below.)

The last two points above basically look at the relationship between ends and means.

Culture

Does the strategy fit the culture and values of the organization?

E–V–R congruence

Summarizing the above points, is there congruence between the environment, values and resources?

Simplicity

Is the strategy simple and understandable? Is the strategy one which could be communicated easily, and which people are likely to be enthusiastic about? These factors are also aspects of desirability.

Feasibility

Change demands – issues of implementation

Is the strategy feasible in resource terms? Can it be implemented effectively? Is it capable of achieving the objectives it addresses?

Can the organization cope with the extent and challenge of the change implied by the option?

Finance and other resource availability

A lack of any key resource can place a constraint on certain possible developments.

Ability to meet key success factors

A strategic alternative is not feasible if the key success factors dictated by the industry and customer demand, such as quality, price and service level, cannot be met.

Competitive advantage

The effectiveness of a strategy will be influenced by the ability of the organization to create and sustain competitive advantage. When formulating a strategy it is important to consider the likely response of existing competitors in order to ensure that the necessary flexibility is incorporated into the implementation plans. A company which breaks into a currently stable industry or market may well threaten the market shares and profitability of other companies and force them to respond with, say, price cuts, product improvements or aggressive promotion campaigns. The new entrant should be prepared for this and ready to counter it.

Timing

Timing is related to opportunity on the one hand and risk and vulnerability on the other. It may be important for an organization to act quickly and decisively once an opening window of opportunity is spotted. Competitors may attempt to seize the same opportunity.

At the same time managers should make sure that they allow themselves enough time to consider the implications of their actions and organize their resources properly. Adaptive incremental change in the implementation of strategy can be valuable here. An organization may look to pursue a new strategy, learn by experience and improve by modification once they have gone ahead.

Strategic leadership and the structure, culture and values of the organization are therefore important. Case 21.1 shows how a timely change of leadership at Walt Disney led to new opportunities being seized.

Timing is also an implementation issue; Case 21.2 provides one illustration of its significance. Next introduced a number of successful strategic changes which resulted in growth and increased profitability, but then over-stretched themselves by pursuing strategies for which they had insufficient resources at the time. This theme relates to the theory of growth and the existence of the receding managerial limit suggested by Edith Penrose (1959), which was discussed in Chapter 5.

Desirability

Strategic needs; the planning gap

The ability of the strategy to satisfy the objectives of the organization and help close any identified planning gap are important considerations. Timing may again be an important issue. The ability of the strategy to produce results in either the short term or the longer term should be assessed in the light of the needs and priorities of the firm.

The level of returns expected

Synergy Effective synergy should lead ideally to a superior concentration of resources in

---

In my experience those who manage change most successfully are those who welcome it in their own lives and see it as an opportunity for stimulation and learning new things. Implicit is the willingness to take risks, including making intelligent mistakes. I am much more interested in important failures that prepare the way for future success than I am in cautious competence and maintaining the status quo.

Robert Fitzpatrick, Président Directeur Général,
Euro Disneyland SA

Case 21.1
WALT DISNEY CORPORATION

Walt Disney's fame and early success was based substantially upon films, books and comics featuring such cartoon characters as Mickey Mouse and Donald Duck. To further exploit these characters, which Disney saw as resources, and to capitalize upon increased leisure spending (a window of opportunity) the first Disneyland theme park was opened in 1955 in Anaheim, California. Within one year Disneyland contributed 30% of the company's revenue.

Although Walt Disney himself died in 1966 his strategies were continued. The Magic Kingdom was opened in Florida in 1971, followed 11 years later by Epcot. These have proved immensely successful, but were not seen as 'really new'. In the 1980s the environment for leisure businesses was perceived to be changing dramatically, but Disney was no longer regarded as a trend setter. Revenues, profits and stock prices all fell.

Disney appointed a new strategic leader, Michael Eisner, in 1984, and he has successfully opened several new windows of opportunity for the corporation. He introduced more aggressive marketing (together with price increases) at the theme parks, and throughout the 1980s the numbers of visitors, including foreigners, grew steadily. Additional attractions, including a film studio, were added, together with a support infrastructure including Disney resort hotels. New marketing and licensing opportunities for Disney characters have been sought. Disney has established a new film company, Touchstone Pictures, to enable it to make movies with more adult themes for restricted audiences without affecting the Disney name and family image. They have also invested in videos and satellite television. One single theme pervades all the developments – the hidden wealth of the Disney name and characters. The result has been renewed growth and prosperity.

Disney's American success, though, has yet to be fully transferred to Europe. The initial revenue and profit projections for EuroDisneyland, near Paris, have been revised downwards after the first trading year. The recession is partially to blame. However, it would also appear that European employees are not as yet able to replicate the enthusiasm of their American counterparts, and the total service package is not the same.

---

relation to competitors. The prospects for synergy should be evaluated alongside the implications for the firm's strategic perspective and culture, which were included in the section on appropriateness. These factors in combination affect the strategic fit of the proposal and its ability to complement existing strategies and bring an all-round improvement to the organization. Diversification into products and markets with which the organization has no experience, and which may require different skills, may fit poorly alongside existing strategies and fail to provide synergy.

Risk It has already been pointed out that risk, vulnerability, opportunity and timing are linked. Where organizations, having spotted an opportunity, act quickly, there is always a danger that some important consideration will be overlooked. The risk lies in these other factors, many of which are discussed elsewhere, which need careful attention in strategy formulation.

☐ The likely effect on competition.
☐ The technology and production risks, linked to skills and key success factors. Can the organization cope with the production demands and meet market requirements profitably? Innovation often implies higher risks in this area, but offers higher rewards for success.
☐ The product/market diversification risk. The risk involved in over-stretching resources through diversification has been considered earlier in this chapter.
☐ The financial risk. The cash flow and the firm's borrowing requirements are sensit-

ive to the ability of the firm to forecast demand accurately and predict competitor responses.
☐ Managerial ability and competence. The risk here involves issues of whether skills can be transferred from one business to another when a firm diversifies, and whether key people stay or go after a take-over.
☐ Environmental risks. It is also important to ensure that possible adverse effects or hostile public opinion are evaluated.

Many of these issues are qualitative rather than finite, and judgement will be required. The ability of the organization to harness and evaluate the appropriate information is crucial, but again there is a trade-off. The longer the time that the

---

Case 21.2
NEXT

At the end of 1988 George Davies lost the chairmanship of Next, the retail company he had built, which had experienced rapid growth and success during the 1980s. Recent strategic changes had failed to provide the desired level of success. Arguably the speed of the growth and the extent of the diversification had been too great for Next's resources, and profits had fallen as a result.

Over four years, and with a series of strategic moves, Davies had transformed the relatively dowdy menswear retailers J Hepworth into Next, a group which was innovative, design led and fashion oriented. Next segmented the retail market, selling fashionable clothing to younger men and women, as well as jewellery and furniture. In addition Next had diversified into general mail order by the acquisition of Grattan, one of the largest catalogue retail operations.

The moves which proved problematical occurred in 1987 and 1988. In 1987 Next took over Combined English Stores (CES), a large and already diversified retail group which included Biba (the West German fashion retailer), Zales (jewellery), Salisbury's (luggage, handbags and the like), a chain of chemist's shops, a carpet business and a holiday company. This gave Next a substantial high street presence, together with the problem and expense of converting a large number of stores to the fashionable Next image and format, which was regarded as a key factor in their record of success. Critics argued that Next had acquired too many stores, however, and Zales and Salisbury's were in fact sold to Ratners in autumn 1988. This reduced the extent of Next's diversification, and helped reduce the gearing from 125%.

Continued overleaf

In January 1988 the Next Directory, an exclusive mail-order catalogue, was sold to potential customers through advertising and direct mail. Catalogues are normally free. The product range in the Directory was designed to appeal to upmarket buyers, not the traditional mail-order customers, who could specify when they wanted their goods delivered. The launch and the new concept proved less successful than forecasts and expectations. Moreover, in 1988 there was growing friction between Next and Grattan. Grattan disagreed with Next's plans to re-develop their product line. Davies has claimed that in October 1988 there were serious discussions about splitting Next and Grattan, as happened with Asda and MFI.

At the end of 1988 Next's profitability had declined, their strategy was not co-ordinated, and there were concerns about a fall in demand in 1989 as a result of increased interest charges and inflation.

Had the diversification into mail order and the acquisition of Combined English Stores been appropriate and feasible?

Next were unable to provide all the necessary resources at the time they were required; and George Davies was quoted in the *Financial Times* on 5 December 1988 as saying, 'The lesson that I've learnt this year is that you must stick to the markets you know'.

Next, also, were a highly innovative company, but Davies was seen as an autocratic strategic leader who had failed to develop an appropriately supportive team of managers and an organization which was sufficiently decentralized.

Since Davies' departure Next has concentrated on two principal businesses:

- ☐ Retailing ladies', men's and children's clothing, accessories and home furnishings. The remaining retail businesses have been divested, and there are now 330 shops which provide some 75% of Next's turnover.
- ☐ The Next Directory, with 400 000 customers. Grattan has been sold to Otto Versand, the German mail-order company.

organization spends in considering the implications and assessing the risks, the greater the chance it has of reducing and controlling the risks. However, if managers take too long, the opportunity or the initiative may be lost to a competitor who is more willing to accept the risk.

Stakeholder needs and preferences

This relates to the expectations and hopes of key stakeholders, the ability of the organization to implement the strategy and achieve the desired results, and the willingness of stakeholders to accept the inherent risks in a particular strategy. These points are illus-trated in Case 21.3 on Waring and Gillow. The company management was unable to achieve the results demanded by the institutional shareholders who were ultimately in control. Whilst the strategies chosen may have seemed appropriate they were poorly implemented because they were insufficiently robust to withstand setbacks.

Strategic changes may affect existing resources and the strategies to which they are committed, gearing, liquidity, and organization structures, including management roles, functions and systems. Shareholders, bankers, managers, employees and customers can all be affected; and their relative power and influence will prove significant.

The willingness of each party to accept particular risks may vary. Trade-offs may be required. The power and influence of the strategic leader will be very important in the choice of major strategic changes, and his or her ability to convince other stakeholders will be crucial.

Strategic leaders may have ambitions to develop the organization in particular directions and in terms of growth targets. Strategies to achieve these preferences may be pursued because they are regarded as desirable by people who are able to exercise power and influence. They may not be the most appropriate or feasible strategies in the context of the factors discussed in this chapter. Again there may be a trade-off between appropriateness, feasibility and desirability.

It is important to stress again that a strategy must be implemented before it can be considered effective. The formulation may be both analytical and creative, and the strategy may seem excellent on paper, but

the organization must then activate it. The value of commitment and support from the strategic leader, managers and other employees should not be under-estimated.

When organizations are evaluating possible strategic changes in terms of appropriateness, feasibility and desirability it is unlikely that any one alternative will score the highest mark for every criterion. The best overall choice is therefore being sought. See Case 21.4, which considers a number of strategic changes at British Steel.

Whilst evaluation techniques can assist in strategic decision making, individual subjectivity and judgement will also be involved. Consequently we conclude this chapter by examining the role of judgement.

JUDGEMENT

Strategic changes can be selected by an individual manager, often the strategic

---

Case 21.3.
WARING AND GILLOW

Waring and Gillow became a private furniture company in May 1985 when the shares in the existing public company were bought by an external management consortium for £25 million. The managers had institutional backing. The company, as such, had been in existence for several decades. New directors introduced a number of strategic changes in an attempt to return the company to profitability. In the year to September 1985 the company lost £2.6 million pre-tax. Costs were to be cut and stock levels tightened; a new management reporting and control system was to be introduced; and a key objective was to re-position the company in the volume furniture retailing industry.

The strategy appeared to bring results quickly. In the year to September 1986 pre-tax profits of £4.1 million were achieved, and a 50% increase was forecast for the following year. Towards the end of 1986 a new group of institutional investors paid £45 million to acquire 89% of the equity, thereby valuing the company at twice its May 1985 price.

One year later the company recorded a loss of £7.2 million pre-tax. By May 1988 the gearing was 300% and many supplier accounts were overdue. What had gone wrong?

Continued overleaf

☐ In January 1987 Waring and Gillow paid £7.3 million to acquire Wades, a chain of 43 furniture stores serving roughly the same market as their own. But during 1987 demand for their products fell dramatically, partly as a result of bad publicity for inflammable upholstery. Heavy price discounting hit margins.

☐ Internally a major computer failure resulted in decisions being made with unreliable financial information. This difficulty was exacerbated by an inconsistency and mismatch between the information systems at Waring and Gillow and at Wades.

☐ A refurbishment programme cost £7 million but had no discernible effect on sales. There was an argument that the disruption actually resulted in lost business.

☐ Accurate information on progress was not being fed back to the institutional investors who were picking up signals concerning the problems. At their request, in January 1988, the chairman and chief executive both resigned.

Cyril Spencer (non-executive chairman) contended that the investors were taking a view which was too short term. The refurbishment, he argued, was crucial because many of the stores had received no direct investment for some 50 years. He claimed: 'Institutional investors . . . don't see the longer view. They are concerned with instant returns which don't always come. The new management team [appointed after Spencer resigned] has not made any fundamental changes to the strategy we pioneered.'

In reality the new managers:

☐ cut staff levels
☐ put on hold the new computer management information system
☐ disposed of property worth £17 million.

The result was a profit of £200 000 in the year to September 1988. In 1989 two-thirds of the group was sold to Asda. See Case 17.6.

Had the strategy been appropriate, feasible and desirable?

leader, or a team of managers, and Vickers (1965) stresses that three contextual aspects have a critical impact on the decision:

☐ the decision makers' skills and values together with aspects of their personality (*personal factors*)
☐ their authority and accountability within the organization (*structural factors*)
☐ their understanding and awareness (*environmental factors*).

Related to these, the decisions taken by managers are affected by their personal judgemental abilities, and understanding judgement can, therefore, help us explain why some managers appear to 'get things right' whilst others 'get things wrong'.

Vickers suggests that there are three types of judgement:

☐ *Reality judgements*
Strategic awareness of the organization and its environment and which is based upon interpretation and meaning systems.
☐ *Action judgements*
What to do about perceived strategic issues.
☐ *Value judgements*

Case 21.4
BRITISH STEEL

Since it was privatized in 1988 British Steel (BSC) has increased its profits and later traded at a loss. In 1989/90 pre-tax profits were a record £733 million – followed a year later by a £254 million profit and then a loss of £55 million in 1991/2. The successes have been attributed to effective strategic management; the losses to the world recession and severe over-capacity in world steelmaking. Between 1989 and 1992, for example, European steel prices fell by 20%.

Sir Robert Scholey was Chief Executive from 1973 (and Chairman from 1986) until his retirement in 1992. Both before and after privatization, cost cutting and rationalization were key aspects of the strategy. BSC was restructured around a smaller number of large, concentrated sites which achieved high turnover and lower costs. Output per man doubled between 1981 and 1991. This was seen as essential as world competition was intensifying. Many basic steel products are commodity products and available from Third World countries at competitive prices. This strategy was clearly appropriate, and it proved feasible. As the industry became increasingly global many factors were beyond the control of any individual company – BSC acted decisively in areas that could be tackled at company level. However, it was not seen as wholly desirable by all interested stakeholders. Many jobs have had to be sacrificed. The workforce and the trade unions have accepted the changes reluctantly, persuaded that they were fundamental to the future of BSC. Scotland has been particularly hard hit, the result of the collapse of the Scottish shipbuilding and motor industries.

A focus on quality, service and adding value has been another aspect of the strategy. Related to this, BSC has sought to invest downstream in order to establish closer links with steel users. In 1990 BSC acquired C Walker, the largest UK steel stockholder and a major customer.

BSC decided to concentrate on structural steel products, but seek niche opportunities for differentiation and adding value – structural steels are basically commodity products. The appropriateness of this focus has been queried by some commentators, who have pointed out that many leading steel companies have instead followed a strategy of selective diversification. New materials are an appropriate choice, particularly as plastic car bodies and glass fibre components for certain structural applications are real threats to the steel industry. To implement their strategy BSC looked for international partners, and the logic behind this was not disputed. There is 'chronic over-capacity', especially in Europe, and although BSC has made small acquisitions in Germany and Spain it remains substantially dependent on the UK. France and Italy are dominated by State-owned producers; and Germany is seen by BSC as a 'closed club'. Expansion within the heart of Europe has not therefore been feasible, although BSC has made a number of approaches.

Consequently, BSC looked to America and Japan. In 1991 a joint venture was proposed with Bethlehem Steel, producer of structural steels and the 'only American integrated steel manufacturer not in a joint venture with a Japanese partner'. The proposal was appropriate, but again it was not seen as wholly desirable. Some BSC

Continued overleaf

managers were wary of the deal and anxious about financial and other implications. In the end it proved not to be feasible either, mainly because of workforce resistance in America, but also because the two companies could not finally agree on particular aspects of implementation.

As a result, BSC turned again to Europe, proposing, in 1992, a joint venture with the Swedish stainless steel manufacturer, Avesta. The stainless steel production and distribution facilities of BSC (centred on Sheffield) would be merged with Avesta, thereby creating the largest stainless producer in Europe, with 40% of the stainless plate market. BSC would own 40% of the new company; the owners of Avesta (mainly institutions and construction and trading companies) would have a controlling share – roughly in line with existing turnover contributions. The business would be called Avesta Sheffield but with headquarters in Stockholm. The deal needed ratification by both the European Commission and Avesta's shareholders. The aim was further rationalization and cost savings. Would this prove to be appropriate, feasible and desirable?

concerning expected and desired results and outcomes from the decision.

Figure 21.2 shows how these are interconnected. Decision makers need to understand 'what is' (reality), 'what matters' (values) and 'what to do about it' (action). Their choice will be based upon a conceptualization of what might or what should be a better alternative to the current situation. Ideally it will incorporate a holistic perspective, implying either an understanding or a personal interpretation of the organization's purpose or mission, and it also requires an appreciation that what matters is a function of urgency and time horizons. A company with cash difficulties, for example, might need a strategy based upon immediate rationalization or consolidation; a liquid company evaluating growth options has greater flexibility. The choice will also be affected by managers' relative power and influence, their perception of the risks involved, and their willingness to pursue certain courses of action.

Having considered a number of possible frameworks through which organizations might formulate their strategies and changes in strategies (Chapter 16) and a variety of strategic alternatives in Chapters 17–20, in this chapter we have considered the criteria which determine the effectiveness of strategies. It has been emphasized that effective strategies take account of both formulation and implementation issues. Implementation is therefore the subject of the remaining chapters of the book.

SUMMARY

In this chapter we have addressed the questions: What constitutes a good strategic choice? What can the organization do and What can it not do? What should the organization seek to do and what should it not seek to do?

In simple terms the effective strategy is the one which (a) meets the needs and preferences of the organization, its key decision makers and influencers – ideally better than any alternatives – and (b) can be implemented successfully.

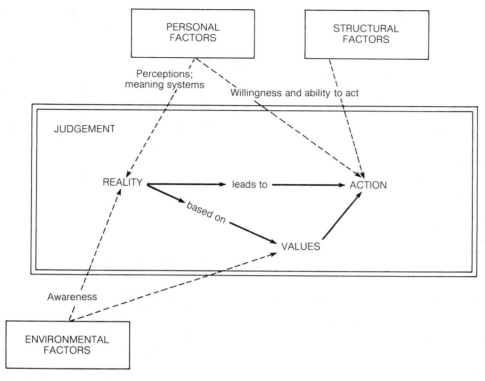

Figure 21.2 Judgement and strategic decision making.

A number of issues which determine the effectiveness of a strategy have been considered under the headings of appropriateness, feasibility and desirability. These include strategic fit, E–V–R congruence, risk, synergy and the ability to be an effective competitor. In addition the value of simplicity and the importance of support from managers and other employees has been emphasized.

Evaluation techniques, which have been discussed in earlier chapters and which have an important contributory role to play in strategy selection, have been summarized and reviewed.

Specifically we have

☐ briefly looked at strategy evaluation in its widest context, how strategies might be measured in terms of their ability to meet

the objectives they were designed to satisfy, and which strategic alternatives might be the most appropriate in particular circumstances;

☐ reviewed ten evaluation techniques;

☐ highlighted a number of key strategic principles which might usefully be sought in any strategy;

☐ discussed effective strategies under three headings: appropriateness, feasibility and desirability;

☐ emphasized that there are trade-offs between these factors, in that the most desirable strategy may not be the most feasible and so on;

☐ concluded by commenting that the preference of the strategic leader will have a significant influence on the choice and by exploring the role of judgement in strategic decision making.

CHECKLIST OF KEY TERMS AND CONCEPTS

You should feel confident that you understand the following terms and ideas:

- ☐ The ten evaluation techniques summarized in Table 21.3
- ☐ Key strategic principles
- ☐ Evaluation criteria included under the headings of
  - ☐ appropriateness
  - ☐ feasibility
  - ☐ desirability

  and the possible trade-offs involved
- ☐ Judgement.

QUESTIONS AND RESEARCH ASSIGNMENTS

Text related

1. Which of the evaluation techniques featured in Table 21.3 do you feel are most useful? Why? How would you use them? What are their limitations?
2. From your experience and reading, which evaluation criteria do you think are most significant in determining the effectiveness of strategies?

   List examples of cases where the absence of these factors, or the wrong assessment of their importance, has led to problems.

Library based

3. The performance of Storehouse, the retail group which began originally as Habitat and subsequently acquired, first, Mothercare and later BHS (British Home Stores), deteriorated during the later 1980s.

   Research the company and determine where the problems have arisen. Were the strategy and the acquisitions ill-conceived? Were there implementation difficulties which prevented the anticipated synergy being achieved? Assess the most recent strategic changes in terms of appropriateness, feasibility and desirability. How successful have they been?

4. In 1983 Tottenham Hotspur became the first English football club to be listed on the Stock Exchange. Subsequently the club diversified, acquiring a number of related leisure companies. The intention was to subsidize the football club with profits from the new businesses. Initially this happened, but in the recession of the late 1980s football had to prop up the other activities. Businesses were closed or divested, and the ownership of Tottenham Hotspur changed hands in 1991.

   Research the various changes and evaluate the strategies. Was it appropriate and desirable for Tottenham to become a public limited company?

RECOMMENDED FURTHER READING

Hofer and Schendel (1978) and Tilles (1963) are both useful sources of further detail.

REFERENCES

Hofer, C W and Schendel, D (1978) *Strategy Evaluation: Analytical Concepts*, West.

Penrose, E (1959) *The Theory of the Growth of the Firm*, Blackwell.

Rumelt, R (1980) The evaluation of business strategy. In *Business Policy and Strategic Management* (ed. W F Glueck), McGraw-Hill.

Thompson, A A and Strickland, A J (1980) *Strategy Formulation and Implementation*, Richard D Irwin.

Tilles, S (1963) How to evaluate corporate strategy, *Harvard Business Review*, July–August.

Vickers, G (1965) *The Art of Judgement: A Study of Policy Making*, Chapman and Hall.

PART FIVE

STRATEGY IMPLEMENTATION

AN INTRODUCTION TO STRATEGY IMPLEMENTATION AND CONTROL

It was emphasized in the previous chapter that to be considered effective a chosen strategy must be implemented. The prospects for effective implementation are clearly dependent upon the appropriateness, feasibility and desirability of the strategy. Some strategies are not capable of implementation. In this last section of the book therefore we consider issues of strategy implementation and control. Reed and Buckley (1988) suggest that new strategies are selected because they offer opportunities and potential benefits, but that their implementation, because it involves change, implies risk. Implementation strategies should seek to maximize benefits and minimize risks. How might this be accomplished?

The major implementation themes concern organization structures, policies and control systems related to the management of resources; and the management of strategic change. The fundamental questions are as follows.

☐ How appropriate is the organization structure, given the diversity of the strategic perspective and the interrelationships between the various business units, products and services?
☐ How effectively are we managing our resources? Are the various functions and activities co-ordinated and contributing towards clearly understood objectives?

This last question relates to both implementation and control, and the ability of the organization to answer it is determined by the effectiveness of the information system and the strategic awareness of managers.

☐ How do we manage changes in strategy, appreciating that cultural and behavioural changes may be required?

These questions provide the themes of the next three chapters, but before examining them in greater detail it is useful to consider a number of general aspects of implementation.

Strategy → structure or structure → strategy?

The notion of a strategy statement was developed in Chapter 16 and illustrated in Figure 16.11. It was suggested that the overall mission and corporate strategy should be used to develop a series of competitive strategies for each business unit, product/market and service/market. Functional strategies are designed to implement the competitive strategies, and related to these will be a series of action plans.

At the same time the structure of the organization is designed to break down the work to be carried out, the tasks, into discrete components, which might comprise business units and functional departments. People work within these divisions and functions, and their actions take place within a defined framework of objectives, plans and policies which are designed to direct and control their efforts. In designing the structure and making it operational it is important to consider the key aspects of empowerment, employee motivation and reward. These points are illustrated in the top half of Figure V.1.

The information and communication systems within the organization should ensure that efforts are co-ordinated to the appropriate and desired extent and that the strategic leader and other senior managers are aware of progress and results. In other words, the structure is designed to enable the implementation of strategies; or the structure in existence should be capable of implementing strategic decisions. Resources are managed within the framework provided by the structure, results are measured, and control mechanisms are used to establish where changes might be needed.

However:

☐ **personal objectives** are likely to be evident (their significance was discussed in Chapter 5);
☐ there will be a need for *adaptive strategic change* in response to environmental opportunities and threats, and the climate within the organization should encourage and allow managers to make necessary changes;
☐ the activities and decisions which take place within the structure, as a result of the way managers behave individually and work with each other, lead to emergent functional, competitive and in turn corporate strategies.

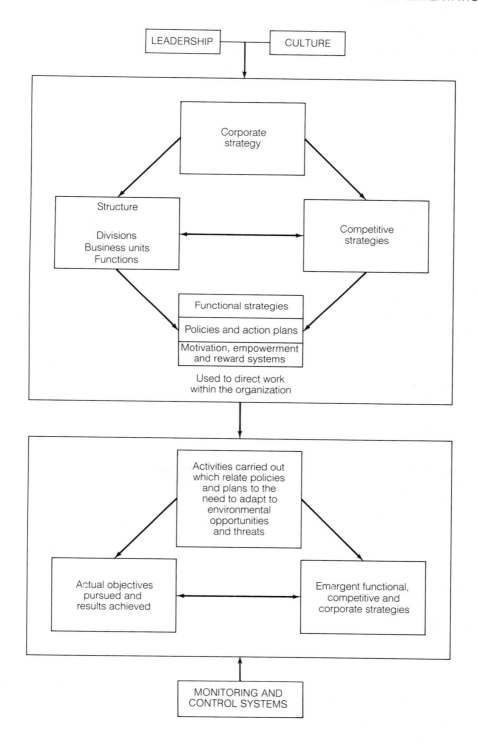

Figure V.1 The relationship between strategy and structure.

This is illustrated in the bottom half of Figure V.1. Hence, whilst structures are designed to implement strategies, and should be capable of implementing strategic decisions effectively, the behaviour of people within the structure leads to emergent strategies. There is a continual circular process:

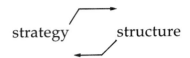

strategy   structure

Consequently, whilst issues of structure and implementation are being considered at the end of this book, they should not be thought of as the end point in the strategy process. They may be the source of strategic change.

The outcome, in terms of effective strategic management and organizational success, is dependent upon:

☐ the direction provided by the strategic leader;
☐ the culture of the organization;
☐ the extent to which managers throughout the company understand, support and **own** the mission and corporate strategy, and appreciate the significance of their individual contribution;
☐ the effectiveness of the information, monitoring and control systems.

Implementation and change

Implementation incorporates a number of aspects, some of which can be changed directly and some of which can only be changed indirectly. The latter aspects are more difficult for the strategic leadership to control and change. The success of the strategic leader in managing both the direct and indirect aspects influences the effectiveness of

☐ the implementation of strategies and strategic changes which are determined through the planning and entrepreneurial modes of strategy creation and
☐ the ability of the organization, and its managers, to respond to changes in the environment and adapt in line with perceived opportunities and threats.

Aspects of implementation which can be changed directly

☐ The organization structure (the actual, defined structure, not necessarily the way people behave within the structure)

☐ Management systems
☐ Policies and procedures
☐ Action plans and short-term budgets
☐ Management information systems.

Aspects of implementation which are changed indirectly

Communication systems   Whilst the management information system can affect formal information flows, the network of informal communications truly determines awareness. Such communications are affected by, and influence, the degree and spirit of co-operation between managers, functions and divisions.

Managing and developing quality and excellence   Attention to detail, production on time and to the appropriate quality, and the personal development of managers and other employees are all factors in this. As well as developing managers' skills and capabilities generally, it is important to consider the quality of management in particular areas and the cover for managers who leave or who are absent. The organization structure should provide opportunities for managers to grow and be promoted.

Manifested values and the organization culture   This involves the way things are done: standards and attitudes which are held and practised.

The fostering of innovation   The willingness of people to search for improvements and better ways of doing things, their encouragement and reward is very much influenced by the strategic leader, with leadership by example often proving significant.

Those aspects which can be changed directly generally imply physical changes in the way that resources are allocated. Behavioural aspects, which imply changes in beliefs and attitudes, can only be modified indirectly. Both are considered in the forthcoming chapters.

Problems of successful implementation

Owen (1982) contends that in practice there are four problem areas associated with the successful implementation of strategies.

☐ At any time strategy and structure need to be matched and supportive of each other. Products and services need to be managed independently, or in linked groups or business units, if they are to be matched closely and effectively with their environments. There may be good reasons for having a structure which does not separate the products, services and business units in this way. The strategic leader might prefer a centralized structure without delegated responsibilities, for example. The organization might possess certain key skills and enjoy a reputation for strength in a particular area, and this might be influential in the design of the structure. Equally, certain skills might be absent and have to be compensated for. Related to this might be the willingness or reluctance of managers to change jobs or location within the structure. Structures cannot be created and activated independently of the people involved; their individual skills may provide either opportunities or constraints. Changing attitudes and developing new skills is accomplished indirectly, as pointed out above, and takes time.

It is also possible that related products may be produced in various plants nationally or internationally, when a geography-oriented structure, which keeps the plants separate, is favoured for other sound reasons. In addition it may not prove feasible to change the structure markedly every time there is a change in corporate strategy, and instead, acceptable modifications to the existing structure are preferred to more significant changes.

☐ The information and communications systems are inadequate for reporting back and evaluating the adaptive changes which are taking place, and hence the strategic leader is not fully aware of what is happening. Hence the performance of the existing structure is not monitored properly, and as a result control mechanisms may be ineffective.

☐ Implementing strategy involves change, which in turn involves uncertainty and risk. New skills may have to be developed, for example. Whilst managers may agree in meetings to make changes, they may be more reluctant in practice to implement them. Motivating managers to make changes is therefore a key determinant.

☐ Management systems, such as compensation schemes, management development, communications systems and so on, which operate within the structural framework will have been developed to meet the needs of past strategies. They may not be ideal for the changes which are taking place currently, and again it is difficult to modify them continually.

Alexander (1985) argues that additional factors are also significant, especially:

☐ the failure to predict the time and problems which implementation will involve

☐ other activities and commitments that distract attention and possibly cause resources to be diverted

☐ the bases upon which the strategy was formulated changed, or were forecast poorly, and insufficient flexibility has been built in.

All these problems presuppose that the formulated strategic change is sound and logical. A poorly thought out strategy will create its own implementation problems.

Successful implementation

To counter these problems Owen suggests the following.

☐ Clear responsibility for the successful outcome of planned strategic change should be allocated.
☐ The number of strategies and changes being pursued at any time should be limited. The ability of the necessary resources to cope with the changes should be seen as a key determinant of strategy and should not be overlooked.
☐ Necessary actions to implement strategies should be identified and planned, and again responsibility should be allocated.
☐ 'Milestones', or progress measurement points, should be established.
☐ Measures of performance should be established, and appropriate monitoring and control mechanisms.

These, Owen argues, can all be achieved without necessarily changing the structural framework but rather changing the way people operate within it.

In addition, Alexander contends that the involvement and support of people who will be affected by the changes in strategy must be considered, and that the implications of the new strategies and changes should be communicated widely, awareness created, and commitment and involvement sought. Incentives and reward systems under-pin this.

In building societies we have moved from a situation in which 'change' was not the norm to one where it is. From being little changed from their formation to the late 1970s, over the past ten years societies have changed immeasurably. We now expect change. Moving on from expecting change, we must desire it. It must be seen as necessary for competitive advantage and success. But to realize competitive success it will be necessary to manage the change – not just to react to it or even to be proactive – but actually to inspire and then manage the changes to ensure competitive success for the Halifax. In managing change, we must then ensure we remain in control – controlling change is an essential part of managing it.

Richard Hornby, Chairman, Halifax Building Society

In just the same way that no single evaluation technique can select a best strategy, there is no best way of implementing strategic change. There are no right answers, as such. A number of lessons, considerations and arguments, however, can be incorporated into the thinking and planning; and these are the themes of the next three chapters.

Three final points need to be mentioned to conclude this introduction. First, although there are no right answers to either strategy formulation or strategy implementation, the two must be consistent if the organization is to be effective. Arguably, **how** the organization does things, and manages both strategy and change, is more important than the actual strategy or change proposed.

Second, the style of strategic leadership will be very influential. It was argued in the previous chapter that the preference of the strategic leader affects the desirability of particular strategic alternatives. The structure of the organization, the delegation of responsibilities, the freedom of managers to act, their willingness to exercise initiative, and the incentive and reward systems will all be determined and influenced by the strategic leader. These in turn determine the effectiveness of implementation. The strategic leader's choices and freedom to act, however, may be constrained by any resource limitations and certain environmental forces.

Third, the timing of when to act and make changes will also be important. In this context, for example, Mitchell (1988) points out that timing is particularly crucial in the implementation decisions and actions which follow acquisitions. Employees anticipate changes in the organization, especially at senior management level, and inaction, say beyond three months, causes uncertainty and fear. As a result, there is greater hostility to change when it does occur. The dangers of hasty action, such as destroying strengths before appreciating that they are strengths, are offset. Mitchell concludes that it is more important to be decisive than to be right, and then learn and adapt incrementally.

In the next chapter we examine issues of structure, considering both the design of the framework and the management and control of the activities which operate within the framework. This is followed by an assessment of action plans, policies and control mechanisms, and finally an assessment of the issues involved in change and the management of change.

REFERENCES

Alexander, L D (1985) Successfully implementing strategic decisions, *Long Range Planning*, **18** (3).

Mitchell, D (1988) *Making Acquisitions Work: Lessons from Companies' Successes and Mistakes*, Report published by Business International, Geneva.

Owen, A A (1982) How to implement strategy, *Management Today*, July.

Reed, R and Buckley M R (1988) Strategy in action – techniques for implementing strategy, *Long Range Planning*, **21** (3).

STRATEGY AND STRUCTURE

22

LEARNING OBJECTIVES

After studying this chapter you should be able to

☐ discuss the advantages and disadvantages of centralization and decentralization and explain the concept of empowerment;
☐ identify and describe five basic structural forms which an organization might adopt;
☐ explain why structures evolve and change as organizations develop and grow;
☐ summarize the main determinants of organization structure;
☐ distinguish between the alternative control mechanisms which large diverse organizations might use;
☐ discuss the role and skills of general managers in large multi-business organizations;
☐ explain the importance of the appropriate reward system in organizations.

In this chapter we look at the linkages between strategy and structure by examining a number of alternative structural forms and by considering the key issue of centralization and decentralization. The forces which influence and determine the structure are discussed, and there is an assessment of the role of general managers in large multi-divisional organizations.

INTRODUCTION

Lawrence and Lorsch (1967) have argued that the organization should be structured in such a way that it can respond to pressures for change from its environment and pursue any appropriate opportunities which are spotted. Given that strategies are concerned with relating the organization's resources and values with the environment, it follows that strategy and structure are linked. Structure, in fact, is the **means** by which the organization seeks to achieve its strategic objectives and implement strategies and strategic changes. Strategies are formulated and implemented by managers operating within the current structure. Thompson and Strickland (1980) comment that whilst strategy formulation requires the abilities to conceptualize, analyse and judge, implementation involves working with and through other people and instituting change. Implementation poses the tougher management challenge.

The essential criteria under-pinning the design of the organization structure are first, the extent to which decision making is **decentralized**, as opposed to centralized, and second, the extent to which policies and procedures are **formalized**. Decentralization to some degree is required if adaptive strategic change is to take place; and the issue of centralization/decentralization is explored as a key concept early in this chapter. Formality is linked to the extent to which tasks and jobs are specialized and defined, and their rigidity, i.e. the period of time over which jobs have remained roughly the same. The longer the period is, arguably, the greater will be the resistance to changing them.

Centralization and formality in the structure yield economies but at the same time remove initiative from managers who are most closely in touch with the organization's customers and competitors. This is likely to affect motivation and slow down the firm's sensitivity to changes in the environment. Decentralization therefore allows decisions to be made by the people who must implement the changes, and informality allows these managers to use their own initiative and change things in a dynamic turbulent environment.

These criteria create four extreme types of structure. First, those which are centralized and formal, which tend to be bureaucratic, slow to change and efficient in stable circumstances. Companies which are centralized and informal tend to be small, with power concentrated in the hands of one central figure. Decentralized formal organizations are typically large businesses divided up into divisions and business units. Power is devolved to allow adaptive change, but formal communication systems and performance measures are required for co-ordination. Finally decentralized and informal organizations tend to be groups or teams of people who are put together for a specific purpose and then abandoned once the task is accomplished. Film crews would be an example, as would special project groups within large firms.

The challenge for most organizations is to find the appropriate degrees of decentralization and informality to enable them to maintain control whilst innovating and managing change in a dynamic and turbulent environment. In turn this requires that managers are **empowered**. (Empowerment is defined later in Key Concept 22.2.)

These structural types will be evidenced in the organization frameworks and structural designs which are explored in detail in this chapter. It is important to appreciate that structure involves more than the organization chart or framework which is used for illustrative purposes and to explain where businesses, products, services and people fit in relation to each other. Charts are static; structures are dynamic and involve behaviour patterns.

In this chapter five popular structural forms, namely the entrepreneurial, functional, divisional, holding company and matrix structures, will be described and evaluated. From these outline frameworks the determining forces of structure will be explored in greater detail, and the research work of such authors as Greiner and Mintzberg will be discussed. The relationship of structure and management style, particularly in relation to large diversified businesses, will be used as a basis to examine the role of strategic leaders and general managers in greater detail. Finally a consideration of the issues involved in rewarding performance within the structure will conclude the chapter.

STRUCTURAL FORMS

There are a number of discrete structural forms which can be adapted by an organization when attempts are made to design an appropriate structure to satisfy its particular needs. The following are described in this section:

☐ the entrepreneurial structure
☐ the functional structure
☐ the divisional structure
☐ the holding company structure
☐ the matrix structure.

This is not an exhaustive coverage in the sense that personalized varieties of each of these alternatives can easily be developed.

Chandler (1962) and subsequent authors such as Salter (1970) have suggested that as firms grow from being a small business with a simple entrepreneurial structure, a more formal functional structure evolves to allow managers to cope with the increasing complexity and the demands of decision making. As the organization becomes diversified, with a multiplicity of products, services or operating bases, a different structure is again required, and initially this is likely to be based on simple divisionalization. In other words there are stages of structural development which evolve as strategies change and organizations grow. Chandler contends, though, that whilst strategy and structure develop together through a particular sequence, structures are not adapted until pressures force a change. The pressures tend to relate to growing inefficiency resulting from an inability to handle the increasing demands of decision making. Matrix organizations have been designed to cope with the complexities of multi-product, multi-national organizations with interdependences which must be accommodated if synergy is to be achieved. However, matrix organizations are difficult to manage and control.

It has been emphasized earlier that many organizations fail to achieve the anticipated synergy from strategies of diversification and acquisition, and as a result divest the businesses they cannot add value to. Implementation difficulties are often linked to a failure to absorb the new acquisition into the existing organization, and this is likely to involve changes in the structure.

It is important to appreciate that the structural forms described in this section are only a framework, and that the behavioural processes within the structure, the way that resources are managed and co-ordinated, really determines effectiveness. In turn this is related to the way that authority, power and responsibility is devolved throughout the

---

In my experience, the key to growth is to pick good managers, involve them at the outset of discussions on strategy and objectives, and then devolve as much responsibility as they will accept. That's the only way you know if they are any good.

Michael Grade, Chief Executive,
Channel Four Television

Autonomy is what you take, not what you are given.

Roy Watts, Chairman, Thames Water

Organisational flexibility is essential. Rates of change have speeded up. The hierarchical organisation is slow to respond. Decisions taken at the centre are too far away from the coal face. While the centre seeks local and relevant understanding, delays in decision making result.

In today's turbulent business environment speed of decision making is critically important . . . decisions should be pushed down the organisation and as close to the customers as possible.

Sir John Harvey-Jones MBE, quoted in
The Responsive Organisation, *BIM, 1989*

Key Concept 22.1
CENTRALIZATION AND DECENTRALIZATION

Centralization and decentralization relate to the degree to which the authority, power and responsibility for decision making is devolved through the organization. There are several options, including the following.

☐ All major strategic decisions are taken centrally, at head office, by the strategic leader or a group of senior strategists. The size of any team will depend upon the preference of the overall strategic leader together with the size, complexity and diversity of the organization. Strictly enforced policies and procedures will constrain the freedom of other managers responsible for business units, products, services and functional areas to change competitive and functional strategies. This is centralization.

☐ Changes in the strategic perspective are decided centrally, but then the organization is structured to enable managers to change competitive and functional strategies in line with perceived opportunities and threats.

☐ The organization is truly decentralized such that independent business units have general managers who are free to change their respective strategic perspectives. In effect they run a series of independent businesses with some co-ordination from the parent headquarters.

The role of general managers in charge of divisions and business units is explored later in this chapter.

The extent to which true decentralization exists may be visible from the organization's charted structure. It is useful to examine the membership of the group and divisional/business unit boards, regardless of the number and delineation of divisions. The organization is likely to tend towards decentralization where there is a main board and a series of subsidiary boards, each chaired by a member of the main board. The chief executive/strategic leader, who is responsible for the performance of each subsidiary, will not necessarily have a seat on the main board. The organization will tend towards greater centralization where the main board comprises the chairmen/chief executives of certain subsidiaries, generally the largest ones, together with staff specialists. Hence decentralization and divisionalization are **not** synonymous terms.

___

THE TEN MAIN DETERMINANTS

☐ The size of the organization
☐ Geographical locations, together with the
  ☐ homogeneity/heterogeneity of the products and services
  ☐ technology of the tasks involved
  ☐ interdependences

☐ The relative importance and stability of the external environment, and the possible need to react quickly
☐ Generally, how fast decisions need to be made
☐ The work load on decision makers
☐ Issues of motivation via delegation, together with the abilities and willingness of managers to make decisions and accept responsibility
☐ The location of competence and expertise in the organization. Are the managerial strengths in the divisions or at headquarters?
☐ The costs involved in making any changes
☐ The significance and impact of competitive and functional decisions and changes
☐ The status of the firm's planning, control and information systems.

ADVANTAGES AND DISADVANTAGES

There are no right or wrong answers concerning the appropriate amount of centralization/decentralization. It is a question of balancing the potential advantages and disadvantages of each as they affect particular firms.

Horovitz and Thietart suggest that companies which achieve and maintain high growth tend to be more decentralized, and those which are more concerned with profits than growth are more centralized. The highest performers in terms of both growth and profits tend to retain high degrees of central control as far as the overall strategic perspective is concerned. Child (1977) contends that the most essential issue is the degree of internal consistency.

Advantages of centralization

☐ Consistency of strategy
☐ Easier to co-ordinate activities (and handle the interdependences) and control changes
☐ Changes in the strategic perspective are more easily facilitated.

Disadvantages of centralization

☐ May be slow to respond to changes which affect subsidiaries individually rather than the organization as a whole, depending upon the remoteness of head office

☐ Easy to create an expensive head office who rely on management information systems and become detached from customers, and for whom there are too many diverse interests and complexities
☐ General managers with real strategic ability are not developed within the organization. Instead the organization is dependent on specialists and as a result the various functions may not be properly co-ordinated. Does this achieve a fit between the organization and its environment?

Advantages of decentralization

☐ Ability to change competitive and functional strategies more quickly
☐ Improved motivation
☐ Can develop better overall strategic awareness in a very complex organization which is too diverse for a head office to control effectively.

Disadvantages of decentralization

☐ May be problems in clarifying the role of head office central services which aim to co-ordinate the various divisions and business units and achieve certain economies through and centralization of selected activities
☐ Problems of linking the power which general managers need and the responsibility which goes with the power. General managers must have the freedom to make decisions without referrals back.

organization, and whether generally the firm is centralized or decentralized. These themes are explored in Key Concept 22.1, where it is emphasized that decentralization and divisionalization are not synonymous, and Key

Concept 22.2 on empowerment. The establishment of a divisionalized structure does not necessarily imply that authority to adapt competitive and functional strategies is freely delegated; the firm could remain centralized.

Key Concept 22.2
EMPOWERMENT

Empowerment means freeing employees from instructions and controls and allowing them to take decisions themselves. Total quality management implies constant improvement; to achieve this employees should be contributing to the best of their ability. Proponents argue that rules stifle innovation and that future success relies not on past results but on the continuing ability to manage change pressures. Managers must be free to make appropriate changes in a decentralized structure.

There are three main **objectives** of empowerment:

☐ to make organizations more responsive to external pressures
☐ to 'de-layer' organizations in order to make them more cost effective. British Airways, for example, now has five layers of management between the chief executive and the front line who interface with customers. It used to be nine. Managers become responsible for more employees who they are expected to coach and support rather than direct
☐ to create employee networks featuring teamworking, collaboration and horizontal communications. This implies changes in the ways decisions are made.

It is neither feasible nor appropriate to decentralize all decisions, and therefore the important empowerment questions are why, how and when. The leading retailers, for example, benefited from increasing centralization throughout the 1980s. Information technology has enabled cost savings and efficiencies from centrally controlled buying, store and shelf layouts, stocking policies and re-ordering. In the 1990s there is little support for changing this in any marked way and delegating these decisions to store level.

At the same time individual stores will be judged in part on the quality of service they provide to their customers; and it is in this area that there is considerable scope for empowering managers and other employees.

As empowerment is increased it is important that employees are adequately informed and knowledgeable, that they are motivated to exercise power, and that they are rewarded for successful outcomes. In flatter organization structures there are fewer opportunities for promotion.

There are three **basic empowerment options**:

☐ Employees can be encouraged to contribute ideas. We saw in Chapter 16 how several important new product ideas for McDonald's have come from individual franchisees. In reality this may represent only token empowerment.
☐ Employees work in teams which share and manage their own work, but within clearly defined policies and limits. This should increase both efficiency and job satisfaction.
☐ More extensive decentralization where individuals are much freer to change certain parameters and strategies. Evaluating outcomes is seen as the important control mechanism rather than rules and guidelines. This requires strong leadership, a clear mission and effective communications. Information must flow openly upwards and sideways as well as down. In many organizations there is a tendency for 'bad news' to be selectively hidden, with perhaps two-thirds not flowing up to the next layer. Many potential threats are thereby not shared within the company. This would be unacceptable in an empowered organization.

An example: Banc One

Banc One, whose headquarters are in Columbus, Ohio, has quickly grown into one of America's leading banks. During 1991 and the first half of 1992 Banc One acquired 12 other banks. The company deliberately avoids the property sector and concentrates on personal accounts. Their strategy implementation blends decentralized decision making with group-wide guidance and advice. Individual managers cannot choose their own product portfolio, but they are free to set their own marketing and pricing strategies. There is an elaborate reporting system and IT is harnessed to share relative successes and results amongst the 1300-plus branches. Managers can quickly compare their own performances. In addition, a team of internal consultants visits the branches to provide support and advice, and spread best practices.

For many organizations empowerment implies that the core organization strategies are decided centrally, with individual managers delegated a discretionary layer around the core:

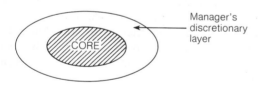

Manager's discretionary layer

It is crucial, first, to find the right balance between the core and discretionary elements and, second, to ensure that managers support and **own** the core strategy.

The deciding factors

☐ The competitive strategies and the relative importance of close linkages with customers in order to differentiate and provide high levels of service. When this becomes essential empowerment may imply an inverted pyramid structure. The structure exists to support front-line managers:

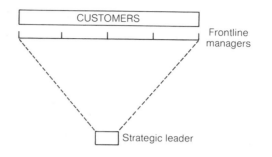

Successful empowerment means putting the 'right' people in place and ensuring they are able to do their job – which they understand and own. In this way they feel important.

☐ The extent to which the environment is turbulent and decisions are varied rather than routine.
☐ The expectations and preferences of managers and employees, and their ability and willingness to accept responsibility. Not everyone wants accountability and high visibility. If empowerment is mishandled it is possible that work will be simply pushed down a shorter hierarchy as managers seek to avoid responsibility.

Successful empowerment requires appropriate skills, which in turn frequently implies training. The appropriate style of management is coaching. Moreover it is important to link in monitoring systems together with rewards and sanctions. Finally empowerment must be taken seriously and not simply limited to non-essential decisions. Empowerment implies risk taking, and any mistakes, whilst not overlooked, must be handled carefully.

Empowerment is a powerful motivator as long as it does not suddenly stop when the really important and interesting decisions have to be taken.

(Jeremy Soper, ex Retail Sales Director, W H Smith)

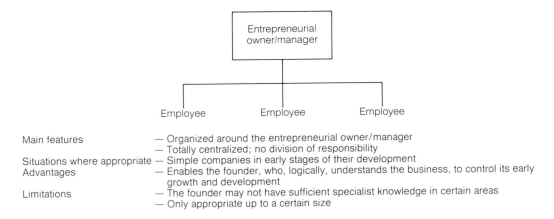

Main features	— Organized around the entrepreneurial owner/manager
	— Totally centralized; no division of responsibility
Situations where appropriate	— Simple companies in early stages of their development
Advantages	— Enables the founder, who, logically, understands the business, to control its early growth and development
Limitations	— The founder may not have sufficient specialist knowledge in certain areas
	— Only appropriate up to a certain size

Figure 22.1 The entrepreneurial structure.

The entrepreneurial structure

The entrepreneurial structure, built around the owner/manager and typically utilized by small companies in the early stages of their development, is illustrated in Figure 22.1. The structure is totally centralized. All key decisions are made by the strategic leader, and employees refer everything significant back to him or her. It is particularly useful for new businesses as it enables the founder, who normally will have some expertise with the product or service and whose investment is at risk, to control the growth and development.

There is an argument that this is not really a formal structure as all responsibility, power and authority lies with one person. However, in some small companies of this nature, selected employees will specialize and be given job titles and some limited responsibility for such activities as production, sales or accounting. In this respect the structure could be redrawn to appear more like the functional organization discussed below. The functional form only really emerges when **managers** are established with genuine delegated authority and responsibility for the functions and activities they control.

New firms with entrepreneurial structures are likely to be established because the owner/manager has contacts and expertise in a particular line of business and, for whatever reason, wishes to establish his or her own business. Whilst the entrepreneur will want to control the early stages of growth, it does not follow that he or she will have expertise in all aspects of the business. Many start-ups occur because the founder understands the technology and production or operational aspects of the business. Marketing, sales and financial control may well be areas of potential weakness with a consequent reliance on other people together with an element of learning as the business develops. This need can prove to be a limitation of the entrepreneurial structure.

Another limitation relates to growth. At some stage, dependent upon both the business and the founder, the demands of decision making, both day-to-day problem decisions and longer-term planning decisions, will become too complex for one person, and there will be pressure to establish a more formal functional organization. The owner/manager relinquishes some responsibility for short-term decisions and has greater opportunity to concentrate on the more strategic aspects of the business. This can prove to be a dilemma for some entrepreneurs, however, particularly those who started their own business because they

Case 22.1
WESTWOOD ENGINEERING

Westwood Engineering was formed by Gerry Hazlewood in 1969, and after 18 years it was the leading manufacturer of garden tractors in the UK. The company's products held a 70% market share. Turnover in 1987 was £12 million and the company employed 300 people.

Hazlewood became convinced that as chief executive he was too involved in operational decisions for a business of this size. Areas of the business were being neglected as he 'was running everything personally'. In February 1987 he announced that he was giving away 25% of the company's equity to 35 loyal employees and that three of his most senior managers were being promoted. They would assume executive control of the business and he would step aside to a more strategic role related to the development of special projects and new ventures. It was assumed that there would be a change to a more formal professional style of management away from his 'quirky, entrepreneurial style'.

Development opportunities had already been spotted, but resources had not been allocated to them. Westwood, for instance, was vertically integrated, manufacturing many of their own parts in an attempt to be self-sufficient. To achieve this they had developed some special welding techniques and Hazlewood was convinced that there was an external market for this.

Source: Oates, D (1987) Out to grass, *The Director*, February.

wanted total control over something, or because they were frustrated with the greater formality of larger companies. Although the company was beyond this early stage of development, Case 22.1, Westwood Engineering, provides an example of this issue.

The functional structure

The functional structure, illustrated in Figure 22.2, is commonplace in small firms which have outgrown the entrepreneurial structure and in larger firms which produce only a limited range of related products and services. It is also the typical internal structure of the divisions and business units which comprise larger diversified organizations. It is more suitable in a stable environment than a turbulent one as it is generally centralized with corporate and competitive strategies again being controlled substantially by the strategic leader.

The structure is built around the tasks to be carried out, which tend to be split into specialist functional areas. Managers are placed in charge of departments which are responsible for these functions, and they may well have delegated authority to change functional strategies. Consequently the effectiveness of this structure is very dependent on the ability of these specialist managers to work together as a team and support each other and on the ability of the strategic leader to co-ordinate their efforts.

The functional structure can be highly efficient with low overheads in comparison with divisional structures, which have to

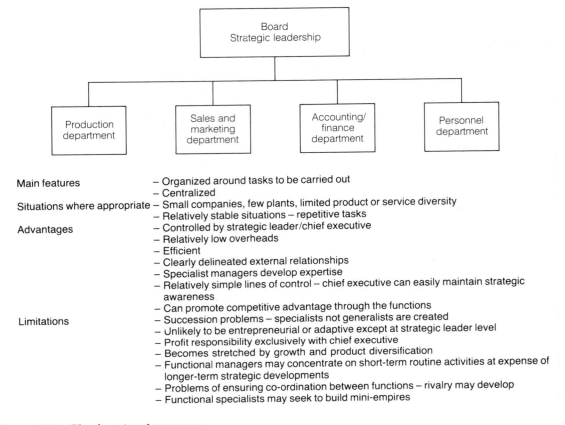

Figure 22.2 The functional structure.

address the issue of functions duplicated in the business units and at head office. Functional managers will develop valuable specialist expertise which can be used as a basis for the creation of competitive advantage, and the relatively simple lines of communication between these specialists and the strategic leader can facilitate a high degree of strategic awareness at the top of the organization.

There are a number of limitations, however. The concentration on the functions tends to lead to managers with greater specialist expertise rather than a more corporate perspective. General managers who can embrace all the functions are not developed, and consequently any internal successor to the chief executive is likely to have a particu-

lar specialist viewpoint, which may involve cultural change. This might conceivably mean a change from a financial orientation to a customer-led organization, for example, or vice versa.

Functional organizations are less likely to be entrepreneurial throughout the company than is the case in more decentralized forms, although the strategic leader could be personally dynamic and entrepreneurial. Because corporate and competitive strategy changes are generally the responsibility of the strategic leader, functional managers may concentrate on short-term issues at the expense of longer-term strategic needs. The tendency for profit responsibility to lie primarily with the strategic leader compounds this. Functional managers may seek to build mini-empires around their specialism, and this can lead to rivalry between departments for resources and status and make the task of co-ordination and team-building more difficult.

The structure is stretched and becomes more inefficient with growth and product or service diversification. As the firm grows from a limited range of related products to unrelated ones, co-ordination proves increasingly difficult. Hence a need grows for some form of divisionalization, together with a revised role for the strategic leader. The strategic leader is now responsible for co-ordinating the strategies of a series of business units or divisions, each with a general manager at their head, rather than co-ordinating specialist functional managers into a cohesive and supportive team. Financial management skills become increasingly necessary. Adaptive changes in competitive strategies are now likely to be delegated.

Galbraith and Nathanson (1978) contend that the corporate strategy formulated by an organization at the functional stage of development indicates which new structural form is likely to be most appropriate. They suggest the following development path:

Strategy	Next logical structural form
Vertical integration	More sophisticated, centralized functional organization
Internal growth and related diversification	Divisional
Unrelated diversification	Holding company

The divisional structure

One example of a divisional structure is illustrated in Figure 22.3, using product groups as the means of divisionalizing. Geographic regions are another means that are frequently used, and sometimes both geo-graphy and product groups are used in conjunction. Vertically integrated organizations might divisionalize into manufacturing, assembly and distribution activities.

The primary features are as follows:

- a set of divisions or business units which themselves are likely to contain a functional structure, and which can be regarded as profit centres
- each division will be headed by a general manager who is responsible for strategy implementation and to some extent strategy formulation within the division
- decentralization of limited power, authority and responsibility.

Divisional structures are found when complexity and diversity increases and where turbulent environmental conditions make it appropriate to decentralize some responsibility for making sure that the organization is responsive and possibly proactive towards external forces in a variety of different industries. They are also useful where there are major differences in needs and tastes in the company's markets around the world.

The major advantage of this structure is that it can facilitate the ability of the organization to manage the strategies of a number of disparate products and markets effectively. The major difficulty lies in designing the most appropriate structure, as the following example illustrates.

When British Steel Corporation (BSC) was formed in 1967, with the nationalization of much of the UK steel industry, a number of separate and already diversified steel companies were brought together. After a series of closures and rationalization programmes 36 identifiable plants remained in 1988 when BSC was privatized once more. These plants are shown in Table 22.1 allocated into four product groups and seven geographical regions. This particular product grouping, which was used by the corporation, means that a product such as a steel plate can be manufactured by both the general steels product group and the stainless steels product

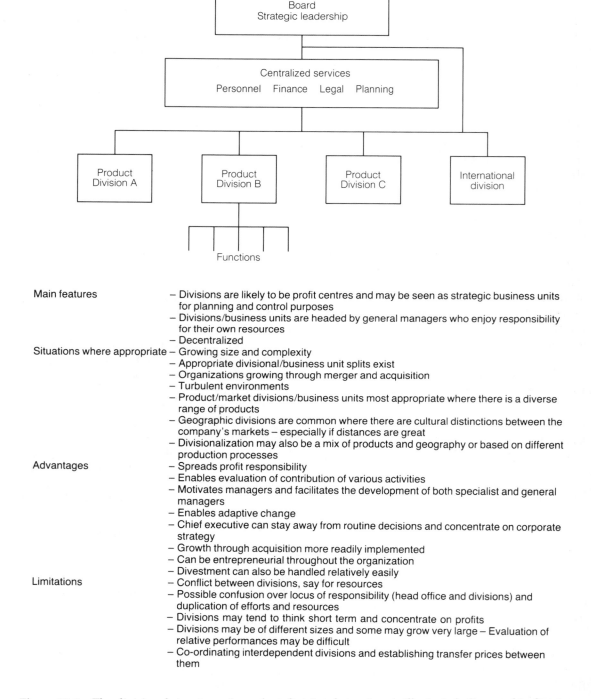

Main features   – Divisions are likely to be profit centres and may be seen as strategic business units
                                   for planning and control purposes
                                 – Divisions/business units are headed by general managers who enjoy responsibility
                                   for their own resources
                                 – Decentralized
Situations where appropriate   – Growing size and complexity
                                 – Appropriate divisional/business unit splits exist
                                 – Organizations growing through merger and acquisition
                                 – Turbulent environments
                                 – Product/market divisions/business units most appropriate where there is a diverse
                                   range of products
                                 – Geographic divisions are common where there are cultural distinctions between the
                                   company's markets – especially if distances are great
                                 – Divisionalization may also be a mix of products and geography or based on different
                                   production processes
Advantages   – Spreads profit responsibility
                                 – Enables evaluation of contribution of various activities
                                 – Motivates managers and facilitates the development of both specialist and general
                                   managers
                                 – Enables adaptive change
                                 – Chief executive can stay away from routine decisions and concentrate on corporate
                                   strategy
                                 – Growth through acquisition more readily implemented
                                 – Can be entrepreneurial throughout the organization
                                 – Divestment can also be handled relatively easily
Limitations   – Conflict between divisions, say for resources
                                 – Possible confusion over locus of responsibility (head office and divisions) and
                                   duplication of efforts and resources
                                 – Divisions may tend to think short term and concentrate on profits
                                 – Divisions may be of different sizes and some may grow very large – Evaluation of
                                   relative performances may be difficult
                                 – Co-ordinating interdependent divisions and establishing transfer prices between
                                   them

Figure 22.3   The divisional structure. A product divisional structure is illustrated. Geographic divisions, or a mixture of the two, are also used.

Table 22.1 British Steel plants by geographical location and product type at time of privatization in 1988

	Region						
	Scotland	Northeast	Sheffield/ Rotherham	Lincs	Midlands including Staffs	North Wales	South Wales
General steels, e.g. girders, bars, strip plates, rail sections (non-stainless)	2	5	1	1	1		
Strip products (including wide sheet in coils, again non-stainless)	1	1			1	1	9
Stainless plates, sheets, coils, strips etc.			5				1
Tubes	2	2			3		

group, depending upon the type of steel and the end use. The plates will sell to different customers. The first organization structure designed by BSC was based on geographic regions, although these were not exactly the seven shown in the table. This lasted until 1970 when the corporation was re-structured by products, loosely those shown in the table. In 1976 there was a reversion to geographic divisions (profit centres), each containing a number of discrete product units. Similar to the 1960s period, there was a corporation-wide allocation policy of the orders for various products to alleviate direct competition between plants in different divisions which produced essentially the same product. This 1976 re-structuring allowed BSC, under pressure from government, to identify which parts of the corporation were profitable and which were losing money. Geographical profit centres allowed clear identification (in political terms) of loss-making plants and areas. In the past the consolidated accounting procedures adopted by BSC had prevented such public identification. In 1982 another structure based on product divisions was introduced, and this remained in existence until the strategic changes described in Case 21.4.

In summary, there is no one best way of dividing a business into divisions, especially if the composition of the whole corporation changes with acquisitions, divestments and closures. Large companies will change their structures periodically in an attempt to improve both efficiency and effectiveness. Structural changes of this nature imply changes in the power structure, the relative amount of decentralization and in managers' jobs, and for these reasons they may prove disruptive.

Other advantages of divisional structures are that profit responsibilities are spread between the divisions or business units. This helps to motivate managers who can be given authority and responsibility for profit, and enables an evaluation of the contribution of each activity to the organization as a whole. Responsibility for changes in competitive and functional strategies can be delegated to the general managers in charge of each division or business unit; and it is feasible for these managers also to have responsibility for changes in the corporate strategy of their divisions. In this way the strategic leader of the corporation can concentrate substantially on corporate strategy and avoid involvement in routine decisions. Acquisitions and divestments can be handled so that only parts of the firm are affected directly. Finally this structure facilitates innovation and intrapreneurialism throughout the corporation if

Table 22.2 W H Smith, group structure in 1991

Retailing activities	
W H Smith retail (high street stores + airports and stations)	500 outlets
Our Price (specialist sounds retailing)	305 outlets
Waterstone's (specialist booksellers)	83 outlets
Our Price Video (video retailing)	27 outlets
Paperchase (cards and fashion stationery)	21 outlets
Do It All (DIY superstores – joint venture with Boots)	234 outlets
W H Smith retail – USA	305 outlets – mainly small variety stores in hotels and airports
Wee Three Records (specialist sounds retailing – USA)	84 outlets
Non-retailing activities	
W H Smith News (newspaper and magazine distribution)	96 houses serving 24 000 outlets
Heathcote Books and D Services (distribution of books and related products to retailers, schools, libraries)	
5 suppliers of commercial stationery and office products	

There are plans to open up to 20 Waterstone's specialist bookshops in the USA.
Source: Company accounts.

there is encouragement for this by the strategic leader.

In addition to the difficulty of designing an appropriate structure, there are also problems of implementation. It was highlighted above that divisions are normally seen as profit centres, and consequently their profit targets will be used as a basis for assessing performance and effectiveness. There may be problems in establishing profit targets which are seen as equitable, given that divisions (a) may well be of uneven sizes, (b) are likely to be operating in markets which differ in their attractiveness, (c) may have strong or weak relative market shares, (d) be interdependent upon each other and (e) have to compete with each other for scarce corporation resources. Where there are interdependences the corporation policy on transfer prices will favour certain divisions at the expense of others, which again can cause conflict. Wherever profits are a key measure, buying divisions will look for discounts and favourable treatment from within the corporation; selling divisions will expect other parts of the company to pay the going market price, or they will prefer to sell outside. Such profit orientation may also encourage divisions to think in terms of short-term financial measures rather than address more strategic issues.

Where an organization has a variety of different products, all of which depend on core skills and technologies, the challenge is to harness and improve the skills (which are, in effect, corporate resources) whilst ensuring competitiveness and operating efficiency for each product range. We saw in Chapter 1, for example, that Canon have developed a range of discrete products (cameras, copiers, printers etc.) around three core competencies: precision mechanics, fine optics and microelectronics.

Finally each division is likely to contain a functional structure, and there is also likely to be functional support from headquarters. The corporation as a whole may be able to negotiate better borrowing terms than an individual division could; personnel policies may need to be consistent throughout the firm; and head office planners may provide support to divisional planners. Reconciling

Case 22.2
BRITISH RAIL (BR)

Prior to nationalization in 1948 the railways in Britain were run by regionally based companies. For 40 years after nationalization the structure of BR was based upon these regions.

In 1988 five new business sectors were established: Inter City, Network South East, Provincial (later re-named Regional), Railfreight and Parcels. Trains, tracks and stations were still provided by the existing regional divisions, and hired by the business sectors. Whilst this was a clear attempt to set up measurable profit centres, the difficulties in properly allocating costs to activities made it a complex structure.

The structure was changed again in 1992. The business sectors were each divided up into a number of smaller profit centres. Inter City, for example, has the East Coast and West Coast main lines to Scotland and the Great Western route to the southwest amongst its profit centres. Each profit centre owns its own tracks and services. Other divisions of BR therefore have to hire tracks and stations from the relevant profit centre if they need to use them. Network South East, for example, hires part of Kings Cross Station from Inter City East Coast which owns it. The Railfreight and Parcels divisions own very little track. The intention was to make it easier to pinpoint responsibilities and accountability, say for late running.

When the first details of the proposed privatization plans were released in 1992 it emerged that a nationalized BR would retain ownership of the basic infrastructure, including tracks and signalling equipment. Private operators would be able to bid to run services and stations. The need remains for effective cost and information systems to co-ordinate all the activities.

any conflicts between these divisional and head office groups, together with the need to minimize the potential waste from duplicate resources, can be a limitation of this structural form. The problem can be more difficult to resolve where there are layers of divisions, as discussed below.

Where organizations grow very large, complex and diversified it may be necessary to establish a number of layers of divisions or business units within larger divisions. Each business unit or subdivision may also be a profit centre with its own general manager. By way of illustration, the W H Smith Group contained 16 discrete activities or business units in 1991, as described in Table 22.2. The company was less diversified than it had

been three years earlier, having divested its travel agencies and television interests. Whilst it would be possible to have 16 divisions, they would be of significantly different sizes. Moreover, there are strong links between some of the business units. Eight of them are clearly retailing, and the others all involve distribution of a product or service, for example. Of the retailing activities, books, sounds and stationery feature in seven of the business units, but two of these are in the USA. The retailing and distribution activities involve basically the same products. There are therefore any number of ways of splitting the group into divisions with business units reporting to divisional heads. The appropriate support and co-ordination roles for both head office and divisional staff will depend on the structure which is preferred. For example the purchasing of books, records and stationery for wholesale and retail could usefully be centralized, and the same electronic point-of-sale (EPOS) system could be relevant for all the retail activities. As in the example of British Steel above, there is no one right answer to the W H Smith structure problem.

British Rail have similar problems, and these are described in Case 22.2.

As organizations develop globally the structural issues are compounded. We saw in Chapter 17 that Porter (1990) and Ohmae (1990) disagree about how a company should transform itself into a successful global firm. Ohmae argues it should shake off its origins; Porter thinks they must be preserved. Ohmae advocates decomposing the central head office into a number of regional head-quarters, with the control of different functions (marketing, production etc.) being dispersed to different extents and to different

locations. The approaches of IBM and Nestlé are featured in Case 22.3.

The traditional divisionalized structure may prove inadequate for coping with the complexities of diversity and globalization. Whilst the holding company and matrix structures provide alternatives (the choice depending upon interdependences and synergy needs), some organizations will eventually choose to split up into smaller, less diverse parts. Courtaulds (see Case 10.1)was split in 1990; ICI (Case 22.4) has stated an intention to split in 1993. Since 1990 both Courtaulds companies have 'out-performed the stock market'. The arguments for such splits are:

☐ the whole is worth less than the sum of the parts – the complexity is preventing individual businesses from achieving their true potential; and
☐ being part of a large organization prevents or delays important decisions.

Case 22.3
TWO TRANSNATIONALS: IBM AND NESTLÉ – DECENTRALIZATION IN A DIVISIONALIZED STRUCTURE

The challenge for these multi-product, multi-national businesses is to design and implement a structure which enables them to be sensitive to different customer requirements whilst containing costs. The successful competitors, especially in a recession, are those which can deliver high service and quality at low cost.

IBM

IBM is the largest manufacturer of computer hardware and software in the world. The company became over-centralized and over-bureaucratic and was slow to change in the economic recession. Profits fell. IBM entered into a series of strategic alliances with related American, Japanese and German companies; and recently the corporation has been re-structured and decentralized. IBM is now a federation of 13 independent (yet interdependent) companies, comprising six hardware manufacturing divisions, three software divisions, and four regional sales companies. The largest three (in terms of annual turnover) are two sales companies and the division which manufactures mainframe computers. Basically the hardware and software divisions manufacture and wholesale; the regional sales companies are retailers. Whilst the corporation is vertically integrated, manufacturing semiconductors and disc drives as well as final products, the divisions are under no obligation to trade with each other. The divisions are internally competitive, and consequently any transfer prices tend to be at market rates. The intention is to:

☐ divorce corporate and competitive strategies;
☐ speed up decision making and the lead times for new product/service developments;
☐ give each division a 'real opportunity to become the lowest cost manufacturer of state-of-the-art information systems'.

Each divisional general manager has to agree targets for:

☐ revenue growth
☐ profit
☐ return on assets
☐ cash flow
☐ customer satisfaction
☐ quality
☐ employee morale.

Notably these measures cover both efficiency and effectiveness targets. This issue is developed further in Chapter 23. Managers' rewards are partially based upon the success of their division; failure to achieve corporate financial targets affects future corporate investment, and increases the possibility of either divestment or joint venture.

The global headquarters of one division (which manufactures communications systems) has been relocated from the US to the UK. IBM is not alone in moving decision-making responsibility for global competitive strategies away from the home base. Unilever, Procter and Gamble and Philips are amongst the pioneers, and Nestlé have also recently followed.

The re-structuring at IBM involves major changes to the culture of the organization, and it is still not clear just how sucessful the changes are. Initially the morale of some managers deteriorated because they felt more exposed and threatened. After declaring a substantial trading loss IBM's chief executive stepped down early in 1993.

NESTLÉ

Nestlé produces and sells in over 100 countries, many of which have strong local preferences. Their corporate headquarters has been slimmed down in the early 1990s in an attempt to be more innovative and more customer-focused. There are seven new strategic business units (including coffee and beverages; foods; etc.) which have worldwide strategic responsibility. Operations in the various countries are co-ordinated through a regional network.

Each strategic business unit is free to operate in the most appropriate way – there is no longer a 'central way of doing things'. The style and approach will vary with the degree of novelty/maturity of the business, its market share and technological intensity, and the need to be localized. The intention is to establish the most appropriate cost structure and decision-making procedures. The requirements for E–V–R congruence vary between the divisions. There are, however, in-built mechanisms to try and spread best practices and to overcome a past tendency to resist adopting ideas developed in other countries.

Case 22.4
ICI

ICI's strategic and structural problems are partially a result of the range and diversity of its products. These range from bulk chemicals (including chlorine and petrochemicals [plastics from oil and gas]) to more sophisticated products such as pharmaceuticals and pesticides. The prospects for bulk chemicals are traditionally dependent upon the world economic cycle, and consequently profits vary dramatically from year to year. Drugs are classically immune from the economic cycle, and they are also cash generative. ICI's dilemma concerns the utilization of its profits for research and development and capital investment, and whether to cross-subsidize or treat the businesses separately. During the boom years of the mid-1980s chemicals and related products were very profitable; but in the recession of 1991 they contributed just 30% of ICI's profits from 70% of the turnover.

Between 1980 and 1985, chaired by Sir Maurice Hodgson and later Sir John Harvey-Jones, ICI reduced its global workforce from 225 000 to 175 000 and purged its costs. The early 1980s were also recession years. ICI's competitive position strengthened. The company was also re-structured into seven global product divisions co-ordinated through nine regional territories. Financial responsibilities were split amongst the divisions and the regions. UK inflation later in the 1980s meant that ICI's costs started to rise again, and faster than those of its main competitors. The workforce was further reduced (to 132 000 in 1990) and productivity improved – but it was still not enough.

In 1990 ICI was re-structured again in an attempt to place greater emphasis on the global nature of its businesses, increase the financial accountability of the divisional business managers, and focus greater attention on improving shareholders' wealth. The head office was slimmed down, and the number of regional chairmen was reduced to three. The regions lost any managerial responsibility over individual businesses. The product division heads became autonomous, and they could spend up to £10 million without reference to the main Board. In comparison, business chiefs in Hanson must seek executive approval for all capital expenditures over £500 or $1000. When Hanson acquired 2.8% of ICI's shares in Spring 1991, and raised the threat of a hostile take-over bid, the company was encouraged to evaluate again both its strategy and structure. No bid materialized, but Hanson and external analysts questioned whether ICI was effectively exploiting its assets.

ICI decided to concentrate on businesses where it could achieve a strong global position – see Case 9.3. The fibres operations were swapped for the acrylics businesses of Du Pont early in 1992 – see Chapter 17.

In July 1992 ICI's Board announced plans to split the company into two separate businesses in 1993 – ICI and ICI Bioscience – later renamed Zeneca. Shareholders in ICI would be given an equivalent shareholding in the new company. ICI would retain industrial chemicals, paints and explosives, it would have 88 000 employees world wide and be the seventh largest chemical company in the world (relegated from fifth). Zeneca would comprise the drugs and agrochemicals businesses and be the ninth largest pharmaceutical company in the world. There would be 35 500 employees. It was assumed that most of ICI's cash reserves would remain with the bulk chemicals when it was announced that Zeneca would have an early rights issue.

Each of the new groupings would enable each company to respond better to future opportunities. ICI now comprises two distinct families of businesses with the same values, but very different technologies, operating requirements and market needs.

(Company spokesman)

Arguably ICI would be less vulnerable to any future hostile take-over bid. ICI would prove unattractive; Zeneca too expensive.

The holding company structure

The holding company structure, illustrated in Figure 22.4, is ideal for diversified conglomerates where there are few interdependences between the businesses. The small head office acts largely as an investment company, acquiring and selling businesses and investing money as appropriate. The subsidiaries, which may or may not be wholly owned, are very independent, and their general managers are likely to have full responsibility for corporate strategy within any financial constraints or targets set by headquarters. It is quite common to find that the subsidiaries trade under individual names rather than the name of the parent organization, especially where they are acquisitions who may at any time be sold again.

The holding company structure is particularly appropriate for companies pursuing restructuring strategies, buying, rationalizing and then selling businesses when they can no longer add further value.

BTR (See Case 23.3) and Lonrho are examples of organizations with a holding company structure. BTR is an acquisitive industrial conglomerate whose products include Dunlop tyres, Slazenger sports equipment and Pretty Polly tights, all of which trade under their original names. Lonrho is a genuine multi-product, multi-national with a series of unrelated businesses, although there are clear links between some of them. Their interests include mining and refining, agriculture (farming and ranching in Africa and the USA), hotels (Metropole group in the UK, Princess group in the Caribbean), motor vehicle distribution (VW–Audi, Jaguar, Mercedes–Benz and Seat), printing and publishing (the Observer Group), oil and gas, engineering, textiles (manufacturing and retailing), international trading, and freight. Lonrho's chief executive is Roland 'Tiny' Rowland, who has built the group over a period of 25 years through a series of entrepreneurial acquisitions. General managers are delegated considerable responsibility, although Rowland stays strategically very aware and is clearly responsible for the overall corporate strategy.

The advantages of this structural form are that it implies low central overheads and considerable decentralization but enables the head office to finance the subsidiaries at a favourable cost of capital. Risks are spread across a wide portfolio, and cross-subsidization is possible between the most and least profitable businesses. This again raises the issue of ascertaining a fair reward structure for the general managers.

The limitations relate, first, to the vulnerability that general managers may feel if they suspect that their business may always be for

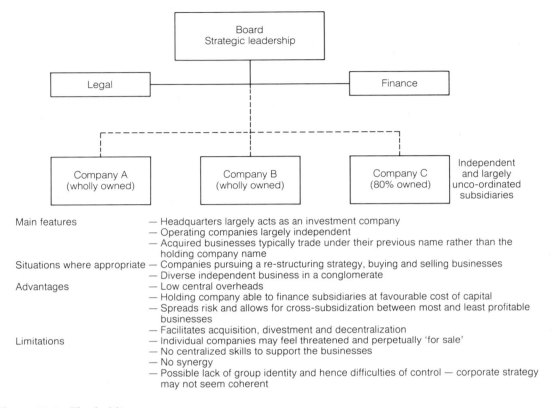

Main features
— Headquarters largely acts as an investment company
— Operating companies largely independent
— Acquired businesses typically trade under their previous name rather than the holding company name

Situations where appropriate
— Companies pursuing a re-structuring strategy, buying and selling businesses
— Diverse independent business in a conglomerate

Advantages
— Low central overheads
— Holding company able to finance subsidiaries at favourable cost of capital
— Spreads risk and allows for cross-subsidization between most and least profitable businesses
— Facilitates acquisition, divestment and decentralization

Limitations
— Individual companies may feel threatened and perpetually 'for sale'
— No centralized skills to support the businesses
— No synergy
— Possible lack of group identity and hence difficulties of control — corporate strategy may not seem coherent

Figure 22.4   The holding company structure.

sale at the right price. There are fewer centralized skills and resources supporting the businesses, little co-ordination and therefore few opportunities for synergy. In addition there may be no real group identity amongst the business units and a lack of coherence in the corporate strategy. The potential benefit to headquarters lies in their being able to earn revenue and profits from the businesses, ideally in excess of pre-acquisition earnings, and being able to sell for a real capital gain.

A number of control issues which face head offices of divisionalized and holding company structures have been mentioned in the above sections, and these will be explored in greater detail later in the chapter.

The matrix structure

Matrix structures are an attempt to combine the benefits of **decentralization** (motivation of identifiable management teams; closeness to the market; speedy decision making and implementation) with those of **co-ordination** (achieving economies and synergy across all the business units, territories and products). They require dual reporting by managers to, say, a mix of functional and business unit heads or geographic territory and business unit general managers.

The matrix structure is found typically in large multi-product, multi-national organizations where there are significant interrelation-

Case 22.5
ABB – ASEA BROWN BOVERI

ABB was formed in 1988 when the Swedish company Asea merged with Brown Boveri of Switzerland to create a global electrical engineering giant. ABB has since acquired a series of smaller businesses. The Chief Executive is Percy Barnevik, and he sees a challenge in maintaining drive and dynamism whilst digesting large acquisitions. He is committed to a matrix structure and his aim is to make ABB the global low-cost competitor.

ABB has been divided up into 1300 identifiable companies and 5000 profit centres. These are aggregated into eight business segments and 59 business areas. The segments are responsible for organizing manufacture around the world and for product development. Horizontally ABB is divided up into a mix of countries and regions. There is a 12-member executive Board representing products, regions and corporate operations, and a slim head office in Zürich. 'ABB is a multi-national without a national identity.' Financial reporting and evaluation is on a monthly basis.

The basic structure, therefore, is based on small units (of 50 people each on average) supported by good communications and information technology. Although ABB comprises distinct businesses, both technology and products are exchanged. Every employee has a country manager and a business sector manager. Dual responsibilities such as this are often key issues in matrix structures which fail. However, Barnevik insists that ABB's version is 'loose and decentralized' and that it is easily recognized that the two bosses are rarely of equal status.

Barnevik has also commented that the biggest problem has been 'motivating middle and lower level managers and entrenching corporate values – particularly a customer and quality focus'. He believes that his executives should see the business as their number one priority and assumes that highfliers will spend up to 30 hours a week (in addition to their regular tasks) travelling, attending conferences and evening seminars and lectures.

ships and interdependences as illustrated in Figure 22.5 and Case 22.5, and in small sophisticated service businesses such as a business school. The matrix structure in Figure 22.5 illustrates an organization which is split into a series of divisions, based on both products and geographic territories. The product groups would be responsible for co-ordinating the production and marketing of their particular products in a series of plants which might be based anywhere in the world. The geographic divisions would have responsibility for co-ordinating the sales, marketing and distribution of all the corporation's products, regardless of where they are manufactured, within their territorial area. The operating units would be the production plants, who were members of one or more product groups, depending upon the range of products manufactured in the plant, and whose products are marketed in more than one territory or geographic region. Consequently the general manager in charge of each operating unit is responsible in some

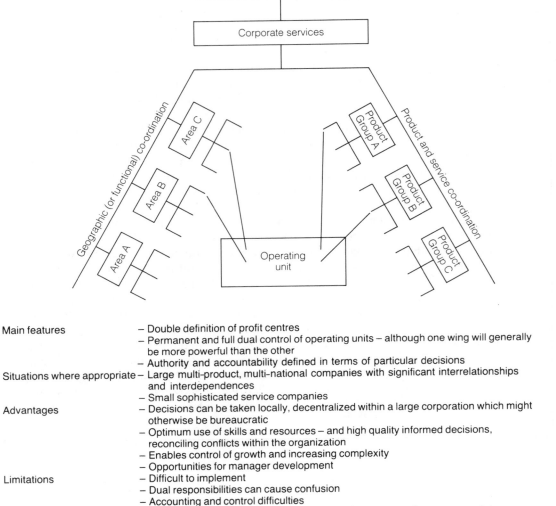

Main features	– Double definition of profit centres – Permanent and full dual control of operating units – although one wing will generally be more powerful than the other – Authority and accountability defined in terms of particular decisions
Situations where appropriate	– Large multi-product, multi-national companies with significant interrelationships and interdependences – Small sophisticated service companies
Advantages	– Decisions can be taken locally, decentralized within a large corporation which might otherwise be bureaucratic – Optimum use of skills and resources – and high quality informed decisions, reconciling conflicts within the organization – Enables control of growth and increasing complexity – Opportunities for manager development
Limitations	– Difficult to implement – Dual responsibilities can cause confusion – Accounting and control difficulties – Potential conflict between the two wings, with one generally more powerful – High overhead costs – Decision making can be slow

Figure 22.5 The matrix structure.

way to a series of product and territory chiefs (four in the illustration), all of whom will have profit responsibility. The matrix is designed to co-ordinate resources and effort throughout the organization. Structures such as this evolved in the 1960s and 1970s because of the need to establish priorities in multi-product, multi-national organizations. Should the resources and efforts be concentrated on the product groups or in the geographic territories? The ideal answer is both.

Figure 22.6 is a more straightforward illustration of how the staff in a business school

	Human resources	Marketing	Operations	Finance and accounting	Business policy/ strategy	Economics
Undergraduate courses						
Postgraduate and post-experience courses						
Research						
Executive courses						

Figure 22.6 Possible matrix structure for a business school.

might be organized. It is assumed that all the academic staff would have a specialization which would fit into one of the six columns shown, and that expertise and development in their subject specialism would be important to the staff. At the same time the business school would offer a series of 'products' or services which are shown as four rows. Staff from each subject group would be allocated to each of these areas. Each product group, and possibly each course within the group, would have a leader with responsibility for delivering a quality product and earning revenue; each subject group would also have a leader responsible for allocating resources and ensuring that staff develop academically.

The potential advantages of a matrix are that responsibility and authority are delegated and spread throughout a complex organization and the stifling tendencies of a bureaucracy are avoided. Because of the flows of information, and the establishment of priorities, decisions are informed and quick. Conflicts between the various groups are reconciled within the structure by the establishment of the priorities and objectives. In addition there are numerous specialist and generalist development opportunities for managers.

Also in theory changes in priorities can be readily accommodated. A typical large accountancy practice, for example, will specialize in audit work, tax, consultancy etc., and their work for different clients and industrial sectors will be co-ordinated. Some commentators believe that in the future 'clients must come first' and any internal, parochial boundaries built around specialisms must be destroyed.

However, the limitations have tended to ensure that these advantages have rarely been achieved. Dual responsibilities are difficult to handle; conflicts are not very easily reconciled; and as a result decision making can be slow. In addition the overhead costs can be quite high. It is also very difficult to establish the appropriate objectives and targets for the general managers, and to get priorities agreed. As a result it has often been the case that one wing of the matrix has enjoyed greater power than the other. A typical conflict might arise in the case of a special variant of a product for a particular market segment. The territory manager might be keen to market this product in order to offer a comprehensive range and support other, possibly completely different, products from other product groups within the corporation. The product chief, responsible for production of the product, might feel that the volume in question was too small and insignificant and that the product should not be produced. The locus of power within the matrix, together with any political activity by the managers concerned, would determine the decision reached.

Temporary matrices

As an alternative to the full matrix, and in an attempt to gain some of the benefits and avoid the drawbacks, some organizations make use of temporary project teams. In such cases groups or teams of managers are brought together from various parts of the organization to work on a particular project for a period of time before returning to their normal jobs. Such groups are very useful for the management of change, and they can be superimposed on any basic structure. Peters and Waterman (1982), in *In Search of Excellence*, pointed out that such teams are frequently in evidence in the most successful large corporations. The major advantage of these groups is that they are less costly than the complete matrix form, with its high overheads, but there are again limitations. There might be a tendency to seek to use the best managers quite frequently; and in such instances conflicts will be created within the organization when they are taken away from their other responsibilities.

Where there is a rigid hierarchy, specializa-

tion and narrow functional perspectives which prevent managers taking a holistic approach, the structure will inhibit managers from pursuing the organization's purpose effectively. Crises are likely to result. A typical response would be a task force to deal with the problem. As a result strong informal relationships will be formed, and these networks are likely to survive after the project team is disbanded and be used to overcome structural rigidities.

Alternatives to the matrix

In many cases, then, the matrix has proved to be too complicated to be effective. The primary reason has been the inability to deal with the issues of dual responsibility. Henri Fayol (1916) established a number of basic management principles, one of which was 'unity of command', the need to be responsible to only one manager; and the matrix has challenged this premise. Fayol's contention, however, has not been overturned. Decisions have been stifled by confusion, complexity and delay because managers have not been sufficiently sophisticated to operate effectively within this theoretically ideal structure. The need for a structural form which offers the potential advantages of the matrix to large complex multi-product, multi-national organizations, and which can be implemented, remains. If an organization is unable to design and operate a structure which enables the effective linking of a diverse range of related interests to achieve synergy, and at the same time permits the various business units to be responsive to environmental change, the organization may need to be split up.

Hunsicker (1982) quotes Philips, Ciba-Geigy and Texas Instruments as examples of multi-nationals who have retreated from the pure matrix structure. Hunsicker argues that matrices were designed to co-ordinate activities, and that the real strategic need has now become the development of new initiatives. This suggests a greater emphasis on temporary project teams, and the development and encouragement of managers within the organization so that they are more innovative and intrapreneurial. This implies that attention is focused more on changes in behaviour than on changes in the structural framework.

Pitts and Daniels (1984) list the following opportunities for obtaining the benefits of a matrix-type structure within more unitary forms:

- ☐ Strengthen corporate staffs to look after corporate strategic developments. They might, for example, search for new opportunities which existing business units could exploit.
- ☐ Rotate managers between functions, business units and locations. This increases their awareness and provides inputs of fresh ideas.
- ☐ Locate those executives responsible for product co-ordination in geographic territories physically closer to those managers responsible for production of the key products. Quite often such territory managers are based in their territories, close to their customers and somewhat divorced from manufacturing.
- ☐ Create some form of liaison groups which meet periodically and whose brief is to co-ordinate related issues. Such a group might attempt to co-ordinate the global strategies of a number of related products in a search for synergy and mutual benefits.
- ☐ Build the notion of agreed contributions between business units into both the management by objectives systems and the compensation schemes.
- ☐ Periodically review and amend the constitution of the divisions without restructuring the whole organization.

These suggestions again concentrate more on the processes within the structure than on the framework itself. We have therefore considered a number of basic structural forms and it is now appropriate to look in greater detail at the needs and considerations underpinning the design of a structure which is appropriate for both the strategies and the people who must implement these strategies.

STRUCTURE: DETERMINANTS AND DESIGN

In this section we draw together the key points concerning the determination and design of effective organization structures. Many of the points have been incorporated in the discussion of structural forms.

Determinants of structure

There are four main determinants of the design and effectiveness of an organization structure: size, tasks, environment and ideology.

Size

The previous section on alternative structural forms illustrated that, as the organization grows larger and becomes increasingly complex and diverse, the structure needs to change to allow for effective communication and co-ordination.

Tasks

The need for co-ordination is linked to the complexity, diversity and interdependence of the tasks that the organization must carry out. Where the businesses are unrelated, for example, the holding company structure can be appropriate. Where the business units are interdependent and particularly where there is considerable trading activity within the organization between the various activities, a divisional or matrix structure will be needed. The structure must take account of the information needs and exchanges which are required for effective decision making.

Environment

The key environmental issues concern the nature of the pressures for change and the speed at which the organization must be able to respond and act. These in turn relate to the nature of the industry, competition, and the general sensitivity of demand to environmental forces and changes. The extent of centralization/decentralization is therefore important in dealing with this issue, together with the readiness and willingness of managers to accept and implement change.

Ideology

Ideology can be either a driving force or a limiting force with regard to certain structural alternatives. It could be argued that, the longer an existing structure has existed, the more difficult it will be to make changes because people will be used to particular jobs and responsibilities. The preference of the strategic leader to retain a particular structure, or experiment with new forms, and his or her views on the appropriate amount of decentralization will also have a significant bearing.

The basic logic behind the design of the structure is to make the complexity manageable so that the organization can perform effectively with existing strategies and deal with the formulation and implementation of strategic change. Organization structures should be designed with this in mind, and the above four factors should be taken into consideration. It will not be possible, however, to predict whether a particular structural change will be more or less effective than the present structure. Much depends

upon the reaction of managers and other employees to the changes implied, and their ability to deal with the communication and decision-making needs.

Greiner's development model

These requirements apply at all stages in the development and growth of an organization, and different structural forms are more or less likely to satisfy them in certain circumstances. Greiner (1972) suggests that over time firms evolve and grow in a series of stages. Each period of evolvement has a dominant management style and a given structure, which is used to achieve the growth. At various times the current structure and strategies being pursued cease to be matched. Management problems and conflicts result from this mismatch. In response there is what Greiner calls an internal revolution when the structure and style of management are changed deliberately to cope with the demands of the present strategy. Greiner's model is illustrated in Table 22.3.

Initially the organization grows via the creativity of the entrepreneur who tends to direct all the work of the organization with an informal style of management. At some stage, dependent upon the abilities and commitment of the strategic leader and the particular strategies being followed, the style of management and the informality is no longer appropriate. The functional organization replaces the entrepreneurial style, bringing more formal systems and professional specialist managers. This is appropriate until the formality and systems prove restrictive and stifle initiative.

Greater decentralization follows, profit centres are created, and the strategic leader concentrates mostly on the corporate strategy. However, it is still necessary to co-ordinate the activities and business units, and as the company becomes more diverse and divisionalized the relationships between head office and the business units must be

Table 22.3 Evolution and revolution as organizations grow

	Growth via	Crisis of	
The entrepreneurial driving force, and informal direction	Creativity		
		Leadership	Does the entrepreneur stay or go as formality is required?
The functional organization	Direction		
		Autonomy	The centralized hierarchy becomes cumbersome. Even leaders lost touch with the expertise of specialists
Decentralization to motivate downwards – profit centres	Delegation		
		Control	Head office loses control of fiercely competitive and individual subsidiaries
Decentralized units have to be brought together, say in product groups. Investment centres. Review of centralized functions	Co-ordination		
		Red-tape	Line and staff conflicts over responsibilities and power. Who is responsible to whom? Bureaucracy and procedures create problems
Collaborative teams become useful for problem solving	Collaboration		

Each phase lasts a few years. Organizations must change and adapt to new circumstances. Those that do not, fail. Developed from Greiner, L E (1972) Evolution and revolution as organizations grow, *Harvard Business Review*, July–August.

clearly established. Interdivisional rivalries and parochial attitudes, together with the possibility that head office may feel that they are losing control because of the necessary adaptive changes which are taking place, cause the crisis and the next revolution. Formal systems to achieve greater co-operation result, such as the introduction of more formal planning systems, together with greater centralization.

Conflicts are then likely to arise between the staff specialists at headquarters and the line managers in the business units concerning responsibilities and relative power. The increasing tendency towards bureaucracy because of the formality and the systems can stifle innovation once again. Collaboration is the answer, whether achieved through a formal matrix structure or through more informal project and liaison groups.

The length of life of each stage is dependent on the speed of growth of the organization and the changes in strategy which take

place. Greiner developed his model before the problems of implementing matrix structures become apparent, and consequently he is only speculative about the crisis which follows the collaboration stage. Greiner suggests that managers might become exhausted by the demands for teamwork and innovation. The organization, he suggests, might conceptualize an alternative dual structure. Part of the structure will be designed to ensure that essential tasks are carried out as required; the other parallel structure will be 'reflective' and consider future options. Managers might be seconded periodically to this reflective role.

Also, since Greiner developed his model many organizations have become less diversified and IT has introduced new structural opportunities. Handy (1989) believes that a suitable new structural framework, which he terms a 'shamrock organization', can be based upon a core of essential and full-time executives, who receive and co-ordinate support from contractors, part-time employees and specialist out-workers (people who work from home but are linked to the organization by a computer terminal).

Structural design

Lorsch and Allen (1972), building on earlier work by Lawrence and Lorsch (1967), contend that the design of the structure must accommodate two requirements: the need to differentiate and separate the various groups which comprise the organization, and the need to integrate their respective contributions.

The need for differentiation is influenced by the different attitudes, values and behaviour of the various groups. Whilst total quality and consumer satisfaction are important considerations for all managers, the objectives of a production department, a sales department and the finance department could be expected to differ. Production might be concerned with simplifying the demands on production control and reducing costs through efficiency. Their flexibility would be increased if they were allowed to hold high levels of raw material and components stock, but this would increase costs and possibly cause conflicts with the accountants. A sales department might prefer to choose which customers and orders should receive priority, regardless of production costs, and suggest high levels of finished goods stock to allow

---

The management style of the future is the flattened pyramid. It's not a trick, but a fantastic invention: you don't order people from the top, you lead them. You give them vision and help. You must let the manager do his own thing. If you do not, the company cannot run fast enough.

Jean-Marie Descarpentries,
President, CMB Packaging

---

instant deliveries. In a similar way the various product groups might operate in environments which place quite different pressures on them. The values and styles of management appropriate in each case might lead to inconsistencies of style within the organization as a whole.

Integration is concerned with the collaboration and co-ordination between the various activities, and conflict reduction. The various functions within a business unit must be integrated so that their differences are reconciled and objectives and priorities are agreed. The need for integration between business units will relate to interdependences.

Dividing and separating tasks

The division of work is normally achieved in two ways: first, by the way in which the tasks are separated and grouped into functions or divisions – the basic structural forms described earlier in this chapter – and, second, by the shape of the departmental and divisional structures within the organization. Shape is concerned with the number of levels in the management hierarchy and the span of control of each manager. Generally, as the number of levels increases the span of control decreases, and vice versa. These points are illustrated in Figure 22.7. The tall pyramid on the left could represent an organization with a number of divisional layers or a department with several levels of management. This shape can lead to delays and increasing formality as there is a greater separation of the top and bottom levels. However, it does offer an increased number of promotional opportunities for managers. The flatter shape on the right illustrates fewer layers of management, but greater demands on individual managers as their span of control, the numbers of people reporting directly to them, increases. Communications are likely to be easier and more informal, but there will be fewer promotional opportunities. Generally,

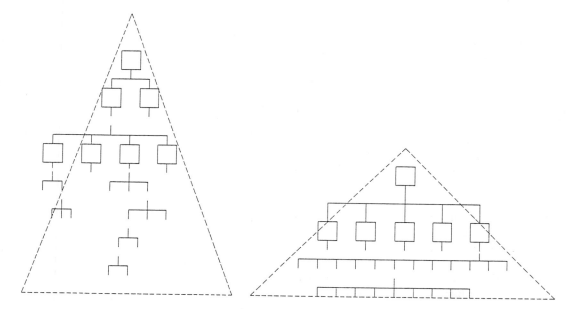

Figure 22.7 Alternative structural shapes.

there is now a tendency for structures to become flatter.

Co-ordinating and integrating work

The various alternatives, listed below, have all been discussed in greater depth already:

☐ linking related profit centres into appropriate strategic business units
☐ partial centralization
☐ clearly defined policies
☐ special task forces and liaison groups
☐ management by objectives and performance management
☐ team briefing
☐ manager rotation
☐ communicated mission and core values.

Case 22.6 summarizes aspects of the approach used by General Electric in America.

Mintzberg's co-ordinating mechanisms

Mintzberg (1979) also considers that it is necessary for an organization to divide the whole task into smaller subtasks in order to achieve the benefits of specialization and division of labour. In order to accomplish the total task Mintzberg agrees that the subtasks must then be co-ordinated and integrated, and argues that there are five main co-ordinating mechanisms:

☐ **mutual adjustment** – essentially informal communication systems
☐ **direct supervision** whereby managers take responsibility for the work of others, controlling and monitoring activity
☐ **standardized work processes** – the content of tasks is specified clearly, say through detailed job instructions
☐ **standardized outputs** – expected results are specified and manager performance is evaluated against these targets (this is a performance-oriented mechanism)
☐ **standardized skills** where the training and experience required to do jobs effectively is specified.

Standardized skills incorporates the notion of specific qualifications being required for particular specialist positions. Co-ordination

---

Case 22.6
GENERAL ELECTRIC

General Electric (GE), which manufactures aircraft engines, defence electronics and household consumer goods, provides financial services and owns NBC Television in America, has annual revenues in excess of $50 billion.

The company is decentralized and employees are encouraged to speak out and pursue ideas. The Chief Executive Officer, John F Welch, believes 'the winners of the 1990s will be those who can develop a culture that allows them to move faster, communicate more clearly, and involve everyone in a focused effort to serve ever more demanding customers'. Integration strategies aim to 'inject down the line the attitudes of a small fast-moving entrepreneurial business and thereby improve productivity continuously'.

There is a developed strategy of moving managers between businesses to transfer ideas and create internal synergy together with a reliance on employee training (Welch regularly attends training courses to collect opinion and feedback) and GE's *work out* programme. This involves senior managers presenting GE's vision and ideas to other managers and employees, and then later reconvening to obtain responses and feedback on perceived issues and difficulties. External advisers (such as university academics) monitor that communications are genuinely two-way.

If we are to get the reflexes and speed we need, we've got to simplify and delegate more – simply trust more. We have to undo a 100 year old concept and convince our managers that their role is not to control people and stay on top of things, but rather to guide, energize and excite. But with all this must come the intellectual tools, which will mean continuous education of every individual at every level of the company.

(John F Welch)

---

is achieved through workers and managers understanding what is expected of each other and making effective contributions naturally. An anaesthetist and a surgeon, for example, appreciate each other's roles and contributions.

In addition there is a sixth mechanism which results from mutual adjustment and adaptive changes in strategy. Mintzberg refers to this as the **standardization of norms** where employees share a set of common beliefs. This is a cultural issue which evolves as mutual adjustment and informal communications lead to adaptive changes and the establishment of new norms of behaviour. The evolution of a road through a forest from a well-trodden path would constitute an analogy.

Mintzberg argues that small entrepreneurial firms rely mainly on direct supervision by the owner/manager, and that as the organization grows and becomes more complex standardized work processes, outputs and skills become increasingly popular in a sequential and ascending order. Mutual adjustment is the favoured mechanism in what Mintzberg terms adhocracies, and which are discussed later in this section. Each

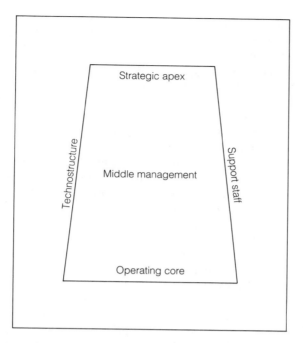

Figure 22.8   The basic parts of the organization. Developed from Mintzberg, H (1983) *Structure in Fives*, Prentice Hall.

structural type and style of management has a most appropriate co-ordinating mechanism, and this is explored below.

Mintzberg's structural configurations

Mintzberg (1983) has described five structural configurations, each of which is suitable for organizations at certain stages of development and in particular environmental circumstances. Each structural configuration achieves co-ordination and congruence of environment, values and resources in different ways. Moreover, whilst each configuration comprises five basic parts or sets of resources, as outlined below, the relative size and importance of these parts varies between the configurations.

The five constituent parts of the organization

Mintzberg's five parts are illustrated in Figure 22.8 and are as follows.

☐ The **operating core** relates to those employees who carry out the various tasks involved in the primary activities of the value chain, which include securing inputs, transforming the inputs into outputs by adding value and then distributing the outputs.

☐ The **strategic apex**: the strategic leader and his or her colleagues who are responsible for developing the corporate strategy, managing relations with the environment, designing the structure and allocating resources.

☐ The **middle management**: middle managers, with authority, link the strategic apex with the operating core. They manage the tasks carried out by the operating core, applying any policies and systems established by the strategic apex, and feed information up and down the organization.

☐ **Support staff**: support activities occur at various levels in the hierarchy and provide assistance to both middle managers and the operating core. Such activities would include research and development, public relations and certain aspects of the personnel function such as running the payroll.

☐ The **technostructure** comprises analysts who affect the work of others, such as work study analysts, planners and the training and recruitment staff in personnel. Galbraith (1969) uses the expression 'technocrats' to describe the experts and specialists who control much of the activity in large, powerful and growth-oriented corporations. Some of Galbraith's ideas were summarized in Chapter 5.

The five configurations

Mintzberg's five configurations are discussed below, and the salient points are compared in Table 22.4. These configurations do not match completely with the structural forms outlined earlier but they are clearly related.

The simple structure Mintzberg's first configuration relates very closely to the entrepreneurial structure. It is typically small, and has no technostructure and little formal planning. Decision making is centralized with the chief executive or owner/manager, and performance is very dependent on the strategic leader.

The machine bureaucracy Machine bureaucracies are generally found where the work is routine, with standardized production processes. Jobs are tightly defined and regulated, and there is a powerful technostructure to search for efficiencies and cost control oppor-

tunities. This configuration is typical of mass production assembly systems.

Some power is decentralized to the specialist functional managers, but strategic change decisions are largely centralized. As the specialists implement the proposed changes, strategy formulation and implementation is separated. The machine bureaucracy is relatively slow to change, and therefore more suitable for stable environmental conditions. In a number of respects it is similar to the functional structure.

The professional bureaucracy The professional bureaucracy is typically found in organizations which rely heavily on administrators and administration systems, such as hospitals and universities. It is bureaucratic but not centralized, and power lies with specialist professionals and professional managers. Where professionals are in evidence they are likely to hold formal qualifications; and standardized skills will be the main co-ordinating mechanism. Support administrators are unlikely to be as well qualified as the professionals. However, in the late 1980s there has been an increasing tendency for administrators in some of these organizations to study for high-level management qualifications.

The polytechnics in the UK were examples of professional bureaucracies which had to change their structures. Until 1989 their administrative systems provided a link between the powerful academic structure, comprising highly qualified academics and heads of department, and the respective local authorities who controlled their financial affairs. Since the polytechnics were in effect privatized in April 1989, when they became independent higher education corporations with plc status, new administrative and financial structures have been introduced with additional layers of management. Because new funding arrangements have been introduced commercial considerations and market orientation have also increased in significance. The polytechnics became 'new

Table 22.4 Selected features of Mintzberg's five configurations

	Simple structure	Machine bureaucracy	Professional bureaucracy	Divisionalized form	Adhocracy
Key co-ordinating mechanism	Direct supervision	Standardization of work	Standardization of skills	Standardization of outputs	Mutual adjustment
Key part of organization (resource concentration)	Strategic apex	Technostructure	Operating core	Middle management	Support staff
Roles of strategic apex/leadership in addition to responsibility for corporate strategy	All administration	Co-ordination and conflict resolution	External liaison and conflict resolution	Strategic perspective and control of performance	External liaison, conflict resolution and project monitoring
Centralization/decentralization	Centralized	Limited horizontal decentralization	Decentralized	Decentralized vertically	Decentralized
Environment	Simple and dynamic	Simple and stable	Complex and stable	Relatively simple and stable but diverse	Complex and dynamic
Power and values	Controlled by strategic leader – possibly owner/manager	Technocratic and sometimes external control	Professional manager control	Middle management control, i.e. general managers	Expert control
Typical examples	Small firms Young organizations	Processing companies Assembly companies	Hospital University	Diversified or multi-product organization	Management consultants

universities' in 1992 and it was necessary for them to review their distinctive mission and market niche. Does this structural configuration encourage or inhibit change?

Adaptive change is likely to be evident and influenced significantly by external professional organizations. Committee structures will restrict the freedom of the professionals to change things, but the changes will still prove difficult to co-ordinate in many instances. More substantial strategic changes are difficult to implement as the structure tends to be inflexible. Performance measures relating to effectiveness, rather than to the efficient utilization of resources, are difficult to establish and monitor because of the nature of the service.

The divisionalized structure This configuration represents any structure based on autonomous divisions or business units co-ordinated by a central administrative structure. It typically develops out of a machine bureaucracy when there is diversification. Power and responsibility is devoted to the divisions, creating a key strategic role for the general managers who head the divisions. These general managers, who comprise Mintzberg's middle line in this configuration, are responsible for changes in competitive strategies; but the extent of the decentralization in the organization as a whole may be restrained. General managers, for example, may centralize the power within their divisions.

Divisions will be expected to agree objectives and targets with the strategic leader; and measures of effective performance related to these will be used for monitoring and control purposes. Hence the standardization of outputs is the most appropriate co-ordination mechanism.

Recapping on points made previously, the overall strategic leader in a divisionalized structure is responsible for managing and co-ordinating a portfolio of businesses. General managers at lower levels in the hierarchy are responsible for portfolios of business units or product/markets. If they are to accomplish this effectively they must be able to reach informed decisions concerning resource allocation, especially finance. The technocracy therefore provides an important support function.

The adhocracy An adhocracy is an informal and innovative organization which features teams of specialists and decentralized power. An advertising agency or a management consultancy group would be a typical example. Liaison between groups of experts is very important, and some variant of the matrix structure, such as temporary project teams or liaison groups, is likely to be evident. Expertise lies throughout the organization, the operating core and support staff being particularly important.

Adaptive strategic changes, originating anywhere within the organization, are likely to be commonplace and encouraged as this configuration is attempting to deal with a complex and dynamic environment. The pursuit of personal objectives and organizational politics (considered in greater detail in

---

The constituent companies [in LVMH, Moët Hennessy. Louis Vuitton] have asked for the following: simplified structures, autonomy for the operational units and a method of administration in keeping with their particular culture.

I am convinced that the success of our group and its subsidiaries is due to the fact that we trust the operational teams to carry out their own quest for quality.

We keep these companies autonomous at middle management level so that they can have the advantages of medium size companies as well as the advantage of belonging to a powerful group that can fund their development.

Bernard Arnault, Group Chairman, LVMH, Moët Hennessy. Louis Vuitton

---

Chapter 24) are facilitated and must be monitored and controlled. Decision making may be slowed down where people are very active politically. Linked to these issues, conflict will also be present, and resolving this will be a key role for the strategic leader.

It is quite possible to find more than one configuration present in an organization where diverse interests mean that E-V-R congruence cannot be achieved effectively with only one style of management. A newspaper, for example, may have an adhocracy for dealing with editorial aspects and a machine bureaucracy for printing. A university overall is likely to be a professional bureaucracy, but the business school within it may well be more of an adhocracy and built around a matrix, as described earlier.

At this stage it would be useful to review the Key Reading 14.1, Chapter 14. Drucker (1988) argues that the organization of the future will have fewer managers and fewer layers in the management hierarchy. Information technology will lead to more autonomy for individual managers and more informed decision making when specialists have decentralized responsibility for key activities within the organization. Strategy co-ordination will still constitute a major challenge.

STRUCTURE AND STYLES OF MANAGEMENT: MANAGEMENT STYLE AT THE CORPORATE LEVEL

Corporate management styles

The questions addressed in this section are the following: What is the appropriate role for corporate headquarters in divisionalized organizations? How much power should be centralized? How independent should the divisions and business units be? These relate to the difference between the divisional and the holding company structures and styles of management, and the themes of integration

and behavioural processes within the structural framework are explored further.

In relation to these issues Goold and Campbell (1988) have contrasted the views of Sir Hector Laing, Chairman of United Biscuits, with those of Lord Hanson. Laing contends that it takes a number of years to build a business, and that during this period corporate headquarters should help the general managers of business units to develop their strategies. Hanson argues that it is more appropriate for head office to remain detached from operations, and instead of involvement to set strict financial targets. All Hanson businesses are for sale at any time. Both approaches have been shown to work, but with different levels of overall performance and strategic growth patterns. These two approaches represent two ends of a spectrum – a third approach is a compromise between the two. Goold and Campbell have categorized large UK companies following these three approaches as follows.

Strategic planning companies

United Biscuits, together with BP, Lex and Cadbury Schweppes, fall into this category. The basic premise is that head office should be actively involved in the development of business unit strategies. Whilst achievement targets are set, there is a generally flexible approach and understanding if external circumstances make the targets difficult to achieve. Corporate headquarters is more concerned with the long-term strategic development of the business and the overall strategic perspective than with short-term financial targets. This approach is particularly applicable when there are strong interdependences between the business units which need fostering if synergy is to be achieved.

Financial control companies

Financial control companies include Hanson, BTR and GEC. They feature a small headquarters staff who are not involved in the detailed planning activity of the business units. Generally there will be fewer inter-dependences and links between the business units. General managers throughout the organization are given financial rather than strategic targets with typically a short-term focus. Twelve months would be normal. Success is rewarded, but general managers who fail to achieve their targets are vulnerable.

Strategic control companies

Strategic control companies such as Courtaulds, ICI and Plessey fall between the other two approaches. Here corporate head-quarters will assist business units in the development of their strategies, but delegate much of the responsibility. Corporate managers foster strategic thinking by general managers, and audit their proposals, but remain detached. They play the role of the 'fully aware shareholder'. Strategic objectives, such as the launch of a particular new product by a certain date and measured improvements in customer service or quality, are agreed together with financial targets.

The merger of two organizations who currently follow different approaches will necessitate changes in the style of management. In the light of this it is interesting that a number of what Gray and McDermott (1989) term 'mega-mergers' in the UK in recent years have involved companies with different corporate styles. The failed bid by BTR for Pilkington in 1986 featured two companies with opposing styles and cultures; and in 1986 Hanson successfully fought United Biscuits to acquire the Imperial Group. In 1986 the Monopolies and Mergers Commission blocked the 1985 bid by GEC for Plessey. In 1989 GEC, in conjunction with Siemens of western Germany, again sought to acquire Plessey.

Levels of success

Goold and Campbell studied 16 large UK companies, including those given as examples above, and concluded that each style has both advantages and disadvantages and that no one style is outstandingly the most successful.

Strategic planning companies proved to be consistently profitable during the 1980s, mainly through organic growth. Head office corporate staff tend to be a quite large group and differences of opinion with general managers sometimes cause frustration within the divisions and business units. **Financial planning companies** exhibited the best financial performance. In a number of cases, particularly BTR and Hanson, this resulted from acquisition and divestment rather than organic growth. Short-term financial targets were felt to reduce the willingness of general managers to take risks. There were few trade-offs whereby short-term financial targets were sacrificed for long-term growth. A general manager, for example, might consider a programme of variety reduction and product rationalization with a view to developing a more consistent and effective portfolio. In the short term this would result in reduced revenue and profits before new orders and products improved overall profitability. This temporary fall might be un-acceptable in the face of short-term financial targets. **Strategic control companies** also performed satisfactorily but experienced difficulties in establishing the appropriate mix of strategic and financial targets for general managers. Financial targets, being the more specific and measurable ones, were generally given priority.

Goold and Campbell conclude that whilst the style of management adopted within the structure determines the strategic changes which take place, the overall corporate strategy of the company very much influences the choice of style. Large diverse organizations, for example, will find it difficult to adopt a strategic planning approach. Equally, where the environment is turbulent and competitive, increasing the need for adaptive strategic change, the financial planning approach is less appropriate. Not unexpectedly Hanson's main acquisitions have been of companies in mature slow growth sectors.

Whilst each of the above approaches will constitute the dominant style of an organization, they can be mixed within the same firm. Lorenz (1988) points out that Kingfisher use a strategic control approach for B & Q (their do-it-yourself chain) and a financial planning approach for their recently acquired drug-stores, whilst controlling the Woolworth chain stores directly from head office.

One question left unanswered concerns the extent to which the conclusions of Goold and Campbell are a result of British management strengths, weaknesses and preferences. Certain Japanese companies appear to grow organically at impressive rates whilst maintaining strict financial controls and directing corporate strategic change from the centre. This tendency, however, is affected by legislation which restricts the ability of Japanese companies to grow by acquisition and merger. Without this control Japanese firms may have followed different strategies.

Corporate management roles

Reinton and Foote (1988) have identified a number of roles for headquarters in relation to business units:

☐ developing or improving competitive and functional strategies; general managers may be good operational managers but less effective strategic thinkers
☐ motivating managers to perform with agreed objectives, targets and rewards
☐ upgrading the quality of management throughout the organization; poor performers are removed or demoted (and possibly retrained) and successful achievers are promoted

☐ exploiting real synergies; this requires that the best opportunities are identified and exploited, and implies that resources may need to be shared within the organization
☐ re-defining divisions and business units in line with changes in the industry and competition. European car producers have ceased to operate only in single countries and have developed businesses which span several European countries. As a result Ford of Europe, as a subsidiary of its American parent, has been made responsible for production and marketing throughout Europe. Previously the plants in individual countries had this responsibility, and the European headquarters provided co-ordination. Individual country operations now control sales and servicing.

Which roles are needed and how they are executed will vary between organizations, and consequently the appropriate links between head offices and business units need careful evaluation. Reinton and Foote, like Goold and Campbell, conclude that this relationship influences strategic change in a major way and that the portfolio of businesses is more easily changed than is the style of managing the corporation. The issues involved in the management of change are discussed in Chapter 24.

Having considered the relationship between head office and general managers, it is now appropriate to explore the role and function of general managers in greater depth.

STRUCTURE AND STYLES OF MANAGEMENT: THE ROLE OF GENERAL MANAGERS

General management in perspective

Basically general managers co-ordinate the work of subordinate specialist managers;

they are responsible for the management of strategy implementation and, in certain cases, strategy formulation. Clearly the chief executive or managing director of the company, the overall strategic leader, is a general manager. So too are the heads of divisions and business units, and the heads of operating units in a matrix structure. Their task is to match effectively the resources they control with their particular environment and to achieve E-V-R congruence.

Divisionalized organizations were examined in the previous section, where it was shown that the degree of decentralization and the power, authority and responsibility enjoyed by general managers will be affected by their relationship with head office and headquarters corporate staff. Whatever the extent of the decentralization from head office to business units, the business units themselves might be highly centralized. It depends upon the style of management adopted by the particular general manager in charge.

Each division or business unit is part of a larger organization and corporate structure, and consequently it is not fully autonomous. Whilst the organization as a whole has an external environment comprising customers, suppliers, competitors and shareholders amongst other influences, each division will have corporate headquarters as part of its environment. Business units may have both divisional headquarters and corporate head office in their environment. General managers in divisions and business units therefore do not have full responsibility for strategy creation and implementation. They can be pressurized by corporate headquarters, and they can turn to head office in their search for additional finance and other resources. The provision of finance within the organization may operate differently from the external market, but justification should still be required.

The relationship between general managers and head office will determine whether they are free to change their portfolios of business units and products or just adapt competitive and functional strategies. Performance measures and expectations will also affect this, as mentioned in the previous section. Where specific short-term objectives and targets are set, and monitored strictly, general managers are less likely to focus on corporate changes and instead will concentrate on more immediate changes which can yield faster results. Their flexibility to make changes will increase as their targets become more vague and directional and less specific. Even though the general managers of business units may not be responsible for the formulation of changes in the corporate strategy which will affect their sphere of influence, they will invariably be responsible for the implementation of the changes.

General management skills and values

It has been established, then, that effective strategic management concerns issues of formulation and implementation. Strategic choices concern

☐ the nature and orientation of the organization – the strategic perspective
☐ the deployment of its resources, ideally to achieve and sustain competitive advantage.

The strategic choice is implemented by the strategic leader, either the chief executive, the owner/manager in the case of a small business, or a general manager. It was pointed out in Chapter 3 that different strategic leaders (a) exhibit different patterns of behaviour and styles of management and (b) will have different technical skills and biases as a result of their background. Arguably alternative general managers would seek to implement basically the same strategy in different ways. The views of a number of authors concerning the relationship between general manager skills and particular strategies are discussed below.

Herbert and Deresky (1987) have examined

the issue of match between the general manager and the strategy, concluding that the orientations and styles given at the foot of the page were important for particular strategies.

Herbert and Deresky contend that financial skills are important for all strategies, with marketing skills being particularly important at the development stage and production and engineering skills invaluable for stabilizing strategies. This raises three issues. Which specialist functional managers might be most appropriate for promotion to general management in particular circumstances? Is a change of general manager appropriate as products and businesses grow and decline and need changes in their strategies? As strategies evolve and change should general managers adapt their styles of management accordingly?

Dixon (1989) suggests that **innovatory** general management skills are most required in the early and late stages of the life of a business or product in its present form. These skills are required to establish or recreate competitive advantage and, in the case of terminal decline, to find an alternative product, service or business. These changes are often best accomplished by outsiders with fresh ideas. Correspondingly the constant search for efficiencies and improvements whilst an established product or business is maturing is normally best carried out by specialists.

A major problem with this type of innovation lies in the fact that changes in senior management, structure or values may be involved. The outlook and styles of general managers are likely to be different, and their responses to different sets of expectations and performance targets will vary. Again this raises the issue of which managers are most appropriate for managing particular strategies.

Developing this argument further, Rosabeth Moss Kanter (1989) has researched the general management skills required to run businesses effectively in the competitive environment of the late 1980s and the 1990s. Large companies, she contends, must be able to match corporate discipline with entrepreneurial creativity in order to become 'leaner' and more efficient whilst being committed to both quality and innovation.

Three strategies are particularly important:

☐ re-structuring to improve synergy from diverse businesses
☐ the development of joint ventures and strategic alliances to input new ideas
☐ the encouragement of intrapreneurship within organizations.

These points are explained in greater detail in Key Reading 22.1.

Kanter's main conclusion is that **process is more important than structure**. She suggests that:

☐ general managers must be able to balance maintenance and entrepreneurial skills;
☐ internal competition (typically fostered in organizations which are divided into discrete divisions and business units) can be harmful and impede synergy;
☐ incentive and reward schemes should

Strategy	Styles and qualities required
Development (start-up and growth)	Aggressive, competitive, innovative, creative and entrepreneurial
Stabilizing (maintaining competitive position)	Conservative, careful and analytical
Turnaround	Autonomous, risk and challenge oriented and entrepreneurial

Key Reading 22.1
COMPETITIVENESS IN THE 1990s

Future success lies in the **capability** to change and to accomplish key tasks by using resources more efficiently and more effectively. Organizations must be innovative and, at the same time, control their costs. Sustainable competitive advantage, however, does not come from either low costs, or differentiation, or innovation alone. It needs the **whole organization** to be *focused, fast, flexible and friendly*.

Being **focused** requires investment in core skills and competences, together with a search for new opportunities for applying the skills. Intrapreneurship should be fostered to constantly improve the skills; and managers throughout the organization should be strategically aware and innovative. They should own the organization's mission, which, by necessity, must be communicated widely and understood.

Fast companies move at the right time, and are not caught out by competitors. New ideas and opportunities from the environment will be seized first. Ideally they will be innovating constantly to open up and sustain a competitive gap, because gradual improvements are likely to be more popular with customers than are radical changes. But 'instant success takes time' – the organization culture must be appropriate.

Flexibility concerns the search for continual improvement. The implication is a 'learning organization' where ideas are shared and collaboration between functions and divisions generates internal synergy. This, in turn, suggests that performance and effectiveness measures – and rewards – concentrate on outcomes.

Internal synergy can be achieved with cross-functional teams and special projects, and by moving people around the organization in order to spread the best practices. General Motors allows components and assembly workers, who work in separate plants in different locations, to contact each other by telephone to sort out problems and faults without relying on either written communications or messages which go 'up, across and down again'. These workers see each other as 'colleagues in the *whole organization*'. It is important that internal constraints (imposed by other functions and divisions) and which restrain performance are highlighted and confronted. To be effective this requires a clear and shared vision and purpose for the organization, decentralization and empowerment (see Key Concepts 22.1 and 22.2).

Friendly organizations are closely linked to their suppliers and customers to generate synergy through the added value chain. Such external collaboration may be in the form of strategic alliances.

Summarized from: Kanter, Rosabeth Moss (1989) *When Giants Learn To Dance*, Simon and Schuster.

reflect the need for co-operation and support between business units;
- [ ] the increasing incidence of joint ventures, which requires the forging of closer links with other external businesses, suggests that structures may need revision if the potential and desired synergy is to be achieved.

There are similarities and differences in these conclusions, reflecting again that there is no one best answer. The issue of match between general manager and strategy is important, and consequently one might expect that changes in one will lead to changes in the other.

In this section we have introduced the subject of performance targets and expectations for general managers, which is likely to be linked to rewards and recognition. In the final part of the chapter we look deeper into this subject.

MEASURING AND REWARDING PERFORMANCE

It is important to emphasize that, in assessing and designing an appropriate structure, the process aspects must incorporate the need for measuring and rewarding performance. In the previous section on structure and styles of management, it was emphasized that the attention of general managers might be focused on either strategic or financial performance targets or a mix of the two, depending on the control systems which prevail. Their rewards should be related to the expectations that the overall strategic leader has for performance in their divisions and business units. In turn the specialists who support the general managers will need performance targets and appropriate rewards.

As well as being a financial issue rewards influence the culture of the organization as they affect motivation and commitment and the interactions and rivalry between managers. In addition some of the benefits will be non-financial and will affect the lives of managers outside their working environment. Free holidays for the managers, or possibly all the employees, of the operating units which achieve the highest levels of performance would be an example. Promo-

tion can also be a reward, and this will bring increased status as well as more money. In addition to assessing performance in conjunction with rewards, performance appraisal should also evaluate the ability of managers to make their intended contributions. This may highlight specific development and training needs.

There are a number of important considerations when assessing the appropriate reward system for any organization.

☐ Are there any incentives and bonuses linked to success and performance? If so, should they involve money, promotion, status or other non-financial benefits? Equally, are there sanctions for underachievement?

☐ Are general managers and other executives rewarded for their individual performances, their business unit performance, or the success of the organization as a whole? It could be a mix of these rather than just one.

☐ If it is linked to individual business units, can there be a fair system, given that the various business units will have different opportunities to perform well. Some will be in growth industries; others might face intense competition leading to tight margins and low profitability.

In addition, can the interdependences required for synergy be developed and inter-divisional rivalry be avoided? Would an organization-wide approach be better for fostering interdependences and co-operation?

Reward systems are likely to be based on specific performance targets, but these could relate to growth in revenue, absolute profits or profitability ratios. Stonich (1982) has suggested that business units might be categorized as having high, medium or low growth potential. Four factors could be used in evaluating their relative performances: return on assets; cash flow; strategic development programmes; and increases in market share. The relative weighting attributed to each of these four factors would be changed to reflect their specific objectives and whether they were of high, medium or low growth potential. Return on assets and cash flow would be critical for low growth business units, and market share and strategic development programmes most important for those with high growth potential. The factors would be weighted equally for medium growth. This approach would be particularly relevant where general managers were changed around to reflect their particular styles of management and the current requirements of the business unit.

If there are individual reward systems for functional managers, then again the performance measures selected will have to reflect the different types of expectation and contribution. Whilst sales, marketing and production managers can be given specific targets relatively easily, the same is not true of research and development managers.

☐ How might the long-term strategic aspects be incorporated? Short-term performance measures provide a system which is easy to operate, but is there a risk that they might focus attention on the short term at the expense of longer-term needs? Linked to this, it was pointed out in the previous section that qualitative measures are more likely to encourage managers to take risks than are short-term financial measures.

The system, then, must satisfy the needs of individual managers and of the organization as a whole.

As a final thought on this issue it is interesting to reflect upon the possible effect of the changes in performance measures which are being introduced in the public sector and which were mentioned in Chapter 6. Market-oriented measures, some of them qualitative, are replacing the concentration on the efficient use of resources, bringing such not-for-profit organizations closer to the private sector culture. Nevertheless, the vast majority of employees are on rigid pay scales with only limited opportunities for performance-related rewards. There may well be pressures to change this.

I believe that this is likely to become an increasingly significant issue. Tens of thousands of people in such organizations as the Health Service currently remain on rigid pay scales whilst the most senior managers have been moved on to performance-related salaries, and in many cases have enjoyed substantial rises. In the education sector there are moves to make a proportion of teachers' salaries dependent upon their contribution and performance. Establishing and agreeing the most appropriate measures is difficult.

In the latter part of this chapter we have considered structural processes and reward systems. Both these are related to the expectations that managers at every level have of their subordinates, and to aspects of behaviour and culture, including the way that things are done inside the organization. Policies and action plans for the allocation and management of resources are also important aspects of measurement and control mechanisms, and they are linked to these factors. They are the subject of the next chapter.

SUMMARY

The introduction to this chapter emphasized that, whilst organization structures are designed to ensure that strategies can be implemented effectively, the processes within the structure affect the formulation of future strategies. Particularly significant is the location of power, responsibility and authority in the organization and the extent to which these are centralized and decentralized. In large organizations the relationship between head office and the business units relates to this issue. In this chapter we have explored the links between strategies and structure.

Specifically we have

☐ looked at the determinants, advantages and disadvantages of centralization and decentralization and examined the concept of empowerment;

☐ examined five structural forms – the entrepreneurial structure, the functional structure, the divisional structure, the holding company structure and the matrix structure – in terms of (a) their main features, (b) where they are most appropriate, (c) their advantages and (d) their limitations;

☐ within this section, highlighted (a) the alternative approaches to divisionalization, (b) why matrix organizations are difficult to implement and manage, despite being theoretically very attractive, and (c) that the behavioural processes within the structural framework are an essential consideration;

☐ considered how structures might evolve and change as organizations grow larger, more complex and more diversified, quoting in particular the research of Chandler and Greiner;

☐ discussed the four main determinants of structure: size, tasks, environment and ideology;

☐ considered how the major requirements of the structure, namely that the tasks to be carried out can be effectively divided and integrated, might be accomplished;

☐ described the five co-ordinating mechanisms, the five component parts of the organization and the five structural configurations identified by Mintzberg;

☐ looked at the different control mechanisms and management styles in large companies, differentiating between the strategic planning, financial planning and strategic control approaches;

☐ discussed the role, skills and values of general managers;

☐ briefly considered the important issues under-pinning reward systems.

CHECKLIST OF KEY TERMS AND CONCEPTS

You should feel confident that you understand the following terms and ideas:

☐ The strategy → structure, structure → strategy issue
☐ Centralization and decentralization
☐ Empowerment
☐ The five structural forms: entrepreneurial, functional, divisional, holding company, matrix
☐ Greiner's developmental model
☐ The division and integration of tasks in structural design
☐ Mintzberg's five co-ordinating mechanisms; five parts of the organization: operating core, strategic apex, middle management, support staff, technostructure
☐ Five structural configurations: simple structure, machine bureaucracy, professional bureaucracy, divisionalized, adhocracy
☐ Strategic planning, financial planning and strategic control as links between head offices and business units
☐ The role of general managers
☐ The key issues in measuring and rewarding performance.

QUESTIONS AND RESEARCH ASSIGNMENTS

Text related

1. It was stated in the text that decentralization and divisionalization are not synonymous. What factors determine the degree of decentralization in a divisionalized organization?

2. For an organization with which you are familiar, obtain or draft the organization structure. How does it accord with the structural forms described in the text. Given your knowledge of the company's strategies and people, is the structure appropriate? Why? Why not? If not, in what way would you change it?

3. 'Sophisticated innovation requires a configuration that is able to fuse experts drawn from different disciplines into smoothly *ad hoc* project teams' (Henry Mintzberg discussing adhocracies).

    Do you agree? Can innovation not be incorporated into the alternative structures?

    Do you believe the adhocracy approach will overcome the perceived drawbacks of the matrix structure?

Library based

4. Obtain a current organization chart for the W H Smith Group, and consider how the various businesses featured in Table 22.2 are integrated. Do you feel that this is the most suitable structure?

5. Evaluate the divisionalized or holding company structure of a large diverse multi-product multi-national, considering the main board status of the key general managers. Does this suggest centralization or decentralization?

    If you are familiar with the company, do your findings accord with your knowledge of management styles within the organization?

6. Investigate the role of:
    (a) general managers in the Health Service;
    (b) the heads of financial services (whatever they might be called) in universities.

How has their role changed and developed in the last five years? How is, and how might, their performance be assessed? What are the most appropriate measures of effectiveness, and why? Are they rewarded in line with measures of performance?

RECOMMENDED FURTHER READING

The second edition (1984) of Child's book *Organization: A Guide To Problems and Practice* is an ideal source of further information.

Mintzberg (1979) contains more detail on structural forms.

The texts by Galbraith and Nathanson (1978), Mintzberg (1983) and Thompson and Strickland (1980) are also worthy of further study.

The article by Drucker on 'The coming of the new organization' (1988) is provocative reading.

REFERENCES

Chandler, A D (1962) *Strategy and Structure: Chapters in the History of the American Industrial Enterprise*, MIT Press.

Child, J A (1977) *Organization: A Guide to Problems and Practice*, Harper and Row. (A more recent edition is now available.)

Dixon, M (1989) The very model of a mythical manager, *Financial Times*, 10 May.

Drucker, P F (1988) The coming of the new organization, *Harvard Business Review*, January–February.

Fayol, H (1916) *General and Industrial Administration*, Pitman, 1949 (translation of French original).

Galbraith, J K (1969) *The New Industrial State*, Penguin.

Galbraith, J R and Nathanson, D A (1978) *Strategy Implementation: The Role of Structure and Process*, West.

Goold, M and Campbell, A (1988) *Strategies and Styles*, Blackwell.

Gray, S J and McDermott, M C (1989) *Mega-merger Mayhem: Takeover Strategies, Battles and Controls*, Paul Chapman Publishing.

Greiner, L E (1972) Evolution and revolution as organizations grow, *Harvard Business Review*, July–August.

Handy, C (1989) *The Age of Unreason*, Hutchinson.

Herbert, T T and Deresky, H (1987) Should general

managers match their business strategies, *Organizational Dynamics*, **15**(3), pp. 40–51.

Hunsicker, J Q (1982) The matrix in retreat, *Financial Times*, 25 October.

Kanter, Rosabeth Moss (1989) *When Giants Learn to Dance*, Simon and Schuster.

Lawrence, P R and Lorsch, J W (1967) *Organization and Environment*, Richard D Irwin.

Lorenz, C (1988) How the discriminating parent should behave, *Financial Times*, 5 December.

Lorsch, J W and Allen, S A (1972) *Managing Diversity and Interdependence*, Division of Research, Harvard Business School.

Mintzberg H (1979) *The Structuring of Organizations*, Prentice Hall.

Mintzberg, H (1983) *Structure in Fives: Designing Effective Organizations*, Prentice Hall.

Ohmae, K (1990) *The Borderless World*, Harper.

Peters, T J and Waterman, R H Jr (1982) *In Search of Excellence: Lessons from America's Best Run Companies*, Harper and Row.

Pitts, R A and Daniels, J D (1984) Aftermath of the matrix mania, *Columbia Journal of World Business*, Summer.

Porter, M E (1990) *The Competitive Advantage of Nations*, Free Press.

Reinton, S and Foote, N (1988) Why parents must be more particular, *Financial Times*, 17 June.

Salter, M S (1970) Stages in corporate development, *Journal of Business Policy*, Spring.

Stonich, P J (1982) *Implementing Strategy*, Ballinger.

Thompson, A A and Strickland, A J (1980) *Strategy Formulation and Implementation*, Richard D Irwin.

RESOURCE MANAGEMENT AND CONTROL

23

LEARNING OBJECTIVES

After studying this chapter you should be able to

☐ define the operational aspects of strategy implementation;
☐ distinguish between resource allocation issues at corporate and business unit level;
☐ explain the importance of functional interrelationships;
☐ describe different types of budget and explain their contribution to strategy implementation;
☐ list the important aspects of measurement and control systems;
☐ identify the main issues in crisis management.

In this chapter we look at the operational aspects of strategy implementation, examining issues involved in the management and co-ordination of resources.

INTRODUCTION

The allocation of resources has to be planned, controlled and evaluated if strategies are to be implemented and objectives achieved. This fundamental requirement applies at every level in the organization. It is perhaps obvious to state that the strategic leader plans; but at the lower levels of the management hierarchy the allocation of employees and their time, together with components and raw materials, is planned as part of a continuous scheduling activity. These various plans, though, are basically statements of intent. Strategies are only implemented when resources have been allocated and used.

It is therefore important to ensure that daily activities are directed by the strategy. Until the work of individual salespeople and shopfloor workers is affected by strategic decisions, the strategies will not be implemented. This requires effective communication and management information systems; specific projects and programmes for implementing corporate and competitive strategies; and action plans for the relevant functions.

Resources are mainly allocated through the budgeting process. How they are used is either controlled or affected by policies, depending upon the rigidity of the policies in question. Control mechanisms are required to evaluate whether the resources are being allocated according to the plans and whether the plans and the actions are proving efficient and effective and enabling the organization to achieve its desired objectives. These activities constitute the operational aspects of strategy implementation, and they are the subject of this chapter.

After exploring this outline of the main issues in greater detail, resource planning at both the corporate and functional levels will be examined. Policies, which were first introduced in Chapter 5, Key Concept 5.1, will then be discussed, and this will be followed by an examination of the budgeting process and different types of budget. We then consider further issues of measurement and control, and finish the chapter with an examination of crisis management.

THE OPERATIONAL ASPECTS OF STRATEGY IMPLEMENTATION

Corporate and competitive strategies are formulated in the light of both organizational objectives and the opportunities and threats perceived in the environment. Implementation requires that the possible strategies are matched with the resources that the organization already has or could develop or obtain, and corporate values. Effective strategic management requires congruence between environment, values and resources. Ishikawa (1985) uses the term 'strategic budgeting' to describe the linking of internal resources with external strategic plans. It has

been mentioned earlier that strategy formulation can be based on the search for new opportunities to capitalize on existing strengths or the development of internal resources in order to capitalize on environmental trends. Once formulated, though, the strategy must be implemented successfully. The resources on which the strategy depends must be allocated and used as necessary. Case 23.1 on Amstrad illustrates how resource difficulties can result in a failure to implement a basically creative strategy. (Readers may already have researched the background to the growth of Amstrad if they tackled the question on Alan Sugar at the end of Chapter 3.)

In this chapter we build on the notion of the strategy statement featured in Chapter 16 and illustrated in Figure 16.11, and concentrate on the derivation of detailed functional strategies and action plans. The measurement of performance, and assessment of how successful the organization is, relates to the issues discussed in Chapter 6. This process is very dependent upon the effectiveness of information management within the organization, and it is this which really links together the concepts of strategic awareness and strategic change decisions. Figure 2.4 (Chapter 2), which provided a diagrammatic summary of the content of this book, illustrates this point.

Figure 23.1 illustrates how detailed action plans are created and evaluated, and summarizes the content of this chapter. The allocation of resources at either the corporate or the functional levels may well imply change, and the issues involved in the management and implementation of change are discussed in the next chapter.

The first stage illustrated in Figure 23.1 relates to decisions concerning where resources will be required and allocated on a corporate basis, specifically:

☐ the future strategic perspective of the organization;

Case 23.1
AMSTRAD – PART A

Amstrad, the UK-based producer of personal computers and other electrical equipment, including dishes for satellite television and, from 1989, facsimile machines, is run by its founder, entrepreneurial businessman Alan Sugar. Sugar formulated a creative strategy which has not been implemented to the desired level of success. The main reason for this has been problems in controlling resources.

The strategy

Alan Sugar identified new electronics products with mass market potential and designed cheaper models than those his main rivals were producing. Manufacturing was to be by low cost suppliers, mainly in the Far East, supported by aggressive marketing in the West. Expenditure on high profile marketing was possible because little or no capital was tied up in plant and machinery. Central overheads were kept low and potential suppliers were 'played off against each other in order to reduce direct costs'.

Implementation problems

In 1988 the flexibility which Amstrad had built into the strategy turned from a strength to a weakness. There were five main reasons for this.

☐ In 1987 there was a worldwide shortage of memory chips, essential components for Amstrad. Some chip prices were doubled and others trebled, and in order to maintain production Amstrad had to pay whatever suppliers asked. The production of certain products was cut back deliberately.
☐ The launch of a new personal computer was delayed because a sophisticated chip, designed by Amstrad, failed to work when full production began.
☐ Labour shortages in Taiwan led to a reduced supply of audio products.
☐ A joint venture with Funai of Japan for the production of videos in the UK took off more slowly than anticipated. Previously all Amstrad's videos had been manufactured for them in Japan, by Funai.
☐ Amstrad established its own distribution network in western Germany, replacing an existing agreement with a third party. However, the previous distributor was left with surplus unwanted stock which it sold off cheaply, undercutting Amstrad's own price.

Changes to the strategy

Gradually production was moved to higher cost locations in Europe, and Amstrad became more involved in manufacturing.
[The Amstrad story is updated in Case 23.4.]

Source: Dixon, H (1989) The wizard loses some of his magic, *Financial Times*, 15 February.

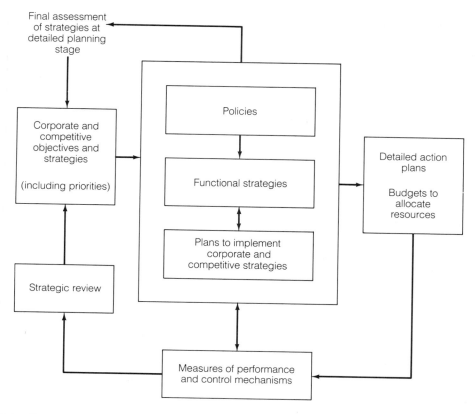

Figure 23.1 Operational aspects of strategy implementation.

☐ which existing divisions and business units are to be seen as priority areas;

☐ proposed new developments at corporate (acquisition, for example) and competitive levels.

These strategies are then operationalized through policies, functional strategies and detailed action plans. Functional strategies and action plans relate to an examination of what tasks must be carried out, how and when, if competitive and corporate strategies are to be implemented successfully and objectives achieved. To carry out these tasks functional managers will require resources: people, skills, facilities, money and so on. Where the resources are not currently available within the functional department they will need to be provided from either business

unit, divisional or corporate level. If the necessary resources are neither available nor obtainable the proposed strategy will need to be reviewed.

Policies guide and constrain decision makers and should ensure that the various functional strategies are integrated and complementary. This planning process, then, provides a check that the corporate and competitive strategies that have been formulated are both appropriate and feasible in the sense that they can be implemented.

There are two outcomes from the planning process: first, detailed budgets through which resources are allocated to individual functions and activities; and, second, measures of performance. These performance measures can be used as targets against which results can be evaluated. Information is then fed back and assessed and current strategies are evaluated. The assessment will certainly form part of any formal planning system operated by the organization, but ideally the strategic decision makers will maintain a constant awareness of how well the organization is performing.

Before considering the allocation of resources at corporate and functional levels in greater detail two points need to be emphasized. First, this type of planning is based on the notion of dividing the organization's requirements into functional objectives and tasks that can be agreed with individual managers and that are designed to provide particular contributions to an organization-wide plan. It was mentioned in the introduction to the book that it is important for the functional managers to be able to think strategically and maintain an overall strategic awareness of the organization's progress, rather than concentrating exclusively on their area of personal responsibility. Second, although detailed budgets are prepared to establish how resources should be allocated to functions, activities and managers, there should be sufficient flexibility to allow functional managers, with or without reference to their managers, to make adaptive changes as needs and opportunities arise.

CORPORATE RESOURCE PLANNING

Corporate resource planning relates to the allocation of resources between the various parts of the organization together with corporate investment decisions concerning the acquisition of additional resources. If investment funds are limited their allocation will be based on the strategic importance of the various spending opportunities as well as financial evaluations of the viability of each project. If funds are not available and need to be borrowed to finance possible projects, the return on the investment should exceed the cost of capital.

Organizations should seek the best possible returns from investments because, as Seed (1983) suggests, they can be seen as an undesirable but necessary freezing of corporate funds. However, some general and functional managers, especially if they have a technical background, may see investments in new plant and equipment as a reflection of status, preferring the best and most modern technology. Where this happens there could be a suboptimal allocation of corporate resources. This argument can also be applied to the purchase of large luxurious city-centre head offices.

The organization structure, whichever form it might take, will form the basis for the allocations. Where the organization is multidivisional, the extent to which power and responsibility are decentralized will determine how much freedom is given to general managers to allocate resources amongst their functional managers and departments. Where the power to change functional or competitive strategies is delegated to general managers, they will also require delegated authority to change resource allocations. This may imply moving resources within their area of responsibility. Equally it may necessitate the acquisition of additional resources from elsewhere within the organization or from outside. In functional organizations resources must be allocated to those areas that are most significant in the creation of competitive advantage.

Where any strategic resources are located centrally and used by the various divisions and business units their effectiveness will need to be carefully monitored. The extent of their use is an efficiency measure; effectiveness relates to their allocation to the areas in which they can yield most benefit for the organization.

The allocation of resources at a corporate level is closely tied in to the planning system through which priorities must be established. Alternative approaches to planning, together with a number of planning techniques, were considered in Chapter 16. Portfolio analyses such as the directional policy matrix may well be used to help to determine which products and business units should receive priority for investment funding; and any new developments which are proposed will require resources. An acquisition, for example, will need to be financed, but the integration of the new business after the purchase may also involve the transfer of managers and other resources.

Corporate resource planning and organization growth

Corporate resources may be allocated in different ways in line with the speed of growth of the organization and the degree of instability in the environment.

Rapid growth

Where the business overall, or selected business units within it, are growing rapidly the resource allocation process must be able to accommodate this growth and the consequent and possibly continual demand for additional resources. The process could be either centralized or decentralized, or a mixture of the two, influenced by the management style of the overall strategic leader and the interdependences between the various parts of the organization.

If it is centralized priorities will be established by head office corporate staff using some formal planning system and periodic review of the potential of all business units. Business units will need to provide the necessary information. With a decentralized approach the priorities would again be decided centrally but after allowing all divisions and business units to formulate their own preferred strategies and make their case for the corporate resources that they would require to implement their preferences. A mixed approach would involve resources for continuing activities being allocated through centralized mechanisms and incremental additions funded through a bidding process.

In all cases the decisions should balance the potential financial gains with the strategic logic implied. Whilst divisions or business units may be making individual requests for resources to support certain programmes, the opportunities for synergy, sharing activities and transferring skills across activities should be assessed. In addition the desirability of the implications of the various proposals for the overall strategic perspective of the organization should be considered.

Limited change and stability

Where businesses are growing more steadily and in a relatively stable environment, resource allocation for continuing programmes could be a straightforward extrapolation of previous budgets, incorporating an allowance for inflation. This basic approach was postulated when strategy formulation in local authorities was considered in Chapter 16. The assumption has often been that existing local government services should be continued as a first priority, with additional services added where resources could be found. The approach has certain drawbacks; and as a result zero-based budgeting, discussed later, is being used increasingly in local authorities. The basic premise of this approach is that a mere continuation of present strategies without evaluation and proper review may lead to ineffectiveness.

Established policies, such as fixing advertising budgets at an agreed percentage of projected sales revenue or maintaining particular levels of stocks, are likely to be a key feature of this approach.

Decline situations

Where businesses or business units are in decline some quite tough decisions often have to be taken. Where the organization as a whole is in difficulty the strategic leader must search for new opportunities for re-deploying resources. In the case of selected business units that are experiencing decline, unless there are opportunities for turnaround, resources should be transferred to activities with better growth and profit potential. In both cases the decisions are likely to be centralized, particularly as there may have to be structural changes to accommodate the rationalization, divestment or other strategic changes.

Once resources are allocated to divisions, business units and functions there will be further allocations to individual managers within each area; and this to a greater or lesser extent will be delegated to the general manager or functional manager in charge of each one. This is known as functional or operational resource planning; in the process it is important not to overlook any interdependences between the budget holders.

FUNCTIONAL RESOURCE PLANNING: AN INTRODUCTION

When resources are allocated to functions, and to particular activities within functions, there are a number of essential considerations.

☐ First, it is important to consider the relative importance of each function; the concept of the value chain, discussed in Chapter 15, could prove helpful in establishing this.
☐ Second, competitive advantage is established within functional activities; consequently an appreciation of key success factors and competitive opportunities is crucial if the resource allocation is to lead to strategic effectiveness.

The following anecdote is a useful illustration of the need to understand key success factors and manage resources in line with consumer demand. A few years ago it was established that buses on the Hanley to Bagnall route in Staffordshire were often failing to stop in order to pick up passengers. One passenger complained that he had been in a queue of 30 people and a bus with empty seats had simply driven past. When the matter was investigated one local councillor commented that 'if these buses stopped to pick up passengers they would disrupt the time-table'.

☐ Third, the important linkages between functions, which are the sources of potential synergy, should be considered. Any appropriate sharing of resources should be encouraged.
☐ Fourth, where there are sequential dependences, the whole resource allocation process must take account of these. For example, if activity Z is dependent upon activity X which precedes it, then it is both inefficient and ineffective to allocate resources to Z unless adequate resources are also given to X. An obvious application of this would be production activities which must be built around any bottlenecks. Similarly the capacity of hospital operating theatres should be consistent with the number of beds available for recuperation.

In addition, it is important to ensure that the necessary resources are available or can be made available before establishing competitive strategies. One small electronics company in the UK wished to expand its radio business but found that it could not obtain the appropriate engineers for researching and designing the products. Such engineers were being trained in the universities and polytechnics but they were being attracted by large companies, especially American and Japanese firms.

Similarly, poor resource planning by Ford of Europe reduced its competitiveness. Done (1992) reports that Ford failed to equip its Halewood (Merseyside) plant with the facility to assemble left-hand-drive Escorts and Orions. During 1991 the recession in the UK led to a collapse in demand for these models;

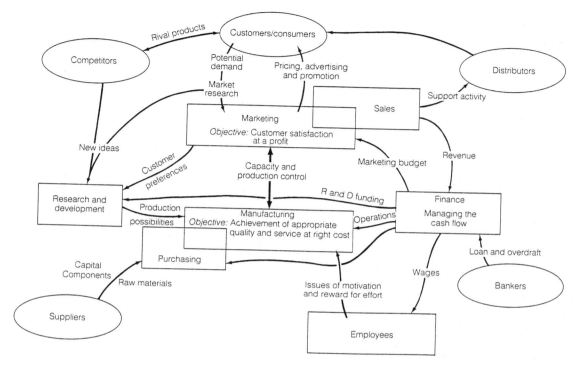

Figure 23.2 Functional interrelationships.

but sales potential remained buoyant in Germany. Because Halewood could not satisfy the demand it was reduced to three-days-a-week working. At the same time German customers were reluctantly having to accept engines without catalytic converters because of supply problems.

Functional interrelationships

The principle of functional links is illustrated in Figure 23.2, which features the various functions of the organization in a series of rectangles and the external stakeholders with whom they deal in ovals. The flows of information, money and resources which link them are indicated by the lines. The vital link between production and marketing is at the heart of the model. The following commentary considers the impact on these functional

activities of the development of a new product. The development of any new venture such as this has to be planned in detail and costed. Time, money and other resources have to be acquired and allocated to the project; and consequently an analysis of the impact on other continuing activities in the organization is essential.

Market research must be undertaken to establish potential demand for the new product and to assess its viability. This would be funded out of the marketing budget, which also covers the selling, advertising and promotion of all existing products and services. Research and development would be provided with ideas by marketing, and their budget would fund the development of the concept and a prototype for testing. Research and development are unlikely to be involved in only one new development, and consequently a decision has to be taken concerning how much money and time, and which staff and facilities, should be allocated to this particular project. Assuming that the project develops satisfactorily the marketing budget will also be required to finance the necessary test marketing. If this proves successful, and the projected figures for demand, prices and costs indicate a potentially profitable venture, the project is then handed over to production. They will be charged with producing the product to the appropriate quality standards within certain cost constraints which are derived from potential pricing possibilities. Their costs will include labour and materials. An advertising and promotion campaign will be required to launch the product.

Of course all this planning and expenditure could be wasted if the necessary distribution network is not properly established.

All these activities must take place before the product is able to earn any revenue, except for the sales in test marketing. Moreover, the new product is unlikely to break even financially until demand and sales have been properly established. Consequently the allocation of time, money and other resources for developing new ideas and future strategic changes must be planned alongside existing activities which to some extent will be used to fund them. It is the role of the finance department to manage the cash flow and any necessary borrowing to facilitate this. In just the same way as it is necessary to establish priorities between established and continuing products and services, it is also important to establish the appropriate allocation for the development of 'tomorrow's products and services'.

Certain techniques, such as network analysis, can be very useful in planning a project such as this and establishing the resource needs. The whole project should be managed for efficiency, with time and resources being saved wherever appropriate. Nevertheless, as Robert Burns said, 'The best laid schemes o' mice an' men . . . Gang aft a-gley'. In the early 1960s it was decided to introduce into

the UK a successful American car wax. The decision was made to launch the product initially within the Granada television region, using limited television advertising and concentrating distribution only in selected garages. The commercials were scheduled in the middle of a late-night magazine programme with a relatively small audience. However, in the event an important European football match featuring Manchester United was re-programmed at short notice and the car wax advertisements filled the half-time commercial break. A demand for the car wax was generated which the importers simply could not supply. The situation was made worse by people asking for the product in outlets other than garages.

Efficiency and effectiveness in resource allocation and management

It is important to consider both efficiency and effectiveness measures in relation to the allocation and deployment of resources, as has been pointed out earlier when the utilization of resources for competitive advantage and SWOT analyses were discussed. An examination of the way in which resources are employed and managed in the production and marketing of existing products and services can be used to search for improvements. Savings in time and costs (without threatening quality) lead to higher productivity, higher profits and the freeing up of resources which can be deployed elsewhere. This is essentially a search for greater efficiency.

At the same time it is also useful to consider whether resources are being allocated to those products, services and activities which are most important for the organization as a whole and for the achievement of its objectives. This analysis is applicable at organizational, divisional and business unit level – wherever there is an opportunity cost of the resources in question. If resources are finite and limited to the extent that choices have to be made concerning which products to concentrate resources on and which to give low priority to, then the opportunity cost of the resources should be considered. If growth or profitability or both are important objectives, the resources should be allocated to those products and services which can best fulfil the objectives. This is an assessment of effectiveness. However, as discussed above, it is important to ensure that sufficient resources are allocated to development programmes that will lead to growth and profits in the future.

If decisions are made to alter resource allocations and concentrate them in different areas, issues of managing change arise; these are considered in Chapter 24. It should be appreciated that particular business units, products and services are likely to have their champions within the organization. Resource reductions in favour of alternative products may be resisted by certain managers. Their ability and willingness to resist change pressures from higher management will be related to their power bases and their ability to influence decisions. These issues also are considered in Chapter 24.

It is now appropriate to consider in more detail how resources are allocated to managers and how policies influence the way that resources are used. Put simplistically, managers are allowed certain resources, which represent costs to the organization, and are then expected to use them to generate revenues and profits. The budgeting process determines how many of what resources managers are allocated. Their agreed objectives and targets concerning particular products and services determine how the resources are further deployed, and established policies influence the way they are deployed and managed. These are the subjects of the next two sections.

POLICIES, PROCEDURES, PLANS AND BUDGETS

Policies

Policies are designed to guide the behaviour of managers in relation to the pursuit and achievement of strategies and objectives. They can guide either thoughts or actions or both by indicating what is expected in certain decision areas. Over time they establish the way that certain tasks should normally be carried out, and place constraints upon the decision-making freedom that managers have. In this respect they imply that the implementation of strategies formulated by strategic leaders is a planned activity, and recognize that managers may at times wish to make changes and pursue objectives which are personally important to them. Policies, therefore, should be related to stated objectives and strategies and assist in their implementation; at the same time they should not restrict managers to the extent that they are unable to make adaptive changes when these are appropriate or necessary. Managers should be offered sufficient inducements to comply with organizational policies, and sanctioned when they fail to comply without justification.

Policies need not be written down or even formulated consciously. They may emerge as certain behaviour patterns become established in the organization and are regarded as a facet of values and culture. A policy can exist simply because it is the perceived way that something has always been done. Policies are particularly significant in the case of recurring problems or decisions as they establish a routine and consistent approach.

Policies can be either advisory, leaving decision makers with some flexibility, or mandatory, whereby managers have no discretion. Koontz and O'Donnell (1968) suggest that mandatory policies should be regarded as 'rules' rather than policies. They argue that mandatory policies tend to stop managers and other employees thinking about the most efficient and effective ways to carry out tasks and searching for improvements. Policies should guide rather than remove discretion.

Koontz and O'Donnell further argue that advisory policies should normally be preferred because it is frequently essential to allow managers some flexibility to respond and adapt to changes in both the organization and the environment. Moreover, mandatory policies are unlikely to motivate managers whilst advisory guides can prompt innovation.

The creation and use of policies

It has already been mentioned that policies may be created both consciously and unconsciously. This complex issue needs to be explored in greater detail before we consider the criteria that affect the soundness and viability of policies and look at a number of examples in different functional areas.

The main stated policies are those which the managers of the company draw up in relation to their areas of discretionary responsibility. Certain key policies will be established by the overall strategic leader and will be filtered down the organization. It is important that when general managers create policies for their divisions and business units, and functional managers for their departments, there is some consistency between them.

Some policies will be forced on the company by external stakeholders. Government legislation upon contracts of employment, redundancy terms and health and safety at work all affect personnel policies, for example. The design of certain products will have to meet strict criteria for safety and pollution. The fabric used for airline seats in the UK must be fire-resistant, and there are similar restrictions upon the type of foams that can be used in furniture. Car engines must be designed to meet certain emission regulations. In some cases financial policies can be dictated by powerful shareholders or bankers.

It is useful, then, if the major functional areas of the business are covered by explicit policies which are known to all employees who will be affected by them. Where they exist in this form they provide a clear framework in which decisions can be made; and they also allow people to understand the behaviour patterns that are expected of them in particular circumstances. However, the policies should not be too rigid and prevent managers making important change decisions. Changes in strategies may require changes of policy if they are to be implemented successfully.

Principles of good policy

Koontz and O'Donnell (1968) suggest that the following principles determine the potential effectiveness of policies in relation to strategy implementation.

☐ *Policies should reflect objectives* The existence of a policy can only be justified if it leads to the achievement of the company's objectives. To this end policies should be reviewed from time to time and assessed whenever strategies are changed in any significant way. Policies which have evolved unconsciously and become the normal way of doing things may remain in existence for long periods if they are not carefully evaluated; and they may not contribute positively towards company objectives. In fact they may have the opposite effect and make the objectives harder to achieve.

☐ *Policies should be consistent* Policies which conflict with each other should be avoided. Whilst this appears to state the obvious, it may not be easy to ensure that it does not happen. A company might, for example, establish a strategy of cutting the number of indirect employees in order to achieve the objective of reduced overheads

Contributory policies might include not replacing people who leave and asking for volunteers for redundancy. At the same time the reduced workforce will have to be more productive if output is to be maintained, and a policy to support this might include the recruitment of more work study engineers. Work study engineers are indirect employees.

☐ *Policies should be flexible* In general policies should neither be ignored nor departed from indiscriminately. However, it is unhelpful if they are seen as mandatory and inflexible when there is a clear need to make changes. Whilst regular reviews and changes when necessary will provide the appropriate flexibility in a turbulent environment this can defeat one purpose in having policies.

Policies exist to provide consistent guides to decision making and to advise managers how to behave in particular circumstances. This allows managers to predict how their colleagues will behave. Where the advice changes constantly this understanding will disappear.

It is useful to qualify policies with a statement that limited discretion should be exercised when the occasion demands it, and also to encourage decision makers to refer back to their superiors when the policy seems inappropriate for current circumstances. This brings us to the next principles.

☐ *The extent to which a policy is mandatory, as opposed to advisory, should be clear.*
☐ *Policies should be communicated, taught and understood* The existence of a set of policies in a policy document will not guarantee that they are followed and that strategies are implemented as desired. It is important to ensure that employees understand the existence and meaning of policies, and appreciate why they exist. They are then more closely tied in with the performance objectives that are agreed with managers.
☐ *Policies should be controlled* Stated policies

can be assessed and controlled as part of any formal planning system and strategic review, but the evaluation may fail to take non-stated, emergent, policies into account. The importance of informal information systems, feedback and the strategic awareness of functional and general managers, and the strategic leader, can be emphasized again in this respect.

Examples of functional policies

Policies can exist for any functional task undertaken by the organization, and consequently the following examples are merely indicative.

In **finance** the dividend policy discussed in Chapter 13 constitutes one example. Similarly there may be policies for assessing the viability of proposed investments and ranking a set of alternatives. Where the firm has a financial strategy of investing cash balances on a short-term basis there may well be policies and criteria for evaluating appropriate opportunities.

Personnel policies would include the following:

☐ the type and qualification of employees for particular jobs
☐ the recruitment activities and procedures which will take place
☐ the training and development of particular skills and competences in relation to specified jobs
☐ communicating to employees how well (or poorly) the company is performing
☐ policies concerning overtime and bonuses.

Policies with regard to quality and meeting delivery dates are examples from the **operations** function. Policies may also establish who has the authority to change production schedules; and in a retail organization there are likely to be policies concerning the reordering of stock, the refilling of shelves, and

Case 23.2
BRITISH TELECOM

BRITISH TELECOM

In July 1989 British Telecom announced their proposals for increasing prices later in the year. Their **objective** was to increase their revenue within the constraints imposed on them (their freedom to raise prices is limited by their regulator), and at the same time to favour business users rather than domestic customers.

The pricing **strategy** was one of discrimination, raising certain prices, particularly for those services which are relatively more important for non-business users, by more than the overall average and leaving others unaffected. The overall weighted price increase, based on forecast demand, was to be 3.2% for all services, but domestic users would face 5.5% increases.

The detailed pricing **policies** were as follows:

☐ rental and connection charges for all users up by 10%
☐ the charge for local calls to increase by roughly 6%
☐ the charge for national, or long distance, calls would stay the same
☐ local calls from payphones would cost 40% more for the same time unit, but again long-distance calls would stay the same.

the ways in which merchandise should be displayed both in-store and in the windows.

Marketing policies are related to the four components of the marketing mix: product, price, promotion and distribution. One product policy of a car manufacturer might establish which models are made in anticipation of sale and displayed in distributor showrooms and which ones are only made when orders have been placed for them. A pricing policy of certain retailers is to reduce prices to the level of their competitors when customers highlight the differential. A preference for advertising in certain magazines or the use of a particular layout would constitute examples of promotional policies. The willingness of Marks & Spencer to exchange goods on demand, regardless of whether they are faulty, is a merchandising policy.

All these policies are designed to implement chosen strategies and further the achievement of desired objectives. See Case 23.2.

Procedures

A procedure is a type of plan designed to establish the steps that employees should follow in carrying out certain, normally routine, tasks. If a customer complains, for example, there may be an established procedure for gathering the required information and dealing with the complaint. Where products fail inspection there may be procedures for establishing the cause. Algorithms, whereby a series of questions are posed and the answer to one question determines the next question asked, can be used to provide an appropriate framework for diagnosing faults. These again would constitute a formalized procedure.

In the same way that policies help clarify expectations, a well-conceived and straightforward procedure can ensure that the necessary action in certain circumstances is clear to everyone. In addition, procedures can provide a useful control mechanism.

Functional and single-use plans

When strategic planning was discussed in general terms in Chapter 16 and alternative approaches were considered, it was pointed out that the thinking process was often more important than the production of a definite rigid plan. The tasks to be carried out by certain divisions, business units and functional managers must be clarified through a planning process if the resources required for their implementation are to be allocated efficiently. Certain functional activities, however, lend themselves to detailed planning and specific plans. The scheduling of production, of operator hours and of the receipt of supplies under a just-in-time (JIT) system are examples.

In addition there are single-use plans which are self-explanatory, designed to meet specific contingencies and generally detailed. The plan for the launch and development of a new product, discussed earlier in this chapter, the plans for the installation of a new piece of equipment, and the change-over plans linked to the implementation of a new organization structure are all examples of single-use plans. The value of single-use plans lies in forcing managers to set down the steps which are required to accomplish specific tasks and at the same time to examine the impact on all the people who are in some way affected.

Whilst techniques such as network analysis and Gantt charts (activity flow charts) can prove helpful in single-use planning, the logical approach which under-pins these techniques is important. A typical thought pattern would be as follows:

☐ Decide what specific actions are necessary to achieve the objective, and state these as a series of steps.
☐ Place the steps in the chronological order in which they must be carried out, noting where steps must be performed sequentially and where there are opportunities to perform steps in parallel.

☐ Allocate each step to an individual who will be held responsible for its completion by a certain date, and possibly within a certain budget limit. This is important for control and for gaining the individual commitment of key managers.
☐ Allocate the necessary resources for each step to the managers who are responsible for their completion, and ensure that they have the authority to use them.
☐ Establish an information system which will allow all participants to co-ordinate their efforts and facilitate changes to the plan if the target completion dates for any steps are missed.

Budgets

The allocation of resources through a budgeting process is expanded below. Budgets, quite simply, are plans expressed in numerical terms, usually in financial terms. They will indicate how much should be spent, by which departments, when, and for what purpose.

Budgets are in common use in organizations as a way of managing and controlling resources. Where budgets are properly part of strategy implementation, resources will be allocated to ensure that formulated strategies can be implemented effectively and to enable managers to make any necessary changes to them. However, budgets involve the allocation of resources to individual managers who are responsible for the completion of particular tasks and to individual products and business units. These managers may naturally wish to see their responsibilities and products growing and prospering rather than declining, and as a result will press for additional resources. Unless the future prospects and viability of products and business units are evaluated objectively, and the opportunity-cost of the resources they consume considered, budgeting may become more financially oriented than strategic.

ALLOCATING RESOURCES

All the resources utilized by an organization need to be allocated to individual managers, and this process needs planning and controlling. Most organizations will seek to quantify the allocation process and use some form of budgeting. Budgets are financial statements of the resources required to achieve a set of finite objectives or put into action a formulated strategy. It was mentioned earlier that when this detailed implementation planning takes place it may prove necessary to review the feasibility of certain strategies. Budgeted earnings from sales and budgeted expenses, once agreed with managers, will normally be used as a basis for measuring performance against expectations. Before looking at the budgeting process in greater detail, a number of points need to be made.

Pearce and Robinson (1985) distinguish between three types of budget. **Capital budgets** concern the allocation of resources for investment in buildings, plant and equipment. These new resources will be used to generate future revenues. **Sales budgets** reflect the anticipated flow of funds into the organization based on forecast sales; and **revenue or expense budgets** concern the operating costs that will be incurred in producing these products and services. Because of such factors as seasonal demand, the need to hold stock, and the fact that the final payment for goods and services is likely to occur after all operating expenses have been paid, the flows of cash in and out of the business need to be controlled through these budgets.

Budgeting the direct costs of producing certain products and services requires an estimate of the raw materials, components, labour and machine hours that are likely to be needed. Standard costing techniques usually form the basis of this, with analyses of any variances being used to measure both performance and the reliability of the standard costs.

People are a crucial strategic resource, and their physical contribution in terms of hours of work can be budgeted. Work study and other techniques will be used to establish the standard times required to complete particular tasks, which can then be costed. Whilst such standards, and the wage rates which are used to determine the payment for these inputs, are likely to be common throughout the organization, and in many cases agreed centrally, the selection and training of the people in question are likely to be decentralized. Whilst the skills and capabilities of staff should be considered when the budgets are quantified, the process of budgeting can be useful for highlighting weaknesses and deficiencies.

Developing from this, another expense which needs to be budgeted is training and management development programmes. This involves the utilization of funds which are currently available to improve the long-term contribution and value of people. Training and development should therefore be seen as an investment. However, the anticipated returns will be difficult to quantify, and as a result the investment techniques considered earlier may be of only limited use. Moreover, the contribution of people will also depend upon their commitment to the organization, which in turn will be influenced by the overall reward and incentives packages which are offered and the ability of the organization structure to harness and co-ordinate their various contributions.

The budgeting process

All managers who spend money, and whose departments consume resources, should ideally be given a budget. These budgets should represent agreed targets which relate closely to the manager's objectives, again agreed with his or her superior. In the same way that individual manager objectives contribute towards the objectives for departments, business units, divisions and ultimately the organization as a whole, individual budgets will be part of a master budget. Activities which constrain other activities, because they involve scarce resources for which demand exceeds supply capability, should be budgeted early.

Budgets and objectives are clearly related, and consequently resources should be allocated to those areas and activities in the organization which are seen as priorities. If important objectives are to be achieved, and priority strategies implemented, resources must be provided. Where growth and profits are important organizational objectives, those business units and products which are best able to contribute to their achievement should be funded accordingly. This approach suggests that the strategies being implemented have been formulated to satisfy corporate objectives, and personal objectives have been contained. However, the process of budgeting can facilitate the ability of managers to pursue personal objectives. Moreover, budgeting can be perceived as a technique for short-term financial management rather than a key aspect of strategy implementation. These contentions are expanded below.

Where resources are available and new developments are being considered, the previous record and contribution of managers is likely to have an influence. Rather than select strategies on merit and then allocate the most appropriate managers to implement them, the strategies championed by successful managers may be preferred.

Furthermore, the ability of certain managers to exercise power and influence over resource allocations within the organization, issues which are discussed in the next chapter, may result in allocations to areas and activities which potentially are not the most beneficial to the organization as a whole. Bower (1970) points out that where the objectives of the organization are difficult to agree and quantify, as is the case in many not-for-profit organizations, the political ability of managers to defend existing allocations

and bid for additional resources grows in importance. Wherever this is evident, the resource allocation process becomes a determinant of the objectives and strategies pursued by organizations.

Flexibility

The budgeting process will normally take place on an annual basis, but as the targets will be utilized for regular performance reviews there should be scope to adjust budgets either upwards or downwards. Whilst sales and revenue budgets are by nature short term, capital budgets have long-term implications. Investments may be paid for in instalments, and their returns are likely to stretch over several years. The budgets, of course, are interrelated. Once capital investment decisions have been taken there are immediate implications for revenue to support them.

The allocation of resources to managers is dependent upon the strategies which the organization has decided to continue and develop, but adaptive changes require flexibility which must be accounted for. Where resources are limited and finite, strategic opportunities may be constrained. New alternatives may only be feasible if other activities are divested.

Flexed budgets, discussed below, can assist in providing flexibility.

Measuring performance against budgets

Budgeting is one key means of monitoring and controlling the allocation and use of resources throughout the organization. Agreed objectives and performance targets can be used to monitor the progress of individual managers, departments and business units, and draw comparisons. However, for this to be valuable, the targets should be agreed rather than imposed and any in-built advantages and disadvantages should be

Box 23.1
BUDGETING: CONTROLLING THE PROCESS AND THE ADVANTAGES OF BUDGETING

CONTROLLING THE BUDGETING PROCESS

Successful budgeting is essentially people oriented, and the following considerations are important.

☐ There needs to be communication, co-operation and co-ordination between budget holders, especially where there are interdependences.
☐ Targets should be agreed by budget holders and their superiors, and perceived to be both realistic and attainable.
☐ The objectives agreed with individual managers should be consistent with the overall objectives in the master budget.
☐ The budgets, and the feedback reports, should increase in detail as they cascade down the organization.
☐ Feedback should be constructive; and reports for individual budget holders should emphasize variances between targets and results.
☐ These reports should be produced within a time-scale which allows managers to act quickly on problem areas, but they should be accurate or otherwise confidence in the system will be reduced.

THE ADVANTAGES OF BUDGETING

Budgets are time consuming to prepare and review, but they can be essential for the effective allocation and control of resources. Where budget targets are imposed rather than agreed some of the advantages listed below will not be achieved.

☐ Budgeting enables the organization's objectives to be stated clearly in financial terms.
☐ Key actions which must be taken are specified.
☐ Responsibilities for carrying out these actions are allocated to individual managers.
☐ Performance measures are specified.
☐ The budgeting process generates an overview of the entire activities of the organization and, where resources are limited, allows for decisions concerning priorities and trade-offs.
☐ Conflict between departments can be reduced.
☐ Problems can be flagged quickly and dealt with.
☐ Handled well, budgeting and the allocation of target expectations, resources and responsibilities can be a positive motivator.

clarified. These points are covered in greater detail in Box 23.1 which summarizes the potential advantages of budgeting and the key issues involved in controlling the process in order to achieve the advantages.

Measuring the returns on the resources allocated and used is a measure of efficiency. Effectiveness depends upon whether the initial allocation of resources to activities has been objectively evaluated and whether the best interests of the organization, related to corporate objectives, have been satisfied. Unless the opportunity cost of supporting the various corporate, competitive and functional strategies is reviewed regularly, this may not happen.

Resource allocations which preserve the budget of certain business units and continue existing strategies without objective evaluation may lead to suboptimal allocations. In the case of departments and activities which **support** the direct production and selling activities of one or more products, services or business units, it can be convenient to base future budgets on previous budgets. This is especially true if performance and returns are 'satisfactory' and if managers are politically competent in defending their budgets. In addition, as budgets can be seen as short-term detailed financial planning, certain organizations will hand over budgeting responsibility to a finance department who may use the past as a basis for extrapolating the future. Budget allocations are therefore related more to past achievements than to future potential. The term traditional budgeting is often used to describe the approach whereby the annual budgets of many centres with no manufacturing responsibility are based on the previous year's budget.

A strategic approach to budgeting, which considers existing and possible new corporate, competitive and functional strategies simultaneously, forms the most appropriate base for effective resource allocation. **Strategic budgeting** (Ishikawa, 1985) requires that the strategic planning process consistently seeks congruence between resource allocation and environmental opportunities and is used to establish budgets throughout the organization. The notion of zero-base budgeting for evaluating existing strategies is related to this, and is discussed below.

Zero-base budgeting

Where a traditional approach to budgeting is adopted, once the continued production of a product or service has been assumed or decided, demand prospects are forecast. Against these are set expense budgets based on standard costs. Overhead contributions are most probably adjusted for volume changes and inflation. Previous experiences are therefore carried forward and used as a base. With zero-base budgeting no previous experience is assumed, and every proposed activity must be justified afresh.

It was suggested earlier that many local authorities have, historically, sought to continue with existing service provisions, supplemented by new and additional services when resources could be found to fund them. Local authorities who make use of zero-base techniques start with the assumption that all services must be justified and priorities established on merit. Existing services might well be replaced rather than continued simply because they already exist, or better ways of providing the services might be found.

Under traditional budgeting methods it is easy to carry forward past inefficiencies which result in over-spending. Zero-base budgeting should prevent this and offer opportunities for reducing expenses by searching for improved efficiencies. Moreover, the establishment of priorities on merit can result in greater effectiveness, depending on the assessment criteria selected for evaluation. Zero-base approaches essentially become strategic budgeting when the priorities are established in terms of the overall corporate objectives rather than the most efficient use of resources.

Zero-based budgeting in Strathclyde, for example, has led to nursery education being established as a new high priority area and to refurbishment of existing local authority council houses being preferred to a more expensive new building programme.

Both strategic and zero-based budgeting are conceptually very attractive as they distinguish between high and low priority areas and contain the pursuit of personal objectives by managers. Their implementation presents a number of difficulties, however, which often result in traditional budgeting being preferred. The most serious problems concern the administration, paperwork and time required to implement them effectively and establish priorities objectively. In large complex organizations the decision-making burden concerning low level priorities, which individually may not be very significant, can draw senior management attention away from the overall strategic needs of the organization. Finally zero-based budgeting implies that any job might be declared redundant at any time, and this causes both uncertainty and increased political activity.

Flexed budgeting

Flexed budgets are designed to allow for changes in the level of activity, which might result from adaptive changes in functional and competitive strategies. Managers would realize that, if they were able to sell in excess of their targets, then resources would be found to facilitate increased production. The assumption would be that more sales equals more profit, which may well be true. However, if the implication is that resources would be diverted from other activities,

---

Continuous business success is built when the solid foundations are strong, open relationships throughout an organization. It is not built upon systems or management techniques – they are tools which will be used by people working well together for one another.

Businesses which nurture good, open relationships will encourage, welcome and survive change. Businesses driven by systems and characterized by fear and anxiety will do none of these things.

Change is about people. The management of change is therefore about the management of people.

Patrick Byrne, Group Chief Executive Officer,
Waterford Wedgwood plc

---

issues of opportunity cost are again relevant; and the resources should only be diverted from activities which are either less profitable or strategically less important to the organization in the long term.

In this section on budgeting, the need for measures of both efficiency and effectiveness has been featured. Both are important. Resources allocated to particular managers, departments and business units should be utilized as efficiently as possible. At the same time the long-term interests of the organization and the overall strategic perspective should be reviewed. This requires an assessment of whether the resources are being allocated and deployed in the most effective way. This was illustrated earlier in Figure 16.7.

ISSUES OF MEASUREMENT AND CONTROL SYSTEMS

The need to measure and evaluate performance, and to make changes when necessary, applies at all levels of the organization. Budgets establish quantitative targets for individual managers, departments, business units and divisions. Progress against these targets can be measured through the information system; and the feedback should be both fast and accurate to enable any corrective actions to take place quickly. The ability of all these budget holders to achieve their targets will be useful when reviewing their futures. The system used by BTR is described in Case 23.3. However, it is important when looking ahead to consider the current match between products, services and business units and their respective environments. Future prospects do not necessarily rely on past performance.

The ability to achieve targeted strategic milestones is the normal control measure. Case 23.4, an up-date of the earlier Amstrad case, shows how competitive strategies can

---

Case 23.3
BTR

BTR is an acquisitive and diversified conglomerate, and their strategy was outlined in Chapter 13. During the 1980s BTR took over:

☐ Tilcon (the UK aggregates company) — BTR also owns Grahams Builders' Merchants;
☐ Newey and Eyre (the leading electrical wholesaler in the UK);
☐ DCE (an international dust control company); and
☐ Dunlop Slazenger.

In 1991 BTR also acquired Hawker Siddeley. BTR was identified as a *financial control* company in Chapter 22.

BTR operates with 500 profit centres directed by a head office with fewer than 50 staff and four regional offices.

BTR . . . allows its operations a large degree of autonomy within a carefully designed system of financial controls. The control system 'enables BTR to build its business both by investment in existing companies and through acquisitions, which it integrates rapidly and successfully'.   (BTR offer document for Hawker Siddeley)

The control system is built around two documents:

☐ *The Annual Profit Plans* These are fed through the regional office structure and ultimately approved by one designated main Board director — because of the number of profit centres, the profit plans have to be spread amongst the whole Board. The profit plan encapsulates corporate investment, and the objectives for each profit centre are negotiated to a level where they are thought to be achievable but not too easily.

  Profit centre general managers are delegated considerable autonomy whilst ever their targets are attained.
☐ *Monthly Management Reports* These contain some 17 pages of detailed analysis, with a strong emphasis on cash flow management. A working capital target of between 20 and 25% is set, and general managers are charged interest by the centre if they exceed their target.

The two documents characterize BTR's strong internal discipline, and they require that all profit centre managers are competent financially. The obvious attention to detail relies upon large quantities of carefully reported, accurate and honest information.

  The efficiency aspects of the BTR system are clear; the attainment of potential internal synergies is less obvious.

---

become inappropriate in a changing environment.

  Also when establishing budgets and performance targets it is important to ensure that the attention of managers is not focused too narrowly on only their areas of responsibility. Their contributions to other managers and their commitment to the overall interests of

---

Case 23.4
AMSTRAD – PART B

Amstrad Part A (earlier in this chapter) featured the company's supply problems; the recession of the early 1990s raised questions about the appropriateness of Amstrad's corporate and competitive strategies.

In 1991 Amstrad traded at a loss for the first time. The recession had hit sales of its personal computers. Manufacturers of higher quality and more expensive machines, including IBM and Compaq, slashed their prices to try to stimulate demand and Amstrad's competitive edge (its price advantage) was lost. Alan Sugar's dilemma was that if he withdrew from the market he had nothing really new to replace PCs.

Amstrad had earlier withdrawn from computer games, unable to compete successfully with the aggressive Nintendo. Satellite dishes, however, seemed safer with continental sales buoyant; and the increasing involvement of BSkyB in major sporting activities (exclusive coverage of the cricket world cup and live football from the Premier League) augured well for the 1990s. [Alan Sugar is also Chairman of Tottenham Hotspur.] Amstrad's word processors and fax machines were continuing to sell satisfactorily; and although demand for VCRs (video cassette recorders) had fallen, Amstrad had successfully innovated a new double-decker machine which allows users to edit their own tapes and to record from two television channels at the same time. The company had launched a new lap-top computer in 1991.

Sugar's initial reaction was to consolidate and to minimize inventories in order to strengthen Amstrad's balance sheet. He commented: '. . . no intention of moving into technology-led businesses or the high end of the market. Our vocation is always in the lower end of the market.'

The appropriateness of the strategy for the 1990s remained an unanswered question.

Although such new products as a notepad computer (a user-friendly personal organizer/word processor/calculator), a compact telephone-fax machine and a consumer videophone are in the pipeline, Amstrad's basic problem is that the markets in which it competes are already crowded.

Source: Nakamoto, M (1992) A desperate need for hits in an intensive price war, *Financial Times*, 12 February.

---

the organization are the sources of synergy. Whilst these measures of individual performances are crucial, the effectiveness of all functional, competitive and corporate strategies and their abilities to achieve corporate objectives are the ultimate measures.

The effectiveness of the contribution of such activities as research and development is difficult to assess, but this is no excuse for not trying.

Figure 23.3 charts a number of possible performance measures – those on the right focus on efficiency and reflect a financial control culture; those on the left are crucial indicators of a commitment to service, quality and excellence. The culture of the organization

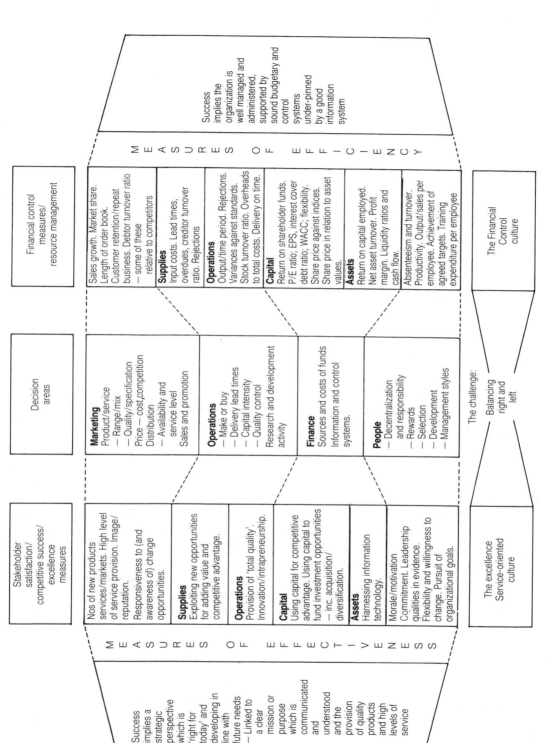

Figure 23.3 Some possible measures of performance.

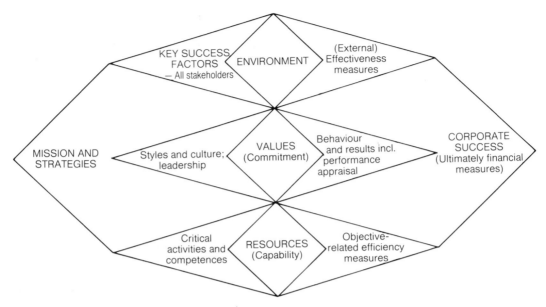

Figure 23.4   Performance measurement: What should we be measuring?

will dictate which measures are given priority. It has been pointed out earlier that establishing such excellence measures requires a real attempt to reconcile the different expectations of the stakeholders. Where there is no common agreement, the objectives and measures selected will reflect the relative power of the various stakeholders. In any case, commercial pressures invariably focus attention on resource management and efficiencies, which are easier to set and monitor. There is then always the danger that because efficiency measures are possible, and often straightforward, they may become elevated in significance and, as a result, begin to be seen as the foundation for the objectives. In other words, measurement potential rather than stakeholder satisfaction dictates objectives.

Figure 23.4 takes this argument a stage further and relates back to the model of E–V–R congruence. Whilst environment, values and resources are separated within the diamond, rather than overlaid, the need for congruence is implicit. There are two premises to this model:

☐ Corporate success is concerned with the mission and purpose of the organization, but frequently it will be assessed by financial measures of some form. Commercial businesses are judged on profitability and growth, although profits, *per se*, are really a means, not an end. Not-for-profit organizations must be commercially viable, for they can only spend what they can raise. Charities are dependent upon their fund raising, and consequently will measure their success on their ability to raise increasing amounts of money. Long-term success is built around a cycle comprising the ability to raise money, to spend it wisely and effectively, to be seen to be doing this and to be doing it efficiently, and on the strength of this to raise even more money.

☐ Long-term strategic success therefore requires that the interests of stakeholders are met, and are seen to be met; that this is accomplished efficiently with capable resources; and that there is a commitment to the mission reflected in organizational values.

The implication is that in addition to resource efficiency and stakeholder satisfaction organizations should also attempt to **measure values** to ensure that the culture is appropriate.

Organizations which attempt this will first need to clarify which values and behaviours are critical for carrying out corporate and competitive strategies, and pursuing the mission, both now and in the future. In 1991 Yorkshire Water determined that their key values were: trust, loyalty, pride, honesty, integrity, endeavour, quality, service/excellence and competitiveness. Adherence to these values would be manifested in a number of behaviour traits. It was seen as important that employees were committed to, and confident about, their roles, and that they were suitably empowered and rewarded. Effective communications networks were also thought to be vital.

Research can capture a snapshot of currently held values and the extent to which particular behaviours are being manifested. Some organizations will prefer to use volunteers from amongst the workforce rather than select a sample. The findings should be evaluated against a set of expectancies, and follow-up research can track both positive and negative developments. The organization must then decide what action to take if there is any deterioration or the initial absence of a critical value or behaviour pattern. Changing the culture of the organization is dealt with in Chapter 24.

Performance expectations

Arguably the central issue in measurement and control is what is communicated to managers in terms of performance expectations, and how they are rewarded and sanctioned for their success or failure to achieve their targets. The two issues are linked, and resources should be allocated to enable managers to perform as required and, at the same time, to motivate them.

Reed and Buckley (1988) argue that when this is handled effectively then strategy implementation through action plans can be proactive, and strategies can be adapted in line with changes in the environment. Where it is poorly thought through there is likely to be more reaction to events and external threats. Research indicates that this aspect of implementation is difficult to achieve, however.

Wernham (1984) contends that managers benefit from an appreciation of 'superordinate organizational goals' and the overall strategic perspective, and that any perceived internal inconsistencies between the performances expected of different managers can be demotivating. Communication and information systems should therefore seek to make managers aware about where the organization is going strategically and how well it is doing. Wernham's argument also implies that resource allocations and strategic priorities should be seen as fair and equitable, and that political activity to acquire or retain resources for the pursuit of personal objectives, or to support ineffective strategies, must be contained.

McMahon and Perrit (1973) have demonstrated that the effectiveness of managers in achieving their objectives is enhanced when the control levers are high, but Lawrence and Lorsch (1967) indicate that these controls also need to be loose and flexible if the environment is volatile.

It has been argued that resources are allocated through the budgeting process and that this establishes a quantitative short-term link between expectations and resources. It has also been argued that managers need to be aware of wider strategic issues, and that their attention should be focused on long-term strategies as well as short-term tactics and actions designed to bring immediate results. This necessitates that managers are aware of the key success factors for their products and business units, and of how their competitive environments are changing. Whilst it is important to achieve budget targets, it is also important that there is a continuing search for new ways of creating, improving and sustaining competitive advantage.

Reed and Buckley (1988) suggest that implementation can be made more effective by addressing the following issues:

☐ establishing the **strategic benefits** that the organization is hoping to achieve from particular strategic options – both immediate and long-term benefits
☐ clarifying the managerial actions which will be required if these benefits are to be attained, and using these as a basis for action plans
☐ incorporating the matching of resources with key success factors, and the development of sustainable competitive advantage, in the objectives and targets which are agreed with managers
☐ appraising and rewarding the ability of managers to contribute to the development of sustainable competitive advantage and not merely their ability to meet short-term budget targets
☐ ensuring that sufficient flexibility is built in.

These arguments emphasize that, whilst budgeting is essential for allocating resources on a short-term basis and progress against budget targets is a vital efficiency measure, organizational effectiveness also depends on longer-term flexibility. New developments and strategies, and improved ways of doing things, must also be considered. These may well involve changes in structures and policies as well as in the status of individual business units and managers. Issues in the implementation and management of change are the subject of Chapter 24.

The final section of this chapter looks at the deployment and commitment of resources to deal with crises.

CRISIS MANAGEMENT

Crisis management concerns the management of certain risks and future uncertainties.

Organizations should be ready to deal with both opportunities and surprises – resources should be managed to cope with unexpected and unlikely events in the organization's environment. E–V–R congruence again. It is important strategically because failure to deal effectively with crises can lead to losses of confidence, competitiveness, profits and market share.

Crisis management involves elements of planning and management. Planning constitutes crisis prevention or avoidance – the search for potential areas of risk, and decisions about reducing the risks. Management is being able to deal with crises if and when they occur.

The word *crisis* covers a number of different issues. Fires, fraud and computer failure are typical crises which might affect any organization almost any time. Poisoning scares or contamination with food products, and oil or chemical spillages, are foreseeable crises for particular companies. In relation to these there is an obvious logic in making contingency plans and being prepared.

In a different way, strategic changes can also lead to crises of confidence, particularly amongst employees. Rumours that a firm might be taken over often imply redundancies; falling sales and profits suggest possible cutbacks or closure. Good internal communications and openness are required to minimize the potential damage, especially as competitors might see these situations as competitive opportunities.

Decision areas

Simplified, there are three decision areas in determining the crisis strategy:

1. Decisions concerning what can go wrong, the probability of it happening, and the impact it will have if it does happen.
2. Crisis planning. Decisions about investing in prevention in order to reduce or minimize the risk. Invariably this implies cost

increases; and for this and other reasons less is often done than conceivably could be done.

3. Mechanisms for contingency management.

The decisions involve trade-offs between costs and risks in an attempt to find the best balance between areas 2 and 3. The successful management of crisis situations involves both awareness and the ability to deal effectively with unexpected change pressures.

Fire provides a useful example of these points. Fires are caused by such events as smoking, over-heating machinery and electrical faults. All of these are predictable. The likelihood of a fire happening will differ from situation to situation, and the potential damage will similarly vary. Smoking can be banned and all conceivable safety measures can be invested in, if necessary, in order to minimize the risks. However, these may not always be practical or affordable, and consequently detectors, sprinklers and fire doors to isolate areas are used as contingency measures. Nuclear power generation and airlines are examples of businesses which invest substantially in safety and prevention, often led by legislation. Situations are, however, frequently unclear. In 1991, following research after the 1985 fire on board a Boeing 737 at Manchester Airport, the Civil Aviation Authority ruled out the use of passenger smoke hoods on aircraft. The CAA argued they delayed the time required to evacuate an aircraft and thereby risked causing more deaths. The Consumers' Association is one group who disagreed, saying it was 'outraged' at the decision.

Crisis management

There are a number of identifiable steps in attempting to manage crises effectively:

☐ Initially it is necessary to identify the most obvious areas of risk.

☐ Following on from this, firms should establish procedures and policies for ensuring that risks do not become crises. Discussing possible scenarios, training sessions and actual rehearsals can all contribute, in addition to the investment in physical prevention.

☐ A crisis management team should be identified in advance, trained and prepared to step aside from all normal activities in the event of a crisis occurring. Experience suggests that the expertise required will be primarily communications and public relations, financial and legal. Clear leadership of the team by the strategic leader will be expected; and personnel, operations and marketing skills can be added as required. Secretarial support is sometimes overlooked.

☐ Building the team is one aspect of a planning process which should also cover how to get hold of key people over weekends and during holidays, how to restore critical facilities which might go down, and how to gain fast access to important regulatory bodies.

☐ Stakeholder analysis is another crucial aspect of the planning. It is vital to clarify which stakeholders are most likely to be affected by particular crises – and how. After a crisis customers either exhibit loyalty or switch to competitors; the confidence of distributors and the banks may also prove important. The media often play a significant role and their stance is likely to influence the confidence of other stakeholders. Where stakeholder perspectives and expectations differ it may be necessary to deal with each group on an individual basis.

Insurance brokers Sedgwick (1991) state that whilst 75% of Britain's largest companies claim to have contingency plans for dealing with sudden crises when they occur, few had plans to cover the follow-up implications. Plans should also be in hand for re-launching products which might have to be withdrawn and for dealing with investors and possible litigation. 'Most companies only find out about the cost of a crisis once it's over.'

☐ Finally, a clear communications strategy is essential. Ethical issues may be involved, and the company will be expected to be co-operative, open, honest, knowledgeable and consistent. They must be seen to be in control and not attempting to cover up. The media will want to know what has happened, why, and what the company intends to do about the situation. 'No comment' may well be interpreted as defensive or incompetent.

An effective information system will be required for gathering and disseminating the salient facts.

Strategies and examples

The most proactive strategy for crisis management can be compared with the notion of total quality management. The organization is looking for a culture where all employees think about the implications and risks in everything they do.

Reactions when a crisis has happened can prove to be effective or ineffective. Effective management is likely to mean that confidence is maintained and that there is no long-term loss of customers, market share or share price. Booth (1990) quotes research which indicates that this is more likely to happen in an open, flexible structure than it is in one which is bureaucratic.

Sandoz, the Swiss chemical company, was perceived as handling a crisis in 1986 ineffectively. Water used to fight a fire in a warehouse, possibly caused by arson, drained into the River Rhine because the local 'catch basins' were too small for the volume of water involved. The river was polluted. When pressed by the media Sandoz did not have important details readily available; and the company, the local authority and the

Swiss government put out contradictory statements. Considerable ill-feeling was manifested against the company; and it has been suggested that the incident led to a medium-term loss of confidence in both Sandoz and the Swiss chemical industry.

Kabak and Siomkos (1990) offer a spectrum of four reactive approaches. At one extreme (and normally ineffective) is denial of responsibility, arguing that the company is an innocent victim or that no harm has been done. Similarly, some organizations will attempt to pin the blame on identified individuals (who possibly did make mistakes), or argue that the general public must share the risks. Where individual errors do lead to crises there may well be a lack of effective organizational control systems; and equally the public can only be expected to share the risk if they have available all the information required for decision making. Much of this is likely to be exclusive to the company, and quite possibly buried away in files.

A better, but still ineffective, approach is involuntary regulatory compliance. Exxon's reluctant acceptance of responsibility after their tanker *Exxon Valdez* ran aground and spilled oil off north Alaska in 1989 is given as an example. The incident was the result of human error rather than poor systems, but the company is still held accountable.

Kabak and Siomkos offer Perrier as an excellent example of the third strategy – voluntary compliance. Here there is a positive company response towards meeting its responsibilities (see Case 23.5). The incident highlights that even though companies may have crisis management strategies a number of unforeseen difficulties are likely to be encountered.

The other extreme strategy is the so-called super effort, whereby the company does everything it can, openly and honestly, and stays in constant touch will all affected stakeholders. In 1982 an extortionist succeeded in introducing cyanide to packs of Tylenol in America. Tylenol is manufactured by Johnson and Johnson and at the time it was the country's leading pain-killer with a 35% market share. Six people died. All stocks were recalled immediately 'to contain the crisis and demonstrate responsibility'. The media were provided with constant up-to-date information. The product was re-launched in tamperproof containers and the associated heavy advertising featured the new containers rather than simply claiming the product was safe. The incident was costly, but market share was quickly regained. Some had suggested that Johnson and Johnson should drop the Tylenol brand name, but this was resisted. Interestingly the name *Townsend Thoresen* has been dropped by their parent company, P & O, after their ferry, *Herald of Free Enterprise*, capsized off Zeebrugge in 1987.

Whilst there is little argument against the logic of planning ahead of a crisis, some organizations are cautious about the extent to which one should attempt to plan.

> The scale of the Bhopal [Union Carbide chemical plant in India] disaster [gas leak in 1984] was unimaginable. There is simply no way anyone could have anticipated it.
> (Union Carbide Director of Corporate Communications quoted in Nash (1990))

Whilst the extent and magnitude of a disaster may be unexpected, events like Bhopal are predictable, often because there have been similar incidents in the past. Union Carbide argued that they tried to be as honest as they could, but they were limited by the lack of hard facts from a remote area of India. Nash

---

Case 23.5
PERRIER

In 1989 Perrier was the world leader in the fast-growing market for bottled water. In the UK, for example, the Perrier brand accounted for over one-third of the market for sparkling water, which represented 20% of the whole market. Perrier also own Buxton, which is second to Evian in the still-water segment. The name 'Perrier' had become synonymous with bottled water.

In February 1990 minute traces of Benzene were discovered in a sample during routine tests in North Carolina, America. The trace, six parts per billion, did not represent any discernible health risk. Within one week every Perrier brand worldwide had been withdrawn from sale. This amounted to 160 million bottles in 110 countries.

Even if it is madness, we decided to take Perrier off the market everywhere in the world. I don't want the least doubt, however small, to tarnish our product's image of quality and purity.

(Gustave Leven, then Chairman, Perrier)

[Leven, 77 years old in 1990, had built Perrier from a run-down business to world leadership over 40 years. He retired later in 1990.]

Perrier had created crisis management strategies some years earlier . . . 'Everyone knew what they were supposed to do . . . in spite of this we never, ever, imagined a worldwide withdrawal. We'd never dreamed of a problem of such magnitude.' Only Tylenol had previously been withdrawn on such a scale; and in that crisis people had died.

Continued overleaf

Actions in the UK

Local tests were arranged as soon as news spread from America. The tests took a normal 48 hours, and Benzene was again found in the sample. Unfortunately during this period a Perrier spokesman in Paris speculated prematurely that a greasy rag might have introduced the wrong cleaning fluid onto bottling equipment. Moreover, when the worldwide withdrawal was announced to the world's press in Paris – rather than local press conferences – the room was too small for the press and television crews attending.

On the following day advertisements appeared around the world, explaining the situation, and clarifying what people, including retailers, should do. The 24-hour emergency telephone network in the UK 'received mostly friendly calls'.

A major problem in the UK concerned the disposal of all the water and the further disposal or recycling of the bottles. A large proportion of the stocks were in the distinctive Perrier green glass, which, recycled, has few alternative uses.

The source of the contamination was quickly traced to a filter at the bottling plant in France, a filter used to purify carbon dioxide being added to the water. This revelation suggested that Perrier is not 100% naturally carbonated, although the label on the bottles stated 'naturally carbonated natural mineral water'. It transpired that the gas used is collected underground with the water and added back after purification. Only the gas, not the water, is purified. Nevertheless the publicity caused Sainsbury's to refuse to stock Perrier for a period after it was re-launched in April 1990.

One month after the re-launch Perrier was already selling at half its previous volume; and market leadership was quickly regained. The worldwide cost was estimated to be £125 million.

Competitors had not attempted to exploit the situation, possibly believing they might spread a scare by association and affect the market for all bottled water.

It has been suggested that the very popularity of Perrier had caused the problem. Demand world wide had put pressure on the supply side. Some years earlier, and before the increased consumer awareness and concern with health issues, the problem would probably have been contained on a smaller scale.

The balance of opinion seems to be that Perrier got the big decisions right. It adopted a worst case scenario, acted fast, and spoke out honestly.

Sources: Butler, D (1990) Perrier's painful period, *Management Today*, August; Caulkin, S (1990) Dangerous exposure, *Best of Business International*, Autumn.

comments that the organization appreciated the need to act quickly and develop effective communications, but, after the event, remained sceptical about establishing rigid guidelines, arguing that one can never be certain in advance about the actual nature and detail of any crisis.

SUMMARY

In this chapter we have considered a number of issues in the way that resources are allocated and controlled. Resources are required for strategy implementation, and their availability is a determinant of the

feasibility of a particular strategic option. However, the existence of resources does not guarantee the effective implementation of strategies. The way that resources are used and managed is also important. Policies are designed to guide the use of resources by managers; and budgets are used to allocate resources for particular activities and tasks. Budgets, however, are often short term in scope, and the measurement of performance against budget targets may be more an evaluation of efficiency than of longer-term strategic effectiveness.
Specifically we have

☐ considered how policies, functional strategies and action plans constitute the operational aspects of strategy implementation, and provide a means of measuring performance;
☐ discussed the need for corporate resource allocation to divisions, business units and functional departments, based on opportunity cost and designed to lead to the achievement of the overall corporate objectives;
☐ pointed out that the appropriate style of allocating corporate resources may be influenced by the rate of growth of the organization;
☐ examined the interrelationships between functions and illustrated the need to consider their interdependences when allocating resources;
☐ distinguished between policies, procedures, functional plans and budgets;
☐ looked at how policies might be created and used, the principle of good policies, and examples of policies in a number of functional areas;
☐ explored the role of budgeting in the allocation of resources, highlighting the thinking behind strategic and zero-base budgeting;
☐ considered a number of issues underpinning measurement and control systems;

☐ identified the main issues in crisis management.

CHECKLIST OF KEY TERMS AND CONCEPTS

You should feel confident that you understand the following terms and ideas:

☐ How strategies are made operational
☐ Corporate and functional resource planning
☐ Policies
☐ Budgets
☐ Efficiency and effectiveness issues in measurement and control
☐ Crisis management.

QUESTIONS AND RESEARCH ASSIGNMENTS

Text related

1. Should top management policies be essentially broad and general, and lower level policies narrow, explicit and rigid? Why? Why not?
2. What are the contributions and limitations of budgeting and the measurement of performance against budgets in the implementation of strategy and the monitoring of strategic effectiveness?
3. Referring back to Table 4.3, do you believe Amstrad has historically been an 'excellent' company, using the criteria suggested by Peters and Waterman in *In Search of Excellence*? Are they now moving away from the essence of the original business and the strengths upon which they grew?

Research and assignment based

4. For an organization that you are familiar with, ascertain the main stated policies for finance, production, personnel and marketing.

   How are these policies used? How were they created? How do they rate in terms of the principles of good policies discussed in the text?

5. Ascertain the budgeted resources and targets allocated to one manager you are able to interview.

   What measures of performance are utilized? What feedback is provided? What does the manager do with the feedback?

   What do you believe is the personal impact of the budget and measures of performance on the manager? Is he or she motivated? Rewarded or sanctioned for success or failure?

6. By contacting either a local councillor or a financial executive ascertain how planning and budgeting is managed in your local authority. What have been the priority areas in the past? What are the current priorities? How have the changes in priority been decided?

7. In November 1991 (event: 13 November; Press reports: 14 November) SmithKline Beecham withdrew Lucozade from shops in the UK following a contamination alert.

   Research the incident and assess how effectively the crisis was handled.

RECOMMENDED FURTHER READING

The following two books are useful references on the conversion of strategies into operational and functional plans:

Murdick, R G, Eckhouse, R H, Moor, R C and Steiner, G A (1979) Strategic Planning, Free Press, Chapters 11–13.

Zimmerer, T W (1976) Business Policy: A Framework for Analysis, Grid.

REFERENCES

Booth, S (1990) Dux at the Crux, Management Today, May.

Bower, J L (1970) Managing the Resource Allocation Process: A Study of Corporate Planning and Investment, Division of Research, Harvard Business School.

Done, K (1992) Winter of despair, spring of hope, Financial Times 17 February.

Ishikawa, A (1985) Strategic Budgeting: A Comparison Between US and Japanese Companies, Praeger.

Kabak, I W and Siomkos, G J (1990) How can an industrial crisis be managed effectively? Industrial Engineering, June.

Koontz, H and O'Donnell, C (1968) Principles of Management, 4th edn, McGraw-Hill.

Lawrence, P R and Lorsch, J W (1967) Organisation and Environment, Richard D Irwin.

McMahon, J T and Perrit, G W (1973) Toward a contingency theory of organisational control, Academy of Management Journal, 16.

Nash, T (1990) Tales of the unexpected, The Director, March.

Pearce, J A and Robinson, R B (1985) Strategic Management, 2nd edn, Richard D Irwin.

Reed, R and Buckley, M R (1988) Strategy and action: techniques for implementing strategy, Long Range Planning, 21 (3).

Sedgwick (1991) Research quoted in de Jonquières, G (1991) Taking the drama out of a crisis, Financial Times, 14 November.

Seed, A H (1983) New approaches to asset management, Journal of Business Strategy, Winter.

Wernham, R (1984) Bridging the awful gap between strategy and action, Long Range Planning, 17.

MANAGING CHANGE

24

LEARNING OBJECTIVES

After studying this chapter you should be able to

☐ describe the major forces for change and types of change situation;
☐ explain why people frequently resist change;
☐ summarize alternative ways of overcoming resistance;
☐ identify a number of different approaches to the planned management of change;
☐ contrast planned change with emergent change in a learning organization;
☐ assess the importance of power and how it is used in change situations;
☐ describe ways in which managers can improve their political effectiveness in organizations.

In this chapter we look at various issues and problems in the management of change. It is stressed that organizations must be reactive to external change pressures and proactive in seeking to take advantage of opportunities and shape their environment if they are to be effective strategically. Cultural and power considerations are important variables in the management of change.

INTRODUCTION

There is nothing more difficult to take in hand, more perilous to conduct, or more uncertain in its success than to take the lead in the introduction of a new order of things.
(Machiavelli)

Organizations and managers face change on a continuous basis, especially in volatile environments. Some changes are reactions to external threats; others are proactive attempts to seize opportunities and manage the environment. Organizations should seek to obtain and maintain a congruence between their environment, values and resources, making changes when there are pressures from either the environment or their resources. It is crucial that organizations seek to create and sustain competitive advantage, and wherever possible innovate to improve their competitive position. This implies a readiness to change within the organization and the ability to implement the proposed changes.

At times there will be a perceived need to try and change values and culture. In the last decade of the twentieth century the pressures for change in a wide cross-section of businesses are clearly visible. Food manufacturers and distributors are affected by changing consumer attitudes to their diets and by the public reaction and concern to the growing awareness of incidences of food poisoning. Building societies and banks are responding to changes in the competitive regulations which directly affect them, generally seeing the changes as opportunities. The water authorities and electricity industries have followed a number of other corporations into privatization, which is forcing major changes of strategy, resource management and culture. Organizations within the umbrella of the National Health Service are responding to new proposals and legislation on controls and performance measures. Some National Health Service employees see the changes as threats, others as opportunities.

Effective organizations must be able to **manage change,** with managers and employees supportive rather than resistant or hostile. When strategies change, there are often accompanying changes in structures and responsibilities, and people are clearly affected. Kotter and Schlesinger (1979) and Waterman (1987) suggest that most companies or divisions need to make moderate organizational changes at least every year, with major changes every four or five years.

Whilst organizational changes can be reactive and forced by external change, effective strategic management really requires **learning.** Managers must be aware of their environment, assessing trends and deciding in advance what should be done about perceived opportunities and threats. Planning activities and systems should ensure that the future is considered, and the result-

ant plans should encompass the implementation aspects of any proposed changes and the need to be flexible to accommodate unexpected changes. Moreover, innovation should be possible within the organization. Managers should be constantly looking for ways of being more effective and able to proceed with appropriate changes.

Hence the implementation of change requires:

☐ **a perceived need for change** – this can originate with either the strategic leader or managers throughout the company who are aware of the possibilities;
☐ **the necessary resources** – which involves aspects of skills as well as physical resources, and the ways in which managers use power to influence the allocation and utilization of resources;
☐ **commitment** – the culture of the organization will influence the extent to which managers are responsive and innovative.

The forces for and against change and the types and implications of change will be discussed first, and the various issues involved in implementing change successfully will be explored. We consider a number of alternative strategies for the management of change and examine the crucial underpinning aspects of power and politics. Managers who wish to make changes, and through these changes adapt strategies, must be strategically aware and politically effective. Sources of personal power and political tactics will be examined.

ISSUES IN THE MANAGEMENT OF CHANGE

It was mentioned in the introduction that organizations face change pressures from the environment, and the significance, regularity and impact of these pressures will be determined by the complexity and volatility of the environment. At the same time managers may see opportunities and wish to adapt existing strategies. There are therefore a number of forces which encourage change, and a variety of different change situations. Change, though, affects people, their jobs and responsibilities and their existing behaviour patterns. It can also lead to changes in the underlying culture of the organization. For these reasons people may be wary or even hostile. This is increasingly likely if they fail to understand the reasoning behind the proposed changes and if they personally feel that they are losing rather than gaining from the changes. The various forces for change, the reasons why people resist change, and an outline framework for the effective management of change are considered in this section.

Forces for change

Five major forces for change are as follows.

☐ *Technical obsolescence and technical improvements* Technical change pressures can stem from outside the organization in the form of new developments by competitors and the availability of new technologies which the organization might wish to harness. Internal research and development and innovatory ideas from managers can generate technical change internally. In high technology companies and industries, and particularly where product life cycles are becoming shorter, this can be a very significant issue. Some organizations follow product strategies built around short life cycles, product obsolescence (both physical and design) and persuading customers to replace the product regularly. A number of service businesses also find this a useful strategy.

☐ *Political and social events* Many of these change pressures will be outside the control of the firm, but companies will be forced to respond. In the mid-to-late 1980s there had been considerable pressure on companies not to trade with South Africa,

and in the late 1980s increased public awareness of environmental issues placed pressure on certain firms. Government encouragement for the use of lead-free petrol, in the form of both media coverage and price advantages from lower taxation, has forced car manufacturers to respond. New cars are capable of running on both leaded and lead-free petrol; conversion kits for older cars have had to be developed. The impact of the European market in 1992 has been a well-publicized change pressure, and whilst some organizations made very few changes in preparation others considered major changes in corporate and competitive strategies.

☐ *The tendency for large organizations and markets to become increasingly global* Whilst this again has provided opportunities and new directions of growth for many organizations, others have been forced to respond to changing competitive conditions. The growing incidence of joint ventures and strategic alliances, discussed in Chapter 18, is a feature of this.

☐ *Increases in the size, complexity and specialization of organizations* The growth of organizations, linked to internal changes of structure, creates pressure for further changes. Large complex specialist organizations have made increasing use of information technology in their operations, introducing automation and JIT systems. These create a need for greater specialist expertise from both managers and other employees, possibly necessitating training and changes in their jobs. Effective use of these technological opportunities also requires greater co-operation and co-ordination between functions and managers.

Good figures are like bayonets. You can't just sit on them.

Sir Peter Gibbings, Chairman, Anglia Television

Table 24.1 Levels of change

Need	Level of change	Approaches/tactics
New mission; different 'ways of doing things'	Values; culture; styles of management	Organizational development
New corporate perspective/ strategy	Objectives; corporate strategy	Strategic planning
	Organization structure	New organization design
Improved competitive effectiveness (existing products and services)	Competitive strategies; systems and management roles	Empowerment; management by objectives; performance management; job descriptions; policies
Improved efficiencies	Functional strategies; organization of tasks	Method study; job enrichment

☐ *The greater strategic awareness and skills of managers and employees* Able and ambitious managers, and employees who want job satisfaction and personal challenges, need opportunities for growth within the organization. These can be promotion opportunities or changes in the scope of jobs. Such changes require both strategic development and growth by the company, and appropriate styles of non-autocratic leadership.

From considering these general change forces we now briefly mention a number of issues which have a significant contemporary impact on the competitive activity of organizations.

The current dynamics of change

The strategic environment, especially competitive forces, determines how proactive and change oriented an organization must be if it is to be effective. Whilst the forces and their relative intensity vary between industries and organizations, Peters (1989) suggests that several factors require that most organizations must be receptive to the need for change. Specifically he highlights the following.

☐ The general dynamics and uncertainty of world economies.
☐ Time horizons, which he argues can be a strategic weapon in the face of uncertainty. It was discussed earlier how successful retailers are using information technology to monitor demand changes very quickly and to build distribution systems which allow them to respond to changes. As product life cycles shorten, the development time for new products must also be cut.
☐ Organization structures must be designed to enable decisions to be made quickly.
☐ Quality, design and service – which must be responsive to customer perceptions and competitor activities – are essential for competitive advantage.

Levels of change

Change decisions can be categorized in terms of their significance to the organization and the appropriate level of intervention. See Table 24.1. The five levels form a vertical hierarchy, and it is crucial to clarify and tackle needs and problems appropriately. If the problem is one of operating efficiencies, then the intervention should be at functional strategy level – but this alone would be inadequate for dealing with higher order needs. As one ascends the hierarchy the challenges and difficulties increase – as we saw in Chapter 4, changing the culture of the organization can be slow and problematical. Structural changes can sometimes be difficult to implement as well, particularly where individuals perceive themselves to be losing rather than benefiting.

In recent years the recession-hit high street banks have introduced major changes in an attempt to protect and consolidate their profits, and these have systematically moved up to the highest level. A variety of approaches have been used to improve productivity and reduce costs, but this alone was inadequate. The services provided to customers have been reviewed, resulting, for example, in new branch interiors and the introduction of personal bankers and specialist advisers. These changes have been linked to re-structuring, the closure of some small branches, job losses and increased market segmentation of business clients. More recently the banks have re-thought their corporate strategies, having pursued growth through diversification and overseas expansion during the early 1980s. Concentration on core activities is now preferred. Finally it is anticipated that during the 1990s the cultural focus will see a reduced emphasis on image and marketing and a return to the more productive utilization of assets, harnessing information technology, in order to improve margins.

A number of the high street clearing banks provide excellent illustrations of how companies in the financial services sector, which diversified in an attempt to benefit from new opportunities in the 1980s, were exposed in the recession. Departures from their mainstream activities proved costly. Following deregulation in 1986 National Westminster, aiming to become a truly global bank, opened County Nat West (an investment bank) in the UK and also entered the American market. Compounded by the 1987 stock market crash, County was unprofitable. Like Midland Bank (which lost heavily after acquiring Crocker [bank] in the US) Nat West's American venture was unsuccessful. TSB similarly entered merchant banking by buying Hill Samuel in 1987 – initial profits became losses in 1990 and 1991.

Case 24.1, National Power, categorizes the changes which followed privatization. Concentration is again preferred to diversification.

Types of change

Summarizing these points, Daft (1983) specifies four basic types of change which affect organizations:

☐	**Technology**	production processes
☐	**The product or service**	the output of the business
☐	**Administrative changes**	structure; policies; budgets; reward systems
☐	**People**	attitudes; expectations; behaviour

Invariably a change in one of these factors will place demands for change on one or more of the others.

When an organization decides to launch a new product it may also need to invest in new technology, modify its existing production plant and either acquire people with, or train existing employees in, the new skills required.

Major changes in the strategic perspective, say the acquisition of a similar sized firm, will force changes in the organization structure, which in turn necessitates changes in jobs and behaviour patterns.

However necessary the changes may be, and however ready the organization might be to implement them, the outcomes will not necessarily be positive for everyone affected.

Case 24.1
NATIONAL POWER

National Power is the larger of the two electricity **generating** companies created when the industry was privatized in 1991. The rival company is Powergen. Electricity **distribution** to domestic and business customers is the responsibility of 12 regional companies which were sold to private shareholders.

The privatization necessitated a series of changes which affected the whole organization:

Culture	Prior to privatization electricity generation was seen as bureaucratic and committee-led. Engineers and engineering considerations took priority over the interests of customers. The new culture is more commercial and entrepreneurial, service receives high priority and managers are empowered.
Corporate strategy	There has been a switch of emphasis from coal-fired stations to gas; and some coal-burning stations have already been closed. In addition, more imported coal is being used, which increases the impact upon British Coal. When the industry was nationalized political interests and pressures protected the domestic coal industry. Nuclear power stations, incidentally, were not included in the privatization.
Structure	National Power was organized into 35 separate power stations, each a profit centre. The station managers were made more accountable. The idea is that National Power acts as a sort of middleman, fulfilling demand from its customers (the distribution companies) by buying from selected power stations. Each power station in the organization bids by offering electricity at a certain price – National Power then starts with the lowest price bid and works up until it can satisfy all its customers. The price it actually pays all the selected power stations is that of the highest bid it accepts.
Competitive strategy	A monopoly has been replaced by two rival generating companies who compete for the same business. In the new competitive market anyone may seek a licence to generate electricity and sell it into the distribution system. 'The prices offered by the generating companies are determined mainly by competitive forces now operating in the marketplace.'
Functional strategies	Cost cutting is in progress to improve productivity. The number of jobs was reduced from 16 000 to 15 000 at privatization with further reductions to follow.

Case 24.2
APPLE COMPUTER

Apple was started in 1976 by two young entrepreneurs, Steven Jobs and Stephen Wozniak, who began by making personal computers in a garage. In 1983 the company's turnover, from essentially one model – the distinctive Apple computer – was approaching $1 billion. At this stage in the company's development Wozniak had already left and Jobs had been quoted as saying that he was no longer able to do what he most enjoyed – working with a small group of talented designers to create new innovative products. To overcome his frustration with an increasingly bureaucratic organization Jobs had formed a new team of designers and set about developing the company's second major product, the Apple Macintosh, away from corporate headquarters and the production plant. The Macintosh was regarded as very user friendly and featured an illustrated screen menu and a hand-held mouse unit for giving instructions. It was launched in 1984 and sold immediately.

John Sculley was appointed Apple President in 1983 and took over executive control. His initial priorities were to co-ordinate product development activities, which he felt were fragmented, and to integrate these developments with existing programmes. To achieve this, power was centralized more than it had been in the past and was supported by formalized reporting procedures and new financial control systems.

Sculley was regarded as being more marketing oriented than Jobs, and their business philosophies clashed. Jobs resigned in 1985, together with a number of other key employees, deciding to concentrate his efforts on the development of sophisticated personal computers for university students in a small, entrepreneurial organization environment.

Despite the increased business discipline, Sculley has attempted to preserve important aspects of the original Apple culture. Informal dress codes, a 'fun working environment' and elaborate celebrations when targeted milestones are reached were all considered important. Apple has retained a structure with few layers of management, few perks and few status-carrying job titles.

Sculley's challenge was to move the company away from an informal and entrepreneurial management style to a more functional and more recently (1988) a divisionalized structure, whilst retaining the important aspects of the culture. In addition Sculley felt that Apple needed to be re-positioned in the market in order to overcome the competitive threats from the Far East.

With new versions of the Macintosh, Apple has moved from an education and home computer base into a business computer company which also sells to schools and universities. Apple was a major innovator in desk-top publishing, pioneering the market in advance of competition from IBM and Xerox.

Apple prospered in the late 1980s, but its strategy began to appear inappropriate for the recession and the 1990s. Apple had concentrated on, and succeeded with, high-margin products which were substantially differentiated. However, Sculley claimed Apple's ideas were being copied and used in cheaper rival products – Apple has a

Continued overleaf

legal action pending against Microsoft's *Windows* software for allegedly using ideas from the Macintosh. Moreover, personal computers are becoming more of a commodity product in a maturing market.

In 1991 Apple agreed a series of strategic alliances, mostly with IBM, historically its main rival. The alliances concentrate on areas where Apple lacks either development skills or the ability to fund the research and development independently. New personal computer technology and operating systems software are key areas.

Coincidental with their agreements with the global IBM, Apple's culture has been changing. Empowerment, flexibility and freedom will remain important, but 'there must be more discipline. Our cost structure was out of line. We did not know how to meet schedules. We were a benevolent company that sponsored people to work on things they were interested in' (Sculley).

Apple has reduced the prices of its existing products, hoping for higher volumes which will more than compensate for the lower margins, and introduced a range of cheaper, lower-performance Macintosh machines. In terms of new products Apple was said to be two years late with its lap-top computer but now has a number of innovatory ideas in the pipeline. Future new products will concentrate on personal electronics devices and include a notebook computer and electronic books. In addition, Apple's *Newton* is scheduled for launch in 1993. Essentially Newton is a 7″ × 4½″ black box with a 5″ × 3″ screen. Users jot down ideas on the screen and draw sketches as they talk and think, and record notes and appointments. The machine can translate the images, store and organize. In addition, electronic data, such as a map, can be input.

Sources: A profile on Steven Jobs in Gray, E R and Smeltzer, L R (1989) *Management: The Competitive Edge*, Macmillan; Thomas, D (1987) And then the hard part, *Financial Times*, 27 July; Oram, R (1988) Apple decentralises into four autonomous groups, *Financial Times*, 24 August; Kupfer, A (1992) Apple's plan to survive and grow, *Fortune*, 4 May; Kehoe, L (1992), Feel the force, *Financial Times*, 29 May.

Case 24.2, Apple Computer, considers the changes which Apple had to make to deal with the problems created, first, by its own growth and success, and more recently by a loss of competitiveness. These changes appear to have been beneficial to the organization as a whole, but have caused the company's founder to leave and establish a new venture, as well as involve Apple in alliances with a leading (and stronger) competitor.

The change process

Change frequently disrupts normality. Job security seems threatened; existing behaviour patterns and values are questioned; people are required to be more flexible and to take more risks. Whilst the organization may be facing strong external pressures it is unrealistic to expect managers and other employees not to query or resist the need to change. This is particularly true if individuals feel threatened, or perceive themselves to be losing out rather than benefiting or not being rewarded in some way for co-operating.

It is important to encourage people to recognize the need for change, the benefits, and the external threats from not changing. Managed change should be planned and evolutionary, although some organizations have attempted to become more flexible such that people not only accept change, but constantly seek new opportunities for change and improvement. Although change can be speedy and dynamic – normally when it is forced by powerful external influences – managing change positively in a growth situation, taking advantage of opportunities rather than responding to threats, requires that the process begins gradually and on a limited scale, and then spreads. Advancement needs consolidation and learning. The innovation stage, which can easily go wrong, requires that the change agents (who will not always be the strategic leader) find powerful and influential allies and supporters. Time and effort must be invested in explaining, justifying and persuading. Trial and error leads to incremental learning. Early supporters should be visibly rewarded for their commitment, and this will encourage others and begin to consolidate the changes. Conservative people are inevitably going to be late joiners; and some older people, together with those who are very set in their ways, are likely to be laggards. Because changes can be slow to take off they often appear to be failing once the process is well under way. This will renew opposition and resistance. During the process it is important to continue to monitor the environment. The programme may need amendment if circumstances alter.

Resistance to change

There are a number of reasons why change pressures might be resisted, and certain circumstances where the implementation of change will have to be planned carefully and the needs of people considered.

☐ Some resistance can be expected where people have worked out ways of doing things which are beneficial to them in terms of **their** objectives and preferences. They may see change as a threat. Simi-

larly, when people have mastered tasks and feel in control of their jobs and responsibilities, they are likely to feel relatively safe and secure personally. Again change may be perceived as a threat to their security, although the aim might be to ensure the security of the organization as a whole.

☐ Resistance to 'sideways change' (expanding certain activities whilst contracting elsewhere) is likely unless the people affected are fully aware of the reasons and implications.

☐ Where particular policies, behaviour patterns and ways of doing things have been established and accepted for a long time and in effect have become part of the culture of the organization, change will require careful implementation. The need for change may not be accepted readily.

☐ It is not unusual for people to have some fear of the unknown and to feel comfortable with situations, policies and procedures they know. Awareness and understanding is therefore an important aspect of change.

☐ The organization itself, or particular managers, may resist external pressures if the change involves considerable expense, investment in new equipment and the associated risks. This issue can be exacerbated where there has previously been substantial investment in plant and equipment which technically is still satisfactory. Although demand may be falling there may be a reluctance to sell or close.

☐ Resistance is likely to be forthcoming where there are perceived flaws or weaknesses in the proposal. Change decisions

---

Remember, it is not always the man on the shopfloor who opposes change. It can be the second or third tier of management who are the most reactionary.

Sir Peter Gibbings, Chairman, Anglia Television

may be made by the strategic leader and then delegated for implementation. Managers who are closer to the market may have some justified reservations if they have not been consulted during the formulation process.

The opposition may be to the change itself, or to the proposed means of implementation. Both can and must be overcome if changes are to be implemented successfully.

Casualties are, however, possible and sometimes inevitable. Some people will leave because they are uncomfortable with the changes.

Kotter and Schlesinger (1979) have identified six ways of overcoming resistance to change, and these are described in Box 24.1. They suggest that each method has both advantages and disadvantages and can be appropriate in particular circumstances. Issues raised by some of these alternatives are developed further in this chapter. Organizational development is considered as an approach to gaining support through active participation by managers on a continuous basis; manipulative approaches are discussed as a 'machiavellian' use of power and influence. In the next section we consider a number of general aspects in the management of change before specific strategies are discussed in more detail.

Implementing change: a general overview

Effective change occurs when managers and employees modify their behaviour in a desired or desirable way, and when the important changes are lasting rather than temporary.

Lewin (1947) contends that permanent changes in behaviour involve three aspects: unfreezing previous behaviour, changing, and then refreezing the new patterns. These three stages are crucial if changes in culture are required.

Unfreezing is the readiness to acquire or learn new behaviour. People are willing to accept that existing strategies and ways of doing things could be improved and made more effective. Normally this needs a trigger such as declining sales or profits, or the threat of closure or acquisition.

Change occurs when people who perceive the need for change try out new ideas. The changes could be introduced gradually or they may be more dramatic. Choosing the appropriate change strategy once the need is clarified may involve the selection of one from a number of alternatives, and consequently there are opportunities for involving the people who are most likely to be affected. Power structures are likely to be altered and consequently resistance might be evident from certain people.

Particularly where the pressures for change are significant, and the likely impact of the changes will be dramatic and felt widely throughout the organization, the change strategy will need a champion. Organizations in difficulty quite often appoint a new strategic leader to introduce fresh ideas and implement the changes. Newcomers are unlikely to be associated with the strategies which now need changing. Similarly, general managers might be moved to different business units when strategic changes are necessary.

No positive changes will occur within a company unless the Chief Executive realizes that people are basically opposed to change. A climate for change must be created in people's minds.

Changes need to be planned and everyone must be reassured that these changes will be for the betterment of the company, its employees, customers and shareholders.

Changes have therefore to be managed against a set of objectives and to a timetable.

Jacques G. Margry, Group Chief Executive, Parker Pen Ltd

Box 24.1
SIX WAYS OF OVERCOMING RESISTANCE TO CHANGE

EDUCATION AND COMMUNICATION

Education and communication should help people understand the logic and the need for change. A major drawback can be the inherent time delays and logistics when a lot of people are involved. It also requires mutual trust.

PARTICIPATION AND INVOLVEMENT

The contention is that people will be more supportive of the changes if they are involved in the formulation and design. Again it can be time consuming; and if groups are asked to deliberate and make decisions there is a risk that some decisions will be compromises leading to suboptimization.

FACILITATION AND SUPPORT

This can involve either training or counselling but there is no guarantee that any resistance will be overcome.

NEGOTIATION AND AGREEMENT

Negotiation and agreement are normally linked to incentives and rewards. Where the resistance stems from a perceived loss as a result of the proposed change, this can be useful, particularly where the resisting force is powerful. However, offering rewards every time changes in behaviour are desired is likely to prove impractical.

MANIPULATION AND CO-OPTATION

This encompasses covert attempts to influence people, for example by the selective use of information and conscious structuring of events. Co-optation involves 'buying-off' informal leaders by personal reward or status. These methods are ethically questionable, and they may well cause grievances to be stored for the future.

EXPLICIT AND IMPLICIT COERCION

The use of threats can work in the short run but is unlikely to result in long-term commitment.

Source: Kotter, J P and Schlesinger, L A (1979) Choosing strategies for change, *Harvard Business Review*, March–April.

Refreezing takes place when the new behaviour patterns are accepted and followed willingly. People are supportive and con-vinced of the wisdom of the changes; ideally the new approaches become established within the culture. Rewards are often

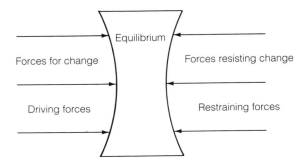

Figure 24.1   Force field analysis. Derived from Lewin, K (1951) *Field Theory in Social Sciences*, Harper and Row.

influential in ensuring that refreezing does in fact take place.

Throughout the change process it is important that people are **aware** of why changes are being proposed and are taking place, and that they **understand** the reasons. The key issues are participation, involvement and commitment.

Margerison and Smith (1989) suggest that the management of change exhibits four key features:

☐ **dissatisfaction** with the present strategies and styles
☐ **vision** of the better alternative – a clear picture of the desired state which can be communicated and explained to others (this again emphasizes the need for a champion of the change)
☐ a **strategy** for implementing the change and attaining the desired state
☐ **resistance** to the proposals at some stage.

Force field analysis

Lewin (1951) has proposed that changes result from the impact of a set of driving forces upon restraining forces. Figure 24.1 illustrates Lewin's theme of a state of equilibrium which is always under some pressure to change. The extent to which it does change will depend upon whether the driving forces or the restraining forces prove to be stronger.

The driving forces, which may be external or internal in origin, are likely to have economic aspects. There may be a need to increase sales, to improve profitability, to improve production efficiencies, to generate new forms of competitive advantage. Corporate, competitive and functional strategies may appear in need of change, but existing strategies may have people who are loyal and committed to them. People will be affected and may feel concerned. Any resistance will constitute a restraining force, seeking to abandon or modify the change proposals.

Although the driving forces will be concerned with improving organizational efficiency and effectiveness, the opposition is more likely to stem from personal concerns than from disagreement that improved efficiency and effectiveness are desirable. Lewin suggests that the driving forces are

A nursing team in a geriatric hospital wanted the seats of the toilets raised for the comfort of their patients. Hospital management was silent to their pleas. The team re-presented their request and argued that the change would reduce the amount of laundry and in turn the laundry bills. The proposal was approved and implemented.

Anecdote told by Christine Hancock,
General Secretary, Royal College of Nursing

based more on logic and the restraining forces on emotion. However, people who are aware of the situation may seek to argue their opposing case in relation to the relative ability of the change proposal to achieve the required improvements. As a result the ensuing debate concentrates on these issues. The opponents may choose not to be honest and open about their personal fears, feeling that their arguments must concentrate on the economic issues. When this happens the decision, whatever it might be, has not encompassed important underlying behavioural issues.

Effective managers of change situations will be clearly aware of both the driving forces and the real restraining forces. They will seek to strengthen the justifications by communication and explanation and diffuse opposition by exploring the likely impact with the people affected.

In this section we have looked generally at the issues which affect and under-pin the management of change. Lewin's force field analysis is particularly helpful for establishing a holistic view of the change situation in terms of cause and likely effect. From this a clearer strategy for implementing the change can emerge. A number of strategies are explored in the following section. Where the extent of the change is substantial, and changes in culture are involved, it is important to ensure that the new behaviour patterns are permanent rather than temporary.

STRATEGIES FOR IMPLEMENTATION AND CHANGE

It is possible to view implementation as an activity which follows strategy formulation – structures and systems are changed to accommodate changes in strategy. However, implementation, instead of following formulation, may be considered in depth at the same time as the proposed strategy is thought through and before final decisions are made. This is more likely to happen where a number of managers, especially those who will be involved in implementation, are consulted when the strategy is evaluated. Strategies, as has been pointed out earlier, may evolve from the operation of the organization structure. Where managers are encouraged to be innovatory and make incremental changes, elements of trial and error and small change decisions are often found. Implementation and formulation operate simultaneously; the changes are contained rather than dramatic and resistance may similarly be contained. Innovatory organizations can develop change orientation as part of the culture. People expect things to change regularly and accept changes.

Bourgeois and Brodwin (1984) have identified five distinct basic approaches to strategy implementation and strategic change.

☐ The strategic leader, possibly using expert planners or enlisting planning techniques, defines changes of strategy and then hands over to senior managers for implementation. The strategic leader is primarily a thinker/planner rather than a doer.

☐ The strategic leader again decides major changes of strategy and then considers the appropriate changes in structure, personnel, and information and reward systems if the strategy is to be implemented effectively. Quinn (1988) contends that the strategic leader may reveal the strategy gradually and incrementally as he or she seeks to gather support during implementation. This theme is developed later in this section.

In both these cases the strategic leader needs to be powerful as both involve top-down strategic change.

☐ The strategic leader and his or her senior managers (divisional heads, business unit general managers or senior functional managers) meet for lengthy discussions with a view to formulating proposed strategic changes. All the managers are briefed and knowledgeable, and the aim is to reach decisions to which they will all be committed. Strategies agreed at the meetings are then implemented by the managers who have been instrumental in their formulation. Whilst this approach involves several managers it is still primarily centralized.

☐ The strategic leader concentrates on establishing and communicating a clear mission and purpose for the organization. He or she seeks to pursue this through a decentralized structure by developing an appropriate organization culture and establishing an organization-wide unity of purpose. Whilst the strategic leader will retain responsibility for changes in the strategic perspective, decisions concerning competitive and functional strategy changes are decentralized to general and functional managers who are constrained by the mission, culture and policies established by the strategic leader.

Case 24.3, Trafalgar House, provides an interesting example of an organization which clearly separates the creation and implementation of changes in the corporate strategy and strategic perspective from on-going operational issues. Whilst the chairman is the key thinker behind the strategies, his chief executive is responsible for on-going performance

---

To many, uncertainty is a shadow of the unknown, to be avoided; far better, as we are stuck with an uncertain world, is to look upon it as the spice of life.

Sir Peter Holmes, Chairman, Shell UK

Teach people that change is inevitable and, if embraced, can be fun.

Leslie Hill, Chairman and Chief Executive, Central Independent Television plc

---

matters. Features of the first and fourth approaches above are both evident.

☐ Managers throughout the organization are widely encouraged to be innovative and come up with new ideas for change. The strategic leader establishes a framework for evaluating these proposals – recognizing that those which are accepted and resourced result in increased status for the managers concerned.

These basic approaches highlight a number of general themes and ideas which are considered below.

Ideas for change can start at the bottom of the organization rather than always at the top; and change can be seen as both a clearly managed process and the incremental outcome of the decisions taken in an innovative, change-oriented organization where managers are empowered. The term **learning organization** (see Box 24.2) is often used to describe the latter. The issues involved in trying to create an effective learning organization are explored in Case 24.4.

Top-down strategic change

A number of approaches can be involved in drawing up the strategic plans for the organization, but changes in strategy are ultimately centralized decisions. This approach can be both popular and viable as long as the strategies which are selected can be implemented effectively. It was mentioned earlier that resistance can be expected if managers who are charged with carrying out changes in strategy feel that there are flaws in the proposals. It is important to ensure that the appropriate level of consultation takes place during formulation.

Capable managers are needed throughout the organization to deal with operational issues, and the quality of the information systems which under-pin the planning is a

Case 24.3
TRAFALGAR HOUSE

This case describes the implementation aspects of the Trafalgar House strategy outlined in Case 18.1.

Trafalgar House was begun in the 1950s by Sir Nigel Broackes as a property company. After diversifying through acquisition into construction, Trafalgar merged with another construction company, Bridge Walker, in 1967. Bridge Walker was owned by Victor Matthews, and the financial director was Eric Parker. Both joined Trafalgar. Matthews became Chief Executive, a post which he held until 1982 when he was succeeded by Parker. Matthews left when Trafalgar floated off Fleet Holdings, the division based on the acquisition of Beaverbrook Newspapers (*Daily Express* and *Sunday Express*) and a diversification which had proved unpopular with shareholders.

The three men had very different backgrounds, personalities, interests and skills, but they have been able to work together effectively. By making distinct and individual contributions they have ensured that over a lengthy period both strategy creation and implementation have been generally effective − but separated.

Sir Nigel Broackes has been the chief creator of strategy throughout 30 plus years of the company and the entrepreneurial driving force behind the acquisitions and diversification. He is reported to have had little interest in day-to-day operational aspects. Matthews (who became Lord Matthews) was a strong hands-on manager who enjoyed both operational details and challenges. He was particularly skilled at turning around companies which were under-performing. Parker was originally a management accountant and he has been responsible for a set of control systems which allows divisions and subsidiary businesses to operate autonomously with their own boards and chief executives. Trafalgar House retains only a small head office structure, but reporting back by the decentralized units takes place frequently.

Although Matthews enjoyed running certain of the newly acquired businesses for a limited period until they were effectively turned around, the Trafalgar House implementation strategy involves performance targets and control systems which encourage managers to act independently. Typically on acquisition Trafalgar has dismissed the most senior managers and promoted others that they have identified as promising. These promotions, rewards and performance targets are used as motivators, and non-performance is likely to be sanctioned. As a result Broackes has been free to pursue a number of other external interests. From 1979 to 1984 he was Chairman of the London Docklands Development Corporation.

Case 18.1 describes how Trafalgar House became vulnerable to acquisition itself and why Hongkong Land posed a threat late in 1992. As part of TH's defensive strategy Sir Nigel Broackes relinquished the Chairmanship and became Life President, effectively an honorary consultant. Sir Eric Parker stepped down as Chief Executive, to be replaced internally.

crucial issue. The approach is attractive to strategic leaders who are inclined more towards the analytical aspects of strategy than they are towards behavioural issues.

Quinn's incremental model

Whilst Quinn's model is another primarily top-down approach it suggests a high degree of political skill on the part of the strategic leader, who appreciates the difficulties involved in implementing change. These

---

The management of Change within *any* company usually fails for only one reason: an inadequate understanding on the part of top management of how much continuing effort – in years, not months – is needed from all senior managers on the basis of personal, engaged, hands-on commitment rather than just soothing memoranda. Without the willingness for this engagement, do not even think of embarking on the harnessing of Change to bring positive results within any company.

Sir Colin Marshall, Chief Executive, British Airways plc

---

skills are discussed in detail towards the end of the chapter.

Quinn (1988) argues that the hardest part of strategic management is implementation as transition and change impacts structures and systems, organization culture and power relationships. The strategic leader is critical in the process because he or she is either personally or ultimately responsible for the proposed changes in strategy, and for establishing the structure and processes within the organization.

Quinn's approach is as follows.

☐ The strategic leader will develop his or her own informal information and communication channels, both within and external to the organization, and will draw on this as much as using the formal systems.
☐ The strategic leader must generate **awareness** of the desired change with the appropriate managers within the organization. This involves communication and cultural issues.
☐ The strategic leader will seek to legitimize

Box 24.2
THE LEARNING ORGANIZATION

The basic arguments:

☐ In a decade when quality, technology and product/service variety are all becoming widely available at relatively low cost, speed of change is essential for sustained competitive advantage. See Chapter 15.
☐ If an organization, therefore, fails to keep up with, or ahead of, the rate of change in its environment it will either be destroyed by stronger competitors, or lapse into sudden death or slow decline. The ideal is to be marginally ahead of competitors – opening up too wide a gap might unsettle customers.

☐ An organization can only adapt if it is first able to learn, and this learning must be cross-functional as well as specialist.

Hence a learning organization 'encourages continuous learning and knowledge generation at all levels, has processes which can move knowledge around the organization easily to where it is needed, and can translate that knowledge quickly into changes in the way the organization acts, both internally and externally' (Senge, 1991). Strategically important information, together with lessons and best practice, will thus be spread around; and ideally this learning will also be protected from competitors.

Essential requirements

☐ Systemic thinking. Decision makers will be able to use the perspective of the whole organization; and there will be significant environmental awareness and internal co-operation. See Chapter 16. For many organizations the systemic perspective will be widened to incorporate collaboration and strategic alliances with other organizations in the added value chain.

☐ Management development and personal growth – to enable effective empowerment and leadership throughout the organization, and in turn allow managers to respond to perceived environmental changes and opportunities.

☐ A shared vision and clarity about both core competences and key success factors. Changes should be consistent through strategic and operational levels.

☐ Appropriate values and corporate culture – to fully exploit core competences and satisfy key success factors.

☐ A commitment to customer service, quality and continuous improvement. Kotter and Heskett (1992) argue that the appropriate culture is one which is capable of constant adaptation as the needs of customers, shareholders and employees change.

☐ Team learning within the organization through problem sharing and discussion.

These points have been used to develop the following matrix

	Individuals and tasks	Teams and integration
Empowerment and development	Effectiveness oriented Focus on problem-solving approach CHANGE ACCEPTED	The learning organization Innovative; intrapreneurial; risk taking CHANGE INITIATED
Orientation towards efficiency and results	Concentration on resource efficiency Consistent and systematic CHANGE RESISTED	Supportive organization Cross-functional co-operation RESPONSIVE TO CHANGE PRESSURES

CULTURE AND VALUES

STRUCTURAL FOCUS

Case 24.4
BRITISH PETROLEUM

Robert Horton was promoted to the chairmanship of BP in March 1990 and almost immediately began to implement Project 1990, a programme of development and cultural change. The preparatory work for Project 1990 had been initiated by Horton and begun during 1989. The programme had already received Board approval.

In the 1980s we learned how to manage change. In the 1990s we shall need to manage surprise.
(Horton)

BP has worldwide interests in crude oil, natural gas, minerals and coal, it refines and distributes petrol, and it manufactures associated products such as chemicals, detergents and animal foods. One of the UK's largest companies, it is structured around four main business areas: exploration; oil (refining and distribution); chemicals; and nutrition. There had been major structural changes during the 1980s, following financial difficulties at the beginning of the decade. As a result of these changes BP had become extensively bureaucratic 'with a plethora of committees'. Horton's own reputation and progress had been built within BP's American operations, which he had successfully reorganized and turned around.

Project 1990

In 1989 Horton had formed a seven-man investigative team which began by interviewing 500 BP managers around the world. This was followed by a questionnaire survey of all BP's managers. The sample was one in every six managers; and the response rate was 65%. Late in 1989 the team concluded that there was a need for a more open, learning organization and began to plan appropriate changes. In December a large team of senior managers met away from the organization to discuss the findings and agree an outline implementation programme. A 'culture change' team was then formed and new vision and values statements prepared.

The aims of Project 1990

- ☐ Build on identified strengths, conquer some weaknesses, and 'equip BP for outstanding success in the 1990s'
- ☐ Reduce complexity and speed up decision making
- ☐ Greater autonomy for the four business areas
- ☐ Reduced power of regional (co-ordinating) managers
- ☐ Reduce the size of BP's Head Office and re-define its role (over 1000 jobs were quickly cut)
- ☐ Increased mobility of managers throughout the whole of BP
- ☐ Enhanced willingness of managers to accept responsibility – linked to appraisal and reward
- ☐ Greater emphasis on cross-functional and cross-business team working, and keeping other managers informed
- ☐ A culture of management by walking and talking
- ☐ Whilst flattening the structure by a limited amount, open up the existing one.

The various changes would only succeed if BP 'changed its underlying culture – the ways employees relate to each other, to customers, to the communities in which BP operates, and to shareholders' (Horton).

Some managers and commentators felt that Horton himself constituted one of the problem areas. He was described by a colleague as a 'natural Theory X manager: autocratic and impatient with people who don't make up their minds quickly', a man who enjoys leading from the front and demands involvement in every strategic decision.

Nevertheless, Project 1990 was launched with full support and enthusiasm from all BP's senior executives. Upwards of £20 million was invested in a myriad of workshops, communications and training programmes, and new human resource initiatives. Incremental learning within the programme highlighted a need for personal development plans (known as PDPs).

Outcomes

Greater empowerment was achieved relatively quickly. Ideas for change soon began to feed upwards through the organization. The approaches differed between the four divisions – in BP Exploration, for example, managers were being appraised by their subordinates. A plethora of new anecdotes emerged and these served to re-inforce the training and cultural change.

Some two dozen senior executives, including Horton, met regularly outside working hours to discuss progress and share ideas and feelings.

However, in the world recession in 1991 profits slumped dramatically. More jobs had to go, but this was not seen as questioning the validity of Project 1990. PDPs were cynically re-titled Personal Departure Plans by those who negotiated early retirement packages. The Project 1990 meetings for senior executives became less frequent, and the number attending was halved.

In June 1992 Horton resigned, 'ousted by BP's non-executive directors with at least the tacit compliance of his senior executives' (*Financial Times*).

A number of reasons were suggested. It was possible that the cultural change programme, accepted and manifestly supported by senior executives, did not have their full, underlying commitment. Perhaps some preferred the more formal style of the 1980s. This argument seems hard to justify given the evidence of the positive progress. It was more probably Horton's forceful management style.

In the event it will take a much longer period of time to clarify whether the new behaviour patterns emergent during 1991–2 have led to a significant and lasting change in BP's culture, and whether the changes really are right for the turbulent 1990s. Nevertheless, in February 1993 BP claimed that its recent cost cutting measures had proved effective. The debt burden had been reduced and profitability increased.

the new approach or strategy, lending it authority, if not, at this stage, credibility.

☐ He or she will then seek to gather key supporters for the approach or strategy.

☐ The new strategy may be floated as a minor tactical change to minimize resistance, and possibly keep the ultimate aim unclear. Alternatively the strategy may be floated as a trial or experiment.

☐ Opposition will be removed by, for example, ensuring that supporters chair key committees, and that stubborn opponents are moved to other parts of the organization.

☐ The strategy will be flexible so that incremental changes can be made in the light of the trials. There will be a strong element of learning by doing, so that any unexpected resource limitations, such as a shortage of key skills, will be highlighted.

☐ Support for the change will harden.

☐ The proposals will be crystallized and focused.

☐ Finally, the proposed changes will be formalized and ideally accepted within the organization. This should involve honest evaluation and attempts to improve upon the original ideas. It is particularly important to look ahead and consider how the new strategy might be developed further in the future.

Quinn's approach incorporates an appreciation of the likely impact upon people and the culture, and pragmatically searches for a better way of doing things once the decision to change has been made. In this respect it links closely to the soft systems approach.

Soft systems thinking

The possible contribution of soft systems ideas to strategy formulation was explored in Chapter 16. The usefulness of this approach is that resource constraints and the feasibility and difficulties of implementing possible strategic changes are evaluated fully during formulation. The ultimate decisions may not achieve the strategic leader's hopes and vision fully, but they are likely to be realistic.

The effects on people, and their expected reactions, will have been considered and these can be assimilated within the plans for change.

Organizational development and innovation

The basic underlying theme of organizational development (OD) is that developing an appropriate organizational culture will generate desirable changes in strategy.

Beckhard (1969) defined OD as effort which is 'planned, organization-wide, and managed from the top, designed to increase organizational effectiveness and health through planned interventions in the organization's processes, using behavioural science knowledge'.

OD is, in essence, planned cultural change. The model which has been used to provide the structure for this book shows strategic leadership and culture as being central to both strategic awareness and decision making. The appreciation by managers of the effectiveness of the current match between

---

The essential pre-requisite for an effective change of direction is to create a climate throughout the organization where change is regarded positively. Professor Hague, when he was at Manchester Business School, made the following remark which I have always remembered: 'The successful manager will expect and understand change; the outstanding manager will anticipate and create it.'

Once the right climate exists, change must be preceded and accompanied by effective and honest communication, meaningful consultation and sound decision making. It is not easy and requires genuine top management commitment.

Tom W Cain, ex-Director, Human Resources,
The Channel Tunnel Group Ltd

resources and the environment, their ability and willingness to make adaptive changes to capitalize on environmental changes, and the formulation and implementation of major changes in corporate strategy are all influenced by the culture of the organization and the style of strategic leadership. Hence it is crucial for the strategic leader to develop the appropriate culture for the mission and purpose he or she wishes to pursue. OD helps to develop a co-operative and innovative culture.

The aim of OD is to establish mechanisms which encourage managers to be more open, participative and co-operative when dealing with problems and making decisions. Specifically the objectives are:

☐ improved organizational effectiveness and, as a result,
☐ higher profits and better customer service (in its widest context)
☐ more effective decision making
☐ the ability to make and manage changes more smoothly
☐ increased innovation
☐ reduced conflict and destructive political activity
☐ greater trust and collaboration between managers and business units.

Organized OD programmes involve activities such as team-building and collaborative decision making, bringing managers together and encouraging them to share and discuss problems and issues. The thinking is that when managers learn more about the problems which face the organization as a whole, and other managers who may have different technical or functional perspectives, they become more aware of the impact of the decisions they make. In addition, if they collaborate and share responsibilities, they are more likely to feel committed to joint decisions.

Whilst one aim is to change the attitudes and behaviour of people in organizations, OD can also allow and encourage the same people to initiate and implement changes through their discussions. Establishing the programmes is likely to involve outside experts who can be seen as objective. OD programmes are not normally a response to specific problems but rather a general approach to the management of change in the longer term.

Given that one idea behind OD is collaboration and collective responsibility, a key theme is the reduction of conflict between managers, functions, business units or divisions within the organization. A reduction in the use of manipulative styles of management, or dysfunctional political activity, whereby managers pursue personal goals in preference to the wider needs of the organization, is also implied. Functional and dysfunctional political activity is explored in the last section of this chapter where we look at the bases and uses of power by managers.

Power and influence: introductory comments

The management of change requires that managers have the requisite power to implement decisions and that they are able to exert influence. There are several bases of power, both organizational and individual, which constitute resources for managers. The processes they adopt for utilizing these power bases, their styles of management, determine their success in influencing others. The ability of managers to exert power and influence is manifested in a number of ways, including:

☐ budgets
☐ rewards
☐ organization structure and positions
☐ promotions and management development
☐ information systems
☐ symbols of power and status.

POWER AND POLITICS

Managers who regularly attempt to get things done, both with and through other people, and introduce changes have the problem of generating agreement, consent or at least compliance with what should be done, how and when. Typically opinions and perspectives will differ. Disagreements may or may not be significant, and can range from the polite and friendly to those involving threats and coercion. Each side, quite simply, is attempting to influence the conduct of the other. In this section we consider the power resources which managers are able to use and how they might use them.

Checkland (1986) defines organizational politics as the process by which differing interests reach accommodation. These accommodations relate to the dispositions and use of power and influence, and behaviour which is not prescribed by the policies established within the organization. It will be shown later that political activity by managers in order to influence others, and ensure that their decisions and strategies are carried out, is essential. Politics can be legitimate and positive, although it can also be more negative and illegitimate. In the latter case managers are seeking to influence others in order to achieve their personal goals. This is often described as machiavellianism and is discussed at the end of this section.

The relative power of the organization

The need for change is affected by the relative power and influence of external stakeholders in relation to the organization. Powerful customers, powerful suppliers, and changes in government legislation would all represent potential threats and demands for change. In turn, the management and implementation of change is affected by the relative power of the organization. Some proposed strategies can be implemented because the organization possesses the appropriate power to acquire the resources which are needed and to generate consumer demand. Others may not be feasible.

At the same time the decisions taken within organizations concerning changes of corporate, competitive and functional strategies are influenced by the disposition of relative power between functions, business units or divisions, and the ways in which managers seek to use power and influence.

Internal and external sources of power are discussed further in the Key Reading 24.1 based on the work of Mintzberg (1983).

Political activity

Farrell and Petersen (1982) classify political activity in terms of three dimensions:

☐ legitimate or illegitimate
☐ vertical or lateral
☐ internal or external to the organization.

For example, a complaint or suggestion by an employee directly to a senior manager, bypassing an immediate superior, would be classified as legitimate, vertical and internal. Discussions with fellow managers from other companies within an industry would be legitimate, lateral and external – unless they involved any illegal activities such as price fixing. Informal communications and agreements between managers are again legitimate, whilst threats or attempts at sabotage are clearly illegitimate.

Power and politics are key aspects of strategy implementation because they can enable managers to be proactive and to influence their environment rather than being dominated and manipulated by external events. The issues affect managers at all levels of the organization and decisions concerning both internal and external changes.

Key Reading 24.1
INTERNAL AND EXTERNAL SOURCES OF POWER

Mintzberg (1983) contends that it is essential to consider both internal and external sources of power, and their relative significance, when assessing the demands for, and feasibility of, certain strategic changes.

The organization's stakeholders will vary in terms of their relative power and the ways in which they exert influence. The interests of the owners of the firm, for example, are legally represented by the board of directors. Whilst large institutional shareholders may exert considerable influence over certain decisions, many private shareholders will take no active part. Employees are represented by external trade unions, who again may or may not exert influence.

The power relationships between the firm and its stakeholders are determined by the importance and scarcity of the resource in question. The more essential and limited the supply of the resource, the greater the power the resource provider has over the firm. According to Mintzberg these external power groups may be focused and their interests pulled together by a dominant power, or they may be fragmented.

Where there are very strong external influences, the organization may seek to establish close co-operation or mutual dependence, or attempt to reduce its dependence on the power source. The relationship between Marks & Spencer and many of its suppliers is a good example of mutual dependence of this nature. Marks & Spencer have encouraged many of their clothing suppliers to invest in the latest technology for design and manufacturing in order that they can both succeed against international competition. Marks & Spencer are typically the largest customer of their suppliers, buying substantial quantities as long as both demand and quality are maintained. However, it is important that their suppliers are aware of fashion changes because they bear the risk of over-production and changes in taste.

Internal power is linked to the structure and configuration of the organization. Following from the issues discussed in Chapter 22, it is clear that the relative power of the strategic apex, middle management, operators, technocrats and support staff needs to be assessed.

Internal power is manifested in four ways:

□ the personal control system of the strategic leadership
□ rules, policies and procedures
□ political activities external to these two factors
□ cultural ideologies which influence decision makers.

External and internal power sources combine to determine a dominant source of power at any time, and Mintzberg suggests six possibilities.

□ A **key external source**, such as a bank or supplier, or possibly the government as, say, a key buyer of defence equipment – the objectives of the source would normally be clearly stated and understood.
□ **The operation of the organization structure**, and the strategies and activities of general and functional managers who are allocated the scarce resources: the relative power of business units is influenced by the market demand for their products and services, but generally external sources exert indirect rather than direct influence; functional managers can enjoy power if they are specialists and their skills are in short supply.
□ **Strong central leadership**.
□ **Ideologies**: certain organizations, such as charities or volunteer organizations, are often dominated by the underlying ideologies related to helping others.
□ **Professional constraints**: accountants' and solicitors' practices, for example, have established codes of professional

Continued overleaf

practice which dictate and influence behaviour. On occasions this can raise interesting issues for decision makers. A frequently used example is the television journalist or news editor working for the BBC or ITN and able to influence reporting strategies and policies. When assessing sensitive issues does the person see himself or herself as a BBC or ITN employee or as a professional journalist, and do the two perspectives coincide or conflict?

☐ **Active conflict** between power sources seeking dominance: whilst this can involve either or both internal and external sources it is likely to be temporary, as organizations cannot normally survive prolonged conflict.

The dominant source of power becomes a key feature of the organizational culture, and a major influence on manager behaviour and decision making.

Source of the basic arguments: Mintzberg, H (1983) *Power In and Around Organizations*, Prentice Hall.

The bases of power

Seven bases of manager power were introduced and described in Chapter 4: reward; coercive; legitimate; personal; expert; information; and connection. The extent to which managers and other employees in organizations use each of these sources of power is a major determinant of corporate culture.

Reward and **coercive power** (the ability to sanction and punish) are two major determinants of employee motivation, and both can be very significant strategically. Thompson and Strickland (1981) argue that motivation is brought about primarily by the reward and punishment systems in the organization; and Blanchard and Johnson (1982) suggest that effective management involves three key aspects: establishing clear objectives for employees, and rewarding and sanctioning performance against objectives appropriately. Strategic leaders who dominate their organizations and coerce their senior managers can be effective, particularly when the organization is experiencing decline and major changes in strategy are urgently required.

Legitimate power is determined primarily by the organization structure, and conse-quently changes of structure will affect the power, influence and significance of different business units, functions and individual managers. **Personal power**, which can lead to the commitment of others to the power holder, can be very important in incremental changes. Managers who are supported and trusted by their colleagues and subordinates will find it easier to introduce and implement changes.

Expert power can also be useful in persuading others that proposed changes in strategy are feasible and desirable. Whilst expert power may not be real, and instead be power gained from reputation, it is unlikely that managers who genuinely lack expertise can be successful without other power bases. Moreover, expertise is job related. An expert specialized accountant, for example, may lose expert power temporarily if he or she is promoted to general manager. Consequently an important tactic in the management of change is to ensure that those managers who are perceived to be expert in the activity or function concerned are supportive of the proposed changes.

Information and related **connection power** are becoming increasingly significant as information technology grows in importance.

Invisible power

These seven power bases are all visible sources. There is, in addition, invisible power. One source of invisible power is the way in which an issue or proposal is presented, which can influence the way it is dealt with. Managers who appreciate the objectives, perspectives and concerns of their colleagues will present their ideas in ways that are likely to generate their support rather than opposition. Second, membership of informal, but influential, coalitions or groups of managers can be a source of power, particularly if the people involved feel dependent on each other. Third, information which would create opposition to a decision or change proposal might be withheld. In the same way that access to key information can be a positive power source, the ability to prevent other people obtaining information can be either a positive or a negative source of power.

Lukes (1974) has identified three further important aspects of power, namely:

☐ the ability to prevent a decision, or not make one
☐ the ability to control the issues on which decisions are to be made
☐ the ability to ensure that certain issues are kept off agendas.

The use of such power by individuals can inhibit changes which might be in the long-term best interests of the organization.

Political effectiveness

Hayes (1984) contends that effective managers appreciate clearly what support they will need from other people if proposed changes are to be carried through, and what they will have to offer in return. In such cases they reach agreements which provide mutual advantages. It is important for the organization as a whole that general and functional managers are effective and politically competent if personal objectives are to be restrained and undesirable changes, championed by individual managers, prevented. Problems can occur where some managers are politically effective and able to implement change, and others are relatively ineffective and reach agreements with other managers whereby their personal interests, and the interests of the organization, are adversely affected.

Allen *et al.* (1979) and Dixon (1982) point out that certain sources of personal power are essential for managers who are effective politically and able to influence others. In addition they suggest certain tactics for managing change. These are featured in Table 24.2. It is important that managers are perceived by others to have expertise and ability, and it is useful if they have a reputation built on past successes. Depending on the relative power of outside stakeholders, such as suppliers or customers, external credibility can also prove valuable. It is essential to have access to information and to other powerful individuals and groups of managers.

It can be a disadvantage for a manager to be perceived as a radical agent of change, as this can arouse fear and uncertainty, possibly leading to opposition, in others. As discussed earlier, it can sometimes be valuable to implement a change of strategy gradually and incrementally, allowing people to make adaptive changes as the learning experience develops. At the same time it is important to ensure that opposition is manifested and brought out into the open rather than being allowed to develop without other people being aware.

Managers who are effective and successful politically, and able to implement their decisions and proposed changes, will generally appreciate and understand organizational processes and be sensitive to the needs of others. It is extremely useful if the strategic leader is an able politician. The type and incidence of incremental changes in strategies throughout the organization will also be

Table 24.2   Political power bases and tactics

Bases of personal power

Expertise	Particularly significant where the skill is in scarce supply
	It is possible to use mobility, and the threat of leaving, to gain support for certain changes of strategy – again dependent upon the manager's personal importance to the firm
Assessed stature	A reputation for being a 'winner' or a manager who can obtain results
	Recent successes are most relevant
Credibility	Particularly credibility with external power sources, such as suppliers or customers
Political access	Being well known around the organization and able to influence key groups of managers
Control over information	Internal and external sources
	Information can be used openly and honestly or withheld and used selectively – consequently it is crucial to know the reliability of the source
Group support	In managing and implementing change it is essential to have the support of colleagues and fellow managers

Political tactics to obtain results

Develop liaisons	As mentioned above, it is important to develop and maintain both formal and informal contacts with other managers, functions, and divisions
	Again it is important to include those managers who are most powerful
Present a conservative image	It can be disadvantageous to be seen as too radical an agent of change
Diffuse opposition	Conflicts need to be brought out into the open and differences of opinion aired rather than kept hidden
	Divide and rule can be a useful strategy
Trade-off and compromise	In any proposal or suggestion for change it is important to consider the needs of other people whose support is required
'Strike while the iron is hot'	Successful managers should build on successes and reputation quickly
Research	Information is always vital to justify and support proposals
Use a neutral cover	Radical changes, or those which other people might perceive as a threat to them, can sometimes be usefully disguised and initiated as minor changes. This is linked to the next point
Limit communication	A useful tactic can be to unravel change gradually in order to contain possible opposition
Withdraw strategically	If things are going wrong, and especially if the changes are not crucial, it can be a wise tactic on occasions to withdraw – at least temporarily

Politically successful managers understand organizational processes and they are sensitive to the needs of others.

Effective political action brings about desirable and successful changes in organizations – it is functional. Negative political action is dysfunctional, and can enable manipulative managers to pursue their personal objectives against the better interests of the organization.

The strategic leader needs to be an effective politician.

Source: Allen, R W, Madison, D L, Porter, L W, Renwick, P A and Mayes, B T (1979) Organisational politics: tactics and characteristics of its actors. *California Management Review*, **22**, Fall; Dixon, M (1982) The world of office politics, *Financial Times*, 10 November.

affected by the political ability of managers. Those with ability will be instrumental in introducing changes. Where the strategic leader wishes to encourage managers to be adaptive and innovative it is important to consider the political ability of the managers concerned. Political ability relates to the use of power and influence in the most appropriate way in particular circumstances. This is the subject of the next section.

Uses of power and influence

MacMillan (1978) argues that introducing and implementing change frequently requires the use of power and influence, which he examines in terms of the control of situations and the ability to change people's intentions. Where a person wishes to exercise control over the behaviour of other people, either within the organization or external to it, he or she has two basic options. First, he can **structure the situation** so that others comply with his wishes; second, by communicating with other people, he can seek to change their perceptions so that they see things differently and decide to do as he suggests. In other words he succeeds in **changing their intentions**. Both of these approaches are categorized as strategies of manipulation.

Where a manager is concentrating on structuring the situation he is using certain power bases as enabling resources; where he is attempting to change intentions he is seeking to use influence. Power, in particular personal power, is again important as a source of influence.

The outcome from both the situational and intentional approaches can be either positive or negative. When the effect is positive the other people feel that they are better off as a result of the changes; the effect is negative if they feel worse off.

MacMillan identifies four tactics in relation to these points.

Inducement   Inducement implies an ability to control the situation, and the outcome is perceived as beneficial by others involved. A large retail organization with several stores might require managers to be mobile as a condition of their employment, and reward them with improved status, salary increases and relocation expenses every time they move. The situation is controlled; ideally the managers concerned feel positive about the moves.

Coercion   The situation is again controlled, but the outcome is perceived negatively. In the above situation the same managers might be threatened with no further promotions unless they agreed to certain moves within the company.

Persuasion   The manager does not try to control or change the situation but argues that the other people can or will benefit by behaving in certain ways. The desired outcome is positive. People might be persuaded to agree to a change which is not immediately desirable by suggestions that future rewards will be forthcoming.

Obligation   Obligation is another intentional tactic, but the outcome is negative. People are persuaded to behave in a certain way by being made to feel that they have an obligation. It might be suggested that people

☐ owe the company something for the money that has been invested in their previous training, or
☐ owe particular managers a favour for something which has happened in the past, or
☐ are obligated to the group of people that they have been working with for some years and should not let them down.

In particular cases, individual managers may or may not have a number of alternative tactics to select from. Tactics which have positive outcomes must normally be preferable to those which cause negative feelings if both are available and likely to yield the desired results. At times managers whose power bases are limited and who need speedy results may have little option but to coerce or obligate people. Kanter (1983) emphasizes that successful managers of change situations are able to keep their power invisible both during and after the change. Participation in the change is then perceived to stem from commitment or conviction rather than from power being exercised over people. Kanter contends that it is very important for middle managers in organizations to be skilful in managing change as they implement the detailed strategies, and that it is important for strategic leaders to ensure that they have support from their middle managers for the overall corporate strategy.

Machiavellianism

Machiavellianism is the term often used to describe coercive mangement tactics. Marriott (1908), translating Machiavelli's book *The Prince* written in the sixteenth century, uses the expression to cover 'the ruthless use of power, particularly coercive power, and manipulation to attain personal goals'. Whilst coercive power can be used effectively by managers it may not always be easy to justify, especially if other alternatives are available. Coercion may not be practical on a repeat basis; and any fear of threats not carried out quickly recedes.

Jay (1967), however, contends that Machiavelli also offers much useful advice for ethical managers. Basing his arguments on Machiavelli's views on strategies and tactics for annexing and ruling nations, Jay argues that chief executive strategic leaders should concentrate their efforts outside the organization, developing and strengthening the strategic perspective. In order for them to feel able to do this, the internal structure and systems must be sound and effective, and managers must be supportive of proposals from the top. General and functional managers should be free to operate and feel

able to make certain changes, but their overall power should be contained. They should exercise leadership, which is based on power. This power yields the freedom to decide how things should be done. Managers, though, should be afraid to pursue personal goals against the interest of the organization as a whole. Achieving this requires a clear awareness of what is happening throughout the organization and the appropriate punishment of offenders. Successful managers, of course, should be rewarded. Trafalgar House, discussed earlier in this chapter, provides an interesting illustration of these basic points.

Pearce and DeNisi (1983) stress that most organizations are managed partially by informal coalitions or groupings of managers superimposed on the formal structure. It is particularly important that managers in key positions in the organization, those in charge of important resources or responsible for products upon which the profits or reputation of the organization depends, are known to be committed and loyal to the strategic leader. Moreover, any informal and powerful coalitions which develop should also be supportive. To achieve both these it may be appropriate for the strategic leader to remove or switch senior managers occasionally as a reminder of his or her overall power. This is particularly likely to happen after an acquisition, during a re-structuring exercise, or on the appointment of a new strategic leader.

Strategic coalitions can be a major force behind strategy formation, especially where the overall strategic leader is relatively weak. An effective leader will therefore seek to use coalitions which already exist, and encourage the formation of other loyal ones.

In considering the feasibility of changes and how to implement them, it is very important to examine the underlying political abilities and behaviour within the firm: who has power, how it is manifested, how it is used. Without taking these into account, implementation is likely to prove hazardous.

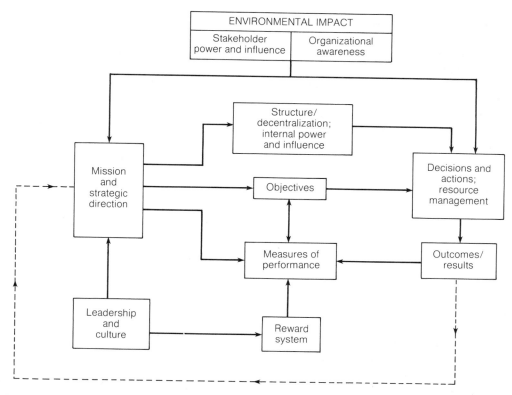

Figure 24.2   The strategic change process.

SUMMARY

In this chapter we have explored a number of issues involved in the effective management of change. These are synthesized in Figure 24.2. It has been emphasized that, in volatile environments in particular, organizations face constant pressures for change. Some organizations are proactive and seek to manage their environments; others are reactive and changes are forced on them. However powerful the economic forces for change, people who are affected by the proposed changes are likely to resist them. The management of change is influenced by the relative power of external forces and of managers and groups of managers inside the organization. Power may arise in a number of ways and different managers are more able

than others to use their power to influence and affect the behaviour of others.

Specifically we have

☐ described the major forces for change and types of change situation, and the most common reasons why people resist change;

☐ summarized six ways of overcoming resistance;

☐ considered Lewin's work on the forces for and against change, and his arguments concerning the stages involved in achieving permanent changes in behaviour;

☐ discussed the five basic approaches to the management of change summarized by Bourgeois and Brodwin, exploring in greater depth the notion of top-down strategic change, Quinn's incremental model, the contribution of soft systems thinking, and organizational development and innovation;

☐ explained what is meant by the term 'learning organization';
☐ highlighted the significant role of power and political activity;
☐ reviewed the seven bases of power introduced in Chapter 4 and introduced the idea of invisible power;
☐ considered the relative importance of external and internal power;
☐ discussed how managers might seek to be effective politically, and how power and influence can be used to achieve results with either positive or negative connotations;
☐ concluded briefly with some ideas developed from the sixteenth-century writings of Machiavelli.

CHECKLIST OF KEY TERMS AND CONCEPTS

You should feel confident that you understand the following terms and ideas:

☐ Types of change situation
☐ Lewin's force field analysis
☐ Unfreezing, changing and refreezing behaviour
☐ Learning organization
☐ Quinn's model of incremental change
☐ Organizational development
☐ Organizational politics
☐ Visible and invisible power
☐ Machiavellianism.

QUESTIONS AND RESEARCH ASSIGNMENTS

Text related

1. Describe an event where you have personally experienced forces for change, and discuss any forces which were used to resist the change. What tactics were adopted on both sides?
2. Describe a strategic leader (any level in an organization of your choice) whom you consider to be a powerful person.

    What types of power does he or she possess?
3. Describe a manager whom you believe is successful at using organizational politics. On what observations and experiences are you basing your decision? How might you measure political effectiveness and the elements within it?
4. As a manager, what are your personal power bases? How politically effective are you? How could you increase your overall power and improve your effectiveness?

Library and assignment based

5. Select an industry or company and ascertain the forces which have brought about changes in the last ten years. How proactive/reactive have the companies been, and with what levels of success?
6. Analyse the news broadcasts of both the BBC and ITN and evaluate whether their reporting of industrial and business news is similar or dissimilar. Are they reporting to inform or to persuade about, say, the merits or demerits of government policy? To what extent are they constrained by government?

RECOMMENDED FURTHER READING

For a short and straightforward introduction to the management of change, see Plant, R (1989) *Managing Change and Making It Stick*, Fontana. A more detailed introduction can be found in Basil, D C and Cook, C W (1983) *The Management of Change*, McGraw-Hill. In addition Mintzberg (1983) and

Argyris, C (1985) *Strategy, Change and Defensive Routines*, Pitman, are useful general texts.

Readers who are specifically interested in organizational development are referred to Beckhard (1969) and Schein, E H and Bennis, W G (1967) *Personal and Organisational Change Through Group Methods*, Wiley.

MacMillan (1978) provides a useful perspective on politics and change. Jay's book *Management and Machiavelli* (originally published in 1967, and reissued recently) is also thought provoking on this topic.

REFERENCES

Allen, R W, Madison, D L, Porter, L W, Renwick, P A and Mayes, B T (1979) Organisational politics: tactics and characteristics of its actors, *California Management Review*, **22**, Fall.

Beckhard, R (1969) *Organisation Development: Strategies and Models*, Addison Wesley.

Blanchard, K and Johnson, S (1982) *The One Minute Manager*, Morrow.

Bourgeois, L J and Brodwin, D R (1984) Strategic implementation: five approaches to an elusive phenomenon, *Strategic Management Journal*, **5**.

Checkland, P B (1986) The politics of practice, Paper presented at the IIASA International Round-table 'The Art and Science of Systems Practice', November.

Daft, R L (1983) *Organisation Theory and Design*, West.

Dixon, M (1982) The world of office politics, *Financial Times*, 10 November.

Farrell, D and Petersen, J C (1982) Patterns of political behaviour in organisations, *The Academy of Management Review*, **7** (3), July.

Hayes, J (1984) The politically competent manager Journal of General Management, **10** (1), Autumn.

Jay, A (1967) *Management and Machiavelli*, Holt, Rinehart and Winston.

Kanter, R M (1983) The middle manager as innovator. In *Strategic Management* (ed. R G Hamermesch), Wiley.

Kotter, J P and Heskett, J L (1992) *Corporate Culture and Performance*, Free Press.

Kotter, J P and Schlesinger, L A (1979) Choosing strategies for change, *Harvard Business Review*, March–April.

Lewin, K (1947) Frontiers in group dynamics: concept, method and reality in social science, *Human Relations*, **1**.

Lewin, K (1951) *Field Theory in Social Sciences*, Harper and Row.

Lukes, S (1974) *Power: A Radical View*, MacMillan.

MacMillan, I C (1978) *Strategy Formulation: Political Concepts*, West.

Margerison, C and Smith, B (1989) Shakespeare and management: managing change, *Management Decision*, **27** (2).

Marriott, W K (1908) Translation into English of *The Prince* written by N Machiavelli in the 1500s.

Mintzberg, H (1983) *Power In and Around Organisations*, Prentice Hall.

Pearce, J A and DeNisi, A S (1983) Attribution theory and strategic decision making: an application to coalition formation, *Academy of Management Journal*, **26**, March.

Peters, T (1989) Tomorrow's companies: new products, new markets, new competition, new thinking, *The Economist*, 4 March.

Quinn, J B (1988) Managing strategies incrementally. In *The Strategy Process: Concepts, Contexts and Cases* (eds J B Quinn, H Mintzberg and R M James), Prentice Hall.

Senge, P (1991) *The Fifth Discipline: The Art and Practice of the Learning Organization*, Doubleday. (European edition by Century Business, 1992.)

Thompson, A A and Strickland, A J (1981) *Strategy and Policy: Concept and Cases*, Business Publications.

Waterman, R H Jr (1987) *The Renewal Factor*, Bantam.

FINAL THOUGHTS 25

LEARNING OBJECTIVES

After studying this chapter you should be able to

☐ list nine major themes from this book;
☐ from these, summarize five principles which determine the effectiveness of an organization's corporate strategy;
☐ identify a number of strategic issues which pose challenges for the future.

In this final chapter we recap the major themes of the book and summarize the essential aspects of effective strategic management.

We have attempted to illustrate that there is no simple or prescriptive approach to strategic management. Whilst the overall strategic leader is ultimately responsible for changes in corporate strategy, or the strategic perspective, general and functional managers spread throughout the organization will have some involvement in, and responsibility for, changes in competitive and functional strategies. The nature of their role and responsibilities will depend upon the structure of the organization and the extent to which power and authority are decentralized. These issues will also be determined by the strategic leader.

Hence the processes involved in formulating and implementing strategies and strategic changes will depend on the structural framework and management systems preferred by the strategic leader. They will also be influenced by the culture of the organization. Certain changes of strategic direction will need changes in the organizational culture if they are to be implemented effectively. Equally the culture, and changes in the culture, will influence adaptive and incremental changes continuously.

A number of alternative strategies have been discussed. In particular circumstances all of them can prove effective; in different circumstances they may be inappropriate. The key aspects relate to the ability to match the environment, values and resources, and for the timing to be right. At any time an organization might be pursuing clearly defined strategies which are proving very successful, but unless they adapt and innovate as the environment changes, say through competitor activity, the strategies may no longer appear timely and may become ineffective.

Also at any time certain strategies may seem more appropriate than others for the general economic environment. In the late

1980s and early 1990s joint ventures and strategic alliances grew in popularity. Management buy-outs were appropriate for the 1980s. The logic of diversification strategies involving acquisitions has been questioned because of implementation difficulties. Although a number of companies have failed to achieve the synergy they anticipated from pursuing this strategic alternative, others have implemented it effectively. It is a risky strategy but success can be rewarding.

Quite simply, different organizations pursue different objectives and strategies. Whilst there are some lessons to be learnt from the experiences of other organizations, there is no best way of managing strategies, no ideal set of objectives, and no guaranteed prescription for evaluating which strategy from a number of alternatives is likely to prove most effective. The important aspect, which applies to all organizations, is strategic awareness. It is essential for the strategic leader and other managers to understand how well the organization is doing, and why, and where the current and future opportunities and threats are. Managers should appreciate how their job and area of responsibility fit into the organization as a whole, and the impact on other managers of the decisions they take. Ideally they will also be responsive to change pressures and ready and able to innovate.

Our intention in this final chapter is to summarize the ideas, themes and concepts introduced and discussed in the book. The material is presented in a way that should enable readers to be able to consider the overall strategic effectiveness of an organization.

THE MAJOR THEMES

The major themes upon which this book has been based are summarized below.

The effective allocation and management of resources requires strategies, the pursuit of excellence and innovation

Strategies relate to the notion of a clear mission, a vision of the future, a direction for growth and means of achieving objectives.

Excellence implies striving to do the important things well and achieving effectiveness as well as efficiency.

Innovation deals with renewal and change. It is important to persuade employees that currently successful strategies are not infinite, and that changes are required before the company gets into difficulties.

E–V–R congruence

Strategies concern the effectiveness of the fit, or match, between the environment, the organization's resources and its values. When planning future strategies these three aspects must all be considered.

Competitive advantage

It is important to create and sustain distinctiveness and competitive advantage for every product, service and business.

There are three levels of strategy: corporate, competitive, and functional

Competitive strategies for each product, service and business comprise the corporate strategy. When reviewing these it is important to consider how well the company is doing with each activity, where it is going, and whether the activities are interrelated and generating synergy.

Functional strategies support competitive strategies. Competitive advantage originates in the functions, which should be co-ordinated and supportive of each other.

There are three essential modes of strategy formulation: planning, entreprenurial, and adaptive

Planning systems can make use of the analytical techniques discussed in this book; entrepreneurial strategies reflect vision and drive; and adaptive strategic changes imply continuous learning. All are important and they are not mutually exclusive.

Hamel and Prahalad (1989) argue that the most defensible competitive advantage is an organization's ability to improve its existing skills, learn new ones and adapt its strategies.

Synergy

The various products, services and businesses which comprise the organization should all benefit from being part of the organization, and there should be tangible benefits from their combination.

Strategic management involves awareness and decision making, and the formulation and implementation of strategies

Techniques can be of assistance. SWOT analyses help increase awareness; the planning gap and portfolio analyses, for example, are useful in the formulation and evaluation of strategies. Implementation involves aspects of organization structure and de-centralization.

Culture and leadership

The qualities, strengths, style and ambitions of the strategic leader, and the culture of the organization, are vital influences in every aspect of strategic management. They influence the objectives, the choice of direction and strategies, the ways in which strategies are implemented, the contribution of managers and other employees, and the overall success.

The principles under-pinning strategic management are applicable for every organization

Certain aspects are, of course, more important for certain types of business. In the case of many small firms the issues discussed under the headings of competitive and functional strategies are more important than the notion of changes in corporate strategy. Their scope and perspective is limited, and they need to improve their competitive advantage. For public sector organizations, measures of effective performance are a major concern.

Box 25.1 summarizes these themes and recaps the model of E–V–R congruence.

ESSENTIAL ASPECTS OF CORPORATE STRENGTH

These nine themes, and the issues they raise, can be summarized as a set of essential aspects which determine the effectiveness of an organization's corporate strategy. These are:

Direction

☐ The existence of a clear mission and purpose
☐ The need for the broad aspects of this to be communicated throughout the organization
☐ A need for some consistency amongst the activities which comprise the organization.

Box 25.1

E–V–R CONGRUENCE AND STRATEGIC EFFECTIVENESS

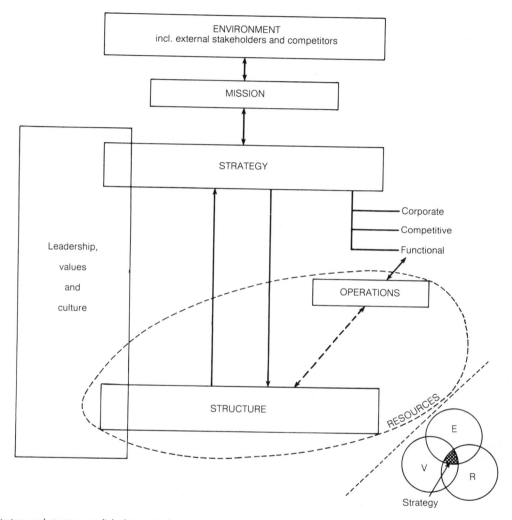

ENVIRONMENT
incl. external stakeholders and competitors

MISSION

STRATEGY

Corporate
Competitive
Functional

Leadership,
values
and
culture

OPERATIONS

STRUCTURE

RESOURCES

E

V   R

Strategy

Strategy and structure are linked in a circular interrelationship which impacts upon strategy formulation and implementation.

There are three levels of strategy: corporate, competitive and functional.

The operations within the structure determine functional strategies.

The effectiveness of these linkages is affected significantly by the style of management and strategic leadership, values and culture.

Successful organizations achieve a close match between their strategies and the (changing) needs and expectations of the external environment.

This requires a clear and understood mission and purpose, which may evolve alongside changes to the corporate perspective.

Effective strategic change requires that a systemic view of customers and competitors, structure and operations, and leadership and values is taken.

Pascale (1992) uses the word 'transformational' to describe those organizations which succeed in changing all these variables either sequentially or simultaneously. Such organizations, which essentially 're-invent themselves' are more likely to sustain the process of change and thereby maintain strategic effectiveness. They must be able to develop an awareness of the current situation and continuously monitor changes. Pascale argues that two such companies are British Airways (see Cases 4.2, 7.6 and 14.4) and Grand Metropolitan (Case 17.8).

Areas of involvement

☐ The industries in which the organization competes, and its levels of success in each
☐ The relative attractiveness of each industry
☐ The degree of diversification
☐ The need for competitive advantage with each activity.

Aspects of growth

☐ The future prospects of current activities
☐ The existence of any planning gap
☐ The need for innovation
☐ A recognition that diversification and acquisition involve higher risks than organic growth.

Relatedness

☐ An appreciation that synergy is elusive and that some strategies are likely to be more effective than others in creating it
☐ The argument that businesses should be built on existing strengths and competences
☐ The importance of looking for opportunities for developing and sharing existing skills.

The management of strategy

☐ The realization that assets and resources have opportunity costs, and that they should be allocated where they can provide the highest returns
☐ An understanding of risk, so that risks are spread and balanced with rewards
☐ The need for managers to be innovative, ready to change, and willing to take appropriate risks
☐ The need for some power to be decentralized to an appropriate extent to enable decisions to be made by those people with the information needed
☐ The significance of corporate culture.

STRATEGIC EFFECTIVENESS

Establishing how well these essential aspects are being applied will assist an evaluation of strategic effectiveness. The following questions are designed to focus attention on the main issues.

☐ Is there a clear and established mission and sense of corporate direction?
☐ What are the corporate objectives, both long term and short term?
☐ Which business(es) is the company competing in today, and which does it want to be in in the future?
☐ Taking into account the company, the competition and the industry as a whole, does the current corporate strategy seem to be optimal in the light of the company's strengths and weaknesses and its competitive environment? Are future changes in the environment being addressed?
☐ Do all the contributory activities (products, services and businesses) fit logically, generate synergy and benefit from

---

Change is a permanent feature of the National Health Service – new diseases, new technology, changing patterns of delivery of care and changing political priorities. The key to coping with constant change is good communications with staff. Without good communications staff will become confused, frightened and demoralized by change.

A. Randall, District General Manager, Worthing District Health Authority being part of the organization? Does the structure facilitate or inhibit this?

☐ How is the company positioned in each of its businesses? How is it differentiated from each of its key competitors? What future plans for creating and sustaining further competitive advantage does it have?

☐ Has the company clearly identified the key success factors for each business, and is it able to satisfy them? Are resources deployed effectively in relation to their opportunity cost?

☐ Have significant aspects of the corporate strategy been communicated effectively to all levels of personnel in the organization? Are the majority of employees in broad agreement with the company's mission and long-term objectives?

☐ Are there clearly established functional policies which are integrated and which address the key success factors? Do these policies ensure that employees have guidelines and incentives which make their long-term interests consistent with those of the organization?

☐ Does the company have people with the necessary vision, and innovatory and entrepreneurial skills to implement and develop competitive and functional strategies on an on-going basis?

FINAL THOUGHTS: THE CHALLENGE FOR THE FUTURE

Organizations which prove to be effective strategically in the future must address three critical issues. First, there is a need for **strategic leadership**. This applies throughout the organization and encapsulates general and functional managers who are responsible for adaptive changes in competitive and functional strategies as well as the overall strategic leader. Change management, empowerment, innovation and intrapreneur-ship (the application of entrepreneurial skills) will all be critical.

Second, managers must **learn to manage uncertainty** in such a way that they are always reactive to events, and in effect managed by uncertainty. The environment is generally becoming increasingly volatile, competitive and international.

These two points imply that the organization and its managers are able to **deal with strategic disturbance**. They should be able to deal with such disturbances as the loss of an existing market, the failure of a new product, or, as in the case of Amstrad, the failure of a supplier to deliver an important component. Appropriate policies and control systems should allow for contingency actions which overcome the difficulties in some way. The presence and success of these will differentiate a good business (strategically) from a poorly directed one.

Third, the organization must be able to **manage complexity and diversity**. There is a clear need to build a sound organization structure which enables managers to be both motivated and rewarded. These managers must understand their businesses and be able to make the complex simple. This implies empowerment which must not be at the expense of control, productivity and efficiency.

All of these require **strategic awareness and learning**, which really develops through the organization structure and culture. Employees should know what matters in terms of creating strategic success; what their company stands for; how well it is doing, and why; and what contribution is expected from them.

REFERENCES

Hamel, G and Prahalad, C K (1989) Strategic intent, *Harvard Business Review*, May–June.
Pascale, R T (1992) Paper presented at the Strategic Renaissance Conference, Strategic Planning Society, London, October.

AUTHOR INDEX

Abell, D.F. 16, 190, 299, 467
Ackoff, R.L. 61, 80, 126, 133–4,
  145, 407, 415, 454, 488
Adair, J. 370, 371
Alexander, L.D. 616
Allen, D. 393
Allen, R.W. 721, 722
Allen, S. 407
Allen, S.A. 648
Altman, E.I. 234, 235
Amdahl Executive Institute 413
Ansoff, H.I. 9, 21, 23, 240, 262,
  461
Anthony, R.N. 408, 409
Argenti, J. 228, 235, 459
Armistead, C.G. 340
Ashcroft, J. 53
Austin, N. 344, 370, 372

Barney, J.B. 98
Bartlett, C. 513, 514
Batchelor, C. 576, 580, 582, 587
Baumol, W.J. 132
Beck, P. 7
Beckhard, R. 716
Belbin, R.M. 363–4
Bennis, W. 51
Berry, D. 100, 104
Biggadike, R. 533
Binter, M.J. 344
Blanchard, K. 365, 370, 720
Bleackley, M. 550
Bolwijn, P.T. 333
Booms, B. 344
Booth, S. 692
Bourgeois, L.J. 709
Bower, J.L. 681
Boyle, D. 53
Braddick, B. 53
Brady, C.J. 352
Brewin, D. 480
Brigham, E.F. 383
Brodwin, D.R. 709
Brown, R. 359

Broyles, J.E. 385
Buckley, M.R. 611, 689, 690
Burgman, R. 533, 543
Burlingham, B. 102
Business International 538
Business Week 296
Butler, D. 694
Buzzell, R.D. 473

Campbell, A. 126, 655, 656, 657
Caulkin, S. 333, 334, 336, 694
CBI (Confederation of British
  Industries) 97, 269
Chaffee, E.E. 19, 20
Chandler, A.D. 20, 514, 623
Channon, D.F. 439, 525
Checkland, P.B. 264, 482,
  483–5, 718
Child, J.A. 625
Chiplin, B. 589
Clarke, C.J. 377, 399
Clifford, D.K. 568
Clutterbuck, D. 97, 126
Cohen, K.J. 459, 463
Cohen, P. 13, 133
Confederation of British
  Industries (CBI) 97, 269
Connell, D.C. 546
Constable, J. 6, 134, 474
Constable, C.J. 187, 480, 526–7
Cooper, R.G. 314
Coopers and Lybrand 576, 579,
  580
Cope, N. 62, 513
Coulson-Thomas, C. 359
Cowling, K. 531
Coyne, J. 575
Cubbin, J. 531
Cummings, L.L. (Shull et al.) 65
Cummings, T.G. 363
Cyert, R.M. 131, 459, 463

Daft, R.L. 701
Daniels, J.D. 645

Davidson, J.H. 294
Davis, G.B. 404
Davis, J.V. 563
Davis, S.M. 92
Deal, T. 90, 104, 105
De Jonquières, G. 72, 513, 534
Delbecq, A.L. (Shull et al.) 65
DeNisi, A.S. 724
Deresky, H. 658–9
Devine, P.J. 191
Devlin, G. 550, 563, 567
Dickel, K.E. (Rowe et al.) 471,
  472
Dixon, H. 513, 668
Dixon, M. 659, 721, 722
Dodsworth, T. 269
Donaldson, G. 391
Done, K. 672
Drucker, P.F. 152, 175, 240,
  291, 352, 352–3, 354, 367,
  413, 414–15, 537, 655
Dumaine, B. 441
Duncan, R. 248
Dunnette, M.D. 58
Dyas, G.P. 525

Earl, M.J. 408
Eason, K.D. 413
EC (European Community)
  271, 277
Economist 29, 103, 163, 202, 224,
  500
Edmonds, P. 187
Edwards, P.K. (Marginson et
  al) 369
Ettinger, J.C. 70
Etzioni, A. 66
European Community (EC)
  271, 277
Eustace, P. 577, 580
Evans, P. (Stalk et al) 15

Fahey, L. 255
Fallon, I. 233

Farrell, D. 718
Fayol, H. 644
Fisher, A. 534
Foote, N. 657
Forrester, J. 406
Fowler, A. 368
Foy, P. 352
Franks, J.R. 385
Frederick, W.C. 154
Freeman, R.E. 129
French, J.R.P. 90
Friedman, M. 152, 242
Fuller, J. 435

Galbraith, J.K. 132, 133, 652
Galbraith, J.R. 411, 412, 631
Gale, B.T. 473
Gapper, J. 26
Garnett, N. 269, 338, 346
Ghoshal, S. 513, 514
Gitman, L.J. 383
Glueck, W.F. 261, 262, 459, 464
Golde, R.A. 367
Goldratt, E. 335
Goldsmith, W. 97, 126
Goold, M. 655, 656, 657
Gray, J. 342
Gray, S.J. 656
Greiner, L.E. 646, 647
Grey, E.R. 704
Griffiths, J. 353

Hackman, J.R. (Porter et al.) 365
Halevi, S. 506
Hamel, G. 15, 108–9, 314, 429,
  730
Hamermesch, R. 469
Hamilton Fazey, I. 278
Hammond, J.S. 190, 467
Hampden-Turner, C. 81, 91
Handy, C. 372, 414, 647
Handy, C.B. 83
Harrigan, K.R. 569–71
Harris, C. 499
Harrison, R. 83
Harvey-Jones, J.H. 454, 482
Hatvany, N. 105, 107
Hayes, J. 721
Hayes, R.H. 339
Haylett, R. 335
Henderson, B. 23
Henderson, B.D. 309
Henderson, D. 57
Herbert, T.T. 658–9
Hersey, P. 365, 370
Hertzberg, F. 364
Heskett, J.L. 713
Hill, R. 109

Hill, T. 327
Hilton, A. 527
Hitchens, R.E. 469
HMSO 188, 193
Hofer, C.W. 20, 413, 597
Hogarth, R.M. 255
Hopwood, A.G. 408
Houlden, B. 153, 155
Houston, J.E. 154
Huey, J. 242
Hunsicker, J.Q. 644
Hussey, D. 459
Hussey, D.E. 458

Ishikawa, A. 667, 683

Jackson, C. 423
Jackson, P. 176
Jauch, L.R. 261, 262, 459, 464
Jay, A. 724
Jenkinson, T. 543
Johnson, G. 32, 482
Johnson H.T. 439
Johnson, S. 720
Jones, R.M. (Devine et al.) 191
Jonquières, G. de 72, 513, 534

Kabak, I.W. 692
Kakabadse, A. 90
Kanter, R.M. 259, 659, 660, 724
Kaplan, R.S. 439
Kay, J.A. 510
Kearney, A.T. 347
Kehoe, L. 704
Kelly, F.J. 264
Kelly, H.M. 264, 265
Kennedy, A. 90, 104, 105
Kets de Vries, M.F.R. 53
King, R. 255
King, R.R. 533
Kitching, J. 532, 533
Knowlton, C. 315
Kolb, D.A. xii
Koontz, H. 675, 676
Kotler, P. 299, 316, 320
Kotter, J.P. 369, 698, 706, 707,
  713
KPMG Peat Marwick 583
Kumpe, T. 333
Kupfer, A. 704

Laing, H. 135
Lander, R. 580
Lawler, E.E. (Porter et al.) 365
Lawler, E.E. III 428
Lawrence, P.R. 621, 648, 689
Leadbeater, C. 84, 278

Lee, J. 7
Lee, N. (Devine et al.) 191
Levitt, T. 292, 297, 315
Lewin, K. 706, 708
Lindblom, C.E. 65, 368
Lipton, M. 137
Litterer, J.A. 367
London, S. 175
Lorenz, C. 293, 315, 440, 531,
  657
Lorsch, J. 407
Lorsch, J.W. 391, 621, 648, 689
Lowe, J.F. 331, 475
Lucas, H. 404
Luffman, G. 532
Luffman, G.A. 129, 130
Lukes, S. 721
Lynch, R. 276

McClelland, D. 70, 364
McDermott, M.C. 656
McFarlan, F.W. 416, 421
McGregor, D.M. 365
McKenny, J.L. (McFarlan et al.)
  421
McLean, R.J. 544
McMahon, J.T. 689
MacMillan, I.C. 723
Madison, D.L. (Allen et al.)
  721, 722
Makridakis, S. 255
March, J.G. 131
Margerison, C. 708
Marginson, P. 369
Marriott, W.K. 724
Marris, R. 132
Marsh, P. 275, 498
Martin, R. (Marginson et al.) 369
Mason, R.O. (Rowe et al.) 471,
  472
Mayeda, K. 439
Mayer, C. 543
Mayes, B.T. (Allen et al.) 721,
  722
Meeks, J. 532
Miles, R.E. 82
Millar, V.E. 418, 421, 422
Miller, M.H. 387
Mills, D.Q. 467
Mintzberg, H. 21, 22, 69, 80,
  251, 353, 369, 408, 474,
  475–6, 649–54, 718, 719–20
Mitchell, D. 618
Modigliani, F. 387
Monkton, C. 233
Morrison, R. 7, 49
Myddleton, D.R. 166

Nakamoto, M. 686
Nash, T. 53, 693
Nathanson, D.A. 631
Nayak, P.R. 348
Nesbitt, S.L. 533
New, C.C. 333, 334, 336, 338
Newbould, G.D. 129, 130

Oates, D. 629
Odiorne, G. 367
O'Donnell, C. 675, 676
OECD 407
Ohmae, K. 11, 110, 184, 268,
   282, 284, 307, 316, 429, 457,
   514, 549, 636
Olsen, M. 404
Onkvisit, S. 308
Oram, R. 704
Ouchi, W. 112
Owen, A.A. 615, 617

Palmer, C. 419
Palmer, R. 176
PA Management Consultants
   346, 415–16
Pascale, R.T. 731
Pass, C. 400
Paton, R. 411
Pavy, D. 348
Pearce, J.A. 680, 724
Pearson, E.A. 347
Penrose, E. 132, 520, 599
Perrit, G.W. 689
Perrow, C. 148
Peters, T. 370, 372, 422, 700
Peters, T.J. 81, 93, 95, 96, 344,
   347, 496, 532, 644
Petersen, J.C. 718
Pfeffer, J. 141
Pike, R.H. 391, 400
Pilditch, J. 313
Pitts, R.A. 645
Pope, N.W. 320
Porter, L.W. 365, (Allen et al.)
   721, 722
Porter, M.E. 10, 184, 198, 208,
   210, 213, 224, 397, 417, 418,
   421, 422, 429, 454, 455, 458,
   514, 533, 540, 571, 595, 636
Prahalad, C.K. 15, 108–9, 314,
   429, 730
Press, G. 85
Prowse, M. 198
Pucik, V. 105, 107
Pumpin, C. 15, 16, 18, 91
Purcell, J. (Marginson et al.) 369
Pyburn, P. (McFarlan et al.) 421

Quinn, J.B. 12, 21–2, 65, 368,
   709, 712

Ramsay, J. 539
Rapoport, C. 304
Rappaport, A.S. 506
Raven, B. 90
Rawsthorn, A. 53
Rawsthorne, P. 499
Reed, R. 532, 611, 689, 690
Reid, W. 166
Reinton, S. 657
Reis, A. 294, 295
Renwick, P.A. (Allen et al.)
   721, 722
Richards, M.D. 123
Ringbakk, K.A. 467
Robbie, K. 575, 589
Robinson, J. 456
Robinson, R.B. 680
Robinson, S.J.Q. 469
Rock, S. 262
Rodger, I. 242
Rowe, A.J. 471, 472
Rudd, R. 84
Rumelt, R. 593
Rumelt, R.P. 532

Sadler, P. 95, 259
Salter, M.S. 532, 623
Saporito, B. 535
Sasseen, J. 202
Schein, E.H. 14, 92, 365, 378,
   413, 415
Schendel, D. 597
Schlegelmilch, B.B. 154
Schlesinger, L.A. 698, 706, 707
Scholes, K. 32
Schonberger, R.J. 110
Schwartz, H. 92
Sedgwick 691
Seed, A.H. 670
Senge, P. 712
Shaw, J.J. 308
Shull, F.A. 65
Shulman, L.E. (Stalk et al.) 15
Simon, H.A. 64, 131
Siomkos, G.J. 692
Sisson, K. (Marginson et al.) 369
Skapinker, M. 360
Skinner, W. 326, 339
Slatter, S. 228, 555, 556, 558
Smeltzer, L.R. 704
Smiley, T. 373
Smith, B. 708
Smith, R. 258
Snow, C.C. 82

Snyder, N.H. (Rowe et al.) 471,
   472
Spear, R. 405
Stalk, G. 15
Steiner, G. 467
Stewart, R. 413
Stoneman, P. 531
Stonich, P.J. 661
Stopford, J.M. 187
Storey, D. 136
Strickland, A.J. 123, 594, 622,
   720

Taffler, R.J. 234
Taylor, A. III 214
Taylor, B. 458
Taylor, R.N. 58
Tetreault, M.S. 344
Thanheiser, H.T. 525
Thomas, D. 151, 704
Thompson, A.A. 123, 594, 622,
   720
Thompson, J.L. 60
Tilles, S. 597
Touche Ross 150
Trout, J. 294, 295
Tyson, S. 361
Tyson, W.J. (Devine et al.) 191

Urry, M. 220

Vickers, G. 604
Vroom, V. 68

Wade, D.P. 469
Waterman, R.H., Jr, 93, 95, 96,
   496, 532, 644, 698
Weick, K.E. 20
Weinhold, W.A. 532
Wernham, R. 689
Weston, J.F. 383
Wheelwright S.C. 333, 334, 339
White, G. 137
Whittingham, R. 569
Wild, R. 327
Williamson, O.E. 132
Wilson, I.H. 256
Winner, L. 406
Winter, D. 70
Wood, S. 103
Wrapp, H.E. 368
Wright, M. 575, 589

Yetton, P. 68
York, A. 361

Zaleznik, A. 369

SUBJECT INDEX

References in bold type are to 'Key Concept' and 'Key Reading' boxes. References in italics are to 'Case' boxes.

ABB–Asea Brown Boveri, global matrix structure *641*
Accounts, financial, 164–6
Achievement motivation 70
Acid test (liquidity) ratio 173
Acquisitions 393–7, 515–16
  advantages and disadvantages 524
  American research findings 533
  British research findings 532
  effective strategies 537–45
  guidelines for success 538–9
  key considerations 536–7
  poor choice of, as cause of decline 229
  reasons for 528
  reasons for failure 533–6
  relative success of 531–2
  search for 539–43
  unwelcome bids 543
  see also Mergers
Action-centred leadership 370, 371
Action plans, selection of, as step in systematic planning 463–4
Activities of organizations, as theme of strategic management 6–7
Adaptability, in production 327
Adaptive change 482–4
Adaptive strategy **20**, 80–1, 82, 477–9
Added value, opportunities for 18, 19
Adhocracy 653, 654–5
'Admired companies' 163
Advertising 318–19

emphasis on, as turnaround strategy 562–3
Affiliation motivation 70
Aggregation, as step in systematic planning 463
Agreement, in overcoming resistance to change 707
Agriculture, UK, diversification in *249*
Aims, *see* Missions
Aircraft industry
  case examples on risk *59–60*
  see also British Aerospace; Hawker Siddeley; Norman Aeroplane Company; Optica
Airline industry
  international, deregulation of *211–12*
  see also British Airways; GPA; Laker Airways; SAS
Airtours, an opportunity seized *570*
Alliances, strategic 545
  advantages and disadvantages 524
  definition 545
  forms and examples of 545–9
  key issues in 549–50
Allied Textiles, and divestment *565*
Alsthom, Siemens and GEC, difficulties in international alliance *547–8*
America, *see* United States of America
Amstrad
  resource problems *668*

strategies and changing environment *686*
AMT (automated manufacturing technology) 336
Analysis, strategic 10, 32, 33–4
  see also Environmental analysis; Financial analysis; Situation analysis; Strategy evaluation techniques
Apple Computer, changes in strategy *703–4*
Appraisal, *see* Performance appraisal
Appropriateness of strategy 597–8
Asda–MFI
  difficulties after buy-out 577
  merger and de-merger *507–8*
  merger and diversification *541*
Asea, *see* ABB–Asea Brown Boveri
Ashley, Laura, rationalization, *562*
Assessment, *see* Situation assessment
Asset reduction 560
  see also Divestment
Asset swaps 510
Assets, in financial accounts 165–6
Automated manufacturing technology (AMT) 336
Awareness, strategic
  case examples *40*, *41–3*
  definition xiv
  and information 403
  question areas 35, 37, 39

Awareness, strategic – *cont.*
  see also Situation analysis;
  Situation assessment

BA (British Airways), change of
  culture 93, *94–5*
Babcock International, *see* FKI–
  Babcock
BAe (British Aerospace),
  opportunities and threats
  260
Balance sheets 165–6
Balance sheet valuation 392
Banc One, and empowerment
  627
BAT (British American
  Tobacco), bid by
  Hoylake *398–9*
BCG, *see* Boston Consulting
  Group
Behaviour, counter-intuitive 406
Behaviour, modification of
  changing 706
  refreezing 707–8
  unfreezing 706
Behavioural theory 131
Belief, as basis for success 90
Benetton
  and global products *317*
  speed and competitive
    advantage *441*
Berghaus, and differing
  national tastes 273
Beta of a company 386
'Bird approach' to strategic
  management 13
'Blurred boundary
  management' 373
BMW, focus differentiation
  strategies *219*
Board of Directors
  non-executive directors 48, 50
  responsibilities of 47–8
  roles of chairman and chief
    executive 48–9
Body Shop
  and culture-based
    competitive advantage
    101–2
  and success factors 258
Borrowing, *see* Loan capital
Boston Consulting Group
  (BCG) growth-share
  matrix 309–11, 468
  application to retail trade 312
  and resource allocation 333
  uses and limitations 311–12

Boston matrix, *see* Boston
  Consulting Group
Bounded discretion, in decision
  making 65
Bounded rationality, in
  decision making 65
Branding **298**
Braun, marketing and
  manufacturing principles
  329
Breakeven analysis 206, 595–6
Brewery industry
  analysis of 209
  a concentrated industry
    192–3
Britain, *see* United Kingdom
British Aerospace (BAe),
  opportunities and threats
  260
British Airways (BA)
  change of culture 93, *94–5*
  and information technology
    416–17
British American Tobacco
  (BAT), bid by Hoylake
  398–9
British Gas, and effectiveness
  177
British Petroleum, creating a
  learning organization
  714–15
British Rail (BR), structure *635*
British Salt, investigation by
  the Monopolies and
  Mergers Commission 197
British Steel
  pre-privatization divisional
    structure 631, *633*
  strategic changes *605–6*
British Telecom
  efficiency and effectiveness
    160
  functional policy
    implementation *678*
British Tourist Authority (BTA),
  objectives and
  performance measures
  162
British Vita, and quality of
  strategies *100*
Brooke, Margaret, strategic
  questions and answers
  40, *41–3*
Brown Boveri, *see* ABB–Asea
  Brown Boveri
Bruce, David and
  entrepreneurship *73–4*

BTA (British Tourist Authority),
  objectives and
  performance measures
  162
BTR plc
  and acquisitions 393, 396
  control system *685*
Budgets 679
  advantages of budgeting 682
  controlling the process 682
  flexed 684
  flexibility in 670, 681
  measuring performance
    against 681–3
  as outcome from planning
    669–70
  the process 680–1
  and resource allocation 680–1
  strategic budgeting 683
  types of 680
  zero-base 683–4
Building Societies
  change of strategy xv
  and cultural change *105–6*
  and recovery *564*
  and success factors 257
Bulmer, H.P., Holdings,
  company objectives 139
Burton Group
  change of strategy xv
  and temporary recovery *556–7*
Business ethics, *see* Ethics
Buy-backs 577–8
Buyers
  bargaining power, effect on
    profitability 198–9, 203–5,
    209
  of a business, *see* Divestment
  see also Customers
Buy-ins 575, 587–90
Buy-outs, *see* Management buy-
  outs

CAD (computer-aided design),
  and store layouts *420–1*
Camcorders, innovation in
  Japan 111
Capabilities, as base for
  strategic success 15
Capability, production 327,
  332–3
  and resource allocation 333
Capacity, production 327, 332–3
Capital
  cost of, *see* Cost of capital
  equity 379–80
  loans 379, 380–1

Capital asset pricing model (CAPM) 386
Capital budgets 680
Capital markets 253
  threats and opportunities 254
Capital requirements, as barrier to entry to an industry 199
CAPM (capital asset pricing model) 386
Car industry
  challenges in the EC 272
  innovation in Japan 111
  internationalization 267
  plastic car bodies 353
  see also BMW; General Motors; Nissan UK; Toyota; Volvo
Car ownership, increase in 270
Cash cows (product or business type)
  in BCG growth-share matrix 310, 311
  and portfolio analysis 468–9
  and resource allocation 333
Cash flow
  analysis of 595–6
  discounted 389–90
  importance of 173–4
  methods of improving 174
Caterpillar, and advanced manufacturing systems 338
Cathedrals, and finance 144
Cement production, end of price-fixing agreement 196
Centralization 622, 624–5
Centre for Management Buy-out Research (CMBOR) 580
Chairman, role of 47, 49
Challenges for the future 8, 733
Champagne industry, barriers to entry 202
Change
  adaptive 482–4
  attitudes towards 14
  case examples, xv, 23, 24–5, 26, 27–9, 517, 518–19
  and culture 100, 102
  definition xiv
  dynamics of 700
  force field analysis 708–9
  forces for 699–700

implementation, an overview 706–8
incremental model 712, 715–16
levels of 700–1, 702
logical incrementalism 21
management of 18–23, 698–709
need for 161
open systems thinking 716
opportunities for 12–13
organizational development and innovation 716–17
and people 359
planning 484–8
the process 704–5, 725
question areas 36, 38, 39
questions, case example 40, 41, 43
requirements for 698
resistance to 705–6, 707
role of strategic leader 47, 55–6
strategies for 709–10
and systems thinking 482–8
top-down 710–17
types of 704
Charities
  efficiency vs effectiveness 160
  objectives 144
Chemical industry
  research and development in Europe 351
  see also ICI
Chief executives, see Leader, strategic
Chocolate, a concentrated industry 193
Choice, strategic 32–3, 487
  question areas 36, 38, 39
  questions, case example 40, 41, 43
Chrysalis Group, examples of SWOT analysis
  capabilities and values 281
  key success factors and situation analysis 283
Club culture 83–4
Club Méditerranée, change of strategy 103
CMBOR (Centre for Management Buy-out Research) 580
Coercion, to accept change 707, 723, 724
Coercive power 89, 720

Coloroll, changing fortunes of chief executive 52–3
Combination strategies 500–1
Communication
  and culture 81
  of decisions 68
  as Japanese management technique 106, 107
  in overcoming resistance to change 707
  and the strategic leader 47, 68–9
Companies, see Organizations
Competencies, see Skills
Competition 184
  anti-competitive behaviour 197–8
  attributes for success 185, 207–8
  as cause of decline 231–3
  in concentrated industries 191
  diamond of national advantage 222–3
  in the European Community 271
  international competitiveness 222–4
  in Japanese culture 108–10
  market model characteristics 127–9
  monopoly power 188
  regulation of, in UK 194–8
  role of government 208, 210
  UK policy on 195
  see also Rivalry
Competition Act (1980) 197–8
Competitive advantage 11, 11–12
  analysis of, as base for strategy 8
  basic choices 210, 212–13
  creation of, and information technology 418–22
  and culture 98–9
  derived from any part of the business 427–8
  and design 429
  as determinant of strategy 595
  and effectiveness of strategy 599
  examples of, and information technology 423
  and finance 397, 399–400
  and information technology 415–23

Competitive advantage – *cont.*
and investment priority 8
links with other
organizations 430
major purpose 429
model of 213
from operations management
326
and resources 287–9
sources of, examples 428
and speed 439–42
sustaining, difficulties with
185, 440
and the value chain 434–9
and working capital 400
Competitive gap analysis 282
Competitive opportunities
exploitation of 8
and information technology
422
Competitive scope, and the
value chain 433–4
Competitive strategies 10, 184,
213–15, 217
cost leadership 213, 214–16,
217
differentiation strategies 213,
216–21
focus strategies 213, 216–18
timing, importance of 185–6
Competitiveness
in the 1990s **660**
international **222–4**
maximizing, in
manufacturing strategy
342
requirements for 207–8
Competitor analysis 302–4
Competitors
anticipation of their
responses 8
and competitive advantage 12
'good' and 'bad' 221
information about 221
threats and opportunities 254
Complacency 2
Computer-aided design (CAD),
and store layouts *420–1*
Computer integrated
manufacturing 336
Computers
hand-held 418, 420
networking, advantages of
420
see also Information
technology

Concentration (measure of
control)
by acquisition 193–4
aggregate 188
concentrated industries 191–4
market 188, 191
by mergers 193–4
ratios 188, 191, 192–3
sectoral 188, 191
in the UK 193–4
Concentration strategy 496–7
and market growth and
competitive position 594
Concentric diversification 505–6
Conglomerate diversification
506, 525
and market growth and
competitive position 594
Connection power 89, 720
Consumers
increase in knowledge and
sophistication 270
increase in spending power
269–70
needs of, and marketing
291–2
stakeholder interests of 130
see also Customers
Control of industry by
organizations, *see*
Concentration
Co-optation, in overcoming
resistance to change 707
Co-ordinating mechanisms for
work division 649–51
Core competencies, required to
meet success factors 15
Corporate governance 47–9
Corporate management
roles 657
styles 655–7
Corporate strategy 10–11, 184
and the European
Community 274, 276–8
evaluation of 593–4
Corporate strength, essential
aspects 730, 732
Corporations, *see* Organizations
Cost advantages
as barrier to entry to an
industry 200, 203
see also Economies of Scale
Cost breakdown,
manufacturing and
service businesses 436
Cost control, common

problems in value chain
analysis 436–7
Cost disadvantages, as cause of
company decline 230–1
Cost drivers, and the value
chain 434–6
Cost leadership strategy, and
the value chain 434
case examples *214–15, 435*
and competitive advantage
213, 215–16, 217
Cost management, as focus of
management philosophy
86
Cost of capital
capital asset pricing model
(CAPM) 385–6
and gearing 386–7
optimal capital structure
(OCS) 385
weighted average cost of
capital (WACC) 385, 386
Cost of equity 385
Cost of long-term debt 385
Cost reduction
impact of information
technology 418, 420–1
in retrenchment 559–60
Costs (selling and
administration) to sales
ratio 170–1, 172
Cost structures, relationship
with breakeven points
and profits 206
Counter-intuitive behaviour 406
Courtaulds Textiles, and
market segmentation *301*
'Crafting strategy' 251
Crisis management 690
decision areas 690–1
steps in 691–2
strategies and examples
692–4
Critical mass 526
Crown Berger Paints, product
differentiation 219, *220*
Culture
aspects of 91–2
changes in, case examples
93, *94–5*
changing 99–102, **104**
club culture 83–4
communication- and
learning-based 81
and competitive advantage
98–9
and decision making 78